Ferdico's Criminal Law and Justice Dictionary

D0024440

Ferdico's Criminal Law and Justice
Dictionary

John N. Ferdico

West Publishing Company

St. Paul   New York   Los Angeles   San Francisco

Copyediting: Mary McKee Lopez

Text Design: Jose Delgado

Cover Design: Peter Thiel, Peter Thiel Design

Composition and Film: Wiest Publications Management

Production, Prepress, Printing, and Binding by West Publishing Company.

West's Commitment to the Environment

In 1906, West Publishing Company began recycling materials left over from the production of books. This began a tradition of efficient and responsible use of resources. Today, up to 95 percent of our legal books and 70 percent of our college texts are printed on recycled, acid-free stock. West also recycles nearly 22 million pounds of scrap paper annually—the equivalent of 181,717 trees. Since the 1960s, West has devised ways to capture and recycle waste inks, solvents, oils, and vapors created in the printing process. We also recycle plastics of all kinds, wood, glass, corrugated cardboard, and batteries, and have eliminated the use of styrofoam book packaging. We at West are proud of the longevity and the scope of our commitment to our environment.

Copyright © 1992   By West Publishing Company
610 Opperman Drive
P.O. Box 64526
St. Paul, MN 55164-0526

All rights reserved.

Printed in the United States of America

99 98 97 96 95   8 7 6 5 4 3 2 1

ISBN: 0-314-93310-7
Library of Congress Cataloging–in–Publication Data
Ferdico, John N.
    [Criminal law and justice dictionary]
    Ferdico's criminal law and justice dictionary / John N. Ferdico.
        p.   cm.
    ISBN 0–314–93310–7
    1. Criminal law—United States—Dictionaries. 2. Criminal justice, Administration of—United States—Dictionaries.   I. Title.
KF9217.F47   1992
345.73'003—dc20
[347.30503]   92–2956

CIP

To my Mom and Dad

Elsie and John

on the occasion of their

50th

year of marriage

Contents

Preface

The idea of writing a dictionary of criminal law and justice terms came to me for the first time in the mid-1970s. At that time I was researching and writing the first edition of my book *Criminal Procedure for the Criminal Justice Professional* (West Publishing Co., 1989). While engaged in that work, I noticed not only that there were no criminal law and justice dictionaries in publication, but that other legal dictionaries and glossaries in other criminal law and justice texts were woefully inadequate. They were either incomplete, inaccurate, out-of-date, or insufficiently specific or detailed with respect to criminal law and procedure.

When I finished work on my criminal procedure book, I decided that my next big project would be to write a complete and comprehensive criminal law and justice dictionary. I interested a publisher in the project and proceeded to spend the next five years, off and on, researching and writing the dictionary. Unfortunately, my publishing contract called for completion of the dictionary in two years and the publisher cancelled the contract for failure to comply with its terms. I therefore found myself with a nearly completed dictionary on several thousand index cards and no publisher.

For various reasons, including other writing projects and other demands on my time, the dictionary lay dormant for nearly 10 years. It was never totally out of mind, however, and, in 1989, when I was discussing potential book projects with Susan Tubb, my editor at West Publishing Co., I suggested reviving the dictionary. The idea appealed to everyone concerned and I soon had another contract, nearly 15 years after my original contract with a different publisher. I immediately transcribed the index cards onto my computer and have spent the last few years updating, supplementing, polishing, and redesigning that original into this finished product.

The primary purpose of my dictionary is to provide a comprehensive, concise definition of every word or term that a person likely would encounter in dealing with the criminal justice system, from pretrial investigation and detection of crime through corrections, appeals, and postconviction remedies. Every definition is written in plain English and is designed to be understood by the average person without a formal legal education. Cross-references appear within and at the end of definitions to complement the definitions and to provide additional information. (See *HOW TO USE THIS DICTIONARY* for an explanation of the use of bold, italic, and all capitals for emphasis and cross-reference.) The words and terms defined in the dictionary were selected from a multitude of sources and from my over-20-years-experience in preparing educational materials for the criminal justice community. The dictionary is written in gender neutral language.

I designed the dictionary primarily for criminal justice personnel and others who deal regularly with the criminal justice system, but who do not have a formal legal education. This audience includes law enforcement officers, probation and parole officers, corrections personnel, court personnel such as clerks and court reporters, legislators, social workers, family crisis personnel, expert witnesses from other disciplines such as medicine and psychology, paralegal and parajudicial personnel, students, and, of course, persons accused of crime. The dictionary is also useful to lawyers, since many of the definitions are interspersed with quotations and citations from court decisions and are useful to refresh recollection or to assist further research.

I have many people to acknowledge for their support and encouragement during the long period of development of this dictionary. First of all, thanks to my family and friends for bolstering my enthusiasm when the project looked bleak and overwhelming and, especially during the long fallow period, for their assurances that the dictionary would indeed see the light of day. In particular, I would like to acknowledge Mary Lou Leahy, my companion during the early stages of researching and writing the dictionary, for her patience and understanding during some lean times. I owe gratitude to the entire staff of the Maine State Law and Legislative Reference Library in Augusta for their always friendly and helpful service and for granting me a lot of leeway in terms of extended use of library materials and resources. I would like to acknowledge particularly my friend and former head Maine state law librarian Edith Hary for her support and for the use of her grand old oak desk, which I was allowed virtually to usurp as my own during the early development of the dictionary in the mid-1970s. I could not have completed the dictionary without the friendly and able assistance of Theresa J. Lippert and John M. Lindley and their colleagues at West Publishing Company. They were always patient with my delays and always professional and supportive in working through problems. Thanks also to Mary Lopez for a superb job of copy editing. Finally, and most importantly, I want to express my deepest appreciation to my dear friend Abbie Sewall. She not only did a supremely professional job transcribing and editing my sometimes indecipherable index card manuscript, but she has been my most vocal and supportive cheerleader during the entire last 2 and 1/2 years of bringing the dictionary to fruition.

This is the first edition of the dictionary and its ultimate value and usefulness can only be tested by its practical application in the criminal justice system. In closing, therefore, I would like to welcome comments and suggestions from users for the improvement of future editions of this dictionary. Please direct all correspondence to West Publishing Company, Legal Publications—College Division, 610 Opperman Drive, Eagan, MN 55123.

John N. Ferdico
Dresden, Maine

How to Use This Dictionary

This dictionary is designed to be easy to use and self-explanatory. Nevertheless, an explanation of some of the conventions used may facilitate more efficient use of the dictionary.

The term to be defined appears in **BOLD ALL CAPITALS**.

Terms appearing in ALL CAPITALS regular type within a definition are defined elsewhere in the dictionary and are either essential or very important to an understanding of the term being defined. Terms appearing in **bold** upper and lower case within a definition are defined elsewhere in the dictionary and are helpful in understanding the meaning of the word defined.

Terms with more than one meaning are defined using **1.**, **2.**, **3.**, etc. to designate the different meanings. The numbering of the definitions is not designed to indicate degrees of importance or preference but simply to distinguish the definitions and indicate how many different definitions there are.

Terms with more than one grammatical form are defined using **n.**, **v.**, **adj.**, etc. to designate the different grammatical forms. When more than one definition appears under a particular grammatical form, they are designated **adj. 1.**, **adj. 2.**, **adj. 3.**, etc.

Foreign language terms are indicated by the designation *Latin, French,* etc. appearing in italics. If the definition following the language designation is in "quotations," it is a direct translation of the foreign language term. Otherwise it is simply a definition of the term.

References designated "see" or "see also" whether capitalized, italicized, or set in regular type are used to refer the reader elsewhere in the dictionary for a variety of purposes, including reference to synonyms, antonyms, related and contrasted terms, other grammatical forms of words, explanatory material, and further information. The purpose of the "see" reference should be obvious from its context.

Abbreviations for defined terms are introduced by the designation *Abbreviation*: in italics.

Examples are introduced by the designation *Example*: in italics.

Other names for a defined term are introduced by the designation *Also called*: in italics.

Court decisions that are not main dictionary entries are set in italics, e.g., *Duncan v. Louisiana*. Whenever a court decision is mentioned in this dictionary, its complete citation is included so the reader can refer to the decision for further information.

Words that are spelled the same, but pronounced differently, appear as two separate dictionary entries, with the accented syllable underlined in each entry. For example, **CONVICT** the noun appears as a separate entry from **CONVICT** the verb.

All entries have been alphabetized letter by letter rather than word by word. Therefore, for example, **AB INITIO** appears between **ABIDING FAITH** and **ABJURE**, rather than at the beginning of the dictionary.

Ferdico's Criminal Law and Justice Dictionary

ABANDON. To desert; to give up completely; to discard. In the law of search and seizure, to abandon property means to intentionally and voluntarily relinquish all title, possession, and claim to it with no intention of reasserting a claim. Law enforcement officers may, without **probable cause**, **warrant**, or other legal justification, seize property that has been abandoned by its owner. Such a **seizure** is legal and does not violate the Fourth Amendment to the Constitution.

AB ANTE. *Latin.* "From before." Before; in advance.

AB ANTIQUO. *Latin.* Since ancient times.

ABATE. **1.** To put an end to. **2.** To reduce in amount, degree, or intensity; to lessen.

ABBREVIATION. A shortened form of a word or phrase used to represent the complete form. *Example*: U.S. is an abbreviation for United States; misc. is an abbreviation for miscellaneous.

ABDICATE. To give up, abandon, or renounce a right, office, authority, or trust.

ABDUCTION. **1.** Taking and carrying away by force. **2.** The unlawful taking and carrying away by fraud, persuasion, or force of any child, ward, or woman for marriage, prostitution, concubinage, or other unlawful purpose. In its more limited sense, abduction refers to the taking and carrying away of a woman under a certain age. *See*: KIDNAPPING.

ABET. To assist, command, counsel, or encourage another person to commit a crime. Abet implies criminal intent, knowledge of the wrongful purpose of the perpetrator of the crime, and actual or constructive presence at the commission of the crime, without actual participation in the commission of the crime. The word abet is usually used as part of the phrase aid and abet. See PARTY for a list of related terms.

ABETTOR. One who **abets**.

ABEYANCE. Temporary inactivity or suspension with an expectation of revival. *See*: LATENT.

ABIDE. **1.** To accept the consequences of. **2.** To await or remain in waiting for a prolonged period.

ABIDE BY. To obey; to conform to; to comply with.

ABIDING CONVICTION. A settled and fixed belief.

ABIDING FAITH. Belief or confidence in the guilt of one accused of crime that remains or continues in the minds of the jury.

AB INITIO. *Latin.* "From the beginning."

ABJURE. To solemnly repudiate, reject, or avoid.

ABODE. The place where a person dwells; a **residence.** Abode differs from **domicile** in that an abode may be a temporary residence, whereas a domicile is a person's permanent and legal home.

ABOLISH. To do away with; to put an end to; to repeal; to make void.

ABORTION. The destruction or bringing forth prematurely of the human fetus before it is capable of sustaining life on its own. Laws limiting or prohibiting abortions in practically all the states, the District of Columbia, and the territories were invalidated by *Roe v. Wade*, 410 U.S. 113, 93 S.Ct. 705, 35 L.Ed.2d 147 (1973), which recognized a right of personal privacy protected by the due process clause that included a qualified right of a woman to determine whether to bear a child or not. On the basis of its analysis of the competing individual rights and state interests, the United States Supreme Court discerned a three-stage balancing of rights and interests extending over the full nine-month term of pregnancy.

> "(a) For the stage prior to approximately the end of the first trimester, the abortion decision and its effectuation must be left to the medical judgments of the pregnant woman's attending physician.

> "(b) For the stage subsequent to approximately the end of the first trimester, the State, in promoting its interest in the health of the mother, may, if it chooses, regulate the abortion procedure in ways that are reasonably related to maternal health.

> "(c) For the stage subsequent to viability, the State in promoting its interest in the potentiality of human life may, if it chooses, regulate, and even proscribe, abortion except where it is necessary, in appropriate medical judgment, for the preservation of the life or health of the mother." 410 U.S. at 164-65, 93 S.Ct. at 732, 35 L.Ed.2d at 183-84.

A lengthy history of the medical and legal views of abortion apparently convinced the Court that the prohibition of abortion lacked the solid foundation necessary to preserve the prohibitions from constitutional review. Similarly, a review of the concept of "person" as protected in the due process clause and in other provisions of the Constitution established to the Court's satisfaction that the word "person" did not include the unborn and therefore that the unborn lacked federal constitutional protection. Without treating the question in more than summary fashion, the Court announced that "a right of personal privacy, or a guarantee of certain areas or zones of privacy, does exist in the Constitution" and that it is "founded in the Fourteenth Amendment's concept of personal liberty and restrictions upon state action." 410 U.S. at 152-53, 93 S.Ct. at 726-27, 35 L.Ed.2d at 176-77. "This right of privacy . . . is broad enough to encompass a woman's decision whether or not to terminate her pregnancy." 410 U.S. at 153, 93 S.Ct. at 727, 35 L.Ed.2d at 177.

Following the *Roe v. Wade* decision, a so-called "right to life" movement has arisen and has, through demonstrations, proposed legislation and constitutional amendment, and a multitude of subsidiary court cases, attempted to overturn or lessen the effect of *Roe v. Wade*. In *Webster v. Reproductive Health Services*, 492 U.S. 490, 109 S.Ct. 3040, 106 L.Ed.2d 410 (1989), the U.S. Supreme Court upheld a Missouri law that bars the use of public money, medical personnel, or facilities in performing abortions and requires doctors to conduct tests to determine the viability of a fetus at least 20 weeks old. The *Webster* decision is generally viewed as evidence that a dramatic shift against abortion rights has taken place in the Supreme Court. The decision opens the door to state legislation regulating abortion, including provisions requiring parental notification, consent of the husband, waiting periods, and mandatory counseling before abortion. Future court decisions and other developments will determine the continuing validity and vitality of *Roe v. Wade*. *See*: INFANTICIDE; PROLICIDE; RIGHT OF PRIVACY.

ABOUT. **1.** Approximately; nearly; almost. **2.** In the vicinity of; around.

ABOUT TO. Ready or prepared to; on the verge of.

ABOVE. **1.** Higher in rank or power. *Example*: Appeal to the court above. **2.** Appearing earlier in the same document or text. *Example*: Refer to the figures quoted above. **3.** Superior to; more than; in preference to.

ABRIDGE. To diminish; to reduce; to lessen; to curtail.

ABROGATE. To abolish, repeal, or annul by authoritative act.

ABSCOND. **1.** To intentionally and unlawfully absent or conceal oneself in order to avoid **arrest**, **prosecution**, or other legal **process**. The time period of a defendant's unlawful absence is discounted in measurements of time elapsed between filing and court disposition of cases for purposes of determining court efficiency or meeting speedy trial requirements. Fleeing to avoid prosecution or the execution of a sentence can result in prosecution for **contempt of court** under state law. Flight across a state or national border to avoid prosecution is a federal crime. *Also called:* **flee from justice**. **2.** In the law of corrections, to depart without authorization from a geographical area or jurisdiction in violation of the conditions of **probation** or **parole**. To abscond from probation or parole supervision is a violation of individually specified conditions of probation or parole, not a violation of statute, and is thus not a crime. Such behavior, however, may cause a current probation or parole status to be revoked. *See:* ABSENT WITHOUT LEAVE; ESCAPE; FUGITIVE FROM JUSTICE; WANTED PERSON.

ABSENT.   Not **present**; missing.

ABSENTEE.   **1.** One who is absent. **2.** One who is permanently absent from a place; a nonresident.

ABSENT WITHOUT LEAVE.   A designation applied to a person who has failed to return from an authorized **temporary release** from a correctional facility. Some states do not formally register a person as absent without leave until the absence has continued long after the required time of return. Some penal codes explicitly include absent without leave in the crime of **escape**, but others do not. *Abbreviation:* **A.W.O.L.** See ABSCOND for a list of related terms.

ABSOLUTE.   Complete; final; without exception, qualification, or condition.

ABSOLUTE PARDON.   Same as FULL PARDON.

ABSOLVE.   **1.** To pronounce not guilty or free from blame; to acquit. **2.** To set free or release, as from some duty, obligation, or responsibility.

ABSQUE.   *Latin.* "Without."

ABSTENTION.   A federal court's exercise of its discretion to decline to exercise its **jurisdiction** in a legal action and to allow a state court to resolve the matter. Abstention is used when a case can be resolved by application of state law and the federal court can avoid the unnecessary decision of constitutional questions also presented by the facts of the case. See JURISDICTION for a list of related terms.

ABSTRACT.   **n.** A summary of the important points of a statement, document, speech, etc. *Example:* An abstract of a record is a statement of the substantial contents of a record *See:* COPY; DUPLICATE; EXEMPLIFICATION; SUMMARY; SYLLABUS; SYNOPSIS; TRANSCRIPT. **v.** To withdraw; to take away; to remove.

ABSTRACTION.   The taking or withdrawing of the funds or property of another with the intent to defraud or injure. *See:* BLACKMAIL; BURGLARY; COMPOUND

LARCENY; DEFALCATION; EMBEZZLEMENT; EXACTION; EXTORTION; FALSE PRETENSES; GRAND LARCENY; LARCENY; LARCENY BY BAILEE; LARCENY BY TRICK; MISAPPROPRIATION; PETIT LARCENY; RECEIVING STOLEN PROPERTY; ROBBERY; SHOPLIFTING; SIMPLE LARCENY; STEAL; THEFT; THEFT OF SERVICES.

ABSURD. Contrary to reason or common sense; ridiculous; nonsensical.

ABUSE. **1.** To use wrongly or improperly; to misuse. **2.** To assail with contemptuous, coarse, or insulting words.

ABUSE OF DISCRETION. *See*: DISCRETION.

ABUSE OF PROCESS. Improper use of criminal or civil PROCESS (definition 2) after it has been issued, for a purpose other than that intended by the law. Abuse of process is a wrong committed during the course of litigation. *See*: BARRATRY; CHAMPERTY; COMPOUNDING CRIME; FALSE ARREST; FALSE IMPRISONMENT; MAINTENANCE; MALICIOUS ABUSE OF PROCESS; MALICIOUS ARREST; MALICIOUS PROSECUTION; OBSTRUCTING JUSTICE; THEFTBOTE.

ABUTTING. Touching or bordering on. If two objects are abutting, one object terminates at the other. See PROXIMITY for a list of related terms.

A/C. Abbreviation for ACCOUNT.

ACCEDE. **1.** To give assent; to consent; to agree. *Example:* Justice Blackmun acceded to Justice White's point of view. **2.** To arrive at or enter into an office or position.

ACCEPT. To receive with approval; to agree to; to consent to.

ACCESS. **1.** Opportunity to or means of approach. **2.** Right to enter or make use of.

ACCESSORY. Generally, a person who **aids**, promotes, or contributes to the commission of a crime. An accessory before the fact is a person who aids and abets the **principal** in the first degree before the commission of the crime, but is not present at the commission of the crime. "The sole distinction between a principal in the second degree and an accessory before the fact is the matter of presence. The principal in the second degree is present at the perpetration of the felony, either actually or constructively, whereas the accessory before the fact is absent. The same aid, command, counsel, procurement or encouragement which will make one a principal in the second degree if he is present at the time a felony is committed, will make him an accessory before the fact if he is absent." *State v. Mower*, 317 A.2d 807, 811 n.3 (Me. 1971). An accessory after the fact is a person who, knowing that another person has committed a crime, advises, assists, harbors, conceals, or comforts the person to help him or her avoid apprehension, conviction, or punishment. In many jurisdictions, accessories after the fact are recognized as a separate group only in relation to felonies. In some of these jurisdictions a person who knowingly aids a misdemeanant is treated as a principal to the misdemeanor. In others, the person does not commit any offense. See PARTY for a list of related terms.

ACCIDENT. **1.** Any unforeseen and undesirable event. **2.** Under the motor vehicle laws, an accident is an unforeseen and undesirable occurrence involving the operation of a motor vehicle that results in injury to a person or to property.

ACCIDENTAL. Happening by chance or unexpectedly.

ACCIDENTAL HOMICIDE. A killing of a person resulting from a lawful act performed in a lawful manner with a belief that no harm is possible. See HOMICIDE for a list of related terms.

ACCOMPANY. To go along with.

ACCOMPLICE. A person who, with the intent to promote or facilitate the commission of a crime, gives assistance or encouragement to the principal offender or fails to perform a legal duty to prevent the crime. Accomplice includes a **principal** in the first or second degree and an **accessory** before the fact. See PARTY for a list of related terms.

ACCOMPLICE WITNESS. A **principal**, **accomplice**, or **accessory** in a crime who is called to testify at the trial for that crime. Ordinarily, a conviction cannot be based solely on the testimony of an accomplice witness without evidence from an independent source to **corroborate** that testimony. See WITNESS for a list of related terms.

ACCORD. To be in agreement or harmony.

ACCORDANCE. Agreement; conformity.

ACCOUNT. A verbal or written statement of particular events, transactions, or conduct. *Example:* The accused robber gave a complete account of his activities on the night in question. *Abbreviation:* **a/c**.

ACCOUNTABLE. Responsible; liable.

ACCOUNTANT. A person who keeps, audits, and inspects financial records and prepares financial and tax reports.

ACCOUNT FOR.   To give a reason for or explanation of.

ACCRETION.   An increase in size or extent by natural growth or by gradual external addition.

ACCRUE.   **1.** To come into existence as an enforceable claim or right. *Example:* A charge of murder accrues on the date the victim dies, not on the date the injury is inflicted. **2.** To come by way of increase or advantage; to arise in due course. *Example:* Many benefits accrue to society from freedom of the press.

ACCUMULATE.   To increase by continuous or repeated additions.

ACCUMULATIVE JUDGMENT.   A **judgment** imposed upon a person already **convicted** and **sentenced**, which takes effect after the completion of the earlier sentence. See JUDGMENT and SENTENCE for lists of related terms.

ACCUMULATIVE SENTENCE.   Same as CONSECUTIVE SENTENCE.

ACCUSATION.   A formal **charge** against a person, brought before a court or magistrate, to the effect that the person is guilty of a crime. Accusation is a general term for all charges in criminal cases. *See:* AFFIDAVIT; CHARGING DOCUMENT; COMPLAINT; INDICTMENT; INFORMATION; PRESENTMENT.

ACCUSATORY INSTRUMENT.   Same as CHARGING DOCUMENT.

ACCUSE.   To bring a formal **charge** against a person before a court or magistrate to the effect that the person is guilty of a **crime**.

ACCUSED.   A person against whom a criminal **charge** is brought in a legal proceeding. A person becomes an accused when formally charged with a **crime** or when subjected to actual restraint by formal **arrest**. *See:* ALLEGED OFFENDER; APPELLANT; APPELLEE; ARRESTEE; CONVICT; CORESPONDENT; DEFENDANT; DEFENDANT IN ERROR; DETAINEE; EX-OFFENDER; INMATE; OFFENDER; PERPETRATOR; PETITIONER; PLAINTIFF; PLAINTIFF IN ERROR; PRISONER; RESIDENT; RESPONDENT; SUSPECT; WANTED PERSON.

ACCUSTOMED.   Usual; habitual.

ACCUSTOMED TO.   In the habit of; used to.

ACKNOWLEDGE.   **1.** To accept as legally binding. **2.** To admit the existence, reality, or truth of.

ACKNOWLEDGMENT. A formal declaration made before an authorized official or witness by a person who has executed a document that it is the person's free act and genuine expression of intent.

ACQUAINTANCE. **1.** Personal knowledge that is less than thorough, but more than superficial. **2.** A person with whom one is familiar but not intimate; a person with whom one has less frequent contact and less personal interest than a friend.

ACQUIESCE. To agree or comply silently or without protest. *See:* ASSENT; CONSENT.

ACQUIRE. To gain possession of; to obtain.

ACQUISITION. The act of acquiring. *See:* ACQUIRE.

ACQUIT. To discharge, release, or set a person free from an accusation of crime. *See:* ACQUITTAL.

ACQUITTAL. A **judgment** of a court, based either on the **verdict** of a **jury** or of a **judicial officer** in a **nonjury trial**, that the defendant is not guilty of the offense for which he or she has been tried. An acquittal on all charges is a final court disposition terminating **criminal jurisdiction** over the defendant. See DISMISSAL and JUDGMENT for lists of related terms.

ACT. **1.** The **Model Penal Code** defines act or **action** as "a bodily movement whether voluntary or involuntary." The fundamental premise for all criminal liability is that the guilt of the defendant be based upon **conduct** and that the conduct include a voluntary act or an **omission** to perform an act of which the defendant was physically capable. Section 2.01 (2) of the Model Penal Code states that the following are not voluntary acts: "(a) a reflex or convulsion; (b) a bodily movement during unconsciousness or sleep; (c) conduct during hypnosis or resulting from hypnotic suggestion; (d) a bodily movement that otherwise is not a product of the effort or determination of the actor, either conscious or habitual." Under Section 2.01 (4) "[p]ossession is an act . . . if the possessor knowingly procured or received the thing possessed or was aware of his control thereof for a sufficient period to have been able to terminate his possession." **2.** Something done or performed; a deed. Act usually refers to something done momentarily or instantaneously. **3.** A decision or determination of a court that is reduced to writing, such as a judgment, an order, a decree, or a rule. **4.** A written law that has been formally enacted by a legislature and duly signed by an executive officer. *See:* BILL; LAW; LEGISLATION; MEASURE; ORDINANCE; REGULATION; RULE; STATUTE.

ACTING. Temporarily assuming the duties or authority of.

ACTIO. *Latin.* "Action." *Example:* An actio criminalis is a criminal action.

ACTION. **1.** Same as ACT (definition 1). **2.** Something done or performed; an act; a deed. **3.** A judicial proceeding instituted and maintained by one party against another for the enforcement or protection of a right, the redress or prevention of a wrong, or the punishment of a crime. The term action applies to both criminal and civil matters, although it is used more commonly for civil matters. *Example:* The State brought a civil action for forfeiture of the automobile used to transport drugs. *See:* CIVIL ACTION; CRIMINAL ACTION.

ACTIONABLE. Furnishing grounds for a legal action.

ACTIVE. In action; in actual motion or progress.

ACTIVE SUPERVISION. *See:* SUPERVISED PROBATION.

ACT OF GOD. An unavoidable and unforeseeable occurrence caused exclusively by nature and not by any human agency. *Example:* An earthquake; a tornado. *Also called:* **act of nature**; **act of providence**.

ACT OF LAW. The operation of legal rules upon given facts, resulting in consequences independent of the will of the parties involved.

ACT OF NATURE. Same as ACT OF GOD.

ACT OF PROVIDENCE. Same as ACT OF GOD.

ACTUAL. Real; existing in fact. As opposed to possible, theoretical, or **constructive**.

ACTUAL AGENCY. An AGENCY in which the AGENT has ACTUAL AUTHORITY to act for or represent the PRINCIPAL. *See:* IMPLIED AGENCY.

ACTUAL AGENT. An AGENT who has ACTUAL AUTHORITY.

ACTUAL AUTHORITY. AUTHORITY (definition 1) intentionally conferred by a PRINCIPAL upon an AGENT or the authority that a principal allows an agent to believe he or she possesses. Actual authority includes both **express authority** and **implied authority**.

ACTUAL FRAUD. Fraud originating from an actual evil design to deceive others to their detriment. *Also called:* **fraud in fact; moral fraud; positive fraud**. *See:* CONSTRUCTIVE FRAUD.

ACTUAL NOTICE.   Notice conveyed directly or personally to, and actually received by, a person. Actual notice includes both **express notice** and **implied notice**. See NOTICE for a list of related terms.

ACTUS.   *Latin.* "Act; action."

ACTUS REUS.   *Latin.* The deed of crime committed by the offender. There are two major components to every crime—the actus reus and the **mens rea**. The actus reus is the objective, physical act of someone producing social harm. The mens rea is the mental element. *Example:* The actus reus of murder is homicide, whereas the mens rea is malice aforethought. See CRIME for a list of related terms.

AD.   *Latin.* To; at; for; on; concerning; until.

ADAPT.   To make suitable for a specified use or situation.

ADD.   To unite or join so as to increase in size, quantity, or importance.

ADDENDUM.   Something added or to be added. *Example:* A supplement to a book is an addendum. *See:* APPENDIX; SUPPLEMENT.

ADDICT.   A person who has a habit of using a substance (such as alcohol or drugs) to the extent that he or she no longer has reasonable control of that use.

AD DIEM.   *Latin.* "At the day."

ADDLED.   Muddled; confused.

ADDRESS.   To speak to with an implication of formality and clear purpose and with a suggestion of speaking at some length. *Example:* To address the court. *See:* ADDUCE; ADVANCE; AFFIRM; ALLEGE; ALLUDE; ASSERT; AVER; AVOUCH; AVOW; CITE; CLAIM; COMMENT; CONTEND; DECLARE; DEMAND; DETAIL; IMPLY; MAINTAIN; NARRATE; OFFER; POSE; PROFESS; PROFFER; PROPOSE; PROPOUND; PROTEST; QUOTE; RECITE; RECOUNT; REFER; RELATE; REPORT; SUBMIT; TENDER; TESTIFY.

ADDUCE.   To propose or bring forward (facts, evidence, arguments) for consideration in support of a contention; to present; to offer; to introduce. *Example:* To adduce evidence in court. See ADDRESS for a list of related terms.

ADEEM.   To take away; to revoke.

ADEQUATE.   Sufficient; enough; satisfactory.

ADEQUATE PROVOCATION. In the law of **homicide**, a provocation that a reasonable person would find extreme, causing such an emotional disturbance or **heat of passion** that the person would lose his or her self-control. Such circumstances, if proven, will reduce an intentional killing of another from **murder** to **voluntary manslaughter**. *Also called:* **sufficient provocation**. See HOMICIDE for a list of related terms.

ADEQUATE REMEDY. A legal remedy that provides sufficient and just relief.

AD FINEM. *Latin.* To the end; at the end.

ADHERENCE. Steady attachment; close following. *Example:* Rigid adherence to the rules.

AD HOC. *Latin.* For this; for this purpose. *Example:* An ad hoc committee is a committee formed for a special limited purpose.

AD HOMINEM. *Latin.* "To the person." *Example:* An ad hominem argument is one that appeals to a person's emotions, prejudices, and personal interests rather than to the person's reason or intellect.

AD IDEM. *Latin.* To the same effect or point.

AD INFINITUM. *Latin.* Without end; limitless.

AD INTERIM. *Latin.* Meanwhile; in the meantime.

ADJACENT. Close but not necessarily touching. If two objects are adjacent, they are so situated that nothing of the same kind comes between them. See PROXIMITY for a list of related terms.

ADJECTIVE LAW. Same as PROCEDURAL LAW.

ADJOINING. Touching at some line or point. See PROXIMITY for a list of related terms.

ADJOURN. To put off or defer to another time. The term adjourn is applied to all situations in which public bodies separate for a brief period with the idea of meeting again. If the time of the next meeting is not specified, the term adjourn **sine die** is used.

ADJUDGE. To judicially determine or decide. The term adjudge does not necessarily refer to a final judgment or determination, but may also be applied to interlocutory orders or decrees of court. Adjudge is often used interchangeably with ADJUDICATE.

ADJUDICATE. To judicially determine or decide. The term adjudicate usually refers to a final disposition of an issue made after deliberation upon evidence presented. Adjudicate is often used interchangeably with ADJUDGE.

ADJUDICATION. **1.** Generally, the act, process, or result of adjudicating (see **adjudicate**). **2.** The judicial decision terminating a criminal proceeding by judgment of **conviction** or **acquittal**, or a **dismissal** of the case. See JUDGMENT for a list of related terms. **3.** The juvenile court decision, terminating an **adjudicatory hearing** that the **juvenile** is either a **delinquent, status offender**, or **dependent,** or that the **petition is not sustained**. An adjudication that a juvenile is a delinquent is similar to a **conviction** in a criminal court, in that a court has made a finding that the juvenile has committed an act that could be prosecuted as a crime if the juvenile were an adult. An adjudication that the petition is not sustained is similar to an **acquittal** in a criminal court. See JUVENILE for a list of related terms.

ADJUDICATION WITHHELD. A court decision at any point after filing of a criminal **complaint**, to continue court **jurisdiction** but stop short of pronouncing **judgment**. The usual purpose in stopping criminal proceedings short of judgment is avoidance of the undesirable effects of conviction, including unnecessary harm to the offender and unnecessary expense or harm to the public interest. Withholding adjudication places the subject in a status where the court retains jurisdiction but will not reopen proceedings unless the person violates a condition of behavior.

ADJUDICATORY HEARING. In juvenile proceedings, the fact-finding process wherein the **juvenile court** determines whether or not there is sufficient evidence to **sustain** the allegations in a **juvenile petition**. An adjudicatory hearing occurs after a juvenile petition has been filed and after a **detention hearing**, if one is necessary. If the petition is not sustained, no further formal court action is taken. If the petition is sustained, the next step is a **disposition hearing** to determine the most appropriate treatment or care for the juvenile. These last two stages of judicial activity concerning juveniles are often combined in a single hearing, referred to as a **bifurcated hearing**, meaning a process that encompasses both adjudication of the case and disposition of the person. An adjudicatory hearing concerning an alleged **delinquent** is analogous to the **trial** in criminal proceedings, since both proceedings determine matters of fact concerning alleged acts in violation of criminal law. An adjudication that a juvenile is a delinquent requires proof **beyond a reasonable doubt**. An adjudication that a juvenile is a **status offender** requires that the **preponderance of the evidence** supports the allegations in the petition. See HEARING, JUVENILE, and TRIAL for lists of related terms.

AD JUDICIUM. *Latin.* To judgment; to court.

ADJUNCT. Something added to another thing, without becoming an essential part of it.

ADJURATION. A swearing upon oath.

ADJUST. To settle; to place in order; to bring to a satisfactory state.

AD LITEM. *Latin.* For the purposes of the suit. *See:* GUARDIAN AD LITEM.

AD MANUM. *Latin.* At hand; ready for use.

ADMINICULAR. Auxiliary; subordinate; corroborative.

ADMINISTER. **1.** To manage; to conduct; to direct. *Example:* Administer a drug rehabilitation program. **2.** Furnish; apply; give; dispense. *Example:* Administer an oath. Administer poison.

ADMINISTRATIVE. **1. Ministerial**; leaving nothing to discretion. **2.** Pertaining to the managing, conducting, or directing of persons or things. When administrative is applied to the managing of government, it refers to the duties of the executive department, which carries out the policies and purposes already declared by the legislative department, plus other inherent duties of the executive.

ADMINISTRATIVE AGENCY. An organ of government, other than a court or legislature, which carries out laws and policies enacted by legislative bodies and which may affect the rights of private parties through either adjudication or rule-making. An administrative agency may be called an administration, agency, board, bureau, commission, corporation, department, division, or office.

ADMINISTRATIVE LAW. The law governing the powers and procedures of **administrative agencies**.

ADMINISTRATIVE PROCEDURE. The methods and processes followed by **administrative agencies** in carrying out the law. Administrative procedure is different from and usually more informal than **civil procedure** or **criminal procedure**.

ADMINISTRATIVE REMEDY. A remedy provided by an **administrative agency**. An administrative remedy is not a **judicial remedy**.

ADMIRALTY. Pertaining to all transactions and proceedings relative to commerce and navigation and to damages and injuries upon the sea.

ADMISSIBLE. Pertinent and proper to be considered in reaching a decision. *See:* ADMISSIBLE EVIDENCE.

ADMISSIBLE EVIDENCE. Evidence of such character that a court is bound to receive it or allow it to be introduced to prove a fact in issue. In order to be admissible, evidence must be **competent**, **relevant** (see **relevant evidence**), **material**, and the circumstances surrounding the obtaining and offering of the evidence must not violate public policy. See EVIDENCE for a list of related terms.

ADMISSION. **n. 1.** Generally, a statement or acknowledgment of a fact that is against the interest of the party making it. **n.2.** A statement or acknowledgment of a fact by a person tending to incriminate the person but not sufficient of itself to establish guilt of a crime. An admission, alone or in connection with other facts, tends to show the existence of one or more, but not all, of the **elements of a crime**. *See:* CONFESSION. **n. 3.** The act or state of being accepted or received. *Examples:* Admission to the bar is the formal acceptance of an attorney to the practice of law. Admission of **evidence** is the acceptance of evidence for consideration by the court or jury. **n.4.** In correctional usage, the entry of an offender into the legal **jurisdiction** of a **corrections agency** and/or physical custody of a **correctional facility**. **v.** ADMIT.

ADMONITION. **1.** Oral advice given by a **court** to a **jury** regarding the jurors' duties or conduct, the admissibility of evidence, or limitations on the purposes for which evidence may be considered. **2.** A statement by a judge, before accepting the **plea** of an accused, informing the accused of the consequences of a **guilty plea**. **3.** A warning or reprimand from a judge to a person being discharged from an accusation that a repetition of the unlawful behavior will result in a more severe punishment.

ADOPT. To accept formally; to endorse and assume official responsibility for. *See:* RATIFY.

ADOPTIVE ADMISSION. An accusatory statement made in the presence of a person, which is deemed to be adopted or acquiesced in by the person because of his or her silence or equivocal response. *Also called:* **tacit admission**.

ADULT. **1.** A person who, because he or she has attained a certain age, usually eighteen, is considered under the law to be able to manage his or her own affairs. **2.** A person who is within the **original jurisdiction** of a criminal, rather than a juvenile, court because his or her age at the time of an alleged criminal act was above a statutorily specified limit. The assumption of jurisdiction by a criminal or juvenile court is based on the person's age at the time of the occurrence of the alleged offense or offenses, and not the age at the time of **arrest** or of initiation of court proceedings. A juvenile court may waive jurisdiction and transfer a juvenile to a criminal court for prosecution as an adult. However, the available sentencing dispositions may exclude commitment to adult prisons. The age at which a person becomes an adult varies among the different states. *See:* JUVENILE; YOUTHFUL OFFENDER.

ADULT AUTHORITY. *See:* PAROLE AUTHORITY.

ADULTERATE.   To make something impure or inferior by adding a foreign or improper substance.

ADULTERY.   Voluntary **sexual intercourse** between a married person and someone not his or her spouse. Statutory definitions of the offense called adultery vary. Sometimes only a married participant has committed an offense. In some jurisdictions, this type of behavior is not criminal. See SEX OFFENSES for a list of related terms.

AD VALOREM.   *Latin.* In proportion to the value.

ADVANCE.   **1.** To propose or bring forward something contentious (a theory, a claim, an argument) for acceptance or consideration. See ADDRESS for a list of related terms. **2.** To supply something before it is due. **3.** To move forward; to hasten.

ADVANCE SHEETS.   Paperback pamphlets containing recently decided opinions of federal or state **appellate courts** in a particular region. Cases appearing in advance sheets are eventually published in hardbound volumes. The National Reporter System, published by West Publishing Company, St. Paul, Minnesota, is the most comprehensive collection of appellate court decisions of state and federal courts.

ADVANTAGE.   A favorable condition or circumstance.

ADVENTITIOUS.   Acquired by accident or by chance.

ADVENTURE.   A hazardous undertaking of uncertain outcome.

ADVERSARY.   Opponent; the opposite party in a legal action.

ADVERSARY JUDICIAL CRIMINAL PROCEEDING.   Same as ADVERSARY JUDICIAL PROCEEDING.

ADVERSARY JUDICIAL PROCEEDING.   A contested proceeding having opposing parties. In the criminal law, an adversary judicial proceeding is initiated by formal **charge**, **preliminary hearing**, **indictment**, **information**, or **arraignment**. The determination of the point of initiation of an adversary judicial criminal proceeding is important because a suspect's Sixth Amendment right to **assistance of counsel** attaches at that time. *Kirby v. Illinois*, 406 U.S. 682, 92 S.Ct. 1877, 32 L.Ed.2d 411 (1972).

ADVERSARY SYSTEM.   A judicial system characterized by opposing parties who contend against each other for a result favorable to themselves in the presence of a **judge**, who acts as an independent referee rather than as a **prosecutor**. The competing parties have the principal responsibility for gathering **evidence**, formulating legal theories, and presenting the evidence and theories at trial. The justice system of the United States is an adversary system. See TRIAL for a list of related terms.

ADVERSE. Opposed; against; hostile.

ADVERSE PARTY. **1.** In an **appeal**, a party to an action whose interests would be adversely affected by a **reversal** or **modification** of the judgment or order on appeal. An adverse party is entitled to notice of appeal. **2.** The party on the opposite side of a legal action.

ADVERSE WITNESS. A witness who exhibits hostility or prejudice toward the party calling the witness on **direct examination**. The general rule is that a witness cannot be cross-examined by the party calling the witness. There is an exception to the rule, however, where a witness is determined by the court to be an adverse witness. *Also called:* **hostile witness**. See WITNESS for a list of related terms.

ADVICE. **n.** Opinion; recommendation; suggestion; counsel. Advice does not require obedience. **adj.** ADVISORY

ADVISE. To offer or give ADVICE.

ADVISEMENT. Careful consideration; deliberation. A court takes a case under advisement after it has heard the arguments of opposing counsel but before it renders a decision.

ADVISORY. In the nature of ADVICE.

ADVISORY OPINION. A formal opinion prepared by a court on a question of law submitted by a legislative body, a governmental official, or other interested party, but not actually presented in a concrete legal action. Advisory opinions are not **precedents** and are not **res judicata**. Many courts refuse to issue advisory opinions for policy reasons. Federal courts do not issue advisory opinions because their jurisdiction is limited to cases and **controversies**. See OPINION for a list of related terms.

AD VITAM. *Latin.* "For life."

ADVOCATE. **v.** To speak in favor of; to support or recommend publicly. **n. 1.** One who assists, defends, or pleads for another. **n. 2.** An ATTORNEY AT LAW.

AD VOLUNTATEM. *Latin.* "At will."

ADW. Abbreviation for ASSAULT WITH A DEADLY WEAPON.

AESTHETIC. Pertaining to that which is beautiful or in good taste.

AFFECT. To influence; to act on; to change.

AFFIANT. A person who makes and signs an AFFIDAVIT.

AFFIDAVIT. A written statement sworn to or affirmed before an officer authorized to administer an oath or affirmation. An affidavit may be distinguished from a deposition in some contexts in that an affidavit requires no notice to the adverse party or opportunity for cross-examination. In the criminal law, affidavits are used by law enforcement officers and others to provide information to a magistrate to establish **probable cause** for the issuance of an **arrest warrant** or a **search warrant**. An affidavit need not be prepared with any particular formality. If a law enforcement officer knowingly and intentionally, or with reckless disregard for the truth, makes false statements in an affidavit supporting a request for a search warrant, the warrant may not be issued or evidence seized under the warrant may be suppressed. *Franks v. Delaware*, 438 U.S. 154, 98 S.Ct. 2674, 57 L.Ed.2d 667 (1978). In addition, if a warrant application is so lacking in indicia of probable cause as to render official belief in its existence unreasonable, the officer making the affidavit may be held liable for damages in a **civil action**. See ACCUSATION, ARREST, and SEARCH for lists of related terms.

AFFILIATION. Close association; alliance.

AFFINITY. **1.** A natural liking for or attraction to a person or thing. **2.** The relationship between a spouse and the blood relations of the other spouse. *See:* CONSANGUINITY.

AFFIRM. **1.** To state positively and with firm conviction. See ADDRESS for a list of related terms. **2.** To testify or declare by AFFIRMATION (definition 2). **3.** To ratify; to confirm. When an appellate court affirms a judgment, decree, or order of a lower court, it declares that that judgment, decree, or order is valid and correct and must stand as decided.

AFFIRMANCE. **1.** A confirmation by an appellate court of the validity and correctness of a judgment, decree, or order of a lower court. **2.** A decision by a person to deal with an unauthorized act done in his or her behalf as though it were authorized.

AFFIRMANT. A person who testifies on AFFIRMATION (definition 2).

AFFIRMATION. **1.** A positive statement. **2.** A solemn declaration made under the penalties of **perjury** by a person who conscientiously declines to take an **oath**. *See:* FALSE OATH; FALSE SWEARING; FORSWEAR; OATH; PERJURY; SUBORNATION OF PERJURY; UNSWORN FALSIFICATION.

AFFIRMATIVE. Asserting that the fact is so; positive; assertive; the opposite of negative.

AFFIRMATIVE DEFENSE. A substantive law **defense** by which a defendant avoids liability for a crime by showing that he or she did not have the mental state required for the crime charged, the behavior was justified, or the behavior fell within a statutory exception to a particular crime. Examples of affirmative defenses are **insanity** (lack of required mental state), **self-defense** (justification), and marriage to a rape victim (statutory exception). In an affirmative defense, the defendant does not simply deny the accusation, but offers new evidence that is claimed to be legally sufficient to excuse the defendant.

AFFIRMATIVE PROOF. **Evidence** establishing a fact in dispute by a **preponderance of the evidence**, regardless of whether the evidence is direct or circumstantial. See EVIDENCE for a list of related terms.

AFFIRMATIVE STATUTE. A **statute** that declares what shall be done or directs the performance of an act. See STATUTE for a list of related terms.

AFFIX. **1.** To attach securely or physically. **2.** To attach in any way; to connect to; to impress upon; to inscribe.

AFFLICTION. A condition of pain, suffering, or distress.

AFFORCE. To strengthen; to increase; to add to.

AFFRAY. The fighting of two or more persons in a public place causing terror to the public. An affray is a type of **disorderly conduct** and is a **breach of the peace**. An affray differs from a **riot** or a **duel** in that an affray is not premeditated. *See:* CRIMINAL MISCHIEF; DISORDERLY CONDUCT; DISORDERLY HOUSE; DISTURBING THE PEACE; DUEL; INCITING TO RIOT; LOITER; RIOT; ROUT; UNLAWFUL ASSEMBLY; VAGRANT.

AFFRONT. A personally offensive act or statement.

AFORESAID. Previously said or mentioned. *Also called:* **foresaid**; **said**.

AFORETHOUGHT. Premeditated; deliberate; thought of beforehand for any length of time. *See:* MALICE AFORETHOUGHT.

A FORTIORI. *Latin.* For a still stronger reason; all the more. This term is used before a statement that is more certain or more necessary than a comparable statement preceding it.

AFTER.   Following in time or place; later than; behind; below in rank.

AFTERCARE.   The status or program membership of a **juvenile** who has been committed to a treatment or confinement facility, conditionally released from the facility, and placed in a supervisory and/or treatment program. In a few states, aftercare status does not exist for juveniles. *Also called:* **juvenile parole**. See JUVENILE and PAROLE for a list of related terms.

AFTER-DISCOVERED EVIDENCE.   Same as NEWLY DISCOVERED EVIDENCE.

AGAINST.   Opposed to; contrary to; in resistance to; contrasted to.

AGAINST THE WILL.   With utmost reluctance; with the greatest resistance. Against the will is an essential element of the crime of **rape**. *Also called:* **without consent**.

AGE.   **1.** The length of time a person has lived. **2.** Same as AGE OF MAJORITY. **3.** The particular period of life at which one becomes naturally or conventionally qualified or disqualified for something. *Example:* Past the age for military service.

AGENCY.   **1.** A legal relationship entered with the mutual consent of two parties in which one party (the AGENT) acts for or represents the other party (the PRINCIPAL) by authority of the principal. *See:* GENERAL AGENCY; SPECIAL AGENCY. **2.** The place of business of an agent. **3.** *See:* ADMINISTRATIVE AGENCY.

AGENT.   A person authorized by another person (the PRINCIPAL) to act for or represent him or her. An agent of a corporation or unincorporated association is defined by Section 2.07(4)(b) of the **Model Penal Code** as "any director, officer, servant, employee or other person authorized to act in behalf of the corporation or association and, in the case of an unincorporated association, a member of such association."

AGE OF CONSENT.   The age at which a female is legally capable of consenting to **sexual intercourse**, so that a male who has sexual intercourse with her cannot be prosecuted for **statutory rape**.

AGE OF MAJORITY.   *See:* MAJORITY.

AGGRAVATED.   More severe; more offensive; more serious; heavier.

AGGRAVATED ASSAULT.   **1.** An ASSAULT committed with the intention of committing some other crime (such as murder, rape, or robbery). **2.** An assault committed under particularly outrageous circumstances. Under modern statutes that include **battery** within the definition of assault, aggravated assault may include the unlawful intentional inflicting of **serious bodily injury** with or without a **deadly**

weapon or the unlawful intentional attempting or threatening of serious bodily injury or death with a deadly weapon. Police agencies customarily count as an aggravated assault any assault causing an injury that requires medical treatment beyond first aid, such as broken bones, loss of teeth, internal injuries, injuries requiring stitches, and loss of consciousness. See ASSAULT for a list of related terms.

NOTE: The term aggravated assault is not only subject to varying definitions, but the behavior that it encompasses is given different names in different jurisdictions. Examples of terms that may be synonymous or nearly synonymous with aggravated assault are **aggravated assault and battery**, **aggravated battery**, **assault with a deadly weapon**, **assault with intent to commit murder or manslaughter**, **atrocious assault**, **attempted murder**, and **felonious assault**.

AGGRAVATED ASSAULT AND BATTERY. See note under AGGRAVATED ASSAULT.

AGGRAVATED BATTERY. See note under AGGRAVATED ASSAULT.

AGGRAVATED MISDEMEANOR. *See:* SERIOUS MISDEMEANOR.

AGGRAVATED SENTENCE. A SENTENCE in which the penalty is greater than the norm for the offense. See SENTENCE for a list of related terms.

AGGRAVATING CIRCUMSTANCES. Circumstances accompanying the commission of a crime that increase its seriousness or outrageousness and are above and beyond the essential **elements** of the crime. Examples of aggravating circumstances are causing **serious bodily injury**, using a **deadly weapon**, or accidentally or intentionally committing one crime in the course of committing another crime or as a means to commit another crime. Aggravating circumstances may be formally or informally considered by a judge or paroling authority in deciding the **sentence** for a convicted person within the penalty range provided by statute for a given offense.

The behavior and circumstances that constitute an aggravated form of an offense are also often explicitly defined in penal codes and provided with a more severe penalty range than that of the basic offense. One way this is expressed is through the structure common to most penal codes establishing different **degrees** within a given type of offense, with different penalties attached. Another way is through the provision of separate code sections defining "aggravated" offenses, for example, "aggravated robbery" vs. "robbery." In some codes both structures appear. *Also called:* **aggravation**. *See:* DANGEROUS PERSON; MANDATORY SENTENCE; MITIGATING CIRCUMSTANCES.

AGGRAVATION. Same as AGGRAVATING CIRCUMSTANCES.

AGGREGATE. The combination of many persons or things united together; the complete whole; the total amount.

AGGREGATE MAXIMUM RELEASE DATE. The calendar date on which a given offender should be fully discharged on all **sentences** currently in effect in that jurisdiction. See SENTENCE for a list of related terms.

AGGRESSOR. The party who first offers force or violence.

AGGRIEVED. **1.** Substantially wronged or offended. **2.** Treated unjustly with respect to a substantial right by a court or other legal authority.

AGGRIEVED PARTY. **1.** A person who is entitled to bring a lawsuit against another because the person's legal rights have been violated. **2.** A party whose rights have been directly and substantially injured by a court's action.

AGITATOR. One who stirs up others to arouse their interest in a cause.

AGONY. Extreme physical or mental suffering.

AGREE. To concur; to harmonize; to be of one opinion; to come to an understanding.

AGREED STATEMENT OF FACTS. A statement of facts, accepted by the parties as true and correct, to be submitted to a court for a ruling on the law of the case. See FACT for a list of related terms.

AGREEMENT. **1.** A coming together of minds on a given proposition. **2.** Mutual assent of two or more persons to do something. **3.** An expression of understanding and intention between two or more parties with respect to their relative rights and duties. *See:* CONTRACT.

AGUILAR v. TEXAS. *See*: ILLINOIS v. GATES.

AID. To render assistance. To aid in the commission of a crime is, while present at the time and place of the crime, to render assistance to the actual **perpetrator** of the crime without taking part in the commission of the crime. To aid in the commission of a crime does not necessarily require criminal **intent**. See PARTY for a list of related terms.

AID AND ABET. Same as ABET.

AID AND COMFORT. Support; assistance; encouragement. Giving aid and comfort to enemies of the United States is an intentional act strengthening or tending to strengthen those enemies or weakening or tending to weaken the power of the United States to resist and attack those enemies. Giving aid and comfort to enemies of the United States is an element in the crime of **treason**.

AIDER. One who aids. *See:* AID.

AIDER BY VERDICT. The correction, by the rendering of the **verdict**, of technical errors or defects in a **pleading**, **indictment**, or **information** that might have been objected to before the verdict. Rules of criminal procedure permit aider by verdict only when the errors or defects are immaterial and do not impair a defendant's constitutional rights. See ERROR and VERDICT for lists of related terms.

AIM. **n.** Purpose; object. **v.** With intent and careful calculation, to turn or direct toward the exact spot or object intended to be hit. *Example:* To aim a pistol at a target. *See:* POINT.

AIRCRAFT PIRACY. "[A]ny seizure or exercise of control, by force or violence or threat of force or violence, or by any other form of intimidation, and with wrongful intent, of an aircraft within the special aircraft jurisdiction of the United States." 49 U.S.C. §1472(i).

A.K.A. Abbreviation for "also known as." *See:* ALIAS.

ALCOHOL. A product of the fermentation of starches and sugars. Alcohol is the basis for all intoxicating liquors. See INTOXICATION for a list of related terms.

ALCOHOLIC. **adj.** Pertaining to or containing alcohol. **n.** A person who habitually lacks self-control as to the use of alcoholic beverages, or uses alcoholic beverages to the extent that the person's health is substantially impaired or endangered or the person's social or economic function is substantially disrupted.

ALCOHOLISM. A chronic disease with both physical and mental symptoms resulting from the excessive use of intoxicating liquors.

ALCOHOL, TOBACCO AND FIREARMS, BUREAU OF. The Bureau of Alcohol, Tobacco and Firearms in the **Department of the Treasury** was established by Treasury Department Order No. 221, effective July 1, 1972. The order transferred the functions, powers, and duties arising under laws relating to alcohol, tobacco, firearms, and explosives from the Internal Revenue Service to the Bureau. On December 5, 1978, Treasury Department Order No. 120-1 assigned to the Bureau responsibility for enforcing chapter 114 of title 18 of the United States Code (18 U.S.C. §2341 et seq.) relating to interstate trafficking in contraband cigarettes. With passage of the Anti-Arson Act of 1982, the Bureau was given the additional responsibility of addressing commercial arson nationwide.

Bureau headquarters is located in Washington, D.C., but since the Bureau is decentralized, most of its personnel are stationed throughout the country, where many of its operational functions are performed. The Director is appointed by the Secretary of the Treasury and is under the supervision of the Assistant Secretary (Enforcement).

The Bureau is responsible for enforcing and administering firearms and explosives laws, as well as those covering the production, use, and distribution of alcohol and tobacco products. The objective of the Bureau's programs is to maximize compliance and investigate violations of those laws. To achieve these goals, the Bureau is divided into two basic functions: law enforcement and compliance operations.

The objectives of the law enforcement activity are to:

—eliminate illegal trafficking, possession, and use of firearms, destructive devices, and explosives;

—investigate and prevent arson-for-profit schemes;

—investigate narcotics traffickers who use firearms and explosives as tools of their trade;

—suppress interstate trafficking in contraband cigarettes; and

—assist federal, state, and local law enforcement agencies in reducing crime and violence.

The compliance operations activity:

—determines and ensures full collection of revenue due from legal alcohol, tobacco, and firearms industries;

—fulfills the Bureau's responsibility in product integrity, health warning statements, the prevention of commercial bribery, consumer deception, and other improper trade practices in the beverage alcohol industry;

—assists other federal, state, and local governmental agencies in the resolution of problems relating to revenue protection;

—ensures that persons prohibited by law from manufacturing, importing, or dealing in alcohol, tobacco, firearms, and explosives do not obtain a license or permit;

—ensures that storage facilities for explosives are safe and secure, to avoid presenting a hazard to the public, and that explosives are properly stored in such facilities; and

—ensures that the audit trail is preserved to permit the tracing of firearms used in the commission of crimes and full accountability for explosive materials.

ALFORD PLEA.   A common law **plea** under which a defendant pleads **guilty** with the acknowledgment that the plea is not due to guilt but is made for other considerations, such as the promise of prosecutorial leniency.

ALIA.   *Latin.* "Other things."

ALIAS.   *Latin.* **n.** Any name used for an official purpose that is different from a person's correct legal name. In criminal history records, an alias may be designated by A.K.A., an abbreviation for "also known as." An alias is a false name that has been substituted for a correct legal name on such documents as a driver's license or a check, or a false name established for the purpose of such a substitution. **adj.** At another time. The term alias is used as an adjective to refer to various judicial writs or orders. Thus, an alias **execution**, **subpoena**, **summons**, **warrant**, or **writ** is one issued after the original has not accomplished its purpose.

ALIAS DICTUS. *Latin.* "Otherwise called."

ALIBI. The defense of a person accused of crime that he or she was not at the place where the crime was committed at the time of its commission.

ALIEN. A person born outside of the United States and not naturalized under our Constitution and laws; a noncitizen.

ALIENATE. To voluntarily convey or transfer (title, property, or right) to another.

ALIENIST. A doctor who specializes in mental diseases; a psychiatrist.

ALI INSANITY TEST. Same as SUBSTANTIAL CAPACITY TEST.

ALIKE. Similar to another. *See:* IDENTICAL.

ALITER. Otherwise.

ALIUNDE. *Latin.* From elsewhere; from another source. With respect to documents, evidence aliunde is evidence from sources beyond the language of the document itself that explains the document, when the document's provisions are unclear or ambiguous

ALIVE. **1.** Living. **2.** In force or operation; active.

ALL. **adj.** The entire number, amount, or quantity of. **n.** The whole number; the totality.

ALLEGATION. **1.** A statement of a party to an action, made in **pleading**, setting out what he or she intends to prove. **2.** A statement in a **complaint**, **indictment**, or **information** that the accused has violated a particular law. **3.** Something alleged. *See:* ALLEGE.

ALLEGE. **v.** To bring forward or state without offering proof. The term allege sometimes conveys doubt about or disclaimer of responsibility for the truth of the matter stated. **n.** ALLEGATION. See ADDRESS for a list of related terms.

ALLEGED DELINQUENT. A JUVENILE, **alleged** but not **adjudged** to have committed a **delinquent act**. See JUVENILE for a list of related terms.

ALLEGED OFFENDER. A person who has been charged with a specific criminal offense by a law enforcement agency or court, but whose case has not reached judgment. See ACCUSED for a list of related terms.

ALLEGED STATUS OFFENDER. A JUVENILE **alleged** but not **adjudged** to have committed a **status offense**. See JUVENILE for a list of related terms.

ALLEGIANCE. The obedience or fidelity a citizen owes to the government under which he or she lives.

ALLEN CHARGE. An INSTRUCTION to a **jury** having a difficult time reaching a **verdict** that each juror should consider the arguments and reasons of the other jurors and not take an inflexible position. An Allen charge is given to encourage deadlocked juries to reach agreement. *Also called:* **dynamite charge**; **nitroglycerin charge**; **shotgun instruction**; **third-degree instruction**. See INSTRUCTION for a list of related terms.

ALL FOURS. *See:* ON ALL FOURS.

ALLOCATE. **1.** To designate for a particular purpose or to a particular place. **2.** To give out shares or portions to members of a group by someone in authority according to a plan. *See:* ALLOT; APPORTION; ASSIGN; CIRCULATE; DEAL; DISPENSE; DISTRIBUTE; DIVIDE; DOLE; PORTION; PRORATE; RATION.

ALLOCUTION. A formal inquiry by a judge to a person convicted of a crime as to whether the person can show any legal cause why **judgment** should not be pronounced against him or her on the **verdict**, or whether the person has anything to say to the court before sentencing. *See:* SENTENCE.

ALLOT. To give out shares or portions to members of a group by someone in authority, with the implication of matching items on one list with those on another, but with no suggestion of fair or equal distribution. See ALLOCATE for a list of related terms.

ALLOW. **1.** Permit. **2.** To admit or acknowledge.

ALLUDE. To refer indirectly or casually. See ADDRESS for a list of related terms.

ALTER. To modify; to change something without converting it into something else or destroying its identity.

ALTERCATION. A heated quarrel or controversy.

ALTERNATIVE. Affording a choice of two or more mutually exclusive things.

ALTERNATIVE PLEADING. A PLEADING that alleges mutually exclusive facts, claims, or defenses so that it cannot be determined upon which the pleader intends to rely. Modern rules governing pleading in courts specifically allow alternative pleading. This allows both parties to plead in the alternative and leaves it to the court to decide from all the facts and theories presented. See PLEADING for a list of related terms.

ALTERNATIVE WRIT. A **writ** commanding the person to whom it is issued to perform a specified act or to **show cause** to the court why he or she should not be compelled to do it.

A.M. Abbreviation for ANTE MERIDIEM.

AMBIGUOUS. Uncertain; doubtful; susceptible to more than one meaning.

AMBULATORY. **1.** Revocable; capable of being altered or changed. **2.** Moving from place to place; movable.

AMBUSH. To attack from a concealed position.

AMELIORATION. Improvement.

AMENABLE. **1.** Accountable; answerable. **2.** Willing to follow advice or suggestion.

AMEND. **1.** To improve; to correct; to rectify. **2.** To alter (a pleading or legislative bill, for example) by adding, deleting, or rephrasing. *See:* DEROGATION; REPEAL.

A MENSA ET THORO. *Latin.* "From bed and board." A term used to describe a limited type of divorce, sometimes called a legal separation. In this type of divorce, the parties remain legally married and neither may legally remarry, but they are relieved from all obligations and rights as to cohabitation.

AMERCEMENT. **1.** A money penalty imposed arbitrarily. **2.** A money penalty imposed by a court upon its own officers for some misconduct or neglect of duty. *See:* FINE.

AMICABLE ACTION. Same as CASE AGREED ON.

AMICUS CURIAE. *Latin.* "Friend of the court." A person interested in, but not a **party** (definition 2) to, an action, who volunteers or is allowed to give advice to the court upon some matter pending before it. The written argument submitted by such a person is called an amicus curiae **brief**.

AMNESIA. Loss of memory.

AMNESTY. A kind of **pardon** granted by a sovereign authority, often before any **indictment**, **trial**, or **conviction**, to a group of persons who have committed offenses against the government, which not only frees them from **prosecution** or **punishment**, but has the effect of removing all legal recognition that the offenses occurred. A pardon is distinct from an amnesty in that the former applies to only one person, and does not necessarily include the abolition of all legal recognition that the offense occurred. An amnesty is sometimes called a **general pardon** because it applies to all offenders of a given class, or all offenses against a given statute or during a certain time period. The sovereign authority may be executive or legislative. See CLEMENCY for a list of related terms.

AMONG. **1.** In the midst of; in the company of; intermingled with. **2.** To each of; for distribution to. **3.** Involving; concerning. *Example:* A choice among several alternatives. Among is sometimes said to be the equivalent of **between**, but among implies more than two objects, whereas between implies only two.

AMPLIATION. The action of a judge in deferring a cause for further examination. *See:* CONTINUANCE.

ANAESTHESIA. Insensibility to pain or other sensation. *Also spelled*: **anesthesia**.

ANALOGOUS. Similar in some way or ways.

ANARCHY. A state of society in which there is no government or law or in which there is violent resistance to the existing government resulting in political disorder and lawlessness. Criminal anarchy is the doctrine that organized government should be destroyed by violence and other unlawful methods.

ANCIENT. Old; existing from a long time ago.

ANCILLARY. Auxiliary to or subordinate to that which is principal or primary.

ANCILLARY JURISDICTION. The authority of a court to hear and decide matters that are incidental to the exercise of the court's primary authority to act in a particular case and that the court would not otherwise be authorized to hear and decide if independently presented. See JURISDICTION for a list of related terms.

AND. Added to; together with; joined with; as well as.

ANESTHESIA. Same as ANAESTHESIA.

ANEW. From the beginning; once more. *Example:* To try a case or issue anew implies that it has been tried before.

ANGER. A strong passion or emotion of displeasure caused by a real or supposed injury or insult.

ANGUISH. Extreme pain or distress.

ANIMAL. A living creature, other than a human, with the power of voluntary motion.

ANIMATE. Living; alive; possessing life.

ANIMUS. *Latin.* "Mind; intention."

ANIMUS FURANDI. *Latin.* "Intent to steal."

ANNEX. To physically join; to attach; to fasten.

ANNOTATION. A note explaining, commenting upon, or criticizing a passage in a book or other writing. *Example:* In statute books, an annotation is a commentary on the meaning of the wording of a statute.

ANNOUNCE. To proclaim officially; to make known publicly. *Example:* A court's decision has been announced when the court makes the decision formally known either by oral declaration or written publication.

ANNOYANCE. Irritation; discomfort.

ANNUAL. Yearly; performed or happening every year.

ANNUL. **1.** To make void; to cancel; to abolish. **2.** To obliterate; to annihilate.

ANOMALOUS. Abnormal; irregular; deviating from the normal rule or order.

ANON. Abbreviation for ANONYMOUS.

ANONYMOUS. Having or giving no name; of unknown or unnamed origin.

ANOTHER. **1.** Additional. **2.** Different; distinct.

ANSWER. In **civil actions** the formal written statement in response to the plaintiff's complaint, by which a defendant either denies the allegations of the complaint or acknowledges them and asserts additional reasons why the plaintiff should be prevented from recovering on the facts alleged.

ANTE. *Latin.* "Before."

ANTECEDENT. Preceding; prior.

ANTEDATE. **1.** To precede in time. **2.** To assign a date earlier than the actual date. *Example:* To antedate a check.

ANTE MERIDIEM. *Latin.* "Before noon." The time period from twelve midnight to twelve noon. *Abbreviation:* **A.M.**

ANTICIPATE. **1.** To do something before the proper or normal time. **2.** To foresee; to realize beforehand.

ANTICIPATORY OFFENSE. Same as INCHOATE OFFENSE.

ANTINOMY. Contradiction; opposition.

ANTITRUST DIVISION. The Antitrust Division of the **Department of Justice** is responsible for promoting and maintaining competitive markets by enforcing the federal antitrust laws. Such enforcement, which is the principal function of the division, involves investigating possible antitrust violations, conducting grand jury proceedings, preparing and trying antitrust cases, prosecuting appeals, and negotiating and enforcing final judgments. The antitrust laws affect virtually all industries and apply to every phase of business, including manufacturing, transportation, distribution, and marketing. They prohibit a variety of practices that restrain trade, such as price-fixing conspiracies, corporate mergers likely to reduce the competitive vigor of particular markets, and predatory acts designed to achieve or maintain monopoly power. The division prosecutes serious and willful violations of the antitrust laws by filing criminal suits that can lead to large fines and jail sentences. Where criminal prosecution is not appropriate, the division seeks a court order forbidding future violations of the law and requiring steps by the defendant to remedy the anticompetitive effects of past violations.

ANUM. Same as ANUS.

ANUS. The excretory opening at the lower end of the alimentary canal, located between the buttocks.

ANY. **1.** All; every; each. **2.** Some; several; one or more. **3.** A; an; either; one out of many.
NOTE: The term any has several meanings and its meaning in a given situation depends on the context in which it is used.

APARTMENT. A room or suite of rooms, designed for dwelling purposes, in a building containing other such rooms or suites.

APARTMENT HOUSE. A building containing **apartments** and having certain conveniences such as heat, light, and elevator services furnished in common.

A POSTERIORI. *Latin.* Based upon experimental data or actual observation. This term is used to describe a type of reasoning (also called **inductive reasoning**) that proceeds from facts or particulars to general principles or from effects to causes. *See:* A PRIORI.

APPARATUS. Implements or equipment used for the accomplishment of some purpose. *Example:* Gambling apparatus.

APPARENT. **adj.** Plain; evident; obvious; clearly understood.

APPARENT AGENCY. An AGENCY in which the AGENT has APPARENT AUTHORITY to act for or represent the PRINCIPAL.

APPARENT AGENT. An AGENT who has APPARENT AUTHORITY.

APPARENT AUTHORITY. AUTHORITY (definition 1) not actually conferred by a PRINCIPAL upon an AGENT, but which the principal knowingly allows the agent to exercise or which the principal holds the agent out to others as possessing. *Also called:* **ostensible authority**.

APPARENT DANGER. In the law of **self-defense**, apparent danger is a set of circumstances created by the unlawful acts of an aggressor that cause a person to reasonably believe that he or she must use **deadly force** against the aggressor to prevent the person's own death or **serious bodily injury**. *Also called:* **apparent necessity**.

APPARENT NECESSITY. Same as APPARENT DANGER.

APPEAL. An application to or proceeding in an **appellate court** for review or re-hearing of a **judgment**, **decision**, or **order** of a lower court or other tribunal in order to correct alleged **errors** or injustices in the trial below. A successful appeal results in the **reversal** or **modification** of the lower court judgment, decision, or order. An appeal may be either on the record of the proceedings below or **de novo**. In an appeal on the record only, matters of law may be reviewed. In an appeal de novo, matters of fact as well as law may be reviewed.

The rules governing circumstances in which an appeal is permitted, and in which a hearing is guaranteed, are complex and differ from state to state. They vary according to the type of case (e.g., civil vs. criminal), whether the appeal is by the defendant or by the plaintiff or prosecution, and the specific grounds for appeal.

The major steps in appeal proceedings are:

1. The appeal is initiated by the filing of a formal document in the **appellate court**.

2. A record of the original proceedings in the trial court (**transcript**) is obtained by the appellate court.

3. **Briefs** are filed in court by the opposing parties (**appellant** and **respondent**).

4. If there are to be oral arguments, a hearing is scheduled and the arguments heard.

5. Following completion of arguments or submission of briefs, the court deliberates, reviewing the record of the earlier proceedings and considering the allegations and arguments of the parties, and announces its decision in the case.

6. The possible decisions are (a) the appeal is **dismissed**; (b) the trial court judgment is **reversed**, **affirmed**, or **modified**; or (c) the case is **remanded** to the trial court for entry of a proper judgment, for further proceedings, or for a **new trial**. A given criminal appeal case disposition may be a combination of these alternatives, for example, reversed and remanded. This decision may be embodied in an **opinion** which also gives the reasons for the decision

See: ADVERSE PARTY; APPEAL OF RIGHT; APPELLANT; APPELLATE; APPELLATE BRIEF; APPELLATE COURT; APPELLATE JUDGE; APPELLATE JURISDICTION; APPELLEE; ASSIGNMENT OF ERRORS; AUTOMATIC APPEAL; BILL OF EXCEPTIONS; BRIEF; COLLATERAL ATTACK; COURT OF APPEALS; COURT OF LAST RESORT; DEFENDANT IN ERROR; DIRECT ATTACK; DISCRETIONARY REVIEW; ERROR; EXCEPTION; HABEAS CORPUS; INTERLOCUTORY APPEAL; INTERMEDIATE APPELLATE COURT; JUDGMENT ON THE MERITS; LAW OF THE CASE; NOTICE OF APPEAL; OBJECTION; OPINION; PETITION; PLAINTIFF IN ERROR; POSTCONVICTION REMEDY; REMAND; RESPONDENT; SENTENCE REVIEW; TAKE AN APPEAL; TRIAL; TRIAL DE NOVO; UNITED STATES COURT OF APPEALS; UNITED STATES SUPREME COURT; WRIT OF CERTIORARI; WRIT OF ERROR; WRIT OF PROBABLE CAUSE.

APPEAL OF RIGHT. An **appeal** that the **appellate court** must hear and decide on its merits, at the request of an **appellant**. In criminal cases, **defense** appeals of trial court final judgments are most frequently appeals of right; that is, a defendant's right to appeal from a conviction is generally guaranteed by law. See APPEAL for a list of related terms.

APPEAR. To make an APPEARANCE.

APPEARANCE. **1.** An overt act by which a party submits to the **jurisdiction** (definition 3) of the court, either personally or through an **attorney**. *See:* GENERAL APPEARANCE; INITIAL APPEARANCE; SPECIAL APPEARANCE. **2.** The conduct of an attorney indicating to a court that the attorney will represent a particular client in a particular **action**.

APPEARANCE BOND.   A person's written obligation to pay a specified amount of money to a court if the person does not **appear** in **court** as required.

APPELLANT.   The person or party who initiates an **appeal**. The appellant is the person who contests the correctness of a court order, judgment, or other decision and who seeks review and relief in an **appellate court**, or the person in whose behalf this is done. Used broadly, the term appellant includes a **plaintiff in error**.

The appeal process may begin by petitioning for leave to appeal. At this point there is no **respondent**; that is, the court does not conduct an adversary proceeding to determine whether or not to hear the appeal. Later, as an appeal case is being processed, when **briefs** must be submitted and arguments presented, the party who answers the claims and allegations of the appellant is the respondent (also called the **appellee**). In appeal proceedings relating to criminal cases, the appellant is usually a defendant who has been convicted, and consequently the respondent is the **people** of a state or of the United States, represented by the **prosecution**. See ACCUSED and APPEAL for lists of related terms.

APPELLATE.   Pertaining to or concerning an APPEAL. See APPEAL for a list of related terms.

APPELLATE BRIEF.   A BRIEF filed with an **appellate court** so that it may evaluate the decision of a lower court. The **appellant's** brief will attempt to persuade the appellate court to **reverse** or **vacate** the lower court's decision because of some error or impropriety that occurred during trial. The **appellee's** brief will argue that the lower court acted properly in its decision and request its **affirmance**. See APPEAL for a list of related terms.

APPELLATE COURT.   A court that hears APPEALS of decisions of lower courts but does not try cases in the first instance. An appellate court may hear appeals from a **court of general jurisdiction**, or in some cases may hear appeals directly from a **court of limited jurisdiction**. The term appellate court includes **intermediate appellate courts** and **courts of last resort**. In special cases an appellate court may have **original jurisdiction**. For example, the U.S. Supreme Court has original jurisdiction in controversies involving two or more states. An appellate court is commonly called a **court of appeals, supreme court,** or **supreme judicial court**. *Also called:* **court of appellate jurisdiction**. See APPEAL, COURT, and JURISDICTION for lists of related terms.

APPELLATE JUDGE.   A judge of an APPELLATE COURT. See APPEAL for a list of related terms.

APPELLATE JURISDICTION.   Lawful authority or power of a court to review a decision made by a lower court or to hear an **appeal** from a judgment of a lower court. See APPEAL and JURISDICTION for lists of related terms.

APPELLEE.   The person or party against whom an **appeal** is taken. Used broadly, the term appellee includes a **defendant in error**. See ACCUSED and APPEAL for lists of related terms.

APPEND.   To add; to attach.

APPENDIX.   Material added after the end of a book that provides useful information but is not necessary to the completeness of the book. *See:* ADDENDUM; SUPPLEMENT.

APPERTAIN.   **v.** To belong to; to have relation to; to be incident to. **adj.** APPURTENANT.

APPLICABLE.   Capable of being applied; appropriate; relevant; pertinent; suitable. *See:* APPLY.

APPLICANT.   One who applies. *See:* APPLY.

APPLICATION.   *See*: APPLY.

APPLY.   **1.** To make a formal request, usually in writing. *Example:* To apply for a pardon. **2.** To put to use for some practical purpose. *Example:* To apply payments toward a debt. **3.** To bring to bear. *Example:* To apply the law to a particular set of facts. **4.** To be pertinent or relevant. *Example:* That case does not apply to this fact situation.

APPOINT.   To select a public officer by one legally authorized to do so, such as a governor or the President. *Example:* She was appointed an Assistant Attorney General by the Attorney General. *See:* ELECT.

APPORTION.   To give out shares or portions to members of a group by someone in authority, with the suggestion of a just and fair distribution based on some objective standard. *Example:* Congress apportions the number of representatives for each state based on the census. See ALLOCATE for a list of related terms.

APPREHENSION.   **1.** Generally, **seizure** and holding under restraint or in custody under authority of the law. **2.** Same as ARREST. See ARREST for a list of related terms.

   NOTE: Apprehension is a nontechnical word of varying meanings. In criminal law, arrest is the proper technical term and is preferred to apprehension.

APPURTENANT.   *See*: APPERTAIN.

A PRIORI. *Latin.* Valid independently of factual study or observation. This term is used to describe a type of reasoning that puts forth a general principle or accepted truth as a cause and proceeds to derive from it the effects that must necessarily follow. Another name for this method of reasoning is **deductive reasoning.** *See:* A POSTERIORI.

APT. **1.** Suitable; appropriate. **2.** Likely; inclined. *Example:* He is apt to get into trouble.

ARBITER. Same as ARBITRATOR, but less commonly used.

ARBITRARY. Not governed by fixed rules or principles; without regard for the facts and circumstances presented; capricious.

ARBITRARY AND CAPRICIOUS. Without rational basis; unsupported by substantial evidence. *See:* CAPRICIOUS.

ARBITRARY PUNISHMENT. A punishment determined by a judge rather than defined by statute.

ARBITRATION. The process by which parties submit for determination a disputed matter to an impartial third party appointed by mutual consent or by law. The parties agree ahead of time to comply with the **arbitrator's** decision, which is issued after a hearing at which both parties have an opportunity to be heard.

ARBITRATOR. A neutral person appointed or chosen to hear arguments and settle a controversy between parties.

ARCHAIC. Antiquated; outmoded; no longer current or useful. *Example:* Much of the common law is now archaic.

ARGUENDO. In the course of argument. A statement or observation made for the purposes of illustration, but not directly bearing on the issue at hand, is said to be made arguendo. *Example:* Let us assume arguendo that the witness's testimony is true.

ARGUMENT. **1.** A reason or reasons, expressed in words, aimed at demonstrating the truth or falsity of some proposition. **2.** An address to a jury or court to persuade them to support or overthrow some proposition or to render a favorable verdict. *See:* CLOSING ARGUMENT; OPENING ARGUMENT. **3.** A discussion in which disagreement is expressed on some issue.

ARGUMENTATIVE PLEADING. **1.** A **pleading** in which a statement relied upon by the pleader is **implied** rather than expressed. **2.** A pleading that states, in addition to the facts establishing a cause of action or a defense, reasoning or arguments that should be reserved for presentation at trial. See PLEADING for a list of related terms.

ARISE. To originate; to come into being; to become operative.

ARMED. Furnished or equipped with a weapon of offense or defense.

ARMED ROBBERY. *See*: ROBBERY.

ARMS. **1.** In its broad sense, the term arms means every **weapon** or instrument that can be used offensively or defensively. **2.** In the sense of the constitutional guaranty of the right to bear arms, the term arms means weapons used in civilized warfare and that constitute the military equipment of an ordinary soldier, including modern day equivalents of weapons used by colonial militiamen and weapons used for personal defense. It does not include modern weapons used exclusively by the military nor "those used by a ruffian, brawler or assassin." *State v. Swainton,* 629 P.2d 99 (Ariz.App. 1981).

AROUND. **1.** In the vicinity of. **2.** About; approximately.

ARRAIGN. To bring a defendant before the court in order that the **charge** may be read and that the defendant may PLEAD to the charge. *See:* ARRAIGNMENT.

ARRAIGNMENT. The **hearing** before a court having jurisdiction in a criminal case, in which the identity of the defendant is established, the defendant is informed of the charge and of his or her rights, and the defendant is required to enter a **plea**. The defendant's entering of a plea is the crucial distinguishing element of the arraignment. Besides the pleas of **guilty** or **not guilty**, courts of many states and the federal courts permit pleas of **nolo contendere** and some accept pleas of **not guilty by reason of insanity** or **former jeopardy**.

In **misdemeanor** cases where the offense is minor, all actions constituting adjudication are often taken on the first and only occasion on which the defendant appears before the court. In more serious misdemeanor cases the arraignment may be the subject of a separate hearing. In **felony** cases the arraignment occurs after proceedings are begun in the trial court by filing of an **information** or **indictment**. In jurisdictions where **probable cause** is determined in a lower court and trial takes place in a higher court, there may be a preliminary arraignment in the lower court. See HEARING for a list of related terms.

ARRAY. **v.** To arrange or set forth in order. *Example:* The jury was arrayed for the trial of the case. **n.** The entire body of **jurors** as they are arranged on the **panel** and from which is selected a smaller body of jurors to form a **petit jury** or a **grand jury**. See JURY for a list of related terms.

ARREST. The taking of a person into the custody of the law for the purpose of charging the person with a criminal offense or a delinquent act or status offense. The basic elements necessary to constitute a **formal arrest** are:

1. a purpose or intention of a law enforcement officer to effect an arrest;
2. a law enforcement officer acting under real or pretended authority;
3. an actual or constructive seizure or detention of the person to be arrested by an officer having the present power to control the person; and
4. an understanding by the person to be arrested that it is the intention of the arresting officer then and there to arrest and detain him or her.

In order to make a lawful formal arrest without a warrant, a law enforcement officer must either have **probable cause** to believe that the person to be arrested is committing or has committed a **felony** or the person to be arrested must be committing a **misdemeanor** in the officer's presence.

Even though an officer does not intend to make a formal arrest, a court may find that the officer's actions are tantamount to an arrest if they are indistinguishable from an arrest in important respects. If an officer seizes (see **seizure**, definition 1) or detains a person significantly, beyond a mere **stop** or other minor investigatory detention, the seizure or detention may nevertheless be considered an arrest for purposes of the Fourth Amendment, even if the officer does not comply with all the requirements of a formal arrest. As such, the seizure or detention will be ruled illegal unless it is supported by probable cause. *Dunaway v. New York*, 442 U.S. 200, 99 S.Ct. 2248, 60 L.Ed.2d 824 (1979).

An arrest may also be made by persons other than law enforcement officers. A **citizen's arrest** is the taking of a person into physical custody, by a person other than a law enforcement officer, for the purpose of delivering the person to the physical custody of a law enforcement officer or agency so that the person can be charged with a crime. *See:* AFFIDAVIT; APPREHENSION; ARRESTEE; ARRESTEE DISPOSITION; ARREST OF JUDGMENT; ARREST RECORD; ARREST REGISTER; ARREST REPORT; ARREST WARRANT; BLOTTER; BOOKING; CITATION; COMPLAINT; CUSTODIAL ARREST; DETAIN; DETENTION; FRESH PURSUIT; LAW ENFORCEMENT OFFICER; MALICIOUS ARREST; PRESENCE OF AN OFFICER; PROBABLE CAUSE; RESISTING ARREST; SEARCH INCIDENT TO ARREST; SEIZURE; STOP AND FRISK; SUMMONS; WANTED PERSON.

ARRESTEE. A person who has been **arrested**. See ACCUSED and ARREST for lists of related terms.

ARRESTEE DISPOSITION. A law enforcement or prosecutorial action that terminates or provisionally suspends proceedings against an arrested person before a charge has been filed in court. Examples of arrestee dispositions are:

—police release of the arrestee after booking because of a law enforcement agency decision not to request a **complaint**.

—if a complaint is requested, rejection of the complaint by the **prosecutor** because he or she declines to prosecute on grounds such as insufficient evidence, lack of witnesses, or interests of justice.

—suspension of proceedings by the prosecutor, conditional on the behavior of the arrestee, with or without referral to a **probation agency** or other agency.

See ARREST and DISPOSITION for lists of related terms.

ARREST OF JUDGMENT.   The refusal of a court to enter **judgment** in a case after **verdict** because of **error** appearing on the face of the **record**. Entry of judgment is refused because the error would make the judgment reversible on **appeal**. This action is often taken by a court in response to a **motion in arrest of judgment**. In criminal proceedings, the defendant makes a motion in arrest of judgment when the **indictment** or **information** fails to charge the defendant with an offense or when the court lacks **jurisdiction** (definition 3) of the offense charged. See ERROR and JUDGMENT for lists of related terms.

ARREST RECORD.   **1.** The official form completed by a **law enforcement agency** when a person is **arrested**. **2.** The cumulative history of the instances in which a particular person has been arrested. See ARREST for a list of related terms.

ARREST REGISTER.   The document containing a chronological record of all **arrests** made by members of a given law enforcement agency, containing at a minimum the identity of the arrestee, the charges at time of arrest, and the date and time of arrest. In some agencies the information is entered directly into an electronic processing system. See ARREST for a list of related terms.

ARREST REPORT.   The document prepared by the arresting officer describing an arrested person and the events and circumstances leading to the **arrest**. Arrest reports are the basic source of information for a variety of other records and functions, depending on the procedures in a given jurisdiction. Information in an arrest report may be the basis for the **complaint** filed by the prosecutor. See ARREST for a list of related terms.

ARREST WARRANT.   A written order issued by a **magistrate** or other proper **judicial officer**, upon **probable cause**, directing a law enforcement officer to ARREST a particular person. An arrest warrant is issued on the basis of a sworn **complaint** charging that the accused person has committed a crime. The arrest warrant must identify the person to be arrested by name and/or other unique characteristics and must describe the crime. When a warrant for arrest does not identify a person by name, it is sometimes called a **John Doe warrant** or a **no name warrant**. *See:* BENCH WARRANT; BODY EXECUTION; CITATION; COMPLAINT;

COMPULSORY PROCESS; CORAM NOBIS; EXECUTION; GENERAL WARRANT; HABEAS CORPUS AD SUBJICIENDUM; HABEAS CORPUS AD TESTIFICANDUM; MANDAMUS; MITTIMUS; MONITION; NE EXEAT; PRECEPT; PREROGATIVE WRIT; PROCESS; QUO WARRANTO; SCIRE FACIAS; SEARCH WARRANT; SEIZURE; SUBPOENA; SUMMONS; SUPERSEDEAS; VENIRE DE NOVO; VENIRE FACIAS; WARRANT; WRIT; WRIT OF ASSISTANCE; WRIT OF CERTIORARI; WRIT OF ERROR; WRIT OF PROBABLE CAUSE; WRIT OF PROHIBITION; WRIT OF REVIEW; WRIT OF RIGHT.

ARSON.   The **common law** definition of arson is the **malicious** burning of the **house** or **outbuilding** of another. A typical modern statutory definition of arson is the intentional damaging or destruction, by means of fire or explosion, of the property of another without the consent of the owner, or of one's own property or that of another with intent to **defraud**. Some modern statutory definitions of arson divide the crime into **degrees** and some include under arson burning or destruction for any unlawful purpose, such as concealing evidence of crime. Statutory definitions of arson vary greatly from jurisdiction to jurisdiction.

ART.   *See*: TERM OF ART.

ARTICLE.   **1.** A material or tangible object.   **2.** A separate and distinct part of a writing (document, book, set of laws or rules, etc.) that contains several parts.

ARTICLES.   A system of rules or laws; a contractual document containing terms of agreement. *Example:* Articles of Confederation; articles of incorporation.

ARTICULABLE SUSPICION.   The constitutional standard under which a brief investigatory **stop** is permitted. Articulable suspicion is "less than **probable cause** to make an **arrest** or conduct a **search**, but must be more than mere caprice or arbitrary harassment." *Pullano v. State*, 312 S.E.2d 857, 860 (Ga.App. 1984). Articulable suspicion has also been defined as "the ability to surmise from the information at hand that a **crime** was in progress or had occurred. . . . a substantial possibility that criminal conduct has occurred or is about to occur." *State v. Kennedy*, 726 P.2d 445, 448 (Wash. 1986).

ARTICULATED PLEADING.   A **pleading** in which the facts are stated in separate paragraphs, separately numbered. See PLEADING for a list of related terms.

ARTIFICE.   A clever or deceptive trick or scheme to achieve a desired result.

ARTIFICIAL.   **1.** Not genuine; made in imitation of something natural.   **2.** Created by and deriving its force and effect from the law. *See:* ARTIFICIAL PERSON.

ARTIFICIAL PERSON. A group of human beings considered as a legal unit, which has the lawful capacity to defend rights, incur obligations, prosecute claims, or which can be prosecuted or adjudicated. Examples of an artificial person are a state, a territory, a government, a country, a corporation, and a partnership.

AS. **1.** Like; similar to; in the same manner. **2.** When; while. **3.** Since; because. **4.** For instance.

ASCERTAIN. To learn definitely by investigation; to determine with certainty.

ASK. **1.** To request. **2.** To seek information; to inquire.

ASPERSION. A derogatory criticism.

ASPHYXIA. Unconsciousness or death caused by lack of oxygen and excess of carbon dioxide in the blood.

ASPORTATION. The carrying away of goods from one place to another. Asportation is one of the elements required to establish the crime of **larceny** under the **common law**.

ASSASSINATE. To MURDER by stealth or treachery and often for a reward. The term assassinate often implies the murder of a person in governmental or political power.

ASSAULT. Under the **common law**, an assault is an unlawful intentional **attempt** to inflict **bodily injury** or offensive physical contact upon another person under circumstances creating a well-founded fear of imminent danger, coupled with the present ability to carry out the attempt, if not prevented. Some modern statutes have changed the common law meaning of assault to include **battery**. A modern definition of assault would be the unlawful, intentional inflicting, or attempted or threatened inflicting, of bodily injury or offensive physical contact upon the person of another. Some statutes establish different degrees of assault. *See:* AGGRAVATED AS-SAULT; ASSAULT ON A LAW ENFORCEMENT OFFICER; BATTERY; EX-CUSABLE ASSAULT; INDECENT ASSAULT; MAYHEM; MUGGING; SEXUAL ASSAULT; SIMPLE ASSAULT.

ASSAULT AND BATTERY. Same as BATTERY.

ASSAULT ON A LAW ENFORCEMENT OFFICER. A **simple assault** or an **aggravated assault** where the victim is a **law enforcement officer** engaged in the performance of his or her duties. This type of assault is usually distinguished in statutes from other assaults by a separate, higher penalty range. Many statutory definitions of this offense require that the officer be engaged in the performance of official duties

· at the time of the assault and that the perpetrator be aware of this fact. In many jurisdictions a higher penalty is also established for assaults on other government officials, such as firefighters and corrections officers. See ASSAULT for a list of related terms. *See also:* RESISTING AN OFFICER; RESISTING ARREST.

ASSAULT WITH A DEADLY WEAPON. See note under AGGRAVATED AS-SAULT. *Abbreviation:* **ADW**

ASSAULT WITH INTENT TO COMMIT MURDER OR MANSLAUGH-TER. See note under AGGRAVATED ASSAULT.

ASSAY. To examine or analyze a substance.

ASSEMBLY. The meeting together of a large number of persons at the same place. *See:* ASSEMBLY AND PETITION; UNLAWFUL ASSEMBLY.

ASSEMBLY AND PETITION. The right guaranteed by the First Amendment to the United States Constitution that permits a peaceful gathering of persons for nearly any lawful objective. American citizens, whether they are meeting for political activity, religious services, or other purposes, have the right to assemble peaceably. Public authorities cannot impose unreasonable restrictions on these assemblies, but they can impose limitations reasonably designed to prevent fire, hazard to health, or a traffic obstruction. The U.S. Supreme Court emphasized that freedom of assembly is just as fundamental as freedom of speech and press. Thus, while no law may legitimately prohibit demonstrations, there may be laws or other governmental actions that legitimately restrict demonstrations to certain areas or prohibit the obstruction and occupation of public buildings. Assembling for the purpose of picketing may be reasonably regulated to prevent pickets from obstructing movement onto and from the property involved. Picketing on private property has been upheld, but only where the property is open to the public and the picketing relates to the business being conducted on the property. The right of petition is designed to enable citizens to communicate with their government without obstruction. When citizens exercise their First Amendment freedom to write or speak to their senator or representative, they partake of "the healthy essence of the democratic process."

ASSENT. To express understanding and agreement or concurrence. *See:* ACQUI-ESCE; CONSENT.

ASSERT. To state positively and with conviction but without proof. See ADDRESS for a list of related terms.

ASSESS. **1.** To evaluate; to appraise. **2.** To set or determine the amount of. *Example:* The court assessed a fine of $100.

ASSETS. Real or personal property that has value and that can be made available for the payment of debts.

ASSIGN. v. 1. To give out shares or portions to members of a group by someone in authority with the implication of arbitrariness. The thing assigned is more often a task or role rather than objects or money. The term assign carries no suggestion of fair or equal distribution. See ALLOCATE for a list of related terms. **v. 2.** To transfer (property, rights, or interests). **v. 3.** To point out; to specify; to particularize. *Example:* To assign errors on a writ of error. **v. 4.** To set apart for a particular purpose; to appoint; to designate. **n.** ASSIGNMENT.

ASSIGNATION. An appointment for a meeting for illicit sexual relations.

ASSIGNATION HOUSE. Same as HOUSE OF PROSTITUTION.

ASSIGNED COUNSEL. A DEFENSE ATTORNEY, not regularly employed by a government agency, assigned by the court on a case-by-case basis to represent in court indigent defendants and offenders. An assigned counsel may be, but is not necessarily, paid by a government agency for his or her work on a particular case. See ATTORNEY AT LAW for a list of related terms.

ASSIGNMENT. The act, process, or result of assigning. *See:* ASSIGN.

ASSIGNMENT OF ERRORS. The **pleading** of the **appellant** in the **appellate court** which calls that court's attention to **errors** allegedly committed by the **trial court**. See APPEAL, ERROR, and PLEADING for lists of related terms.

ASSIST. To aid; to help.

ASSISTANCE OF COUNSEL. Under the Sixth Amendment to the United States Constitution, every person accused of a crime is guaranteed the effective assistance of **counsel** for his or her **defense**. For many years, the Sixth Amendment was interpreted to mean only that defendants had a right to be represented by a lawyer if they could afford one. In the case of *Gideon v. Wainwright*, 372 U.S. 335, 83 S.Ct. 792, 9 L.Ed.2d 799 (1963), however, the U.S. Supreme Court held that the amendment imposed an affirmative obligation on the part of the federal and state governments to provide at public expense legal counsel for those who could not afford it, in order that their cases could be adequately presented to the court. The Supreme Court held that this right extended even to cases involving petty offenses if there is a chance that a jail sentence might result. The indigent are entitled to counsel at any "critical stage of the adjudicatory process." Thus, courts have accorded this right at **custodial interrogations**, at police **lineups** conducted at or after the initiation of **adversary judicial proceedings**, and at all stages of the trial process.

ASSOCIATE.   **v.** To join with others in a common purpose or activity. **adj.** Joined with another or others and having equal or nearly equal status. *Example:* The judges of an appellate court, other than the chief or presiding judge, are sometimes called associate judges or associate justices.

ASSOCIATION.   An organized body of people who have some purpose, activity, or interest in common.

ASSUME.   **v. 1.** To undertake; to take upon one's self; to adopt. **v. 2.** To accept as true without proof or demonstration. **n.** ASSUMPTION.

ASSUMPTION.   *See:* ASSUME.

ASSURANCE.   **1.** A declaration intended to inspire full confidence or belief; a promise. **2.** Freedom from doubt; certainty.

ASYLUM.   Shelter; refuge; protection from prosecution or persecution. *See:* ASYLUM STATE.

ASYLUM STATE.   The state to which a person charged with a crime in another state has fled from justice. *See:* EXTRADITION.

AT.   The term at has many meanings, depending upon the context in which it is used. Among the possible meanings are: in; near; on; about; toward; after; to; by; during; as early as; within; into; in the vicinity of; not later than; when; under; over; through; from.

AT BAR.   Before the court. *Example:* The case at bar.

AT CHAMBERS.   Acting out of court. *Example:* A judge at chambers is a judge acting upon matters that do not have to be decided or handled in court. *See:* CHAMBERS.

AT INTERVALS.   From time to time; now and then; occasionally.

AT ISSUE.   Affirmed on one side and denied on the other.

AT LARGE.   **1.** Not limited to any particular place, person, or matter. *Example:* An ambassador at large is one not assigned to any particular country. **2.** Unrestrained; free. *Example:* Some local laws do not allow domestic animals to run at large. **3.** In detail; comprehensively. *Example:* He spoke at large on the crime problem.

AT LEAST.   Not less than; clearly.

AT LENGTH.   To the full extent.

AT MOST.   No more than; not to exceed.

AT ONCE.   **1.** Immediately; without delay. **2.** All together; simultaneously.

AT PLEASURE.   With wide discretion; without requirement of notice, hearing or cause. *Example:* Power to revoke a license at pleasure.

ATROCIOUS.   **adj.** Extremely wicked or cruel. **n.** ATROCITY.

ATROCIOUS ASSAULT.   See note under AGGRAVATED ASSAULT.

ATROCITY.   An **atrocious** deed or thing.

ATTACH.   **1.** To connect; to unite; to join; to fasten. **2.** To seize or take possession of a person or property by virtue of a **writ, summons,** or judicial **order** and bring the person or property within the custody of the court. The term attach is used to describe seizures of persons or property in civil actions whereby the terms **arrest** and **stop** are used to describe seizures of the person and the term **seizure** is used to describe the taking into custody of items of property in criminal actions. See SEIZE for a list of related terms. **3.** To come into legal operation; to **vest.**

ATTACK.   To set upon with force or weapons.

ATTAIN.   **1.** To reach or accomplish by continued effort. **2.** To arrive at.

ATTAINDER.   Under the common law, attainder was the loss of all civil rights and property that took place when a person who had committed **treason** or a **felony** received a death sentence for the crime. *See:* BILL OF ATTAINDER; CIVIL DEATH.

ATTEMPT.   An **intent** to commit a crime together with an apparent ability to commit the crime and an act in direct movement toward it that goes beyond mere **preparation** but falls short of the actual commission of the intended crime. Attempts are sometimes accorded the same penalties as the completed offenses. See INCHOATE OFFENSE and PARTY for lists of related terms.

ATTEMPTED MURDER.   See note under AGGRAVATED ASSAULT.

ATTENDANT.   Accompanying; immediately following; connected with. *Example*: Attendant circumstances.

ATTENUATE.   To lessen the amount, force, effect, or value of; to weaken.

ATTENUATION OF TAINT. *See*: FRUIT OF THE POISONOUS TREE DOC-TRINE.

ATTEST. **v.** To bear witness to; to affirm to be true or genuine; to certify. **n.** ATTESTATION.

ATTESTATION. *See*: ATTEST.

ATTESTING WITNESS. *See*: WITNESS (definition 3).

ATTORNEY. **1.** In its broad sense, attorney means an agent or one who acts on behalf of another. **2.** An ATTORNEY AT LAW.

ATTORNEY AT LAW. A person trained in the LAW, admitted to practice before the bar of a particular jurisdiction, and authorized to advise other persons in legal matters, draft legal documents, and represent others in legal proceedings. An attorney at law may be referred to as **advocate**, **attorney**, **counsel**, **counselor**, or **lawyer**. An attorney may represent private individuals, corporations, or the government. The attorney acting on behalf of the government (the **people**) in a criminal case is the **prosecutor**. *See:* ASSIGNED COUNSEL; ATTORNEY GENERAL; ATTOR-NEY OF RECORD; DEFENSE ATTORNEY; PUBLIC DEFENDER; RETAINED COUNSEL.

ATTORNEY GENERAL. The chief law officer and head of the legal department of the federal government or the government of a state. The Attorney General of the United States, as the head of the **Department of Justice** and chief law enforcement officer of the federal government, represents the United States in legal matters generally and gives advice and opinions to the President and to the heads of the executive departments of the Government when so requested. The Attorney General appears in person to represent the Government in the U.S. Supreme Court in cases of exceptional gravity or importance. See ATTORNEY AT LAW for a list of related terms.

ATTORNEY OF RECORD. A duly licensed **attorney at law** who has entered an **appearance** in a case on behalf of his or her client and whose name appears on the formal documents involved in the case. *Also called:* **counsel of record**. See ATTORNEY AT LAW for a list of related terms.

ATTRIBUTE. To regard as originating with or belonging to someone or something; to ascribe.

AUDIT. An official examination of records or accounts to determine their accuracy.

AUTHENTIC. **1.** Genuine; real; reliable; trustworthy. **2.** Executed with the proper formalities.

AUTHENTICATE. To establish as genuine.

AUTHORITY. **1.** The power to act for or represent another. *See:* ACTUAL AU-THORITY; APPARENT AUTHORITY; EXPRESS AUTHORITY; GENERAL AUTHORITY; IMPLIED AUTHORITY; SPECIAL AUTHORITY. **2.** The right and power to command people, enforce laws, demand obedience, or adjudicate disputes; a person or body having such right and power. **3.** A public agency with administrative powers limited to a specific field. *Example:* Housing Authority. **4.** A person or book that is an accepted source of expert information or advice. **5.** A **statute**, text, or judicial **decision** that sets forth a principle of law that can be used as a **precedent** or guide in decisionmaking. Primary authorities are statutes, governmental rules and regulations, and court decisions that have the force of law and must be applied by the court in deciding issues in dispute. Secondary authorities are textbooks and scholarly treatises that do not have the force of law and may be disregarded by the court.

AUTHORIZE. To give a right or power to act.

AUTO-LOADING FIREARM. A **firearm** that reloads itself after each shot, but requires that the trigger be pulled for each shot. *See:* AUTOMATIC FIREARM.

AUTOMATIC. Acting or operating independently of human control or influence; self-acting. *Example:* An automatic pistol is one that repeatedly ejects the shell, inserts a new one, and prepares the pistol to be fired, all without human manipulation.

AUTOMATIC APPEAL. An APPEAL initiated as a matter of course, without action of either party, and which the **appellate court** must hear and decide. A typical situation for which an automatic appeal is provided by law is the pronouncement of the death sentence on a defendant. See APPEAL for a list of related terms.

AUTOMATIC FIREARM. A firearm that will continue to fire so long as the trigger is held back. *See:* AUTO-LOADING FIREARM.

AUTOMOBILE EXCEPTION. *See*: CARROLL DOCTRINE.

AUTOPSY. The examination of a dead body to determine the cause of death. *Also called:* **necropsy; post-mortem examination**. See DEATH for a list of related terms.

AUTREFOIS ACQUIT. *French.* "Formerly acquitted." A **plea** to **bar** further criminal **prosecution** on the ground that the defendant has already been tried and **acquitted** of the same offense. *Also called:* **former acquittal**. *See:* DOUBLE JEOPARDY.

AUTREFOIS CONVICT. *French.* "Formerly convicted." A **plea** to **bar** further criminal **prosecution** on the ground that the defendant has already been **convicted** of the same offense. *See:* DOUBLE JEOPARDY.

AUXILIARY. Giving aid or support. The term auxiliary usually implies subordinate rank or status. *Example:* Auxiliary troops.

AVAILABLE. Accessible; usable; at the disposal of.

AVER. v. To state positively with complete confidence and certainty of proof. **n.** AVERMENT. See ADDRESS for a list of related terms.

AVERMENT. **n.** A positive statement or allegation of facts or claims in a **pleading**. **v.** AVER.

AVOID. **1.** To invalidate; to make void or ineffective; to cancel. **2.** To shun; to keep away from; to escape the consequences of. The term avoid implies no wrongful or unlawful intent. *See:* EVADE.

AVOUCH. To state positively from personal knowledge or authority. See ADDRESS for a list of related terms.

AVOW. To state openly and emphatically. The term avow implies that the speaker takes personal responsibility for the statement. See ADDRESS for a list of related terms.

AWARD. A judgment or decision upon a disputed matter submitted for determination.

A.W.O.L. Abbreviation for ABSENT WITHOUT LEAVE.

AXIOM. **1.** A self-evident or universally recognized truth. **2.** An established law, rule, or principle.

BACK.   Toward the rear; in a reverse direction.

BACKLOG.   The number of cases awaiting disposition in a court that exceeds the court's capacity for disposing of them within a period of time considered appropriate.

BAD.   Not good; defective; inadequate; inferior; imperfect; unfavorable.

BAD BEHAVIOR.   Generally, conduct punishable under the law. Opposite of GOOD BEHAVIOR.

BAD CHECK.   Same as CHECK FRAUD.

BAD FAITH.   Willful and malicious failure or refusal to fulfill obligations; intent to deceive or mislead another; dishonesty; fraud.

BAD MOTIVE.   A person acts with a bad motive when he or she intentionally does a wrongful act, knowing at the time that it is wrongful.

BAIL.   **v. 1.** In the criminal law, to bail means to obtain the **release** from custody of an arrested or imprisoned person by pledging money or other property as a guarantee of the person's appearance in court at a specified date and time. The purposes of bail are to prevent the imprisonment of an accused prior to trial and to ensure his or her **appearance** at trial. The court may or may not require that the pledge of money or property be secured. Pledges may be secured in several ways. The most common way is by employment of a **bail bondsman,** to whom a nonrefundable fee is paid. In other cases the court can require a deposit of money before the person is released. The requirement can be for the full amount pledged, or for a percentage of the amount pledged.

The amount of money or property pledged to guarantee appearance can be changed during the course of proceedings. Bail can be reduced when, for example, the defendant shows that his or her community ties will ensure appearance in court. Bail can be increased when the likelihood that the defendant might **abscond** increases, as when he or she has been convicted and is awaiting sentencing or has been charged with another crime.

v. 2. To deliver possession of property to another (the BAILEE) for storage, hire, or other special purpose, without the transfer of ownership.

n. 1. The money or property pledged to the court or actually deposited for the release from custody of an arrested or imprisoned person as a guarantee of the person's appearance in court at a specified date and time. **n. 2.** Same as SURETY.

See: BAILABLE; BAILABLE OFFENSE; BAIL BOND; BAIL BONDSMAN; BAIL FORFEITURE; BAILMENT; BAIL REVOCATION; BIND OVER; EXCESSIVE BAIL; JUMP BAIL; JUSTIFY BAIL; PROOF EVIDENT; RECOGNIZANCE; RELEASE; RELEASE ON BAIL; RELEASE TO THIRD PARTY; SURETY.

BAILABLE. **1.** Eligible for **bail**; capable of being set free on bail. **2.** Admitting of bail. *Example*: Is manslaughter a bailable offense? See BAIL for a list of related terms.

BAILABLE OFFENSE. An offense for which an accused may be admitted to **bail**. See BAIL for a list of related terms.

BAIL BOND. A document guaranteeing the **appearance** of the defendant in court at a specified date and time as required, and recording the pledge of money or property to be paid to the court if he or she does not appear. The bail bond is signed by the person to be released and by his or her **surety**. If the accused appears in court as required, the bail bond becomes void and the surety receives back his or her payment. If the accused does not appear in court as required, the payment is forfeited. See BAIL for a list of related terms.

BAIL BONDSMAN. A person, usually licensed, whose business it is to effect releases on **bail** for persons charged with offenses and held in custody, by pledging to pay a sum of money if a defendant fails to appear in court as required. A bail bondsman is a type of SURETY. See BAIL for a list of related terms.

BAILEE. The party to whom property is delivered under a contract of BAILMENT (definition 2).

BAIL FORFEITURE. The court decision that the defendant or **surety** has lost the right to the money or property pledged to guarantee court appearance or the fulfillment of another obligation, or has lost the right to the sum deposited as security for the pledge, and that the court will retain it. Bail forfeiture is not automatic; it is a court decision requiring a hearing. See BAIL for a list of related terms.

BAILIFF. A **law enforcement officer**, similar to a sheriff or deputy sheriff, whose duties are to execute judicial **processes**, make **arrests**, keep order in the court, and the like. The term bailiff is applied especially to the court attendant who is responsible for the custody of persons before the court, protection of the jurors, seating of witnesses, announcing the judge's entrance into the courtroom, and other duties relating to the

Bb

maintenance of order in the court. In some jurisdictions, the person who performs bailiff and often other duties is called a **court officer**. Federal court bailiffs are U.S. **marshals**. See COURT and LAW ENFORCEMENT OFFICER for lists of related terms.

BAILIWICK. **1.** The **jurisdiction** or office of a BAILIFF. **2.** In its broader sense, the term bailiwick means a person's specific area of operation, authority, skill, or interest. See JURISDICTION for a list of related terms.

BAILMENT. **1.** The process of providing BAIL for an accused person. See BAIL for a list of related terms. **2.** The delivery of property to another (the **bailee**) under a contract requiring the bailee to carry out a special purpose with regard to the property and then to return the property or otherwise account for it. *Example*: They made a bailment of their yacht to the marina for repairs and winter storage.

BAILOR. The party who delivers goods to another (the **bailee**) under a contract of BAILMENT (definition 2).

BAIL REVOCATION. The court decision withdrawing the status of **release on bail** previously conferred upon a defendant. Bail status may be revoked if the defendant fails to appear in court when required, or is arrested for another crime, or violates a condition of the bail release, such as a requirement that he or she remain within a certain **jurisdiction**. Bail revocation is not automatic, but is a court decision requiring a hearing. See BAIL for a list of related terms.

BAIT AND SWITCH. A deceptive sales technique that involves advertising a low-priced product or service to attract customers and then persuading them to purchase a more expensive version by disparaging the advertised product or service or failing to have an adequate supply available. Statutes prohibit this practice in many states.

BALANCE OF SENTENCE SUSPENDED. A type of **sentencing disposition** consisting of a **jail commitment** or **prison commitment**, which credits the defendant for time already spent in confinement awaiting adjudication and sentencing, suspends the execution of the time remaining to be served, and results in the **release** from confinement of the defendant. This type of disposition and **sentenced to time served** are functionally equivalent from the defendant's standpoint, since both provide credit for time previously spent in confinement and result in release of the defendant from confinement at the time of sentencing. See RELEASE and SENTENCE for lists of related terms.

BALANCING. A judicial method of determining constitutional issues by weighing competing values or interests. Balancing usually involves weighing a private right against the public good, but may involve competing public interests or competing private interests. *Example*: In determining the reasonableness of stop and frisk procedures, the U.S. Supreme Court balanced the individual's right to privacy and right to be free from unreasonable searches and seizures against the public need for effective crime prevention and detection and the safety of law enforcement officers. *See*: TERRY v. OHIO.

BALLOON TEST. A breath analysis test for alcoholic intoxication.

BAN. To prohibit.

BAND. A relatively small group pursuing the same purpose.

BANDIT. An outlaw; a robber.

BANISHMENT. A punishment inflicted upon a criminal, forcing him or her to leave a place for a specified period of time, or for life.

BANKED CASE. *See*: SUPERVISED PROBATION.

BAR. **n. 1**. The place in the courtroom where a prisoner stands at his or her trial. **n. 2**. A certain court or system of courts. *Example*: She practices at the Massachusetts bar. **n. 3**. The members of the legal profession considered collectively. **n. 4.** A railing in a courtroom separating the judge, jury, attorneys, defendant, witnesses, etc. from the general public. **n. 5**. Impediment, obstacle, prohibition. *Example*: The judgment of not guilty was a bar to further prosecution. **n. 6.** An objection that nullifies a claim or action. **v. 1.** To obstruct; to impede; to prevent. **v. 2.** To nullify a claim or action by legal objection.

BARE. Mere; just sufficient. *Example*: The bare necessities.

BARRATRY. At **common law** and in some state statutes, the crime of frequently stirring up quarrels between persons either at law or otherwise. Barratry is most commonly applied to an **attorney** who repeatedly attempts to bring about lawsuits that will be profitable to the attorney. Since few cases are prosecuted, barratry is generally considered to be an **archaic** crime. See ABUSE OF PROCESS for a list of related terms.

BASE. **1.** Impure; adulterated. **2.** Inferior; low.

BASELESS COMPLAINT. Same as UNFOUNDED REPORTED OFFENSE.

BASELESS OFFENSE. Same as UNFOUNDED REPORTED OFFENSE.

BASIC. Fundamental.

Bb

BASTARD. A child of a married woman and a man who is not the husband of the mother. The term bastard is also sometimes used to designate any illegitimate child.

BATTERY. The unlawful intentional infliction of **bodily injury** or offensive physical contact upon another. Every battery includes **assault**. The requirement of touching another person may be satisfied not only by contacts with the body, but also by contacts with anything closely connected with the body or an item carried in the hand. Examples of batteries are spitting in someone's face, knocking a glass out of someone's hand, or whipping a horse on which someone is sitting, causing the person to fall and be injured. See ASSAULT for a list of related terms.

BAWDYHOUSE. Same as HOUSE OF PROSTITUTION.

BEAR. **1.** To carry; to support. **2.** To render; to relate. *Example*: To bear witness. **3.** To produce; to yield. *Example*: The investigation bore unexpected results. **4.** To endure; to tolerate. *Example*: He could not bear the pain. **5.** To visibly exhibit. *Example*: Bearing a scar on his cheek. **6.** To assume as a responsibility. *Example*: To bear the blame.

BEAT. To unlawfully strike or hit.

BECOME. To pass from one state or condition to another.

BEFORE. **1.** Earlier than; previous to. **2.** In front of; ahead of. **3.** In the presence of. **4.** By; at. **5.** In preference to; rather than. *Example*: He would quit before compromising his beliefs.

BEG. To ask for as charity; to solicit alms.

BEGIN. **1.** To start; to commence; to institute. **2.** To come into existence; to arise; to originate.

BEG THE QUESTION. To assume the truth of the very point being argued.

BEHAVIOR. Manner of acting; conduct; demeanor.

BELIEF. *See*: INFORMATION AND BELIEF.

BELONG. To be the property of; to be a part of.

BELOW. **1.** Of inferior jurisdiction; in a lower rank or class. *Example*: The court of appeals reversed the decision of the court below. **2.** In a lower place; beneath. **3.** At a point further along on a page or in a book. *Example*: See the explanation below.

BENCH. **1.** The whole body of judges, considered collectively. **2.** The office or position of a judge. *Example*: He was appointed to the bench. **3.** The seat for judges in a courtroom.

BENCH TRIAL. Same as NONJURY TRIAL.

BENCH WARRANT. A **warrant** initiated by and issued from the bench or court directing a **law enforcement officer** to bring a specified person before the court. A bench warrant is used, among other purposes, when a person has failed to appear in response to a **subpoena**, **summons**, or **citation**; when a person is first named as a defendant in an **indictment**; when an accused person needs to be transferred from jail to court for trial; and when failure to obey a court order is **contempt of court**. A bench warrant is so called to distinguish it from an **arrest warrant** issued by a magistrate on the basis of a **complaint** and **affidavit** prepared by a law enforcement officer or other person. A bench warrant is sometimes called a **capias** or an **alias warrant**. See ARREST WARRANT for a list of related terms.

BENEFICIARY. **1.** A person who receives a benefit, profit, or advantage. **2.** A person to whom another person owes a **fiduciary** obligation, whether as an agent, an attorney, a trustee, a guardian, a partner, or the like.

BENEFIT. Anything that is good for a person or thing; advantage; profit; privilege; gain.

BESIDE. By the side of. See PROXIMITY for a list of related terms.

BESIDES. In addition to; over and above; moreover.

BEST EVIDENCE. Original or firsthand **evidence** that provides the best authority for or greatest certainty of a fact in question. *Example*: A ransom note itself is the best evidence of the existence and contents of the ransom note. *Also called*: **primary evidence**. See EVIDENCE for a list of related terms.

BEST EVIDENCE RULE. A rule of EVIDENCE that requires a party to a case to introduce the highest possible degree of proof of a fact, considering the nature of the case, and assuming that such proof is accessible. *Example*: A written document is always regarded as the best evidence of its existence and contents. A copy of the document or testimony about it would be inadmissible in court under the best evidence rule, unless it were shown that the document itself could not be obtained. See EVIDENCE for a list of related terms.

BESTIALITY. **Sexual intercourse** between a human and an animal. At common law, bestiality was considered a crime against nature and was punishable by death.

B b

Under modern statutes, bestiality is prohibited as a form of **sodomy**. See SEX OFFENSES for a list of related terms.

BET. An agreement between two or more persons that a sum of money or other thing of value shall be paid or delivered to one of them on the occurrence or nonoccurrence of an uncertain event; a wager.

BETWEEN. **1.** Intermediate to (in time, quantity, or degree). *Example*: Between two and three o'clock. **2.** Connecting. *Example*: A path between the house and barn. **3.** Involving; concerning. *Example*: A choice between two courses of action. *See*: AMONG.

BEYOND A REASONABLE DOUBT. An accused person is presumed innocent until proven guilty beyond a reasonable doubt. Beyond a reasonable doubt requires little interpretation, although many courts have attempted to formulate somewhat involved definitions that add little to the plain meaning of the term. Some examples of these definitions are "fully satisfied," "entirely convinced," "reasonably certain," and "satisfied to a moral certainty." Suffice it to say that proof beyond a reasonable doubt requires that the fact be established to a reasonable, but not absolute or mathematical, certainty. A possibility or probability is not sufficient.

In the U.S. Supreme Court decision holding that due process required the use of the reasonable doubt standard in criminal prosecutions, Justice John M. Harlan concurred, writing: "I view the requirement of proof beyond a reasonable doubt in a criminal case as bottomed on a fundamental value determination of our society that it is far worse to convict an innocent man than to let a guilty man go free." *In re Winship*, 397 U.S. 358, 372, 90 S.Ct. 1068, 1077, 25 L.Ed.2d 368, 380 (1970). In the *Winship* decision, the Court also decided that the Fourteenth Amendment required proof beyond a reasonable doubt in state juvenile delinquency proceedings during the adjudicatory stage, when the juvenile was charged with an act that would constitute a crime if committed by an adult. Furthermore, the *Winship* decision held that due process requires "proof beyond a reasonable doubt of every fact necessary to constitute the crime with which [the defendant] is charged." 397 U.S. at 364, 90 S.Ct. at 1073, 25 L.Ed.2d at 375. This means that the prosecution must establish every **element of a crime** beyond a reasonable doubt. The **burden of persuasion** never shifts to the accused to prove that an element of the crime was not established. See EVIDENCE for a list of related terms.

BIANNUAL. Occurring twice a year.

BIAS. A predisposition or inclination of the mind that prevents a person from impartially evaluating facts presented for determination. *See*: PREJUDICE.

BIENNIAL. Occurring once every two years.

BIFURCATED HEARING. *See*: ADJUDICATORY HEARING.

BIFURCATED TRIAL. A special two-part trial proceeding in which the issue of **guilt** is tried in the first step, and, if a **conviction** results, the appropriate **sentence** or applicable sentencing statute is determined in the second step. The two steps of a bifurcated trial generally take place in separate hearings. The second step occurs following the **verdict** and pronouncement of **judgment**. Typical issues in the second step of a bifurcated trial are whether the **insanity** defense is applicable and whether the death penalty should be imposed. See SENTENCE and TRIAL for lists of related terms.

BIGAMY. The offense of unlawfully entering into marriage by a person who, at the time of the marriage, knows himself or herself already to be legally married. In many jurisdictions, an unmarried person who knowingly enters into marriage with a person who already is legally married also commits bigamy. In some jurisdictions, **cohabitation** without legal marriage is also bigamy if one of the persons is legally married to someone else.

BILL. **1.** A formal written statement in the nature of a declaration, complaint, or petition, presented to a court. *See*: BILL OF INDICTMENT. **2.** A **draft** of a proposed **statute** submitted to a legislature for its adoption or rejection. See ACT for a list of related terms. *See also*: PRIVATE BILL; PUBLIC BILL. **3.** An itemized statement of particular details. *See*: BILL OF PARTICULARS. **4.** A special enactment of a legislature in the exercise of a quasi-judicial power. *Example*: Bill of impeachment. **5.** A written statement of the terms of a contract or transaction. *Example*: Bill of lading. **6.** An account for goods sold, services rendered, or work done. **7.** A piece of paper money.

BILL OF ATTAINDER. A special legislative enactment directed against a particular person, pronouncing the person guilty of an alleged **felony** or **treason**, without following the established rules of procedure, and passing sentence of death and **attainder** upon the person. In its constitutional sense, a bill of attainder includes a **bill of pains and penalties**. Article 1, Section 9, Clause 3 of the United States Constitution prohibits bills of attainder.

BILL OF EXCEPTIONS. A formal written statement of **exceptions** taken to rulings, decisions, or instructions of the trial judge during a trial. A bill of exceptions is presented to an **appellate court** for **review** of the trial judge's actions. *Also called*: **bill of review; certificate of evidence.**

BILL OF INDICTMENT. A formal written document prepared by a **prosecuting attorney** accusing a specified person of having committed a specified crime and presented to a **grand jury** for their action. *See*: INDICTMENT.

BILL OF PAINS AND PENALTIES.   A special legislative enactment directed against a particular person, pronouncing the person guilty of a **felony** or **treason**, without following the established rules of procedure, and inflicting a punishment other than death upon the person. *See*: BILL OF ATTAINDER.

BILL OF PARTICULARS.   A written statement prepared by the **prosecution** giving the accused more specific details of the crime charged in the **indictment** or **complaint**. The purpose of a bill of particulars is to help the accused prepare a **defense**, avoid prejudicial surprise at trial, and intelligently raise pleas of **double jeopardy** and the bar of the **statute of limitations**. *Also called*: **statement of particulars**.

BILL OF REVIEW.   Same as BILL OF EXCEPTIONS.

BILL OF RIGHTS.   The first ten amendments to the U.S. Constitution, guaranteeing that the people have certain rights and liberties. Included in the bill of rights are the guarantees of **freedom of assembly and petition, freedom of religion, freedom of speech, freedom of the press**, the right against compelled **self-incrimination**, and the prohibition against unreasonable **search and seizure**.

BILL, PRIVATE.   *See*: PRIVATE BILL.

BILL, PUBLIC.   *See*: PUBLIC BILL.

BIND.   To place under legal obligation.

BINDING PRECEDENT.   *See*: PRECEDENT.

BIND OVER.   **1.** The decision by a **court of limited jurisdiction** that a person charged with a **felony** appear for **trial** on that charge in a **court of general jurisdiction** or be subject to **grand jury** proceedings. The decision to bind over is the result of a finding of **probable cause** at a **preliminary hearing** in the limited jurisdiction court. When a court binds over a defendant for trial, he or she may be required to put up **bail** or enter into a **recognizance** guaranteeing appearance as required. **2.** Bind over is sometimes used to refer to the **juvenile court** process of TRANSFER TO ADULT COURT.

BLACK JACK.   A small leather-covered club, weighted at the head and having an elastic shaft.

BLACK LIST.   A list of persons or organizations marked out for special avoidance, antagonism, censure, or discrimination or placed under suspicion.

BLACKMAIL.   Same as EXTORTION. Sometimes the term blackmail is reserved for the kind of extortion where the threat is not physical but relates to exposing some secret or true or alleged fact that would do harm to the personal circumstances of a person, or damage his or her reputation. See ABSTRACTION for a list of related terms.

BLACK MARIA.   A closed vehicle used for transporting prisoners to and from jail.

BLANKET.   Covering a group or class of things rather than one or more things mentioned individually. *Example*: The governor issued a blanket prohibition on all smoking in government buildings.

BLASPHEMY.   An abusive or contemptuous act, utterance, or writing concerning God or religion. Blasphemy is a **common law** offense and an offense under **statute** in some jurisdictions. Blasphemy statutes are rarely, if ever, enforced today.

BLOOD MONEY.   Money paid as a **reward** for the apprehension and conviction of a person charged with a **capital** crime.

BLOTTER.   A police agency's daily record of **arrests** and other occurrences.

BLUDGEON.   A short, heavy club, with one end loaded or thicker than the other, used as a weapon.

BLUE LAW.   Any law restricting or regulating activities on Sunday.

BLUE-SKY LAW.   A popular name for a law regulating and supervising investment companies in order to protect the community from investing in fraudulent companies.

BOARD.   **1.** An official body of persons who direct or supervise some activity. *Example*: Board of Directors; Parole Board. **2.** Daily meals. *Example*: He was provided with room and board.

BOARD OF PARDONS AND PAROLE.   *See*: PAROLING AUTHORITY.

BOARD OF PAROLE.   *See*: PAROLING AUTHORITY.

BOARD OF PROBATION AND PAROLE.   *See*: PAROLING AUTHORITY.

BODILY HARM.   Same as BODILY INJURY.

BODILY INJURY.   Section 210.0 (2) of the **Model Penal Code** defines bodily injury as "physical pain, illness or any impairment of physical condition." The term bodily injury may be defined differently in different jurisdictions. *Also called*: **bodily harm**.

BODY.   **1.** A person, organization, or other legal entity. **2.** The part of the person to which the head and limbs are attached; the trunk. The term body is also used to

Bb

describe the entire physical person, including the head and limbs. **3.** The main part of a written instrument, as distinguished from the **recital**, **title**, **jurat**, **caption**, etc. **4.** A number of persons or things considered collectively. *Example*: A body of laws; the body of judges.

BODY EXECUTION.   A writ or order directing that the body of the named defendant be **seized** and taken into custody. See ARREST WARRANT and SEIZURE for lists of related terms.

BODY OF THE CRIME.   Same as CORPUS DELICTI.

BOMB.   An explosive device fused to detonate under specified conditions.

BOMBING INCIDENT.   The detonation or attempted detonation of an explosive or incendiary device with willful disregard of risk to the person or property of another or for a criminal purpose.

BONA FIDE.   **1.** In good faith; without fraud or deceit; honestly. **2.** Authentic; genuine. *See*: MALA FIDE.

BONA FIDES.   Good faith; honesty. *See*: MALA FIDES.

BONA VACANTIA.   *Latin.* "Vacant goods." Personal property without an owner; unclaimed property. *Also called*: **vacantia bona**. *See*: ABANDON.

BOND.   **1.** Generally, any written obligation, especially one that requires payment of a specified amount of money on or before a specified date. **2.** A certificate or evidence of corporate or governmental debt in which the issuing company or governmental body promises to pay the bondholders a specified amount of interest for a specified amount of time and to repay the loan on the expiration date. **3.** A BAIL BOND.

BONDSMAN.   Same as SURETY.

BOOKING.   A police administrative procedure officially recording an **arrest** in a police register. Booking involves, at the minimum, recording the name of the person arrested, the officer making the arrest, and the time of, place of, circumstances of, and reason for the arrest. The meaning of booking, however, is sometimes expanded to include other procedures that take place in the station house after an arrest. Booking may include a **search** of the arrested person, including in some cases a search of body cavities, fingerprinting, photographing, a **lineup**, or other identification procedures.

Booking is usually completed before the arrested person is taken for his or her **initial appearance** before the magistrate. Booking may, however, take place after the initial appearance, or part of the booking procedures may take place before and part after the initial appearance. Booking procedures vary in different states and in different law enforcement agencies within states. *Also called*: **logging in**; **slating**.

BOOKMAKING. Unlawfully receiving, recording, and paying off **wagers** on uncertain events. As defined in some penal codes, this offense includes casual operations such as office football pools. Prosecution, however, is highly unlikely in such instances. The usual criminal case relates to a continuous, professional operation conducted entirely for the purpose of making profits. See GAMBLING for a list of related terms.

BOOTLEG. To make, sell, or transport intoxicating liquor illegally. The term bootleg may also refer to illegal dealing in other types of **contraband**.

BORDERING. Having a common border or boundary with. See PROXIMITY for a list of related terms.

BOUNDARY. A line or object indicating the limit or furthest extent of a tract of land or territory.

BOUNDING. Having a boundary on. See PROXIMITY for a list of related terms.

BOUND OVER. *See*: BIND OVER.

BOUNTY. A payment promised to induce several persons to perform certain services (such as the destruction of predatory animals). Each person who performs the requested act is entitled to the promised compensation. *See*: REWARD.

BOYCOTT. To abstain, either alone or in combination with others, from doing business with another person or party as a means of protest or to compel some action.

BRAWL. A noisy quarrel in a public place that creates a disturbance of the public peace.

BREACH. A violation or nonfulfillment of an obligation.

BREACH OF PRISON. Same as PRISON BREAKING.

BREACH OF THE PEACE. Same as DISTURBING THE PEACE.

BREAK. In the law relating to **housebreaking** and **burglary**, to break means to use force to gain entry without actually entering. Even the slightest application of force, such as lifting a latch or opening a window, is sufficient to constitute breaking. "It

Bb

is enough to constitute a breaking, if an unlocked window, whether or not partially opened, is raised or further opened to admit a person's body, or if a door, even though unlocked or ajar, is opened for the same purpose." *State v. Kohlfuss,* 211 A.2d 143, 149 (Conn. 1965). Using force to get out of a building after unlawfully entering it is also considered breaking. *See*: BREAKING AND ENTERING.

BREAKING AND ENTERING.   Introducing any part of a person or any implement or projectile into a building after breaking. *See*: BREAK.

BRIBE.   Something of value given to a holder of public office or a person in a position of trust for the purpose of improperly influencing the person's action.

BRIBERY.   Giving or accepting a BRIBE.

BRIEF.   A concise written statement prepared by a party interested in an **appeal**, **motion**, **trial**, or other proceeding, and presented to the court. The purpose of a brief is to inform the court of the essential facts and issues of the case and the points of law the party wishes to establish, and to give reasons and legal authorities to support the party's contentions. Copies of briefs must also be submitted to the opposing party. *See*: APPELLATE BRIEF; MEMORANDUM.

BRING AN ACTION.   To initiate a legal ACTION (definition 3). *Also called*: **bring suit**.

BRING SUIT.   Same as BRING AN ACTION.

BROAD INTERPRETATION.   An interpretation of a law that looks to the intent of the law rather than dwelling on technicalities and minor distinctions.

BROTHEL.   Same as HOUSE OF PROSTITUTION.

BUG.   A small microphone or other listening device used for **eavesdropping**.

BUGGERY.   Anal intercourse between a man and either a woman or another man. The term buggery sometimes also means copulation between a human and an animal. The term buggery is often used interchangeably with SODOMY. See SEX OF-FENSES for a list of related terms.

BUILDING.   Any manmade edifice or structure designed to stand more or less permanently and intended for the shelter of persons or property or some other human use or convenience.

BULGE.   A swelling; a hump; a rounded protuberance.

BULLET.   A small rounded or pointed metal projectile designed to be fired from a pistol, rifle, or other small firearm.

BURDEN OF EVIDENCE.   Same as BURDEN OF PRODUCTION OF EVIDENCE.

BURDEN OF GOING FORWARD WITH EVIDENCE.   Same as BURDEN OF PRODUCTION OF EVIDENCE.

BURDEN OF PERSUASION.   The duty of the party with the **burden of proof** to convince the **trier of fact** of all the elements of the party's case to the degree required. In a criminal case, the **prosecution**, in order to convict the defendant, must convince the trier of fact of the existence of each **element** of the crime **beyond a reasonable doubt**. The burden of persuasion remains with the prosecution throughout a criminal case. *Also called*: **persuasion burden**. See EVIDENCE for a list of related terms.

BURDEN OF PRODUCTION OF EVIDENCE.   The duty of a party during trial to make a **prima facie** showing on a particular issue, sufficient to warrant submitting the issue to **jurors**. In a criminal case, the **prosecution**, in order to avoid a **directed verdict**, must produce sufficient evidence of each **element** of the crime charged. The **defendant** must produce evidence in support of his or her **affirmative defenses** (e.g., **insanity**, **self-defense**). The burden is met if the court determines that there is sufficient evidence to support a finding by the **trier of fact** in favor of the party with the burden of production. The burden of production of evidence may shift between the parties during the trial. *Also called*: **burden of evidence**; **burden of going forward with evidence**; **production burden**. See EVIDENCE for a list of related terms.

BURDEN OF PROOF.   The duty to establish a particular issue or proposition by the quantity of evidence required by law. In a criminal case, the burden of proof involves both the BURDEN OF PRODUCTION OF EVIDENCE and the BURDEN OF PERSUASION. The **prosecution** has the burden of proof to establish every **element** of the crime charged **beyond a reasonable doubt**. See EVIDENCE for a list of related terms.

BUREAU OF ALCOHOL, TOBACCO AND FIREARMS.   *See*: ALCOHOL, TOBACCO AND FIREARMS, BUREAU OF.

BUREAU OF JUSTICE ASSISTANCE.   The Bureau of Justice Assistance in the **Office of Justice Programs** provides financial and technical assistance to state and local units of government to control drug abuse and violent crime and to improve the criminal justice system. The Anti-Drug Abuse Act of 1988 (42 U.S.C. §3750), which established the Edward Byrne Memorial State and Local Law Enforcement Assistance Programs, authorizes the bureau to make grants for the purpose of enforcing

Bb

state and local laws that establish offenses similar to those established in the Controlled Substances Act and to improve the functioning of the criminal justice system, with emphasis on violent crime and serious offenders. The states are required to prepare a statewide anti-drug and violent crime strategy as part of their applications for Formula Grant funds. Federal funds from fiscal year 1990 and prior fiscal years may be used for up to 75 percent of the total project costs. Fiscal year 1991 and subsequent year appropriations may be used for up to 50 percent of the total project costs.

The bureau uses the Discretionary Grant program to provide state and local criminal justice agencies with state-of-the-art information on innovative and effective programs, practices, and techniques through demonstration projects, training, and technical assistance. For example, the bureau is demonstrating effective ways of depriving drug traffickers of the profit of their activities through the seizure and forfeiture of drug-related assets, financial investigations, and the use of civil statutes. Criminal justice agencies are provided assistance in addressing new issues and problems, such as the spread of "crack" cocaine, disruption of clandestine laboratories, and drug testing. The bureau also supports programs that are national or multistate in scope, such as the National Crime Prevention (McGruff) Campaign. Discretionary Grant funds are awarded directly by the bureau and do not require matching funds.

Direct assistance is also provided by the bureau through programs such as the Public Safety Officers' Death Benefits Program, the Emergency Federal Law Enforcement Assistance Program, the Regional Information Sharing System, the Mariel Cuban Reimbursement Program, the Federal Surplus Property Transfer Program, and the Prison Industry Certification Program.

BUREAU OF JUSTICE STATISTICS. The Bureau of Justice Statistics in the **Office of Justice Programs** is responsible for collecting, analyzing, and disseminating statistical information about crime, its perpetrators and victims, and the operation of the criminal justice system at the federal, state, and local levels of government. The bureau assists state governments in developing capabilities in criminal justice statistics and investigates information policy on such issues as the confidentiality and security of data.

The bureau provides the President, the Congress, other officials, and the public with timely and accurate data about crime and the administration of justice. The bureau's *Report to the Nation on Crime and Justice* presents comprehensive statistical information about crime and the justice system in a format suitable for the general public. It publishes concise *Special Reports* and periodic *Bulletins* that provide up-to-date information about various aspects of criminal justice. In addition, lengthier volumes present detailed analyses of specific topics.

The **National Crime Survey** is the largest ongoing statistical series currently conducted by the bureau. Using interviews from a large sample of U.S. households, the survey measures the rates at which the nation's population is victimized by crimes of violence and theft. Other statistical series cover prison and jail inmates, probation and parole, adjudication, processing offenders as they move through the criminal justice system, criminal justice expenditure and employment, and the federal justice system. The bureau supports a statistical component in the **National Criminal Justice Reference Service**. The Justice Statistics Clearinghouse provides reference services for people requesting information, maintains a mailing list, and distributes bureau publications. The bureau also manages the **Drugs and Crime Data Center and Clearinghouse,** which gathers and evaluates existing data on drugs and the justice system; identifies drug enforcement data gaps; operates a clearinghouse/reference center that serves as a single source for those in need of drug statistics; and prepares special reports and tabulations of existing drug data.

BUREAU OF PRISONS. The mission of the Bureau of Prisons in the **Department of Justice** is to protect society by carrying out the judgments of the federal courts through providing confinement services to committed offenders and providing program opportunities to all inmates who qualify and who wish to participate. This confinement function complements other sentencing options available to federal judges. The bureau's mission includes the responsibility to maintain secure, safe, and humane correctional institutions for persons placed in the care and custody of the Attorney General; develop and operate correctional programs that seek a balanced application of the concepts of punishment, deterrence, incapacitation, and rehabilitation; and provide, primarily through the National Institute of Corrections, assistance to state and local correctional agencies.

The Executive Office of the Director provides overall direction for agency operations. In addition to typical administrative functions performed by an agency head, Offices of General Counsel, Internal Affairs, Research, Strategic Planning, and Public Affairs (congressional, media, and communications functions) are within this office and report to the director through the chief of staff.

—The Administrative Division develops plans, programs, and policies concerning the acquisition, construction, and staffing of new facilities, as well as budget development, financial management, procurement, contracting, and information and inmate systems management.

—The Correctional Programs Division is responsible for managing the correctional services (security) operations in bureau institutions, community corrections programs, and case and unit management, as well as religious and psychological services.

—Federal Prison Industries (trade name UNICOR) is a wholly owned government corporation whose mission is to provide employment and training opportunities for inmates confined in federal correctional facilities. UNICOR manufactures a wide range of items, including furniture, electronics, textiles, and graphics. Services performed by UNICOR's inmates include data entry, printing, and

Bb

furniture refinishing. The corporation funds selected preindustrial, vocational, and experimental training programs.

—The Health Services Division has oversight responsibility for all medical programs and environmental, health, safety, and sanitation services in bureau institutions. This division is also responsible for food services, farm operations, and inmate accident compensation programs.

—The Human Resources Division provides personnel, training, and labor management within the agency. Its functions also include pay and position management and recruitment.

—The National Institute of Corrections provides advisory and technical support to state and local correctional agencies throughout the country. The institute also operates the National Academy of Corrections, the Institute Information Center, and the National Jail Center, all of which are currently located in Boulder, Colorado. The institute receives logistical support from the Bureau of Prisons, but is a separate budget entity.

—The Program Review Division is responsible for oversight of agency audit functions and manages an internal control branch for training of auditors and coordinating the year-end assurance statement to the Attorney General. This division has a program analysis branch, coordinating in-depth analysis of audit outcomes and recommending necessary management changes in accord with those findings. The inmate grievance (administrative remedy) procedure is operated out of this division.

The bureau is subdivided into six geographic regions, each staffed with field-qualified personnel who are responsible for policy development and oversight, providing operational guidance to field locations, and providing support functions in areas such as auditing, technical assistance, budget, and personnel. Each regional office is headed by an experienced career bureau manager who is a full member of the bureau's executive staff.

BURGLARY.   Under the common law, burglary is the trespassory **breaking and entering** of a dwelling house of another at night with the intent to commit a **felony** therein. Some modern criminal statutes have expanded the definition of burglary to include any unlawful entry, with or without force, of any building, structure, vehicle, or vessel with intent to commit any crime. Statutory definitions of burglary vary from state to state. See ABSTRACTION for a list of related terms.

BURN.   To consume with or by fire.

BUSINESS RECORDS EXCEPTION.   Records kept in the routine course of business are admissible as exceptions to the **hearsay rule**. In this context, business includes any profession, occupation, institution, or association, whether or not conducted for profit. Therefore, police or hospital records could qualify as business records.

In order to qualify for the exception the record must have been: (1) kept in the course of a regularly conducted business activity; (2) kept as a regular practice of the business; (3) made at or near the time of the act or event in question; and (4) made by a person with personal knowledge of the act or event in question or transmitted to the record maker in the regular course of business by a person with personal knowledge of the act or event. See HEARSAY RULE for a list of other exceptions.

BUT.   Except; except that; on the contrary; nevertheless; yet; however; still.

BY.   **1.** Not later than; before. *Example*: Do it by March 3. **2.** Through the means of; with. *Example*: To enter by force. **3.** Next to; beside. *Example*: He stood by the table. See PROXIMITY for a list of related terms. **4.** Past. *Example*: They walked by the store. **5.** To the extent of. *Example*: It was longer by two inches. **6.** According to. *Example*: By her own admission, she was guilty.

BY REASON OF.   On account of; because of.

BYSTANDER.   A person who is present at an event but does not participate and has no personal interest in it; a spectator; an observer.

CADAVER.   A dead human body; a corpse.

CALABOOSE.   A colloquial term for JAIL.

CALAMITY.   A disaster that produces deep distress or misfortune.

CALCULATE .   **1.** To compute mathematically. **2.** To intend; to plan.

CALCULATED.   **1.** Intended; likely. *Example*: Language calculated to produce anger. **2.** Adapted; fitted; suited. *Example*: A weapon calculated to produce death.

CALENDAR.   A list of cases awaiting **trial** by a court.

CALENDAR CALL.   A court session during which the cases awaiting **trial** are called to determine their current status and to assign trial dates.

CALL.   **1.** To command or request to come. *Example*: To call a witness. **2.** To bring under consideration; to bring to action. *Example*: To call a case for trial. **3.** To convoke; to convene. *Example*: Call a meeting. **4.** To announce; to declare. **5.** To demand payment. *Example*: To call a bond.

CALL THE DOCKET.   To publicly announce the **docket** or list of cases at the beginning of a term of court for the purpose of setting times for **trial** or entering **orders**.

CALUMNY.   A false and malicious statement designed to injure a person's reputation.

CAMARA v. MUNICIPAL COURT.   The 1967 U.S. Supreme Court case that, together with its companion case of *See v. City of Seattle,* 387 U.S. 541, 87 S.Ct. 1737, 18 L.Ed.2d 943 (1967), held that the warrant requirement of the Fourth Amendment applies to administrative inspections of private premises, including both dwellings and commercial premises. Because administrative searches differ in nature and purpose from criminal searches, however, the **probable cause** standard for the issuance of an administrative **search warrant** differs in nature and is less stringent than the standard for the issuance of a criminal search warrant. The Court said:

"The warrant procedure is designed to guarantee that a decision to search private property is justified by a reasonable governmental interest. But reasonableness is still the ultimate standard. If a valid public interest justifies the intrusion contemplated, then there is probable cause to issue a suitably restricted search warrant." 387 U.S. 523, 539, 87 S.Ct. 1727, 1736, 18 L.Ed.2d 930, 941.

CAMERA. A judge's **chambers**. *See*: IN CAMERA.

CAMOUFLAGE. The art of disguising or concealing the nature of objects.

CAN. **1.** To be enabled by law to; to have a right to. **2.** To be competent to.

CANCEL. To annul; to terminate; to obliterate; to revoke. *See*: DELETE; EXPUNGE; OBLITERATE; PURGE; STRIKE.

CANNABIS. Same as MARIJUANA.

CANNABIS SATIVA. Same as MARIJUANA.

CANNOT. **1.** To be unable to. **2.** The term cannot is sometimes used as the equivalent of "shall not" or "may not."

CAPABLE. **1.** Having legal power or capacity; qualified; competent. **2.** Susceptible; open to. *Example*: An error capable of correction.

CAPACITY. **1.** The mental and physical ability to act with purpose and to be aware of the certain, probable, or possible results of one's conduct; the legal ability of a person to commit a criminal act. Whether a person possesses capacity at the time of an act or during judicial proceedings determines whether **prosecution** is legally possible (e.g., children cannot be prosecuted), whether prosecution must halt (e.g., the defendant is found **incompetent to stand trial**), and sometimes the nature of the finding (e.g., **not guilty by reason of insanity**). Some of the bases for incapacity are youth, **insanity**, involuntary intoxication, unconsciousness, and **coercion**. **2.** Potential ability to do something satisfactorily. Capacity, in this sense, and **competence** are often used interchangeably. **3.** Legal qualification or authority. *Example*: A deputy sheriff has the capacity to arrest.

CAPAX DOLI. *Latin*. Capable of criminal intent; having sufficient intelligence and comprehension to be held criminally responsible for one's acts.

CAPIAS. *See*: BENCH WARRANT.

CAPITA, PER. *See*: PER CAPITA.

CAPITAL. Punishable by death. *Example*: A capital crime is one that may, but need not necessarily, be punished by death. See DEATH for a list of related terms.

CAPRICIOUS. Apt to change suddenly; impulsive; unpredictable. *See*: ARBITRARY AND CAPRICIOUS.

CAPTION. The standardized heading or introduction of a **pleading**, **indictment**, or other court document, which shows the name of the court, name of the judge, name of the parties, docket or file number, and other like information.

CAPUT. *Latin.* "Head."

CARE. 1. Caution; diligence; prudence; serious attention. *Example*: She acted with ordinary care under the circumstances. 2. Custody; safekeeping; protection; responsibility. *Example*: He embezzled funds under his care.

CAREER CRIMINAL. A person having a past record of multiple **arrests** or **convictions** for serious crimes, or an unusually large number of arrests or convictions for crimes of varying degrees of seriousness. The term has varying definitions in different jurisdictions and is sometimes used as a synonym for **habitual criminal**. See CRIME for a list of related terms.

CARELESS. Failing to exercise reasonable CARE; negligent.

CARNAL. Pertaining to the flesh or body, its passions, and its appetites; sensual; sexual.

CARNAL ABUSE. An act of assault of the female sexual organs with the male sexual organ that does not amount to **penetration**.

CARNAL KNOWLEDGE. Same as SEXUAL INTERCOURSE. The slightest penetration of the sexual organ of the female by the sexual organ of the male constitutes carnal knowledge.

CARNAL KNOWLEDGE OF A CHILD. Same as STATUTORY RAPE.

CARRIER. One who transports or delivers persons or property.

CARROLL DOCTRINE. The search and seizure doctrine, originating in the case of *Carroll v. U.S.*, 267 U.S. 132, 45 S.Ct. 280, 69 L.Ed. 543 (1925), that a warrantless **search** of a **motor vehicle** under **exigent circumstances** by a law enforcement officer who has **probable cause** to believe that the vehicle contains items subject to seizure is not unreasonable under the Fourth Amendment. The doctrine is sometimes referred to as the **automobile exception** to the search warrant requirement. "As a general rule, [the U.S. Supreme Court has] required the judgment of a magistrate on the probable cause issue and the issuance of a warrant before a search is made. Only in exigent circumstances will the judgment of the police as to probable cause serve as a sufficient authorization for a search." *Chambers v. Maroney*, 399 U.S. 42, 51, 90 S.Ct. 1975, 1981, 26 L.Ed.2d 419, 428 (1970). Usually, exigent circumstances are established by demonstrating specific facts showing either that the vehicle may be moved to an unknown location out of the jurisdiction, making a search under authority of a warrant impossible, or that items subject to seizure may be removed from the vehicle and concealed or destroyed. The U.S. Supreme Court has held, however, that this is not necessary and that the exigent circumstances requirement is automatically satisfied in the case of a motor vehicle stopped on the road. "It is thus clear that the justification to conduct such a warrantless search does not vanish once the car has been immobilized; nor does it depend upon a reviewing court's assessment of the likelihood in each particular case that the car would have been driven away, or that its contents would have been tampered with, during the period required for the police to obtain a warrant." *Michigan v. Thomas*, 458 U.S. 259, 261, 102 S.Ct. 3079, 3081, 73 L.Ed.2d 750, 753 (1982).

CARRY. **1.** To have on or about one's person; to hold; to bear. *Example*: The statute made it unlawful to carry a weapon. **2.** To transport; to convey.

CARRY AWAY. In the definition of **larceny**, carry away means to move the property of another from one place to another. The property need only be moved a slight distance and need not be removed from the owner's presence or premises.

CARRY ON. To conduct; to engage in.

CASE. **1.** Generally, a civil or criminal **action** brought before a court for adjudication; a set of facts that is the occasion for the exercise of the **jurisdiction** of a court, and that is handled by the court as a procedural unit. In civil proceedings, individual case designations are usually based on filings of complaints or petitions. In criminal proceedings, case is usually defined as a single **charging document** filed in a court containing one or more **charges** against one or more **defendants** and constituting the unit of action in court activity following the filing. However, the charges in two or more charging documents are sometimes combined, or the charges or defendants in one charging document separated, for purposes of adjudication. In some jurisdictions a case is defined as a single defendant charged with one or more crimes. **2.** Same as CAUSE OF ACTION. **3.** At the level of police or prosecutorial investigation, a case is a set of possibly criminal circumstances under investigation involving one or more persons. *Example*: Fred and Wally were assigned to investigate the murder case. **4.** In juvenile or correctional proceedings, a case is a person who is the object of agency actions. *See*: CONTROVERSY.

CASE AGREED ON. A written and agreed upon statement of facts submitted to a court in order to obtain a decision of law upon the facts stated without a **trial**. *Also* *called*: **amicable action; case stated; friendly suit**. See FACT for a list of related terms.

CASE FLOW. The process by which a **case** or cases move through the court from the time the case is **filed** to its **disposition**.

Cc

CASE LAW. Law derived from reported court **decisions** (rather than from **statutes** or other sources of law); judge-made law.

CASELOAD. **1.** The total number of **cases** before a given court or judicial officer during a specified time period. Caseload includes cases pending at the beginning of the reporting period, new cases filed, cases reopened or reinstated, and cases transferred from other courts, during the reporting period. *See*: PENDING CASELOAD. **2.** The total number of clients registered with a **correctional agency** or agent on a given date or during a specified time period. In the correctional context, caseload usually refers to those persons for whom a **probation agency** or **parole agency** has supervisory responsibility. Persons in the custody of a **confinement facility** typically are not considered part of a caseload. If, however, a correctional counselor within a confinement facility has responsibilities limited to a specific group of **inmates**, he or she may be considered to have a caseload.

CASE MADE. Same as CASE RESERVED.

CASE OR CONTROVERSY. *See*: CONTROVERSY.

CASE RESERVED. A written statement of facts drawn up and agreed upon by the attorneys for the respective parties and certified by the trial judge for the purpose of having certain undecided points of law determined upon full argument before the full bench. *Also called*: **case made**. See FACT for a list of related terms.

CASE STATED. Same as CASE AGREED ON.

CASUAL. Occurring by chance; accidental; occasional; irregular.

CASUALTY. **1.** A sudden, unforeseen event; an unfortunate accident. **2.** One who is injured or killed in an accident.

CATASTROPHE. A great misfortune; a disaster.

CATEGORICAL. Without exception; absolute; certain.

CAUSA. *Latin*. **n.** "Cause." **prep.** On account of; in anticipation of; in contemplation of. *Example*: Causa mortis means in anticipation of death.

CAUSA PROXIMA. *Latin.* "PROXIMATE CAUSE."

CAUSE. **1.** Justifiable or sufficient reason. *See*: PROBABLE CAUSE. **2.** That which brings about an event, effect, or result. **3.** A legal **action**. *See*: CAUSE OF ACTION.

CAUSE OF ACTION. "A 'cause of action' is a situation or state of facts which entitles a party to sustain an **action** *and* gives him the right to seek judicial interference in his behalf. . . . Thus, a cause of action consists of two elements: the operative facts and the right or power to seek and obtain redress for the infringement of a legal right which the facts show." *Fraticelli v. St. Paul Fire and Marine Insurance Co.,* 375 F.2d 186, 188 n.6 (1st Cir. 1967).

CAUTION. **v.** To warn; to give notice to. **n.** Care; prudence.

CAUTIONARY INSTRUCTION. A part of the INSTRUCTION to the jurors warning them about or explaining to them some aspect of their deliberations. A cautionary instruction may relate to such subjects as **burden of proof**, **credibility** and **weight of the evidence**, **admissions**, **expert evidence**, and the function and duty of the **jury**. The giving or refusing of a cautionary instruction is largely a matter of **judicial discretion** and will not be a ground for **reversal** unless that discretion is grossly abused to the prejudice of a party. See INSTRUCTION for a list of related terms.

CAVEAT. *Latin.* "Let him or her beware." **1.** A warning; a notice. **2.** A formal notice given by an interested party to a judicial officer requesting that a proceeding be postponed until the party is heard.

CAVITY. A hollow area within the body.

CEASE. **v.** To stop; to discontinue; to put an end to. **n.** CESSATION.

CEDE. **v.** To formally surrender possession of. **n.** CESSION.

CELATION. Concealment of pregnancy or childbirth.

CENSORSHIP. The forbidding of **publication** (definition 2) in advance of publication.

CENTRAL INTELLIGENCE AGENCY. The Central Intelligence Agency (CIA) collects, evaluates, and disseminates the vital information on political, military, economic, scientific, and other developments abroad needed to safeguard national security. The CIA was established under the National Security Council by the National Security Act of 1947, as amended (50 U.S.C. 401 et seq.). It now functions under that statute, Executive Order 12333 of December 4, 1981, and other laws, regulations, and directives. The agency has no police, subpoena, or law enforcement powers or internal security functions.

CEPIT. *Latin.* "He took." A technical term sometimes used in **indictments** for **larceny**.

CERTAIN. **1.** Free from doubt; precise; exact; definite; inevitable. **2.** Known but not specified or identified. *Example*: Certain persons were seen in the neighborhood. **3.** Limited; small but meaningful. *Example*: To a certain degree.

CERTIFICATE. A written statement assuring that something has been done or that certain facts are true.

CERTIFICATE OF DEATH. The official document listing the identity of the deceased, the time, date, cause, and circumstances of death, information on burial, and other vital statistics. See DEATH for a list of related terms.

CERTIFICATE OF EVIDENCE. Same as BILL OF EXCEPTIONS.

CERTIFICATION. *See*: TRANSFER TO ADULT COURT.

CERTIFICATION HEARING. Same as TRANSFER HEARING.

CERTIFIED JUVENILE. *See*: TRANSFER TO ADULT COURT.

CERTIFIED PUBLIC ACCOUNTANT. A public **accountant** who has received a **certificate** stating that he or she has met certain legal requirements.

CERTIFY. To testify to or vouch for in writing; to formally guarantee the truth, accuracy, or authenticity of.

CERTIORARI. *See*: WRIT OF CERTIORARI.

CESSATION. *See*: CEASE.

CESSION. *See*: CEDE.

CF. Abbreviation for COMPARE.

CFR. Abbreviation for CODE OF FEDERAL REGULATIONS.

CHAIN OF CUSTODY. "[A]n indirect method of proving the identity and integrity of **evidence** by showing its continuous whereabouts. Such a showing negates any substantial likelihood of substitution or alteration of the evidence. The establishment of a chain of custody is necessary where the nature of the evidence is such that it lacks identifiable characteristics or where the evidentiary purpose to be served by the item requires assurance that the evidence has not been subjected to tampering which could not be detected by human perception. Where the evidence is such that it may be recognized and identified by witnesses, and where tampering or alteration relevant to the purpose to be served by the evidence is not a realistic threat, no chain of custody need be established." *Johnson v. State*, 370 N.E.2d 892, 894-95 (Ind. 1977). *Also called*: **chain of possession**. See EVIDENCE for a list of related terms.

CHAIN OF POSSESSION.   Same as CHAIN OF CUSTODY.

CHALLENGE.   A formal **objection**. *See*: CHALLENGE FOR CAUSE; CHALLENGE TO THE ARRAY; CHALLENGE TO THE FAVOR; CHALLENGE TO THE POLLS; PEREMPTORY CHALLENGE.

CHALLENGE FOR CAUSE.   A formal **objection** to a prospective **juror** directed toward the qualifications of that juror. The party exercising a challenge for cause has an unlimited number of such challenges. Each challenge for cause, however, must be supported by a satisfactory reason or the judge will not dismiss the challenged juror. A general challenge for cause is an objection that the prospective juror is unqualified to serve in any case because of conviction of crime, unsoundness of mind, etc. A special or particular challenge for cause is an objection that the juror is unqualified to serve in the case to be tried because the juror has formed an opinion in the case, has a bias toward one of the parties, etc. See CHALLENGE for a list of related terms.

CHALLENGE TO THE ARRAY.   A formal **objection** to all the prospective jurors collectively because of some defect in the form or manner of making up the entire **panel**. A challenge to the array is usually based on a charge of bias or some default of the sheriff or other officer who summoned the jury. *Also called*: **challenge to the panel**; **challenge to the venire**. See CHALLENGE and JURY for lists of related terms.

CHALLENGE TO THE FAVOR.   A formal **objection** to a prospective **juror** because of a suspicion of **bias** in the mind of the juror. See CHALLENGE for a list of related terms.

CHALLENGE TO THE PANEL.   Same as CHALLENGE TO THE ARRAY.

CHALLENGE TO THE POLLS.   A formal **objection** to an individual prospective **juror**. See CHALLENGE for a list of related terms.

CHALLENGE TO THE VENIRE.   Same as CHALLENGE TO THE ARRAY.

CHAMBERS.   The office or private room of a **judge** where he or she holds hearings, makes orders, signs papers, and performs other judicial tasks when a session of the court, such as a trial, is not being held. Business transacted in this private setting is said to be done in chambers or **in camera**. *See*: AT CHAMBERS.

CHAMPERTY.   At **common law**, an agreement to share in the proceeds of litigation between a party to the litigation and a nonparty who carries on or defends the suit at the nonparty's own expense.

NOTE: Some states still recognize champerty and **maintenance** as offenses, but in most states they have been replaced with the civil actions of **abuse of process**, **malicious abuse of process**, and **malicious prosecution**. See ABUSE OF PROCESS for a list of related terms.

CHAMPION.   One who engages in a contest; one who acts or speaks on behalf of a person or cause; an advocate.

CHANCE.   That which is unplanned, uncontrolled, or unexplained.

CHANCELLOR.   **1.** A nonspecific title given to certain judges or other high officials. **2.** In some states, the presiding judge in a court of **equity** or **chancery**.

CHANCERY.   Same as EQUITY (definition 1).

CHANCE VERDICT.   A VERDICT determined by lot or chance as distinguished from a verdict based on the deliberate conclusions of the **jury** based on their reflections and interchange of ideas. Although formerly acceptable, chance verdicts are now unlawful. See VERDICT for a list of related terms.

CHANGE.   To alter; to make different; to put one thing in place of another.

CHANGE OF VENUE.   The **transfer** of a case from one court to another court that has the same **subject matter jurisdiction** but is in a different geographical location. The most frequent reason for a change of venue is a judicial determination that an **impartial jury** cannot be found within a particular geographic area, usually because of widely publicized prejudicial statements concerning the events that are the basis for the case. *See*: VENUE.

CHARACTER.   The combination of actual moral or ethical qualities and traits that belong to a person as evidenced by his or her habitual conduct. *See*: REPUTATION.

CHARACTER EVIDENCE.   **Evidence** relating to a person's moral standing, habits, traits, and reputation in the community. A defendant might attempt to reduce the probability that he or she committed a particular crime by introducing evidence of good character or propensity for not committing the crime. Ordinarily, this evidence will be limited to testimony concerning the particular character trait in issue. For example, evidence of the defendant's peaceful nature might be relevant in a case involving a violent crime. See EVIDENCE for a list of related terms.

CHARGE. **v. 1.** To formally accuse a specified person of committing a specific crime. **v. 2.** To give a **general instruction** to a **jury**. **v. 3.** To place a defendant's fate in the hands of a jury. *Example*: A jury is charged when it has been impaneled and sworn. **v. 4.** To place a burden on; to entrust with a duty or responsibility. **v. 5.** To command. **v. 6.** To attack or rush at violently. **v. 7.** To hold liable for payment; to demand payment from. **v. 8.** To load; to fill up. **n. 1.** A formal **accusation** that a specified person has committed a specific crime, recorded in a document such as a record of an **arrest**, a **complaint**, an **information** or **indictment**, or a **judgment** of **conviction**. **n. 2.** A COUNT in an indictment or information. *Example:* The indictment contained charges of robbery and assault. **n. 3.** Same as GENERAL INSTRUCTION. **n. 4.** An address of a court to a **grand jury** explaining their duties. **n. 5.** Care; custody; supervision. *Example*: The sheriff has charge of the jail. **n. 6.** A person or thing entrusted to one's care or management. *Example*: The orphan girl became a public charge. **n. 7.** A quantity of explosives to be set off at one time.

CHARGING DOCUMENT. A formal written **accusation**, filed in court, alleging that a specified person has committed a specific offense. The types of charging document are the **complaint**, the **indictment**, and the **information**. In **misdemeanor** cases the complaint may be the only charging document filed. In **felony** cases prosecution usually commences with an accusation called a complaint filed in a lower court. If **probable cause** is found by a **magistrate** or **grand jury**, an accusation called an information or indictment will be filed in the felony trial court. *Also called*: **charging instrument**. See ACCUSATION for a list of related terms.

CHARGING INSTRUMENT. Same as CHARGING DOCUMENT.

CHARLATAN. A person who claims to have more knowledge or skill than he or she possesses; a quack.

CHASTE. Having never voluntarily had unlawful **sexual intercourse**.

CHATTEL. Every tangible thing, whether movable or immovable, that is not **real property**. The term chattel includes both animate and inanimate things.

CHEAT. To fraudulently obtain another person's money or property.

CHECK FRAUD. The issuing or passing of a check, draft, or money order that is a legally effective document, signed by the legal account holder, but with the knowledge that the bank or depository will refuse to honor it because of insufficient funds or a closed account. *Also called*: **bad check**; **insufficient funds check**. *See*: COUNTERFEITING; FORGERY; KITING.

CHICANERY.   Deception by trickery.

Cc

CHIEF JUDGE.   Same as PRESIDING JUDGE (definition 2).

CHIEF JUSTICE.   Same as PRESIDING JUDGE (definition 2).

CHIEF OF POLICE.   A local **law enforcement officer** who is the appointed or elected head of a police department. See LAW ENFORCEMENT OFFICER for a list of related terms.

CHILD ABUSE.   A willful act or acts causing physical harm to a child by a person responsible for the child. In some jurisdictions, child abuse is a separate criminal offense. It may include mental or emotional injury or impairment, sexual abuse or exploitation, deprivation of essential needs, or lack of protection from these dangers. A juvenile court determination that child abuse has occurred can be a reason for adjudicating the child a **dependent**. *See*: CHILD NEGLECT.

CHILD IN NEED OF SUPERVISION.   A class of **juveniles** often consisting of **status offenders** but variously defined in different jurisdictions. A typical definition is a child who is habitually disobedient of the reasonable and lawful commands of his or her parent, guardian, or other custodian, is ungovernable or incorrigible, and is in need of care or rehabilitation. A child in need of supervision has not committed an offense against society, but only against his or her own best interests. *Abbreviation*: **C.H.I.N.S.** *Also called*: **juvenile in need of supervision**; **minor in need of supervision**; **person in need of supervision**. See JUVENILE for a list of related terms.

CHILD NEGLECT.   Willful failure by the person responsible for a child's welfare to provide adequate food, clothing, shelter, education, and supervision for the child. In some jurisdictions, child neglect is a separate criminal offense. A juvenile court determination that neglect has occurred can be a reason for adjudicating the child a **dependent**. *See*: CHILD ABUSE.

CHILLING EFFECT.   Any law or practice that has the effect of seriously dissuading the exercise of a constitutional right, such as freedom of speech, is said to have a chilling effect on that right.

CHIMEL v. CALIFORNIA.   *See*: SEARCH INCIDENT TO ARREST.

C.H.I.N.S.   Abbreviation for CHILD IN NEED OF SUPERVISION.

CHOATE. Perfected; complete; certain.

CHRONIC. Prolonged, lingering; continuing.

CIA. Abbreviation for CENTRAL INTELLIGENCE AGENCY.

CIRCA. *Latin.* "About; around." The term circa is commonly used before approximate dates and figures. *Example*: circa 1900.

CIRCUIT. A division of a state or of the United States for judicial business. The United States is divided into 12 judicial circuits, including the District of Columbia, each of which has a **court of appeals**. There is also a Court of Appeals for the Federal Circuit, which has nationwide jurisdiction defined by subject matter, for a total of 13 federal judicial circuits. *See*: UNITED STATES COURTS OF APPEALS.

CIRCUIT COURT OF APPEALS. *See*: UNITED STATES COURTS OF APPEALS.

CIRCUIT JUDGE. A judge of one of the circuits of the UNITED STATES COURTS OF APPEALS.

CIRCUIT JUSTICE. The justice of the U.S. Supreme Court who is assigned to one of the UNITED STATES COURTS OF APPEALS in one of the 13 federal judicial circuits.

CIRCULATE. To pass from one person or place to another; to distribute; to disseminate. See ALLOCATE for a list of related terms.

CIRCUMSTANCES. Conditions or **facts** surrounding a central fact or event and having some bearing upon it. The words circumstances and facts are frequently used interchangeably. See FACT for a list of related terms.

CIRCUMSTANTIAL EVIDENCE. **Evidence** that does not directly prove a fact in issue, but raises a strong **inference** or suggestion as to the truth of that fact. *Example*: Possession of stolen goods shortly after a robbery is strong circumstantial evidence that the person possessing the goods committed the robbery. *Also called*: **indirect evidence**; **presumptive evidence**. See EVIDENCE for a list of related terms.

CITATION. **1.** A written order issued by a **law enforcement officer** notifying a defendant to voluntarily appear in court at a specified time to answer the **charge** against him or her. The failure to voluntarily appear may result in **arrest**. A citation may also provide a procedure for the defendant to enter a **guilty plea** to the offense and **waive appearance** in court by paying a **fine** or forfeiting **bail**. A citation is used for minor offenses and **infractions** in lieu of arrest and **booking**. See ARREST

WARRANT for a list of related terms. **2.** A shorthand reference to the location of a legal authority in law books. *Example*: The citation for the *Miranda* case is *Miranda v. Arizona*, 384 U.S. 436, 86 S.Ct. 1602, 16 L.Ed.2d 694 (1966).

CITE. To bring forward or refer to something concrete, specific, and authoritative in support of a proposition. The term cite allows for paraphrasing the source and does not require the use of exact words, whereas the term **quote** requires the use of exact words. *Example*: The prosecutor cited the *Terry* case to back up his argument. See ADDRESS for a list of related terms.

CITIZEN. A person either born or naturalized in a country. A citizen of a country owes allegiance to the country and is entitled to its protection and to certain rights. United States citizens are also citizens of the state wherein they reside. A corporation or a municipality may be a citizen for certain purposes.

CITIZEN'S ARREST. *See*: ARREST.

CITIZENSHIP. The status of a **citizen**, with its attendant rights and duties.

CITY COURT. A **court** whose **territorial jurisdiction** is limited to a particular city. *See*: COURT OF LIMITED JURISDICTION.

CIVIL. Pertaining to the private rights and remedies of persons, as distinguished from criminal, political, or military rights and remedies.

CIVIL ACTION. An **action** for the enforcement or protection of private rights or the redress or prevention of private wrongs; any noncriminal action. An example of a private right is the right to be free from trespassers on one's land.

CIVIL COMMITMENT. **1.** Generally, the action of a **judicial officer** or administrative body ordering a person to be placed in an institution or program for custody, treatment, or protection, usually one administered by a health service. **2.** A nonpenal **commitment** to a treatment facility resulting from findings made during criminal proceedings, either before or after a **judgment**. A civil commitment may follow a court determination that an alleged offender cannot be prosecuted because **incompetent to stand trial** or a determination of **not guilty by reason of insanity**. It may also follow, for example, a successful criminal prosecution for a drug law violation, where the offender is committed to a special institution for the treatment of drug addiction, instead of a penal institution. Although a person may be deprived of liberty by a civil commitment, it is in principle not done for the purpose of punishment, but rather for the welfare of the subject or others. **3.** In **civil actions**, a civil commitment may refer either to the court-ordered jailing of a person who refuses to obey a **court order** or to the involuntary commitment of a person to a medical or mental health facility because the person is a danger to self or to others, or cannot care for himself or herself because of mental disability. See COMMITMENT for a list of related terms.

CIVIL DEATH.   The forfeiture of rights and privileges of a person who has been convicted of a serious crime. Civil death is provided for by statute in some states. It may involve loss of privileges to vote, to hold public office, to obtain occupational licenses, and to enter into certain contracts. *Also called*: **infamy**. *See*: ATTAINDER.

CIVIL LIABILITY.   Legal accountability in a civil **action**. *Example*: A police officer who has made an illegal arrest may be subject to civil liability.

CIVIL LIBERTY.   *See*: LIBERTY (definition 2).

CIVIL PROCEDURE.   The methods and rules governing the bringing and defending of **civil actions**. The law of civil procedure deals with matters such as **jurisdiction**, **venue**, **process**, **pleading**, **discovery**, **evidence**, **trial**, **judgment**, and **appeal**. Each state establishes its own form of civil procedure by statute and by **rules of court**. Practice in the federal courts is governed by the Federal Rules of Civil Procedure and by rules of court for each federal court. *See*: ADMINISTRATIVE PROCEDURE; CRIMINAL PROCEDURE; PROCEDURAL LAW.

CIVIL RIGHTS.   Generally, the constitutionally guaranteed rights of a person by virtue of the person's status as a member of civil society, except those rights involving participation in the establishment, support, or management of the government. Examples of civil rights are those rights to personal liberty established by the bill of rights and by the 13th and 14th Amendments to the Constitution and other congressional acts. *See*: CIVIL RIGHTS DIVISION; POLITICAL RIGHTS.

CIVIL RIGHTS DIVISION.   The Civil Rights Division of the **Department of Justice** was established in 1957 in response to the need to secure effective federal enforcement of civil rights. The division is responsible for enforcing federal civil rights laws that prohibit discrimination on the basis of race, national origin, religion, and, in some instances, sex or handicap, in the areas of voting, education, employment, housing, credit, the use of public facilities and public accommodations, and in the administration of federally assisted programs. The division also has the obligation to enforce specific criminal statutes, including those concerning willful deprivation of constitutional rights under color of law or through conspiracy, involuntary servitude, and violent interference with federally protected activities (18 U.S.C. §§241, 242, 245, 1584). The Civil Rights Division is composed of eight major organizational sections and an administrative component. Each of the eight litigating sections has jurisdiction over particular subject areas and related statutes, except for the appellate section, which handles most appeals involving all areas of division litigation.

CIVIL SUIT.   Same as CIVIL ACTION.

CIVIL VIOLATION.   A noncriminal offense for which a statutorily defined fine, forfeiture, or other penalty may be recovered in a **civil action** brought by an appropriate public official. Some states have designated certain offenses of minimal seriousness civil violations in order to move them out of the criminal law and to make them subject to the simpler and more flexible rules and laws of civil procedure.

Cc

CIVIL WRONG.   Same as PRIVATE WRONG.

CLAIM.   v. 1. To state as factual, recognizing the possibility of argument. *Example:* He claimed he was elsewhere on the night of the riot. See ADDRESS for a list of related terms. **v. 2.** To demand as one's legal right. **n.** A set of facts giving rise to a right enforceable in the courts.

CLANDESTINE.   Secret; concealed.

CLASS.   1. A group of persons or things having common characteristics. *Example*: Middle class. **2.** Any division of persons or things according to rank or degree. **3.** Same as DEGREE (definition 1).

CLASSIFICATION.   Grouping according to CLASS.

CLASSIFICATION CENTER.   Same as DIAGNOSIS CENTER.

CLAUSE.   A subdivision of a legal document, usually a paragraph, sentence, or part of a sentence.

CLEAR.   Obvious; plain; evident; unambiguous.

CLEAR AND CONVINCING PROOF.   A standard of proof used under certain circumstances in **civil actions** requiring a firm belief or conviction in a person's mind that a fact is much more likely to be true than not. Clear and convincing proof is a higher standard than the common standard in civil actions of **preponderance of the evidence**, but is a lesser standard than the common standard in criminal actions of **beyond a reasonable doubt**. See EVIDENCE for a list of related terms.

CLEAR AND PRESENT DANGER.   A test created by the U.S. Supreme Court for determining whether a statute or other act of government is invalid because it abridges the First Amendment to the Constitution (free speech). "[T]he character of every act depends upon the circumstances in which it is done. . . . The most stringent protection of free speech would not protect a man in falsely shouting fire in a theatre and causing a panic. It does not even protect a man from an injunction against uttering words that may have all the effect of force. . . . The question in every case is whether the words used are used in such circumstances and are of such a nature as to create a clear and present danger that they will bring about the substantive evils that Congress has a right to prevent." *Schenck v. U.S.*, 249 U.S. 47, 52, 39 S.Ct. 247, 249, 63 L.Ed. 470, 473-74 (1919).

CLEMENCY. **1.** Executive or legislative action by which the severity of punishment of a person or group of persons is reduced or the punishment stopped, or a person is exempted from prosecution for certain actions. Grounds for clemency include **mitigating circumstances**, postconviction evidence of innocence, dubious guilt, illness of prisoner, reformation, services to the state, turning **state's evidence** (definition 1), the need to restore civil rights, and corrections of unduly severe sentences or injustices stemming from imperfections in penal law or the application of it. The chief forms of clemency are **pardon** (full and conditional), **amnesty**, **commutation**, **reduced sentence**, **reprieve**, and **remission of fines and forfeitures**. **2.** Mercy; leniency.

CLERICAL. Pertaining to clerks or office workers.

CLERICAL ERROR. An error committed in the performance of clerical work rather than in the exercise of judicial **discretion**. A clerical error may be a typographical error or the unintended addition or omission of a word, phrase, or other item. An error of this nature may be corrected by the court **sua sponte** or on the **motion** of either party. See ERROR for a list of related terms.

CLERK OF COURT. An elected or appointed court officer responsible for maintaining the written records of the court and for supervising or performing the clerical tasks necessary for conducting judicial business; also, any employee of a court whose principal duties are to assist the court clerk in performing the clerical tasks necessary for conducting judicial business. The typical duties of a court clerk are receiving documents to be filed in the court record, assigning case numbers, scheduling cases on the court calendar, entering judgments and orders in the court record, preparing **writs** and **warrants**, and keeping the court records and seal. See COURT for a list of related terms.

CLIENT. A person who hires an attorney to give legal advice, to appear for the person in court, or to act for the person generally in legal matters.

CLOSE. **v. 1.** To finish; to conclude; to terminate. **v. 2.** To bar entrance or access; to shut or seal up. *Example*: The law required the saloon to be closed on Sunday. **adj. 1.** Near in time, space, or relation. See PROXIMITY for a list of related terms. **adj. 2.** Nearly even or equal. *Example*: A close decision. **adj. 3.** Thorough; strict; not deviating from the subject under consideration. *Example*: Pay close attention.

CLOSED SEASON. The time of the year when hunting, fishing, or trapping is prohibited.

CLOSING ARGUMENT. The part of a **trial** after all the **evidence** has been presented and the **jury** has been instructed (see **instruction**) in which each party recapitulates the facts and evidence it has presented and attempts to convince the judge or jury of the correctness of its position. *Also called*: **summation**. See EVIDENCE and TRIAL for lists of related terms.

Cc

CO-. A prefix meaning joint or together. *Example*: codefendant; cocounsel.

CODE. A systematic and comprehensive body of laws, rules, or regulations compiled and classified according to subject matter.

CODE OF FEDERAL REGULATIONS. The Code of Federal Regulations (CFR) is the annual cumulation of executive agency regulations published in the daily **Federal Register**, combined with regulations issued previously that are still in effect. Divided into 50 titles, each representing a broad subject area, individual volumes of the Code of Federal Regulations are revised at least once each calendar year and issued on a staggered quarterly basis. In the back of each CFR volume under the heading "Finding Aids" appears a table of CFR titles and chapters and an alphabetical list of agencies appearing in CFR. The Code is a convenient and comprehensive reference source for general and permanent federal regulations.

CODIFY. To collect and arrange laws into a CODE.

COERCION. Compelling a person either to do something he or she does not have to do or to fail to do something the person may legally do, by threat, force, restraint, or other illegal means. The threat, force, or restraint may be directed against the child, spouse, or parent of the person coerced. Coercion is a recognized **affirmative defense** in prosecutions for crimes other than **murder**. A defendant who can establish that he or she committed a crime as a result of coercion imposed by another will be acquitted on the charge as a matter of law. Under Section 2.09 of the **Model Penal Code** "[i]t is an affirmative defense that the actor engaged in the conduct charged to constitute an offense because he was coerced to do so by the use of, or a threat to use, unlawful force against his person or the person of another, that a person of reasonable firmness in his situation would have been unable to resist." Coercion is also an element of various crimes such as **rape**. *Also called*: **duress**.

COGNIZABLE. Capable of being tried or examined before a particular tribunal; within a particular court's or judge's **jurisdiction**. *Example*: Shoplifting offenses are cognizable before a district court judge. See JURISDICTION for a list of related terms.

COGNIZANCE. **1.** The power and ability to take notice of and decide a matter. *Example*: A justice of the peace has no cognizance over criminal matters. **2.** JUDICIAL NOTICE.

COHABITATION. Living together under the representation or appearance of being married. The term cohabitation has several meanings depending on how it is used. It may or may not imply **sexual intercourse**. It may be used to describe promiscuous and casual relations without continuous living together. However, cohabitation is generally applied to situations in which a man and a woman live together in a sexual relationship as man and wife, but are not legally married.

COITUS. SEXUAL INTERCOURSE.

COLD-BLOODED. Willful, deliberate, and premeditated with no **mitigation** or **justification**. *Example*: A cold-blooded murder.

COLLATERAL. Related to but not strictly a part of the main thing or matter under consideration; supporting; accompanying; supplementary.

COLLATERAL ATTACK. An attempt to avoid or defeat a **judgment** indirectly through a proceeding separate from the original action or from an **appeal** from the original action. **Habeas corpus** is a collateral attack on a judgment in a criminal case. *Also called*: **indirect attack**. *See*: DIRECT ATTACK.

COLLATERAL ESTOPPEL. An ESTOPPEL that bars a second **action** between the same parties on an identical issue raised and decided in a previous action. *Also called*: **estoppel by judgment**. *See*: RES JUDICATA.

COLLATERAL FACT. A **fact** outside of or not directly connected with the main issue under consideration. See FACT for a list of related terms.

COLLISION. Striking together; violent contact.

COLLUSION. An agreement between two or more persons to **defraud** another person or to obtain something prohibited by law.

COLOR. The outward appearance or semblance of a thing as distinguished from the thing itself. *Example*: The statute punished anyone who, under color of law, deprived another of his or her rights.

COMBAT. A physical fight or battle entered into by two or more persons voluntarily.

COMBINATION. An agreement between two or more persons for a common purpose. Sometimes used as a synonym for CONSPIRACY.

COME. To participate in legal proceedings; to appear. *Example*: Now comes the defendant.

COMITY. The practice of one **court** giving effect to the laws and judicial decisions of another court on a like question, although not legally obligated to do so.

COMMENCE. To begin; to institute; to perform the first act of. *Example*: A criminal prosecution is commenced when the complaint is filed.

COMMENT. To express an opinion for the purpose of explanation, illustration, or criticism. See ADDRESS for a list of related terms.

COMMENT ON THE EVIDENCE. A statement by a judge to a jury revealing the judge's personal opinion on the truth or falsity of **evidence** or on the **merits** of the case. Judges are prohibited from commenting on the evidence. See EVIDENCE for a list of related terms.

COMMERCIAL PAPER. A written instrument such as a check, draft, or promissory note evidencing the pledge of one person to pay money to another.

COMMINGLE. To mix or blend together.

COMMISSION. **1.** Written authority granting the right to hold and discharge the duties of a certain office. **2.** Perpetration; act of doing. *Example*: Commission of a crime. **3.** One of the names given to a government bureau or agency. *Example*: Liquor Commission.

COMMISSIONER. *See*: JUDICIAL OFFICER.

COMMIT. **1.** To do; to perform; to perpetrate. **2.** *See*: COMMITMENT.

COMMITMENT. The action of a **judicial officer** ordering that a person subject to judicial proceedings be placed in a particular kind of **confinement facility** or **residential facility**, for a specific reason authorized by law. More specifically, for purposes of the criminal law, commitment refers to the process of placing a person who has been convicted of a crime into **jail** or **prison**. *See*: CIVIL COMMITMENT; COMMITMENT AFTER INSANITY DEFENSE; DETENTION; DIAGNOSTIC COMMITMENT; JAIL COMMITMENT; NEW COURT COMMITMENT; PLACEMENT; PRISON COMMITMENT; RELEASE; RELEASE AFTER INSANITY COMMITMENT; RESIDENTIAL COMMITMENT; SENTENCE; VOLUNTARY COMMITMENT.

COMMITMENT AFTER INSANITY DEFENSE. An accused who has been found **not guilty by reason of insanity** may be committed to a mental institution. Some jurisdictions require automatic, mandatory commitment. In other jurisdictions, commitment is determined by **judge** or **jury** or in a special proceeding. Although the test to determine whether a person should be committed following a successful insanity defense varies from jurisdiction to jurisdiction, the most common grounds for commitment are that the person's **insanity** continues or that he or she is dangerous. See COMMITMENT for a list of related terms.

COMMITTED IN THE PRESENCE OF AN OFFICER.   *See*: PRESENCE OF AN OFFICER.

COMMITTING MAGISTRATE.   A judicial officer authorized to conduct a **preliminary examination** of persons charged with crime. If the committing magistrate finds **probable cause** to believe the accused committed the crime charged, the magistrate may either commit the accused to jail to await action by the **grand jury** or admit the accused to **bail**. If the committing magistrate does not find probable cause, the accused must be **discharged**. *Also called*: **examining court**.

COMMON.   **1.** Ordinary; usual; frequent; customary. **2.** Belonging to many or the majority; public.

COMMON CARRIER.   A person or company in the business of transporting the public or goods for hire.

COMMON INTENDMENT.   The customary or usual interpretation; the plain or natural meaning. *Also called*: **common intent**.

COMMON INTENT.   Same as COMMON INTENDMENT.

COMMON KNOWLEDGE.   That which is generally accepted as true or generally known through the ordinary experience and learning of humankind. A court may take **judicial notice** of matters of common knowledge.

COMMON LAW.   The system of law, originated and developed in England, based on court decisions and on custom and usage, rather than on written laws created by legislative enactment. "The common law does not consist of absolute, fixed, and inflexible rules, but rather of broad and comprehensive principles based on justice, reason, and common sense. It is of judicial origin and promulgation. Its principles have been determined by the social needs of the community and have changed with changes in such needs. These principles are susceptible of adaptation to new conditions, interests, relations and usages as the progress of society may require." *Miller v. Monsen*, 37 N.W.2d 543, 547 (Minn. 1949).

COMMON-LAW CRIME.   A crime punishable under the **common law** as opposed to a crime punishable under a criminal **statute**. Most states and the federal government have made all crimes statutory and no longer have common-law crimes. See CRIME for a list of related terms.

COMMON-LAW MARRIAGE.   A marriage effected by the mutual agreement of the parties to live together as man and wife without a formal ceremony, an officiating officer, or a license.

COMMON NUISANCE.   Same as PUBLIC NUISANCE.

COMMONWEALTH.   The official title of several states of the United States, such as Kentucky, Massachusetts, Pennsylvania, and Virginia.

COMMUNICATION.   A transmission of thoughts, opinions, or information from one person to another. *See*: CONFIDENTIAL COMMUNICATION.

COMMUNITY.   The locality where a person resides and has established a reputation.

COMMUNITY FACILITY.   *See*: RESIDENTIAL FACILITY.

COMMUTATION.   An executive act changing a punishment from a greater to a lesser penalty. Examples of commutations are the reduction of a prison term from a longer to a shorter term and the change from a sentence of death to a term of imprisonment. See CLEMENCY for a list of related terms.

COMPACT.   An **agreement** or **contract**.

COMPARE.   To examine two or more things in order to discover similarities and differences. *Abbreviation:* **Cf.**

COMPATIBLE.   Capable of existing or being exercised together without conflict or disharmony. *Example*: Are the offices of Chief of Police and member of the state legislature compatible?

COMPEL.   **v.** To force; to constrain; to oblige. *Example*: The witness was not compelled to testify against himself within the meaning of the Fifth Amendment. **n.** COMPULSION.

COMPETENCE.   **1.** Legal qualification, fitness, or capability to do something satisfactorily. *Example*: The competence of a witness must be determined by the court before a witness is allowed to testify. *See*: CREDIBILITY; WEIGHT OF THE EVIDENCE. **2.** Sometimes used as a synonym for CAPACITY. *Also called*: **competency**.

COMPETENCY.   Same as COMPETENCE.

COMPETENT.   Legally qualified, fit, or capable of doing something satisfactorily; having sufficient ability or authority.

COMPETENT COURT. A court having lawful **jurisdiction** over the person or property at issue. See COURT and JURISDICTION for lists of related terms.

COMPETENT EVIDENCE. **1. Evidence** that the nature of the fact to be proven requires. A document is competent evidence of the contents of the document. Testimony of an eyewitness to a crime is competent evidence of the crime. In order for testimonial evidence to be competent evidence, it must be shown that the **witness** had the ability to perceive what was going on around him or her and to remember and relate the perceptions to others. Also, the witness must be able to understand the **oath** or **affirmation** and comprehend its significance. **2.** Generally, **evidence** that is relevant and admissible to prove a point in issue. See EVIDENCE for a list of related terms.

COMPETENT TO STAND TRIAL. See INCOMPETENT TO STAND TRIAL.

COMPLAINANT. The person who makes a COMPLAINT against someone in a criminal case.

COMPLAINING PARTY. Same as PROSECUTING WITNESS.

COMPLAINING WITNESS. Same as PROSECUTING WITNESS.

COMPLAINT. **1.** A sworn written statement presented to a **magistrate** or other proper **judicial officer** alleging that a specified person has committed a specified **crime** and requesting **prosecution**. The complaint must state the essential facts constituting the crime charged, including the time and place of its commission and the name or description of the **defendant**. If the defendant has been **arrested** without an **arrest warrant**, the complaint may serve as the **charging document** upon which the **preliminary examination** is held. If the defendant has not been arrested, the complaint serves as the basis for determining whether there is **probable cause** to justify the issuance of a warrant for the arrest. Most jurisdictions call the charging document filed in a **misdemeanor** case or at the first step of a **felony** case a complaint, and the document filed to initiate trial proceedings at the second step of a felony case an **information**. In some jurisdictions, the document filed to **bind over** a defendant until a **grand jury** decides whether or not to issue an **indictment** is also called a complaint. See ACCUSATION for a list of related terms. *See also*: **complaint denied; complaint granted; complaint requested**. **2.** The first document filed by the plaintiff in a **civil action** setting forth the allegations on which the action is based.

COMPLAINT DENIED. The decision by a **prosecutor** not to file a **complaint** or **information** in court, or not to seek an **indictment**. When a request for a complaint against an arrested person is denied, that case against the person is terminated. *Also called*: **complaint rejected**. See DISMISSAL and PROSECUTE for lists of related terms.

COMPLAINT GRANTED.   The decision by a **prosecutor** to grant a request for a **complaint** by filing a complaint or an **information** in court, or by seeking an **indictment** from a **grand jury**. See PROSECUTE for a list of related terms.

COMPLAINT REJECTED.   Same as COMPLAINT DENIED.

Cc

COMPLAINT REQUESTED.   A request by a citizen, **law enforcement agency**, or other government agency that a **prosecutor** seek an **indictment** or file a **complaint** or **information** alleging that a specified person has committed a specified offense. Law enforcement agencies are the primary source of requests for prosecution. The prosecutor's screening process usually consists of examination of police reports and other information about the alleged crime, the reaching of a conclusion about whether to **charge** and which charges will be made in the charging document, and the preparation of the document. See PROSECUTE for a list of related terms.

COMPLICATED LARCENY.   Same as COMPOUND LARCENY.

COMPLICITY.   Any conduct on the part of a person other than the chief actor in the commission of a crime, in which the person intentionally or knowingly serves to further the intent to commit the crime, **aids** in the commission of the crime, or assists the person who has committed the crime to avoid **prosecution** or to **escape** from justice. Where complicity occurs before or during the commission of a given crime, the chargeable offense is usually that crime. Where the complicity occurs only after the commission of a crime, some penal codes have established a separate chargeable offense carrying a lesser penalty. See PARTY for a list of related terms.

COMPLY.   To act in accordance with a command, requirement, request, or wish.

COMPOS MENTIS.   *Latin.* "Sound of mind." Having control of the mental faculties.

COMPOUND.   Composed of or involving two or more parts, elements, or ingredients.

COMPOUNDER.   *See*: COMPOUNDING CRIME.

COMPOUNDING CRIME.   Unlawfully agreeing not to **prosecute** or inform on one who has committed a crime in return for some property or other thing of value. Under Section 242.5 of the **Model Penal Code** (Compounding), "[a] person commits a misdemeanor if he accepts or agrees to accept any pecuniary benefit in consideration of refraining from reporting to law enforcement authorities the commission or suspected commission of any offense or information relating to an offense." Depending on the jurisdiction, a compounder can be a **victim**, **witness**, or **prosecuting attorney** who accepts payment to refrain from assisting in prosecution, or the **offender** who pays or offers to pay someone who can prevent or hinder prosecution. In some states, the only compounding offense is compounding a **felony**. Note that formally authorized payment of **reparation** or **restitution** to a victim is a legitimate alternative to prosecution in some jurisdictions. See ABUSE OF PROCESS and CRIME for lists of related terms.

COMPOUNDING FELONY. *See*: COMPOUNDING CRIME.

COMPOUND LARCENY. LARCENY committed with aggravating circumstances such as violence, taking from one's person, or taking from one's house. See ABSTRACTION for a list of related terms.

COMPRISE. To consist of; to be composed of. Comprise usually implies that all the items of the whole are stated. *Example*: The Union comprises 50 states.

COMPROMISE. To adjust a disputed matter by mutual concession or agreement.

COMPROMISE VERDICT. A VERDICT resulting from the improper surrender of one or more **jurors**' conscientious convictions on a material issue to other jurors in return for like behavior by the other jurors. See VERDICT for a list of related terms.

COMPULSION. **1.** *See*: COMPEL. **2.** An irresistible, irrational impulse to act.

COMPULSORY. Coerced or required by legal process or by force of law.

COMPULSORY PROCESS. Coercive means used by courts to procure the attendance in court of persons wanted as **witnesses** or otherwise. Examples of compulsory process are **subpoenas** and **arrest warrants**. The Sixth Amendment to the U.S. Constitution guarantees a defendant the right to have compulsory process to obtain witnesses in his or her favor. The right makes the subpoena power of the court available to a defendant only with respect to competent, material witnesses subject to the court's process, whose expected testimony will be admissible. See ARREST WARRANT and WITNESS for lists of related terms.

COMPUTER CRIME. A popular name for crimes committed by use of a computer or crimes involving misuse or destruction of computer equipment or computerized information. Computer crime may include specifically theft committed by means of manipulation of a computerized financial transaction system or the use of computer services with intent to avoid payment. Other types of computer crime may include unlawfully accessing a computer resource, unauthorized copying of a computer program or software, and knowingly introducing a computer virus into another's computer resource. See CRIME for a list of related terms.

COMPUTERIZED CRIMINAL HISTORY. **Criminal history record information** concerning an identified **offender** or alleged offender contained in a computerized file. Computerized criminal history is also a common name for the program of computerized files maintained by the **FBI** and several states for the national and state exchange of criminal history record information.

CON. **1.** Against; in opposition to; in disagreement with. **2.** A prefix meaning with or together. **3.** A slang abbreviation for confidence, as in con game (see **confidence game**). **4.** A slang abbreviation for <u>con</u>vict.

Cc

CONCEAL. To hide; to keep from sight; to prevent discovery of.

CONCEDE. **v.** To yield; to admit as true. **n.** CONCESSION.

CONCERN. **1.** To pertain to; to relate to; to affect. **2.** To involve; to engage; to interest. *Example*: All persons concerned in the commission of a felony will be punished.

CONCERTED ACTION. "Action which has been planned, arranged, adjusted, agreed upon, and settled between parties acting together, in pursuance of some design or in accordance with some scheme." *Stone v. Wingo*, 416 F.2d 857, 860 (6th Cir. 1969).

CONCESSION. *See*: CONCEDE.

CONCLUSION. **1.** End; termination; close. **2.** Result; outcome. **3.** An inference from or reaction to undisclosed facts; an unsupported allegation. See FACT for a list of related terms.

CONCLUSION OF FACT. An **inference** drawn from subordinate or evidentiary facts. See FACT for a list of related terms.

CONCLUSION OF LAW. A decision arrived at by applying rules of law to given facts. A conclusion of law will usually describe a legal status, condition, or offense. *Example*: A finding that a person is a habitual offender is a conclusion of law.

CONCLUSIVE. Beyond question or dispute; irrefutable; decisive; final.

CONCLUSIVE EVIDENCE. **Evidence** that is incontrovertible or from which only one reasonable conclusion may be drawn. See EVIDENCE for a list of related terms.

CONCLUSIVE PRESUMPTION. A PRESUMPTION in which the presumed fact must follow from the proven fact or facts. No other evidence is permitted to contradict the presumed fact. The presumption that a child below a certain age has a fundamental inability to consent to sexual relations is a conclusive presumption. *Also called*: **irrebuttable presumption**. See PRESUMPTION for a list of related terms.

CONCRETE. Actually existing; real; specific.

CONCUR. To agree; to have the same opinion.

CONCURRENT. **1.** Acting in conjunction; contributing to the same event or purpose; cooperating. **2.** Running together; contemporaneous. *See*: CONCURRENT SENTENCE. **3.** Agreeing; harmonious; accordant.

CONCURRENT JURISDICTION. JURISDICTION of a **court** held together with or shared with one or more other courts over a particular territory, subject matter, or person. See JURISDICTION for a list of related terms.

CONCURRENT SENTENCE. A **sentence** that is served simultaneously with another sentence, whether or not the sentences begin or end at the same time. Under concurrent sentences, a prisoner is entitled to **discharge** at the expiration of the longest sentence. See SENTENCE for a list of related terms.

CONCURRING OPINION. An **opinion** filed by one of the judges of an appellate court in which the judge agrees with the result of the **majority opinion** but states different reasons for reaching the result. An opinion concurring in the result only merely agrees with the result of the majority, not the reasoning, but states no reasons of its own. See OPINION for a list of related terms.

CONDEMN. To adjudge guilty of a crime and to sentence.

CONDITION. **1.** Restriction; qualification; limitation; prerequisite. **2.** Term; circumstance; stipulation. **3.** A specified standard of conduct imposed on a person who has been placed on PROBATION or PAROLE. A violation of probation or parole conditions may result in a **probation revocation** or a **parole revocation**.

CONDITIONAL. Imposing, depending on, or containing a CONDITION.

CONDITIONALLY SUSPENDED SENTENCE. A **court disposition** of a convicted person specifying a penalty of a **fine** or **commitment** to **confinement**, but holding **execution** of the penalty in **abeyance** upon good behavior. See SENTENCE for a list of related terms.

CONDITIONAL PARDON. An executive act releasing a person from punishment, contingent upon his or her performance or nonperformance of specified acts. See CLEMENCY for a list of related terms.

CONDITIONAL RELEASE. The **release** by executive decision (usually a **paroling authority**) from a federal or state **correctional facility**, of a prisoner who has not served his or her full sentence and whose freedom is contingent upon obeying specified rules of behavior. The two main types of conditional release from prison are RELEASE TO PAROLE and MANDATORY SUPERVISED RELEASE. See PAROLE and RELEASE for lists of related terms.

CONDUCT. **n. 1.** The **Model Penal Code** defines conduct as "an **action** or **omission** and its accompanying state of mind, or, where relevant, a series of **acts** and omissions." **n. 2.** Personal behavior. *Example*: His conduct in the courtroom was reprehensible. **v.** To manage; to direct; to carry on.

CONFEDERACY. A combination of two or more persons for an unlawful purpose. A confederacy is usually referred to as a CONSPIRACY.

CONFEDERATE. A person who, in conjunction with another or others, intentionally contributes to or collaborates in the commission of an unlawful act. See PARTY for a list or related terms.

CONFEDERATION. A compact or alliance for mutual support.

CONFER. To give; to grant; to bestow.

CONFESSION. A statement whereby a person admits facts revealing his or her guilt as to all **elements** of a particular crime. In order for a confession to be admissible in court, it must be VOLUNTARY and it must have been obtained in compliance with the requirements of MIRANDA v. ARIZONA. *See*: ADMISSION.

CONFESSION AND AVOIDANCE. A **pleading** by which the defendant does not deny doing the acts complained of but raises a reason, usually based on public policy considerations, which **bars conviction** and **punishment** notwithstanding that the acts constituting the crime have been established **beyond a reasonable doubt**. **Affirmative defenses** are usually made by way of confession and avoidance.

CONFIDENCE GAME. A popular name for a scheme involving a **false representation** to obtain money or any other thing of value, where the deception is accomplished through the trust placed by the **victim** in the character of the offender. *See*: SWINDLE.

CONFIDENTIAL COMMUNICATION. A COMMUNICATION between persons in a special confidential or **fiduciary** relationship of trust or intimacy. Confidential communications may not be divulged or inquired into in **court** without the **consent** of the party making the communication. Examples of relationships giving rise to confidential communications are attorney and client, husband and wife, and doctor and patient. *Also called*: **privileged communication**.

CONFIDENTIAL RELATIONSHIP.   A relationship between two persons in which one person puts his or her trust and confidence in the skill and integrity of the other person and the other person is duty bound to act in good faith for that person's interest. *See*: FIDUCIARY.

CONFINE.   **1.** To imprison; to incarcerate. **2.** To restrain of freedom of action; to restrict within limits.

CONFINEMENT.   Physical restriction of a person to a clearly defined area from which he or she is lawfully forbidden to depart and from which departure is usually constrained by architectural barriers and/or guards or other custodians. *See*: CONFINEMENT FACILITY; IMPRISONMENT; INCARCERATION.

CONFINEMENT FACILITY.   A **correctional facility** characterized by 24-hour physical restriction of all or most of the facility population to a clearly defined area from which they are forbidden to depart, cannot easily depart because of physical barriers and/or guards, and do not lawfully depart without being in the **custody** of an official. Some confinement facilities send selected prisoners out on **work release programs** or other **temporary release** programs. *See*: IMPRISONMENT; IN-CARCERATION; RESIDENTIAL FACILITY.

CONFIRM.   **1.** To make certain; to remove doubt about. **2.** To make binding or valid by formal or legal act; to ratify.

CONFISCATE.   To seize private property for the use of the state, often as a penalty for using the property illegally, without compensation to the owner.

CONFLICTING EVIDENCE.   **Evidence** that, considered as a whole, presents a fair and reasonable ground for a difference of opinion on the issue in question. See EVIDENCE for a list of related terms.

CONFORMITY.   Correspondence in form or character; agreement; harmony.

CONFRONTATION.   **1.** The right of confrontation is the right of an accused person to come face to face with an adverse **witness** in the court, so the accused person has the opportunity to **object** to the testimony of the witness and to **cross-examine** the witness. The Sixth Amendment to the U.S. Constitution guarantees the right of confrontation to defendants in federal criminal prosecutions. The due process clause of the Fourteenth Amendment makes this Sixth Amendment guarantee applicable to the states. See WITNESS for a list of related terms. **2.** Any presentation of a **suspect** to a **victim** or **witness** of a crime for the purpose of identifying the perpetrator of the crime. The term confrontation includes both **lineups** and **showups**. *See*: EYEWITNESS IDENTIFICATION; IDENTIFICATION.

CONGRESSIONAL RECORD. A daily publication of the federal government that details the proceedings of the Congress when it is in session. The Daily Digest of the Congressional Record, printed on the back of each issue of the Record, summarizes the proceedings of that day in each House, and before each of the committees and subcommittees of each house. *See*: CONGRESS OF THE UNITED STATES.

Cc

CONGRESS OF THE UNITED STATES. The Congress of the United States was created by Article I, Section 1, of the Constitution, adopted by the Constitutional Convention on September 17, 1787, providing that "All legislative Powers herein granted shall be vested in a Congress of the United States, which shall consist of a Senate and House of Representatives." The Senate is composed of 100 Members, two from each state, who are elected to serve for a term of six years. The House of Representatives comprises 435 Representatives. The number representing each state is determined by population, but every state is entitled to at least one Representative. Members of the House are elected by the people for two-year terms. Both the Senators and the Representatives must be residents of the state from which they are chosen. In addition, a Senator must be at least 30 years of age and must have been a citizen of the United States for at least 9 years; A Representative must be at least 25 years of age and must have been a citizen for at least 7 years.

The Vice President of the United States is the presiding officer of the Senate. In his or her absence, the duties are taken over by a president pro tempore, elected by that body, or a designee. The presiding officer of the House of Representatives, the Speaker, is elected by the House. The Speaker may designate any Member of the House to act in his or her absence. The positions of Senate majority and minority leader are elected at the beginning of each new Congress by a majority of the Senators in their political party. In cooperation with their party organizations, leaders are responsible for the design and achievement of a legislative program. This involves managing the flow of legislation, expediting noncontroversial measures, and keeping Members informed regarding proposed action on pending business. Each leader serves as an ex officio member of his or her party's policymaking and organizational bodies and is aided by an assistant floor leader (whip) and a party secretary.

The work of preparing and considering legislation is done largely by committees of both Houses of Congress. There are sixteen standing committees in the Senate and twenty-two in the House of Representatives. In addition, there are special committees in each House, and various congressional commissions and joint committees composed of members of both Houses. Each House may also appoint special investigating committees. The membership of the standing committees of each House is chosen by a vote of the entire body; members of other committees are appointed under the provisions of the measure establishing them. Each bill and resolution is usually referred to the appropriate committee, which may report a bill out in its original form, favorably or unfavorably, recommend amendments, or allow the proposed legislation to die in committee without action. The House Judiciary Committee and the Senate Judiciary Committee are the standing committees that deal with matters relating to criminal law and criminal justice.

All bills and joint resolutions must pass both Houses and must be signed by the President, except those proposing a constitutional amendment, in order to become law, or be passed over the President's veto by a two-third's vote of both Houses. Article I, Section 7, of the Constitution states: "If any Bill shall not be returned by the President within ten Days (Sundays excepted) after it shall have been presented to him, the Same shall be a Law, in like Manner as if he had signed it, unless the Congress by their Adjournment prevent its Return, in which Case it shall not be a Law." When a bill or joint resolution is introduced in the House, the usual procedure for its enactment into law is as follows.

—The bill is assigned to the House committee having jurisdiction.

—If favorably considered, it is reported to the House either in its original form or with recommended amendments.

—In the Senate committee, the bill, if favorably considered, may be reported in the form as received from the House, or with recommended amendments.

—The approved bill or resolution is reported to the Senate, and, if passed by that body, is returned to the House.

—If one body does not accept the amendments to a bill by the other body, a conference committee comprising Members of both bodies is usually appointed to effect a compromise.

—When the bill or joint resolution is finally approved by both Houses, it is signed by the Speaker and the Vice President and is presented to the President.

—Once the President's signature is affixed, the measure becomes a law. If the President vetoes the bill, it cannot become a law unless it is repassed by a two-thirds vote of both Houses.

Article I, Section 8, of the Constitution defines the powers of Congress. Included are the powers to assess and collect taxes—called the chief power; to regulate commerce, both interstate and foreign; to coin money; to establish post offices and post roads; to establish courts inferior to the Supreme Court; to declare war; and to raise and maintain an army and navy. Congress is further empowered "To provide for calling forth the Militia to execute the Laws of the Union, suppress Insurrections and repel Invasions;" and "To make all Laws which shall be necessary and proper for carrying into Execution the foregoing Powers, and all other Powers vested by this Constitution in the Government of the United States, or in any Department or Officer thereof." Another power vested in Congress is the right to propose amendments to the Constitution, whenever two-thirds of both Houses shall deem it necessary. Should two-thirds of the state legislatures demand changes in the Constitution, it is the duty of Congress to call a constitutional convention. Proposed amendments shall be valid as part of the Constitution when ratified by the legislatures or by conventions of three-fourths of the states, as one or the other mode of ratification may be proposed by Congress.

Article I, Section 9, of the Constitution also imposes prohibitions upon Congress. "The Privilege of the Writ of Habeas Corpus shall not be suspended, unless when in Cases of Rebellion or Invasion the public Safety may require it." A **bill of attainder** or an **ex post facto** law cannot be passed. No export duty can be imposed. Ports of one state cannot be given preference over those of another state. "No money shall be drawn from the Treasury, but in Consequence of Appropriations made by Law. . . ." No title of nobility may be granted.

Under Article I, Section 6, Members of Congress are granted certain privileges. In no case, except in **treason, felony**, and breach of the peace, can Members be arrested while attending sessions of Congress "and in going to and returning from the same. . . ." Furthermore, the Members cannot be questioned in any other place for remarks made in Congress. Each House may expel a Member of its body by a two-thirds vote.

CONJECTURE.   An opinion or notion based on inconclusive or incomplete evidence; a supposition; a guess.

CONJUGAL.   Relating or pertaining to marriage.

CONNIVANCE.   Passive or secret encouragement or consent to the commission of an unlawful act by another.

CONSANGUINITY.   Blood relationship. *See*: AFFINITY (definition 2).

CONSCIENCE.   The moral sense in a person by which he or she determines right or wrong.

CONSCIOUS.   Knowing; deliberate.

CONSECUTIVE.   Following one another in uninterrupted sequence.

CONSECUTIVE SENTENCE.   A SENTENCE that begins at the expiration of the term of another sentence. *Also called*: **accumulative sentence; cumulative sentence**. See SENTENCE for a list of related terms.

CONSENT.   To actively and voluntarily comply or agree with what is proposed or requested by another. Consent assumes sufficient mental **capacity** to reason and deliberate on the part of the person giving consent. Consent also assumes freedom from **fraud, coercion**, or other forms of compulsion. Consent may be a **defense** to a criminal charge. Section 2.11 of the **Model Penal Code** states that "[t]he consent of the victim to conduct charged to constitute an offense or to the result thereof is a defense if such consent negatives an element of the offense or precludes the infliction of the harm or evil sought to be prevented by the law defining the offense." *See*:

ACQUIESCE; ASSENT; CONSENT DECREE; CONSENT SEARCH; IMPLIED CONSENT.

CONSENT DECREE.   A binding decree entered into by agreement of the parties with the sanction and permission of the court.

CONSENT SEARCH.   A **search** of a person's body, premises, or belongings conducted by a **law enforcement officer** with the person's permission. A consent search is lawful only if the totality of circumstances surrounding the search indicate that the consent was **voluntary**. "Just as was true with confessions the requirement of 'voluntary' consent reflects a fair accommodation of the constitutional requirements involved. In examining all the surrounding circumstances to determine if in fact the consent to search was coerced, account must be taken of subtly coercive police questions, as well as the possibly vulnerable subjective state of the person who consents. Those searches that are the product of police coercion can thus be filtered out without undermining the continuing validity of consent searches. In sum, there is no reason for us to depart in the area of consent searches, from the traditional definition of 'voluntariness.' " *Schneckloth v. Bustamonte*, 412 U.S. 218, 229, 93 S.Ct. 2041, 2048-49, 36 L.Ed.2d 854, 864 (1973). A person may limit the scope of a consent search by words or actions and may revoke the consent to search at any time. A person may not consent to the search of a third person's premises or property unless the third person has specifically given the person authority to do so or the person possesses "common authority over or other sufficient relationship to the premises or effects sought to be inspected." Common authority rests "on mutual use of the property by persons generally having joint access or control for most purposes, so that it is reasonable to recognize that any of the co-inhabitants has the right to permit the inspection in his own right and that the others have assumed the risk that one of their number might permit the common area to be searched." *U.S. v. Matlock*, 415 U.S. 164, 171 n.7, 94 S.Ct. 988, 993 n.7, 39 L.Ed.2d 242, 250 n.7 (1974).

CONSEQUENCE.   A natural or necessary result.

CONSERVATION CAMP.   *See*: PRISON.

CONSIDER.   **1.** To think carefully about; to deliberate upon. **2.** To determine after careful deliberation; to adjudge.

CONSIDERABLE.   Worthy of consideration; significant; important.

CONSIDERATION.   Something of value given or done in return for something promised or performed by another which has the effect of making an agreement a legally enforceable **contract**.

CONSIDERED.   **1.** *See*: CONSIDER. **2.** Esteemed; regarded.

CONSIDERED DICTUM. A DICTUM that is so well reasoned and influential that it is later adopted in a court opinion as if it were an **authority** (definition 5).

CONSISTENT. Not contradictory; compatible; harmonious.

CONSIST IN. To have as its foundation, substance, or nature. *Example*: Courage consists in standing up for what you believe.

CONSIST OF. To be made up of; to be composed of. The term consist of usually implies that all the items of the whole are stated. *Example*: The class consists of fifteen students.

CONSOLIDATED TRIAL. A **trial** in which two or more **defendants** named in separate **charging documents** are tried together, or where a given defendant is tried on charges contained in two or more charging documents. See TRIAL for a list of related terms.

CONSPIRACY. A voluntary agreement by two or more persons to commit or to effect the commission of an unlawful act, or to use unlawful means to accomplish an act that is not in itself unlawful. In addition some state statutes require some **overt act** in furtherance of the agreement. Generally, there are two mental states required for conspiracy: intent to agree and intent to commit the unlawful act or to commit a lawful act in an unlawful manner.

Under Section 5.03 (1) of the **Model Penal Code** "[a] person is guilty of conspiracy with another person or persons to commit a crime if with the purpose of promoting or facilitating its commission he: (a) agrees with such other person or persons that they or one or more of them will engage in conduct that constitutes such crime or an **attempt** or **solicitation** to commit such crime; or (b) agrees to **aid** such other person or persons in the planning or commission of such crime or of an attempt or solicitation to commit such crime." See INCHOATE OFFENSE and PARTY for lists of related offenses.

CONSTABLE. A **law enforcement officer** of a local governmental unit with powers assigned by state or local law. A constable has powers and duties similar to a **sheriff** but with less authority and smaller **jurisdiction**. See LAW ENFORCEMENT OFFICER for a list of related terms.

CONSTANT. Regular; persistent; steady; invariable.

CONSTITUTION. A written instrument that establishes and limits the fundamental powers of government, distributes those powers among several branches of government, defines the basic principles to which society must conform, and secures and protects the rights of the governed. The U.S. Constitution is the supreme law of the United States.

CONSTITUTIONAL. **1.** Consistent with or in conformance with the U.S. CON-STITUTION. *Example*: The police practice of forcing a confession from a defendant is not constitutional, because it deprives the defendant of rights to due process of law guaranteed by the Constitution. **2.** Established by or operating under a CON-STITUTION. *Example*: Constitutional rights.

CONSTITUTIONAL LAW. The body of law dealing with the establishment and interpretation of the U.S. Constitution or the constitution of a state or other nation and with the testing of the validity of governmental actions and enactments under the criteria of conformity to the constitution.

CONSTITUTIONALLY PROTECTED AREA. An area within which a person has a reasonable expectation of privacy and a right to be free from unreasonable governmental intrusion. *Also called*: **zone of privacy**. See PRIVACY for a list of related terms.

CONSTRAIN. To restrict another by force or threat of force.

CONSTRUCTION. The act, process, or result of construing. *See*: CONSTRUE; LIBERAL CONSTRUCTION; STRICT CONSTRUCTION.

CONSTRUCTIVE. Not actually existing, but having the same legal effects as if it were existing; inferred or **implied** by law. *Example*: He had constructive possession of the house, although he did not live there.

CONSTRUCTIVE FRAUD. FRAUD originating from an act contrary to duty, trust, or good conscience, which operates to the detriment of others but does not originate from an actual evil design to deceive others. Constructive fraud is **implied** or inferred by law from the circumstances. *Also called*: **fraud in law**; **legal fraud**. *See*: ACTUAL FRAUD.

CONSTRUCTIVE MALICE. MALICE inferred or **implied** by the law from the doing of an evil act. *Also called*: **legal malice**.

CONSTRUCTIVE NOTICE. NOTICE that the law presumes a person to have received (even though not actually received) because the person could have acquired it through the exercise of reasonable care. See NOTICE for a list of related terms.

CONSTRUCTIVE SERVICE. Any SERVICE other than **personal service**, such as service by mail, service by publication in a newspaper, or service upon an authorized agent. *Also called*: **substituted service**.

CONSTRUE. v. To ascertain the meaning and the legal effects and consequences of language by examining the written or spoken words, surrounding circumstances, and other authorities and sources and by applying background knowledge and legal skills. Construe is a term of broader scope than **interpret**. **n.** CONSTRUCTION.

CONSUMER FRAUD. Deception of the public with respect to the cost, quality, purity, safety, durability, performance, effectiveness, dependability, availability, and adequacy of choice relating to goods or services offered or furnished, and with respect to credit or other matters relating to terms of sales. Consumer fraud is a generic term indicating the focus of crime prevention or law enforcement activities associated with consumer affairs agencies. Particular instances of consumer fraud are prosecuted as types of **fraud** designated in statutes under a variety of names.

CONTEMNOR. A person guilty of **contempt of court**.

CONTEMPLATE. **1.** To consider thoughtfully; to reflect upon. **2.** To have as a purpose; to intend.

CONTEMPT OF COURT. An act calculated to embarrass, hinder, or obstruct a **court** in the administration of justice or to lessen its authority or dignity, or failure to obey the court's lawful orders. **Criminal contempt** is an offense against the court. A **fine** or **confinement** can be imposed for the purpose of punishment. **Civil contempt** is an offense against the party in whose behalf the mandate of the court was issued. A fine or confinement can be imposed for the purpose of enforcing the court's original order, and the penalty can be avoided by compliance with that order.

    Direct contempt is contempt committed in the immediate presence of the court. **Indirect contempt** is contempt committed outside the presence of the court, usually by failure or refusal to obey a lawful order, injunction, or decree of the court.

CONTEND. To assert in opposition to another's argument. See ADDRESS for a list of related terms.

CONTERMINOUS. Having a common boundary. See PROXIMITY for a list of related terms.

CONTEST. To challenge; to oppose; to dispute; to defend.

CONTEXT. The part of a written or spoken statement that precedes or follows a given passage or word and that is directly connected with it. The context of a legal document is often examined to determine the meaning of an ambiguous or obscure sentence or clause, so that it may be interpreted as the writer intended.

CONTIGUOUS. Touching on one side or a large portion of one side. See PROXIMITY for a list of related terms.

CONTINGENT. **1.** Dependent upon a future event that may or may not happen. **2.** Possible.

CONTINUAL. Repeated frequently and regularly; recurring often.

CONTINUANCE. Postponement of the **trial** of a case from one **term** (definition 2) to the next or until some later date in the same term. In ruling on a **motion** for a continuance, a court examines all the facts and circumstances of the case, including the applicant's good faith, the purpose and necessity for the postponement, the probable advantages to result from the continuance, and the possibility of prejudice to the rights of other parties. Continuances can also be granted on the court's own motion and by operation of law for unanticipated problems, such as the death of the presiding judge. A continuance operates only as a temporary cessation of proceedings, usually for a definitely stated period, after which the matter resumes from the point at which it was discontinued. See TRIAL for a list of related terms.

CONTINUING. Not terminated by a single act or fact; enduring for a definite period; persisting day by day.

CONTINUING OFFENSE. An offense that, because of its nature, is usually not completed in a matter of seconds or minutes, but continues for a period of days, months, or even years. Examples of continuing offenses are possession of stolen property and **conspiracy**. Usually, the **statute of limitations** does not begin to run on a continuing offense until the person discontinues the acts constituting the offense. *Also called*: **continuous crime.** See CRIME for a list of related terms.

CONTINUOUS. Without break or interruption in space or time.

CONTINUOUS CRIME. Same as CONTINUING OFFENSE.

CONTRA-. *Latin.* A prefix meaning: Against; opposed to.

CONTRABAND. **1.** Goods the importation or exportation of which is prohibited. **2.** Goods the possession of which is prohibited. *See*: ITEMS SUBJECT TO SEIZURE.

CONTRACT. An **agreement** between two or more parties creating a legally enforceable obligation. *See*: CONSIDERATION.

CONTRACT FACILITY. A public or private CORRECTIONAL FACILITY or JUVENILE FACILITY that by special contract houses, supervises, or treats persons under the **jurisdiction** of a **court** or **correctional agency**.

CONTRACT PAROLE. Same as MUTUAL AGREEMENT PROGRAM.

CONTRADICT. **1.** To be opposed to; to be inconsistent with. **2.** To deny or challenge the statement of. *See*: IMPEACH.

CONTRARY. Opposed in purpose or character; against; completely different.

Cc

CONTRARY TO LAW. Against or in violation of the principles of law applicable to the particular **case** under consideration. The term contrary to law is ordinarily applied to a **verdict** that is returned in disobedience to or in disregard of the court's **instructions**.

CONTRARY TO THE EVIDENCE. Against the **weight of the evidence**. To say that a **verdict** is contrary to the evidence is the same as saying that the evidence is insufficient to justify the verdict. See EVIDENCE for a list of related terms.

CONTRAVENE. **v.** To come in conflict with; to act counter to; to violate; to infringe. **n.** CONTRAVENTION

CONTRAVENTION. *See*: CONTRAVENE

CONTRIBUTE. **1.** To aid in producing an effect. **2.** To give a share to.

CONTRIBUTING TO DELINQUENCY OF A MINOR. The offense committed by an **adult** who in any manner causes, encourages, or aids a **minor** to commit a **crime** or **status offense**. The status offense will often consist of entering a place where liquor is served, a place where **pornography** is sold or displayed, a place of **gambling**, or a place of **prostitution**.

CONTRIVE. **1.** To plan or plot with cleverness or ingenuity. **2.** To manage or bring about by a device or scheme.

CONTROL. To exercise authority or influence over; to direct; to regulate; to restrain.

CONTROLLED SUBSTANCE. Any **drug** whose possession, distribution, sale, or use is restricted by state or federal controlled substances acts. Substances included in these acts are **narcotics**, stimulants, depressants, hallucinogens, and **marijuana**. The federal act is found at 21 U.S.C. 801 et seq. See DRUG for a list of related terms.

CONTROVERSY. An actual dispute between persons who seek judicial resolution of grievances arising from a conflict of their alleged legal rights. In constitutional law, in order to constitute a **case or controversy** such that the judicial power is capable of acting upon it under Article III of the U.S. Constitution, a dispute "must be one that is appropriate for judicial determination. . . . A justiciable controversy is thus distinguished from a difference or dispute of a hypothetical or abstract character;

from one that is academic or moot. . . . The controversy must be definite and concrete, touching the legal relations of parties having adverse legal interests. . . . It must be a real and substantial controversy admitting of specific relief through a decree of a conclusive character, as distinguished from an opinion advising what the law would be upon a hypothetical state of facts." *Aetna Life Insurance Co. v. Haworth*, 300 U.S. 227, 240-41, 57 S.Ct. 461, 464, 81 L.Ed. 617, 621 (1937). Controversies are distinguished from **cases** in that controversies only include **civil actions**, whereas cases include both civil and **criminal actions**.

CONTROVERT.   To contradict; to deny; to take issue with.

CONTUMACY.   **1.** Willful and obstinate resistance to authority. **2.** A person's intentional failure to obey a **summons** to appear in court to defend against a **charge** or to obey a **court order**.

CONTUMELY.   Insulting and contemptuous rudeness.

CONTUSION.   A bruise that does not break the skin.

CONVENIENT.   Suitable; agreeable; accessible; favorable.

CONVENTIONAL.   **1.** Growing out of or established by mutual agreement of the parties rather than by effect of **law**. **2.** Conforming to accepted standards or established practice; customary.

CONVERSION.   Unauthorized assumption and exercise of rights of ownership over another person's property permanently or for an indefinite time. Conversion requires some serious interference with the owner's rights in the property such as consuming it, selling it, or damaging it. The essence of conversion lies in depriving the owner of the benefit of the property and it makes no difference that the conversion may not be for the direct benefit of the taker.

CONVEY.   **1.** To transfer property or title to property to another. Convey usually refers to transfers of **real property** as opposed to **personal property**. **2.** To take or carry from one place to another.

CONVICT.   **v.** To **adjudge** a person **guilty** of a crime at the end of a criminal **prosecution** or after entry of a **guilty plea** or a plea of **nolo contendere**. *See*: ACQUIT.

CONVICT.   **n.** A person who has been adjudged guilty of a crime, and who is confined in a federal or state **confinement facility**. See ACCUSED for a list of related terms.

CONVICTION.   **1.** A **judgment** of a court, based on the **verdict** of a **jury** or of a **judicial officer** in a **nonjury trial**, or on the **guilty plea** or **nolo contendere** plea of a defendant, that the defendant is guilty of the offense for which he or she has been tried. See DISMISSAL and JUDGMENT for lists of related terms. **2.** A firm or strong belief. **3.** The act of convincing; the state of being convinced.

CONVINCING PROOF. See CLEAR AND CONVINCING PROOF.

Cc

COOL BLOOD. In the law of **homicide**, cool blood is the absence of the **heat of passion** or uncontrollable excitement of mind that interferes with judgment and reason. See HOMICIDE for a list of related terms.

COOLING TIME. In the law of **homicide**, cooling time is the time it takes an ordinary reasonable person to become calm and self-controlled after severe excitement or **provocation**. See HOMICIDE for a list of related terms.

COOPERATE. To act or operate together with another or others toward a common goal.

COORDINATE. **adj.** Equal in rank, importance, or degree. **v.** To combine in harmonious action. *Example*: An officer was assigned to coordinate the investigation.

COORDINATE JURISDICTION. **1.** JURISDICTION held by courts of equal rank, degree, or authority. **2.** Same as CONCURRENT JURISDICTION. See JURISDICTION for a list of related terms.

COPULATE. To engage in **sexual intercourse**.

COPY. A reproduction or double of an original. See ABSTRACT for a list of related terms.

CORAM. *Latin.* "Before; in the presence of."

CORAM JUDICE. *Latin.* "In the presence of a judge." A cause is coram judice when it is presented to a **court** with **jurisdiction** to hear it. *See*: CORAM NON JUDICE.

CORAM NOBIS. *Latin.* "Before us." A **writ** of error coram nobis is a **common law** writ for review of **errors** of fact brought before the same court that is alleged to have committed the error. The writ is sought where the error that is alleged to have occurred does not appear on the **record** of court proceedings. The petitioner asks the court to go beyond the official record to examine the relevant facts. If the petitioner's allegations are sustained, the writ is issued to correct the judgment. See ARREST WARRANT and ERROR for lists of related terms.

CORAM NON JUDICE. *Latin.* "In the presence of a person not a judge." A cause is coram non judice when it is presented to a **court** lacking **jurisdiction** to hear it. Any judgment rendered by a court in such a case is void. *See*: CORAM JUDICE.

CORESPONDENT. A person who, together with another RESPONDENT or respondents, must answer claims alleged in an **appeal**, **motion**, or **petition**. See ACCUSED for a list of related terms.

CORONER. A public officer whose primary duty is to conduct **coroner's inquests** into the cause of violent or suspicious deaths or deaths not clearly due to natural causes. The coroner's office has been replaced in many states by the office of **medical examiner**. See DEATH for a list of related terms.

CORONER'S INQUEST. A judicial investigation into the cause of death by the CORONER with the aid of a **jury**. The purpose of a coroner's inquest is to determine whether the death was caused by a criminal act and, if so, to obtain **evidence** of the crime to furnish the foundation for a criminal **prosecution**. Incident to the coroner's duties is the right to order an **autopsy** when appropriate and essential to ascertain the circumstances and the nature of death.

CORPORAL. Relating to the body; physical.

CORPORAL PUNISHMENT. Physical punishment, such as whipping or beating, as opposed to a fine or other nonphysical punishment for the commission of a wrongful or illegal act. Corporal punishment may or may not include **imprisonment**.

CORPOREAL. Capable of being seen and touched; having physical form and substance.

CORPSE. A dead body, especially of a human being.

CORPUS. **1.** A human or animal body. **2.** The main body or essential element of a thing. **3.** A large or complete collection of writings on a specific subject or of a specific kind.

CORPUS DELICTI. *Latin.* "Body of the crime." Objective proof that a particular **crime** was actually committed and that someone was criminally responsible for it. To **convict** a person of a crime, the **prosecution** must first prove the corpus delicti. The corpus delicti in a criminal case cannot be established by the **confession** of the defendant alone. The prosecution must produce some evidence, besides the confession, to prove that a particular crime was committed by someone before the confession can be admitted. "Some evidence" has been defined as such independent credible evidence as will create a really substantial belief that the crime charged has actually been committed by someone. For example, before the prosecutor can introduce a defendant's admission to setting fire to a building, the prosecutor must offer independent evidence that the fire was intentionally set. This is generally done by offering testimony from a fire marshal or other arson investigator. See CRIME for a list of related terms.

CORRECTIONAL AGENCY. A federal, state, or local criminal or juvenile justice agency, under a single administrative authority, of which the principal functions are the intake screening, supervision, custody, confinement, treatment, or presentence or predisposition investigation of alleged or adjudicated adult offenders, youthful offenders, delinquents, or status offenders. Types of correctional agencies include **probation agencies**, **parole agencies**, and agencies that administer **correctional facilities**.

Cc

CORRECTIONAL DAY PROGRAM. A publicly financed and operated nonresidential educational or treatment program for persons required by a judicial officer to participate in such a program.

CORRECTIONAL FACILITY (ADULT). Generally, a building, part of a building, set of buildings, or area enclosing a set of buildings or structures, operated by a government agency for the physical custody, or custody and treatment, of sentenced persons or persons subject to criminal proceedings. Correctional facilities include both **confinement facilities** and **residential facilities**. *See*: PRISON.

CORRECTIONAL FACILITY (JUVENILE). *See*: JUVENILE FACILITY.

CORRECTIONAL INSTITUTION. *See*: PRISON.

CORRECTIONS. The branch of the criminal justice system that encompasses all government agencies, facilities, programs, procedures, personnel, and techniques concerned with the **intake**, **custody**, **confinement**, **supervision**, or treatment or **presentence investigation** or **predisposition investigation** of alleged or adjudicated **adult offenders**, **youthful offenders**, **delinquents**, or **status offenders**.

CORRELATIVE. Mutually related so that one complements or implies the other.

CORROBORATE. To support or enhance the believability of a fact or assertion by presenting additional information that confirms or strengthens the truthfulness of the fact or assertion. A law enforcement officer applying for a **search warrant** or **arrest warrant** based on information from an **informant** may increase the likelihood of the warrant issuing by presenting in the **affidavit** information that corroborates the information provided by the informant.

CORROBORATING EVIDENCE. **Evidence** supporting or confirming other evidence already given and of a different character from it. See EVIDENCE for a list of related terms.

CORRUPT. Dishonest; depraved; immoral; perverted; unlawful. The term corrupt has many shades of meaning, depending on the context in which it is used.

COTERMINOUS. Same as CONTERMINOUS.

COUNSEL. **1.** Advice, opinion, or instruction given to direct the judgment or conduct of another. **2.** An ATTORNEY AT LAW. *See*: ASSISTANCE OF COUNSEL.

COUNSEL OF RECORD. Same as ATTORNEY OF RECORD.

COUNSELOR. Same as ATTORNEY AT LAW.

COUNT. An allegation charging a distinct offense in a **complaint**, **indictment**, or **information**. A complaint, indictment, or information may contain one or more counts. A single count may name one or more persons and a single person may be named in one or more counts.

COUNTENANCE. To favor; to encourage; to support; to approve.

COUNTER. Opposing; contradicting; adverse.

COUNTERFEIT. Generally, made in imitation of something genuine or original with intent to **defraud**. *Example*: He attempted to pass counterfeit food stamps.

COUNTERFEITING. The manufacture or attempted manufacture of a copy or imitation of a negotiable instrument with a value set by law or convention (such as currency, coins, postage stamps, ration stamps, food stamps, etc.), or the possession of such a copy without authorization, with the intent to **defraud** by claiming the genuineness of the copy. *See*: FORGERY.

COUNTERMAND. To revoke or reverse a command or order.

COUNTERSIGN. To sign in addition to another signature in order to authenticate the other signature.

COUNTY. A political subdivision of a state for governmental purposes.

COUNTY ATTORNEY. A public PROSECUTOR whose jurisdiction is a county. See PROSECUTE for a list of related terms.

COUNTY COURT. *See*: COURT OF LIMITED JURISDICTION.

COUNTY FARM. A CONFINEMENT FACILITY, similar in purpose to a **jail**, for **adults** detained pending **adjudication** or **sentencing** and/or adults who have been sentenced. A county farm is usually under local government administration and its custodial authority is not limited to a maximum of 48 hour detention. Depending on local usage, a county farm may be called an **honor farm**, a **road camp**, or a **work camp**. *See*: PREARRAIGNMENT LOCKUP; PRISON.

COURT. **1.** An agency or unit in the **judicial** branch of government, authorized or established by statute or constitution, and consisting of one or more **judicial officers**, that is responsible for the public administration of justice and that has the authority to decide upon **cases, controversies** in law, and disputed matters of fact brought before it. There are two basic types of courts: **trial courts** having **original jurisdiction** to make decisions regarding matters of fact and law, and **appellate courts** having **appellate jurisdiction** to review issues of law in connection with decisions made in specific cases previously adjudicated by other courts and decisions made by administrative agencies. However, individual courts are frequently authorized to exercise both original and appellate jurisdiction, depending upon the subject matter of individual cases.

In most states there are two levels of trial court: **courts of limited (special) jurisdiction** and **courts of general jurisdiction**. In many states there are two levels of appellate court: **intermediate appellate courts** and **courts of last resort**. Whether a given court deals with criminal cases only depends upon the structure of the court system of a given state; generally, most courts handle both civil and criminal matters.

2. The **judge** or judges presiding over the administration of justice in a particular cause or particular tribunal. *Example*: The court denied the motion to suppress. **3.** The building, hall, or room where justice is judicially administered *See*: ADJUDICATION; AMICUS CURIAE; APPEAL; APPELLATE COURT; BAILIFF; CITY COURT; CLERK OF COURT; COMMITMENT; COMPETENT COURT; CONTEMPT OF COURT; COURT ABOVE; COURT ADMINISTRATOR; COURT BELOW; COURT CALENDAR; COURT DISPOSITION; COURT HOUSE; COURT MARTIAL; COURT OF APPEALS; COURT OF FIRST INSTANCE; COURT OF GENERAL JURISDICTION; COURT OF LAST RESORT; COURT OF LIMITED JURISDICTION; COURT OF RECORD; COURT OF SPECIAL SESSIONS; COURT PROBATION; COURT REPORTER; COURT SYSTEM; DECISION; DISMISSAL; DISTRICT COURT; DOCKET; ERROR; EVIDENCE; FAMILY COURT; FEDERAL COURTS; FULL COURT; HEARING; INFERIOR COURT; INTERMEDIATE APPELLATE COURT; JUDGMENT; JURISDICTION; JURY; JUVENILE COURT; JUVENILE COURT JUDGMENT; MARSHAL; MOOT COURT; MUNICIPAL COURT; NEW COURT COMMITMENT; OFFICER OF THE COURT; OPEN COURT; OPINION; ORDER; OUT OF COURT; POLICE COURT; RULES OF COURT; SENTENCE; SESSIONS; STATE COURT; SUPERIOR COURT; SUPREME COURT; TRANSFER TO ADULT COURT; TRIAL; TRIAL COURT; UNITED STATES COURTS; UNITED STATES COURTS OF APPEALS; UNITED STATES DISTRICT COURTS; UNITED STATES SUPREME COURT.

COURT ABOVE. A **court** to which a case is removed for review. See COURT for a list of related terms.

COURT ADMINISTRATOR. The official responsible for supervising and performing administrative tasks for a given **court**. The duties of a court administrator depend upon the size of the court. They may include assisting the presiding judge in administrative duties; other personnel, budget, and administrative tasks; and statistical reporting. In some small courts, the court administrator also performs some of the duties of a clerk of court, such as assigning case numbers, notifying all parties in a case of dates of court hearings, and assigning cases to the court calendar. See COURT for a list of related terms.

COURT BELOW. A **court** from which a case is removed for review. See COURT for a list of related terms.

COURT CALENDAR. The court schedule; the list of events comprising the daily or weekly work of a court, including the assignment of the time and place for each hearing or other item of business, or the list of matters to be taken up in a given court **term**. See COURT for a list of related terms.

COURT CASE. *See*: CASE (definition 1).

COURT CASELOAD. *See*: CASELOAD.

COURT CLERK. Same as CLERK OF COURT.

COURT DECISION. *See*: DECISION.

COURT DISPOSITION. The judicial decision that terminates a criminal proceeding before judgment is reached, or the judgment itself. Court disposition, in the criminal justice context, means either the immediate result of prosecution (**conviction, acquittal,** or **dismissal**) or the final result in the sense of **sentencing disposition** when the **judgment** is **conviction**. A court disposition terminates the **jurisdiction** of a particular court over a person or case. See COURT, DISPOSITION, JUDGMENT, and SENTENCE for lists of related terms.

COURTESY SUPERVISION. **Supervision** by the **correctional agency** of one **jurisdiction**, of a person placed on **probation** by a **court** or on **parole** by a **paroling authority** in another jurisdiction, by informal agreement between agencies. Courtesy supervision occurs when a receiving agency agrees to supervise a **probationer** or **parolee** through arrangements made without reference to statutory or administratively promulgated rules for the exchange of supervisees (such as **interstate compacts**). The kind of case handled in this fashion is usually one where the offense is not grave, and the practical and rehabilitative needs of the probationer or parolee are best served by residence in a jurisdiction other than the one where adjudication occurred. These informal exchanges are often at the local level, as between one county and another.

Local exchanges can also be the subject of regular, formal agreements. *See*: PAROLE SUPERVISION; SUPERVISED PROBATION.

COURT HOUSE. A building housing judicial **courts**. See COURT for a list of related terms.

COURT MARTIAL. A **court** for the trial and punishment of persons violating military law.

COURT OF APPEALS. A name for an APPELLATE COURT. In some states, the court of appeals is the highest court in the state. In most states and in the federal court system, the court of appeals is an **intermediate appellate court**. See APPEAL and COURT for lists of related terms.

COURT OF APPELLATE JURISDICTION. Same as APPELLATE COURT.

COURT OF COMPETENT JURISDICTION. Same as COMPETENT COURT.

COURT OFFICER. *See*: BAILIFF.

COURT OF FIRST INSTANCE. A **trial court**, as distinguished from an **appellate court**. See COURT for a list of related terms.

COURT OF GENERAL JURISDICTION. Speaking only of criminal courts, a court that has **trial jurisdiction** over all criminal offenses, including all **felonies**, and that may or may not hear **appeals**. A court of general jurisdiction has **original jurisdiction** over all felonies and frequently has **appellate jurisdiction** over the decisions of a **court of limited jurisdiction**. The decisions of a court of general jurisdiction may be reviewed by an **appellate court**. Courts of general jurisdiction are commonly named "superior court," "district court," and "circuit court." The factual determination of a court of general jurisdiction is final. Appeals are on the record and on matters of law rather than on matters of fact. *Also called*: **major trial court**. See COURT and JURISDICTION for lists of related terms.

COURT OF INTERMEDIATE APPEALS. Same as INTERMEDIATE APPEL-LATE COURT.

COURT OF LAST RESORT. A **court** that has final **jurisdiction** over all **appeals** within a state or the United States. There is no appeal from a court of last resort. Nevertheless, issues of law may exist that permit subsequent appeal from a state court of last resort to a federal court. See APPEAL, COURT, and JURISDICTION for lists of related terms.

COURT OF LIMITED JURISDICTION. Speaking only of criminal courts, a court whose **trial jurisdiction** either includes no **felonies** or is limited to less than all felonies, and which may or may not hear **appeals**. A court of limited jurisdiction is limited to a particular class or classes of cases, and cannot try every felony. A court of limited jurisdiction often has jurisdiction over **misdemeanor** or traffic cases, over the initial setting of **bail** and **preliminary hearings** in felony cases, and occasionally over felony trials where the penalty prescribed for the offense is below a statutorily specified limit. In these cases, the **courts of general jurisdiction** maintain **concurrent jurisdiction** over those felonies that the courts of limited jurisdiction are also empowered to try. In some jurisdictions a court of general jurisdiction may hear **appeals** from a court of limited jurisdiction, and in some cases may review decisions of a court of limited jurisdiction **de novo**. In other jurisdictions, appeals from a court of limited jurisdiction are made directly to an **appellate court,** bypassing the court of general jurisdiction. With respect to civil actions, a court of limited jurisdiction may be limited to a certain type of case, or to cases where the amount in controversy is below a statutorily specified limit. Courts of limited jurisdiction are commonly named **city court, county court, district court, domestic relations court, family court, justice court, magistrate court, municipal court, police court, probate court, small claims court,** and **traffic court**. *Also called*: **court of special jurisdiction**. See COURT and JURISDICTION for lists of related terms.

COURT OF ORIGINAL JURISDICTION. Same as TRIAL COURT.

COURT OF RECORD. A **court** whose acts and proceedings are recorded by a duly authorized person and that has the power to **fine** and **imprison**. Decisions of a court of record are **reviewed** on the <u>record</u> (definition 2). Thus, when an **appeal** is taken from a court of record, the **appellate court** bases its findings and decision on the written record rather than hearing the testimony of witnesses and arguments of counsel over again.

Felony trial courts are courts of record. Trial proceedings are supposed to be recorded verbatim. The record, usually in the form of a stenotype or shorthand representation of what has been said and done, but sometimes stored on audiotape, is not necessarily transcribed. The **court reporter** may store such material in the original form and it will not be converted into a typed transcript unless the record pertaining to a case is requested. See COURT for a list of related terms.

COURT OF SPECIAL JURISDICTION. Same as COURT OF LIMITED JURISDICTION.

COURT OF SPECIAL SESSIONS. Any **court** that is not continuous and has no stated **term**, but is constituted for the trial of a particular **case** and becomes powerless after **judgment** in that case is rendered. See COURT for a list of related terms.

COURT ORDER. *See*: ORDER.

COURT PROBATION. A criminal court requirement that a defendant or offender fulfill specified conditions of behavior in lieu of a **sentence** to **confinement**, but without assignment to a **probation agency's** supervisory caseload. Court probation is used as a **sentencing disposition** by some courts to avoid the unnecessary supervisory activity and expense in appropriate cases. Court probation does not, however, amount to an **unconditional release**. As in all instances of **probation orders**, the court retains **jurisdiction** over the case, and probation status can be revoked. The typical **probation violation** that will cause the court to reconsider probationary status and sentence the person to confinement is reappearance in court charged with a new offense, or a new conviction. **Probation supervision** of **juveniles** is frequently performed by an officer of the juvenile court, rather than by a **probation agency** or separate probation subunit within the court system. *Also called*: **unsupervised probation**; **summary probation**; **informal probation**. See PROBATION for a list of related terms.

COURT REPORT. *See*: PRESENTENCE REPORT.

COURT REPORTER. A person who records all testimony and other oral statements during court proceedings by shorthand or stenotype machine and prepares a **transcript** of the proceedings if requested. Court reporters are usually present in the courtroom during court **sessions**. They may also be present during other judicial proceedings held outside the courtroom, e.g., in the judge's **chambers**. See COURT for a list of related terms.

COURT RULE. *See*: RULES OF COURT.

COURTS OF THE UNITED STATES. *See*: UNITED STATES COURTS.

COURT SYSTEM. A judicial agency established or authorized by constitutional or statutory law. A court system may consist of a single **court** or a group of two or more courts in the same judicial district. See COURT for a list of related terms.

COURT TRIAL. Same as NONJURY TRIAL.

COVENANT. A formal, binding agreement between two or more parties to do something or to refrain from doing something.

COVERT. Concealed; secret; hidden.

CREATE. To bring into existence.

CREDIBILITY. Worthiness of belief. After the court has found a **witness** to be **competent**, the **jury** is allowed to consider the witness's credibility. The credibility of a witness is based upon the jury's ability to trust and believe what the witness says, and relates to the accuracy of the witness's testimony as well as to its logic, truthfulness, and sincerity. Personal credibility depends upon the qualities of a person that would lead a jury to believe or disbelieve what the person said, including the person's appearance or demeanor while testifying. See WITNESS for a list of related terms.

CREDIBLE. **adj.** Worthy of belief. **n.** CREDIBILITY. *See*: COMPETENT.

CREDIT CARD FRAUD. The use or attempted use of a credit card to obtain goods or services with the intent to avoid payment.

CREDIT TIME. *See*: SENTENCE CREDIT TIME

CRIER. A court or town official who makes public announcements or proclamations.

CRIME. An act committed or omitted in violation of a law specifically prohibiting or commanding it, for which the possible penalties for an **adult** upon **conviction** include a **fine** and **incarceration**, for which a corporation can be penalized by fine or **forfeiture**, or for which a **juvenile** can be adjudged **delinquent** or transferred to criminal court for prosecution. Crimes are usually divided into **felonies** and **misdemeanors**, but may be otherwise classified in some modern statutory schemes. Generally, a crime consists of conduct that violates the duties a person owes to the community or society, as distinguished from a **private wrong**. *Also called*: **criminal act**; **criminal offense**. *See*: ACCUSED; ACTUS REUS; CAREER CRIMINAL; CIVIL; CIVIL ACTION; CIVIL VIOLATION; COMMON-LAW CRIME; COMPOUNDING CRIME; COMPUTER CRIME; CONTINUING OFFENSE; CORPUS DELICTI; CRIME INDEX; CRIME MALUM IN SE; CRIME MALUM PROHIBITUM; CRIMEN FALSI; CRIMES AGAINST PERSONS; CRIMINAL; CRIMINAL ACT; CRIMINAL ACTION; CRIMINAL CONTEMPT; CRIMINAL DIVISION; CRIMINAL FACILITATION; CRIMINAL FORFEITURE; CRIMINAL HOMICIDE; CRIMINAL JURISDICTION; CRIMINAL JUSTICE; CRIMINAL JUSTICE AGENCY; CRIMINAL JUSTICE SYSTEM; CRIMINAL LAW; CRIMINAL MISCHIEF; CRIMINAL NONSUPPORT; CRIMINAL PROCEDURE; CRIMINAL PROCEEDINGS; CRIMINAL RECORD; CRIMINAL SYNDICALISM; CRIMINATE; CRIMINOLOGY; CULPABILITY; DELINQUENT ACT; ELEMENT OF A CRIME; FEDERAL RULES OF CRIMINAL PROCEDURE; FELONY; FRUIT; HABITUAL CRIMINAL; INCRIMINATE; INCRIMINATING ADMISSION; INCRIMINATING CIRCUMSTANCE; INCULPATORY; INFAMOUS CRIME; INFRACTION; INSTANTANEOUS CRIME; INSTRUMENT OF CRIME; INTENT; LAW ENFORCEMENT; LAW ENFORCEMENT AGENCY;

LIBEL; LOCUS CRIMINIS; LOCUS DELICTI; MENS REA; MISDEMEANOR; MODEL PENAL CODE; NATIONAL CRIME SURVEY; OFFENDER; OFFENSE; ORGANIZED CRIME; PARTY; PENAL LAW; PENOLOGY; PERPETRATOR; PROFESSIONAL CRIMINAL; PROPERTY CRIMES; PROSECUTOR; QUASI-CRIME; RECIDIVISM; RECIDIVIST; SELF-INCRIMINATION; SERIOUS MISDEMEANOR; STATUS OFFENSE; STREET CRIME; SUSPECT; UNIFORM CRIME REPORTING; VICTIM; VIOLATION; VIOLENT CRIMES; WHITE-COLLAR CRIME.

Cc

CRIME AGAINST NATURE. Same as SODOMY.

CRIME INDEX. In **Uniform Crime Reporting** terminology, a set of numbers indicating the volume, fluctuation, and distribution of **crimes** reported to local law enforcement agencies, for the United States as a whole and for its geographical subdivisions, based on counts of reported occurrences of UCR Index Crimes. The UCR Index Crimes are **murder, nonnegligent manslaughter, forcible rape, robbery, aggravated assault, burglary, larceny-theft, motor vehicle theft,** and **arson.** See CRIME for a list of related terms.

CRIME MALUM IN SE. A **crime** involving an act that is immoral or wrong in itself. Examples of crimes mala in se are **murder, burglary,** and **arson.** See CRIME for a list of related terms.

CRIME MALUM PROHIBITUM. A **crime** involving an act that is not inherently evil but is only wrong because prohibited by law. Examples of crimes mala prohibita are driving slightly over the speed limit and keeping slot machines. See CRIME for a list of related terms.

CRIMEN FALSI. *Latin.* "Crime of falsifying." Any **crime** involving an element of **deceit** or **fraud** and that thereby renders a person who committed it incompetent to be a **witness.** Examples of crimen falsi are **forgery** and **perjury.** See CRIME for a list of related terms.

CRIME OF STATUS. Same as STATUS OFFENSE (definition 2).

CRIME RATE. *See:* UNIFORM CRIME REPORTING.

CRIMES AGAINST HOUSEHOLDS. Same as HOUSEHOLD CRIMES.

CRIMES AGAINST PERSONS. A category used in some crime classification schemes to include crimes such as **murder, manslaughter, forcible rape, assault,** and **robbery** or **larceny** against persons. See CRIME for a list of related terms.

CRIMES AGAINST PROPERTY. Same as PROPERTY CRIMES.

CRIMES OF VIOLENCE. Same as VIOLENT CRIMES.

CRIMINAL. adj. Of or pertaining to **crime** or the administration of **criminal justice**. n. A person who has **committed** or has been legally **convicted** of a crime. In some contexts, the meaning of criminal is restricted to a person legally convicted of a crime. See CRIME for a list of related terms.

CRIMINAL ACT. A **crime**. See CRIME for a list of related terms.

CRIMINAL ACTION. An **action** brought by a **prosecutor** in the name of the government, representing the public, against a person accused of **committing** a crime, to **convict** and **punish** the person according to the law. See CRIME for a list of related terms.

CRIMINAL CASE. Same as CRIMINAL ACTION.

CRIMINAL CONTEMPT. *See*: CONTEMPT OF COURT.

CRIMINAL DIVISION. The Criminal Division of the **Department of Justice** formulates criminal law enforcement policies and enforces and exercises general supervision over all federal criminal laws except those specifically assigned to other divisions of the department. The Criminal Division also supervises certain civil litigation incidental to federal law enforcement activities. The Criminal Division contains the following specialized units, sections, and offices:

—The National Obscenity Enforcement Unit spearheads and coordinates federal obscenity and child exploitation prosecutions. It assists federal, state, and local prosecutors with advice, training, and legal resource materials.

—The Organized Crime and Racketeering Section investigates and prosecutes cases to suppress the illicit activities of organized criminal syndicates. Cases handled in this section typically focus on labor-management racketeering, loansharking, extortion, gambling, and prostitution. The section also supervises the use of the **Racketeer Influenced and Corrupt Organizations** (RICO) statute throughout the federal legal system and is responsible for identifying and targeting emerging organized criminal groups.

—The Narcotics and Dangerous Drugs Section investigates and prosecutes high-level drug traffickers and members of criminal organizations involved in the importation, manufacture, shipment, or distribution of illicit narcotics and dangerous drugs, with particular emphasis on litigation attacking the financial bases of those criminal organizations.

—The Internal Security Section investigates and prosecutes cases affecting the national security, foreign relations, and the export of military and strategic commodities and technology. It also administers and enforces the Foreign

Agents Registration Act of 1938 (22 U.S.C. §611) and related statutes. The section has exclusive prosecutorial responsibility for criminal statutes regarding espionage, sabotage, neutrality, and atomic energy.

—The Fraud Section directs and coordinates the federal effort against fraud and white-collar crime, focusing primarily upon frauds against government programs and procurement, transnational and multidistrict fraud, the security and commodity exchanges, banking practices, and consumer victimization. It conducts investigations and prosecutes certain fraud cases of national significance or great complexity.

—The Public Integrity Section investigates and prosecutes corruption cases involving public officials and the elective system at the federal, state, and local levels.

—The General Litigation and Legal Advice Section investigates and prosecutes crimes under a broad spectrum of federal criminal statutes regarding crimes against the government and the public. It also handles certain civil matters, including the defense of civil actions to obtain information on or to interfere with criminal justice and national security operations and the defense of suits against actions taken by the **Bureau of Prisons** and the **United States Parole Commission**.

—The Appellate Section assists the Office of the **Solicitor General** in obtaining favorable constitutional and statutory interpretations in criminal cases being heard on appeal before the **United States Supreme Court** and the 13 **United States Courts of Appeals**.

—The Office of Enforcement Operations oversees the use of sensitive and sophisticated investigative tools, such as witness protection and electronic surveillance. It also assists and supports government prosecutors by reviewing requests for authorization to compel testimony (immunity) and responding to inquiries under the **Freedom of Information Act** and the **Privacy Act**.

—The Office of Special Investigations detects, identifies, and takes appropriate legal action leading to the denaturalization and/or deportation of Nazi war criminals in the United States who were involved in the atrocities committed against civilian populations during the Second World War and who subsequently entered the United States illegally.

The Criminal Division also contains Offices of Administration, Policy and Management Analysis, International Affairs, Legislation, and Asset Forfeiture. See CRIME and PROSECUTE for lists of related terms.

CRIMINAL FACILITATION. Unlawful conduct on the part of a person by which he or she knowingly **aids** another person to commit a **crime**, but without any specific **intent** to participate in or benefit from the crime. In facilitation there is no offense unless a crime has actually been committed by another person. It is generally charged where the defendant acted with a degree of culpability less than that required to convict him or her of the substantive crime as an **accomplice**. Many jurisdictions have no statutory offense of this type. See INCHOATE OFFENSE and PARTY for lists of related terms.

CRIMINAL FORFEITURE.   The government act of taking property without compensation because the property was used or possessed in violation of the law. *Example*: Police seizure of an automobile used to transport illegal drugs is a criminal forfeiture. *See*: FINE; FORFEIT.

CRIMINAL HISTORY RECORD INFORMATION.   Information collected by **criminal justice agencies** about persons, consisting of identifiable descriptions; notations of **arrests**, **detentions**, **indictments**, **informations**, or other formal criminal **charges**, **dispositions**, **sentencing**, correctional **supervision**, and **release**.

CRIMINAL HOMICIDE.   The intentional killing of another person without **justification** or **excuse**, or the unintentional killing of another person with **recklessness** or **gross negligence**. The term criminal homicide includes **murder** and **manslaughter**, but does not include **excusable homicide** or **justifiable homicide**. See HOMICIDE for a list of related terms.

CRIMINAL INTENT.   *See*: INTENT.

CRIMINAL JURISDICTION.   JURISDICTION (definition 3) over criminal cases. See CRIME and JURISDICTION for lists of related terms.

CRIMINAL JUSTICE.   In the strictest sense, the **criminal law**, the law of **criminal procedure**, and the array of procedures and activities having to do with the enforcement of this body of law. The federal Crime Control Act of 1973 defines this term as part of a longer phrase, as follows: " 'Law enforcement and criminal justice' means any activity pertaining to crime prevention, control or reduction or the enforcement of the criminal law, including, but not limited to police efforts to prevent, control, or reduce crime or to apprehend criminals, activities of courts having **criminal jurisdiction** and related agencies (including prosecutorial and defender services), activities of corrections, probation, or parole authorities, and programs relating to the prevention, control, or reduction of juvenile delinquency or narcotic addiction." See CRIME for a list of related terms.

CRIMINAL JUSTICE AGENCY.   Any court with **criminal jurisdiction** and any government agency or identifiable subunit that defends indigents, or that has as its principal duty the performance of criminal justice functions (prevention, detection, and investigation of crime; the apprehension, detention, and prosecution of alleged offenders; the confinement or official correctional supervision of accused or convicted persons; or the administrative or technical support of these functions) as authorized and required by statute or executive order. The five major subclasses of criminal justice agencies as defined for use in this dictionary are **law enforcement agency**, **prosecution agency**, **public defender agency**, **court**, and **correctional agency**. Not included in this definition, but sometimes considered criminal justice agencies are **private rehabilitation agencies**, **private security agencies**, agencies whose jurisdiction is limited solely to juveniles, agencies whose law enforcement activities are incidental to their major activities, such as forestry or fish and wildlife departments and port authorities, and judicial agencies, planning agencies, and other boards, councils, and commissions that have only partial or marginal criminal jurisdiction. See CRIME for a list of related terms.

CRIMINAL JUSTICE SYSTEM. The aggregate of all operating and administrative or technical support agencies that perform **criminal justice** functions. See CRIME for a list of related terms.

CRIMINAL LAW. The branch of **substantive law** that defines **crimes** and provides for their punishment. The basic difference between criminal law and **civil law** is that the former establishes **penalties**, usually fines or deprivation of liberty, for behavior that is thought to injure society (see **crime**); the latter provides principles and methods for resolving disputes between private or corporate persons (see **private wrong**). Also, in criminal proceedings a higher standard of proof is required to decide **guilt** (**beyond a reasonable doubt**); the standard in civil proceedings is **preponderance of the evidence**. See CRIME for a list of related terms.

CRIMINAL LIBEL. *See*: LIBEL.

CRIMINAL MISCHIEF. Intentionally destroying or damaging, or attempting to destroy or damage, the property of another without his or her consent, usually by a means other than burning. Criminal mischief is popularly referred to as **vandalism** and includes behavior such as breaking school windows, slashing tires, and defacing public or private property of any kind. *Also called*: **malicious mischief**; **malicious trespass**. See AFFRAY for a list of related terms.

CRIMINAL NEGLIGENCE. *See*: NEGLIGENCE.

CRIMINAL NONSUPPORT. Willful failure to provide **support** to a spouse, child, or other dependent by a person who is able and legally obliged to provide support.

CRIMINAL OFFENSE. Same as CRIME.

CRIMINAL PROCEDURE. Generally, the body of laws and rules governing the process of detecting and investigating **crime** and gathering evidence against, apprehending, prosecuting, trying, adjudicating, sentencing, and punishing persons accused of crimes. *See*: ADMINISTRATIVE PROCEDURE; CIVIL PROCEDURE; CRIME; CRIMINAL LAW; PROCEDURAL LAW; PROCEDURE; SUBSTANTIVE LAW.

CRIMINAL PROCEEDINGS. Proceedings in a court of law, undertaken to determine whether an adult accused of a **crime** is **guilty** or **innocent**. Criminal proceedings begin with the filing of a **charging document** and end with an **adjudication** (definition 2). See CRIME for a list of related terms.

CRIMINAL RECORD. The cumulative history of the instances in which a particular person has been **convicted** of a **crime**. See CRIME for a list of related terms.

CRIMINAL SYNDICALISM. Advocating or **aiding and abetting** the commission of **crime**, **sabotage**, violence, or unlawful methods of terrorism in order to accomplish industrial or political reform.

CRIMINAL THREATENING. *See*: THREAT.

CRIMINAL TRESPASS. *See*: TRESPASS (definition 2).

CRIMINATE. To INCRIMINATE.

CRIMINOLOGY. The study of the nature of, causes of, and the means of dealing with **crime** and **criminals**. See CRIME for a list of related terms.

CROOK. A dishonest person; a thief; a swindler.

CROOKED. Dishonest, unscrupulous.

CROSS-EXAMINATION. The questioning of a **witness** by the party opposed to the party producing the witness. Cross-examination comes after **direct examination** of the witness by the party producing the witness. The purpose of cross-examination is to discredit the witness's information and impeach the witness's **credibility** as a means of testing the accuracy of his or her testimony. The scope of cross-examination is usually limited to matters covered during direct examination. See EXAMINATION and WITNESS for lists of related terms.

CROSS INTERROGATORIES. INTERROGATORIES prepared and served on a **witness** by the party adverse to the party calling the witness. See INTERROGATORIES for a list of related terms.

CRUEL AND UNUSUAL PUNISHMENT. Any punishment so inhumane, barbarous, or disproportionate to the offense committed as to shock the sense of justice of the community. The Eighth Amendment to the U.S. Constitution and similar provisions of state constitutions prohibit the infliction of cruel and unusual punishments. "The term cannot be defined with specificity. It is flexible and tends to broaden as society tends to pay more regard to human decency and dignity and becomes, or likes to think that it becomes, more humane. Generally speaking, a punishment that amounts to torture, or that is grossly excessive in proportion to the offense for which it is imposed, or that is inherently unfair, or that is shocking or disgusting to people of reasonable sensitivity is a 'cruel and unusual punishment.' And a punishment that is not inherently cruel and unusual may become so by reason of the manner in which it is inflicted." *Holt v. Sarver*, 309 F.Supp. 362, 380 (E.D.Ark. 1970). The U.S. Supreme Court announced that the standard under the Eighth Amendment was that punishments are barred when they are "excessive" in relation to the crime committed. A "punishment is 'excessive' and unconstitutional if it (1) makes no measurable contribution to acceptable goals of punishment and hence is nothing more than the purposeless and needless imposition of pain and suffering; or (2) is grossly out of proportion to the severity of the crime." *Coker v. Georgia*, 433 U.S. 584, 592, 97 S.Ct. 2861, 2866, 53 L.Ed.2d 982, 989 (1977).

CRUELTY TO ANIMALS. The willful, malicious, and unjustifiable infliction of physical suffering upon a living creature other than a human being.

CUI BONO. *Latin.* For whose benefit; for what useful purpose.

CULPABILITY. Generally, blameworthiness or responsibility in some sense for an event or situation deserving of moral blame. More specifically, in the criminal law context, a state of mind on the part of one who is committing an act that makes him or her liable to **prosecution** for that act. The term culpability encompasses the various states of mind that make up the **mens rea** element of crime. Culpability must be proven to **convict** a person of any crime, unless the statute defining the crime otherwise indicates. Section 2.02 (2) (a)—(d) of the **Model Penal Code** divides culpability into four states of mind accompanying the commission of an act.

"A person acts **purposely** with respect to a material element of an offense when: (i) if the element involves the nature of his conduct or a result thereof, it is his conscious object to engage in conduct of that nature or to cause such a result; and (ii) if the element involves the attendant circumstances, he is aware of the existence of such circumstances or he believes or hopes that they exist.

"A person acts **knowingly** with respect to a material element of an offense when: (i) if the element involves the nature of his conduct or the attendant circumstances, he is aware that his conduct is of that nature or that such circumstances exist; and (ii) if the element involves a result of his conduct, he is aware that it is practically certain that his conduct will cause such a result.

"A person acts **recklessly** with respect to a material element of an offense when he consciously disregards a substantial and unjustifiable risk that the material element exists or will result from his conduct. The risk must be of such a nature and degree that, considering the nature and purpose of the actor's conduct and the circumstances known to him, its disregard involves a gross deviation from the standard of conduct that a law-abiding person would observe in the actor's situation.

"A person acts **negligently** with respect to a material element of an offense when he should be aware of a substantial and unjustifiable risk that the material element exists or will result from his conduct. The risk must be of such a nature and degree that the actor's failure to perceive it, considering the nature and purpose of his conduct and the circumstances known to him, involves a gross deviation from the standard of care that a reasonable person would observe in the actor's situation."

These differences sometimes distinguish between offenses (**murder** is purposeful killing; **involuntary manslaughter** is often defined as negligent killing) and sometimes between degrees of an offense (first degree **arson** is purposeful burning; second degree arson is reckless burning). Examples of other terms variously used to describe the culpability element of crime are corruptly, fraudulently, intentionally, maliciously, wantonly, willfully, and with malice aforethought.

CULPABLE. *See*: CULPABILITY

CULPABLE NEGLIGENCE. *See*: NEGLIGENCE.

CUMULATIVE. Adding to or increasing something of the same kind.

CUMULATIVE EVIDENCE. **Evidence** of the same kind and to the same point as that already given. See EVIDENCE for a list of related terms.

CUMULATIVE SENTENCE. Same as CONSECUTIVE SENTENCE.

CUNNILINGUS. A sexual act committed with the mouth and the female sex organ. Cunnilingus is a crime in some states, sometimes punishable as a form of the more encompassing crime of **sodomy**. See SEX OFFENSES for a list of related terms.

CURATIVE. Designed to remedy **errors**, omissions, or other defects. *Example*: The judge's curative instruction mitigated the effect of the prosecutor's comment.

CURFEW. A **law**, **ordinance**, or **order** prohibiting certain classes of people from being on the public streets of a designated area during certain hours.

CURRENT. **1.** Belonging to the present time. *Example*: Current affairs. **2.** In general circulation; commonly accepted; prevalent. *Example*: A current rumor.

CURRENT PAROLE ELIGIBILITY DATE. *See*: ELIGIBLE FOR PAROLE.

CURTAIL. To cut short; to abridge; to reduce.

CURTILAGE. The ground and buildings immediately surrounding a dwelling and used for domestic purposes in connection with the dwelling. Under the Fourth Amendment to the U.S. Constitution, "[t]he right of the people to be secure in their persons, **houses**, papers, and effects, against unreasonable searches and seizures, shall not be violated. . . ." Courts have extended the meaning of houses under the Fourth Amendment to include the curtilage. To determine whether property falls within the curtilage of a house, one must consider "the factors that determine whether an individual reasonably may expect that an area immediately adjacent to the home will remain private." *Oliver v. United States*, 466 U.S. 170, 180, 104 S.Ct. 1735, 1742, 80 L.Ed.2d 214, 225 (1984). The U.S. Supreme Court described those factors in another case: "[W]e believe that curtilage questions should be resolved with particular reference to four factors: the proximity of the area claimed to be curtilage to the home, whether the area is included within an enclosure surrounding the home, the nature of the uses to which the area is put, and the steps taken by the resident to protect the area from observation by people passing by." *United States v. Dunn*, 480 U.S. 294, 301, 107 S.Ct. 1134, 1139, 94 L.Ed.2d 326, 334-35 (1987). The Court emphasized that "the primary focus is whether the area in question harbors those intimate activities associated with domestic life and the privacies of the home." 480 U.S. at 301 n.4, 107 S.Ct. at 1139 n.4, 94 L.Ed.2d at 335 n.4. *See*: OPEN FIELDS; PRIVACY; SEARCH.

CUSTODIAL ARREST. An ARREST in which the person arrested is taken into custody and not merely given a ticket, **citation**, or notice to appear. Whether or not an arrest is custodial is a determining factor in justifying a **search incident to arrest**. The U.S. Supreme Court held that "in the case of lawful custodial arrest, a full search of the person is not only an exception to the warrant requirement of the Fourth Amendment, but is also a 'reasonable' search under that Amendment." *United States v. Robinson*, 414 U.S. 218, 235, 94 S.Ct. 467, 477, 38 L.Ed.2d 427, 441 (1973). See ARREST for a list of related terms.

CUSTODIAL INTERROGATION. *See*: INTERROGATION.

CUSTODY. **1.** Legal or physical control of a person or thing; legal, supervisory or physical responsibility for a person or thing. The term custody has several degrees of meaning, depending on the context in which it is used, and may mean actual imprisonment or the mere power—legal or physical—to imprison or take into physical possession. It ranges from the clearest legal and physical control and responsibility, as when a legally **arrested** person is in the custody of a police officer, to physical control without legal justification, as when a **jail** holds prisoners in its custody who are legally under the **jurisdiction** of a state **prison** system. Custody also applies to physical objects, such as **evidence** taken into custody by law enforcement investigators. *See*: ARREST; DETENTION; SEIZURE; STOP. **2.** A person is in custody for purposes of the MIRANDA v. ARIZONA decision when the person is deprived of freedom of action in any significant way. The U.S. Supreme Court said: "Although the circumstances of each case must certainly influence a determination of whether a suspect is 'in custody' for purposes of receiving *Miranda* protection, the ultimate inquiry is simply whether there is a 'formal arrest or restraint on freedom of movement' of the degree associated with a formal arrest." *California v. Beheler*, 463 U.S. 1121, 1125, 103 S.Ct. 3517, 3520, 77 L.Ed.2d 1275, 1279 (1983). **3.** For definitions of three types of custody in the **corrections** context, see JURISDICTIONAL CONTROL, SUPERVISORY CUSTODY, and PHYSICAL CUSTODY.

CUSTOM.   A long-continued habitual practice or course of conduct that has become so established that it has the obligatory force of **unwritten law**.

CUSTOMS SERVICE, UNITED STATES.   The fifth act of the first Congress, passed on July 31, 1789 (1 Stat. §29), established customs districts and authorized customs officers to collect duties on goods, wares, and merchandise imposed by the second act of the first Congress, dated July 1, 1789 (1 Stat. §24). The Bureau of Customs was established as a separate agency under the **Department of the Treasury** on March 3, 1927 (19 U.S.C. §2071), and, effective August 1, 1973, was redesignated the United States Customs Service by Treasury Department Order 165-23 of April 4, 1973.

The Customs Service collects the revenue from imports and enforces customs and related laws. Customs also administers the Tariff Act of 1930, as amended (19 U.S.C. §1654), and other customs laws. Some of the responsibilities that Customs is specifically charged with are:

—Assessing and collecting customs duties, excise taxes, fees, and penalties due on imported merchandise;

—Interdicting and seizing contraband, including narcotics and illegal drugs;

—Processing persons, carriers, cargo, and mail into and out of the United States;

—Administering certain navigation laws; and

—Detecting and apprehending persons engaged in fraudulent practices designed to circumvent customs and related laws, copyright, patent and trademark provisions, quotas, and marking requirements for imported merchandise.

As the principal border enforcement agency, Customs' mission has been extended over the years to assisting in the administration and enforcement of some 400 provisions of law on behalf of more than 40 Governmental agencies. Today, in addition to enforcing customs statutes, the Customs Service:

—Enforces export control laws and intercepts illegal high-technology exports to Soviet bloc countries;

—Cooperates with other federal agencies and foreign governments in suppressing the traffic of illegal narcotics and pornography;

—Enforces reporting requirements of the Bank Secrecy Act; and

—Collects international trade statistics.

Also, Customs enforces a wide range of requirements to protect the public, such as auto safety and emission control standards; radiation and radioactive material standards; counterfeit monetary instruments; flammable fabric restrictions; animal and plant quarantine requirements; and food, drug, and hazardous substance prohibitions. Customs is extensively involved with outside commercial and policy organizations and trade associations, and with international organizations and foreign customs services.

Headquarters of the U.S. Customs Service is located in Washington, D.C., under the supervision of the Commissioner of Customs, who is appointed by the Secretary of the Treasury. The 50 states, plus the Virgin Islands and Puerto Rico, are divided into seven Customs Regions. Contained within these regions are 44 subordinate district or area offices under which there are approximately 240 ports of entry. The Customs Service also has field offices in many foreign cities.

CUT. To make an incision or a wound with a sharp instrument.

D.A.   Abbreviation for DISTRICT ATTORNEY.

DACTYLOGRAPHY.   The scientific study of fingerprints as a means of identification.

DAGGER.   A short pointed weapon with sharp edges used for stabbing.

DAMAGE.   Loss, injury, or other impairment of person or property.

DAMAGES.   Monetary compensation that may be recovered in court in a **civil action** by a person who has suffered loss or injury to his or her person, property, or rights, through the unlawful act, omission, or negligence of another.

DAMN.   To condemn; to pronounce an adverse **judgment** or **sentence** upon. The term damn is sometimes used in a stronger sense to mean to condemn to eternal punishment.

DANGER.   Exposure or vulnerability to loss or injury; hazard; peril.

DANGEROUS PERSON.   A person who, when at large, is believed likely to cause serious harm to himself or herself or to others. While there is no uniform definition of this term in police usage, the stated grounds for believing that a person is dangerous are usually evidence of past violent behavior, use of weapons, and, of course, actual infliction of injury. Simple resisting of arrest is not grounds for considering a person dangerous. "Dangerousness" may be taken into account in determining the severity of **sentence** after **conviction** for an offense. *See*: AGGRAVATING CIRCUMSTANCES.

DANGEROUS WEAPON.   *See*: DEADLY WEAPON.

DATE OF SERVICE.   The date of the delivery of an **order**, **summons**, or **writ** to the person against whom it is directed.

DAY CERTAIN.   A specified date.

DAY IN COURT.   The opportunity to present or defend one's rights in **court**. A person has his or her day in court when the person has received lawful notice of court proceedings and has been given an opportunity to be heard.

DAYTIME. The time of day during which there is sufficient natural sunlight to be able to recognize a person's facial features. The term daytime has been given various other definitions by different courts and legislatures. *See*: NIGHTTIME.

DEA. Abbreviation for DRUG ENFORCEMENT ADMINISTRATION.

DEADLY FORCE. Under Section 3.11 (2) of the **Model Penal Code**, deadly force "means force that the actor uses with the purpose of causing or that he knows to create a substantial risk of causing death or serious bodily injury. Purposely firing a firearm in the direction of another person or at a vehicle in which another person is believed to be constitutes deadly force." See DEATH and FORCE for lists of related terms.

Dd

DEADLY WEAPON. An instrument designed to inflict **serious bodily injury** or death, or capable of being used for such a purpose. A statutory distinction is sometimes made between a deadly weapon, i.e., one specifically designed to cause serious bodily injury or death, for example, a gun, and a **dangerous weapon**, i.e., one capable under certain circumstances of causing serious bodily injury or death, for example, a knife. However, in many criminal codes and in general usage the two are merged. Section 210.0 (4) of the **Model Penal Code** defines deadly weapon as "any firearm or other weapon, device, instrument, material or substance, whether animate or inanimate, which in the manner it is used or is intended to be used is known to be capable of producing death or serious bodily injury." For example, an automobile is not designed to cause injury or death but it may be considered to satisfy the "deadly weapon" criterion for an **aggravated assault charge**. The essential distinction being made in statutory and other crime definitions making use of the designation "deadly or dangerous" weapon (e.g., armed robbery v. unarmed robbery) is between the presence or absence of an instrument that, if used by the perpetrator, would greatly increase the likelihood that serious bodily injury or death would result. See DEATH for a list of related terms.

DEAD TIME. Time that does not count as prison **time served** towards a required term in confinement, or as time served on **parole** towards total time under correctional jurisdiction. Time elapsed after **escape** and before apprehension is dead time for counting time in confinement. Time spent out of confinement pending an **appeal** decision may also be declared dead time in counting prison time served, depending upon the rules of a jurisdiction, or decisions made in individual cases. *Also called*: **nonrun time**. See SENTENCE for a list of related terms.

DEAL. **v. 1.** To do business; to trade; to traffic. **v. 2.** To give or deliver. *Example*: The officer dealt him a serious blow. **v. 3.** To give out piece by piece to members of a group, with the suggestion that the members have a right to expect it. *Example*: The chief dealt out badges to each new officer. See ALLOCATE for a list of related terms. **n.** A secretly arranged agreement.

DEATH. The cessation of life; the total and permanent cessation of all vital functions. There is no legal definition for the precise moment of death, although several states have enacted statutory definitions. *See*: AUTOPSY; CAPITAL; CERTIFICATE OF DEATH; CIVIL DEATH; CORONER; CORONER'S INQUEST; DEADLY FORCE; DEADLY WEAPON; DEATH SENTENCE; DEATH WARRANT; DECAPITATE; DECEASE; DECEASED; DEMISE; DIE; DYING DECLARATION; EXECUTE; EXECUTION; EXECUTIONER; FATAL INJURY; FORCE; HOMICIDE; IN EXTREMIS; KILL; LETHAL; MEDICAL EXAMINER; MORTAL; NATURAL DEATH; REPRIEVE; RIGOR MORTIS; SELF-DEFENSE; SERIOUS BODILY INJURY; VICTIM; VIOLENT DEATH.

DEATH SENTENCE. The ultimate punishment imposed upon a **convicted criminal** that mandates the forfeiture of the criminal's life. The death sentence is ordinarily reserved only for particularly heinous crimes such as **murder**. In effect, a death sentence is a sentence to the custody of a prison facility while awaiting execution. See DEATH and SENTENCE for lists of related terms.

DEATH WARRANT. A written order, usually issued by the President or the governor of a state, commanding a warden of a prison, a sheriff, or some other appropriate officer to carry out the **execution** of a **death sentence** upon a convicted criminal. See DEATH for a list of related terms.

DEBATABLE. Disputable; subject to controversy; open to question.

DEBAUCH. To carnally know; to deflower; to have illicit **sexual intercourse** with. The term debauch is sometimes used in a broader sense to mean to corrupt or lead astray from sexual moral principles. See SEX OFFENSES for a list of related terms.

DEBAUCHERY. Excessive indulgence in sensual pleasures, especially sexual pleasures.

DE BENE ESSE. *Latin*. Conditionally; in anticipation of future need. *Example*: A **deposition** de bene esse is a conditional deposition in that it may not be used if the witness is available at trial.

DE BONIS ASPORTATIS. *Latin*. "For goods carried away." *See*: TRESPASS DE BONIS ASPORTATIS.

DECAPITATE. To kill by cutting off the head. See DEATH for a list of related terms.

DECEASE. To die. See DEATH for a list of related terms.

DECEASED. A dead person. See DEATH for a list of related terms.

DECEIT. The act or practice of deceiving. *See*: DECEIVE.

DECEIVE. To intentionally mislead another person by trick, falsehood, concealment, or other underhanded practice, causing harm to that person.

DECEPTION. The act or practice of deceiving. *See*: DECEIVE.

DECIDE. To determine or resolve a question or dispute; to come to a conclusion; to form a definite opinion.

DECISION. The determination or resolution of a court after evaluating the facts and the law. The term decision has several shades of meaning, depending upon the context in which it is used and may refer to a **judgment, decree, finding,** or **order.** The term decision is sometimes distinguished from the term **opinion,** in that a decision is the pronouncement of a court's resolution or judgment in a case, whereas an opinion is a statement of the reasons for the court's decision. See JUDGMENT and OPINION for lists of related terms.

DECISION ON THE MERITS. A decision rendered by applying the **substantive law** to the essential facts of a case as opposed to a decision based solely on technical or procedural grounds. A decision on the merits finally determines the status of legal rights contested in a case and bars a subsequent suit on the same **cause of action**.

DECLARATION. In the law of **evidence**, an unsworn statement made out of court. *See*: DECLARATION AGAINST INTEREST; DYING DECLARATION.

DECLARATION AGAINST INTEREST. A statement that, when made, (1) conflicts with the pecuniary or proprietary interest of the person making it, (2) could subject the person to civil or criminal liability, or (3) tends to render invalid a claim of the person against another. Declarations against interest are admissible in evidence as exceptions to the **hearsay rule**. See HEARSAY RULE for a list of other exceptions.

DECLARATION IN EXTREMIS. Same as DYING DECLARATION.

DECLARATORY JUDGMENT. A **judgment** that states the rights, duties, or status of the parties to a **justiciable controversy** or expresses the opinion of the court on a disputed question of law without ordering anything to be done. A declaratory judgment is conclusive and bars a subsequent action between the same parties on the identical matter. See JUDGMENT and OPINION for lists of related terms.

DECLARATORY STATUTE. A **statute** enacted to clarify the **common law** or the meaning of another statute, without enacting any additions or changes. See STATUTE for a list of related terms.

DECLARE. To state positively and openly or publicly; to proclaim; to announce. See ADDRESS for a list of related terms.

DECOY. To entice or lure by trickery, misrepresentation, or temptation.

DECREE. **n.** A final judicial **order**; a **judgment**. See JUDGMENT for a list of related terms. **adj.** DECRETAL.

DECREPIT. Disabled, broken down, or weakened because of old age, illness, or physical disability.

DECRETAL. *See*: DECREE.

DEDUCTION. The process or result of drawing a conclusion from known or assumed facts. See FACT and PRESUMPTION for lists of related terms. *See also*: A PRIORI.

DEDUCTIVE REASONING. *See*: A PRIORI.

DEEM. To consider something as having certain characteristics or a certain status; to treat as if. *Example*: Alcoholic beverages in improper containers shall be deemed to have been illegally acquired.

DEFACE. To injure or mar the face of; to disfigure. The term deface implies outward injuries by scratching, scrubbing, or removing detail.

DE FACTO. *Latin.* "From the fact." In reality; in fact; actually. The term de facto refers to something that is not **legal** or **legitimate** but that must be accepted because it is actually existing or exercising power. *See*: DE JURE.

DEFALCATION. The **misappropriation** or **embezzlement** of money, particularly by a person in a **fiduciary** position. The term is commonly applied to public or corporate officers who misappropriate funds to their own private use. See ABSTRACTION for a list of related terms.

DEFAMATION. Intentional causing or attempting to cause damage to the reputation of another or to decrease the respect, regard, or confidence in which another is held, by communicating false or distorted information about the person's actions, motives, or character. A statutory distinction is often made between **slander**, which is defamation by spoken communication, and **libel**, which is defamation by any nonspoken communication, most commonly by some written or printed matter. Defamation is not a criminal offense in all jurisdictions, but can always be a **cause of action** in a **civil suit**.

DEFAULT. **1.** Failure to perform a required act. **2.** Failure to file **pleadings** or to make a required **appearance** in court. *See*: DEFAULT JUDGMENT.

DEFAULT JUDGMENT. A **judgment** against a party because he or she failed to file **pleadings**, make an **appearance**, or take some other required step in the proceedings. See JUDGMENT for a list of related terms.

DEFEAT. To annul; to terminate.

DEFECT. The lack of something legally required; an imperfection; an insufficiency.

DEFEND. **1.** To represent the **defendant** in a **civil action** or **criminal action**. **2.** To make a DEFENSE. **3.** To protect from attack, danger, or harm. *Example*: A woman has a right to defend herself.

DEFENDANT. The person or party against whom a claim or charge is brought in a legal proceeding. The legal proceeding may be either a **civil action** or a **criminal action**. In a criminal action, the terms defendant and **accused** mean the same thing: a person formally accused of an offense by the filing in court of a **charging document**. A person becomes a defendant when the charging document is entered into the **record** of the court and remains a defendant until the prosecutor withdraws the prosecution, or the court **dismisses** the case or otherwise determines that **judgment** will not be pronounced, or the court pronounces judgment of **acquittal** or **conviction**. See ACCUSED for a list of related terms.

DEFENDANT DISPOSITION. A prosecutorial or judicial action that terminates or provisionally halts proceedings regarding a given **defendant** in a criminal case after **charges** have been filed in court. The following is a list of final or potentially final dispositions regarding the defendant.

Before judgment:

   No true bill; **nolle prosequi**; **dismissal**; transfer to **juvenile court**; **adjudication withheld** (with or without referral); **incompetent to stand trial**; **civil commitment**.

At or after judgment:

   Acquittal; **not guilty by reason of insanity**; **civil commitment**; **conviction**.

See DISPOSITION for a list of related terms.

DEFENDANT IN ERROR. The prevailing party in the lower court against whom an **appeal** is brought by means of a **writ of error**. See ACCUSED for a list of related terms.

DEFENSE. **1.** The **defendant** and his or her **counsel** collectively. *Example*: The jury was not convinced by the arguments of the defense. **2.** A reply to the claims of opposing party that asserts reasons why the claims should be defeated. The defense may involve an absolute denial of the opposing party's factual allegations or may be an **affirmative defense**, which sets forth completely new factual allegations. **3.** The totality of **arguments**, **motions**, **pleas**, and other legal methods used by a defendant in defeating a charge or action brought against the defendant. **4.** The act of resisting or protecting one's self, property, or country from attack, danger, or harm. *See*: SELF-DEFENSE.

DEFENSE ATTORNEY. An **attorney at law** who advises, represents, and acts for the **defendant** in a legal proceeding (or for the **offender** in postconviction proceedings). The three types of defense attorneys are **retained counsel**, **public defender**, and **assigned counsel**. A defendant who acts as his or her own attorney, is said to be acting **pro se** or **in propria persona**. See ATTORNEY AT LAW for a list of related terms.

DEFER. **1.** To deliberately decide to do something later on. **2.** To comply with or yield to the decision or opinion of another.

DEFERRED SENTENCE. Same as SENTENCING POSTPONED.

DEFIANCE. Open and intentional disregard.

DEFILE. To corrupt; to debase; to debauch; to dishonor.

DEFINE. **1.** To state the precise meaning of. **2.** To fix or determine definitely; to specify distinctly.

DEFINITE. Having fixed limits; certain; positive; explicit.

DEFINITE SENTENCE. Same as DETERMINATE SENTENCE.

DEFINITION. An explanation of the meaning or significance of a word, phrase, or term.

DEFINITIVE. Conclusive; determining; definitely settling.

DEFLOWER. To deprive a woman of her virginity.

DEFRAUD. To deprive a person of property or a right by **fraud** or **deceit**.

DEGREE. **1.** A division or classification of a specific **crime** according to the seriousness of the prohibited behavior. *Example*: Murder in the first degree. *See*: GRADED OFFENSE. **2.** Extent; amount; intensity; condition; grade. *Example*: What degree of proof is required?

DEHORS. *French.* Out of; unconnected with.

DE JURE. *Latin.* "From the law." Lawful; legitimate; established or operating in compliance with all requirements of the law. *See*: DE FACTO.

DELAY. **1.** To postpone until later; to defer. **2.** To impede the progress of; to hinder; to retard.

DELEGATE. **n.** A person sent and empowered to act for another. **v.** To authorize another to act as agent or representative.

DELETE. To **cancel**; to erase; to obliterate. *See*: EXPUNGE; PURGE.

DELETERIOUS. Injurious; detrimental; hurtful.

DELIBERATE. **adj.** Arrived at or decided after careful thought and weighing of considerations. **v.** To carefully consider and examine the reasons for and against a proposed action or choice.

DELIBERATION. **1.** In general, "a weighing in the mind of the consequences of a course of conduct, as distinguished from acting upon a sudden impulse without the exercise of reasoning powers." *Davis v. State*, 475 S.W.2d 155, 156 (Ark. 1972). **2.** "Deliberation in the context of the **jury** function means that a properly formed jury, comprised of the number of qualified persons required by law, are within the secrecy of the jury room analyzing, discussing and weighing the **evidence** which they have heard with a view to reaching a **verdict** based upon the **law** applicable to the **facts** of the **case** as they find them to be. Such deliberation can only be carried on by the lawful number of jurors in the presence of all." *Rushing v. State*, 565 S.W.2d 893, 895 (Tenn.Crim.App. 1978). **3.** In the context of a first-degree **murder** statute, "[d]eliberation means an **intent** to kill carried out by the defendant in a cool state of blood, in furtherance of a fixed design for revenge or to accomplish an unlawful purpose and not under the influence of a violent **passion**, suddenly aroused by lawful or just cause or legal **provocation**." *State v. Hamlet*, 321 S.E.2d 837, 842-43 (N.C. 1984).

DELICT. A tort; a wrong; an injury.

DELICTUM. **1.** Same as DELICT. **2.** Culpability; blameworthiness. *See*: IN PARI DELICTO.

DELINQUENT. **n.** A **juvenile** who has been adjudicated by a **judicial officer** of a **juvenile court** to have committed a **delinquent act**. In some jurisdictions a status **offender** who commits repeated **status offenses** can be adjudged a delinquent. See

JUVENILE for a list of related terms. **adj.** Failing to do what is required by law or moral obligation.

DELINQUENT ACT.   An act committed by a **juvenile** for which an **adult** could be prosecuted in a criminal court, but for which a juvenile can either be adjudicated in a **juvenile court**, or be prosecuted in a court having **criminal jurisdiction** if the juvenile is **transferred to adult court**. See CRIME and JUVENILE for lists of related terms.

DELIRIUM TREMENS.   A disorder of the nervous system caused by long and excessive indulgence in intoxicating liquor or the abrupt cessation of such use after protracted drinking. Delirium tremens is characterized by hallucinations, paranoia, trembling, and sleeplessness. It is sometimes called the "DTs."

DELIVER.   To transfer from one person to another.

DELUSION.   A false impression or belief without any real or possible basis in fact. A delusion may be caused by self-deception, deception by others, or mental disorder. *Example*: He suffered from delusions of grandeur. *See*: HALLUCINA-TION; ILLUSION.

DEMAND.   **1.** To ask for firmly with an expectation of compliance; to require with authority. See ADDRESS for a list of related terms.   **2.** To call into court; to summon.

DEMANDING STATE.   In the law of **extradition**, the state that demands from an **asylum state** the return of a person who is charged with a crime in the former state and who has fled from justice and is located in the asylum state.

DEMEANOR.   The manner in which a **witness** appears and behaves or conducts him or herself. Demeanor includes such things as tone of voice, attitude, gestures, facial expressions, and appearance. A witness's demeanor is very important in determining the witness's **credibility**. See WITNESS for a list of related terms.

DEMENTIA.   Irreversible deterioration of mental faculties accompanied by emotional disturbance as a result of organic brain disorder.

DEMI-.   A prefix meaning: **1.** Half. **2.** Inferior; of lesser status.

DE MINIMUS NON CURAT LEX.   *Latin.* "The law does not concern itself with small or trifling matters." This term is sometimes referred to merely as "de minimis." A legal doctrine under which the court refuses to consider trifling matters. In some states a court may dismiss a **prosecution** for de minimis infractions of the law that cause minimal harm. See DISMISSAL for a list of related terms.

DEMISE. Death.

DEMOLISH. To bring down completely; to put an end to; to destroy.

DEMONSTRATE. **1.** To show or explain by experiment or with samples. *Example:* He will demonstrate the operation of the polygraph. **2.** To conclusively prove by reasoning or arguments. *Example*: The attorney demonstrated the fallacy in her opponent's argument. **3.** To reveal; to exhibit; to show.

DEMONSTRATIVE EVIDENCE. **1.** Same as REAL EVIDENCE. **2.** Demonstrative evidence is sometimes used in a more limited sense to distinguish it from real evidence. In this limited sense, demonstrative evidence means evidence such as a model, map, or X ray that has no probative value in itself, but serves merely as an aid to a **jury** in comprehending the **testimony** of a **witness**. See EVIDENCE for a list of related terms.

DEMURRER. An allegation that even if the statements of fact in the opposing party's **pleading** are true, they are insufficient to constitute a **cause of action** or a **defense** (definition 2). The demurrer has been replaced in most jurisdictions by the **motion to dismiss**. See DISMISSAL and PLEADING for a list of related terms.

DENIAL. **1.** A contradiction or refutation of a statement or allegation. **2.** Refusal; rejection; deprivation. *Example*: The illegal search was a denial of his constitutional rights. **3.** A refusal to acknowledge something; a disclaimer of connection with or responsibility for an action or statement. *Example*: Her defense was a denial that she was at the crime scene at the time of the crime.

DENOUNCE. **1.** To declare something to be a crime and to provide a punishment for it. **2.** To accuse; to inform against.

DE NOVO. *Latin.* Anew; over again; a second time. *See*: TRIAL DE NOVO.

DENY. *See* DENIAL.

DEPARTMENT OF JUSTICE. The Department of Justice is the largest law firm in the United States and serves as counsel for its citizens, representing them in enforcing the law in the public interest. Through its thousands of lawyers, investigators, and agents, the department plays the key role in protection against criminals and subversion, in ensuring healthy competition of business in our free enterprise system, in safeguarding the consumer, and in enforcing drug, immigration, and naturalization laws. The department also plays a significant role in protecting citizens through its efforts toward effective law enforcement, crime prevention, crime detection, and prosecution and rehabilitation of offenders. Moreover, the department conducts all suits in the U.S. Supreme Court in which the United States is concerned. It represents the government in legal matters generally, rendering legal advice and opinions upon request to the President and to the heads of the executive departments.

The Department of Justice was established by act of June 22, 1870 (28 U.S.C. §§501,503), with the **Attorney General** as its head. Prior to 1870 the Attorney General was a member of the President's cabinet, but not the head of a department, the office having been created under authority of act of September 24, 1789, as amended (28 U.S.C. §503). The Attorney General supervises and directs the affairs and activities of the department, as well as those of the **United States attorneys** and **United States marshals** in the various judicial districts around the country. The offices, divisions, bureaus, and boards of the Department of Justice that deal significantly with criminal justice matters are listed below and described elsewhere in this dictionary: ANTI-TRUST DIVISION; BUREAU OF PRISONS; CIVIL RIGHTS DIVISION; CRIMINAL DIVISION; DRUG ENFORCEMENT ADMINISTRATION; ENVIRONMENTAL AND NATURAL RESOURCES DIVISION; FEDERAL BUREAU OF INVESTIGATION; OFFICE OF JUSTICE PROGRAMS; PARDON ATTORNEY; SOLICITOR GENERAL; TAX DIVISION; UNITED STATES MARSHALS SERVICE; UNITED STATES NATIONAL CENTRAL BUREAU; UNITED STATES PAROLE COMMISSION.

DEPARTMENT OF THE TREASURY. The United States Department of the Treasury was created by act of September 2, 1789 (31 U.S.C. §1001). Many subsequent acts have figured in the development of the department, delegating new duties to its charge and establishing the numerous bureaus and divisions that now comprise the Treasury. Among those bureaus and divisions are the BUREAU OF ALCOHOL, TOBACCO AND FIREARMS, the FEDERAL LAW ENFORCEMENT TRAINING CENTER, the INTERNAL REVENUE SERVICE, the UNITED STATES CUSTOMS SERVICE, and the UNITED STATES SECRET SERVICE. The Secretary of the Treasury, as a major policy adviser to the President, has primary responsibility for formulating and recommending domestic and international financial, economic, and tax policy; participating in the formulation of broad fiscal policies that have general significance for the economy; and managing the public debt. The Secretary also oversees the activities of the department in carrying out its major law enforcement responsibility; in serving as the financial agent for the U.S. Government; and in manufacturing coins, currency, and other products for customer agencies.

DEPENDENCY. **1.** The state of being dependent for proper care upon the community instead of one's family or guardians. **2.** The legal status of a **juvenile** who has been adjudicated a DEPENDENT. See JUVENILE for a list of related terms.

DEPENDENT. **n.** A **juvenile** over whom a **juvenile court** has assumed jurisdiction and legal control because his or her care by parent, guardian, or custodian has not met a legal standard of proper care. To be a dependent is not an offense but is included here as one possible **juvenile adjudication**, of which the other two major types are

delinquent and **status offender**. The reasons why a juvenile court may find that a juvenile is dependent for proper care upon persons other than his or her parents are unintentional neglect, where the responsible adult is mentally disabled or lacks financial resources, willful **child neglect**, or willful **child abuse**. See JUVENILE for a list of related terms. **adj.** Conditioned or contingent upon someone or something else.

DEPLETE. To lessen or reduce by using up or exhausting.

DEPONENT. A person who makes a DEPOSITION.

Dd

DEPOSE. To make a DEPOSITION.

DEPOSITION. Out-of-court testimony of a **witness**, taken under oath prior to trial and reduced to writing. A deposition is taken either orally or upon written **interrogatories** with notice to the adverse party so that the adverse party may attend and **cross-examine**. If it appears that a prospective witness may be unable to attend or be prevented from attending a trial or hearing, that the witness's testimony is material, and that it is necessary to take the witness's deposition to prevent a failure of justice, the court may, upon motion and notice to the parties, order that the witness's testimony be taken by deposition. At the trial or hearing, the deposition, or any part of it, may be used if the court finds that:

—the witness is dead;

—the witness is out of the jurisdiction, unless the court finds that the absence of the witness was procured by the party offering the deposition;

—the witness is unable to attend or testify because of sickness or infirmity; or

—the party offering the deposition has been unable to procure the attendance of the witness by **subpoena**.

A deposition may also be used by any party for the purpose of contradicting or **impeaching** the testimony of the **deponent** as a witness. *See*: AFFIDAVIT; DE BENE ESSE; WITNESS.

DEPRAVE. To corrupt; to debase.

DEPRAVED MIND. Same as MALICE.

DEPRIVE. **1.** To take away from; to dispossess. With respect to property, under Section 223.0 (1) of the **Model Penal Code** deprive means "(a) to withhold property of another permanently or for so extended a period as to appropriate a major portion of its economic value, or with intent to restore only upon payment of reward or other compensation; or (b) to dispose of the property so as to make it unlikely that the owner will recover it." **2.** To prevent from acquiring, using, or enjoying.

DEPUTY.   A person who acts officially for another.

DEPUTY SHERIFF.   A law enforcement officer employed by a **sheriff's department** who is authorized to act on behalf of the **sheriff** in regard to official business. See LAW ENFORCEMENT OFFICER for a list of related terms.

DERELICT.   **1.** Abandoned; deserted. **2.** Neglectful of duty; remiss.

DERIVATIVE.   Coming or acquired from another.

DERIVATIVE EVIDENCE.   *See*: FRUIT OF THE POISONOUS TREE.

DERIVE.   **1.** To receive or obtain from a source. *Example*: He derived income from his property. **2.** To arrive at by reasoning. *Example*: The judge could only derive one conclusion from the facts.

DEROGATION.   **1.** The partial repeal or abolition of a law, usually by a subsequent act that in some way diminishes its original intent or scope. **2.** The act of taking away, detracting, or disparaging. *See*: AMEND; REPEAL.

DESCRIBE.   To explain or give an account by providing details that give a clear picture or representation of a person, thing, or event. See ADDRESS for a list of related terms.

DESECRATE.   To abuse the sacredness of; to violate the sanctity of. Section 250.9 of the **Model Penal Code** defines desecrate as "defacing, damaging, polluting or otherwise physically mistreating in a way that the actor knows will outrage the sensibilities of persons likely to observe or discover his action."

DESERT.   To leave or **abandon** with an intent to cause a permanent separation.

DESIGN.   Intention; purpose; aim.

DESIGNATE.   **1.** To show; to point out; to indicate. **2.** To select for a particular office or purpose; to **appoint**.

DESPATCH.   Same as DISPATCH.

DESTROY.   To ruin completely; to render useless for the purpose intended; to demolish; to consume.

DETAIL.   **n.** An individual portion; a particular. **v. 1.** To report or relate in particulars. See ADDRESS for a list of related terms. **v. 2.** To appoint and dispatch for a particular duty.

DETAIN.   A general term meaning to restrain from proceeding, to hold in custody briefly, or to delay. Detain has different meanings in different contexts. *See*: ARREST; DETENTION; SEIZURE; STOP.

DETAINEE.   **1.** Generally, a person who is detained. **2.** A person held in local, very short term **confinement** while awaiting consideration for **pretrial release** or **initial appearance** for **arraignment**. The term may also be used to refer to persons held in physical custody for more lengthy periods while awaiting **trial**, **judgment**, or **sentencing**. *Also called*: **detentioner**. See ACCUSED and DETENTION for lists of related terms.

Dd

DETAINER.   An official notice from a government agency to a **correctional agency** requesting that an identified person wanted by the first agency, but subject to the correctional agency's **jurisdiction**, not be **released** or **discharged** without the first agency being notified and given an opportunity to respond. The placing of a detainer is often, but not always, subsequent to the issuing of a **warrant**. Typical reasons for detainers include that the person is wanted for trial in the requesting jurisdiction or is wanted to serve a sentence. A detainer is notification of the existence of a warrant or other official procedural document and cannot be legally ignored by the recipient custodial agency. Methods of implementation of detainers, and the various states' and prisoners' rights and obligations relating to the implementation, are the subject of **interstate compacts** on detainers, usually codified in statute.

DETECT.   To discover; to find out.

DETECTIVE.   A **law enforcement officer** whose duties are investigating **crimes**, obtaining **evidence**, and apprehending offenders. See LAW ENFORCEMENT OFFICER for a list of related terms.

DETENTION.   The legally authorized confinement of a person subject to criminal or juvenile court proceedings, until the point of **commitment** to a **correctional facility** or until **release**. Detention describes the custodial status of persons held in **confinement** after **arrest** or while awaiting the completion of judicial proceedings. Release from detention can occur prior to **trial**, or after trial or adjudication as a result of a **dismissal** of the case, an **acquittal**, or a **sentencing disposition** that does not require confinement. *See*: ARREST; COMMITMENT; CUSTODY; DETAIN; DETAINEE; DETENTION CENTER; DETENTION HEARING; HABEAS CORPUS AD SUBJICIENDUM; PREARRAIGNMENT LOCKUP; PRETRIAL DETENTION; PRETRIAL RELEASE; PREVENTIVE DETENTION; RELEASE; STOP.

DETENTION CENTER.   A short-term JUVENILE FACILITY that provides temporary care in a physically restricting environment for **juveniles** in custody pending **court disposition** and, often, for juveniles who are adjudicated **delinquent** or are awaiting **transfer** to another jurisdiction. See DETENTION and JUVENILE for lists of related terms.

DETENTIONER.   Same as DETAINEE.

DETENTION HEARING.   In juvenile justice usage, a hearing by a **judicial officer** of a juvenile court to determine whether a **juvenile** is to be detained, continue to be detained, or be **released** while juvenile proceedings in the case are pending. A detention hearing must be held to determine the lawfulness of the authority under which a juvenile is confined if detention is to continue for longer than a specified time period (usually 48 hours). A juvenile whose detention is not to be continued is usually released to the custody of a parent or guardian, but in some jurisdictions provision is also made for the setting of **bail**, as in adult criminal proceedings. In some jurisdictions, a decision to detain can only be made after a **petition** has been filed in **juvenile court**. In others, the decision to detain can be made while the **intake** investigation is proceeding, before a decision has actually been made whether to file a petition. If the juvenile is detained, a detention hearing decision must precede an **adjudicatory hearing**. See DETENTION, HEARING, and JUVENILE for lists of related terms.

DETER.   To prevent or discourage someone from acting through fear of consequences or doubt.

DETERMINATE SENTENCE.   A type of SENTENCE to **incarceration** where the commitment is for a specified single time quantity rather than for a range of time. This time quantity is likely to be lower than the limits automatically provided by **statute** or set by the **court** under the **indeterminate sentence** method. Some degree of **paroling authority** discretion, **good time** rules, and the like will still usually determine the actual release and termination dates. *Also called*: **definite sentence**; **flat sentence**. See SENTENCE for a list of related terms.

DETERMINE.   **1.** To decide or settle a question or controversy conclusively and authoritatively. **2.** To put an end to; to terminate.

DETOXIFICATION CENTER.   A public or private facility for the short-term medical treatment of acutely intoxicated persons or drug or alcohol abusers, often functioning as an alternative to **jail** for persons who have been taken into custody.

DETRIMENT.   Damage; harm; loss.

DEVELOP.   To bring out the possibilities or capabilities of; to bring to a more advanced or complete state; to enlarge; to unfold.

DEVEST.   Same as DIVEST.

DEVIATE.   To turn away from a designated course or procedure.

DEVIATE SEXUAL CONDUCT.   *See*: SODOMY.

DEVIATE SEXUAL INTERCOURSE.   Section 213.0 (3) of the **Model Penal Code** defines deviate sexual intercourse as "**sexual intercourse** per **os** [mouth] or per **anum** between human beings who are not husband and wife, and any form of sexual intercourse with an animal."

DEVICE.   **1.** An instrument; a contrivance; an invention. **2.** A plan; a scheme; a trick; an artifice.

Dd

DIAGNOSIS CENTER.   A functional unit within a **correctional facility** or medical facility, or a separate facility, which contains persons held in custody for the purpose of determining whether criminal proceedings should continue, what the appropriate **sentencing disposition** or treatment disposition should be, or which **correctional facility** or program is appropriate for a committed offender. Diagnosis centers are often established as special units within larger state or local correctional facilities, with one or two such centers serving the courts and correctional facility systems of an entire state, but some are housed in facilities entirely separate from other institutions. Persons may be sent to these centers by the court before **court disposition** of the case. They may also be placed in a center after a court disposition of **commitment** to the jurisdiction of a **correctional agency**. The agency then decides which of available alternative facilities and programs is most appropriate for the offender. **Parolees** returned to prison for alleged or confirmed **parole violations** may also be placed in diagnostic facilities. *Also called*: **classification center**. *See*: DIAGNOSTIC COMMITMENT.

DIAGNOSTIC COMMITMENT.   The action of a court ordering a person subject to criminal or juvenile proceedings to be temporarily placed in a **confinement facility**, for study and evaluation of his or her personal history and characteristics, usually as a preliminary to a **sentencing disposition**, **juvenile disposition**, or other disposition of the case. This kind of a **commitment** is usually a provisional one, which will be followed by a final **defendant disposition**. It is usually a commitment to confinement either in a restrictive correctional facility or as an inpatient in a public or private medical facility. It may occur before **judgment** and thus be unrelated to any determination of guilt.

   Diagnostic commitments have various purposes. A court may commit a person for study and observation to determine if he or she is **competent** to be tried, or, if he or she has been found **incompetent to stand trial** or found **not guilty by reason of insanity**, to determine whether the person is a danger to self or others. There is also the diagnostic commitment to advise the court as to what kind of correctional program is most suitable for a person who has been **convicted** of a **crime** or adjudged to be a **delinquent** or **status offender**. In such an instance, the key findings may be whether to confine the person at all, or, given that confinement is necessary, what program is most appropriate. This kind of determination is often made for presentation to the court in a **presentence report** or a **predisposition report**. See COMMITMENT for a list of related terms.

DICTUM. Same as OBITER DICTUM.

DIE. To cease living; to expire. See DEATH for a list of related terms.

DILATORY. Tending or intended to delay, gain time, or defer decision. Dilatory tactics are abuses of the rules of procedure by a party to an **action** in order to delay the progress of the proceedings for that party's benefit. A party found to engage in dilatory tactics may be held in **contempt of court**.

DILIGENCE. Care; prudence; attentiveness.

DIMINISH. **v.** To reduce; to lessen; to detract from. **n.** DIMINUTION.

DIMINISHED CAPACITY. Same as DIMINISHED RESPONSIBILITY.

DIMINISHED RESPONSIBILITY. An abnormal mental condition that is not of a kind or character to support a successful **insanity defense**, but that is admissible if relevant in determining whether the defendant had the required mental state for the offense charged. If diminished responsibility is proven in a criminal trial, the **trier of fact** may consider it a **mitigating circumstance** in determining the **degree** of an offense or in reducing an offense to a **lesser included offense**. *Also called*: **partial insanity**; **partial responsibility**.

DIMINUTION. *See* DIMINISH.

DIPSOMANIA. An insatiable, uncontrollable craving for intoxicating liquors.

DIRECT. **1.** Going straight to or bearing straight on the point or issue; straightforward; not circuitous; not roundabout. **2.** Without intervening persons, conditions, or agencies; immediate; uninterrupted.

DIRECT ATTACK. An attempt to avoid or correct a **judgment** within the original action in which the judgment was obtained, through an **appeal**, request for a **new trial**, etc. *See*: COLLATERAL ATTACK.

DIRECT CAUSE. Same as PROXIMATE CAUSE.

DIRECT CONTEMPT. *See*: CONTEMPT OF COURT.

DIRECTED VERDICT. A NOT GUILTY VERDICT (1) returned by the **jury** at the direction of the **court**, or (2) entered on the record by the court after dismissal of the jury, when the **judicial officer** decides that the case presented against the defendant obviously falls short of that required to establish **guilt**. In a criminal case, a directed verdict only of **acquittal** is possible and is ordered if the prosecution's evidence is insufficient to overcome the **presumption of innocence** in favor the defendant. A directed verdict of **conviction** would be unauthorized because it would violate the defendant's constitutional right to a jury determination of guilt or innocence. A directed verdict may be ordered by the court on its own **motion** or on the motion of the defendant. See VERDICT for a list of related terms.

Dd

DIRECT EVIDENCE. **Evidence** of the precise **fact** in issue, without other intervening facts, **presumptions**, or **inferences** for support. A type of direct evidence is evidence introduced in court through the oral statements of witnesses on the stand testifying to what they saw, heard, smelled, or touched regarding the facts in issue. *Also called*: **positive evidence**. See EVIDENCE and WITNESS for a list of related terms.

DIRECT EXAMINATION. The first interrogation or examination of a **witness** in a **trial** by the party on whose behalf the witness is called. The direct examination consists of specific questions asked by the attorney for the party calling the witness, and the witness is expected to give testimony favorable to the party calling the witness. *Also called*: **examination in chief**. See EXAMINATION and TRIAL for lists of related terms.

DIRECT INTERROGATORIES. INTERROGATORIES served on a **witness** by the party calling the witness. See INTERROGATORIES for a list of related terms.

DIRECTORY. Instructional; advisory. A directory statutory provision is one that does not relate to the essence of the statute and as to which compliance is a matter of convenience rather than substance. A directory provision usually relates merely to the proper and orderly conduct of business. *See*: MANDATORY.

DIRK. A straight pointed knife primarily suited for stabbing.

DISABILITY. Legal incapacity or disqualification from exercising all the legal rights ordinarily possessed by the average person. **Convicts**, **minors**, and **incompetent** persons are regarded as being under a disability.

DISAFFIRM. To repudiate.

DISALLOW. To refuse to allow; to reject. *Example*: The court disallowed the motion for a continuance.

DISAVOW.   To disclaim knowledge of, responsibility for, or association with; to repudiate.

DISBAR.   To permanently take away an **attorney's** license to practice **law** as a result of illegal or unethical conduct by the attorney.

DISCERNIBLE.   Distinguishable; recognizable as distinct or different.

DISCHARGE.   **1.** To liberate from **confinement** or **supervision**. This term is used with various meanings in the criminal justice context. A discharge from **prison** or **parole** is most often, though not always, understood to mean a final separation from the **jurisdiction** of the **correctional agency**. Discharge from **probation** may mean a satisfactory termination or a **revocation** of the probation status. See RELEASE for a list of related terms. **2.** To relieve from an obligation; to fulfill an obligation.

DISCLAIMER.   The repudiation or denial of a claim, power, or responsibility.

DISCLOSE.   To reveal; to make known.

DISCONTINUE.   To terminate; to put an end to.

DISCOVERY.   A procedure by which a party obtains a legal right to compel the opposing party to allow him or her to obtain, inspect, copy, or photograph items within the possession or control of the opposing party. Among the items subject to discovery are tangible objects, tape recordings, books, and papers, including written or recorded statements made by the defendants or witnesses, and the results or reports of physical examinations and scientific tests, experiments, and comparisons. Information usually not subject to discovery includes investigators' notes, lawyers' work product (see **work product doctrine**), and anything that would violate the defendant's constitutional privilege against compelled **self-incrimination**.

The general purpose of discovery is "to promote the orderly ascertainment of the truth" during trial. Ordinarily, to obtain the right to discovery, a party must make a **motion** before the court and must show that the specific items sought may be material to the preparation of its case and that its request is reasonable. A recent development is automatic informal discovery for certain types of evidence, without the necessity for motions and court orders. The state of the law governing discovery is constantly changing, but the trend appears to be in favor of broadening the right of discovery for both the **defense** and the **prosecution**. The federal government and the states have varying statutes and rules relating to the nature and scope of the information required to be disclosed in the discovery process. See EVIDENCE and TRIAL for lists of related terms.

DISCREDIT.   **1.** To impair or destroy the **credibility** or trustworthiness of a person or document. **2.** To disbelieve.

DISCREET.   Showing good judgment; prudent; judicious.

DISCREPANCY.   Disagreement; inconsistency; difference.

DISCRETE.   Separate; detached; distinct.

DISCRETION.   Generally, the right or power to act according to one's own **judgment** (definition 3) or conscience in choosing between two or more alternative courses of action. "The term 'discretion' implies the absence of a hard and fast rule or a mandatory procedure regardless of varying circumstances. 'Discretion' of a court is a privilege allowed a judge within the confines of justice to decide and act in accordance with what is fair and equitable. Thus, judicial action which involves discretion is final and cannot be set aside on appeal except when there is an abuse of discretion." *Preuss v. McWilliams,* 230 N.E.2d 789, 792 (Ind.App. 1967). Abuse of discretion is an unreasonable, arbitrary, or unconscionable action taken without proper consideration of the **law** and the **facts**. *Example*: A new trial will be granted in the court's discretion. *See*: PROSECUTORIAL DISCRETION.

DISCRETIONARY ACT.   An act for which there are no clearly defined rules as to which course of conduct to take, but which requires judgment and choice.

DISCRETIONARY REVIEW.   An **appeal** that the **appellate court** may agree or decline to hear, at its own **discretion**. Procedurally, in these cases, a party wishing to appeal must first make a request to the court for permission to make the appeal, stating the reasons for doing so. The court can grant or deny the request. See APPEAL for a list of related terms.

DISCRIMINATION.   **1.** The ability or power to perceive fine distinctions between things that are very much alike; discernment. **2.** Prejudicial treatment or denial of rights on the basis of such characteristics as sex, race, age, nationality, or religion.

DISCUSS.   To talk over; to debate; to exchange ideas and reasons.

DISFIGURE.   To impair or injure the appearance or shape of; to deform; to mutilate.

DISGUISE.   To change the appearance of in order to conceal identity or to mislead.

DISHONEST.   Disposed to lie, cheat, or steal.

DISINTER.   To dig up; to exhume.

DISINTERESTED.   Impartial; fair-minded; unbiased. A disinterested **witness** is one who has no personal interest in the case being tried or the matter at issue and is legally **competent** to give testimony.

DISMISSAL. **1.** In judicial proceedings generally, the disposal of an **action, petition, motion,** or the like without trial of the issues; the termination of the **adjudication** process of a case before the case reaches judgment. **2.** The decision by a court to terminate adjudication of all outstanding charges in a criminal case, or all outstanding charges against a given defendant in a criminal case, thus terminating court action in the case and permanently or provisionally terminating court **jurisdiction** over the defendant in relation to those charges. In criminal proceedings, a dismissal of a given charge or entire case can be initiated by motion of the **defense** or **prosecution,** or on the court's own motion. The common reasons for dismissals include insufficient evidence to support **arrest** or prosecution, evidence illegally obtained, errors in the conduct of the proceedings or failure to proceed as quickly as required, and failure of the **jury** to agree on a **verdict.** *See*: ACQUITTAL; COMPLAINT DENIED; CONVICTION; COURT DISPOSITION; DE MINIMIS NON CURAT LEX; DEMURRER; DISMISSAL FOR WANT OF PROSECUTION; DISMISSAL IN THE INTEREST OF JUSTICE; DISMISSAL WITH PREJUDICE; DISMISSAL WITHOUT PREJUDICE; FINAL JUDGMENT; HUNG JURY; JUDGMENT; MISTRIAL; MOTION FOR ACQUITTAL; MOTION TO DISMISS; NOLLE PROSEQUI; PETITION NOT SUSTAINED; SPEEDY TRIAL; TRIAL.

DISMISSAL FOR WANT OF PROSECUTION. The judicial termination of a case against a defendant, occurring after the filing of a **charging document** but before the beginning of a **trial,** on grounds that **prosecution** has not been continued. A court may dismiss a case for want of prosecution on the **motion** of the **defense** or on its own motion. In some jurisdictions, such dismissals are automatic in cases that have not been brought to trial within a specified period of time following the filing of a charging document, unless a defendant has **waived** the right to have the trial during the period. See DISMISSAL and PROSECUTE for lists of related terms.

DISMISSAL IN THE INTEREST OF JUSTICE. The judicial termination of a case against a defendant, on the grounds that the ends of justice would not be served by continuing **prosecution.** See DISMISSAL for a list of related terms.

DISMISSAL WITHOUT PREJUDICE. A DISMISSAL that does not affect the existing rights of the parties and that leaves open the possibility of subsequent **prosecution** on the same matter. Only nonconstitutional grounds that do not adversely affect the rights of the defendant, such as the crowding of court calendars, might be sufficient to warrant the dismissal of a criminal action without prejudice. See DISMISSAL for a list of related terms.

DISMISSAL WITH PREJUDICE. A DISMISSAL that is an adjudication on the **merits** and that operates as a **bar** to subsequent **prosecution** on the same matter. A defendant cannot be subsequently be reindicted (see **indictment**) because of the constitutional guarantee against **double jeopardy.** See DISMISSAL for a list of related terms.

DISORDER. A disturbance of public peace and order.

DISORDERLY CONDUCT. All acts and conduct that disturb the public peace, corrupt the public morals, or outrage the sense of public decency. Disorderly conduct is usually considered a broader term than **breach of the peace** and, under some statutes, breach of the peace is an element of disorderly conduct. The meaning of the term disorderly conduct is variable, except when defined by statute. Section 250.2 of the **Model Penal Code** defines disorderly conduct as follows.

"A person is guilty of disorderly conduct if, with purpose to cause public inconvenience, annoyance or alarm, or recklessly creating a risk thereof, he:

(a) engages in fighting or threatening, or in violent or tumultuous behavior; or

(b) makes unreasonable noise or offensively coarse utterance, gesture or display, or addresses abusive language to any person present; or

(c) creates a hazardous or physically offensive condition by any act which serves no legitimate purpose of the actor."

See AFFRAY for a list of related terms.

DISORDERLY HOUSE. Any house or building to which people resort to habitually violate the law, to disturb the tranquility and order of the neighborhood, or to otherwise injure the public health, morals, convenience, or safety. Examples of a disorderly house are a **house of prostitution**, a house of gambling, and a place where drugs are habitually bought and sold. See AFFRAY for a list of related terms.

DISORDERLY PERSON. A person who violates the public peace and order.

DISPATCH. **v.** To send off on specific business or to a specific destination. **n.** A written message sent with speed. *Also spelled*: **despatch.**

DISPEL. To drive away; to scatter; to dissipate.

DISPENSATION. A relaxation or suspension of a law in a particular case.

DISPENSE. **1.** To give out in carefully weighed or measured portions to members of a group according to what is considered due or proper or according to need. *Example*: A judge's duty is to dispense justice equally. See ALLOCATE for a list of related terms. **2.** To administer.

DISPENSE WITH. To abolish; to do away with; to suspend.

DISPOSE. To arrange; to put in proper order.

DISPOSE OF. To get rid of; to settle finally and definitely.

DISPOSITION. **1.** The action by a **criminal justice agency** or **juvenile justice agency** that signifies that a portion of the justice process is complete and **jurisdiction** is terminated or transferred to another agency; or that signifies that a decision has been reached on one aspect of a case and a different aspect comes under consideration, requiring a different kind of decision. *See*: ARRESTEE DISPOSITION; COURT DISPOSITION; DEFENDANT DISPOSITION; DISPOSITION HEARING; JUVENILE DISPOSITION; SENTENCE; SENTENCING DISPOSITION. **2.** The act or power of dealing with properly or orderly. **3.** Arrangement. **4.** Tendency; inclination. **5.** Attitude; temperament.

DISPOSITION HEARING. A **hearing** in juvenile court, conducted after an **adjudicatory hearing** and the subsequent receipt of the report of any **predisposition investigation**, to determine the most appropriate form of custody and/or treatment for a juvenile who has been adjudged a **delinquent**, a **status offender**, or a **dependent**. The possible dispositions of juveniles over whom a court has assumed jurisdiction range from placement of a juvenile on **probation** or in a foster home to commitment of the juvenile to **confinement**. A disposition hearing occurs after an adjudicatory hearing and **juvenile court judgment** and terminates with a **juvenile disposition**. See DISPOSITION, HEARING, and JUVENILE for lists of related terms.

DISPROVE. To prove to be false or wrong; to refute.

DISPUTABLE PRESUMPTION. Same as REBUTTABLE PRESUMPTION.

DISPUTE. A controversy between two or more parties about their respective rights and obligations toward one another.

DISREGARD. To pay no attention to; to ignore.

DISREPUTE. Lack or loss of reputation; discredit; disgrace.

DISSENT. **v.** To differ in opinion; to disagree. **n.** *See*: DISSENTING OPINION.

DISSENTING OPINION. The OPINION of one or more judges who disagree with the decision or result of the majority. A dissenting opinion usually points out the deficiencies of the majority opinion and explains the reasons for arriving at a contrary conclusion. *Also called*: **dissent**. See OPINION for a list of related terms.

DISSIPATE. To cause to spread out or spread thin; to diffuse; to dissolve.

DISSIPATION OF TAINT. *See*: FRUIT OF THE POISONOUS TREE DOCTRINE.

DISSOLUTE. Morally unrestrained; licentious; recklessly abandoned to sensual pleasures.

DISSOLUTION. *See*: DISSOLVE.

DISSOLVE. **v.** To terminate; to cancel; to annul. **n.** DISSOLUTION.

DISSUADE. To prevent a person from doing something by advice or persuasion.

DISTILLERY. A place where alcoholic liquors are distilled or manufactured.

DISTINCT. **1.** Different; unlike; individual. **2.** Easily perceived by the senses or mind; clear; well-defined.

Dd

DISTINGUISH. **1.** To perceive or point out a difference. *Example*: To distinguish between cases means to show that a case cited as applicable to a case in dispute is really inapplicable because the two cases are different. **2.** To perceive clearly; to discern; to recognize.

DISTRIBUTE. **1.** To give out in portions or units to each member of a group. See ALLOCATE for a list of related terms. **2.** To scatter or spread over a particular area.

DISTRICT. A defined portion of a country, state, county, or other political subdivision or geographical territory for administrative, judicial, or political purposes.

DISTRICT ATTORNEY. *See*: PROSECUTOR.

DISTRICT CLERK. A clerk of a DISTRICT COURT.

DISTRICT COURT. A **court** serving a judicial district in the federal system or in many state systems. A district court is usually a **court of general jurisdiction** but may be a **court of limited jurisdiction**. See COURT for a list of related terms.

DISTRICT JUDGE. A **judge** of a **district court**.

DISTURBING THE PEACE. An offense, defined in different ways in different jurisdictions, involving the interruption of the peace, quiet, and order of a neighborhood or community. Acts that commonly constitute the offense are: public fighting, violent behavior in public, use of offensive or abusive language or making offensive gestures in public, making unreasonable noise, disrupting religious or other public meetings, and failing to move on or to disperse in accordance with a police order. *Also called*: **breach of the peace**. See AFFRAY for a list of related terms.

DIVERS. Several; various.

DIVERSION. The official suspension of formal criminal or juvenile justice proceedings against an alleged offender at any legally prescribed processing point after a recorded initial processing step (e.g., **arrest**, police **referral to intake**, **initial appearance** in court), but before the entry of **judgment**, combined with referral of that person to a treatment or care program administered by a public or private non-justice agency or no referral. Diversion ordinarily refers to formal, organized efforts that offer program alternatives to continued criminal justice system processing.

DIVEST.   To take away. *Also spelled*: **devest**.

DIVIDE.   To give out in shares to members of a group, usually with the implication that the shares are equal. See ALLOCATE for a list of related terms.

DIVISIBLE OFFENSE.   An offense that includes one or more **lesser included offenses**. **Murder** is a divisible offense in that it includes offenses such as **assault**, **battery**, and others. *See*: MERGER.

DIVULGE.   To disclose; to reveal.

DOCK.   The place in the courtroom where the **defendant** stands or sits in a criminal trial.

DOCKET.   **1.** A book containing the formal written record of all important court actions in a case, from its beginning to its conclusion. **2.** Sometimes used as a synonym for COURT CALENDAR. See COURT for a list of related terms.

DOCTOR.   **n. 1.** A person licensed to practice medicine; a physician. **n. 2.** A person who has achieved the highest academic degree awarded by a university in a particular discipline. *Example*: A Doctor of Laws. **v.** To falsify; to change; to tamper with. *Example*: He attempted to doctor the evidence.

DOCTRINE.   A legal principle, rule, or theory. *Example*: The weapon was seizable under the plain view doctrine.

DOCUMENT.   Any written or printed paper that furnishes **evidence** or conveys information. Examples of documents are deeds, letters, licenses, certificates, contracts, and affidavits.

DOCUMENTARY EVIDENCE.   EVIDENCE supplied by **documents**, records, and any other writings. *Example*: A forged check is documentary evidence. See EVIDENCE for a list of related terms.

DOCUMENT EXAMINER.   An expert in the field of handwriting, typewriting, inks, and the like.

DOLE. To give out to members of a group, usually with the suggestion of reluctance and of niggardliness or scantiness in the amount dispensed. See ALLOCATE for a list of related terms.

DOLI CAPAX. *Latin.* Capable of criminal intent.

DOLI INCAPAX. *Latin.* Incapable of criminal intent.

DOMAIN. **1.** The complete and absolute ownership and control over the use of land. **2.** Territory under control; realm.

Dd

DOMESTIC. Pertaining or belonging to the family or household.

DOMESTICATE. To tame; to convert to family or household use.

DOMESTIC RELATIONS COURT. *See*: COURT OF LIMITED JURISDICTION.

DOMICILE. A place where a person has his or her permanent **legal** home. Domicile is to be distinguished from a **residence** used for only temporary or special purposes. Domicile is the place that a person intends to establish as a permanent home for an unlimited or indefinite period and to which the person intends to return whenever he or she is absent. A person may have several residences, but can only have one domicile. *Also called*: **legal residence**.

DOMINANT CAUSE. Same as PROXIMATE CAUSE.

DOMINION. Control; power or right to exercise authority or to govern.

DORMANT. Inactive; in abeyance; latent; asleep.

DOUBLE JEOPARDY. A legal doctrine that prohibits a second **prosecution** of a **defendant** for the same offense after he or she has once been placed in danger of **conviction** for that offense. The Fifth Amendment to the U.S. Constitution prohibits placing a person in double jeopardy ("nor shall any person be subject for the same offense to be twice put in jeopardy of life or limb"). "Same offense," under two different tests, means either an offense requiring the same **evidence** to sustain a conviction or an offense arising from the same **criminal act** or **transaction**. The stage of the prosecution at which a person is considered to be in danger of conviction differs in different jurisdictions. Generally, however, an accused is in legal jeopardy in a trial at the moment the **jury** is sworn or, in **nonjury trials**, when the first **witness** is sworn.

The constitutional protection against double jeopardy is extended to state prosecutions through the due process clause of the Fourteenth Amendment as a result of the U.S. Supreme Court decision in *Benton v. Maryland*, 395 U.S. 784, 89 S.Ct. 2056, 23

L.Ed.2d 707 (1989). Nevertheless, the double jeopardy clause does not bar a state prosecution of a defendant who was acquitted on a federal charge arising out of the same criminal act. *Also called*: **former jeopardy; second jeopardy; twice in jeopardy**. See PROSECUTE for a list of related terms.

DOUBT. Uncertainty of mind with regard to the truth or reality of anything; undecidedness of opinion or belief. *See*: BEYOND A REASONABLE DOUBT.

DRACONIAN LAW. Any unusually harsh or severe law.

DRAFT. v. To write or compose a legal document. **n.** A preliminary form of any writing, subject to revision. *Also spelled*: **draught**.

DRAMSHOP. Same as TAVERN.

DRAUGHT. Same as DRAFT.

DRAW. 1. To write or compose a legal **document**. **2.** To select the persons who are to compose a **jury**. **3.** To pull or take out a **weapon** for use.

DRIVING UNDER THE INFLUENCE OF ALCOHOL. The operation of any **motor vehicle** after having consumed a quantity of **alcohol** sufficient to potentially interfere with the ability to maintain safe operation. This offense is usually charged on the basis of evidence from a test for blood alcohol level, administered within a reasonable time after **arrest**. The maximum permissible amount of alcohol in the blood is specified by statute, usually as a percentage. In most jurisdictions this offense may be charged regardless of whether the operation of the vehicle was observed to be reckless. Whether a given instance of this type of offense is a **felony** or **misdemeanor** usually depends on whether **bodily injury** to another person results (often called **felony drunk driving**), and whether the person has previously been convicted of the same offense. *Abbreviation:* **DUI** *Also called*: **driving while intoxicated (DWI); drunk driving; operating under the influence (OUI)**. See INTOXICATION for a list of related terms.

DRIVING UNDER THE INFLUENCE OF DRUGS. The operation of any **motor vehicle** while attention or ability is impaired through the intake of a **narcotic drug** or an incapacitating quantity of another drug. In the absence of objective ways to measure some forms of drug addiction, the offense may be charged in certain jurisdictions if the suspect can be determined to be addicted to a drug. See DRUG and INTOXICATION for lists of related terms.

DRIVING WHILE INTOXICATED. Same as DRIVING UNDER THE INFLUENCE OF ALCOHOL.

DRUG.   Generally, a chemical substance (not a food) which produces either a beneficial or harmful change in the body. The term drug is given various different interpretations by different people and groups. There is no universally accepted classification system for determining whether a given substance is a drug or not. The states and the federal government have codified lists of **controlled substances** that exactly specify the drug materials falling within the scope of the criminal law. Most lists are based on the Uniform Controlled Dangerous Substances Act. The **FBI's Uniform Crime Reporting** program collects data on **arrests** for drug abuse violations utilizing four drug type categories:

Dd

(1) opium or cocaine and their derivatives (morphine, heroin, codeine);

(2) marijuana;

(3) synthetic **narcotics**—manufactured narcotics which can cause true drug addiction (Demerol, methadones); and

(4) dangerous nonnarcotic drugs (barbiturates, Benzedrine).

See: DRIVING UNDER THE INFLUENCE OF DRUGS; DRUG ENFORCEMENT ADMINISTRATION; DRUG LAW VIOLATION; DRUGS AND CRIME DATA CENTER AND CLEARINGHOUSE; HALLUCINOGEN; INTOXICATION; NARCOTIC.

DRUG ENFORCEMENT ADMINISTRATION.   The Drug Enforcement Administration in the **Department of Justice** is the lead federal agency in enforcing **narcotics** and **controlled substances** laws and regulations. It's creation in July 1973 merged four previously separate drug law enforcement agencies. The administration's priority mission is the long-term immobilization of major trafficking organizations through the removal of the leaders and assets upon which those organizations depend. Its primary responsibilities include:

—investigation of major narcotic violators who operate at interstate and international levels;

—enforcement of regulations governing the legal manufacture, distribution, and dispensing of controlled substances;

—management of a national narcotics intelligence system;

—coordination with federal, state, and local law enforcement authorities and cooperation with counterpart agencies abroad; and

—training, scientific research, and information exchange in support of drug traffic prevention and control.

The administration manages the El Paso Intelligence Center, a 24-hour-a-day tactical and strategic drug intelligence center that includes all 50 states and 9 other federal agencies. The administration concentrates its efforts on high-level narcotics smuggling and distribution organizations in the United States and abroad, working closely with such agencies as the **United States Customs Service**, the **Internal Revenue Service**, and the Coast Guard. It also chairs the 11-agency National Narcotics

Intelligence Consumers Committee, which develops an annual report on drug production, trafficking, and abuse trends.

On January 21, 1982, the **Attorney General** gave the **Federal Bureau of Investigation** concurrent jurisdiction with the Drug Enforcement Administration over drug offenses. Drug enforcement agents work side by side with FBI agents throughout the country in major drug cases—a significant change in narcotics law enforcement. Nearly 300 administration compliance investigators enforce regulation of the legal manufacture and distribution of prescription drugs. The administration also maintains an active training program for narcotics officers in other federal, state, and local agencies and for foreign police. See DRUG for a list of related terms.

DRUG LAW VIOLATION. The unlawful sale, purchase, distribution, manufacture, cultivation, transport, possession, or use of a **controlled substance** or prohibited **drug**, or attempt to commit those acts. Definitions of specific drug law offenses and penalties for those offenses vary greatly among different jurisdictions. See DRUG for a list of related terms.

DRUGS AND CRIME DATA CENTER AND CLEARINGHOUSE. *See*: BUREAU OF JUSTICE STATISTICS. See DRUG for a list of related terms.

DRUNK. Intoxicated with alcoholic liquors to the extent that physical and mental faculties are impaired.

DRUNKARD. A person who is habitually DRUNK.

DRUNK DRIVING. Same as DRIVING UNDER THE INFLUENCE OF ALCOHOL.

DUCES TECUM. *Latin*. "Bring with you." *See*: SUBPOENA DUCES TECUM.

DUE. Sufficient; adequate; reasonable; proper. *Example*: You are required to exercise due care.

DUEL. A prearranged combat between two persons fought with deadly weapons according to formal procedure. See AFFRAY for a list of related terms.

DUE PROCESS OF LAW. Another name for governmental fair play, i.e., laws and procedures that conform to the rules and principles established in our system of justice for the enforcement and protection of individual rights. Some of the essential elements of due process of law, with respect to criminal justice, are: a law creating and clearly defining the offense and punishment; an impartial tribunal having jurisdictional authority over the case; accusation in proper form; notice and opportunity to appear, to be heard, and to defend against charges; trial according to established procedure;

and discharge from all restraints or obligations unless convicted. The Fifth Amendment to the U.S. Constitution provides that "nor [shall any person] be deprived of life, liberty, or property, without due process of law." This provision applies only to actions of the federal government. The due process requirement was made applicable to the states by the Fourteenth Amendment, Section 1, which states "nor shall any State deprive any person of life, liberty, or property, without due process of law." The meaning of due process of law is not fixed but changes with changing jurisprudential attitudes of fair play. In his concurring opinion in the 1951 case of *Joint Anti-Fascist Refugee Committee v. McGrath*, Justice Frankfurter said:

Dd

> "The requirement of 'due process' is not a fair weather or timid assurance. It must be respected in periods of calm and in times of trouble; it protects aliens as well as citizens. But 'due process,' unlike some legal rules, is not a technical conception with a fixed content unrelated to time, place and circumstances. Expressing as it does in its ultimate analysis respect enforced by law for that feeling of just treatment which has been evolved through centuries of Anglo-American constitutional history and civilization, 'due process' cannot be imprisoned within the treacherous limits of any formula. Representing a profound attitude of fairness between man and man, and more particularly between the individual and government, 'due process' is compounded of history, reason, the past course of decisions, and stout confidence in the strength of the democratic faith which we profess. Due process is not a mechanical instrument. It is not a yardstick. It is a process. It is a delicate process of adjustment inescapably involving the exercise of judgment by those whom the Constitution entrusted with the unfolding of the process." 341 U.S. 123, 162-63, 71 S.Ct. 624, 643-44, 95 L.Ed. 817, 849.

In *Green v. State*, 247 A.2d 117, 121 (Me. 1968), the court said:

> "Due process . . . does not restrict the State to any particular mode of procedure. It protects against the exercise of arbitrary governmental power and guarantees equal and impartial dispensation of law according to the settled course of judicial proceedings or in accordance with fundamental principles of distributive justice."

See: EQUAL PROTECTION OF THE LAWS; PROCEDURAL DUE PROCESS; SUBSTANTIVE DUE PROCESS.

DUI.   Abbreviation for DRIVING UNDER THE INFLUENCE OF ALCOHOL.

DULY.   In a proper manner; according to legal requirements; rightly.

DUMMY.   An imitation of or substitute for a real or original object.

DUPLICATE.   An exact reproduction of an original; a double. See ABSTRACT for a list of related terms.

DUPLICITY. In **pleading**, the uniting of two or more separate and distinct offenses in the same **count** of an **indictment** or **information**. "It is a well established rule of criminal pleading that two or more substantive offenses may not be joined in the same count of an indictment. The underlying reason for the rule is that a person accused of crime has a constitutional right to know from the face of the criminal pleading the exact offense charged against him and each count of an indictment, information or complaint should present only a single issue which, if sustained, subjects the accused to specific punishment readily ascertainable by him." *State v. Smith*, 277 A.2d 481, 484 (Me. 1971). See PLEADING for a list of related terms.

DURESS. Same as COERCION.

DURHAM RULE. A rule for determining a person's mental **capacity** to commit a crime that modified the **common law** M'NAGHTEN RULE. Under the Durham Rule, "an accused is not criminally responsible if his unlawful act was the product of mental disease or defect." *Durham v. U.S.*, 214 F.2d 862, 874-75 (D.C.Cir. 1954). In a later case, *Carter v. U.S.*, 252 F.2d 608 (D.C.Cir. 1957) the court held that an act is a "product" of a mental disease or defect if, but for the mental disease or defect, the accused would not have committed the act. In the *Durham* opinion, the terms "mental disease" and "mental defect" were distinguished only in that a disease, but not a defect, was capable of either improving or deteriorating. A later case, however, stated that "a mental disease or defect includes any abnormal condition of the mind which substantially affects mental or emotional processes and substantially impairs behavior controls." *McDonald v. U.S.*, 312 F.2d 847, 851 (D.C.Cir. 1962). The Durham Rule was rejected in *U.S. v. Brawner*, 471 F.2d 969 (D.C.Cir. 1972) in favor of the **substantial capacity test**. *See*: INSANITY.

DUTY. An obligation to do something.

DWELL. To live in a place; to reside.

DWELLING. Section 3.11 (3) of the **Model Penal Code** defines dwelling as "any building or structure, though movable or temporary, or a portion thereof, that is for the time being the actor's home or place of lodging."

DWI. Abbreviation for DRIVING WHILE INTOXICATED.

DYER ACT. Another name for the National Motor Vehicle Theft Act (18 U.S.C.A. §2311 et seq.), which makes it a crime to transport stolen motor vehicles across state borders in interstate or foreign commerce.

DYING DECLARATION. A statement made by the victim of a **homicide** while about to die, in the expectation of death and without any hope of recovery, concerning the circumstances under which the fatal injury was inflicted. Dying declarations are admissible in court as an exception to the HEARSAY RULE. Dying declarations are admissible only at the criminal **prosecution** of the person charged with having caused the death of the person making the declaration. Some modern evidence codes have modified the dying declaration exception to the hearsay rule in various ways. *Also called*: **declaration in extremis**. See HEARSAY RULE for a list of other exceptions. See DEATH for a list of related terms.

DYNAMITE CHARGE.   Same as ALLEN CHARGE.

Dd

EACH. Every one of two or more persons or things considered individually.

EAR WITNESS. A person who testifies, or is able to testify, to something he or she has heard. See WITNESS for a list of related terms.

EAVESDROP. To listen secretly or clandestinely and without consent to the private conversations of others by:

(1) stationing oneself within the **constitutionally protected area** of another person; or

(2) installing or using a mechanical, electronic, or other device for hearing, recording, amplifying, or broadcasting sounds originating within the constitutionally protected area of another person, which sounds would ordinarily not be audible or comprehensible outside that person's constitutionally protected area; or

(3) installing or using a mechanical, electronic, or other device for intercepting a telephone, telegraph, or other wire communication with respect to which a person has a reasonable expectation of privacy from governmental intrusion.

The use of electronic devices to hear, record, amplify, broadcast, or intercept private conversations is often referred to as electronic eavesdropping or electronic surveillance. Eavesdropping by the government is regulated by the Fourth Amendment to the U.S. Constitution, by federal statutes, and by state constitutions and statutes. See PRIVACY for a list of related terms.

EBRIETY. Alcoholic intoxication; drunkenness.

ECCENTRICITY. An individual peculiarity that distinguishes a person from the normal or average person but does not amount to mental unsoundness or **insanity**.

EDIFICE. A large or imposing building.

EFFECT. **n.** Result; consequence; something produced by a cause or agent. *Example*: The punishment had no effect. **v.** To bring about; to cause to occur; to accomplish. *Example*: Can you effect a change in his behavior?

EFFECTS. Personal belongings and other movable possessions. The term effects is often applied to **personal property** as distinguished from **real property**.

EFFICIENT ADEQUATE CAUSE.   Same as PROXIMATE CAUSE.

EFFICIENT CAUSE.   Same as PROXIMATE CAUSE.

EFFIGY.   A crude image or dummy fashioned to look like a person, often as an expression of hatred or ridicule for the person.

E.G.   Abbreviation for EXEMPLI GRATIA.

EGRESS.   **1.** The act of going out from an enclosed or confined space. **2.** The right or liberty of going out. **3.** The means or place of going out; exit; outlet.

EITHER.   **1.** One or the other of two alternatives. *Example*: You can either accept a plea bargain or go to trial. **2.** One and the other. *Example*: There are good arguments on either side.

EIUSDEM GENERIS.   *Latin.* Of the same type or kind. The eiusdem generis rule states that when general words in a document follow an enumeration of specific persons or things, the general words are to be construed not in their widest sense, but only as applying to things of the same general type or kind as those enumerated. *Also spelled*: **ejusdem generis.**

EJACULATE.   To discharge **semen** during sexual **orgasm.**

EJUSDEM GENERIS.   *See*: EIUSDEM GENERIS.

ELECT.   **1.** To pick out or choose from among a number of alternatives. **2.** To select a public officer by vote of qualified members of a community. *See*: APPOINT.

ELECTROCUTE.   To **execute** a **criminal** by passing a high-voltage electric current through his or her body.

ELECTRONIC EAVESDROPPING.   *See*: EAVESDROP.

ELECTRONIC SURVEILLANCE.   *See*: EAVESDROP.

ELEMENT OF A CRIME.   Any conduct, circumstance, or state of mind that, in combination with other conduct, circumstances, conditions, or states of mind, constitutes a **crime.** Section 1.13 (9) of the **Model Penal Code** defines "element of an offense" as "(i) such conduct or (ii) such attendant circumstances or (iii) such a result of conduct as (a) is included in the description of the forbidden conduct in the definition of the offense; or (b) establishes the required kind of culpability; or (c) negatives an excuse or justification for such conduct; or (d) negatives a defense under the statute of limitations; or (e) establishes jurisdiction or venue." No person may be convicted of a crime unless each element of the crime is proven **beyond a reasonable doubt**. See CRIME for a list of related terms. *See also*: CULPABILITY; INCLUDED OFFENSE; MERGER.

ELIGIBLE FOR PAROLE.   The status of a person committed to the jurisdiction of a federal or state prison system and usually in **confinement** in an institution, who, by a combination of such factors as **sentence effective date**, statutory provisions concerning length of **sentence** to be served in confinement, **sentence credit time** deductions, and individual sentence, can legally be considered for **release** from confinement in prison to PAROLE status. The **minimum parole eligibility date** is the date on which the offender is or was first eligible for parole, as determined at the time of admission to prison or as first set by **paroling authority** action, depending on the statutes and other rules of the jurisdiction. The **current parole eligibility date** is that date on which a given offender is currently eligible for parole, which may or may not be the same as the original minimum parole eligibility date. See PAROLE for a list of related terms.

ELUDE.   1. To EVADE.   2. To escape the understanding or comprehension of. *Example*: The informant's name eludes my memory.

EMBEZZLEMENT.   The **misappropriation** or illegal disposal of legally entrusted property by the person to whom it was entrusted with intent to **defraud** the legal owner or intended **beneficiary**. Embezzlement differs from **larceny** in that the original taking of the property was lawful, or with the consent of the owner, while in larceny the felonious intent must have existed at the time of the taking. In some state criminal codes, embezzlement is treated as a form of larceny in which the property is initially acquired lawfully. See ABSTRACTION for a list of related terms.

EMBRACERY.   The intentional attempt to illegally influence a **juror**.

EMERGENCY.   A serious situation developing suddenly and unexpectedly and demanding immediate action; a pressing necessity; an exigency; **exigent circumstances**.

EMISSION.   The sending forth or discharge from the body of any secretion or other substance (urine, **semen**, etc).

EMPOWER.   To authorize.

ENABLE.   To give legal power or capacity to do something; to authorize; to empower.

ENABLING CLAUSE.   The part of a statutory or constitutional provision that gives government officials the power to enforce or carry out the provision.

ENABLING STATUTE.   A **statute** giving new or extended authority or powers to a person or organization. See STATUTE for a list of related terms.

ENACT.   To bring a **statute** into effect; to decree by legislative process. *Example*: The legislature enacted a new criminal code.

EN BANC.   *French*. "In the bench." A designation referring to the session of a court in which all the judges of the court participate, as opposed to a session presided over by a single judge or a mere quorum of judges. *Also called*: **in bank**.

ENCOURAGE.   **1.** To raise confidence. **2.** To spur to action; to instigate.

ENDORSE.   **1.** To write one's signature on a paper or document. **2.** To write on the back of a paper or document. *Also spelled*: **indorse**.

ENEMY.   *See*: PUBLIC ENEMY.

ENFORCE.   To compel observance of or obedience to; to put into effect or operation. *Example*: The duty of the police is to enforce the law.

ENGENDER.   To produce; to cause; to give rise to.

ENHANCE.   To increase; to make greater. *Example*: Enhanced penalties are provided for crimes committed with firearms.

ENJOIN.   **1.** To order; to direct; to command. **2.** To require a person by INJUNCTION to perform or abstain from some act.

ENJOY.   To have the use or benefit of.

ENJOYMENT.   **1.** The exercise of a right or privilege. **2.** With respect to the enjoyment of property, enjoyment includes "beneficial use, interest, and purpose to which the property may be put, and necessarily implies a right to the profits and incomes therefrom." *In re Lafayette Houses, City of New York*, 220 N.Y.S.2d 109, 112 (N.Y.Sup.Ct. 1961).

ENLARGE.   **1.** To make larger; to add to; to increase. **2.** To extend the time for. **3.** To set free a person who has been imprisoned or in custody.

ENTER.   **1.** To go or come into. **2.** To formally place before the court. *Example*: The defendant entered a plea of guilty. **3.** To make a notation of a transaction, proceeding, action, or other item in a book, register, or record. *Example*: The clerk entered the judgment of the court.

ENTICE. To attract a person to do something by an offer of pleasure or advantage; to lure.

ENTRAPMENT. The act of a law enforcement agent in inducing a person to commit a crime that the person was not otherwise disposed to commit in order to prosecute the person. Entrapment is a defense to criminal charges established by proof (1) that the crime was induced by government action, and (2) that the defendant was not predisposed to commit the crime. Inducement by government action may consist of any of the following: "persuasion, fraudulent representations, threats, coercive tactics, harassment, promises of reward, pleas based on need, sympathy, or friendship, and any other government conduct which would create the risk of causing an otherwise unpredisposed person to commit the crime charged." *U.S. v. Burkley*, 591 F.2d 903, 914 (D.C. Cir. 1978). "Predisposition, 'the principal element in the defense of entrapment,' . . . focuses upon whether the defendant was an 'unwary innocent' or instead, an 'unwary criminal' who readily availed himself of the opportunity to perpetrate the crime." *Matthews v. U.S.*, 485 U.S. 58, 63, 108 S.Ct. 883, 886, 99 L.Ed.2d 54, 61 (1988).

ENTRY. **1.** An intrusion by a person into a building, vehicle, or other structure. If any part of a person or instrument is within the building, it is sufficient to constitute an entry. *Example*: The crime of burglary is based on an illegal entry. **2.** *See*: ENTER (definition 3).

ENTRY OF JUDGMENT. The formal recording of the court's JUDGMENT of **conviction** or **acquittal**, making the result effective for purposes of enforcement or commencing an **appeal**. Entry of judgment occurs after **rendition of judgment** and is the ministerial act of recording the final conclusion reached by the court as to matters of fact and law. See JUDGMENT for a list of related terms.

ENTRY TO PAROLE. Same as RELEASE TO PAROLE.

ENUMERATED. Specifically named; expressly designated.

ENURE. Same as INURE.

ENVIRONMENTAL AND NATURAL RESOURCES DIVISION. The Environmental and Natural Resources Division of the **Department of Justice** represents the United States in litigation involving public lands and natural resources, environmental quality, Indian lands and claims, and wildlife resources. The fastest growing area of responsibility involves civil and criminal enforcement of environmental statutes. Although the cases filed by the division in the area of hazardous chemical wastes are the most visible and complex, enforcement of the clean air and water laws is also a prominent part of the docket. Thus, the division brings civil and criminal enforcement cases primarily on behalf of the Environmental Protection Agency for the control and abatement of pollution of air and water resources and the regulation and control of toxic substances, as well as the environmental hazards posed by hazardous wastes. The Division is also responsible for prosecuting and defending criminal and civil cases arising under the federal wildlife laws and laws concerning the conservation and management of marine fish and mammals. Prosecutions focus on major smugglers of and black-market dealers in protected species.

EQUAL. Having the same quantity, degree, status, or value; uniform in operation or effect; evenly proportioned or balanced.

EQUAL PROTECTION OF THE LAWS. The Fourteenth Amendment to the U.S. Constitution provides, in part that no state shall "deny to any person within its jurisdiction the equal protection of the laws." This constitutional guarantee prohibits states from denying any person or class of persons the same protection of the law enjoyed by other persons or other classes of persons in similar circumstances. No state may adopt laws, regulations, or policies that establish categories of people receiving unequal treatment on the basis of race, religion, or national origin. Thus, racial segregation in public schools and other public places, laws that prohibit the sale of use of property to certain minority groups, and laws that prohibit interracial marriage have been struck down. Furthermore, the U.S. Supreme Court held that purely private acts of discrimination can be in violation of the equal protection clause if they are customarily enforced throughout the state, whether or not there is a specific law or other explicit manifestation of action by the state.

No specific equal protection clause applies to the federal government, but the federal government is prohibited from denying a person equal protection of federal laws by judicial interpretations of the due process clause (see **due process of law**) of the Fifth Amendment.

EQUITABLE. **1.** Concerned with or existing in EQUITY as distinguished from **statutory law** or **common law**. **2.** In general, fair, even-handed, impartial.

EQUITABLE CONSTRUCTION. Same as LIBERAL CONSTRUCTION.

EQUITABLE ESTOPPEL. An ESTOPPEL that prevents a person from denying words or actions when the person intentionally or negligently induced a second person to believe and rely on those words or actions to the second person's detriment.

EQUITY. **1.** A system of **jurisprudence** supplementing the **common law** whose purpose is to make the administration of justice more complete by providing relief when the remedy in the courts of **law** (definition 8) is lacking or inadequate. Where the common law clearly prefers damages as reparation for wrongful action, equity is designed to provide relief where damages would be inadequate. A court exercising equity jurisdiction may order that something be done or forbidden by means of an **injunction** or **restraining order**. The basic principle of equity is that no right should be without an adequate remedy. Today actions in law and equity are merged and a plaintiff need only draw up a plain statement of facts that seem to justify a legal remedy and a statement of the relief sought from the defendant. One judge may order complete relief for an injured party, even if the relief requires a mix of legal and equitable remedies. *Also called*: **chancery**. 2. In general, fairness; even-handed dealing; impartiality.

EQUIVALENT. Equal in value, amount, degree, meaning, or effect.

EQUIVOCAL. Capable of two or more interpretations; ambiguous.

ERGO. *Latin*. Therefore; thus; consequently.

ERRATUM. An error in writing or printing. *Plural*: ERRATA.

ERRONEOUS JUDGMENT. A **judgment** based upon an incorrect application of legal principles. See JUDGMENT for a list of related terms.

ERROR. In a judicial proceeding, an incorrect belief or statement as to the existence or nonexistence of matters of **fact** (error of fact) or an incorrect application of principles of **law** to facts of a case on **trial** (error of law). *Example 1*: If a court finds that a person accused of committing an offense is an adult, when in fact the person is a juvenile, the court commits an error of fact. *Example 2*: If a court, although correctly finding that a person accused of committing an offense is a juvenile, nevertheless sentences the person as an adult, the court commits an error of law. *See*: AIDER BY VERDICT; APPEAL; ARREST OF JUDGMENT; ASSIGNMENT OF ERRORS; CLERICAL ERROR; CORAM NOBIS; DEFENDANT IN ERROR; FACT; FUNDAMENTAL ERROR; HARMLESS ERROR; MISPLEADING; MISTRIAL; MOTION TO SET ASIDE JUDGMENT; NEW TRIAL; OBJECT (v.); PLAIN ERROR RULE; PLAINTIFF IN ERROR; RECALL A JUDGMENT; REVERSE; REVERSIBLE ERROR; REVIEW; TRIAL; WRIT OF ERROR.

ESCAPE. The intentional unlawful departure of a lawfully confined person from a **confinement facility**, or from lawful **custody** while being transported. A lawfully confined person is a person confined because lawfully **arrested**, **charged**, or **convicted** of a crime. See ABSCOND for a list of related terms.

ESCOBEDO v. ILLINOIS. A 1964 landmark decision of the U.S. Supreme Court which held that where a police interrogation "is no longer a general inquiry into an unsolved crime but has begun to focus on a particular suspect, the suspect has been taken into police custody, the police carry out a process of interrogations that lends itself to eliciting incriminating statements, the suspect has requested and been denied an opportunity to consult with his lawyer, and the police have not effectively warned him of his absolute constitutional right to remain silent, the accused has been denied 'the Assistance of Counsel' in violation of the Sixth Amendment to the Constitution as 'made obligatory upon the States by the Fourteenth Amendment,' ... and that no statement elicited by the police during the interrogation may be used against him at a criminal trial." 378 U.S. 478, 490-91, 84 S.Ct. 1758, 1765, 12 L.Ed.2d 977, 986. The *Escobedo* decision has been largely overshadowed by the Supreme Court's subsequent decision in MIRANDA v. ARIZONA.

ESSENCE.   The indispensable properties, vital constituent element, or intrinsic nature of a thing.

ESSENTIAL.   Indispensable; absolutely necessary; requisite.

ESTABLISH.   **1.** To make firm; to settle; to secure; to confirm. *Example:* An object of the constitution is to establish justice. **2.** To set up on a permanent basis; to institute; to found. *Example*: Congress may not establish a religion. **3.** To prove; to settle beyond dispute. *Example*: The prosecution was unable to establish the necessary facts.

ESTABLISHMENT.   An institution; a business; an association.

ESTOP.   To stop; to prevent; to bar.

ESTOPPEL.   The prevention or stopping of a person from denying the truth of a fact that has been settled by judicial proceedings or by his or her own actions. *See*: COLLATERAL ESTOPPEL; EQUITABLE ESTOPPEL.

ESTOPPEL BY JUDGMENT.   Same as COLLATERAL ESTOPPEL.

ESTOPPEL IN PAIS.   Same as EQUITABLE ESTOPPEL.

ET.   *Latin.* "And."

ET AL.   **1.** Abbreviation for ET ALIBI. **2.** Abbreviation for ET ALII. **3.** Abbreviation for ET ALIUS.

ET ALIBI.   *Latin.* "And elsewhere."

ET ALII.   *Latin.* "And others."

ET ALIUS.   *Latin.* "And another."

ETC.   Abbreviation for ET CETERA.

ET CETERA.   *Latin.* "And others"; and others of like kind; and so forth.

ETHICAL. In accordance with the accepted principles of right conduct or practice governing a particular group or profession.

ETHICS. Rules of conduct or practice applicable to members of a profession regarding their moral and professional obligations. *See* LEGAL ETHICS.

ET SEQ. Abbreviation for ET SEQUENTES and ET SEQUENTIA.

ET SEQUENTES. *Latin.* "And the following."

ET SEQUENTIA. *Latin.* "And the following."

EUTHANASIA. The killing of a person suffering from an incurable and painful disease, usually through painless methods and motivated by concern and compassion. Euthanasia is illegal but is not a distinct crime. It may be prosecuted as either **murder** or **manslaughter**. *Also called*: **mercy killing**.

EVADE. v. To avoid by artifice or subterfuge; to escape from cleverly or underhandedly. The term evade sometimes implies wrongful intent or dishonesty. **n.** EVASION. **adj.** EVASIVE. *See*: AVOID; ELUDE.

EVANESCENT. **1.** Vanishing; transitory; fleeting. **2.** Barely perceptible; infinitesimal.

EVASION. *See*: EVADE.

EVASIVE. *See*: EVADE.

EVASIVE ANSWER. An answer by a person that refuses either to admit or deny something as to which the person is presumed to have knowledge.

EVEN. **adj.** Impartial; fair; just. **adv. 1.** Still; yet; to a higher degree. *Example*: The judge was even stricter than I imagined. **adv. 2.** Nevertheless; notwithstanding; despite. *Example*: Even though the evidence was circumstantial, he was convicted.

EVERY. Each without exception. *Example*: Every citizen must obey the law.

EVIDENCE. Anything offered to a court or jury through the medium of witnesses, documents, exhibits, or other objects, to demonstrate or ascertain the truth of facts in issue in a case; the means by which facts are proved or disproved in court. *See*: ADMISSIBLE EVIDENCE; ADMISSION; AFFIRMATIVE PROOF; ALLEGATION; BEST EVIDENCE; BEST EVIDENCE RULE; BEYOND A REASONABLE DOUBT; BURDEN OF PERSUASION; BURDEN OF PRODUCTION OF EVIDENCE; BURDEN OF PROOF; CHAIN OF CUSTODY; CHARACTER EVI-

DENCE; CIRCUMSTANTIAL EVIDENCE; CLEAR AND CONVINCING PROOF; CLOSING ARGUMENT; COMMENT ON THE EVIDENCE; COMPETENT EVIDENCE; CONCLUSIVE EVIDENCE; CONFLICTING EVIDENCE; CONTRARY TO THE EVIDENCE; CORROBORATING EVIDENCE; CUMULATIVE EVIDENCE; DECLARATION; DEMONSTRATIVE EVIDENCE; DIRECT EVIDENCE; DISCOVERY; DOCUMENTARY EVIDENCE; EVIDENTIARY FACT; EXCLUSIONARY RULE; EXHIBIT; EXPERT EVIDENCE; EXTRINSIC EVIDENCE; FABRICATED EVIDENCE; FACT; FAILURE OF EVIDENCE; FLAGRANTLY AGAINST THE EVIDENCE; FOUNDATION; FRUIT OF THE POISONOUS TREE DOCTRINE; HEARSAY EVIDENCE; HEARSAY RULE; INDISPENSABLE EVIDENCE; INDUBITABLE EVIDENCE; IN EVIDENCE; INTRINSIC EVIDENCE; LAW OF EVIDENCE; MATERIAL; MEDICAL EVIDENCE; MERE EVIDENCE; MORAL EVIDENCE; MOTION TO SUPPRESS; NEGATIVE PROOF; NEWLY DISCOVERED EVIDENCE; OBJECT (v.); OPENING STATEMENT; OPINION EVIDENCE; OPINION RULE; ORIGINAL EVIDENCE; PERPETUATION OF EVIDENCE; POSITIVE PROOF; PREPONDERANCE OF THE EVIDENCE; PRESUMPTION; PRIMA FACIE EVIDENCE; PROBABLE CAUSE; PROOF; PROVE; REAL EVIDENCE; REBUTTAL EVIDENCE; RELEVANT; SATISFACTORY EVIDENCE; SECONDARY EVIDENCE; SELF-INCRIMINATION; STATE'S EVIDENCE; SUBSTANTIAL EVIDENCE; SUBSTANTIVE EVIDENCE; SUFFICIENT EVIDENCE; SUFFICIENT EVIDENCE TO SUPPORT CONVICTION; SUPPRESS; SUPPRESSION HEARING; TAINTED EVIDENCE; TESTIFY; TESTIMONY; TRIAL; TRIER OF FACT; ULTIMATE FACT; WEIGHT OF THE EVIDENCE; WITNESS.

EVIDENCE LAW.   Same as LAW OF EVIDENCE.

EVIDENT.   Plain; obvious; apparent; clear to the understanding.

EVIDENTIARY.   Furnishing **evidence**; having the nature of evidence.

EVIDENTIARY FACT.   A fact that furnishes **evidence** of an ULTIMATE FACT. *Also called*: **primary fact**. See EVIDENCE and FACT for lists of related terms.

EX.   **1.** *Latin.* Out of; from; away from; by; on. **2.** A prefix meaning former. *Example*: Ex-president.

EXACT.   **1.** To compel or force the payment or yielding of. *Example*: The loan shark exacted an excessive rate of interest from him. **2.** To demand; to require; to call for.

EXACTION.   The corrupt collection of a fee by a government official under the color of office when no payment is due. Exaction is less broad than **extortion** because extortion includes the collection of an unlawful fee when some fee is actually due. See ABSTRACTION for a list of related terms.

EXAMINATION. The formal questioning of a **witness** by a party to an action for the purpose of presenting to the court the witness's knowledge of facts and matters in dispute. *See*: CROSS-EXAMINATION; DIRECT EXAMINATION; INTER-ROGATORIES; LEADING QUESTION; PRELIMINARY HEARING; RECROSS-EXAMINATION; REDIRECT EXAMINATION; WITNESS.

EXAMINATION IN CHIEF. Same as DIRECT EXAMINATION.

EXAMINING COURT. Same as COMMITTING MAGISTRATE.

EXAMINING TRIAL. Same as PRELIMINARY HEARING.

EXCEPT. Excluding; but; other than. *Example*: The prosecution proved all elements of the crime except one.

EXCEPTION. A formal objection (see **object** [v.]) to a ruling of a court on a matter of law. An attorney takes an exception to a court's ruling to preserve the matter on the record so that the attorney may seek reversal of the ruling on appeal. In most states, attorneys are no longer required to take exceptions to preserve matters for appeal. *See*: BILL OF EXCEPTIONS.

EXCESSIVE. Exceeding the usual or proper amount or degree; inordinate.

EXCESSIVE BAIL. BAIL set at an amount higher than that reasonably calculated to ensure that a person accused of crime will stand trial and submit to sentence if guilty. Excessive bail is prohibited by the Eighth Amendment to the U.S. Constitution. Courts consider the following in determining the proper amount of bail:
—the defendant's past history and behavior;
—the nature of the crime charged and surrounding circumstances;
—the **weight of the evidence** against the defendant;
—the existence or nonexistence of an **indictment** against the defendant; and
—the defendant's financial ability to post bail.
See BAIL for a list of related terms.

EXCESS OF JURISDICTION. An act that goes beyond a court's lawful authority or power to deal with a matter. See JURISDICTION for a list of related terms.

EXCITED UTTERANCE. *See*: RES GESTAE.

EXCLUDABLE DELAY. *See*: SPEEDY TRIAL.

EXCLUSIONARY RULE. A rule, developed by the U.S. Supreme Court, stating that evidence obtained in violation of a person's constitutional rights by law enforcement officers or agents will be inadmissible in a criminal prosecution against the person whose rights were violated. "The exclusionary rule prohibits introduction into evidence of tangible materials **seized** during an unlawful **search**, *Weeks v. United States*, 232 U.S. 383, 34 S.Ct. 341, 58 L.Ed. 652 (1914), and of testimony concerning knowledge acquired during an unlawful search, *Silverman v. United States*, 365 U.S. 505, 81 S.Ct. 679, 5 L.Ed.2d 734 (1961). Beyond that, the exclusionary rule also prohibits the introduction of derivative evidence, both tangible and testimonial, that is the product of the primary evidence, or that is otherwise acquired as an indirect result of the unlawful search, up to the point at which the connection with the unlawful search becomes 'so attenuated as to dissipate the taint,' *Nardone v. United States*, 308 U.S. 338, 341, 60 S.Ct. 266, 268, 84 L.Ed. 307 (1939)." *Murray v. United States*, 478 U.S. 533, 536-37, 108 S.Ct. 2529, 2532-33, 101 L.Ed.2d 472, 480 (1988). The purpose of the exclusionary rule is to deter law enforcement officers and other government officials from violating the constitutional rights of suspects by removing the incentive for obtaining illegally seized evidence. The rule does not apply to evidence obtained by persons other than government officials. *See*: EVIDENCE; FRUIT OF THE POISONOUS TREE DOCTRINE; GOOD-FAITH EXCEPTION; INDEPENDENT SOURCE; INEVITABLE DISCOVERY; MAPP v. OHIO; MOTION TO SUPPRESS; SEARCH; SEIZURE; WOLF v. COLORADO.

Ee

EXCLUSIVE.   Sole; not shared; not including others.

EXCLUSIVE JURISDICTION.   Sole JURISDICTION, not shared with any other **court** or tribunal, over a particular territory, subject matter, or person. *Example*: The U.S. District Court for the Eastern District of Tennessee has exclusive jurisdiction over trials of federal crimes committed in Knoxville. See JURISDICTION for a list of related terms.

EXCULPATE.   To clear from an **accusation** of **guilt**; to free from blame; to exonerate.

EXCULPATORY.   Tending to clear from **guilt** or blame.

EXCUSABLE ASSAULT.   An ASSAULT committed by accident while acting lawfully and without criminal intent. See ASSAULT for a list of related terms.

EXCUSABLE HOMICIDE.   **Justifiable homicide** or **unintentional homicide** by accident or misadventure without **gross negligence**. Excusable homicide is not a crime.

NOTE: The term excusable homicide is ambiguous, because its statutory definition may include justifiable homicide but is sometimes limited to unintentional homicides without gross negligence. See HOMICIDE for a list of related terms.

EXCUSE.   **v.** To forgive; to pardon; to set free from an obligation; to justify. **n.** A reason offered as a basis for exemption or relief from **guilt**. An excuse is a defense for a person's conduct that is intended to mitigate the person's blameworthiness for a particular act or to explain why the person acted in a particular manner. "[W]hen a defendant prevails on a **justification defense**, no wrongful act occurred; the act itself becomes lawful. If a defendant succeeds on a defense classified as an excuse, a wrongful act occurred; however no criminal liability is attached to the actor." *U.S. v. Lopez*, 662 F.Supp. 1083, 1086 (N.D.Cal. 1987). *Example:* An insane person who robs a bank has an excuse defense to criminal liability. *See*: EXCUSABLE ASSAULT; EXCUSABLE HOMICIDE; JUSTIFICATION.

EXECUTE. **1.** To carry out; to give effect to. *Example*: The duty of the police is to execute the laws. **2.** To put to death according to law; to inflict capital punishment upon. *Example*: They will execute the convicted assassin. See DEATH for a list of related terms. **3.** To make complete; to finish; to accomplish; to fulfill all legal requirements; to perform all necessary formalities. *Example*: The attorney executed the will by signing, sealing, and delivering it.

EXECUTION. **1.** A judicial **writ** issued to a sheriff, marshal, or other officer requiring him or her to carry out the judgment of the court. See ARREST WARRANT for a list of related terms. **2.** The process of putting to death a person who has been convicted of a serious crime and sentenced to death. See DEATH for a list of related terms. **3.** *See*: EXECUTE (definition 3).

EXECUTIONER. A person who puts convicted criminals to death according to the sentence of the court. See DEATH for a list of related terms.

EXECUTIVE. **n. 1.** The branch of government charged with enforcing or carrying out the laws; the administrative branch of government. **n. 2.** The chief officer of a nation, state, or other political division. **adj.** Pertaining to carrying out or enforcing the laws; administrative. *Example:* The governor issued an executive order relating to pardons.

EXECUTIVE WARRANT. Same as EXTRADITION WARRANT.

EXECUTORY. Incomplete; not yet performed or put into effect.

EXEGESIS. A critical explanation or interpretation of a text.

EXEMPLIFICATION. An official and certified **copy** or **transcript** of a document from public records. See ABSTRACT for a list of related terms.

EXEMPLI GRATIA. *Latin.* For example. *Abbreviation*: **e.g.**

EXEMPT. Free from a liability or duty required of others.

EXERCISE. **1.** To put into action or practice; to make use of. *Example*: One cannot be penalized for exercising constitutional rights. **2.** To discharge; to perform. *Example*: She exercised the duties of her office.

EXHIBIT. **v. 1.** To show; to display; to present for inspection. **v. 2.** To formally submit documents or other objects as **evidence** in court. **n.** A document or other object formally submitted as evidence in court.

EXHIBITIONIST. A person who obtains sexual gratification by exposing his or her genitals.

EXIGENCY. Same as EXIGENT CIRCUMSTANCES.

EXIGENT CIRCUMSTANCES. Generally, an emergency, a pressing necessity, or a set of circumstances requiring immediate attention or swift action. In the criminal procedure context, exigent circumstances means "an emergency situation requiring swift action to prevent imminent danger to life or serious damage to property, or to forestall the imminent escape of a suspect or destruction of evidence. There is no ready litmus test for determining whether such circumstances exist, and in each case the claim of an extraordinary situation must be measured by the facts known to the officers." *People v. Ramey*, 127 Cal.Rptr. 629, 637, 545 P.2d 1333, 1341 (Cal. 1976). *See*: CARROLL DOCTRINE.

Ee

EXIST. To be; to live; to be in force or in effect.

EX-OFFENDER. An **offender** who is no longer under the jurisdiction of any **criminal justice agency**. See ACCUSED for a list of related terms.

EX OFFICIO. *Latin.* "By virtue of office; from office." Exercising power by no other authority except by virtue of official position. *Example*: The District Attorney was an ex officio member of the committee.

EXONERATE. To clear of a **charge** of **crime**; to relieve from obligation or responsibility; to **exculpate**.

EX PARTE. By or for one party; on behalf of one party only. A judicial proceeding or order is said to be ex parte when it is held or granted at the request and in the interest of one party only and without **notice** to or **appearance** by any other party.

EXPEDIENT. **adj.** Suitable and appropriate for a particular purpose. **n.** A means to an end; a resource; a device.

EXPEDITE. **1.** To accomplish promptly; to hasten; to facilitate. **2.** To issue a document officially.

EXPEL.   **v.** To drive out; to eject forcefully. **n.** EXPULSION.

EXPERIMENT.   An act or process to discover something unknown, to test a proposition, or to establish or illustrate a known truth.

EXPERT EVIDENCE.   Testimony given about some scientific, technical, or professional matter by an EXPERT WITNESS. See EVIDENCE for a list of related terms.

EXPERT TESTIMONY.   *See*: EXPERT EVIDENCE.

EXPERT WITNESS.   A person who, on the basis of training, work, or experience in a particular science, trade, or art is qualified to speak authoritatively on the standard and scientific facts in that particular field. Before a **witness** can give an **opinion** as an expert, the witness must be qualified as an expert. The party calling the witness must present evidence of the knowledge, skill, education, training, or experience possessed by the witness and must show that the witness is familiar with the particular problem about which the witness is to testify. Also, the subject matter of the expert testimony must be such that the expertise of the witness will assist the **trier of fact** in understanding the **evidence** or in determining a fact in issue. *Also called*: **skilled witness**. See WITNESS for a list of related terms.

EXPIRATION OF SENTENCE.   The termination of the period of time during which an offender has been required to be under the jurisdiction of a **prison** or **parole agency** as the penalty for an offense. A **sentence** to the jurisdiction of a **correctional agency** is said to have expired when the authority of the agency to **confine** or **release** the offender ends. During the time an offender is on **parole** or has other **conditional release** status the sentence has not expired. But once the maximum time set by court or statute as the confinement and/or supervisory period has ended, no **court** or agency can limit that person's freedom without a new **prosecution** and **conviction** for a new offense. See RELEASE and SENTENCE for lists of related terms.

EXPIRE.   **1.** To come to an end; to cease; to terminate. **2.** To die. **3.** To breathe out; to exhale.

EXPLICIT.   Specific; expressed precisely; unambiguous; unequivocal.

EXPLODE.   To burst or expand violently with a loud noise under the influence of suddenly developed internal energy.

EXPLOSIVE.   A substance or combination of substances that, upon rapid decomposition or combustion, will EXPLODE. The term explosive is usually applied to dangerously volatile substances such as gasoline, dynamite, or TNT, rather than to common substances under pressure such as steam or air.

EXPOSE.   **1.** To present to view; to display; to make known; to disclose. *Example*: A careful investigation exposed the crime. **2.** To abandon or put out something (a child, for example) in a place or position so that it is unprotected against danger to its life or health or is subject to the risk of severe suffering or serious bodily harm. **3.** *See*: INDECENT EXPOSURE.

EXPOSITORY STATUTE. A **statute** enacted to explain the meaning of the **common law** or a previously enacted statute. Such a statute acts as a mandate to the courts to construe and apply the law according to legislative judgment. Expository statutes are generally given retroactive operation so as to determine the meaning of the earlier law from its origin. See STATUTE for a list of related terms.

EX POST FACTO. *Latin.* "After the fact." "[A]ny statute which punishes as a crime an act previously committed, which was innocent when done; which makes more burdensome the punishment for a crime, after its commission, or which deprives one charged with crime of any defense available according to law at the time when the act was committed, is prohibited as ex post facto." *Beazell v. Ohio,* 269 U.S. 167, 169-70, 46 S.Ct. 68, 68-69, 70 L.Ed. 216, 217 (1925) *quoted with approval in Collins v. Youngblood,* _U.S._ 110 S.Ct. 2715, 2719, 111 L.Ed.2d 30, 39 (1990). Ex post facto laws are prohibited by Article I, Sections 9 and 10, of the U.S. Constitution and similar provisions of state constitutions.

EXPRESS. Directly and clearly indicated; explicitly and definitely stated. *Example:* Officers must obey the express terms of a search warrant. *See*: IMPLIED.

EXPRESS AGENCY. An AGENCY in which the AGENT has EXPRESS AUTHORITY to act for or represent the PRINCIPAL.

EXPRESS AGENT. An AGENT who has EXPRESS AUTHORITY.

EXPRESS AUTHORITY. AUTHORITY (definition 1) intentionally conferred by a PRINCIPAL upon an AGENT in EXPRESS terms. Express authority is a type of **actual authority**.

EXPRESS MALICE. *See*: MALICE.

EXPRESS NOTICE. NOTICE of a main fact directly obtained either firsthand or by written or oral communication. Express notice is a type of **actual notice**. *Also called*: **personal notice**. See NOTICE for a list of related terms.

EX PROPRIO VIGORE. *Latin.* By its or their own force.

EXPULSION. *See*: EXPEL.

EXPUNGE. v. To strike out; to obliterate; to erase; to cancel. *Example*: To expunge an arrest record is to physically remove it from police or court files by erasure, striking out, or obliteration. *See*: DELETE; PURGE.

EX REL. Abbreviation for EX RELATIONE.

EX RELATIONE. *Latin.* On the relation. When legal proceedings are brought in the name of and on behalf of the state, but at the instigation and on the information of a private person interested in the matter, the proceedings are said to be taken "on the relation" of the private person. Actions of this kind are usually entitled State ex rel. Macri v. Kozak. The private person responsible for the action is called the **relator**. *Abbreviation:* EX REL.

EXTANT. In existence; currently or still existing; not destroyed or lost.

EX TEMPORE. *Latin.* Without premeditation or preparation; on the spur of the moment.

EXTEND. **v.** To expand; to enlarge; to prolong; to lengthen; to widen; to broaden. *Example*: The court extended the time for filing the brief. **n.** EXTENSION.

EXTENSION. *See*: EXTEND.

EXTENT. Amount; degree; range; magnitude; scope.

EXTENUATE. To lessen; to mitigate; to diminish in size or amount.

EXTENUATING CIRCUMSTANCES. Same as MITIGATING CIRCUM-STANCES.

EXTERIOR. Outer; outside; on the surface; at the outer limits.

EXTERNAL. **1.** Outer; outside; beyond; away from. **2.** Visible or perceptible on the surface; apparent; superficial. **3.** Physical or material (as distinguished from mental or spiritual).

EXTINGUISH. To put out; to put an end to; to wipe out; to destroy.

EXTORT. **1.** To compel or coerce by unlawful means; to exact; to wring; to wrest. *Example*: The police extorted a confession from him. **2.** *See*: EXTORTION.

EXTORTION. Under the **common law**, the corrupt collection of an unlawful or excessive fee by a government official under the color of office. Modern statutes have expanded the definition of extortion to include the unlawful obtaining or attempting to obtain something of value from another, with his or her **consent**, by compelling the other person to deliver it by the **threat** of eventual physical injury or other harm to that person or that person's property, or to a third person. In 18 U.S.C. §1951 (b)(2) extortion is defined as the "obtaining of property from another, with his consent, induced by wrongful use of actual or threatened force, violence, or fear, or under color of official right." Extortion differs from **robbery** in that in robbery there is an immediate confrontation between offender and victim, the victim does not consent, and the threatened injury is physical and imminent. Extortion differs from **false pretenses** in that for false pretenses, the money or property is obtained by means of a lie as opposed to a threat. See ABSTRACTION for a list of related terms.

EXTRA. *Latin.* **prep.** Outside; beyond; out of. **adj.** More than or beyond the usual or necessary; additional.

EXTRACT. **v. 1.** To draw or pull out forcibly. **v. 2.** To obtain or draw forth against a person's will. *Example*: They were unable to extract a promise from him. **n.** A passage taken from a writing; an excerpt; a quotation.

EXTRADITION. The surrender of an **accused** or **convicted** person by one state (**asylum state**), to which the person has fled, to the state with **jurisdiction** to try or punish the person (**demanding state**), upon demand of the latter state, so that the person may be dealt with according to its laws. The demand occurs in the form of an **extradition warrant** issued by the governor of the demanding state. The delivery of the person to the demanding state will occur under the executive or judicial authorization of the asylum state. The U.S. Constitution, Article IV, Section 2, requires the officials of a state to **arrest** and return an accused **fugitive** to another state for trial upon demand of the governor of the latter state. Most states have adopted the **Uniform Criminal Extradition Act**, which provides uniform extradition procedures among the states.

EXTRADITION WARRANT. *See*: EXTRADITION.

EXTRAJUDICIAL. Outside the action or authority of the court; outside the course of regular judicial proceedings. *Example*: Her extrajudicial confession was inadmissible in court.

EXTRAJUDICIAL CONFESSION. A CONFESSION made elsewhere than in a **court** or before a **judicial officer**.

EXTRANEOUS. **1.** Coming from the outside; external. **2.** Not belonging; not an integral part; not essential; irrelevant.

EXTRANEOUS OFFENSE. An offense other than the offense for which a person is on **trial**.

EXTRAORDINARY. Beyond the ordinary; unusual; exceptional; exceeding the usual or normal.

EXTRAORDINARY CARE. The highest degree of care; the greatest care.

EXTRAORDINARY GRAND JURY. A GRAND JURY whose scope of investigation is limited. See GRAND JURY for a list of related terms.

EXTREME. **1.** Outermost; farthest. **2.** In the highest degree; far beyond the ordinary or normal; very intense; utmost. **3.** Final; last. **4.** Drastic; of the greatest severity.

EXTREMIS. *See* IN EXTREMIS.

EXTRINSIC. **1.** From or on the outside; external; apart from. **2.** Not essential; extraneous.

EXTRINSIC EVIDENCE. **Evidence** not contained in a document or other object under examination, but derived from outside sources. See EVIDENCE for a list of related terms.

EYEWITNESS. A person who directly perceives an event or thing related to a criminal case. An eyewitness is usually a person other than the **victim**. See WITNESS for a list of related terms.

EYEWITNESS IDENTIFICATION. The determination of the identity of the perpetrator of a crime by a person who observed its commission. *See*: CONFRONTATION; IDENTIFICATION; LINEUP; SHOWUP; WITNESS.

FABRICATE. To make up or invent falsely. *Example*: He fabricated an alibi to protect himself.

FABRICATED EVIDENCE. **Evidence** made up or arranged, with intent to **deceive**, after an act has occurred. See EVIDENCE for a list of related terms.

FACE. **1.** External appearance; outward form; surface; that which is offered to view. *Example*: A search warrant that is not signed by the issuing magistrate is invalid on its face. **2.** Express terms; words in their apparent or obvious meaning. The face of a **document** is the information provided by all the language in the document without reference to any **extrinsic evidence** about the document that does not appear in the document itself. *Example*: A deed may be valid on its face, even though it was signed under duress and no court would uphold it.

FACIES. *Latin*. "Face"; outward appearance.

FACILITATE. To make easier; to free from difficulties or obstacles.

FACILITATION. *See*: CRIMINAL FACILITATION.

FACILITY. *See*: CONFINEMENT FACILITY; CONTRACT FACILITY; CORRECTIONAL FACILITY; JUVENILE FACILITY.

FACSIMILE. A close but usually not exact reproduction of an original. See ABSTRACT for a list of related terms.

FACT. **1.** An act; a deed; an event; an occurrence; a circumstance; a condition; a state. **2.** A truth; a reality; what actually happened; what actually exists. *Example*: Officers should testify to facts and not to their own opinions or conclusions. **3.** An actual event or circumstance to which, in combination with other events or circumstances, principles of **law** are applied in making judicial rulings. *Example*: Whether a person struck another person is a question of fact. Whether the striking constitutes a battery is a question of law. **4.** An item of **evidence**. The terms facts and evidence are sometimes used interchangeably. Evidence is often referred to as those facts that have been found legally **admissible** for consideration by the court in a case. Evidence is also referred to as the means by which facts are proved or disproved in court. *See*: ACCESSORY; AGREED STATEMENT OF FACTS; CASE AGREED ON; CASE

RESERVED; CIRCUMSTANCES; COLLATERAL FACT; CONCLUSION; CONCLUSION OF FACT; DEDUCTION; DE FACTO; ERROR; EVIDENCE; EVIDENTIARY FACT; EX POST FACTO; FACTO; FACTUM; FICTION; FINDING; FINDING OF FACT; FOUNDATION; HYPOTHESIS; HYPOTHETICAL QUESTION; INCRIMINATING CIRCUMSTANCE; INDICIA; IN FACT; INFERENCE; INFERENTIAL FACT; INFORMATION; IPSO FACTO; ISSUE; JUDICIAL NOTICE; KNOWLEDGE; LAW; LOGICAL RELEVANCY; NECESSARY INFERENCE; NEGATIVE PREGNANT; NEGATIVE PROOF; NEW MATTER; NOTICE; OPINION EVIDENCE; OPINION RULE; PHYSICAL FACT; POSITIVE PROOF; PRESUMPTION; PRESUMPTION OF FACT; PROBABLE CAUSE; PROBATIVE FACTS; PROOF; PROVE; PSYCHOLOGICAL FACT; QUESTION OF FACT; THEORY; TRIER OF FACT; ULTIMATE FACTS.

FACT-FINDER.   Same as TRIER OF FACT.

FACTO.   *Latin.* In fact; by the fact; by the act. See FACT for a list of related terms.

FACTUM.   *Latin.* "Act; fact; deed; event." See FACT for a list of related terms.

FAIL.   **1.** To neglect; to omit. *Example*: The defendant failed to appear in court. **2.** To be unsuccessful; to fall short; to be ineffective or inadequate. *Example*: The defense lawyer failed in his attempt to persuade the jury. **3.** To cease functioning properly; to give out.

FAILURE OF EVIDENCE.   An absence of **sufficient evidence** to support a **finding of fact**. See EVIDENCE for a list of related terms.

FAILURE OF PROOF.   A failure to prove sufficient **facts** to support one side of an issue or controversy.

FAIR.   Impartial; just; evenhanded; equitable.

FAIR AND IMPARTIAL JURY.   Same as IMPARTIAL JURY.

FAIR AND IMPARTIAL TRIAL.   Same as FAIR TRIAL.

FAIR COMMENT.   In the law of criminal **libel**, untrue written statements about the conduct of public officials made with the writer's honest and reasonable belief in their truth. If written statements are determined to be fair comment, it is a **defense** to a **prosecution** for criminal libel.

FAIR HEARING.   Generally, a judicial proceeding or hearing conducted in accordance with the fundamental concepts of **justice**, equality, and **due process**. See HEARING for a list of related terms.

FAIR PREPONDERANCE OF THE EVIDENCE. Same as PREPONDERANCE OF THE EVIDENCE.

FAIR TRIAL. A **trial** conducted in substantial conformity to the **law** and that safeguards and respects the **accused's** legal rights. "What is a fair trial? Perhaps no precise definition can be given it, but it certainly must be one where the accused's legal rights are safeguarded and respected. There must not only be a **fair and impartial jury** and a learned and upright **judge** to **instruct** the **jury** and pass upon legal questions, but there ought to be an atmosphere of calm, in which the witnesses can deliver their testimony without fear and intimidation, and in which the attorneys can assert the defendant's rights freely and fully, and in which the truth may be received and given credence without fear of violence. In no case must violence be resorted to— no coerced verdicts—and when **acquittals** are given, there must be no visible appearance of violence." *Fisher v. State*, 110 So. 361, 365 (Miss. 1926). See TRIAL for a list of related terms.

FAITH. Confidence; trust; reliance. Article IV, Section 1, of the U.S. Constitution provides that **full faith and credit** shall be given in each state to the public acts, records, and judicial proceedings of every other state. *See*: BAD FAITH; GOOD FAITH.

FALSE. **1.** Intentionally or knowingly untrue; deceitful. **2.** Untrue. **3.** Not genuine; counterfeit; artificial.

FALSE AFFIRMATION. Same as FALSE OATH. *See*: AFFIRMATION; OATH.

FALSE ARREST. The intentional, illegal restraint of a person's liberty or freedom of movement by another person who purports to act pursuant to legal authority. False arrest is a **tort** for which a **civil action** for damages may be instituted. In some jurisdictions, false arrest may also be a **crime**. See ABUSE OF PROCESS for a list of related terms.

FALSEHOOD. An intentionally untrue statement.

FALSE IMPERSONATION. The crime of unlawfully assuming the character of another person in order to deceive others and thereby obtain some benefit or to cause some detriment to the one impersonated. False impersonation is variously defined in different jurisdictions. *Also called*: **false personation**.

FALSE IMPRISONMENT. Any intentional, illegal restraint of a person's liberty or freedom of movement by another person. False imprisonment is a **tort** for which a **civil action** for damages may be instituted. In some jurisdictions, false imprisonment may also be a **crime**. The terms **false arrest** and false imprisonment are often used interchangeably, but false imprisonment is the broader term and false arrest is a type of false imprisonment. Under Section 212.3 of the **Model Penal Code** a person commits false imprisonment "if he knowingly restrains another unlawfully so as to interfere substantially with his liberty." See ABUSE OF PROCESS for a list of related terms.

FALSE MISREPRESENTATION. *See:* MISREPRESENTATION.

FALSE OATH. A sworn statement, made willfully and corruptly, without an honest belief in its accuracy or truthfulness. See AFFIRMATION for a list of related terms.

FALSE PERSONATION. Same as FALSE IMPERSONATION.

FALSE PRETENSES. The crime of obtaining the money or property of another by means of an untrue representation of a material fact with intent to **deceive**. Many states have extended the scope of false pretenses to include the obtaining of services or other benefits. False pretenses differs from **larceny** in that in larceny, the owner does not intend to part with property, while in false pretenses, the owner does intend to part with property but it is obtained by **fraud**. *Also called*: **false pretext**. See ABSTRACTION for a list of related terms.

FALSE PRETEXT. Same as FALSE PRETENSES.

FALSE REPRESENTATION. An untrue statement made with intent to **deceive**.

FALSE RETURN. A RETURN in which the officer charged with executing a **writ**, **warrant**, or other **mandate** falsely reports that he or she served or executed the document or makes some other false or incorrect statement to the detriment of an interested party.

FALSE SWEARING. The crime of making a FALSE OATH in regard to a **material** matter in a proceeding other than a judicial proceeding in which an **oath** is required by law. See AFFIRMATION for a list of related terms.

FALSE VERDICT. An obviously wrong and unjust **verdict**. See VERDICT for a list of related terms.

FALSE WITNESS. A WITNESS who gives intentionally rather than mistakenly false testimony. See WITNESS for a list of related terms.

FALSIFY. **1.** To make **false** or incorrect; to state untruthfully; to misrepresent. **2.** To make or alter with intent to **deceive**. *Example*: The clerk was accused of falsifying the record. **3.** To avoid; to defeat; to reverse. *Example*: The appeals court falsified the judgment.

FAMILIARITY.   Close acquaintance; moderate understanding. *Example:* He had some familiarity with the criminal law.

FAMILY COURT.   Family court is the name in many court systems for the court or section of a court that adjudicates **juveniles**. The **jurisdiction** of a family court extends over all matters concerning the family and its members as a unit, and can encompass appropriate types of **civil** and **criminal**, adult and juvenile cases. Family courts may hear cases involving criminal acts (such as **child abuse** or **assault** between family members), civil matters (such as adoption or divorce), and juvenile matters. They are called family courts because they specialize in cases that stem from family problems or family issues, or that are limited to members of a given family, although there is no such thing as family jurisdiction. *See*: COURT OF LIMITED JURIS-DICTION.

FARM.   *See*: JUVENILE FACILITY.

FATAL ERROR.   Same as REVERSIBLE ERROR.

FATAL INJURY.   An injury causing or resulting in death. See DEATH for a list of related terms.

FATAL VARIANCE.   A substantial and material VARIANCE that misleads the adverse party to his or her detriment. A variance that substantially misleads the defendant in making a **defense** or prevents a plea of **double jeopardy** is a fatal variance.

FAULT.   **1.** Defect; imperfection; error; mistake; transgression. **2.** Neglect of duty; deviation from right conduct; culpability; negligence.

FBI.   Abbreviation for FEDERAL BUREAU OF INVESTIGATION.

FEAR.   Apprehension or uneasiness caused by a sense of impending harm or danger.

FEASANCE.   The doing or performance of an act, condition, or duty. *See*: MAL-FEASANCE; MISFEASANCE; NONFEASANCE.

FEDERAL.   **1.** Relating to the national government as distinguished from the governments of the states. **2.** Relating to a form of government in which a union of states recognizes a sovereign central authority, but individual states retain certain powers for themselves.

FEDERAL BUREAU OF INVESTIGATION.   The Federal Bureau of Investigation (FBI) is the principal investigative arm of the U.S. **Department of Justice**. It is charged with gathering and reporting facts, locating witnesses, and compiling evidence in cases involving federal jurisdiction. The FBI was established in 1908 by the **Attorney**

General, who directed that Department of Justice investigations be handled by its own staff. The bureau is charged with investigating all violations of federal law except those that have been assigned by legislative enactment or otherwise to another federal agency. Its jurisdiction includes a wide range of responsibilities in the criminal, civil, and security fields. Priority has been assigned to the six areas that affect society the most—organized crime, drugs, counterterrorism, white-collar crime, foreign counterintelligence, and violent crime. On January 28, 1982, the Attorney General assigned concurrent jurisdiction for the enforcement of the Controlled Substances Act (21 U.S.C. §801) to the bureau and the **Drug Enforcement Administration** (DEA). The DEA Administrator reports to the Attorney General through the FBI Director. The bureau also offers cooperative services such as fingerprint identification, laboratory examination, police training, and the National Crime Information Center to duly authorized law enforcement agencies.

The bureau headquarters in Washington, DC, consists of 10 separate divisions, a Deputy Director, two Associate Deputy Directors, an Office of Public Affairs, a Congressional Affairs Office, an Office of Liaison and International Affairs, an Office of Equal Opportunity Affairs, and a Director's staff. The bureau's investigations are conducted through 56 field offices.

FEDERAL COURTS. The courts of the United States government. The federal courts with criminal **jurisdiction** are the **United States District Courts**, the **United States Courts of Appeal**, and the **United States Supreme Court**. See COURT for a list of related terms.

FEDERAL LAW ENFORCEMENT AGENCY. A **law enforcement agency** that is an organizational unit or subunit of the federal government. Examples of federal law enforcement agencies are the **Federal Bureau of Investigation**, the **Secret Service**, and the **Bureau of Alcohol, Tobacco and Firearms**. Federal agency subunits such as the organized crime unit of the U.S. **Department of Justice** and the enforcement unit of the **Internal Revenue Service** are classified as **prosecution agencies** in this dictionary, because their primary purpose is to try cases in court, although many of their personnel may perform law enforcement duties.

FEDERAL LAW ENFORCEMENT OFFICER. An employee of a **federal law enforcement agency** who is an officer sworn to carry out **law enforcement** duties. Examples of federal law enforcement officers are agents of the **Federal Bureau of Investigation** and the **Bureau of Alcohol, Tobacco and Firearms** and the investigative staff of federal organized crime units and tax law enforcement units. See LAW ENFORCEMENT OFFICER for a list of related terms.

FEDERAL LAW ENFORCEMENT TRAINING CENTER. The Federal Law Enforcement Training Center in the **Department of the Treasury** is headed by a Director, who is appointed by the Secretary of the Treasury. The center is an interagency training facility serving 62 federal law enforcement organizations. It conducts its operations at its training facility located at Glynco, Georgia. The major training effort is in the area of basic programs to teach law enforcement skills to police and investigative personnel. The center also conducts advanced programs in areas such as white-collar crime, the use of microcomputers as an investigative tool, advanced law enforcement photography, procurement and contract fraud, marine law enforcement, and several instructor training courses. In addition to the basic and advanced programs, the center provides the facilities and support services for participating organizations to conduct advanced training for their own law enforcement personnel. The center offers selective, highly specialized training programs to state and local officers as an aid in deterring crime. These programs include fraud and financial investigations, juvenile justice topics, marine law enforcement, and arson for profit. The center develops the curriculum content and training techniques for recruit training, and advises and assists the participating organizations in producing, formulating, and operating specialized training materials and equipment.

FEDERAL REGISTER.   The daily publication that makes available to the public federal agency regulations and other legal documents of the executive branch, covering a wide range of government activities. The Federal Register publishes government requirements that involve environmental protection, consumer product safety, food and drug standards, occupational health and safety, and many more areas of concern to the public. Perhaps more importantly, the Federal Register includes proposed changes in regulated areas. Each proposed change published carries an invitation for any citizen or group to participate in the consideration of the proposed regulation through the submission of written data, views, or arguments, and sometimes by oral presentations. The opportunity afforded citizens, through the publication of proposed rules and notices of public meetings, to be informed of and participate in the workings of their government is significant.

FEDERAL RULES OF CRIMINAL PROCEDURE.   A body of rules governing the process by which criminal proceedings are initiated and maintained in **United States courts**. The Federal Rules of Criminal Procedure were promulgated by the U.S. Supreme Court pursuant to authority granted by Congress and are amended frequently. See CRIME for a list of related terms.

FEIGNED.   Pretended; disguised; fictitious; not real.

FELLATIO.   The penetration of a person's mouth by the penis. Fellatio is a crime in some states, sometimes punishable as a form of the more encompassing crime of **sodomy**. See SEX OFFENSES for a list of related terms.

FELON.   A person who has committed a FELONY.

FELONIOUS.   Having the character or nature of a FELONY; done with intent to commit a crime of the seriousness of a felony.

FELONIOUS ASSAULT.   See note under AGGRAVATED ASSAULT.

FELONIOUS HOMICIDE.   Any HOMICIDE that is not an **excusable homicide** or a **justifiable homicide**. See HOMICIDE for a list of related terms.

FELONIOUS RESTRAINT.   According to Section 212.2 of the **Model Penal Code**, a person commits felonious restraint if he or she "knowingly: (a) restrains another unlawfully in circumstances exposing him to risk of **serious bodily injury**; or (b) holds another in a condition of **involuntary servitude**."

FELONY.   In general, a CRIME of a more serious nature than those designated as MISDEMEANORS. Felonies are distinguished from misdemeanors by place of punishment and possible duration of punishment as defined by statute. The statutory definition of felony may differ between states and between the federal government and various states. Typically a felony is a crime with a possible punishment of death or imprisonment in a state or federal prison facility for a period of one year or more. See CRIME for a list of related terms.

FELONY DRUNK DRIVING.   *See*: DRIVING UNDER THE INFLUENCE OF ALCOHOL.

FELONY-MURDER RULE.   The rule stating that the killing of a person is MURDER if the death occurs as a result of the perpetration or attempted perpetration of a FELONY. The modern trend is to limit the application of the felony-murder rule to those killings in which the felony itself is dangerous, the method of perpetration or attempt is dangerous, the killing is foreseeable, or some combination of these factors. See HOMICIDE for a list of related terms.

FELONY PRELIMINARY.   Same as PRELIMINARY HEARING.

FENCE.   A professional RECEIVER who acts as a middleman by relaying stolen property he or she purchases from thieves to various outlets, which sell the goods to the ultimate consumer.

FERAE NATURAE.   *Latin.* "Of a wild nature"; untamed.

FETICIDE.   The destruction of a human FETUS. *Also spelled*: **foeticide**.

FETUS.   An unborn human child developing in the womb. An unborn child is usually referred to as a fetus from about the end of the second month of pregnancy to the moment of birth. *Also spelled*: **foetus**.

FEW.   A small number of; not many.

FEWER.   A smaller number of; not as many. Fewer is preferred to LESS when referring to individual numbers or units. Less refers to something abstract or something considered collectively. *Example*: There were fewer major crimes this year than last. A possible reason is that people were given less opportunity to commit crime.

F.I.   Abbreviation for FIELD INTERVIEW.

FICTION.   Something invented or feigned; something not genuine or nonexistent. See FACT for a list of related terms.

FICTION OF LAW.   An assumption, made by a court and embodied in various legal doctrines for the purposes of the advancement of justice, that something known to be false is true. *Also called*: **legal fiction**.

FICTITIOUS.   **1.** Not real; false; not genuine; nonexistent. **2.** Pretended; feigned; counterfeit; made up with intent to deceive.

FICTITIOUS PERSON.   Same as ARTIFICIAL PERSON.

FIDES.   *Latin.* "Faith; confidence; trust." *See*: BONA FIDES, MALA FIDES.

FIDUCIARY.   **n.** A person who owes a special duty of trust, confidence, or responsibility toward another. Under Section 224.13 of the **Model Penal Code** fiduciary "includes trustee, guardian, executor, administrator, receiver and any person carrying on fiduciary functions on behalf of a corporation or other organization which is a fiduciary." **adj.** Involving confidence, trust, and good faith; confidential. *See*: CONFIDENTIAL RELATIONSHIP.

FIELD INTERROGATION.   The questioning by a **law enforcement officer** in the field of a person who has come under direct suspicion in relation to a particular criminal event. If an **arrest** is not made, a field interrogation report may result from a field interrogation. The report identifies the person questioned and describes the circumstances of the contact. It is used as a source of information on **modus operandi**, on the whereabouts of suspects at the time of a crime, and other matters relevant to crime investigation. If a suspect is in **custody**, and the officer's words or actions are such that the police should know they are reasonably likely to elicit an incriminating response, the officer must satisfy the requirements of MIRANDA v. ARIZONA. Field interrogation has a narrower meaning than FIELD INTERVIEW, but has a broader meaning than CUSTODIAL INTERROGATION.

FIELD INTERVIEW.   Any contact between a private citizen and a **law enforcement officer** acting in official capacity, whether or not relating to suspicion of criminal activity. *See*: FIELD INTERROGATION; INTERROGATION.

FILE. **v. 1.** To enter any document into the official **record** of a court. **v. 2.** To commence a criminal proceeding in court by formal submission to the court of a **charging document** alleging that one or more named persons have committed one or more specified criminal offenses. In **misdemeanor** cases, the initial document, usually called a **complaint**, is ordinarily the only charging document filed. In **felony** cases, one charging document will be filed to initiate the **preliminary hearing** on **probable cause**, and, if the defendant is thereafter held to answer the felony charge, a second document may be filed to initiate the trial stage in a higher court. The second document may be called an **information** if it is filed by a decision of the **prosecutor**, and will be called an **indictment** if it is filed by decision of a **grand jury**. **v. 3.** To commence a **civil action** in court by formal submission to the court of a document alleging the facts of a matter and requesting relief. **n. 1.** The place in the court offices where the official records are kept. **n. 2.** The complete court record of a particular **case**.

FINAL. Last; terminating; decisive; conclusive; that which settles the rights and duties of the parties and leaves nothing open to further dispute. *Example*: The judge will make his final decision tomorrow. *See*: INTERLOCUTORY.

FINAL JUDGMENT. "A final judgment in a criminal case is one which either (1) adjudicates the defendant to have been **convicted** of a criminal offense and imposes, suspends or defers **sentence** or (2) **dismisses** all of the **charges** against the defendant." *State v. Garcia*, 659 P.2d 918, 923 (N.M.App. 1983). See JUDGMENT for a list of related terms.

FINAL ORDER. An ORDER that closes the matter in issue, settles the rights of the parties, and precludes further litigation.

FINAL PLEA. The last **plea** to a given charge entered in a court record by or for a defendant.

FINANCIAL INSTITUTION. Section 223.0 (2) of the **Model Penal Code** defines financial institution as "a bank, insurance company, credit union, building and loan association, investment trust or other organization held out to the public as a place of deposit of funds or medium of savings or collective investment."

FIND. To determine and declare after inquiry. *Example 1*: He expects the jury to find him guilty. *Example 2*: The grand jury found an indictment against him.

FINDING. An official determination, after deliberation, of a **judge**, **jury**, administrative body, etc., on a disputed matter of fact or law. The term finding is more commonly applied to matters of **fact** than to matters of **law**. See FACT and JUDGMENT for lists of related terms.

FINDING OF FACT. A determination, after examining the **evidence**, that a certain fact exists. See FACT for a list of related terms.

FINE. A **penalty** imposed upon a **convicted** person by a court requiring that he or she pay a specified sum of money to the **court**. A fine may be levied in lieu of or in addition to **incarceration**. As a general rule, the court that imposes a fine may also compel its payment by incarceration. This incarceration is only a method to force compliance and is not considered part of the penalty for the offense. Refusal to pay a fine does not result in incarceration. In some criminal statutes, the terms **forfeit** or **forfeiture** are the equivalent of fine. *See*: AMERCEMENT.

FINGERPRINT. The impression made by the ridges of the inner surface of the fingertips. Fingerprints may be lifted from various objects touched by the fingers or may be taken by inking the fingertips and transferring the impression onto paper. Fingerprints are used for purposes of **identification**. *See*: LATENT FINGERPRINT.

FIREARM. Any **weapon** from which a projectile may be propelled by the combustion of gunpowder or other explosive. Examples of firearms are pistols, revolvers, rifles, shotguns, and machine guns.

FIRM. Settled; established; secure; sure; steadfast.

FIRST APPEARANCE. Same as INITIAL APPEARANCE.

FIRSTHAND. From the original source. *Example*: The police had firsthand information from eyewitnesses to the crime.

FIRST IMPRESSION. Presentation of a question of **law** to a **court** for examination for the first time. A case of first impression is one that presents an entirely new question of law for which there is no **precedent**.

FIRST INSTANCE. *See*: COURT OF FIRST INSTANCE.

FIRST OFFENDER. **1.** A person whose violation of the criminal law comes to the attention of law enforcement authorities for the first time. **2.** A person who is prosecuted for a violation of the criminal law for the first time.

FIRST PLEA. Same as INITIAL PLEA.

FISCAL. Pertaining to financial matters.

FISHING EXPEDITION. An activity instituted or carried on to obtain information beyond the fair scope or legal bounds of a particular **action** or proceeding. Examples of a fishing expedition are the overly broad use of the **discovery** process and the loose, vague, unfocused questioning of **witnesses**.

FIT. Appropriate; well suited; proper; qualified; worthy.

FITNESS HEARING.   Same as TRANSFER HEARING.

FIX.   To settle definitely; to determine.

FIXTURE.   An item of **personal property** that is attached to and used in connection with **real property** so that it is considered a part of the real property.

FLAGRANT.   Extremely conspicuous; notorious; glaring; shocking. *Example*: His actions were a flagrant violation of the law.

FLAGRANTE DELICTO.   *Latin*. In the act of committing the crime.

FLAGRANTLY AGAINST THE EVIDENCE.   So contrary to the **weight of the evidence** as to shock the conscience and indicate prejudice.

FLAT SENTENCE.   Same as DETERMINATE SENTENCE.

FLEE.   **v.** To run away. **n.** FLIGHT.

FLEE FROM JUSTICE.   Same as ABSCOND (definition 1).

FLIGHT.   *See*: FLEE.

FOETICIDE.   Same as FETICIDE.

FOETUS.   Same as FETUS.

F.O.I.A.   Abbreviation for FREEDOM OF INFORMATION ACT.

FOLLOW.   To conform to; to adhere to; to act in accordance with; to be governed by. *Example*: The court followed the precedent set by the Second Circuit Court of Appeals. *See*: STARE DECISIS.

FOOTPRINT.   An imprint or impression left on a surface by a foot or a shoe worn by a person.

FOR CAUSE.   *See*: CHALLENGE FOR CAUSE.

FORCE.   **1.** Physical violence; physical strength or power exerted upon an object or person; physical coercion or restraint. *Example*: An officer may use reasonable force in effecting an arrest. **2.** Legal validity; binding power. *Example*: The laws are in full force. *See*: DEADLY FORCE; DEATH; NONDEADLY FORCE; SELF-DEFENSE; UNLAWFUL FORCE.

FORCIBLE ENTRY. The disturbance of one's peaceful possession of **real estate** by entering upon the real estate by **violence** or intimidation.

FORCIBLE RAPE. **Sexual intercourse** with a female against her will, by **force** or **threat** of force. See SEX OFFENSES for a list of related terms.

FORECLOSE. To shut out; to bar; to prevent; to exclude.

FOREIGN. Of another state, nation, or jurisdiction.

FOREMAN. The presiding member and spokesperson of a **jury**. See JURY for a list of related terms.

FORENSIC. Relating to, connected with, or used in **courts** of **law**.

FORENSIC MEDICINE. The application of medical knowledge to the purposes of the **law**. Forensic medicine includes the presentation of medical **expert evidence** given by physicians and other scientists at trials and other hearings. The most common area of forensic medicine is the criminal law. Major areas of concern are the determination of the cause of a victim's death or injury and the identification of defendants, victims, and bodily and chemical substances.

FORESAID. Same as AFORESAID.

FORESEEABLE. Able to be reasonably anticipated; able to be seen or known in advance.

FORESEEN. Anticipated; expected; known or seen beforehand.

FORESTRY CAMP. *See*: JUVENILE FACILITY.

FORFEIT. To lose the right to money or property as a penalty for some crime, fault, error, or omission. In some criminal statutes, the terms forfeit or **forfeiture** are the equivalent of **fine**. *Example*: If he fails to appear in court tomorrow, he will forfeit his bail. *See*: CRIMINAL FORFEITURE.

FORFEITURE. An enforced and involuntary loss or deprivation of property, right, or position as a consequence of a violation of law or a failure to perform an obligation or condition. *See*: CRIMINAL FORFEITURE.

FORGERY. **1.** Generally, the fabrication, construction, or preparation of one thing in imitation of a genuine thing with the intention of **deceiving** others that the **false** is the genuine. **2.** The creation or alteration of a written or printed document that, if validly executed, would constitute a record of a legally binding transaction, with the intent to **defraud** by affirming it to be the act of an unknowing second person. In many statutes, **counterfeiting** is included within the definition of forgery. Where a distinction is made, it rests on the fact that forged materials are of relevance to the legal affairs of specific persons, while counterfeited materials, most typically money, have intrinsic value set by social convention or governmental authority. *See*: CHECK FRAUD. **3.** The creation of an art object with intent to misrepresent the identity of the creator.

FORM. **1.** The technical style or manner of arranging or setting up legal instruments or judicial proceedings. Matters of form generally do not affect the substantial validity or legal sufficiency of documents or proceedings. *Example*: The style of expressing the facts in a search warrant is merely a matter of form. **2.** An outline or skeleton of a legal document containing the necessary technical terms and phrases properly arranged, and providing blanks for insertion of details or information. *Example*: Officers should always use a search warrant application form when applying for a search warrant.

FORMA. *Latin.* "Form."

FORMAL ARREST. *See*: ARREST.

FORMALITY. An established form, rule, or method used in the making of legal documents or in the conduct of legal proceedings to ensure their validity and regularity.

FORMAL PARTY. A person who is not interested in the immediate **controversy** of an **action**, but who is interested in the general subject matter of an action and who may be joined in the action.

FORMA PAUPERIS. *See*: IN FORMA PAUPERIS.

FORMED DESIGN. A fixed and deliberate **intent** to commit a **crime**.

FORMER ACQUITTAL. Same as AUTREFOIS ACQUIT.

FORMER JEOPARDY. Same as DOUBLE JEOPARDY.

FORMULA. A set form of words intended to have legal validity.

FORMULA INSTRUCTION. An **instruction** in a set form of words intended to be a complete statement of the law on a particular subject and upon which a **jury** may base its **verdict**. See INSTRUCTION for a list of related terms.

FORNICATION. Unlawful voluntary **sexual intercourse** between two unmarried persons of the opposite sex. In some jurisdictions, if one of the persons is married and the other not, the offense is **adultery** for the married person and fornication for the unmarried person.

FORSWEAR. To make any **oath** to something that the person swearing knows is untrue. See AFFIRMATION for a list of related terms.

FORTHWITH. 1. Immediately; at once; without delay. **2.** As soon as possible; within a reasonable time under the circumstances.

FORTIORI. *See*: A FORTIORI.

FORTUITOUS. By chance; accidental; unexpected; unplanned.

FORUM. *Latin*. "A court; a tribunal."

FOUND. To base; to ground. *Example*: His opinion was founded on fact.

FOUNDATION. A **fact** or facts that must be established to support the admission of certain **evidence**. When a given species of evidence is admissible only on the condition that some preliminary fact or facts be demonstrated or proven, the preliminary fact or facts are called the foundation. For example, demonstrative evidence is admissible if a foundation is laid by proving that the evidence accurately demonstrates or represents what it purports to demonstrate or represent. Also, a party seeking to offer testimonial evidence must lay a foundation to show that the **witness** was in a position to have firsthand knowledge. See EVIDENCE and FACT for a list of related terms.

FOUR CORNERS. Same as FACE (definition 2).

FOURS, ON ALL. *See*: ON ALL FOURS.

FRAME. 1. To put into words; to compose; to draw up. *Example*: Some of the laws were not carefully framed. **2.** To arrange or adapt for a particular purpose; to phrase. *Example*: The defense attorney's questions were carefully framed to get the answers he wanted. **3.** *See*: FRAME-UP.

FRAME-UP. A plan or plot to **incriminate** an innocent person on **false evidence**.

FRATRICIDE. 1. The killing of one's brother or sister. **2.** One who kills his or her brother or sister.

FRAUD. The intentional **deceiving** of another person in order to induce the person to depart with his or her money or property or to surrender a legal right. Fraud usually does not involve damage to property or injury or threatened injury to persons. Fraud is an element of certain criminal offenses such as **check fraud**, **counterfeiting**, **credit card fraud**, **embezzlement**, and **forgery**.

FRAUD IN FACT. Same as ACTUAL FRAUD.

FRAUD IN LAW. Same as CONSTRUCTIVE FRAUD.

FRAUDULENT. Characterized by, based on, or accomplished by FRAUD.

FRAUDULENT MISREPRESENTATION. *See*: MISREPRESENTATION.

FREE. **1.** Unrestrained; at liberty; discharged from **detention**, **arrest**, or **incarceration**. *Example*: The charges were dropped and he was set free. **2.** Enjoying civil liberty; existing under a government that does not interfere with individual rights. *Example*: We are a free society.

FREEDOM OF ASSEMBLY AND PETITION. *See*: ASSEMBLY AND PETITION.

FREEDOM OF INFORMATION ACT. A federal **statute** (5 U.S.C. §552) that provides for making information about the rules, opinions, orders, records, and proceedings of federal agencies available to the public, unless the information comes within one of the specific categories exempt from public disclosure, such as matters involving an individual's right to privacy, national security or foreign policy interests, or the internal management of an agency. Virtually all agencies of the executive branch of the federal government have issued regulations to implement the Freedom of Information Act. These regulations inform the public where certain types of information may be readily obtained, how other information may be obtained on request, and what internal agency appeals are available if a member of the public is refused requested information. *Abbreviation*: **F.O.I.A.** See PRIVACY for a list of related terms.

FREEDOM OF RELIGION. The right to hold any religious beliefs one wants and to practice any or no religion without any restraints except those lawfully imposed for the general welfare. Freedom of religion is guaranteed by the First and Fourteenth Amendments to the U.S. Constitution.

FREEDOM OF SPEECH. The right to say anything one wants without any restraints except those lawfully imposed for the general welfare. Freedom of speech is guaranteed by the First and Fourteenth Amendments to the U.S. Constitution.

FREEDOM OF THE PRESS. The right to publish anything one wants without any restraints except those lawfully imposed for the general welfare. Freedom of the press is guaranteed by the First and Fourteenth Amendments to the U.S. Constitution.

FREQUENT. To visit often; to be in or about often. *Example*: The suspect is known to frequent the local bars.

FRESH. Recent; newly made. *Example*: We found fresh footprints.

FRESH PURSUIT. Immediate pursuit of a fleeing **criminal** with intent to apprehend him or her. Fresh pursuit generally refers to the situation in which a **law enforcement officer** attempts to make a valid **arrest** of a criminal within the officer's **jurisdiction**, and the criminal flees outside the jurisdiction to avoid arrest, with the officer immediately pursuing. An arrest made in fresh pursuit will be legal if the pursuit was started promptly and maintained continuously. Many states have adopted the Uniform Act on Fresh Pursuit to govern fresh pursuits that take an arresting officer into a neighboring state. See ARREST for a list of related terms. *See also*: HOT PURSUIT.

FRIENDLY SUIT.   Same as CASE AGREED ON.

FRIEND OF THE COURT.   Same as AMICUS CURIAE.

FRISK.   A modified SEARCH consisting of a careful exploration of the outer surfaces of a person's clothing all over his or her body in an attempt to find weapons. The 1968 U.S. Supreme Court case of *Terry v. Ohio* set out the limits on **law enforcement officers'** authority to frisk persons. "[T]here must be a narrowly drawn authority to permit a reasonable search for weapons for the protection of the police officer, where he has reason to believe that he is dealing with an armed and dangerous individual, regardless of whether he has **probable cause** to **arrest** the individual for a crime." 392 U.S. 1, 27, 88 S.Ct. 1868, 1883, 20 L.Ed.2d 889, 909. In a later case, the Court extended the permissible scope of a frisk to include the passenger compartment of an automobile. "[T]he search of the passenger compartment of an automobile, limited to those areas in which a weapon may be placed or hidden, is permissible if the police officer possesses a reasonable belief based on 'specific and articulable facts which, taken together with the rational inferences from those facts, reasonably warrant' the officers in believing that the suspect is dangerous and the suspect may gain immediate control of weapons." *Michigan v. Long*, 463 U.S. 1032, 1049, 103 S.Ct. 3469, 3480, 77 L.Ed.2d 1201, 1220 (1983). *See*: SEARCH; STOP; STOP AND FRISK.

FRIVOLOUS.   Clearly and obviously insufficient and devoid of merit.

FROM.   **1.** Beginning at a specified source or time. *Example*: The footprints led from the back of the building. **2.** Out of; out of the jurisdiction or control of. *Example*: He escaped from prison.

FRUIT.   **1.** Product; result; outcome. **2.** Fruits of **crime** are material objects, such as stolen goods or money, obtained as the result of the commission of a crime and sometimes constituting the subject matter of the crime. See CRIME for a list of related terms.

FRUIT OF THE POISONOUS TREE DOCTRINE.   The doctrine that **evidence** will be inadmissible in court if it was indirectly obtained by exploitation of some prior illegal police activity (such as an illegal **arrest**, **search**, or **confession**). The evidence indirectly obtained is sometimes called **derivative evidence**. The doctrine derives its name from the idea that once a tree is poisoned (illegal police activity), then the fruit of the tree (derivative evidence obtained by exploiting the illegal activity) is likewise poisoned or tainted and should not be used. If, however, evidence is obtained by means sufficiently distinguishable to be purged of the taint of the primary illegality, the primary illegality has not been exploited and the evidence will be admissible. Courts refer to this as **attenuation** or **dissipation** of the taint and require the prosecution to prove at least an intervening act by the defendant or a third party that breaks the causal chain linking the illegality and evidence in such a way that the evidence is not in fact obtained by exploitation of that illegality. *Example*: Assume that the police arrest a man illegally merely because he is walking in an area where a bank robbery has occurred. Then they take him to the bank and the teller identifies him as the robber. The derivative evidence of the teller's identification of the man at the bank would be "fruit of the poisonous tree" and would be inadmissible in court because the identification was obtained by exploitation of the prior illegal arrest. Assume further that the arrested person was **arraigned** and **released** on his own **recognizance**, but returned several days later to make a full **confession** of the robbery. The confession would be admissible because the connection between the arrest and the confession "had become so attenuated as to dissipate the taint." *Wong Sun v. U.S.* 371 U.S. 471, 491, 83 S.Ct. 407, 419, 9 L.Ed.2d 441, 457 (1963). See EXCLUSIONARY RULE for a list of related terms.

FRUITS OF CRIME.   *See*: FRUIT.

FUGITIVE.   *See*: FUGITIVE FROM JUSTICE.

FUGITIVE FROM JUSTICE.   A person who, after committing a **crime**, either departs from the **jurisdiction** where the crime was committed or hides within the jurisdiction in order to avoid **prosecution** or **confinement**. The meaning of the term fugitive from justice varies in common usage and may include both escapees and persons avoiding prosecution or confinement. See ABSCOND for a list of related terms.

FULL AGE.   Same as MAJORITY.

FULL COURT.   A court meeting EN BANC. See COURT for a list of related terms.

FULL FAITH AND CREDIT.   A clause in Article IV, Section 1, of the U.S. Constitution that requires that each state must give full force and effect to the public acts, records, and judicial proceedings of every other state. The U.S. Supreme Court said that "if a judgment is conclusive in the state where it was pronounced, it is equally conclusive everywhere in the courts of the United States." *Christmas v. Russell*, 72 U.S. 290, 302 (1866).

FULL HEARING.   A **hearing** providing a defendant with all rights and protections to which he or she is entitled, including notice of charges, right to present evidence, right to confront witnesses, etc. See HEARING for a list of related terms.

FULL JURISDICTION. Complete JURISDICTION over a given subject matter with no reservations or exceptions. See JURISDICTION for a list of related terms.

FULL LEGAL AGE. Same as MAJORITY.

FULL OPINION. An OPINION in writing, usually lengthy, presenting in detail the reasons and reasoning leading to the court's decision. See OPINION for a list of related terms.

FULL PARDON. An executive act completely and unconditionally absolving a person from all consequences of **conviction** of a crime. A full pardon can imply that **guilt** itself is eradicated. It is an act of forgiveness and is accompanied, generally, by restoration of civil rights. American law tends to use this executive remedy, instead of judicial proceedings, when serious doubt of guilt or evidence of innocence arises after conviction. *Also called*: **absolute pardon**.

FULL-TIME TEMPORARY RELEASE. *See*: TEMPORARY RELEASE.

FUNCTUS OFFICIO. *Latin.* "A task or duty performed." Having accomplished its purpose or function and therefore of no further force or authority. *Example*: A search warrant that has been executed and returned is functus officio.

FUNDAMENTAL ERROR. An ERROR apparent on the **face** of the **record** that goes to the foundation of a case or takes from the defendant rights that are essential to the **defense**. See ERROR for a list of related terms.

FUNDAMENTAL LAW. The basic governing principles or constitution of a nation or state.

FUNGIBLE. Of such a class or kind that one unit or part may be substituted for another equivalent unit or part in satisfaction of an obligation. Examples of fungible goods are grain, oil, and money.

FURANDI ANIMUS. Same as ANIMUS FURANDI.

FURLOUGH. An authorized **temporary release** from a **confinement facility** that is conditioned on compliance with its terms. A furlough may be a full-time temporary release or a part-time temporary release. See RELEASE for a list of related terms.

FURNISH. To supply; to provide; to equip.

FURTIVE. Surreptitious; shifty; clandestine; stealthy; done with intent to escape observation or avoid attention. *Example*: The officer observed the suspect making furtive movements in the front seat of her car.

GAG ORDER. **1.** A court order that an unruly, disruptive defendant be bound and gagged to prevent further interruptions in a trial. The U.S. Supreme Court held such an order constitutionally permissible in *Illinois v. Allen*, 397 U.S. 337, 90 S.Ct. 1057, 25 L.Ed.2d 353 (1970). **2.** A court order, in a highly publicized trial, directing attorneys and witnesses not to discuss the case with reporters, in order to assure the defendant a **fair trial**. **3.** A court order directing reporters not to report public court proceedings in order to protect a defendant from prejudicial pretrial publicity. The U.S. Supreme Court held that such an order violated the constitutional guarantee of freedom of the press in *Nebraska Press Association v. Stuart*, 427 U.S. 539, 96 S.Ct. 2791, 49 L.Ed.2d 683 (1976).

GALLOWS. A structure from which a noose is suspended, used for executing criminals by hanging.

GAMBLING. **n. 1.** Betting money or something of value on the outcome of a game of chance or an uncertain event for the purpose of gaining more than the amount of the bet. **n. 2.** Operating, promoting, or permitting the operation of an unlawful **game of chance** or a wagering establishment. *See*: BOOKMAKING; GAMBLING DEVICE; GAME OF CHANCE; LOTTERY; NUMBERS GAME; POOL; RAFFLE; SLOT MACHINE.

GAMBLING DEVICE. Any implement, apparatus, or machine used for GAMBLING. See GAMBLING for a list of related terms.

GAME OF CHANCE. A game in which a player risks something of value for a chance to win something of greater value and in which an element of chance or luck rather than skill predominantly determines the outcome of the game. See GAMBLING for a list of related terms.

GANGSTER. A member of an organized group of criminals or hoodlums.

GAOL. An archaic term for JAIL.

GATES, ILLINOIS v. *See*: ILLINOIS v. GATES.

GAULT, IN RE. A 1967 landmark decision of the U.S. Supreme Court holding that **juveniles** are entitled to fundamental constitutional due process rights such as representation by **counsel** (at state expense if necessary), **notice** of **charges**, freedom from compulsory **self-incrimination**, and **confrontation** and **cross-examination** of witnesses in juvenile **adjudicatory hearings**. Juveniles do not, however, have a constitutional right to **bail**, **indictment** by a **grand jury**, a **public trial**, or a **jury trial**. The citation for *In Re Gault* is 387 U.S. 1, 87 S.Ct. 1428, 18 L.Ed.2d 527. See JUVENILE for a list of related terms.

GAVEL. A small mallet or hammer used by judges to signal for attention or order.

GENERAL. Relating to or applying to all or to the whole rather than to some or one; not limited or restricted in scope, area, or application; not specific or special.

GENERAL AGENCY. An AGENCY in which the AGENT has GENERAL AUTHORITY to act for or represent the PRINCIPAL.

GENERAL AGENT. An AGENT who has GENERAL AUTHORITY.

GENERAL APPEARANCE. An APPEARANCE made for any purpose other than to attack the **jurisdiction** of court. "Whether an appearance is general or special is determined by the relief sought and if a defendant, by his appearance, insists only upon the objection that he is not in court for want of jurisdiction over his person, and confines his appearance for that purpose only, then he has made a **special appearance**, but if he raises any other question or asks any relief which can only be granted upon the hypothesis that the court has jurisdiction of his person, then he has made a general appearance." *Pease v. City of San Diego*, 209 P.2d 843, 845 (Cal.Dist.Ct.App. 1949). See JURISDICTION for a list of related terms.

GENERAL AUTHORITY. AUTHORITY (definition 1) conferred by a PRINCI-PAL upon an AGENT to act for or represent the principal in all transactions connected with the principal's business. General authority involves the conducting of a series of transactions in the continuous service of the principal.

GENERAL CHARGE. Same as GENERAL INSTRUCTION.

GENERAL INSTRUCTION. The final statement made by a trial **judge** to a **jury** explaining the issues involved in the trial and explaining the law of the case that the jury is required to apply to the facts to reach its **verdict**. See INSTRUCTION for a list of related terms.

GENERAL INTENT. An INTENT to do something prohibited by law without a specific plan or particular result in mind; same as the general notion of **mens rea**. General intent must be proven in prosecutions for all crimes. To prove general intent, it is not necessary to show that the accused intended the precise harm or result. It is sufficient to show that the accused meant to do the act that caused the harm or result. *See*: SPECIFIC INTENT.

GENERAL JURISDICTION.   *See*: COURT OF GENERAL JURISDICTION.

GENERAL OBJECTION.   An OBJECTION that does not identify the ground of the objection.

GENERAL PARDON.   *See*: AMNESTY.

GENERAL TERM.   **1.** The sitting of a court EN BANC. **2.** The ordinary period of time for conducting court business during which **trials** are heard. *See*: SPECIAL TERM.

GENERAL VERDICT.   A VERDICT in which the jury pronounces on all issues of fact and law at the same time. A general verdict is the ordinary form of verdict. *Example*: In a criminal case, a general verdict of guilty means guilty on all counts. *See*: SPECIAL VERDICT. See VERDICT for a list of related terms.

GENERAL WARRANT.   A **search warrant** or **arrest warrant** that fails to specify the person or place to be searched or the person or item to be seized, and that leaves the time and manner of execution to the discretion of the officer executing it. General warrants are forbidden by the Fourth Amendment to the U.S. Constitution and the constitutions of every state. See ARREST WARRANT for a list of related terms.

GESTURE.   A movement of the body, arms, hands, head, or face made to express a thought or feeling or to emphasize speech.

GIBBET.   Same as GALLOWS.

GIDEON v. WAINWRIGHT.   A 1963 landmark decision of the U.S. Supreme Court, which held that a defendant has a constitutional right to **counsel** at his or her criminal trial even if too poor to afford one. The Court ruled that the **due process of law** requirement of the Fourteenth Amendment makes applicable to the states the Sixth Amendment guarantee of the right to counsel in "all criminal prosecutions." The Court made the decision retroactive so that all prisoners who had been tried or sentenced without proper representation were given the right to new trials. The citation for *Gideon v. Wainwright* is 372 U.S. 335, 83 S.Ct. 792, 9 L.Ed.2d 799.

GIST.   The essential ground or substance on which a legal **action** rests.

GOOD.   Valid; legally sufficient; sound. *Example*: It was a good search warrant.

GOOD BEHAVIOR.   Conduct conforming to the law. *Example*: The judge suspended his sentence as long as he maintained good behavior.

GOOD CAUSE.   Legally sufficient reason or ground.

GOOD FAITH.   The honest and sincere intent to deal fairly with others; the absence of any intent to defraud or seek unfair advantage. *See*: BAD FAITH; FAITH; GOOD-FAITH EXCEPTION.

GOOD-FAITH EXCEPTION.   An exception to the EXCLUSIONARY RULE for illegal searches conducted in **good faith**. Under this exception, whenever a law enforcement officer acting with objective good faith has obtained a search warrant from a detached and neutral judge or magistrate and acted within its scope, evidence seized pursuant to the warrant will not be excluded, even though the warrant is later determined to be invalid. In determining what is good faith on the part of an officer, the Court said that "our good-faith inquiry is confined to the objectively ascertainable question whether a reasonably well-trained officer would have known that the search was illegal despite the magistrate's authorization. In making this determination, all of the circumstances—including whether the warrant application has previously been rejected by a different magistrate—may be considered." *United States v. Leon*, 468 U.S. 897, 922-23 n.23, 104 S.Ct. 3405, 3421 n.23, 82 L.Ed.2d 677, 698 n.23 (1984). The good-faith exception has been extended to protect police who acted in good-faith reliance upon a statute (subsequently found invalid) that authorized warrantless administrative searches. *Illinois v. Krull*, 480 U.S. 340, 107 S.Ct. 1160, 94 L.Ed.2d 364 (1987). See EXCLUSIONARY RULE for a list of related terms.

GOOD TIME.   The amount of time deducted from time to be served in prison on a given **sentence** and/or under **correctional agency** jurisdiction, at some point after a prisoner's admission to prison, contingent upon good behavior and/or awarded automatically by application of a statute or regulation. Application of an automatic good-time rule usually reduces the offender's maximum potential term, though in many states it reduces the minimum term and thus affects the **parole eligibility** date. Some states have no good-time provisions. Good time can be lost by misbehavior, unless awarded under a statute or regulation providing otherwise. Good time that is fixed and cannot be lost is called **vested good time**. A variety of other names are used for the various types of good time, most of which are self-explanatory: blood time; earned good time; gain time; industrial good time; mandatory good time; meritorious good time; ordinary good time; statutory good time; work time. The basic division is between good time received by automatic implementation of a rule, and good time earned by some kind of well-performed service or worthy action. See SENTENCE for a list of related terms.

GOVERN.   **1.** To rule, control, or direct; to exercise political authority. **2.** To serve as a principle, law, or precedent for. *Example*: The *Miranda* decision governs this case.

GOVERNMENT.   Section 23.0 (3) of the **Model Penal Code** defines government as "the United States, any State, county, municipality, or other political unit, or any department, agency or subdivision of any of the foregoing, or any corporation or other association carrying out the functions of government."

GOVERNMENT IN THE SUNSHINE ACT. A federal statute (5 U.S.C. §552b) that declares it to be the policy of the United States that the public is entitled to the fullest possible information about the decisionmaking processes of the federal government. The act provides for making this information known by requiring that all meetings of government agencies be open to the public unless they come within one of the specific categories exempt from public disclosure. The act recognizes that openness in government must not impair an individual's right to privacy, the ability of the government to carry out its responsibilities, or national security interests. Virtually all agencies of the federal government have issued regulations to implement the Government in the Sunshine Act, including procedures to be followed in closing meetings to the public. See PRIVACY for a list of related terms.

GOVERNOR. The chief executive of a state of the United States.

GRACE. Temporary immunity from penalties or adverse consequences. *Example:* The legislature allowed a period of grace before the new law went into effect.

GRADE. A degree or level on a scale.

GRADED OFFENSE. An offense that is divided or arranged according to levels of seriousness. The higher the grade of the offense, the more severe is the possible penalty to the offender. *Example*: In some states, arson is a graded offense. *See*: DEGREE.

GRAFT. **1.** The dishonest or unscrupulous use of one's official position to obtain profit or advantage. **2.** The unlawful obtaining of public money through corrupt transactions with public officials.

GRAND JURY. A JURY, usually of 12 to 23 persons, selected according to law and sworn, whose duty is to receive criminal **complaints**, hear the **evidence** put forth by the **prosecution**, and find **indictments** when they are satisfied that there is **probable cause** that an accused person has committed a crime and should be brought to **trial**. Grand juries may also investigate criminal activity generally and investigate the conduct of public agencies and officials. In many states all **felony** charges must be considered by a grand jury before filing in the **trial court**. Ordinarily a prosecutor presents to the grand jury for its consideration a list of charges and evidence related to a specific criminal event. The grand jury may then, after deliberation, decide to indict or not to indict. The grand jury may call witnesses and may even compel witnesses to appear or produce documents by having them served with **subpoenas**. Grand jury proceedings are kept secret for the following reasons:

—to prevent an escape from the jurisdiction of someone who is not yet in custody but whose indictment may be contemplated;

—to provide the utmost freedom for the grand jury in its deliberations and to protect jury members from outside influences;

—to prevent tampering with witnesses who may testify before the grand jury and later appear at the trial of those indicted;

—to encourage the free and unrestrained disclosure of information by persons who have information on the commission of crimes; and

—to protect innocent persons who are exonerated of charges from disclosure of the fact that they were under grand jury investigation.

A **trial jury** is distinguished from a grand jury in that a trial jury hears a case in order to render a **verdict** of **guilty** or **not guilty**. A grand jury only decides whether there is sufficient evidence to cause a person to be brought to trial for a crime. *See*: ARRAY; BILL OF INDICTMENT; BIND OVER; CHARGE; EXTRAORDINARY GRAND JURY; HURTADO v. CALIFORNIA; INDICTMENT; JURY; NO TRUE BILL; PRELIMINARY HEARING; PRESENTMENT; PROSECUTOR; PROSECUTORIAL DISCRETION; TRUE BILL.

GRAND JURY ORIGINAL.   Same as PRESENTMENT (definition 1).

GRAND LARCENY.   LARCENY in which the value of the property stolen exceeds a set statutory limit. See ABSTRACTION for a list of related terms.

GRANT OF PAROLE.   *See*: RELEASE TO PAROLE.

GRANT OF PROBATION.   Same as PROBATION ORDER.

GRAVAMEN.   The essential part of a **charge** or **accusation**; the part of a charge or accusation that weighs most heavily against the accused.

GREAT.   Unusually large; considerable; remarkable; extraordinary; significant; important.

GREAT WRIT.   *See*: HABEAS CORPUS.

GRIEVOUS.   **1.** Causing pain or sorrow. **2.** Very serious; dire; grave; atrocious; flagrant. *Example*: It was a grievous crime.

GROG SHOP.   Same as TAVERN.

GROSS.   **1.** Flagrant; glaring; shameful. *Example*: He suffered a gross injustice. **2.** Complete; whole; total.

GROSS NEGLIGENCE. *See*: NEGLIGENCE.

GROUND. Foundation; basis; reason. The grounds of an **action** are the reasons specified by law that will serve as a basis for demanding relief.

GROUP HOME. A long-term JUVENILE FACILITY in which residents are allowed extensive contact with the community, such as attending school or holding a job. Group home is defined differently in different jurisdictions. See JUVENILE for a list of related terms.

GUARDIAN. A person entrusted by law with the duty of taking care of and managing the property and affairs of a **minor** or other person who is legally **incompetent** to manage his or her own affairs.

GUARDIAN AD LITEM. A person appointed by a court to represent a **minor** or an **incompetent** person in a **lawsuit** involving that person. A guardian ad litem has authority only over matters pertaining to the lawsuit, and the responsibilities cease when the litigation concludes.

GUILLOTINE. A device consisting of a heavy blade that falls freely between two perpendicular grooved posts used for executing convicted criminals by beheading them.

GUILT. Culpability or responsibility for a crime or lesser offense.

GUILTY. Having committed a crime or lesser offense; responsible or culpable for a crime or lesser offense. *Example*: The jury found him guilty. *See*: GUILTY PLEA; GUILTY VERDICT.

GUILTY PLEA. A defendant's PLEA to the charges in a **complaint**, **information**, or **indictment**, admitting that the **charges** are true and that he or she committed the offense charged. A **plea** of **nolo contendere** has the same legal status as a guilty plea.

GUILTY VERDICT. The decision by a **jury** in a **jury trial**, or by a **judicial officer** in a **nonjury** trial, on the basis of the **evidence** presented at trial, that the defendant is **guilty** of the offense or offenses for which he or she has been tried. A guilty verdict indicates that it was concluded that the evidence offered of the defendant's guilt was sufficient to prove guilt **beyond a reasonable doubt**. In entering a **judgment**, a judicial officer may reject a jury verdict of guilty and enter a judgment of **acquittal** if legal requirements have not been satisfied. Thus a guilty verdict does not necessarily result in a judgment of **conviction**. See VERDICT for a list of related terms.

GUN. Any portable FIREARM.

HABEAS CORPUS. *Latin.* "You have the body." The name given to a variety of **writs** whose purpose is to bring a person before a **court** or **judge**. When used alone, the term habeas corpus refers to HABEAS CORPUS AD SUBJICIENDUM.

HABEAS CORPUS AD SUBJICIENDUM. The name of a HABEAS CORPUS **writ** issued by a **court** and directed to a person detaining or confining another (usually the superintendent of a **confinement facility**) commanding him or her to bring the body of the person detained before a **judicial officer** and to show cause whether the detention is legal. Article I, Section 9, Clause 2, of the U.S. Constitution provides that "[t]he privilege of the Writ of Habeas Corpus shall not be suspended, unless when in Cases of Rebellion or Invasion the public Safety may require it." The right of a person to the writ depends on the legality of the detention and not on the person's guilt or innocence. The major grounds for issuance of the writ are lack of **jurisdiction** of the court in which the prisoner was convicted and violation of the petitioner's constitutional rights. Habeas corpus is an extraordinary remedy to be used only in cases of special urgency and not when relief can be obtained by other adequate remedies, such as a **motion** for a **new trial** or an **appeal**. The writ of habeas corpus is also called the **great writ**. See ARREST WARRANT and DETENTION for a list of related terms.

HABEAS CORPUS AD TESTIFICANDUM. The name of a HABEAS CORPUS **writ** whose purpose is to bring a detained or confined person before the **court** so that he or she may give **evidence**. See ARREST WARRANT for a list of related terms.

HABIT. A constant, often unconscious, disposition or tendency to act in a certain way acquired through frequent repetition of the same act; an established condition or inclination of mind or character.

HABITANCY. A settled dwelling place; a fixed and permanent residence. **NOTE**: Habitancy has a similar meaning to **domicile** but does not necessarily carry the connotation of **legal** residence.

HABITUAL. Of the nature of a HABIT; customary; usual; constant.

HABITUAL CRIMINAL. **1.** A person sentenced under the provisions of a statute declaring that persons convicted of a given offense, and shown to have previously been convicted of another specified offense or offenses, shall receive a more severe penalty than that for the current offense alone. The exact meaning of the term varies among jurisdictions, depending on the type and number of crimes for which repeated convictions qualify the offender as habitual. *Also called*: **habitual offender**; **multiple offender**; **repeat offender**. **2.** In general, a person whose previous criminal record and lack of regular employment make him or her subject to suspicion by law enforcement authorities. See CRIME and SENTENCE for a list of related terms. *See also*: CAREER CRIMINAL; RECIDIVIST.

HABITUAL DRUNKARD.   A person who has a fixed habit of frequent excessive use of intoxicating liquor.

HABITUAL OFFENDER.   Same as HABITUAL CRIMINAL.

HALFWAY HOUSE.   A nonconfining RESIDENTIAL FACILITY for adjudicated **adults** or **juveniles**, or those detained pending criminal or juvenile proceedings, intended to provide an alternative to **confinement** for persons not suitable for **probation** or needing a period of readjustment to the community after confinement. Halfway house is defined differently in different jurisdictions.

HALLUCINATION.   An apparently real perception of objects or events through any of the senses, for which there is no external cause or stimulus; a trick of the senses. A hallucination differs from a **delusion** in that a hallucination is usually short-lived whereas a delusion may remain for a long time. *Example*: Certain drugs may cause hallucinations. *See*: DELUSION; ILLUSION.

HALLUCINOGEN.   A **drug** that induces **hallucination**. See DRUG for a list of related terms.

HANDCUFFS.   A pair of hinged, metal, braceletlike bands attached by a short chain, which can be tightened and locked around the wrists. Handcuffs are used on one or both wrists to restrain a prisoner in custody. *Also called*: **manacles**.

HAND DOWN.   To announce or release an **opinion**, **decision**, or **verdict**. *Example:* The Supreme Court will hand down its decision tomorrow.

HANDGUN.   A **firearm** that can be used with one hand.

HANDLE.   **1.** To manage; to control; to command; to direct. *Example*: Officers must learn how to handle crowds. **2.** To deal with; to have responsibility for. *Example*: The new prosecutor will handle white-collar crime cases.

HANDWRITING.   The form or style of writing that distinguishes one person's writing from that of other persons. *Example*: They called an expert on handwriting to examine the signature.

HANG. To execute a person by suspending him or her by the neck from a noose until dead.

HANGMAN. A person who executes condemned criminals by hanging (see **hang**) them.

HARASS. To annoy or trouble by repeated attacks; to disturb or irritate persistently.

HARBOR. To give refuge, shelter, or food to a person for the purpose of concealing the person from someone who has lawful **custody** over him or her.

HARD LABOR. Compulsory physical labor that is imposed along with a sentence of **incarceration** as a punishment for **crime**.

HARM. To injure; to damage; to hurt.

HARMFUL ERROR. Same as REVERSIBLE ERROR.

HARMLESS ERROR. An ERROR committed at a trial that was not prejudicial to the party assigning it, and that does not require granting of a **new trial**, setting aside of the **verdict**, or **reversal** of the **judgment**. Harmless errors are errors that were corrected during the course of the trial or that did not affect substantial rights of the defendant. The classic formulation of the test for harmless error is found in *Kotteakos v. United States,* 328 U.S. 750, 765, 66 S.Ct. 1239, 1248, 90 L.Ed. 1557, 1566-67 (1946): "If one cannot say with fair assurance, after pondering all that happened without stripping the erroneous action from the whole, that the judgment was not substantially swayed by the error, it is impossible to conclude that substantial rights were not affected." See ERROR for a list of related terms.

Hh

HAZARD. A danger; a peril; a risk.

HEADNOTE. Same as SYLLABUS (definition 1).

HEARING. A proceeding in which **arguments**, **witnesses**, or **evidence** are heard by a **judicial officer** or administrative body. In the broadest usage, hearing refers to anything taking place before a judicial or quasi-judicial body exercising decisionmaking powers, in formal or informal circumstances, and including both adversary and nonadversary proceedings. A **trial** is technically a type of hearing, but is rarely referred to as such in criminal proceedings. *See:* ADJUDICATORY HEARING; ARRAIGNMENT; DETENTION HEARING; DISPOSITION HEARING; FAIR HEARING; FULL HEARING; INITIAL APPEARANCE; PAROLE REVOCATION; PRELIMINARY HEARING; PRETRIAL CONFERENCE; PROBATION REVOCATION; REHEARING; REVOCATION HEARING; SENTENCING HEARING; SUPPRESSION HEARING; TRANSFER HEARING; TRIAL; VOIR DIRE; WITNESS.

HEARING OFFICER. *See*: JUDICIAL OFFICER.

HEARSAY EVIDENCE. Evidence of a statement made other than by a **witness** testifying at a **trial** or **hearing** offered to prove the truth of the matter asserted. The statement may be oral or written or may be nonverbal conduct intended as a substitute for words. *Also called*: **secondhand evidence**. *See*: EVIDENCE; HEARSAY RULE.

HEARSAY RULE. The hearsay rule, simply stated, is that **hearsay evidence** is inadmissible. The basis of the hearsay rule is that the **credibility** of the person making a statement is the most important factor in determining the truth of the statement. If a statement is made out of court, there is no opportunity to **cross-examine** the person making the statement or to observe the person's **demeanor**. Without these methods of determining the truth of the statement, the statement may not be admitted into evidence. Many exceptions to the hearsay rule allow the admission of hearsay evidence for various reasons of trustworthiness of the evidence and practical necessity. Some of the exceptions are defined in this dictionary under the following entries: BUSINESS RECORDS EXCEPTION; DECLARATION AGAINST INTEREST; DYING DECLARATION; PAST RECOLLECTION RECORDED; PREVIOUSLY RECORDED TESTIMONY; RES GESTAE; SPONTANEOUS DECLARATION; STATE OF MIND EXCEPTION. *See*: EVIDENCE; HEARSAY EVIDENCE; PERSONAL KNOWLEDGE; UNAVAILABLE.

HEAT OF PASSION. Anger, rage, hatred, resentment, fear, or desperation so extreme that a person's actions are governed by emotional passion rather than reason. A **homicide**, otherwise **murder**, may be reduced to **voluntary manslaughter** if committed in a sudden heat of passion upon **adequate provocation** and if there was no opportunity for the accused to "cool off" or regain self-control during the period between the provocation and the killing. See HOMICIDE for a list of related terms.

HEEDLESS. Careless; unmindful; paying little or no attention. Heedless is almost as strong a word as **reckless** and implies indifference to the rights of others.

HENCEFORTH. From now on; from this time forth.

HEREAFTER. After this in time or order; immediately following; at a future time. *Example*: The legislature enacted the statute, which will be stated hereafter.

HEREBY. By or through this act, decree, or document; by means of this.

HEREIN. In this; into this.

HERETO. To this place, matter, proposition, or document. *Example*: Attached hereto are the affidavits.

HERETOFORE.   Before this time; previously; formerly.

HEREWITH.   **1.** Along with this. **2.** By means of this.

HESTER v. UNITED STATES.   *See*: OPEN FIELDS.

HIGH.   Exalted in rank, character, or quality; of great importance, magnitude, or seriousness; occupying a position of superiority.

HIGH CRIMES AND MISDEMEANORS.   *See*: SERIOUS MISDEMEANOR.

HIGHJACKING.   Same as HIJACKING.

HIGH MISDEMEANOR.   *See*: SERIOUS MISDEMEANOR.

HIGHWAY PATROL.   *See*: STATE HIGHWAY PATROL.

HIJACKING.   Taking control of a vehicle by the use or threatened use of **force** or by intimidation; or, taking a vehicle by stealth, without the use or threatened use of force, in order to steal its cargo. Hijacking is a popular name for behavior that can constitute any of several statutory offenses. Where an occupant of the vehicle is forced to accompany the perpetrator, the chargeable offense can be **kidnapping** or **false imprisonment**. Where a vehicle is taken by force with intent to permanently deprive the owner of the vehicle or any of its parts or contents, the chargeable offense can be **robbery**. Where a vehicle is taken by stealth, the chargeable offense is usually **larceny**.

HIT AND RUN.   Unlawful departure by the vehicle operator from the scene of a motor vehicle accident that resulted in death or injury to a person or damage to the property of another without providing identification or other information required by statute. This behavior is clearly prohibited in almost all states. *Also called*: **leaving the scene of an accident**.

HITHERTO.   Up to this time; until now.

HOC.   *Latin*. "This."

HOLD.   **1.** To decide; to state the ruling of the **court** on a point of law. *Example*: The court held that the arrest was illegal. **2.** To bind; to restrain; to maintain custody or control over. *Example*: The officer held him until help arrived. **3.** To conduct; to carry on; to preside over. *Example*: The judge will hold court tomorrow morning. **4.** To be in possession of; to occupy; to have. *Example*: He holds the office of chief justice.

HOLDING.   The legal principle derived from a **decision** of a **court** resolving an **issue** in a **case**. The holding of a case is relied upon when the case is used as an established **precedent** in deciding a subsequent case. *See*: DICTUM.

HOME.   A settled dwelling place; a permanent residence; the house or place where one regularly lives with his or her family and eats, sleeps, and relaxes.

HOMESTEAD.   A dwelling house with its adjoining buildings and land.

HOMICIDE.   The killing of one human being by another. Homicide is a necessary element of **murder** and **manslaughter**. It is not necessarily a **crime**, however, since homicide may be committed in **self-defense**, in execution of a judicial **sentence**, or in other circumstances excusing or justifying it. *See*: ACCIDENTAL HOMICIDE; ADEQUATE PROVOCATION; COOL BLOOD; COOLING TIME; CRIMINAL HOMICIDE; DEATH; EXCUSABLE HOMICIDE; FELONIOUS HOMICIDE; FELONY-MURDER RULE; HEAT OF PASSION; HOMICIDE BY MISAD-VENTURE; INNOCENT HOMICIDE; INVOLUNTARY MANSLAUGHTER; JUSTIFIABLE HOMICIDE; MANSLAUGHTER; MURDER; NEGLIGENT MANSLAUGHTER; UNINTENTIONAL HOMICIDE; VEHICULAR MAN-SLAUGHTER; VOLUNTARY MANSLAUGHTER; WILLFUL HOMICIDE.

HOMICIDE BY MISADVENTURE.   A type of **excusable homicide** in which a person, doing a lawful act and taking proper precautions to avoid danger to others, unintentionally kills another person. See HOMICIDE for a list of related terms.

HOMOSEXUAL.   A person who has sexual desire for or attraction to other persons of the same sex.

HONOR.   A title of courtesy used in addressing **judges** and other high officials. *Example*: May it please the court, your honor.

HONOR FARM.   *See*: COUNTY FARM.

HORNBOOK.   A book explaining the rudiments or fundamental principles of a particular subject.

HOSTAGE.   A person taken or held by a person or group in order to force a government, a community, or a person to meet certain conditions such as the payment of ransom, the release of prisoners, or some other act. "[T]he term hostage ... implies the unlawful taking, restraining or confining of a person with the intent that the person, or victim, be held as security for the performance, or forbearance, of some act by a third person." *State v. Crump,* 484 P.2d 329, 334-35 (N.M. 1971).

HOSTILE WITNESS.   Same as ADVERSE WITNESS.

HOT PURSUIT. The immediate pursuit by a **law enforcement officer** of a person into a **house** (definition 2) or other **constitutionally protected area** in response to an **emergency**. Examples of emergencies that will justify a hot pursuit are **escape** of a fleeing **felon** or other dangerous person, avoidance of **arrest** by a person suspected of a crime, and prevention of the destruction or concealment of **evidence**. Once inside the house or other constitutionally protected area, officers may **search** the premises if necessary to alleviate the emergency and any items of evidence observed lying open to view may be legally seized under the **plain view doctrine**. *Warden v. Hayden*, 387 U.S. 294, 87 S.Ct. 1642, 18 L.Ed.2d 782 (1967). *See:* FRESH PURSUIT; SEARCH.

HOUSE. **1.** A building designed for human habitation. **2.** For the meaning of house under the Fourth Amendment, see CURTILAGE. *See also:* HOUSE OF ILL FAME; HOUSE OF PROSTITUTION; HOUSE OF REPRESENTATIVES.

HOUSEBREAKING. BREAKING AND ENTERING a **dwelling house** with intent to commit a **felony** therein. When committed at night, this offense is **burglary**. State statutes have modified the meaning of housebreaking and have used other terms to describe the prohibited conduct.

HOUSEHOLD BURGLARY. The unlawful or forcible **entry** or attempted forcible entry of a residence, usually but not necessarily, attended by theft.

HOUSEHOLD CRIMES. A category used in some crime classification schemes to include crimes such as **household burglary**, **household larceny**, and **motor vehicle theft**. See CRIME for a list of related terms.

HOUSEHOLD LARCENY. The **theft** of money or property from a residence or its immediate vicinity. Thefts or attempted thefts from residences that are accompanied by unlawful or forcible **entry** of the residence are classified as **household burglary**.

Hh

HOUSE OF ILL FAME. A house or building in which **prostitution, gambling**, or other illegal or **disorderly conduct** is carried on.

HOUSE OF PROSTITUTION. Section 251.2 (1) of the **Model Penal Code** defines a house of prostitution as "any place where **prostitution** or **promotion of prostitution** is regularly carried on by one person under the control, management or supervision or another." *Also called:* **assignation house; bawdyhouse; brothel; lewd house**. See SEX OFFENSES for a list of related terms.

HOUSE OF REPRESENTATIVES. The lower and more numerous branch of the legislature of the United States and of many states and other nations. *See:* CONGRESS OF THE UNITED STATES.

HUE AND CRY. In earlier times, the pursuit of a **felon** announced by a loud outcry to alert others, who were then legally bound to join in the chase.

HUNG JURY. A **jury** whose members, after long deliberation, are so irreconcilably divided in opinion that they are unable to agree upon any **verdict**. The existence of a hung jury can result in the termination of a **trial** before verdict and **judgment**, when the court is satisfied that the jury is unlikely to agree upon a verdict within any reasonable period of time. Termination of a trial because of a hung jury usually results in a **retrial** on the original charges. The subsequent trial does not constitute a violation of the constitutional prohibition of **double jeopardy**. Occasionally a hung jury is followed by a **dismissal** of the charges. In some jurisdictions, the judicial determination that a hung jury exists is grounds for declaring a **mistrial**. See JURY for a list of related terms.

HURTADO v. CALIFORNIA. A U.S. Supreme Court decision that held that the Fourteenth Amendment guarantee of **due process of law** does not mandate that states comply with the Fifth Amendment provision that a criminal **prosecution** be initiated by an **indictment** by a **grand jury**. The citation for the *Hurtado* case is 110 U.S. 516, 4 S.Ct. 111, 28 L.Ed. 232 (1884). See GRAND JURY for a list of related terms.

HYPOTHESIS. A proposition stated or assumed (without regard to whether it is factual) as a basis for argument or reasoning; a supposition; an assumption. See FACT for a list of related terms.

HYPOTHETICAL QUESTION. A question, proposed to an **expert witness** in a trial, consisting of a mixture of assumed and established facts followed by a request for an **opinion** based on those facts. See FACT for a list of related terms.

IBID. Abbreviation for IBIDEM.

IBIDEM. *Latin*. In the same place; in the same book, chapter, article, or page.

ID. Abbreviation for IDEM.

IDEM. *Latin*. "The same"; the same as previously mentioned. Idem is used primarily in footnotes to indicate a reference previously mentioned.

IDEM SONANS. *Latin*. "Sounding the same." The doctrine of idem sonans states that names that have the same sound are the same for practical purposes. Thus, absolute accuracy in spelling is not required in legal documents or proceedings. If a name, though incorrectly spelled, sounds like the correctly spelled name when pronounced, according to commonly accepted methods, the incorrectly spelled name is a sufficient identification of the person referred to.

IDENTICAL. Exactly the same as another for all practical purposes. *See*: ALIKE.

IDENTIFICATION. **1.** The act or process of identifying (see **identify**). *Example*: The lineup is a reliable method of pretrial identification of suspected criminals. *See*: CONFRONTATION; EYEWITNESS IDENTIFICATION; LINEUP; SHOWUP. **2.** Something that identifies a person or thing. *Example*: The officer asked him for identification and he showed him his driver's license.

IDENTIFY. To establish that a person or thing is the same that he, she, or it is alleged or reputed to be. *Example*: The woman identified him as the robber.

IDENTITY. **1.** Who a person is or what a thing is. *Example*: The police were unable to establish the identity of the person making the obscene calls. **2.** Essential sameness; the fact that a person or thing is the same that he, she, or it is claimed to be. *Example*: The officer established his identity as the man who shot at him.

IDEO. *Latin*. "Therefore."

ID EST. *Latin*. "That is"; that is to say. Id est is used to introduce an explanation of a word or phrase. *Abbreviation*: **i.e.**

I.E. Abbreviation for ID EST.

IGNORAMUS. Same as NO TRUE BILL.

IGNORANCE. Lack of information; absence of knowledge. Ignorance does not refer to the soundness or the mental condition of the mind. *Example*: Ignorance of the law is no excuse. *See*: ERROR; INSANITY.

IGNORANTIA LEGIS NON EXCUSAT. *Latin.* "Ignorance of the law is no excuse." The legal principle that a defendant's ignorance that his or her act was against the law does not prevent the law from punishing the prohibited act.

IGNORE. **1.** To refuse to notice or recognize; to willfully disregard. *Example*: She ignored the warnings she received. **2.** To reject as unsupported or as having insufficient evidence. *Example*: The grand jury ignored the bill of indictment.

ILLEGAL. Not LEGAL.

ILLEGITIMATE. Not LEGITIMATE.

ILL FAME. Bad reputation; notorious bad character. *See*: HOUSE OF ILL FAME.

ILLICIT. Not LICIT; prohibited; proscribed by law.

ILLICIT CONNECTION. Unlawful **sexual intercourse**.

ILLINOIS v. GATES. A U.S. Supreme Court decision holding that a magistrate's determination of probable cause for issuance of a warrant must be based on a practical, commonsense evaluation of the totality of the circumstances set forth in the affidavit. This "totality of the circumstances" test abandoned an approach to determining probable cause through the use of informants that had been established by two previous Supreme Court decisions, *Aguilar v. Texas*, 378 U.S. 108, 84 S.Ct. 1509, 12 L.Ed.2d 723 (1964), and *Spinelli v. U.S.*, 393 U.S. 410, 89 S.Ct. 584, 21 L.Ed.2d 637 (1969). The *Aguilar* and *Spinelli* cases set out a two-pronged test for determining probable cause when the information in an affidavit was either entirely or partially obtained from an informant.

Prong 1—Informant's Basis of Knowledge—The affidavit must describe underlying circumstances from which a neutral and detached magistrate may determine that the informant had a sufficient basis for his or her knowledge and that the information was not the result of mere rumor or suspicion.

Prong 2—Informant's Veracity—The affidavit must describe underlying circumstances from which the magistrate may determine that the informant was credible or that the informant's information was reliable.

In abandoning rigid adherence to the *Aguilar-Spinelli* test, the Court said that the two prongs should be understood as "relevant considerations in the totality of circumstances that traditionally has guided probable cause determinations: a deficiency in one may be compensated for, in determining the overall reliability of a tip by a strong showing as to the other, or by some other indicia of reliability." 462 U.S. at 233, 103 S.Ct. at 2329, 76 L.Ed.2d at 545. The entire process of determining probable cause could, therefore, be simplified as follows.

"The task of the issuing magistrate is simply to make a practical, commonsense decision whether, given all the circumstances set forth in the affidavit before him, including the "veracity" and "basis of knowledge" of persons supplying hearsay information, there is a fair probability that contraband or evidence of a crime will be found in a particular place. And the duty of a reviewing court is simply to ensure that the magistrate had a 'substantial basis for . . . conclud[ing]' that probable cause existed." 462 U.S. at 238-39, 103 S.Ct. at 2332, 76 L.Ed.2d at 548.

See: PROBABLE CAUSE.

ILLITERATE. Unable to read and write.

ILLUSION. A false image or impression of something real caused by the distortion of the real thing in the mind or imagination of the observer. *Example*: He had an illusion that the police officer was an enemy soldier. *See*: DELUSION; HALLUCINATION.

ILLUSORY. Deceptive; of the nature of an ILLUSION.

IMMATERIAL. Not MATERIAL; not essential; not important; insignificant. *Example*: Immaterial evidence is evidence with little probative value.

IMMEDIATE. 1. Without delay; instant; done at once. *Example*: We received an immediate reply. **2.** Having no object, space, time, or agent intervening; close at hand; nearest. *Example*: The rescue party searched the immediate neighborhood.

IMMEDIATE CAUSE. The cause nearest in time and space to a particular result; the last in a series or chain of causes that produces a particular result.

IMMIGRATION AND NATURALIZATION SERVICE. The Immigration and Naturalization Service, in the **Department of Justice**, was created by act of March 3, 1891 (8 U.S.C. §1551 note), and its purpose and responsibilities were further specified by the Immigration and Nationality Act, as amended (8 U.S.C. §1101 note), which charges the **Attorney General** with the administration and enforcement of its provisions. Unique to the service is the dual mission of providing information and service to the general public, while concurrently exercising its enforcement responsibilities. Its mission is divided into five major areas of responsibility:

—facilitating the entry of persons legally admissible as visitors or as immigrants to the United States;

—granting benefits under the Immigration and Nationality Act, as amended, including providing assistance to those seeking permanent resident status or naturalization;

—preventing unlawful entry, employment, or receipt of benefits by those who are not entitled to them;

—apprehending or removing those aliens who enter or remain illegally in the United States and/or whose stay is not in the public interest; and

—strengthening criminal investigations and seeking the most effective deterrents to illegal immigration.

IMMINENT. Likely to occur at any moment; impending; near at hand.

IMMINENT DANGER. In the law relating to justifiable use of **force**, an impending danger that must be met immediately and cannot be prevented by calling for help or for the protection of the law.

IMMOVABLE PROPERTY. Under Section 223.0 (4) of the **Model Penal Code** immovable property is all property that is not **movable property**.

IMMUNITY. An exemption from duty, service, jurisdiction, or liability that is required of or imposed upon others similarly situated; a special privilege. *See*: WITNESS IMMUNITY.

IMPAIR. To diminish in value, quantity, or quality; to make worse; to weaken.

IMPANEL. To make up a list of the **jurors** who have been selected for the trial of a particular case. Impanel is also used to refer to the entire process of determining who will be the proper jurors to sit at the trial of a particular case.

IMPARTIAL. Not favoring one party over another; unprejudiced; disinterested; equitable. The U.S. Supreme Court said: "Impartiality is not a technical conception. It is a state of mind. For the ascertainment of this mental attitude of appropriate indifference, the Constitution lays down no particular tests and procedure is not chained to any ancient and artificial formula." *U.S. v. Wood*, 299 U.S. 123, 145-46, 57 S.Ct. 177, 185, 81 L.Ed. 78, 88 (1936).

IMPARTIAL JURY. A **jury** in which all members are fair, unprejudiced, and disinterested at the beginning of the **trial** and which bases its **verdict** only on legally admissible **evidence** introduced at the trial connecting the **defendant** with the **crime** charged. The Sixth Amendment to the U.S. Constitution provides that "[i]n all criminal prosecutions, the accused shall enjoy the right to a speedy and public trial, by an impartial jury of the State and district wherein the crime shall have been committed. . . ." *Also called*: **fair and impartial jury**. See JURY for a list of related terms.

IMPEACH. **1.** To show that a witness is unworthy of belief; to attack the credibility of a witness. A witness can be impeached through **prior inconsistent statements**, **bias**, **character evidence**, or contradiction of facts. See WITNESS for a list of related terms. **2.** To bring **charges** against a public official for **crimes** or improper conduct in office by means of a written **accusation**, called articles of impeachment, presented to a proper tribunal.

IMPEDE. **v.** To obstruct; to hinder; to stand in the way of. **n.** IMPEDIMENT.

IMPEDIMENT. *See*: IMPEDE.

IMPERATIVE. Expressing a command; demanding obedience or action; mandatory; urgent.

IMPERSONATION. *See*: FALSE IMPERSONATION.

IMPERTINENT. Not PERTINENT; irrelevant.

IMPLICATE. **1.** To involve in a matter or affair. *Example*: They were implicated in a conspiracy. **2.** To IMPLY.

IMPLICATION. **1.** Something suggested or inferred without being expressly stated. **2.** *See*: IMPLICATE. **3.** A resulting condition. *Example*: Consider the implications of your actions.

IMPLIED. Not clearly expressed, but inferred or suggested by the circumstances, general language, or conduct of the persons involved. *See*: EXPRESS.

Ii

IMPLIED AGENCY. An AGENCY in which the AGENT has IMPLIED AUTHOR-ITY to act for or represent the PRINCIPAL. *See*: ACTUAL AGENCY.

IMPLIED AUTHORITY. AUTHORITY (definition 1) not expressly conferred by a PRINCIPAL upon an AGENT but arising out of the language and course of conduct of the principal toward the agent. Implied authority is a type of **actual authority**.

IMPLIED CONSENT. CONSENT not expressly given but inferred from words, actions, or circumstances or created by law.

IMPLIED CONSENT LAW. A law in most states stating that any person who operates or attempts to operate a **motor vehicle** within that state is deemed to have given CONSENT to a chemical test to determine the concentration of alcohol in his or her blood by analysis of his or her blood or breath, if **arrested** for operating or attempting to operate a motor vehicle while under the influence of intoxicating liquor. The wording of the law varies in different states. *See*: DRIVING UNDER THE INFLUENCE OF ALCOHOL.

IMPLIED MALICE.   *See*: MALICE.

IMPLIED NOTICE.   NOTICE of a main fact attributed or charged to a person, because he or she has actual knowledge of collateral facts that is sufficient to create a duty to inquire, and because a reasonable inquiry would inevitably lead to discovery of the main fact. *Also called*: **presumptive notice; record notice**. See NOTICE for a list of related terms.

IMPLY.   To suggest indirectly by language, conduct, or circumstances without stating directly. See ADDRESS for a list of related terms.

IMPOSE.   **v.** To set or announce a penalty; to levy; to assess; to lay upon. *Example*: The court imposed a fine on him. **n.** IMPOSITION. *See*: EXECUTE.

IMPOSITION.   *See*: IMPOSE.

IMPOUND.   To take a vehicle, document, or other object into the custody of the **law** or of a **court** or **law enforcement agency** for safekeeping or examination. The U.S. Supreme Court approved the impounding of motor vehicles under certain circumstances in *South Dakota v. Opperman*.

> "In the interests of public safety and as part of what the Court has called 'community caretaking functions,' automobiles are frequently taken into police custody. Vehicle accidents present one such occasion. To permit the uninterrupted flow of traffic and in some circumstances to preserve evidence, disabled or damaged vehicles will often be removed from the highways or streets at the behest of police engaged solely in caretaking and traffic-control activities. Police will also frequently remove and impound automobiles which violate parking ordinances and which thereby jeopardize both the public safety and the efficient movement of vehicular traffic. The authority of police to seize and remove from the streets vehicles impeding traffic or threatening public safety and convenience is beyond challenge." 428 U.S. 364, 368-69, 96 S.Ct. 3092, 3097, 49 L.Ed.2d 1000, 1005 (1976).

See: INVENTORY SEARCH.

IMPRACTICABLE.   Incapable of being performed or accomplished.

IMPRESSION, FIRST.   *See*: FIRST IMPRESSION.

IMPRISON. **1.** To put in a **prison** or place of **confinement**; to INCARCERATE. **2.** To restrain a person's freedom of movement in any way. **n.** IMPRISONMENT. *See*: FALSE IMPRISONMENT.

IMPRISONMENT. *See*: IMPRISON.

IMPROPER. **1.** Not PROPER; unsuitable; inappropriate. **2.** Abnormal; irregular; inaccurate; erroneous.

IMPULSE. A sudden, involuntary inclination to act without premeditation or reflection; a sudden desire, urge, or drive. *See*: IRRESISTIBLE IMPULSE.

IMPUNITY. Exemption from punishment or penalty.

IMPUTE. **1.** To charge, ascribe, or attribute something discreditable or disadvantageous to another. **2.** To impose, ascribe, or attribute something (e.g., knowledge, notice, or negligence) to a person not because of that person's acts or omissions, but because of the acts or omissions of another for whom the person is responsible.

IMPUTED KNOWLEDGE. **1.** Same as IMPLIED NOTICE. **2.** Knowledge attributed or charged to one person because of his or her relationship to another person. For example, knowledge of certain facts by an **agent** may be attributed or charged to the **principal** if the agent had a duty to report the facts to the principal.

INACTIVE SUPERVISION. *See*: SUPERVISED PROBATION.

INADEQUATE. Not ADEQUATE.

INADMISSIBLE. Not ADMISSIBLE.

INADVERTENT. **1.** Inattentive; heedless; careless. **2.** Unintentional. **3.** Unanticipated; unplanned; unforeseen. *See*: PLAIN VIEW DOCTRINE.

INALIENABLE. Unable to be given up, taken away, or transferred to another. *Example*: We have certain inalienable rights. *Also called*: **unalienable**.

IN BANC. Same as EN BANC.

IN BANK. Same as EN BANC.

IN CAMERA. *Latin*. "In chambers." **1.** In a judge's private room or office. **2.** In a courtroom with all spectators excluded.

Ii

INCAPACITY. Legal disqualification; legal inability to act; prevention by some impediment from exercising a legal right. *Example*: The contract was void because of the child's incapacity to enter into contracts. *See*: CAPACITY.

INCARCERATION. The placing or confining of a person in a **jail** or **prison** under authority of **law**. Incarceration differs from **imprisonment** in that incarceration usually means actually putting a person in a public **confinement facility** according to the procedures of the criminal law, whereas imprisonment may mean to restrain a person's freedom of movement in any way. Also imprisonment does not necessarily imply any legal authority. Incarceration is a more specific term than **confinement** in that incarceration usually means confinement in a jail or prison, not confinement in a **prearraignment lockup**, hospital, or other facility not intended for the serving of sentences.

INCENDIARY. **adj.** Causing or capable of causing fire. *Example*: The rioters threw incendiary bombs. **n.** A person who willfully and maliciously sets fire to a building or other property.

INCEPTION. Beginning; commencement; opening.

INCEST. Unlawful **sexual intercourse** between closely related persons of the opposite sex. Typically, intercourse is prohibited between children and parents, between children and grandparents, between siblings, between half-siblings, and sometimes between aunt and nephew or uncle and niece as well. Frequently the prohibitions are extended to persons related by adoption in addition to those related by blood. See SEX OFFENSES for a list of related terms.

IN CHIEF. Principle; primary. *See*: EXAMINATION IN CHIEF.

INCHOATE. In an early stage; begun but not completed; unfinished; partial; imperfect.

INCHOATE OFFENSE. An offense consisting of an action or conduct that is a step to the intended commission of another offense. Many state penal codes have a chapter entitled "Inchoate Offenses." The criminality of the behavior constituting an inchoate offense arises from the presence of the **intent** to proceed to completion of a **crime**. In some cases, when the intended crime is completed, the inchoate offense may also be charged. But the chief purpose of codification of inchoate offenses is to provide for punishment for criminal behavior that does not accomplish a final criminal purpose. The penalties for inchoate offenses usually depend upon the gravity of the intended crime. *Also called*: **anticipatory offense**. Offenses typically listed under the heading of inchoate offenses are: ATTEMPT; CONSPIRACY; CRIM-INAL FACILITATION; SOLICITATION; THREAT.

INCIDENT. **adj.** Contingent upon or related to some principle thing or event, but subordinate to it. *Example*: The officer conducted a search incident to the arrest. **n.** A relatively minor event, happening, or occurrence.

INCIDENTAL. Casually related to or dependent upon another thing or event, but secondary and nonessential to it. *Example*: We were not charged for incidental expenses incurred in transporting the prisoner.

INCINERATE. To consume by fire; to burn to ashes.

INCISION. A cut; a gash.

INCITE. To stir up; to urge on; to spur on; to provoke to action.

INCITING TO RIOT. The attempt by any person to cause other persons to engage in conduct that would constitute a RIOT. See AFFRAY for a list of related terms.

INCLUDE. To have or contain as a part or member of a whole. Include usually implies that not all the items of the whole are stated. *Example*: The term felony includes crimes such as murder, rape, and arson.

INCLUDED OFFENSE. An offense made up of **elements** that are a subset of the elements of another offense having a greater statutory penalty, and the occurrence of which is established by the same **evidence** or by some portion of the evidence that has been offered to establish the occurrence of the greater offense. The **charge** of which a defendant is convicted will often not be the same as the charge made in the **charging document** that initiates criminal proceedings. This type of alteration of charges, however, occurs within strict limitations with respect to a given case. The convicted offense must be an included offense to the original charge or a **reduced charge** that has a logical relation to the evidence of criminal behavior brought forth in connection with the original charge.

Section 1.07 (4) of the **Model Penal Code** provides:

"(4) <u>Conviction of Included Offense Permitted.</u> A defendant may be convicted of an offense included in an offense charged in the indictment [or the information]. An offense is so included when:

(a) it is established by proof of the same or less than all the facts required to establish the commission of the offense charged; or

(b) it consists of an attempt or solicitation to commit the offense charged or to commit an offense otherwise included therein; or

(c) it differs from the offense charged only in the respect that a less serious injury or risk of injury to the same person, property or public interest or a lesser kind of culpability suffices to establish its commission.

In many jurisdictions it is standard practice for the prosecutor to separately charge all lesser included offenses. However, a person can be found guilty of a lesser included offense even if not specifically charged with it, in any instance where the **judge** so decides in a **nonjury trial** or **instructs** the **jury** as to the possibility in a **jury trial**. When a person is convicted of an included offense in lieu of conviction of the greater offense, it is sometimes said that he or she was convicted of a reduced charge. However, a reduced charge is the result of an optional step in criminal proceedings and is not technically the same as an included offense. *Also called*: **lesser included offense**. *See*: DIVISIBLE OFFENSE; MERGER.

INCOGNITO. With one's identity concealed; in disguise; under an assumed name or character.

INCOMPATIBLE. Not COMPATIBLE.

INCOMPETENT. Not COMPETENT.

INCOMPETENT EVIDENCE. **Evidence** that is not COMPETENT EVIDENCE.

INCOMPETENT TO BE EXECUTED. A person is incompetent to be executed if, as the result of a mental disease or defect, he or she lacks sufficient ability to understand the nature of and reasons for the **conviction** and **execution**. The person may not be executed until he or she recovers from the condition.

INCOMPETENT TO STAND TRIAL. A person is incompetent to stand trial if, as the result of a mental disease or defect, the person (1) lacks sufficient ability to rationally consult with his or her lawyer and provide the lawyer with information to assist in the **defense**; or (2) lacks sufficient ability to understand the significance of the proceedings against him or her and the person's relationship to the proceedings. When a court finds that a given defendant is incompetent to stand trial, criminal proceedings against that defendant are suspended until such time as the defendant may be found competent. Frequently, the court will order periodic examination of the defendant to determine whether competency has been regained. A person declared incompetent to stand trial may be committed to a mental institution (see **civil commitment**) and may not be tried, convicted, or sentenced until he or she recovers.

A plea or finding that a defendant is **not guilty by reason of insanity** differs from a finding that a defendant is incompetent to stand trial. The former is a **defense** to **prosecution** on the grounds that the defendant was mentally incompetent at the time that an alleged crime was committed. The latter concerns only the defendant's mental fitness at the time of **trial**, and is not related to any determination of **guilt**. *See*: CAPACITY.

INCONCLUSIVE. Not CONCLUSIVE.

INCONSISTENT.   Not CONSISTENT; contradictory; incompatible.

INCONTINENT.   Unable to hold back; lacking in self-control.

INCONTROVERTIBLE.   Unquestionable; indisputable.

INCONVENIENT.   Not CONVENIENT; disadvantageous; awkward; troublesome; inopportune.

INCORPORATION BY REFERENCE.   The method of making one **document** become part of another separate document by specifically referring to the former document in the latter and stating that the former shall be considered as part of the latter as if it were completely set out in the latter.

INCORPOREAL.   **1.** Not CORPOREAL; intangible. **2.** Lacking material substance but existing in contemplation of the law. Examples of incorporeal things are a right, an intent, a presumption, and a status.

INCORRIGIBLE.   So firmly fixed in evil ways as to be incapable of being corrected or rehabilitated. *Example*: Hardened criminals who repeatedly violate the law are sometimes referred to as incorrigible.

INCRIMINATE.   **1.** To show or tend to show **guilt** of a **crime**; to expose to an **accusation** of crime. **2.** To charge with a crime. See CRIME for a list of related terms.

INCRIMINATING ADMISSION.   A statement of facts by a person tending to show that the person committed or is committing a **crime**. *Also called*: **incriminatory statement**.

INCRIMINATING CIRCUMSTANCE.   A fact or circumstance that tends to show either that a **crime** was committed or that a particular person committed it. See CRIME and FACT for lists of related terms.

INCRIMINATORY STATEMENT.   Same as INCRIMINATING ADMISSION.

INCULPATORY.   Tending to show **guilt** or blame; incriminating.

INCUMBENT.   A person who presently holds an **office** and who is legally authorized to discharge the duties of the office.

INCUR.   **1.** To bring upon oneself; to become liable to or subject to through one's own action. *Example*: The poorly prepared officer incurred the displeasure of the judge. **2.** To meet with; to run into; to come upon.

INDECENT. Offensive to public morals, modesty, or propriety; unbecoming. Like **obscene**, indecent eludes a precise meaning.

INDECENT ASSAULT. Lewd, obscene, or indecent sexual conduct toward another person causing fear, shame, humiliation, or mental anguish. Indecent assault may be committed without carnal knowledge and without intent to commit **rape**. The conduct must be such as the common sense of society would regard as indecent and improper, but need not involve the private parts of the person assaulted and need not involve direct physical contact. *Also called*: **indecent liberties**. See ASSAULT and SEX OFFENSES for lists of related terms.

INDECENT EXPOSURE. Unlawful, intentional, knowing, or reckless exposing to view of the **genitals** or **anus**, in a place where another person may be present who is likely to be offended or alarmed by such an act. In most jurisdictions, an offense will only be charged against a person who is above a certain age or who has attained a certain degree of physical development. In some states, an age limit for the offense is established by statute. Some statutes specify that the act must be performed in a "lewd or lascivious" manner. See SEX OFFENSES for a list of related terms.

INDECENT LIBERTIES. Same as INDECENT ASSAULT.

INDEFEASIBLE. Unable to be destroyed, revoked, or defeated.

INDEFINITE SENTENCE. Same as INDETERMINATE SENTENCE.

IN DELICTO. *Latin*. In or at fault.

INDEPENDENT SOURCE. An exception to the FRUIT OF THE POISONOUS TREE DOCTRINE that allows the admission of **tainted evidence** if that evidence was also obtained through a source wholly independent of the primary constitutional violation. The independent source exception is compatible with the underlying rationale of the **exclusionary rule**: the deterrence of police misconduct. As stated by the U.S. Supreme Court, "The independent source doctrine teaches us that the interest of society in deterring unlawful police conduct and the public interest in having juries receive all probative evidence of a crime are properly balanced by putting the police in the same, not a *worse*, position than they would have been in if no police error or misconduct had occurred." *Nix v. Williams*, 467 U.S. 431, 443, 104 S.Ct. 2501, 2509, 81 L.Ed.2d 377, 387 (1984). See EXCLUSIONARY RULE for a list of related terms.

INDETERMINATE SENTENCE. A type of SENTENCE to **incarceration** where the commitment, instead of being for a specified single time quantity, such as three years, is for a range of time, such as two to five years, or five years maximum and zero minimum. Generally, a **paroling authority** determines, within limits set by the sentencing **judge** or by **statute**, the exact date of **release** from prison and of termination of correctional jurisdiction. The duration of the sentence is determined by consideration of the previous record of the convicted person, his or her behavior while in prison or while out on **parole**, the apparent prospect of reformation, and other such matters. There are as many patterns of time limits, rules automatically modifying time limits, and rules endowing different authorities with different amounts or types of discretion to alter **time served** in confinement and under correctional jurisdiction, as there are states. Also, some states permit different types of sentence structures to be applied to different offenders or offenses within the same jurisdiction. *Also called*: **indefinite sentence**. See SENTENCE for a list of related terms.

INDEX CRIMES. *See*: CRIME INDEX; UNIFORM CRIME REPORTING.

INDICIA. Facts that give rise to **inferences**; indications, signs, or circumstances that tend to support the probability of a fact but do not prove it to a certainty. *Example*: Some of the indicia of arrest are the use of force, the display of weapons, and the presence of a large number of police officers. See FACT for a list of related terms.

INDICTABLE MISDEMEANOR. *See*: SERIOUS MISDEMEANOR.

INDICTMENT. A formal written **accusation** submitted by a **grand jury** to a **court**, alleging that a specified person has committed a specific offense. An indictment, like an **information**, is usually used to initiate a **felony prosecution**. In some jurisdictions, all felony accusations must be by indictment, but in others felony trials will ordinarily be initiated by the filing of an information by a **prosecutor**. Ordinarily, the prosecutor presents allegations and evidence (often called a **bill of indictment**) to the grand jury, which endorses on it "a **true bill**" if it decides that there is sufficient evidence to sustain the accusation and that a **trial** should be had. The indictment delivered to the court states the facts about the alleged crime as found by the grand jury and cites the penal code sections believed to have been violated. If the grand jury **ignores** the bill of indictment, it endorses "**no true bill**," "not a true bill," or "not found" on it. When a grand jury takes notice of an offense on its own initiative and delivers an indictment, it is sometimes called a **grand jury original** or a **presentment**. *Also called*: **true bill**. See ACCUSATION, GRAND JURY, and PROSECUTE for a list of related terms.

Ii

INDIFFERENT. **1.** Impartial; unbiased; neutral; not preferring one person or thing over another. **2.** Not caring; apathetic; having no interest or concern; without feeling. **NOTE:** Because of the positive and negative meanings of indifferent, it is an ambiguous word and should not be used without clearly specifying which meaning applies.

INDIGENT. Financially poor; without sufficient funds. *Example*: A person cannot be denied his basic constitutional rights because the person is indigent. *See*: GIDEON v. WAINWRIGHT.

INDIRECT.   Not DIRECT; not taking the straight course to an end or desired result; not immediately resulting from a cause or action.

INDIRECT ATTACK.   Same as COLLATERAL ATTACK.

INDIRECT CONFESSION.   A CONFESSION not explicit, but inferred from the conduct of a person.

INDIRECT CONTEMPT.   *See*: CONTEMPT OF COURT.

INDIRECT EVIDENCE.   Same as CIRCUMSTANTIAL EVIDENCE.

INDISPENSABLE.   Absolutely necessary or required; essential; that cannot be done without.

INDISPENSABLE EVIDENCE.   **Evidence** without which a particular fact cannot be proved. See EVIDENCE for a list of related terms.

INDIVIDUAL.   A single human being as distinguished from a group.

INDORSE.   Same as ENDORSE.

INDUBITABLE EVIDENCE.   EVIDENCE that is so strong as to prove the facts alleged beyond a doubt.

INDUCE.   **1.** To successfully lead or move a person to do or believe something by persuasion, influence, or reasoning. *Example*: They induced him to come out of the building with his hands up. **2.** To bring about; to effect; to cause; to produce. *Example*: Certain drugs induce hallucinations.

INDUCEMENT.   **Motive**; incentive; that which leads a person to engage in criminal conduct.

INDUCTIVE REASONING.   *See*: A POSTERIORI.

INDULGE.   To allow oneself to give in to or follow an instinct, appetite, or whim; to gratify.

INEBRIATE.   **v.** To make drunk; to intoxicate. **n.** A habitual drunkard.

IN ESSE.   In being; actually existing.

IN EVIDENCE.   A term used to describe **facts**, **documents**, or **exhibits** that have been introduced before and accepted by the **court** for consideration by the **trier of fact** in making its findings.

INEVITABLE.   Incapable of being avoided or prevented.

INEVITABLE DISCOVERY.   A variation of the **independent source** doctrine allowing the admission of **tainted evidence** if it would inevitably have been discovered in the normal course of events. Under this exception, the **prosecution** must establish by a **preponderance of the evidence** that, even though the evidence was actually discovered as the result of a constitutional violation, the evidence would ultimately or inevitably have been discovered by lawful means—for example, as the result of the predictable and routine behavior of a **law enforcement agency**, some other agency, or a private person.

> "[I]f the government can prove that the evidence would have been obtained inevitably and, therefore, would have been admitted regardless of any overreaching by the police, there is no rational basis to keep that evidence from the jury in order to ensure the fairness of the trial proceedings. In that situation, the State has gained no advantage at trial and the defendant has suffered no prejudice. In-deed, suppression of the evidence would operate to undermine the adversary sys-tem by putting the State in a *worse* position than it would have occupied without any police misconduct." *Nix v. Williams*, 467 U.S. 431, 447, 104 S.Ct. 2501, 2511, 81 L.Ed.2d 377, 389-90 (1984).

See EXCLUSIONARY RULE for a list of related terms.

IN EXTREMIS.   *Latin.* Near death; in the last illness. See DEATH for a list of related terms.

IN FACT.   Actual, real, or positive as distinguished from **implied**, **constructive**, or **legal** (definition 2). *See*: IN LAW.

INFAMOUS.   Shamefully wicked; detestable; disgraceful; abominable.

INFAMOUS CRIME.   A crime punishable by **incarceration** in a prison or penitentiary. The Fifth Amendment to the U.S. Constitution states that "[n]o person shall be held to answer for a **capital**, or otherwise infamous crime, unless on a **presentment** or **indictment** of a **Grand Jury**...." See CRIME for a list of related terms.

INFAMOUS CRIME AGAINST NATURE.   *See*: SODOMY.

INFAMOUS PUNISHMENT.   Punishment either in a prison or penitentiary, or at hard labor, or both.

INFAMY.   **1.** Shameful notoriety; public disgrace; evil fame. **2.** Same as CIVIL DEATH.

INFANCY.   Same as MINORITY.

INFANT. A person who is under the age of legal **majority**; a person not of **full age**; a MINOR. Under the **common law**, the age of legal majority was 21 years. Today, it differs from state to state according to statute.

INFANTICIDE. **1.** The killing of a child shortly after its birth. **2.** One who kills a child shortly after its birth. *See*: ABORTION; PROLICIDE.

INFER. To draw a conclusion from evidence presented or premises accepted.

INFERENCE. A conclusion that may be drawn logically or reasonably from given facts, but is not required to be drawn. "The words 'presumption' and 'inference' are often used synonymously but a distinction exists. A presumption is a conclusion which a rule of law directs shall be made from proof of certain facts but an inference is a **deduction** which reason and logic dictates shall be made from a fact situation. An inference is a deduction as to the existence of a fact which human experience teaches us can reasonably and logically be drawn from proof of other facts. An inference must be based on probability and not on mere possibilities or on surmise or conjecture, and must be drawn reasonably and supported by the facts upon which it rests." *Manchester v. Dugan*, 247 A.2d 827, 829 (Me. 1968). See FACT and PRESUMPTION for lists of related terms.

INFERENTIAL FACT. A fact established by INFERENCE from other facts or evidence. See FACT for a list of related terms.

INFERIOR COURT. **1.** Any court lower than the highest **appellate court** in a particular judicial system. **2.** A COURT OF LIMITED JURISDICTION. See COURT for a list of related terms.

INFERNAL MACHINE. An explosive device maliciously designed to destroy life or property.

INFIRMATIVE. Tending to weaken or invalidate; having a diminishing effect.

INFIRMITY. A flaw, defect, or imperfection that makes a document or transaction legally incomplete or void.

INFORMAL PROBATION. Same as COURT PROBATION.

INFORMANT. **1.** A person who gives information of any sort. **2.** An INFORMER. **NOTE:** Informer and informant are often used interchangeably.

IN FORMA PAUPERIS. *Latin.* "In the form of a pauper"; as a poor person or indigent. This phrase indicates the permission given by a **court** to bring legal **action** without paying **costs** or other court fees because of a lack of financial resources.

INFORMATION.   A formal, written **accusation** submitted to a **court** by a **prosecutor**, without the approval or intervention of a **grand jury**, alleging that a specified person has committed a specific offense. An information is similar in nature and content to an **indictment** and serves as an alternative to the indictment in some jurisdictions to initiate usually **felony prosecutions**. Some jurisdictions initiate felony prosecutions only through indictment and others allow use of the information only after the defendant has **waived** an indictment. See ACCUSATION and PROSECUTE for a list of related terms. **2.** Knowledge about some fact, subject, or event. *Example*: How did the informant obtain his information? See FACT for a list of related terms.

INFORMATION AND BELIEF.   A statement made on information and belief indicates that the person making the statement does not have firsthand knowledge of the information stated but, nevertheless, in **good faith**, has a firm conviction in the truth of the statement.

INFORMER.   **1.** A person who gives information to the police regarding criminal activity. **2.** An INFORMANT.

NOTE: Informer and informant are often used interchangeably.

INFRA.   *Latin.* **1.** Below; under; beneath; inferior to. **2.** Within. **3.** After; later. When infra is used in a book or other document, it means that the matter referred to appears later in the work. *See*: SUPRA.

INFRACTION.   **1.** A violation of a state **statute** or local **ordinance** punishable by **fine** or other penalty, but not by **incarceration**, or by a specified, unusually limited term of incarceration. Some state codes clearly define a specific, named class of offenses not punishable by incarceration, or by incarceration for a limited period, such as up to 15 or up to 30 days. Others do not differentiate so clearly in statute, but in all jurisdictions there is a class comprised of noncriminal offenses such as parking violations, violations of equipment standards, minor violations of health and sanitation codes, and the like, that are disposed of by **citations**, administrative hearing, or other essentially nonadversary procedures. *Also called*: **violation**. See CRIME for a list of related terms. **2.** In the **corrections** context, a statutory offense or a vio-lation of prison or jail administrative regulations committed by an offender while incarcerated or in a **temporary release** program such as work release. The term infraction does not apply to misconduct while on **conditional release**. Alleged infrac-tions of law or institutional rules are recorded in documents usually called "conduct reports" or "disciplinary reports." Opportunity to rebut these allegations is usually offered to the prisoner in a proceeding called an inmate disciplinary hearing or similar name. When it is believed that a **crime** has been committed, a **corrections agency** usually has a certain amount of **discretion** regarding the decision to seek a **judicial disposition** or to treat the matter as an infraction of an institutional rule. *See*: PAROLE VIOLATION. **3.** Generally, the breaking or violation of a law, rule, obligation, or right. *Example*: We see no infraction of rights under the Constitution.

Ii

INFRINGEMENT. **1.** Same as INFRACTION (definition 3). 2. An encroachment; a trespass. *Example*: There was an infringement of copyright.

IN FUTURO. *Latin.* "In the future"; at a future time. *See*: IN PRAESENTI.

IN GENERE. *Latin.* "In kind." Of the same kind or species.

INHABIT. To live or dwell in a place.

INHABITANT. A permanent resident.

INHERENT. Existing as a permanent and essential element or characteristic of something; intrinsic. *Example*: The inherent powers of a court are those that are reasonably necessary for the administration of justice.

INHERENTLY DANGEROUS. Permanently and continuously dangerous because of the essential nature of a condition or instrumentality; intrinsically dangerous. *Example*: A loaded gun is an inherently dangerous instrumentality, whereas a pipe wrench is dangerous only if used irresponsibly.

INITIAL APPEARANCE. The first **appearance** of an **accused** person in the first court having **jurisdiction** over his or her **case**. Various procedural steps may be taken during the initial appearance. In minor **misdemeanor** cases the initial appearance may be the only one, and **judgment** and **penalty**, if any, will be determined at that time. When the charge is more serious, the accused at initial appearance may be informed of the **charges**, a **plea** may be entered and **bail** set, or the accused may merely be informed of his or her rights and of the general nature of the proceedings and it may be determined whether he or she has **counsel**. In any given jurisdiction, the initial appearance may be characterized by the major step taken in that court at that point. Thus, it may be called a preliminary **arraignment**, **preliminary hearing**, magistrate's preliminary hearing, or **presentment** (definition 2). The timing of an initial appearance is largely determined by whether the defendant is in **custody**, and by the laws concerning the maximum period a person can be held in custody without court appearance. In most states an **arrested** person has a right to be brought **forthwith** before a court or magistrate for an initial appearance. *Also called*: **first appearance**. See HEARING for a list of related terms.

INITIAL PLEA. The first **plea** to a given **charge** entered in the court record by or for the defendant. The acceptance of an initial plea by the court indicates that the **arraignment** process has been completed. *Also called*: **first plea**.

INITIATE. To begin; to originate.

IN JUDGMENT. In a **court** of justice; as a **judge** at a **trial**. *Example*: He is one of the finest men to ever sit in judgment. See JUDGMENT for a list of related terms.

INJUNCTION. A judicial **process** or **order**, directed at a particular person, requiring the person to do or refrain from doing a particular thing. A person who violates an injunction may be punished for **contempt of court**.

INJURE. **1.** To violate the legal rights or interests of another. **2.** To harm; to impair; to damage; to wound.

INJURY. Any wrong or damage done to a person's body, rights, reputation, or property.

INJUSTICE. The denial, withholding, or lack of JUSTICE; the violation of a person's rights; a wrong.

IN LAW. **Constructive** or **implied** as distinguished from actual, real, or positive.

IN LIEU OF. In place of; instead of.

IN LOCO. *Latin.* "In place"; instead.

IN LOCO PARENTIS. *Latin.* "In place of a parent"; having the rights and responsibilities of a parent with respect to the care and supervision of a child. *Example*: A guardian stands in loco parentis with respect to his or her ward.

INMATE. A person in physical **custody** in a **confinement facility**. In some jurisdictions, inmate has the further restricted meaning of a person in physical custody in a local **jail**. See ACCUSED for a list of related terms.

INNOCENT. **1.** Not guilty of a specific **crime** charged or alleged. A person accused of a crime is presumed innocent until proven **guilty beyond a reasonable doubt**. **2.** Free from guilt; having done no wrong; blameless. **3.** In the law of **entrapment**, innocent means not having a predisposition or state of mind that readily responds to the opportunity furnished by a government officer or agent to commit a crime. *See*: PRESUMPTION OF INNOCENCE.

Ii

INNOCENT AGENT. A person who commits a **crime** at the solicitation or request of another, but incurs no legal **guilt** because of lack of mental **capacity** or because the person was ignorant of the unlawful intent of his or her **principal**.

INNOCENT HOMICIDE. HOMICIDE that does not involve criminal **guilt**, i.e., either a **justifiable homicide** or an **excusable homicide**. See HOMICIDE for a list of related terms.

INNOCENT MISREPRESENTATION. *See*: MISREPRESENTATION.

INNUENDO. *Latin.* "Meaning." **1.** An explanation or clarification of the meaning of words or statements. Specifically, in an action or prosecution for **libel** or **slander**, the innuendo is the explanation of the meaning of the words alleged to be libelous or slanderous, which might otherwise be considered innocuous or ambiguous. **2.** A subtle, indirect statement, usually derogatory; an insinuation.

IN OPEN VIEW. Freely exposed; affording an unobstructed view; clearly visible. *Example*: The officer seized the gun, which was lying in open view on the couch.

INOPERATIVE. Void; ineffective.

IN PARI DELICTO. *Latin.* "In equal fault." Equally **guilty** or at fault. The term in pari delicto is used to describe **accomplices** to a crime. *Example*: Both parties to the bribe were in pari delicto.

IN PARI MATERIA. *Latin.* "On the same subject matter." Relating to the same person or thing or having a common purpose. **Statutes** in pari materia must be **construed** together in an attempt to harmonize them, even though they contain no reference to each other and were passed at different times.

IN PERSON. **1.** In one's own bodily or physical presence. **2.** Without the assistance of legal **counsel**.

IN PERSONAM. *Latin.* "Against the person." Dealing with or affecting the person or personal rights or interests. A court with in personam **jurisdiction** in a particular case has enough power over the defendant and his or her property to grant a judgment affecting the defendant in almost any way. *See*: IN REM.

IN POSSE. Possible or potential but not in actual existence. *See*: IN ESSE.

IN PRAESENTI. *Latin.* Now; at the present time. *See*: IN FUTURO.

IN PROPRIA PERSONA. *Latin.* Same as PRO SE.

INQUEST. **1.** A legal or judicial inquiry or investigation made by a **jury** or other appointed body of persons. *See*: CORONER'S INQUEST. **2.** A body of persons appointed to make a legal or judicial inquiry.

IN RE. In the matter of; in the case of; concerning. In re is used in the title of some legal proceedings that do not involve adversary parties, but that affect some person or thing about which judicial action must be taken.

IN RE GAULT. *See*: GAULT, IN RE.

IN REM. *Latin*: "Against the thing." Dealing with or affecting property or rights or interests in property. A **court** with in rem **jurisdiction** has power over only the specific real or personal property of the defendant under the control of the court. *See*: IN PERSONAM.

INS. Abbreviation for IMMIGRATION AND NATURALIZATION SERVICE.

INSANITY. Generally, a degree of mental illness or disorder that relieves a person of legal responsibility for his or her actions or negates the person's legal **capacity** to do certain acts. The term insanity has several meanings in the criminal law, depending on the context in which it is used. When insanity is used as a **defense** to a criminal **prosecution**, different tests for insanity are used in different jurisdictions. For four different tests used for this purpose, see the M'NAGHTEN RULE, the IRRESISTIBLE IMPULSE TEST, the DURHAM RULE, and the SUBSTANTIAL CAPACITY TEST. For the insanity test to determine who is **competent** to stand trial, see INCOMPETENT TO STAND TRIAL. For the insanity test to determine who is competent to be executed, see INCOMPETENT TO BE EXECUTED. For the insanity test to determine who is to be committed to a mental institution after a successful insanity defense, see COMMITMENT AFTER INSANITY DEFENSE. And for the insanity test to determine who is eligible for **release** following such a commitment, see RELEASE AFTER INSANITY COMMITMENT. *See*: NOT GUILTY BY REASON OF INSANITY.

INSCRIBE. v. To write on or otherwise mark a surface with words, figures, or symbols, especially in a durable or conspicuous manner. **n.** INSCRIPTION.

INSCRIPTION. *See*: INSCRIBE.

INSPECTION. The examination of the books, papers, documents, photographs, buildings, or other objects or places in the custody or control of the opposing party in a legal **action**, for the purpose of preparing a **case** for **trial**. Inspection is an important element of **discovery**.

Ii

INSTANCE. **1.** Suggestion; request; solicitation; prompting. *Example*: The court recessed at the instance of the defendant. **2.** A case; an example. *Example*: The witness testified as to several instances of police harassment. **3.** A legal proceeding or process. *Example*: A trial court is sometimes called a court of first instance. **4.** Occasion. *Example*: In this instance, I choose not to speak.

INSTANT. **n. 1.** A particular moment; a specific point in time. *Example*: Where were you at the instant of the explosion? **n. 2.** A very short time; a moment. *Example*: She arrived in an instant. **adj. 1.** Immediate. *Example*: The question called for an instant response. **adj. 2.** Impending; imminent; urgent. *Example*: He was in instant danger. **adj. 3.** Present; current; now under consideration. *Example*: The defendant in the instant case is indigent.

INSTANTANEOUS. Occurring or done without a perceptible lapse of time.

INSTANTANEOUS CRIME. A crime that is completed by a single act as distinguished from a crime that involves a series or repetition of acts. An example of an instantaneous crime is murder. See CRIME for a list of related terms.

INSTANTER. **adv.** Immediately; without delay; forthwith; at once. **n.** *See*: SUBPOENA.

INSTIGATE. To stir, urge, or stimulate into action; to incite. Instigate usually implies evil intention. *Example*: He was instigated to commit the crime by his friends.

INSTITUTE. **1.** To initiate; to originate; to commence; to set in operation. *Example*: She instituted a suit against the city. **2.** To establish; to set up; to bring into use or practice. *Example*: We institute laws for our own protection.

INSTITUTION. **1.** The act, result, or process of instituting. *See*: INSTITUTE. **2.** An organization, association, or establishment for the promotion of a particular object, usually some public purpose. *Example*: She was confined to a mental institution.

INSTITUTIONAL FACILITY. *See*: JUVENILE FACILITY.

INSTRUCT. To give an INSTRUCTION.

INSTRUCTION. A direction or explanation given by a trial judge to a **jury** informing them of the law applicable to the case before them. Attorneys for both sides normally furnish the judge with suggested instructions. *See*: ALLEN CHARGE; CAUTIONARY INSTRUCTION; CHARGE; FORMULA INSTRUCTION; GENERAL INSTRUCTION; JURY; MISDIRECTION.

INSTRUMENT. **1.** A formal legal document such as a contract, deed, will, bond, or lease. **2.** A writing evidencing a person's right to collect money, such as a check. **3.** A mechanical device; a tool; an implement; a utensil. **4.** A means; anything which contributes to the accomplishment of an end.

INSTRUMENTAL. Contributing to the accomplishment of an end..

INSTRUMENTALITY. Any property designed or intended for use or which is or has been used as the means of committing a criminal offense. *See*: INSTRUMENT OF CRIME.

INSTRUMENT OF CRIME. Section 5.06 (1) of the **Model Penal Code** defines instrument of crime as "(a) anything specially made or specially adapted for criminal use; or (b) anything commonly used for criminal purposes and possessed by the actor under circumstances that do not negative unlawful purpose." *See*: INSTRUMENTALITY.

INSUFFICIENT. Not SUFFICIENT; inadequate; lacking what is required or necessary.

INSUFFICIENT FUNDS CHECK. Same as CHECK FRAUD.

INTAKE. The process by which a **juvenile** referral is received by personnel of a **probation agency**, **juvenile court**, or special **intake unit**, and a decision made to close the case at intake, or refer the juvenile to another agency, or place him or her under some kind of care or **supervision**, or file a **petition** in a juvenile court. Intake is the first step in decisionmaking regarding a juvenile whose behavior or alleged behavior is in violation of law or could otherwise cause a juvenile court to assume jurisdiction. The official or government unit that makes the intake decision depends on how a given jurisdiction has organized its juvenile services. The screening function is sometimes assigned to **probation officers** attached to the court, sometimes to individuals or a special unit within a probation agency, or to a separate agency. *Also called*: **preliminary screening**; **probation screening**. See JUVENILE for a list of related terms.

INTAKE DECISION. The immediate outcome of the referral of a juvenile case to an **intake unit** or intake officer determining what further actions, if any, will be taken regarding the referred case. Classification and terminology for juvenile intake decisions varies greatly among jurisdictions. A typical set of intake decision categories will include: closed at intake, counseled and released, placed on **informal probation**, referred for testing, referred to another agency, and **petition** filed for formal court action. (In some jurisdictions the **prosecutor** will review petitions alleging **delinquent acts** or **status offenses** after the intake officer or unit has considered the social aspects of the case but before the petition is filed in court, in order to consider the adequacy of the factual basis of the allegations.) Intake decisions that refer the client out of the justice system or away from formal adjudication are now often called **diversion**. See JUVENILE for a list of related terms.

Ii

INTAKE OFFICER. *See*: INTAKE UNIT.

INTAKE UNIT. A government officer, agency, or agency subunit that receives juvenile referrals from police, parents, other government agencies, private agencies, or persons, and screens them, resulting in an **intake decision**. The intake unit is the point of entry into the juvenile justice system. In some jurisdictions, the intake unit may also do **predisposition investigations**. See JUVENILE for a list of related terms.

INTEMPERANCE. **Intoxication** resulting from overconsumption of alcoholic beverages; excessive or habitual use of alcoholic beverages.

INTENDMENT. The true meaning or intention under the law; the sense in which something is understood in the law. *See*: COMMON INTENDMENT.

INTENT. Purpose or design to perform a particular act, either to cause a particular result or with knowledge that a particular result is substantially certain to occur. Intent differs from **motive**. A motive is an inner stimulus that leads a person to form an intent and commit an act. Motive precedes an action; intent is an aspect of an action. Motive is never an **element** of an offense. Intent is an element of most offenses. *Example*: The motive for a murder can be hate or greed. The intent, which makes the action a crime, is the determination to kill. *See*: CRIME; INTENTION; MENS REA; MOTIVE.

INTENTION. A plan to do something or bring something about. Intention is a less definite and less strong word than **intent**. Intent has a specific legal meaning and suggests a more deliberate and clearly defined plan or purpose.

INTENTIONAL. Done **purposely**; willful; deliberate.

INTENTIONAL HOMICIDE. Same as WILLFUL HOMICIDE.

INTER. *Latin*. "Among; between."

INTER ALIA. *Latin*. "Among other things."

INTER ALIOS. *Latin*. "Among other persons."

INTERCEPTION. The seizing, stopping, or cutting off on the way from one place to another. *Example*: Federal laws regulate the interception of communications by wire.

INTERCOURSE. **1.** Dealings or communication between persons. **2.** *See*: SEXUAL INTERCOURSE.

INTERDICT. **v.** To prohibit by authority. **n.** A prohibiting decree.

INTEREST. A right, claim, or legal share in something that may incline a person to favor or disfavor one of the parties to an **action**. Interest is a ground for disqualifying a **judge** or **juror**.

INTERFERE. **1.** To come into opposition; to be an obstacle or hindrance; to get in the way of. **2.** To intrude in the affairs of others; to meddle.

INTERIM. **n.** An intervening time; the meantime. **adj.** Temporary; provisional; done, occurring, or serving in the meantime.

INTERLOCUTORY. Intervening between the beginning and end of a legal **action** and deciding some preliminary or subordinate issue, but not finally disposing of the action or finally settling the rights of the parties.

INTERLOCUTORY APPEAL. A request, made at some point before **judgment** in **trial court** proceedings, that an **appellate court** review a prejudgment **decision** of the trial court before judgment is reached. Unlike **appeals** following completion of trial court proceedings, interlocutory appeals do not challenge the trial court's decision in the case as a whole, but only the correctness of some particular prejudgment decision. The decision being appealed may or may not be one that would have a bearing on the eventual judgment in the case. Where the subject matter of the appeal is such that it would likely have a bearing (for example, an appeal of a decision granting or denying a motion to suppress evidence in a criminal case), the trial court proceedings may be halted pending determination of the appeal. Some states permit interlocutory appeals; others do not. See APPEAL for a list of related terms.

INTERMEDIATE APPELLATE COURT. A court whose **appellate jurisdiction** is limited by law or at the discretion of the **court of last resort** in its jurisdiction. An intermediate appellate court's primary function is to review the judgments of **trial courts** and the decisions of administrative agencies. A higher **appellate court** in the same jurisdiction may review its decisions. Not all states have intermediate appellate courts. *Also called*: **court of intermediate appeals**. See APPEAL, COURT, and JURISDICTION for lists of related terms.

INTERMITTENT SENTENCE. A **sentence** to periods of confinement interrupted by periods of freedom. For example, to allow a person to keep a job, the person may be sentenced to **confinement** on weekends only for a specified period of time. *Also called*: **weekend sentence**. See SENTENCE for a list of related terms.

INTERNAL REVENUE SERVICE. The Internal Revenue Service (IRS) in the **Department of the Treasury** is responsible for administering and enforcing the internal revenue laws and related statutes, except those relating to alcohol, tobacco, and firearms, and explosives. Its mission is to collect the proper amount of tax revenue at the least cost to the public, and in a manner that warrants the highest degree of public confidence in the service's integrity, efficiency, and fairness. The IRS is a decentralized organization consisting of seven regional offices, each headed by a Regional Commissioner, which supervise and evaluate the operations of 62 district offices, 10 service centers, and the Austin Compliance Center, each of which includes criminal investigations of internal revenue law violations among their functions.

INTERNATIONAL CRIMINAL POLICE ORGANIZATION. The International Criminal Police Organization (INTERPOL) is an association of nearly 150 countries dedicated to promoting mutual assistance among law enforcement authorities in the prevention and suppression of international crime. With no police force of its own,

INTERPOL has no powers of **arrest** or **search and seizure**. Instead, INTERPOL serves as a channel of communication among the police of the member countries, and provides a forum for discussions, working group meetings, and symposia to enable police to focus on specific areas of criminal activity affecting their countries.

United States participation in INTERPOL began in 1938 by congressional authorization, designating the **Attorney General** as the official representative to the organization. INTERPOL operations were interrupted during World War II, but resumed in 1947. The Attorney General officially designated the Secretary of the Treasury as the U.S. representative to INTERPOL in 1958, and the **United States National Central Bureau** (USNCB) was established within the Treasury Department in 1969. In 1977, an arrangement was effected between Justice and Treasury officials establishing dual authority in administering USNCB. This memorandum of understanding designates the Attorney General as the permanent representative to INTERPOL and the Secretary of the Treasury as the alternate representative.

INTERPOL. Abbreviation for INTERNATIONAL CRIMINAL POLICE ORGANIZATION.

INTERPRET. To ascertain, clarify, or explain the meaning of language by examining only the written or spoken words and not the surrounding circumstances. *See*: CONSTRUE.

INTERPRETATION. The act, process, or result of interpreting. *See*: INTERPRET.

INTERROGATION. The questioning of a person suspected of a crime with the intent of eliciting **incriminating admissions** from the person. The U.S. Supreme Court explained the meaning of interrogation for purposes of the MIRANDA v. ARIZONA decision as follows: "[T]he *Miranda* safeguards come into play whenever a person in **custody** is subjected to either express questioning or its functional equivalent. That is to say, the term 'interrogation' under Miranda refers not only to express questioning, but also to any words or actions on the part of police (other than those normally attendant to **arrest** and custody) that the police should know are reasonably likely to elicit an incriminating response from the suspect." *Rhode Island v. Innis*, 446 U.S. 291, 300-01, 100 S.Ct. 1682, 1689, 64 L.Ed.2d 297, 307-08 (1980). The Court further refined the definition by stating that an incriminating response is any response—whether inculpatory or exculpatory—that the **prosecution** may seek to introduce at **trial**. Volunteered statements, questions directed at clarifying a suspect's statement, brief, routine questions, spontaneous questions, and questions necessary to protect the safety of the police and public are not considered interrogation for purposes of *Miranda*. *See*: ESCOBEDO v. ILLINOIS.

INTERROGATORIES. A series of formal written questions used in the examination of a **party** or **witness** in connection with a judicial proceeding. Answers to interrogatories must be in writing and signed under oath. Interrogatories are often used in taking **depositions** and as part of the **discovery** process. *See*: CROSS IN-TERROGATORIES; DIRECT INTERROGATORIES; EXAMINATION; SPECIAL INTERROGATORIES.

INTERSTATE COMPACT.   An agreement between two or more states to **transfer** (definition 4) **prisoners, parolees,** or **probationers** from the **physical custody** or **supervisory custody** of one state to the that of another, where the **correctional agency** that first acquired **jurisdiction** over the person usually retains the legal authority to **confine** or **release** the prisoner. Interstate compacts are formal documents setting forth the conditions under which these transfers may take place and the respective powers and duties of the participating agencies. The rules and procedures are frequently expressed in statutes. Interstate compacts relating to **juveniles** usually have among their chief purposes the return of **runaways** or juveniles **absconding** from **supervision** to their homes or to community supervision. This kind of transfer is, however, usually done informally. An interstate compact concerning prisoners may provide for the exchange of prisoners, or for transfer in one direction only, as when state A, having overcrowded institutions, regularly sends some prisoners to state B for housing. Exchanges aimed at protecting prisoners who have been threatened by other inmates are often done informally.

INTERVENING ACT.   Same as INTERVENING CAUSE.

INTERVENING AGENCY.   Same as INTERVENING CAUSE.

INTERVENING CAUSE.   An independent cause, force, or agency that comes into active operation after the act or omission of the original actor to produce a result that would not otherwise have followed and that could not have been reasonably anticipated. An intervening cause breaks the causal connection between the act or omission of the original actor and the result, to negate the original actor's criminal responsibility for the result. *Example*: If a person is burning rubbish in his or her backyard and a 70-mile-per-hour gust of wind suddenly spreads the fire and destroys a neighbor's house, the wind would be an intervening cause, breaking the causal connection between the person's setting of the fire and the destruction of the neighbor's house. *Also called*: **intervening act; intervening agency; intervening force; superseding cause; supervening cause.**

INTERVENING FORCE.   Same as INTERVENING CAUSE.

INTIMIDATE.   To force into or discourage from some action by **threats** or **violence**.

IN TOTO.   In the whole; completely.

INTOXICATION.   Section 2.08 (5) (a) of the **Model Penal Code** defines intoxication as "a disturbance of mental or physical capacities resulting from the introduction of substances into the body." Many jurisdictions allow intoxication to be used as a **defense** to **specific intent** crimes on the rationale that the intoxicated person cannot possess the requisite mental state necessary to establish the offense. With few exceptions, intoxication is not a defense against **general intent** crimes. Intoxication may also be a **mitigating circumstance** in determining the punishment for certain crimes. *See*: ALCOHOL; DRIVING UNDER THE INFLUENCE OF ALCOHOL; DRIVING UNDER THE INFLUENCE OF DRUGS; DRUG; PATHOLOGICAL INTOXICATION; PUBLIC INTOXICATION; SELF-INDUCED INTOXICATION.

INTRA. In; within; inside of.

INTRINSIC EVIDENCE. EVIDENCE derived solely from a **document** or writing without considering any information or circumstances outside of it.

INTRUSION. An encroachment on or invasion of rights or property enjoyed or possessed by another.

INURE. To come into operation; to take effect; to be of use or available. *Example*: The change in the law inured to the benefit of the defendant. *Also spelled*: **enure**.

INVALID. **1.** Not VALID; without legal effect or force; void. **2.** Inadequate; weak.

INVEIGLE. To lead astray or win over by deceitful flattery or artful inducement.

INVENTORY SEARCH. The routine practice of police departments of securing and recording the contents of a lawfully **impounded** vehicle. In *South Dakota v. Opperman*, 428 U.S. 364, 96 S.Ct. 3092, 49 L.Ed.2d 1000 (1976) the U.S. Supreme Court approved this limited type of search for the purposes of protecting the vehicle owner's property while it remains in custody and protecting the police from potential danger and from claims or disputes over lost or stolen property. This inventory procedure is not considered to be a **search** for purposes of the Fourth Amendment because its object is not to find incriminating evidence as part of a criminal investigation. Rather, it is considered to be a routine administrative-custodial procedure, and it may not be used as a pretext to conduct an exploratory search for incriminating evidence in order to circumvent the **warrant** requirement. If, however, incriminating evidence is found under circumstances satisfying the **plain view doctrine**, that evidence may be **seized** and is **admissible** in court. The validity of an inventory search depends on whether the officers conducting the inventory followed standard inventory procedures of their law enforcement agency. See SEARCH for a list of related terms.

INVESTIGATE. To examine and inquire into something systematically and thoroughly. *Example*: Detectives were sent to investigate the murder.

INVOLUNTARY. **1.** Not VOLUNTARY; done against the will; performed under duress. **2.** Unintentional.

INVOLUNTARY MANSLAUGHTER.   Any unintentional **homicide** that is neither **murder** nor **voluntary manslaughter** and that is not justified or excused under the law. Included under involuntary manslaughter are the killing of a human being by committing a lawful act in a reckless or grossly negligent manner, and the killing of a human being by committing an unlawful act **malum in se**, usually a misdemeanor. Homicide caused by reckless or grossly negligent operation of a motor vehicle is involuntary manslaughter. See HOMICIDE for a list of related terms.

INVOLUNTARY SERVITUDE.   The compulsory or involuntary subjection of a person to a master; compelling a person to work for another person against his or her will, regardless of whether or not the person is paid for the labor. The 13th Amendment to the U.S. Constitution states: "Neither slavery nor involuntary servitude, except as a punishment for crime whereof the party shall have been duly convicted, shall exist within the United States, or any place subject to their jurisdiction."

IPSO FACTO.   *Latin.* "By the fact itself; by that very fact."

IPSO JURE.   *Latin.* "By the law itself."

IRREBUTTABLE PRESUMPTION.   Same as CONCLUSIVE PRESUMPTION.

IRREGULARITY.   A violation, by act or omission, of an established rule or practice. Irregularity refers to a formal defect in practice or procedure and is not as strong a word as **illegality**. Although some irregularities are sufficiently serious to require the invalidation and setting aside of a judgment, usually a simple irregularity is **harmless error**.

IRRELEVANT.   Not RELEVANT; not pertinent or applicable to the matter at issue.

IRRELEVANT EVIDENCE.   EVIDENCE that has no tendency either to prove or disprove an issue in a case.

Ii

IRRESISTIBLE IMPULSE.   An abnormally compelling urge to commit a **crime**, which is caused by an impairment of mental condition and which overcomes a person's willpower, self-control, or freedom of choice to resist committing the crime. Irresistible impulse is recognized in some jurisdictions as a **defense** to a criminal charge. *Also called*: **uncontrollable impulse**. *See*: **irresistible impulse test**.

IRRESISTIBLE IMPULSE TEST.   A test supplementing in some states the M'NAGHTEN RULE for determining a person's mental **capacity** to commit **crime**. Under the irresistible impulse test, an accused is not criminally responsible if, at the time the unlawful act was committed, the person had a mental disease that kept the person from controlling his or her conduct. The person is not criminally responsible under this rule even though the person can discern right from wrong and knows and understands the nature of the acts. *See*: INSANITY.

IRREVOCABLE.   Unable to be called back, revoked, withdrawn, or annulled; unalterable; irreversible.

IRS.   Abbreviation for INTERNAL REVENUE SERVICE.

ISSUANCE.   The act, process, or result of issuing. *See*: ISSUE.

ISSUE.   **v.** To send out or put forth officially or authoritatively; to promulgate; to publish. *Example*: The magistrate issued the search warrant. **n. 1.** The act, process, or result of issuing. *See*: ISSUE. **n. 2.** A disputed point or question of fact or law, affirmed by one side and denied by the other. *Example*: The main issue in the case was the validity of the search warrant.

ITEMIZE.   To list or state each item or article separately.

ITEMS SUBJECT TO SEIZURE.   Items for which a **search warrant** may be issued. Federal Rule of Criminal Procedure 41 (b) specifies that "[a] warrant may be issued under this rule to search for and seize any (1) property that constitutes evidence of the commission of a criminal offense; or (2) contraband, the fruits of crime, or things otherwise criminally possessed; or (3) property designed or intended for use or which is or has been used as the means of committing a criminal offense. . . ." Most states have similar rules. *Also called*: **seizable items**. See SEARCH and SEIZURE for a list of related terms.

J. Abbreviation for JUDGE or JUSTICE.

JACKSON v. DENNO. The United States Supreme Court case which held that a defendant's constitutional rights are violated when his or her challenged **confession** is introduced in **evidence** without a prior determination by the trial **judge** of its **voluntariness** after an adequate **hearing**. The citation for *Jackson v. Denno* is 378 U.S. 368, 84 S.Ct. 1774, 12 L.Ed.2d 908 (1964).

JAIL. A **confinement facility** administered by an agency of local government, typically a law enforcement agency, intended for **adults** but sometimes also containing **juveniles**, which holds persons detained pending **adjudication** and/or persons committed after adjudication, usually those committed on **sentences** of a year or less. In jurisdictions where the basic penalty range division is not the usual one year or less versus more than a year, some local confinement facilities for sentenced prisoners have the custodial authority to hold persons sentenced for up to several years.

In a few jurisdictions, all adult confinement facilities are administered at the state level. Facilities administered by state governments are not usually classified as jails. A county jail is usually administered by a sheriff's department; a city jail is usually administered by a city police department. *See*: CORRECTIONAL FACILITY; COUNTY FARM; PREARRAIGNMENT LOCKUP.

JAIL COMMITMENT. A **sentence** of **commitment** to a **confinement facility** system for **adults** that is administered by an agency of local government and of which the custodial authority is usually limited to persons sentenced to a year or less of confinement. Jail commitment is to be distinguished from **prison commitment** and includes commitments to facilities called **jails, county farms, honor farms, work camps**, and **road camps**. A jail commitment is often included as a **condition** of **probation**, meaning that **release** from jail will be followed by a period of probationary status. See COMMITMENT and SENTENCE for lists of related terms.

JAILER. The keeper of a JAIL.

JANE DOE. *See*: JOHN DOE.

JAYWALK. To walk across a street or intersection recklessly or in violation of traffic laws.

J.D.   Abbreviation for JURIS DOCTOR.

JEOPARDY.   **1.** Danger or risk of loss or injury; peril; hazard. **2.** The danger of **conviction** and **sentence** that a criminal **defendant** incurs when he or she has been formally **charged** and a **jury** has been impaneled and sworn (in a **jury** case) or **evidence** has been formally received by the court (in a **nonjury** case). The stage of the criminal proceeding at which jeopardy attaches may differ from state to state. *See*: DOUBLE JEOPARDY; LIFE OR LIMB.

J.I.N.S.   Abbreviation for JUVENILE IN NEED OF SUPERVISION.

J.N.O.V.   Abbreviation for JUDGMENT NON OBSTANTE VEREDICTO.

JOHN DOE.   A fictitious name used in legal proceedings and documents for purposes of argument or illustration or to designate a man until his real name can be determined or revealed. The name Jane Doe is often used for the same purposes when a woman is involved.

JOHN DOE WARRANT.   *See*: ARREST WARRANT.

JOIN.   To bring or come together; to unite; to combine.

JOINDER.   **1.** Generally, the uniting or combining of two or more persons, parties, charges, causes of action, etc. to be considered together. In criminal proceedings, joinder means the naming of two or more **defendants** and/or the listing of two or more **charges** in a single **charging document**. *Example*: The court would not allow a joinder of defendants in the indictment. *See*: CONSOLIDATED TRIAL; MISJOINDER; SEVERANCE (definition 2). **2.** *See*: JOINDER OF ISSUE.

JOINDER OF ISSUE.   The point or stage at which the parties to an action take opposite sides on a disputed question of fact or law.

JOINT.   **1.** Put together; united; combined. **2.** Held by, obligating, or affecting the parties in common or as a unit. *See*: JOINT AND SEVERAL; SEVERAL.

JOINT AND SEVERAL.   Held by, obligating, or affecting the parties both as a unit and separately. *See*: JOINT; SEVERAL.

JOINT INDICTMENT.   A single INDICTMENT in which several participants in the same **crime** are **charged**.

JOINT OFFENSE.   A single offense committed by two or more persons together.

JOURNAL.   A book in which events or experiences are recorded daily or regularly.

JOYRIDING. Unlawful taking of a **motor vehicle** with intent to temporarily deprive the owner of possession. This offense is frequently codified and named **unauthorized use of a motor vehicle**.

J.P. Abbreviation for JUSTICE OF THE PEACE.

JUDGE. **n.** An elected or appointed public official with broad authority granted by statute or constitution to hear and determine **cases** and to administer **justice** in a court of law. Judges preside over **sessions** of **courts of general jurisdiction** and conduct **appellate court** business. The terms judge and **court** are often used interchangeably. *See*: JUDICIAL OFFICER. **v.** To make a decision after evaluating factual **evidence** and applying the **law**.

JUDGE-MADE LAW. Law established by judicial decisions as distinguished from law having its source in **statutes** or administrative rules and regulations.

JUDGE PRO TEM. Abbreviation for JUDGE PRO TEMPORE.

JUDGE PRO TEMPORE. A **judge** who sits in lieu of a regularly appointed or elected judge, and who is appointed with full authority to hear all of the **cases** scheduled for, and to exercise all functions of, the regular judge. A judge pro tempore is appointed to substitute for a regular judge who, for example, is on vacation or is ill. These appointments may be for a day or a week or for up to several months. Judges pro tempore are usually **attorneys**, retired judges, or **judicial officers** from other courts. *Abbreviation*: **judge pro tem.**

JUDGE TRIAL. Same as NONJURY TRIAL.

JUDGMENT. **1.** The statement of a **court's decision** of **conviction** or **acquittal** of a person charged with a **crime**. The date of a judgment of **conviction** is an important item in calculations of elapsed time in those jurisdictions where a **sentence** must be pronounced within a time limit. The count begins the day the judgment is pronounced. Judgment is sometimes used to mean any court decision, such as a judgment of conviction, an **acquittal**, a **court order**, or a **sentence**. *See*: ACCUMULATIVE JUDGMENT; ACQUITTAL; ADJUDICATION; ARREST OF JUDGMENT; CONVICTION; COURT DISPOSITION; DECISION; DECLARATORY JUDGMENT; DECREE; DEFAULT JUDGMENT; DISMISSAL; ENTRY OF JUDGMENT; ERRONEOUS JUDGMENT; FINAL JUDGMENT; FINDING; IN JUDGMENT; JUDGMENT NOTWITHSTANDING THE VERDICT; JUDGMENT ON THE MERITS; JUVENILE COURT JUDGMENT; MANDATE; MEMORANDUM DECISION; MOTION TO SET ASIDE JUDGMENT; OPINION; ORDER; PER CURIAM; PRAECIPE; RECALL A JUDGMENT; RENDITION OF JUDGMENT; REVERSE; SENTENCE; VERDICT. **2.** Generally, the determination or decision of a court upon a matter within its jurisdiction; the final

Ji

conclusion of a court as to matters of **fact** and **law**. Sometimes judgment is used only in the sense of a final or authoritative decision. **3.** The ability to make well-reasoned decisions; wisdom; good sense.

JUDGMENT NON OBSTANTE VEREDICTO. *Abbreviation*: **J.N.O.V.** Same as JUDGMENT NOTWITHSTANDING THE VERDICT.

JUDGMENT NOTWITHSTANDING THE VERDICT. A JUDGMENT opposite to the **verdict** reached by the **jury** because there is neither sufficient **evidence** nor reasonable **inference** from the evidence to support the verdict. In granting a **motion** for judgment notwithstanding the verdict, the court must regard all competent evidence favorable to the party opposing the motion as true and must give that party the benefit of every favorable inference that may reasonably be drawn from the evidence. In a criminal case, a judgment notwithstanding the verdict only of **acquittal** is possible and is ordered if the prosecution's evidence is insufficient to overcome the **presumption of innocence** in favor of the defendant. A judgment notwithstanding the verdict of **conviction** would be unauthorized because it would violate the defendant's constitutional right to a jury determination of guilt or innocence. *Also called*: **judgment non obstante veredicto**. *Abbreviation:* **J.N.O.V.** See JUDGMENT and VERDICT for lists of related terms. *See also*: DIRECTED VERDICT.

JUDGMENT OF ONE'S PEERS. Same as JURY TRIAL.

JUDGMENT ON THE MERITS. A JUDGMENT rendered after presentation of **evidence** and **argument** and determining the substantial or real **issues** between the parties, as distinguished from a judgment based on jurisdictional, procedural, or technical grounds. A judgment on the merits is a **final judgment** and is appealable. A judgment based on procedural or technical grounds or a default judgment is a **dismissal without prejudice** and is not a judgment on the merits. A party whose case is dismissed without prejudice can bring the suit again as long as the procedural errors are corrected. A party who receives a judgment on the merits, however, is barred from relitigating the same issue by the doctrine of **res judicata**. See JUDGMENT for a list of related terms.

JUDICATURE. **1.** The administration of **justice**. **2.** The office, function, or authority of a **judge**. **3.** The **jurisdiction** or extent of jurisdiction of a court or judge. **4.** A body of **judges**; a **court** or courts of justice; a system of courts and judges; the judicial branch of government.

JUDICIAL. **1.** Of or relating to the administration of **justice**, **courts**, or **judges**. **2.** The branch of government charged with interpreting the laws and deciding controversies that arise under the laws. **3.** *See*: JUDICIAL ACT. **4.** Of or pertaining to the **judiciary**.

JUDICIAL ACT. An act that requires the exercise of **discretion** or **judgment** (definition 3) as distinguished from a **ministerial act** or other clerical or routine procedure. A judicial act affects the rights or property of the parties before the court. It involves the interpretation and application of the **law** to a particular set of **facts** contested by the parties in court.

JUDICIAL ACTION. The determination by a **court** of the rights and interests of adverse parties. Judicial action is taken only in **justiciable controversies**.

JUDICIAL ADMISSION. An ADMISSION (definition 1) of a fact made in **court** voluntarily by a party so that the opposing party does not have to prove that fact.

JUDICIAL COGNIZANCE. Same as JUDICIAL NOTICE.

JUDICIAL DISCRETION. *See*: DISCRETION.

JUDICIAL KNOWLEDGE. Same as JUDICIAL NOTICE.

JUDICIAL NOTICE. Recognition by a **court** on its own **motion**, or at the request of a party, of the existence and truth of certain facts without requiring them to be proved, because those facts are universally known and undisputed. Examples of facts of which a court may take judicial notice are historical events and dates, existence of laws, geographical locations and features, etc. *Also called*: **cognizance**; **judicial cognizance**; **judicial knowledge**. See FACT and NOTICE for a list of related terms.

JUDICIAL OFFICER. Any person authorized by statute, constitutional provision, or rules of court to exercise those powers reserved to the **judicial** branch of government. There are a wide variety of judicial officers with varying degrees of authority. Only within a particular jurisdiction is it possible to make a distinction on a consistent basis between those judicial officers commonly called **judges** and those known by other titles. These other judicial officers receive delegated authority through a **court** or in certain cases limited authority by statute. They may also be defined as those officers whose decisions cannot become court orders without confirmation by a judge.

Judicial officers of all types may have special names indicating particular roles or functions within the modern judicial system, or names that reflect historical roles, derived from longstanding tradition. One of the oldest names is **magistrate**. Names for other judicial officers include **justices of the peace**, **masters**, **commissioners**, **referees**, **hearing officers**, and collectively, **parajudicial personnel** or **parajudges**. Some of these parajudicial personnel perform basic functions of the judicial process such as setting **bail** and hearing certain kinds of cases. Others specialize in or are limited to a particular type of proceeding such as probate, juvenile matters, traffic, or domestic relations. Still others are officials such as **paroling authority** members and certain **probation officers**, holding specified, limited judicial powers in relation to the powers and duties of the administrative agencies to which they belong. The

Jj

authority of officials known by these titles in any given jurisdiction depends upon the combination of statutes, administrative rules, and customs governing practice in the particular jurisdiction.

JUDICIAL POWER.   The authority of the **judicial** branch of government to exercise judicial functions. Judicial power includes the ability of **courts** to **punish** persons for committing **crimes**, to declare **laws unconstitutional**, to interpret **statutes**, to resolve **controversies**, to adopt **rules** of court, to issue binding **orders** and **decisions**, and to control the admission of attorneys to the bar. The judicial power of state courts is set out in state constitutions and statutes. The judicial power of federal courts is derived from Article III of the Constitution. *See*: UNITED STATES SUPREME COURT.

JUDICIAL PROCESS.   *See*: PROCESS (definition 2).

JUDICIAL QUESTION.   An issue proper for determination by a court, as distinguished from a political question or a legislative question.

JUDICIAL REVIEW.   "Judicial review is the exercise by **courts** of their responsibility to determine whether acts of the other two branches are illegal and void because those acts violate the **constitution**. The doctrine authorizes courts to determine whether a law is constitutional, not whether it is necessary or useful. In other words, judicial review is the power to say what the constitution means and not whether such a law reflects a wise policy. Adherence to the doctrine of judicial review is essential to achieving balance in our government.... Judicial review, coupled with the specified constitutional provisions which keep the judicial branch separate and independent of the other branches of government and with those articles of the constitution that protect the impartiality of the judiciary from public and political pressure, enables the courts to ensure that the constitutional rights of each citizen will not be encroached upon by either the legislative or the executive branch of the government." *State v. LaFrance*, 471 A.2d 340, 343-44 (N.H. 1983).

JUDICIARY.   **1.** The system of **courts** in a state or country; the body of judges; the bench. **2.** The branch of government responsible for the **interpretation** and **construction** of the **law**, the application of the law in deciding cases, and the administration of **justice** generally.

JUMP BAIL.   To forfeit BAIL by absconding (see **abscond**). See BAIL for a list of related terms.

JURAL CAUSE.   Same as PROXIMATE CAUSE.

JURAT.   The statement at the end of an **affidavit** showing when, where, and before whom the affidavit was sworn.

JURATION. The act of swearing.

JURE. By right or law.

JURIDICAL. Of or relating to the administration of the **law** or **judicial** proceedings.

JURISDICTION. **1.** The territory, subject matter, or person over which lawful authority may be exercised by a **court** or other justice agency, as determined by statute or constitution. *Example*: Criminal cases are not within the jurisdiction of the probate court. **2.** The lawful authority or power of a **court** or an administrative agency to act upon or deal with a matter. *Example*: Police agencies do not have jurisdiction over most private disputes. **3.** The jurisdiction of a **court**, more specifically, is the lawful authority or power to hear or act upon a **case** or question and to pass and enforce **judgment** on it. A particular court can have more than one kind of jurisdiction. *Example*: An appellate court will have appellate jurisdiction over felony cases and original jurisdiction for the issuance of certain writs, but no jurisdiction to conduct trials. *See*: ABSTENTION; ANCILLARY JURISDICTION; APPELLATE COURT; APPELLATE JURISDICTION; BAILIWICK; COGNIZABLE; COMPETENT COURT; CONCURRENT JURISDICTION; COORDINATE JURISDICTION; COURT; COURT OF GENERAL JURISDICTION; COURT OF LAST RESORT; COURT OF LIMITED JURISDICTION; CRIMINAL JURISDICTION; DISPOSITION; EXCESS OF JURISDICTION; EXCLUSIVE JURISDICTION; FAMILY COURT; FULL JURISDICTION; GENERAL APPEARANCE; IN PERSONAM; IN REM; INTERMEDIATE APPELLATE COURT; JUDICATURE; JUVENILE COURT; JUVENILE JURISDICTION; MUNICIPAL COURT; ORIGINAL JURISDICTION; PENDENT JURISDICTION; POLICE COURT; SESSIONS; SITUS; SPECIAL APPEARANCE; SUBJECT MATTER JURISDICTION; SUMMARY JURISDICTION; SUPERIOR COURT; TERRITORIAL JURISDICTION; TRIAL; TRIAL COURT; UNITED STATES COURTS; UNITED STATES COURTS OF APPEAL; UNITED STATES DISTRICT COURTS; UNITED STATES SUPREME COURT; VENUE. **4.** In the **corrections** context, the authority to **confine** or **release** a person, to remove a person from or return a person to a correctional caseload, or to otherwise direct or set conditions for behavior. *Also called*: **jurisdictional control**. *See*: PHYSICAL CUSTODY; SUPERVISORY CUSTODY.

Jj

JURISDICTIONAL CONTROL (CORRECTIONS). Same as JURISDICTION (definition 4).

JURIS DOCTOR. *Latin.* "Doctor of law." The basic law degree given after successful completion of law school. The Juris Doctor degree replaced the Bachelor of Law or LL.B. as the basic law degree.

JURISPRUDENCE. The science or philosophy of **law**, its principles, and its applications.

JURIST. **1.** A person learned or skilled in the **law**; a legal scholar or writer. **2.** A JUDGE.

JUROR. A member of a JURY. See JURY for a list of related terms.

JURY. A body of persons, selected and sworn according to law, to inquire into certain matters of fact and to render a **verdict** or true answer based on **evidence** presented before them. *See:* ADMONITION; ALLEN CHARGE; ARRAY; CHALLENGE TO THE ARRAY; CHARGE; CORONER'S INQUEST; FOREMAN; GRAND JURY; HUNG JURY; IMPARTIAL JURY; INQUEST; INSTRUCTION; JUROR; JURY BOX; JURY COMMISSION; JURY PANEL; JURY POLL; JURY POOL; JURY SENTENCING; JURY TRIAL; JURY WHEEL; NONJURY TRIAL; PACK; POLL THE JURY; RETIRE; SEQUESTER; SPECIAL INTERROGATORIES; STRUCK JURY; TALESMAN; TRIAL; TRIAL JURY; TRIER OF FACT; VENIRE; VENIRE DE NOVO; VENIRE FACIAS; VERDICT; VOIR DIRE.

JURY BOX. The place in a courtroom where the **jury** sits during the trial of a case. See JURY for a list of related terms.

JURY COMMISSIONER or COMMISSION. A public officer or body charged with the duty of ascertaining the names and addresses of persons qualified to act as **jurors** and sometimes of actually selecting by lot a **jury panel**. See JURY for a list of related terms.

JURY PANEL. The group of persons summoned to appear in court as potential **jurors** for a particular trial, or the persons selected from the group of potential jurors to sit in the **jury box**, from which second group those acceptable to the **prosecution** and the **defense** are finally chosen as the **jury**. The group of persons who are asked to sit in the jury box are usually selected by the court clerk by lot. As individuals are dismissed from the box for various reasons, replacements are chosen, also by lot. See JURY for a list of related terms.

JURY POLL. A poll conducted by a **judicial officer** or by the **clerk of court** after a **jury** has stated its **verdict** but before that verdict has been entered in the record of the court, asking each juror individually whether he or she agrees with the stated verdict. A jury poll can be initiated by **motion** of the **prosecution** or the **defense**, or of the court. If the poll determines that all or the required portion of jurors do not agree on a verdict, then the jury in some jurisdictions may be sent back for further deliberation, or in other jurisdictions, discharged. See JURY and VERDICT for lists of related terms.

JURY POOL. The segment of the population within a given jurisdiction that is summoned for **jury** duty, and that must appear as potential **jurors** for a particular **trial**. See JURY for a list of related terms.

JURY SENTENCING.   The recommendation or determination of a **sentence** by the **jury**, after it has rendered a **verdict** of **guilty**. Jury sentencing occurs only in those jurisdictions that have statutes specifically authorizing it, and usually relates only to crimes punishable by death or by life imprisonment. When the jury recommends a sentence, generally the court is not required to accept it. In some jurisdictions, however, the jury by statute makes a final determination of sentence. See JURY and SENTENCE for lists of related terms.

JURY TRIAL.   A TRIAL in which a **jury** determines the issues of **fact** and renders a **guilty verdict** or a **not guilty verdict** and in which a **judge** determines issues of **law**. Article III, Section II, Clause 3 of the U.S. Constitution provides that "[t]he trial of all Crimes, except in cases of Impeachment, shall be by Jury. . ." The Sixth Amendment to the U.S. Constitution provides that "[i]n all criminal prosecutions, the accused shall enjoy the right to a speedy and public trial, by an impartial jury of the State and district wherein the crime shall have been committed. . ." The Fourteenth Amendment guarantees a right of jury trial in all criminal cases that— were they to be tried in a federal court—would come within the Sixth Amendment's guarantee. *Duncan v. Louisiana*, 391 U.S. 145, 88 S.Ct. 1444, 20 L.Ed.2d 491 (1968). Practice varies among jurisdictions in granting the right to a jury trial in cases where a minor offense is charged. The right to a jury trial may be **waived** by the **defense**.

Jury trial comprehends a full and fair hearing upon all relevant issues and a determination by a fair, impartial, and lawfully constituted jury. The jury's determination must be made in the presence of and under the supervision of a judge empowered to **instruct** them on the law, to advise them on the facts, and, except on **acquittal** of a criminal charge, to set aside their verdict if contrary to the law or evidence. *Also called*: **judgment of one's peers**; **trial by jury**; **trial per pais**. See JURY and TRIAL for lists of related terms.

JURY WHEEL.   A revolving mechanism or circular box from which the names of persons to serve as **jurors** may be drawn by chance. See JURY for a list of related terms.

JUS.   *Latin.* "Law." **1.** The **law**, considered abstractly or taken as a whole; the law of the land; the whole body or system of law. **2.** A legal right to something or to do something.

Jj

JUST.   **1.** Legally right or valid; lawful. **2.** Morally right; fair; equitable.

JUSTICE.   **1.** Fair and equal treatment under the **law**. *Example*: People expect justice from the courts. **2.** Rightfulness; lawfulness; validity. *Example*: I see the justice of your claim. **3.** Administration of law or judicial proceedings. *Example*: The university has a department of criminal justice. **4.** The name given to **judges** of the U.S. Supreme Court and to judges of high courts in many states. *Example*: The President announced his nominee for U.S. Supreme Court justice.

JUSTICE ASSISTANCE, BUREAU OF. *See*: BUREAU OF JUSTICE ASSISTANCE.

JUSTICE COURT. *See*: COURT OF LIMITED JURISDICTION.

JUSTICE, DEPARTMENT OF. *See*: DEPARTMENT OF JUSTICE.

JUSTICE OF THE PEACE. A lower **judicial officer** in a state court system who may, depending on the state, decide minor **civil** and **criminal cases**, conduct **preliminary examinations** of persons accused of more serious crimes, solemnize marriages, and administer oaths. The jurisdiction of a justice of the peace is governed by statute and varies from state to state. *Abbreviation*: **J.P.**

JUSTICE PROGRAMS, OFFICE OF. The Office of Justice Programs (OJP) in the **Department of Justice** was established by the Justice Assistance Act of 1984 and reauthorized in 1988 to help foster the cooperation and coordination needed to make the criminal justice system function effectively. The Assistant Attorney General for the Office of Justice Programs, by statute and delegation from the **Attorney General**, carries out policy coordination and general management responsibilities for the office's five components: **Bureau of Justice Assistance**, **Bureau of Justice Statistics**, **National Institute of Justice**, **Office of Juvenile Justice and Delinquency Prevention**, and **Office for Victims of Crime**. While each program bureau or office retains independent authority in awarding funds to carry out programs it sponsors, together these components constitute a single agency whose goal is to implement innovative programs and to foster improvements in the nation's criminal and juvenile justice systems.

The Office of Justice Programs works to form partnerships with state and local governments to help policymakers, practitioners, and the public understand what crime, especially drug abuse, costs in terms of public safety and the social and economic health of communities. Although some research and technical assistance is provided directly by OJP's bureaus and offices, most of the work is accomplished through federal financial assistance to scholars, practitioners, and state and local governments. Program bureaus and offices award formula grants to state agencies, which, in turn, subgrant funds to units of state and local government. Formula grant programs—drug control and system improvement, juvenile justice, victims compensation, and victims assistance—are administered by state agencies designated by each state's governor. Discretionary grant programs usually are announced in the **Federal Register**, and applications are made directly to the sponsoring Office of Justice Programs bureau or office.

JUSTICESHIP. The office of a JUSTICE.

JUSTICE STATISTICS, BUREAU OF. *See*: BUREAU OF JUSTICE STATISTICS.

JUSTICIABLE.   Proper or liable to be tried in a **court**; subject to determination by a court. *See*: JUSTICIABLE CONTROVERSY.

JUSTICIABLE CONTROVERSY.   A genuine or substantial dispute between parties that is capable of being conclusively decided by a **court**. A justiciable controversy is definite and concrete as distinguished from a mere debate or disagreement, from hypothetical questions or disputes, and from moot and academic matters. To be justiciable, a controversy must be ripe. *See*: RIPENESS DOCTRINE.

JUSTIFIABLE.   Capable of being justified (see **justify**); defensible.

JUSTIFIABLE HOMICIDE.   An intentional **homicide** committed in the legal performance of an official duty or in circumstances defined by law as constituting legal **justification**. Examples of homicides committed in the performance of official legal duty are the killing of an enemy under the rules of war and the lawful execution of a sentence of death. Examples of homicides committed with legal justification are a killing by a **law enforcement officer** of a fleeing dangerous **felon** and a killing in defense of oneself or others against an imminent threat of death or great bodily harm. Justifiable homicide is not a **crime**. See HOMICIDE for a listing of various categories of homicide.

JUSTIFICATION.   A reason or excuse that is adequate to free a person from guilt for an act or failure to act that would otherwise be unlawful.

JUSTIFY.   **1.** To demonstrate a good reason or excuse for something done. **2.** To declare free of **guilt**; to absolve. **3.** *See*: JUSTIFY BAIL.

JUSTIFY BAIL.   To prove that a person furnishing **bail** or other **surety** is of adequate financial ability. See BAIL for a list of related terms.

JUVENILE.   A person whose age is below a statutory limit. The statutory age limit varies among states and also, with respect to specified crimes, within states. The generally applicable age limit within a given state is most often the 18th birthday. In statutes establishing criminal trial court jurisdiction over persons below the standard age for specified crimes (usually violent crimes such as murder or armed robbery), the age limit may be lowered to 16 or even less.

For purposes of jurisdiction of a **juvenile court**, a juvenile may be defined as a person subject to juvenile court proceedings because a statutorily defined event or condition caused by or affecting that person was alleged to have occurred while his or her age was below the statutorily specified age limit of original jurisdiction of a juvenile court. Court jurisdiction is determined by age at the time of the event, not at the time of judicial proceedings, and continues in juvenile offender cases until the case is terminated (unless the case is transferred to adult court for prosecution). *See*: ADJUDICATION; ADJUDICATORY HEARING; ADULT; AFTERCARE; AL-

Jj

LEGED DELINQUENT; ALLEGED STATUS OFFENDER; BIND OVER; CHILD ABUSE; CHILD IN NEED OF SUPERVISION; CHILD NEGLECT; DELINQUENT; DELINQUENT ACT; DEPENDENCY; DEPENDENT; DETENTION CENTER; DETENTION HEARING; DIAGNOSTIC COMMITMENT; DISPOSITION HEARING; DIVERSION; FAMILY COURT; GROUP HOME; HALFWAY HOUSE; IN RE GAULT; INTAKE; INTAKE DECISION; INTAKE UNIT; JUVENILE COMPLAINT; JUVENILE COURT; JUVENILE COURT JUDGMENT; JUVENILE DISPOSITION; JUVENILE FACILITY; JUVENILE JURISDICTION; JUVENILE JUSTICE AND DELINQUENCY PREVENTION, OFFICE OF; JUVENILE JUSTICE AGENCY; JUVENILE PETITION; JUVENILE RECORD; PAROLE; PETITION NOT SUSTAINED; PREADJUDICATED; PREDISPOSITION INVESTIGATION; PREDISPOSITION REPORT; PROBATION; PROBATION AGENCY; REFERRAL TO INTAKE; RUNAWAY; SHELTER; STATUS OFFENDER; STATUS OFFENSE; TRAINING SCHOOL; TRANSFER HEARING; TRANSFER TO ADULT COURT; TRUANT; YOUTHFUL OFFENDER.

JUVENILE ADJUDICATION.   Same as JUVENILE COURT JUDGMENT.

JUVENILE COMPLAINT.   A JUVENILE PETITION alleging that a **juvenile** is a **delinquent** or **status offender**. See JUVENILE for a list of related terms.

JUVENILE COURT.   A **court** that has **original jurisdiction** over matters concerning persons statutorily defined as **juveniles**. A juvenile court may be a separately established court, a special division of a court, or a **special session** of a court. Courts dealing with juveniles range in different states from the lowest level of courts to the highest courts of general jurisdiction. See COURT, JURISDICTION, and JUVENILE for lists of related terms.

JUVENILE COURT JUDGMENT.   The **juvenile court decision** terminating an **adjudicatory hearing**, that the **juvenile** is a **delinquent**, **status offender**, or **dependent**, or that the allegations in the **petition** are not sustained (see **petition not sustained**). A **judgment** that a juvenile has committed a **delinquent act** is similar to a **conviction** in a court having **criminal jurisdiction**, in that a court has made a finding that the juvenile has committed an act that could be prosecuted as a **crime** if he or she were **adult**. (The judgments status offender and dependent have no parallel in criminal proceedings.) Petition not sustained is comparable to a **dismissal** or **acquittal**. The **juvenile disposition** follows the judgment, and in the case of juvenile offenders, is similar to an adult **sentencing disposition**. See COURT, JUDGMENT, and JUVENILE for lists of related terms.

JUVENILE DELINQUENT.   *See*: DELINQUENT.

JUVENILE DISPOSITION.   The decision of a **juvenile court** concluding a **disposition hearing** that an adjudicated **juvenile** be committed to a juvenile facility, placed on **probation**, placed in a juvenile residence, shelter, care, or treatment program, required to meet certain standards of conduct, or **released**. A juvenile disposition of an adjudged **delinquent** or **status offender** is similar to an adult **sentence** in that both are decisions that may result in **confinement** or other restrictions on behavior. A juvenile disposition is not necessarily final, since the disposition may include provisions for review of the decision by the juvenile court at a specific later date. See DISPOSITION, JUVENILE, and SENTENCE for lists of related terms.

JUVENILE FACILITY.   A building, part of a building, set of buildings, or area enclosing a set of buildings or structures, that is used for the **custody** and/or care and treatment of **juveniles** who have been administratively determined to be in need of care or who have been formally alleged or judged to be **delinquents**, **status offenders**, or **dependents**. Juvenile facilities may be operated by public agencies or by private organizations.

Juvenile facilities may be classified as **short-term facilities** or **long-term facilities**. Short-term facilities are those that primarily care for juveniles in **detention** awaiting **adjudication**, **commitment**, or **placement**, and/or those being held for diagnosis or classification. Short-term facilities may be called **detention centers**, **shelters**, or reception or **diagnosis centers**. Long-term facilities are those that primarily care for juveniles received following **commitment** or placement by a **juvenile court**, those received as voluntary admissions, and/or those on **probation** or **aftercare**. Long-term facilities may be called **farms, forestry camps, group homes, halfway houses, ranches, reformatories, reform schools**, or **training schools**.

Juvenile facilities may also be classified as **open facilities** and **institutional facilities**. Open facilities are those in which access to the community is relatively frequent, in-house restrictions including physical security features are minimal, and entrances and exits are relatively uncontrolled. Institutional facilities are those with relatively little community access and considerable in-house restrictions in the form of physical restrictions and staff controls. See JUVENILE for a list of related terms. *See also*: CORRECTIONAL FACILITY.

JUVENILE IN NEED OF SUPERVISION.   Same as CHILD IN NEED OF SUPERVISION. *Abbreviation*: **J.I.N.S.**

JUVENILE JURISDICTION.   The authority given to a **court** to hear or act upon a case involving a person statutorily defined as a **juvenile** who is alleged to be a **delinquent, dependent**, or **status offender**. See JURISDICTION and JUVENILE for lists of related terms.

JUVENILE JUSTICE AGENCY.   A government agency whose function is the investigation, **supervision**, **adjudication**, care, or **confinement** of **juvenile** offenders and nonoffenders subject to the **jurisdiction** of a **juvenile court**. In addition to agencies dealing with alleged and adjudicated **delinquents** and **status of-**

Jj

fenders, this definition includes agencies that deal only with **dependents**, who have committed no offense. See JUVENILE for a list of related terms.

JUVENILE JUSTICE AND DELINQUENCY PREVENTION, NATIONAL INSTITUTE FOR. *See*: JUVENILE JUSTICE AND DELINQUENCY PREVENTION, OFFICE OF.

JUVENILE JUSTICE AND DELINQUENCY PREVENTION, OFFICE OF. The Office of Juvenile Justice and Delinquency Prevention, in the **Office of Justice Programs**, was created by the Juvenile Justice and Delinquency Prevention Act of 1974 (42 U.S.C. §5601) in response to national concern about juvenile crime. It is the primary federal agency for addressing juvenile crime and delinquency and the problem of missing and exploited children. The office comprises four divisions:

1. The Training, Dissemination, and Technical Assistance Division is one of two divisions that make up the **National Institute for Juvenile Justice and Delinquency Prevention**. The division sponsors training for juvenile justice practitioners and provides technical assistance in planning, funding, establishing, operating, and evaluating juvenile delinquency programs. It also serves as a clearinghouse for preparing, publishing, and disseminating information about juvenile justice.

2. The Research and Program Development Division, also part of the National Institute, sponsors research about national trends in juvenile delinquency and drug use, serious juvenile crime, the causes of delinquency, prevention strategies, and the juvenile justice system.

3. The Special Emphasis Division provides funds directly to public and private nonprofit agencies and individuals to foster new approaches to delinquency prevention and control and the improvement of the juvenile justice system. The division focuses on such areas as chronic juvenile offenders, gangs and drug-related juvenile crime, school crime, and the victimization of children.

4. The State Relations and Assistance Division oversees the formula grants program. States can receive formula grants to help implement delinquency prevention and system improvement programs, including the mandates of the Juvenile Justice and Delinquency Prevention Act, as amended. These mandates include deinstitutionalizing status offenders, separating juveniles from adult offenders in institutions, and removing juveniles from adult jails and lockups.

Two programs—the Concentration of Federal Efforts Program and the Missing Children's Program—are also under the Office's direction.

—The Concentration of Federal Efforts Program coordinates federal programs dealing with juvenile delinquency and assists federal agencies that have responsibility for delinquency prevention and treatment. It also helps implement programs between departments and agencies that influence the success of the federal juvenile delinquency effort.

—The Missing Children's Program was created in 1984 by the Missing Children's Assistance Act to coordinate federally funded programs relating to missing and exploited children. The program serves as a central focus for research, data collection, policy development, and information about missing and exploited children. It also funds the National Center for Missing and Exploited Children, which operates a national toll-free telephone line and serves as a national information clearinghouse.

See JUVENILE for a list of related terms.

JUVENILE PAROLE. Same as AFTERCARE.

JUVENILE PETITION. A document filed in **juvenile court** alleging that a **juvenile** is a **delinquent**, a **status offender**, or a **dependent**, and asking that the court assume **jurisdiction** over the juvenile, or asking that an alleged delinquent be transferred to a criminal court for **prosecution** as an **adult**. Petitions may be filed by a **prosecutor** or by an officer of an **intake unit**. (In cases of dependency, where the allegations concern the behavior of the adult responsible for the juvenile, petitions may be filed by a social welfare agent or other government officer.) In some states private citizens may also file petitions. A juvenile need not have been taken into custody in order for a petition to be filed. Filing of a petition results in an **adjudicatory hearing** to determine the truth of the allegations, or a **transfer hearing** to determine if jurisdiction should be waived, or both. See JUVENILE for a list of related terms.

JUVENILE RECORD. An official **record** containing information on **juvenile court** proceedings and detention and correctional processes relating to a particular **juvenile**. The nature and content of juvenile records varies from state to state. Statutes usually permit or require the **sealing** or **purging** of juvenile records by court order when the juvenile reaches a certain age. See JUVENILE for a list of related terms.

JUXTAPOSED. Placed side by side (especially for purposes of comparison or contrast). See PROXIMITY for a list of related terms.

Jj

KATZ v. UNITED STATES. *See*: RIGHT OF PRIVACY.

KEEP. **1.** To maintain or cause to continue in some action, position, or condition. *Example*: All vehicles must keep to the right of the center line of the highway. **2.** To carry on; to manage; to conduct. *Example*: It is not against the law to keep a saloon. **3.** To have in possession habitually and continuously; to store. *Example*: The barn where illegal liquor was kept. **4.** To take care of; to support; to provide with the necessities of life and protect from danger. *Example*: She was reprimanded for keeping a dangerous animal. **5.** To maintain by making regular entries. *Example*: The clerk keeps the records of the court.

KIDNAPING. Same as KIDNAPPING.

KIDNAPPING. Transportation or **confinement** of a person without authority of law and without his or her consent, or without the consent of his or her guardian, if a minor. Kidnapping may be accomplished by **force**, **threat**, or **deception** and is often accompanied by a demand for **ransom**. State and federal laws prohibit kidnapping, often with variations in the definition of the crime. Some states place unlawful transportation and unlawful confinement without transportation together in a single penal code section and under a single name, as above. Some states, however, have established two or more separate statutory offenses, only one of which has the name kidnapping. One of the others is often called **false imprisonment**. Some version of the unlawful transport type of offense is sometimes called or defined as **abduction**.

Statutory definitions of kidnapping can be very narrow, as when the elements are unlawful transportation by use of force, with confinement and concealment, for the purpose of **extortion**. But the range of behavior having to do with unlawful transport and/or confinement extends from narrowly defined kidnapping to abduction for the purpose of compelling marriage and the taking of a child from the parent having legal custody by the parent not having legal custody.

An example of a modern definition of kidnapping is section 212.1 of the **Model Penal Code**, which reads as follows:

"Section 212.1 Kidnapping

A person is guilty of kidnapping if he unlawfully removes another from his place of residence or business, or a substantial distance from the vicinity where he is found, or if he unlawfully confines another for a substantial period in a place of isolation, with any of the following purposes:

(a) to hold for ransom or reward, or as a shield or hostage; or

(b) to facilitate commission of any felony or flight thereafter; or

(c) to inflict bodily injury on or to terrorize the victim or another; or

(d) to interfere with the performance of any governmental or political function.

Kidnapping is a felony of the first degree unless the actor voluntarily releases the victim alive and in a safe place prior to trial, in which case it is a felony of the second degree. A removal or confinement is unlawful within the meaning of this Section if it is accomplished by force, threat or deception, or, in the case of a person who is under the age of 14 or incompetent, if it is accomplished without the consent of a parent, guardian or other person responsible for general supervision of his welfare."

KILL. To put to death; to slay; to deprive of life. See DEATH for a list of related terms.

KILLING BY MISADVENTURE. Same as HOMICIDE BY MISADVENTURE.

KITING. The unlawful practice of drawing checks against a bank account containing insufficient funds to cover the checks, with the expectation that sufficient funds will be deposited before the checks are cashed. *See*: CHECK FRAUD; FORGERY.

KLEPTOMANIA. An irresistible desire to **steal** without regard to economic needs.

KNOW. To possess information; to understand; to perceive; to be aware of.

KNOWINGLY. Consciously; intelligently; understandingly; with awareness of facts and circumstances. A person acts knowingly when the person is aware of the facts and circumstances surrounding the person's actions and of the likely results of his or her actions. For the **Model Penal Code** definition of knowingly, see CULPA-BILITY.

KNOWLEDGE. Awareness or understanding of facts or concepts gained through study, investigation, perception, or experience. See FACT for a list of related terms.

KNOWN SPECIMEN. An item of physical evidence obtained from a known source to be compared with a **questioned specimen** in investigating crime. For example, a handwriting sample taken from a person or known to be produced by the person is a known specimen. Handwriting of an unknown source appearing on a bad check or other document or writing under investigation is a questioned specimen.

LACERATE. To severely tear or cut the flesh or skin.

LACHES. An unreasonable or unexplained delay by a party to an **action** in asserting a right or claim, accompanied by a change in conditions or relations between the parties that works to the disadvantage of the other party. Laches will bar the delaying party from bringing an action.

LAPSE. The termination of a right or privilege through neglect to exercise it or through the occurrence or nonoccurrence of some contingent event.

LARCENY. The trespassory taking and carrying away of the personal property of another with the intent to deprive the owner of possession either permanently or for an unreasonable length of time. Trespassory taking originally meant a taking out of the owner's possession without the owner's consent. Over the years, the definition of the term was expanded to include a taking from the owner's **constructive** possession. For example, if an owner of property was induced to give it up by lies or if a **bailee** of property misappropriated the goods, such a taking was held to be larceny despite the voluntary giving up of the property by the owner. Modern statutes tend to abolish many of these distinctions in favor of including any kind of unlawful taking within the definition of larceny. Also, at common law, larceny was limited to the taking of tangible personal property. Modern statutes have broadened the scope of larceny to include intangible personal property (stocks, checks, deeds, contracts, etc.) and certain types of removable real estate (trees, crops, minerals, fixtures, etc.).

Larceny is usually distinguished from **robbery** and **burglary** in that larceny excludes takings that require unlawful **entry**, **force**, or **threat**. Also, the taking of a **motor vehicle** is usually treated as the separate crime of motor vehicle theft. Some modern statutes do away with larceny entirely and include nearly all unlawful takings under a broadly defined crime of **theft**. See ABSTRACTION for a list of related terms.

LARCENY BY BAILEE. The unlawful **conversion** by a **bailee** of another's property, whose possession has been entrusted to the bailee. See ABSTRACTION for a list of related terms.

LARCENY BY TRICK. The obtaining of possession of, but not the title to, property of another by **deception**, fraudulently intending to convert (see **conversion**) the property and later doing so. See ABSTRACTION for a list of related terms.

LASCIVIOUS. Inclined to or tending to incite lust; exciting sexual desires; lewd.

LAST RESORT. *See*: COURT OF LAST RESORT.

LATENT. Present or existing but not visible or apparent; hidden; concealed. *See*: ABEYANCE; PATENT.

LATENT FINGERPRINT. An impression of the skin ridge pattern of a finger or thumb left by the pressing of the finger or thumb against a smooth surface. Latent fingerprints may be either visible, invisible, or plastic. Visible prints are those left in a visible substance such as blood, soot, or powder. Invisible prints are those left when the coating of perspiration, oil, or dirt on the skin ridges comes in contact with a smooth hard surface such as glass or metal. Invisible prints can be made visible by treating them with certain powders and chemicals. Plastic prints are those more durable prints made in substances such as putty, clay, or grease.

Fingerprint identification involves the comparison of unidentified latent prints left at a crime scene with identified inked fingerprints on fingerprint record cards in police files. The reliability of fingerprint comparison evidence is so well established today that most courts will take **judicial notice** of it as a valuable method of positive identification of criminals.

LAW. **1.** A society's means of protecting the persons, rights, and property of its citizens, of enforcing their contracts, of holding them liable for their torts, and of punishing their crimes through rules and governmental machinery to apply, enforce, interpret, and modify those rules. *Example*: Everyone is guaranteed equal treatment under the law. **2.** A written or unwritten rule, principle, or standard governing human conduct established in a constitution or promulgated by a legislative or judicial authority and requiring the compliance of the people governed. *Example*: The state of Maine has completely recodified its criminal laws. See ACT for a list of related terms. **3.** The body of LAWS (definition 2). *Example*: The criminal law changes rapidly. **4.** A STATUTE. *Example*: The legislature enacted several important criminal laws this session. **5.** The proper principle or principles to be applied to a **fact** or set of facts in making judicial rulings. *Example*: Questions of law are decided by the court; questions of fact are decided by the jury. **6.** The science of the LAW (definition 1); the department of knowledge dealing with the principles of the LAW (definition 1); jurisprudence. *Example*: She wants to study law. **7.** The entire governmental machinery and procedure dealing with LAW (definition 1). *Example*: If we can't settle this matter, I am going to resort to the law. **8.** A system of jurisprudence concerned with the **common law**, its origin, theory, and methods, as distinguished from **equity**. *Example*: The object of equity is to render the administration of justice more complete by affording relief where the courts of law are incompetent to give it. **9.** The profession that involves giving legal advice, preparing legal pleadings and instruments, and preparing, managing, and trying cases in courts.

LAW ENFORCEMENT. The generic name for the activities of the agencies responsible for maintaining public order and enforcing the law, particularly the activities

L

of prevention, detection, and investigation of **crime** and the apprehension of **criminals**. The modern preference for law enforcement in many official contexts instead of the older term **police** does not represent a difference in meaning. The **police power** is the inherent power of the state to regulate affairs within its jurisdiction in the interests of the safety and welfare of its citizens. A police force or **law enforcement agency** is the body of professional persons to which a government delegates authority to implement its police power. See CRIME for a list of related terms.

LAW ENFORCEMENT AGENCY. A federal, state, or local **criminal justice agency** whose principal functions are the maintenance of public order; the detection, investigation, and prevention of **crime**; and the apprehension of alleged offenders against the law. Examples of law enforcement agencies are state police agencies; state highway patrols; law enforcement subunits within federal or state regulatory agencies, and within port, bridge, or transit authorities and special districts; campus police departments of publicly financed colleges and universities; sheriff's departments; and city police departments. Examples of agencies that are not law enforcement agencies are **correctional agencies**, **courts**, **prosecution agencies**, and their subunits; agencies primarily concerned with the protection of natural resources or health, such as forestry or fish and wildlife departments or sanitation inspection units; and special prosecutorial subunits such as the organized crime unit of the U.S. **Department of Justice** and the prosecutorial units of regulatory agencies. *See*: CRIME; FEDERAL LAW ENFORCEMENT AGENCY; LOCAL LAW ENFORCEMENT AGENCY; STATE LAW ENFORCEMENT AGENCY.

LAW ENFORCEMENT OFFICER. An employee of a **law enforcement agency** who is an officer sworn to carry out **law enforcement** duties such as maintaining public order, detecting, investigating, and preventing **crime**, and arresting alleged offenders against the law. Sworn personnel are persons formally authorized to make **arrests** while acting within the scope of explicit legal authority. *See*: ARREST; ASSAULT ON A LAW ENFORCEMENT OFFICER; BAILIFF; BOOKING; CHIEF OF POLICE; CITATION; CONSTABLE; DEPUTY SHERIFF; DETECTIVE; FEDERAL LAW ENFORCEMENT OFFICER; FIELD INTERROGATION; FIELD INTERVIEW; FRESH PURSUIT; FRISK; HOT PURSUIT; INTERNATIONAL ASSOCIATION OF CHIEFS OF POLICE; INTERROGATION; LINEUP; LOCAL LAW ENFORCEMENT OFFICER; MARSHAL; PATROLMAN; PEACE OFFICER; POLICE OFFICER; POLICE WITNESS; PRESENCE OF AN OFFICER; PRIVATE PERSON; PROBATION OFFICER; RESISTING AN OFFICER; RESISTING ARREST; RETURN; ROAD BLOCK; SEARCH; SEIZURE; SHERIFF; STATE HIGHWAY PATROL OFFICER; STATE POLICE OFFICER; STOP; STOP AND FRISK; TURNKEY; WARDEN; WARRANT.

LAWFUL. Permitted, authorized, or sanctioned by **law**; not forbidden by law. Lawful and **legal** are sometimes used interchangeably. Lawful, however, usually relates to the substance of the law, whereas legal relates to the form or procedure of the law. For example, a lawful act is an act that is authorized, sanctioned, or not forbidden by the law. A legal act is an act performed in accordance with the formalities, procedures, or technicalities of the law. Also, lawful sometimes implies a reference to ethical considerations or to another, perhaps higher, law such as natural law, moral law, divine law, or **common law**. *Example*: It is your lawful right to speak out against the government.

LAWFUL AGE. Same as MAJORITY.

LAWLESS. **1.** Unrestrained or uncontrolled by the **law**. *Example*: Some underground protest groups are completely lawless. **2.** Contrary to or heedless of the law. *Example*: Taking her automobile was a lawless act.

LAW OF EVIDENCE. The body of rules and principles developed over the years to control the conduct of **trials** with order and efficiency and to govern the admissibility of **evidence**. See EVIDENCE for a list of related terms.

LAW OF THE CASE. "The law of the case doctrine provides: A decision of a legal issue or issues by an **appellate court** ... must be followed in all subsequent proceedings in the same case in the **trial court** or on a later **appeal** in the appellate court, unless [1] the **evidence** on a subsequent trial is substantially different, [2] controlling authority has since made a contrary decision of the law applicable to such issues, or [3] the decision was clearly erroneous and would work a manifest injustice." *U.S. v. Williams*, 728 F.2d 1402, 1405-06 (11th Cir. 1984). The law of the case doctrine differs from the **res judicata** doctrine in that:

(1) the law of the case doctrine merely directs **discretion**, while the res judicata doctrine supersedes discretion and compels **judgment**; and

(2) the law of the case doctrine applies only to the one case, while the res judicata doctrine forecloses parties in one case by what has been done in another case.

LAW OF THE LAND. **1.** Same as DUE PROCESS OF LAW. **2.** The general public **law** applicable to all citizens of a particular state or country.

LAW REPORTS. Books published in a series containing the reported opinions of courts.

LAWSUIT. Same as SUIT.

LAWYER. An ATTORNEY AT LAW.

LAY. Nonprofessional, especially not of the legal or medical profession; not having special knowledge or training; of or relating to the average or common person. *Example*: Some states allowed lay judges to perform certain quasi-legal duties.

LAYMAN. Same as LAYPERSON.

L|

LAYPERSON. A person who is not a member of a particular profession, especially the legal or medical profession.

LAY WITNESS. An ordinary, nonexpert **witness**. See WITNESS for a list of related terms.

LEADING CASE. A court **decision** that establishes an important principle, settles an important question, or is otherwise important in a particular area of the law, so that it is looked to as a guide in deciding subsequent cases. *Example*: *Miranda v. Arizona* is the leading case in the area of admissions and confessions.

LEADING COUNSEL. The one attorney, out of several on one side in a case, who has the principal responsibility for management of the case.

LEADING QUESTION. A question asked a **witness** during a trial or other proceeding that suggests the answer desired by the questioner or that puts words into the witness's mouth to be echoed back. The general rule, subject to well-defined exceptions, is that leading questions may not be used in the **direct examination** of a witness, but may be used on **cross-examination**. Leading questions may be used in the direct examination of a **hostile witness**. See EXAMINATION and WITNESS for lists of related terms.

LEAN. To incline in feeling, opinion, or conduct; to have a tendency or preference; to be somewhat partial or favorable. *Example*: The judge leans toward your interpretation of the law.

LEAVE. Permission; authorization.

LEAVING THE SCENE OF AN ACCIDENT. Same as HIT AND RUN.

LEGAL. **1.** Fulfilling the requirements of the law; conforming to the law; sufficient to be recognized by the law; not contrary to the law. Legal usually relates to the form or procedure of the law rather than the substance of the law. It often refers to compliance with formal or technical rules. Also, legal implies a reference to law as it appears in statutes or as it is administered in the courts, as distinguished from ethical or moral considerations. Legal and **lawful** are sometimes used interchangeably. *Example*: The court held that the arrest was legal. **2.** CONSTRUCTIVE; IMPLIED. *Example*: The attorney's unethical behavior constituted legal fraud. **3.** Of or relating to the law. *Example*: He decided to pursue a legal career.

LEGAL AGE. Same as MAJORITY.

LEGAL CAUSE. Same as PROXIMATE CAUSE.

LEGAL ETHICS. Rules of conduct applicable to members of the legal profession with respect to their duties toward clients, courts, fellow members of the profession, and the public.

LEGAL FICTION. Same as FICTION OF LAW.

LEGAL FRAUD. Same as CONSTRUCTIVE FRAUD.

LEGALIZE. To make LEGAL or LAWFUL; to authorize; to sanction.

LEGAL MALICE. Same as CONSTRUCTIVE MALICE.

LEGAL NOTICE. **1.** Sufficient NOTICE under the law in a particular case or for a particular purpose. **2.** Same as CONSTRUCTIVE NOTICE. See NOTICE for a list of related terms.

LEGAL REALISM. A philosophy of law that holds that other branches of knowledge such as psychology, sociology, and economics should be taken into consideration in making legal decisions.

LEGAL RESIDENCE. Same as DOMICILE.

LEGAL RIGHT. A RIGHT enforceable in the courts.

LEGIBLE. Readable.

LEG IRONS. Two braceletlike rings connected by a chain and fastened around each ankle of a person in order to slow the speed of walking or running.

LEGISLATE. To pass or **enact** a law or laws governing a nation, state, or community. Legislate may include within its meaning to **alter**, to **amend**, or to **repeal** laws.

LEGISLATION. **1.** The act, process, or result of passing or **enacting laws**; lawmaking. **2.** A law or laws enacted by a representative assembly of constitutionally elected members; a **statute** or statutes; an **ordinance** or ordinances. See ACT and STATUTE for lists of related terms.

LEGISLATIVE. **1.** Of or relating to the passing or **enacting** of **laws**. **2.** Of or relating to a LEGISLATURE. **3.** The branch or department of government responsible for the enactment of laws. *See*: EXECUTIVE; JUDICIAL.

LEGISLATIVE INTENT RULE. The doctrine that where the meaning of statutory words or provisions is ambiguous or unclear, or where the application of the **statute** to a particular set of facts is doubtful, **courts** will attempt to give effect to the intent

L|

of the legislature. Legislative intent may be determined by examining the legislative history or by evaluating the conditions that existed prior to the enactment of the law. See STATUTE for a list of related terms.

LEGISLATIVE POWER. The power to enact, alter, amend, or repeal laws.

LEGISLATOR. A person who passes or enacts laws; a member of a LEGISLATURE.

LEGISLATURE. A body of persons selected for the purpose of enacting laws for a political unit.

LEGITIMATE. adj. 1. Recognized by law; according to law; authorized by law. *Example*: A police officer is a legitimate authority to order a crowd to disperse. **adj. 2.** Born in wedlock of parents legally married. **adj. 3.** In accordance with traditional or customary standards; recognized or accepted by proper authorities. **adj. 4.** Genuine; real; authentic. **v.** To make, declare, or establish as LEGITIMATE (adj.).

LESBIAN. A female HOMOSEXUAL.

LESS. Not as much in amount, degree, or value. *See*: FEWER.

LESSER INCLUDED OFFENSE. Same as INCLUDED OFFENSE.

LET. To cause; to allow. Let is often used by **courts** in giving commands. *Example*: Let the warrant issue.

LETHAL. Capable of causing death; deadly. See DEATH for a list of related terms.

LETTER OF THE LAW. The strict and exact meaning of the words of a **statute**, as distinguished from the spirit, purpose, or policy of the statute. See STATUTE for a list of related terms.

LETTERS ROGATORY. A request in writing by one **court** to a court in another **jurisdiction** to obtain and transmit the testimony of a **witness** in that jurisdiction by means of **interrogatories** sent with the request.

LEVY. To impose; to assess. *Example*: The judge levied a heavy fine on her for littering.

LEWD. Grossly and notoriously indecent in sexual matters.

LEWD AND LASCIVIOUS COHABITATION. The open and notorious living together of a man and a woman not married to each other. *See*: COHABITATION.

LEWD HOUSE. A HOUSE OF PROSTITUTION.

LEX. *Latin.* "Law." **1.** Law; the law. Lex is used as a synonym for **jus** (definition 1), but lex does not have the alternative meaning of **right**, as does jus (definition 2). *Example*: Lex talionis, the law of retaliation, requires an eye for an eye and a tooth for a tooth. **2.** A body or system of laws.

LIABILITY. The state of being LIABLE; something for which one is liable.

LIABILITY WITHOUT FAULT STATUTE. Same as STRICT LIABILITY STATUTE.

LIABLE. **1.** Legally obligated; responsible; answerable. *Example 1*: The surety is liable if the defendant jumps bail. *Example 2*: As a citizen, you are liable for jury duty. **2.** Subject; exposed; susceptible. *Example*: She is liable to contempt if she doesn't obey the judge's commands. **3.** Likely; apt. *Example*: You're liable to lose track of the suspect if you quit trailing him now.

LIAISON. A contact or connection between groups or individuals or both for purposes of communication and cooperation.

LIBEL. The **malicious publication** (definition 3) of **defamation** by written or printed words, pictures, or other durable means. Libel is both a **crime** and a **tort**, but the crime is rarely enforced.

LIBERAL CONSTRUCTION. A **construction** of language designed to achieve its plainly disclosed spirit or purpose, without doing violence to the natural and customary meanings of words. A liberal construction of language will resolve all reasonable doubts in favor of making the language applicable to the particular case. *Also called*: **equitable construction**. *See*: STRICT CONSTRUCTION.

LIBERTY. **1.** Generally, freedom from any restriction or control. **2.** In a legal sense, freedom to enjoy all personal rights without any restraints except those reasonably and justly imposed by law for the general welfare. The Fifth and Fourteenth Amendments to the Constitution prohibit the United States or any state from depriving a person of liberty without **due process of law**. In *Allgeyer v. Louisiana*, 165 U.S. 578, 589, 17 S.Ct. 427, 431, 41 L.Ed. 832, 835-36 (1897), the U.S. Supreme Court said: "The 'liberty' mentioned in [the Fourteenth] amendment means, not only the right of the citizen to be free from the mere physical **restraint** of his person, as by **incarceration**, but the term is deemed to embrace the right of the citizen to be free in the enjoyment of all his faculties; to be free to use them in all lawful ways; to live and work where he will; to earn his livelihood by any lawful calling; to pursue any livelihood or avocation; and for that purpose to enter into all contracts which may be proper, necessary, and essential to his carrying out to a successful conclusion the purposes above mentioned." In *Meyer v. Nebraska*, 262 U.S. 390, 399, 43 S.Ct. 625, 626, 67 L.Ed. 1042, 1045 (1923), the Court said: "Without doubt, [liberty] denotes not merely freedom from bodily restraint but also the right of the individual to contract, to engage in any of the common occupations of life, to acquire useful knowledge, to marry, establish a home and bring up children, to worship God according to the dictates of his own conscience, and generally to enjoy those privileges long recognized at common law as essential to the orderly pursuit of happiness by free men."

LICENSE. **1.** Permission given by a competent authority to do or own something that, without permission, would be **illegal**. **2.** Proof of a LICENSE (definition 1) in the form of a document, card, plate, or tag.

LICENTIOUS. Having no regard for the restraints of society in sexual matters; sensually unbridled; libertine.

LICIT. **1.** Allowable; permitted; within the **law**. **2.** Performed in strict conformity with the provisions of the law. *Example*: He was engaged in licit liquor traffic and was not indicted with the others.

LIE. **n.** A deliberate untruth; an intentional misstatement or falsehood. **v.** To be sustainable, maintainable, or admissible. *Example*: Because of the child's tender age, no criminal action will lie against him.

LIE DETECTOR. Same as POLYGRAPH.

LIEN. A charge, hold, or claim of one person upon the property of another until the latter person satisfies some debt or duty owed.

LIEU. *French*. "Place; stead." *See*: IN LIEU OF.

LIFE. Animate existence as distinguished from death. *Example*: It is a crime to deliberately take another's life without excuse or justification.

LIFE OR LIMB. Any criminal penalty. The Fifth Amendment to the U.S. Constitution provides "nor shall any person be subject for the same offence to be twice put in **jeopardy** of life or limb." "Jeopardy of life or limb," as derived from the common law, generally referred to the possibility of capital punishment upon conviction. Now, however, it is settled that "a criminal defendant is placed in jeopardy when he is put to **trial** on an **indictment** or **information** sufficient in form and substance to sustain a **conviction** before a **competent court** and a **jury** has been sworn and charged with his deliverance." *State v. Iglesias*, 374 So.2d 1060, 1062 (Fla.App. 1979). For jeopardy purposes, the commencement of a trial without a jury is deemed the equivalent of one begun with a jury. *See*: DOUBLE JEOPARDY.

LIFE SENTENCE. A **sentence** to **incarceration** for life specified by the **court** at the time of sentencing. A life sentence may be with or without the possibility of **parole**. See SENTENCE for a list of related terms.

LIKE. **1.** Of the same kind, appearance, manner, qualities, etc.; resembling; similar. *Example*: He looks like the man who robbed me. **2.** Equal; equivalent.

LIKELIHOOD. Probability.

LIKELY. **1.** Probable; having an appearance of truth; within the realm of credibility. *Example*: He gave a likely alibi for his whereabouts last Tuesday. **2.** Having or exhibiting an inclination or probability; apt. *Example*: The judge is likely to sentence her to the maximum penalty.

LIMB. A part of the human or animal body distinguished from the head or trunk. Examples of limbs are arms, legs, and wings. *See*: LIFE OR LIMB.

LIMIT. **n.** The final or furthest point or line beyond which something cannot or may not proceed or extend; a boundary. *Example*: The legislature increased the limit of the penalty for rape. **v.** To confine or restrict within limits.

LIMITATION. A condition or circumstance that **limits** (v.); a restriction. *See*: STATUTE OF LIMITATIONS.

LIMITATION OF ACTIONS. Same as STATUTE OF LIMITATIONS.

LIMITED JURISDICTION. *See*: COURT OF LIMITED JURISDICTION.

LINE. **1.** A border or limit. **2.** A series of things that succeed each other chronologically. *Example*: The judge referred to the line of cases on search incident to arrest.

LINEUP. A CONFRONTATION (definition 2) involving the presentation at one time of several persons, including a person suspected of committing a **crime**, to a **victim** or **witness** of the crime for the purpose of **identifying** the **perpetrator** of the crime. The presentation is usually conducted by a law enforcement official or a prosecuting attorney. In *United States v. Wade*, 388 U.S. 218, 87 S.Ct. 1926, 18 L.Ed.2d 1149 (1967), the U.S. Supreme Court held that a pretrial confrontation is a critical stage in the legal proceedings against a suspect and that the suspect has a right to the presence of a **lawyer** at the lineup. Furthermore, if the suspect cannot afford a lawyer, he or she is entitled to have one appointed by the court. In *Kirby v. Illinois*, 406 U.S. 682, 689, 92 S.Ct. 1877, 1882, 32 L.Ed.2d 411, 417 (1972), the Court held that the right to counsel attaches only to lineups held "at or after the initiation of adversary judicial criminal proceedings—whether by way of formal **charge**, **preliminary hearing**, **indictment**, **information** or **arraignment**." Nevertheless, even though a suspect may not have a right to counsel at a confrontation, the due process clause of the Fifth and Fourteenth Amendments to the Constitution forbids any pretrial identification procedure that is unnecessarily suggestive and conducive to irreparable mistaken

L|

identification. *Stovall v. Denno*, 388 U.S. 293, 87 S.Ct. 1967, 18 L.Ed.2d 1199 (1967). If an officer conducts an unnecessarily suggestive identification procedure, the identification evidence will be inadmissible in court unless the identification is otherwise reliable under the totality of the circumstances. Factors to be considered in evaluating the likelihood of misidentification are:

—witness's opportunity to view the criminal at the time of the crime;

—witness's degree of attention;

—accuracy of the witness's prior description of the criminal;

—level of certainty demonstrated by the witness at the confrontation; and

—length of time between the crime and the confrontation.

See: EYEWITNESS IDENTIFICATION; IDENTIFICATION; SHOWUP; WITNESS.

LIQUOR. · An alcoholic beverage manufactured by distillation rather than fermentation.

LIS PENDENS. "Lis pendens simply means a pending **suit**, and the doctrine denotes those principles and rules of law which define and limit the operation of the **common-law** maxim . . . pending the suit nothing should be changed. . . . The object of the doctrine of lis pendens is to keep the subject matter in controversy within the power of the **court** until final decree and to make it possible for courts to **execute** their **judgment**." *Jones v. Jones*, 161 So.2d 640, 643 (Miss. 1964).

LITERAL. Following or complying with the exact or strict meaning of a word or words. *Example*: The judge gave a literal interpretation to the terms of the contract.

LITERAL CONSTRUCTION. Same as STRICT CONSTRUCTION.

LITIGANT. A **party** to a lawsuit.

LITIGATE. **1.** To carry on or be a party to a **lawsuit**. **2.** To dispute or contest a point.

LITIGATION. **1.** The process of carrying on a **lawsuit**. **2.** The lawsuit itself.

LOAN SHARK. A person who lends money at interest rates exceeding the percentage approved by law and who uses **force**, **threats**, or other methods of intimidation to obtain payment.

LOBBY. To attempt to influence a legislator to act in favor of a special interest.

LOCAL. Any level of government that is not clearly federal or state. Local agencies are those belonging to units of general local government (e.g., county, municipal, or township) and agencies or subagencies that are parts of special purpose units of government (special regional agencies; independent school districts; bridge, port, airport, and tunnel authorities; and the like).

LOCAL ACTION. An **action** that may be brought only where the subject matter of the controversy is located. *See*: TRANSITORY ACTION.

LOCAL LAW. A law applicable only to a particular territory or district or to particular persons or things.

LOCAL LAW ENFORCEMENT AGENCY. A **law enforcement agency** that is an organizational unit of local government. Examples of local law enforcement agencies are municipal police departments, sheriff's departments with criminal law enforcement duties, campus police agencies of colleges and universities which are financed and administered by local city and community college districts, and law enforcement units administered by special district limited purpose units of government, such as port and bridge authorities. See LAW ENFORCEMENT OFFICER for a list of related terms.

LOCAL LAW ENFORCEMENT OFFICER. An employee of a **local law enforcement agency** who is an officer sworn to carry out law enforcement duties. Examples of local law enforcement officers are **sheriffs**, **deputy sheriffs**, **chiefs of police**, city **police officers**, campus police officers who are employees of local city and community college districts, and sworn personnel of law enforcement subunits of port and transit authorities.

LOCKUP. *See*: PREARRAIGNMENT LOCKUP.

LOCO. *See*: IN LOCO.

LOCO PARENTIS. *See*: IN LOCO PARENTIS.

LOCUS. A place.

LOCUS CRIMINIS. *Latin.* The place where a **crime** was committed. See CRIME for a list of related terms.

LOCUS DELICTI. *Latin.* The place where a **crime** was committed. See CRIME for a list of related terms.

LOGGING IN. Same as BOOKING.

LOGICAL RELEVANCY. A relationship of one fact to another fact such that the existence of the first fact makes the second fact either probable or improbable. For example, the fact that a person's fresh footprint was found at the scene of a recent crime bears a logical relevancy to the fact that the person committed the crime. See FACT for a list of related terms.

LOITER.   To linger about a place idly or aimlessly. See AFFRAY for a list of related terms.

LONG-TERM FACILITY.   *See*: JUVENILE FACILITY.

LORD'S DAY.   Another name for Sunday.

LOTTERY.   A scheme or arrangement in which tickets or other tokens are purchased for a price in hopes of obtaining something of greater value, and winners are determined in a chance drawing. Usually in a lottery, a person bets a set amount of money by buying a ticket with a unique number on it. Only one person can bet on that number. The amounts to be won are set in advance. In most lotteries the winning numbers are determined by random selection from the numbers on the printed tickets. Some lotteries are legal in some jurisdictions. See GAMBLING for a list of related terms.

LUCRI CAUSA.   *Latin.* For the sake of gain.

LUSTFUL.   Having unlawful or unrestrained sexual desire or craving.

LYING IN WAIT.   Hiding or concealing oneself in order to make a sudden or surprise attack upon a person when he or she arrives upon the scene.

LYNCH.   To **execute** a person (usually by hanging) by a mob or other unofficial group acting without legal authority.

MACE. A chemical substance dispensed by an aerosol container that is sprayed in the face of a person in order to temporarily disable the person without causing permanent injury. Law enforcement officers use mace to defend themselves and to subdue dangerous persons without resorting to **deadly force**. Use of mace is considered to be **nondeadly force**.

MACHINE GUN. An automatic gun that fires small arms ammunition rapidly and continuously when the trigger is pulled.

MAGISTERIAL. Of or relating to a MAGISTRATE or the office of magistrate.

MAGISTRATE. A **judicial officer** of a **court of limited jurisdiction** or with limited or delegated authority. Among the duties of a magistrate are the issuance of **arrest warrants**, **search warrants**, and **summonses**, the setting of **bail**, the ordering of **release on bail**, and the conduct of **arraignments** and **preliminary examinations** of persons charged with serious crimes. A magistrate may also have limited authority to try minor cases or to dispose of cases on a guilty plea. The authority of a magistrate in a particular jurisdiction depends on the statutes, rules, and customs of that jurisdiction. *See*: UNITED STATES MAGISTRATE.

MAGISTRATE COURT. *See*: COURT OF LIMITED JURISDICTION.

MAIL COVER. Surveillance of a person's mail conducted by the U.S. Postal Service at the request of a **law enforcement agency**. The surveillance is conducted by recording all the information on the outside cover of first-class mail, as well as inspecting the contents of any second-, third-, and fourth-class mail. Mail covers are authorized by postal regulations in the interest of national security and crime prevention. Law enforcement agencies requesting a mail cover must apply in writing to the Postal Service, stating reasonable grounds why a mail cover is necessary to protect national security, locate a fugitive, or obtain information about the commission or attempted commission of a crime.

MAIL FRAUD. The federal crime (18 U.S.C. §1341) of making **false representations** through use of the U.S. mail in order to obtain money or other economic benefit from another.

MAIM. To deprive of (or of the use of) a limb or member; to mutilate; to cripple.

MAIN.   Most important; principal; major; chief.

MAINOUR.   Stolen goods found in the possession of the thief.

MAINTAIN.   **1.** To keep in good or proper condition; to keep in good operation; to preserve; to uphold. *Example*: Law enforcement officers are sworn to maintain the public peace. **2.** To state or restate firmly and positively in the face of evidence or arguments to the contrary. *Example*: The defendant maintained his innocence. See ADDRESS for a list of related terms. **3.** To carry on; to keep up; to continue. *Example*: She maintained an action against the state.

MAINTENANCE.   **1.** At **common law**, the assistance in a suit, with money or otherwise, by a person who has no personal interest in the suit. **NOTE:** Some states still recognize maintenance and **champerty** as offenses, but in most states they have been replaced with the civil actions of **abuse of process, malicious abuse of process,** and **malicious prosecution**. See ABUSE OF PROCESS for a list of related terms. **2.** The act or process of maintaining (see **maintain**).

MAJOR.   **adj.** Greater in importance, seriousness, rank, size, or amount. *Example:* The prosecution suffered a major setback. **n.** A person who is of full legal age and is no longer a **minor**. *See*: MAJORITY.

MAJORITY.   **1.** The age at which a person is legally entitled to exercise full civil and personal rights and is recognized by law to be an **adult** rather than a **minor** or **infant**. At the age of majority a person is considered to be capable of managing his or her own affairs and to be responsible for any legal obligations created by the person's actions. *Also called*: **full age; full legal age; lawful age; legal age**. *See*: MINORITY. **2.** A number of people, votes, or other things that is more than half of the total number. *See*: PLURALITY.

MAJORITY OPINION.   An **opinion** (definition 1), written by one member of a **court**, in which a majority of the members of the court join. See OPINION for a list of related terms.

MAJOR TRIAL COURT.   Same as COURT OF GENERAL JURISDICTION.

MAKE.   **1.** To do; to perform. *Example*: The officer made an arrest. **2.** To create; to compose; to draw up. *Example*: The prosecutor made an affidavit. **3.** To cause to become. *Example*: The Attorney General will make him chief of the criminal division. **4.** To compel to. *Example*: They couldn't make her confess. **5.** To provide. *Example*: Make room for one more. **6.** To constitute. *Example*: Ten members make a quorum. **7.** To develop into; to become. *Example*: He will make a fine officer. **8.** To earn; to produce. *Example*: He makes lots of money. **9.** To establish; to enact. *Example*: The legislature makes the laws.

MALA. *Latin.* "Bad; evil."

MALA FIDE. *Latin.* "In bad faith." *See*: BONA FIDE.

MALA FIDES. *Latin.* "Bad faith"; dishonesty. *See*: BONA FIDES.

MALA IN SE. Plural of MALUM IN SE.

MALA PROHIBITA. Plural of MALUM PROHIBITUM.

MALEFACTION. An evil deed; a crime; an offense.

MALEFACTOR. One who commits an evil deed or crime; a criminal.

MALFEASANCE. The performance of an act that is wrongful in itself. *See*: FEASANCE; MISFEASANCE; NONFEASANCE.

MALICE. **Intent**, without **justification**, excuse, or **mitigation**, to cause harm to another or to act in wanton disregard of probable harmful consequences to others; evil intent. **Express malice** is a deliberate intent or formed design to commit a **crime** manifested by external circumstances capable of proof. An example of express malice is the killing of the victim to wreak vengeance or to gratify feelings of animosity, ill will, or hatred. **Implied malice** is intent to commit a crime inferred from the circumstances, such as the intentional use of **deadly force** without **justification** or **mitigating circumstances** or a dangerous act done so recklessly or wantonly as to manifest a disregard for human life.

MALICE AFORETHOUGHT. In the common law definition of murder, malice aforethought means premeditated intent without justification, excuse, or mitigation, to kill, to cause great bodily harm, or to act in wanton disregard of circumstances indicating a strong likelihood of death or great bodily harm to others. *Also called*: **malice prepense**.

MALICE PREPENSE. Same as MALICE AFORETHOUGHT.

MALICIOUS. Characterized by or done with MALICE.

MALICIOUS ABUSE OF PROCESS. Intentional and wrongful initiation of court **process** to accomplish a purpose not intended under the law. See ABUSE OF PROCESS for a list of related terms.

MALICIOUS ACCUSATION. Same as MALICIOUS PROSECUTION.

MALICIOUS ARREST. An **arrest** made intentionally and without **probable cause**. See ABUSE OF PROCESS and ARREST for lists of related terms.

MALICIOUS MISCHIEF.   Same as CRIMINAL MISCHIEF.

MALICIOUS PROSECUTION.   The institution of a prosecution or civil suit against a person without probable cause to believe the charges can be sustained and with malice or with a principal purpose other than that of bringing the person to justice. Malicious prosecution is a tort for which a civil action for damages may be instituted, if the original suit or prosecution is unsuccessful and if there was injury to the person, property, or reputation of the person against whom the suit or prosecution was brought. *Also called*: **malicious accusation**. See ABUSE OF PROCESS for a list of related terms.

MALICIOUS TRESPASS.   Same as CRIMINAL MISCHIEF.

MALLORY v. U.S.   *See*: McNABB-MALLORY RULE.

MALPRACTICE.   Any improper or unethical conduct or unreasonable lack of skill or fidelity in the performance of professional or **fiduciary** duties.

MALT BEVERAGE.   A beverage such as beer or ale that is made by the fermentation of grain. Malt beverages do not include distilled alcoholic beverages or beverages made from fermented grapes, fruits, or berries.

MALUM.   *Latin.* "Wrong; evil; bad."

MALUM IN SE.   *Latin.* "Evil or wrong in itself." The term malum in se is used to describe a public offense that is wrong or immoral in itself. Examples of offenses mala in se are **felonies**, intentional injuries to persons or property, and intentional breaches of the public order. *See*: MALUM PROHIBITUM.

MALUM PROHIBITUM.   *Latin.* "Prohibited wrong." The term malum prohibitum is used to describe an act prohibited by statute but not inherently wrong or evil. Examples of offenses mala prohibita are violations of litter laws and parking laws.

MANACLES.   Same as HANDCUFFS.

MANDAMUS.   *Latin.* "We command." A WRIT issued by a **court** of superior **jurisdiction** commanding an inferior court or tribunal, a person, or an organization to perform a specified legally required act. See ARREST WARRANT for a list of related terms.

MANDATE.   An order or command of a **court**. See ADJUDICATION and JUDGMENT for lists of related terms.

MANDATORY.   Obligatory; requiring obedience. A mandatory statutory provision is one that relates to the essence of the **statute**. A mandatory provision requires compliance or the transaction or proceeding to which it relates will be rendered void. *See*: DIRECTORY.

MANDATORY CONDITIONAL RELEASE. Same as MANDATORY SUPER-VISED RELEASE.

MANDATORY RELEASE DATE. The date marking the end point of the time that a given person may be incarcerated prior to **conditional release**, calculated as the length of institutional **sentence** minus credited **good time**. See SENTENCE for a list of related terms.

MANDATORY SENTENCE. A statutory requirement that a certain **penalty** shall be set and carried out in all cases upon **conviction** for a specified offense or series of offenses. The statute usually provides that an offender convicted of a specified very serious crime or specified series of crimes be confined in prison for a minimum number of years especially established for the particular offense, that the customary alternative of **probation** instead of **incarceration** is not available, and that **parole** is not permitted or is possible only after unusually lengthy confinement. A mandatory sentence is not a type of **sentence**, but rather a statutory requirement for a certain sentence. See SENTENCE for a list of related terms.

MANDATORY SUPERVISED RELEASE. A **conditional release** from prison required by statute when an **inmate** has been confined for a time period equal to his or her full **sentence** minus statutory **good time**, if any. Persons leaving prison by mandatory supervised release are placed on conditional release status until the full sentence expires, or until some other point in time specified by law. They are usually subject to the same conditions as **parolees**, and can be returned by **paroling authority** decision to prison for technical violations of release conditions. The release itself, however is not a paroling authority discretionary decision. The **supervision** is usually performed by a state **parole agency**, or a state probation and parole agency. *Also called*: **mandatory conditional release**. See PAROLE, RELEASE and SENTENCE for lists of related terms.

MANIA. 1. A form of **insanity** characterized by great excitement sometimes amounting to fury and sometimes accompanied by **hallucinations** and **illusions**. **2.** An exaggerated or excessive desire or enthusiasm for something.

MANIFEST. Evident; obvious; clearly revealed; unmistakable; undisputable.

MANN ACT. Same as WHITE SLAVE TRAFFIC ACT.

MANSION HOUSE. A dwelling house.

MANSLAUGHTER. The unlawful killing of a human being that is not **murder**. Statutes in different states recognize various degrees and types of manslaughter. See HOMICIDE for a list of related terms.

MANUAL. adj. Pertaining to the hand or hands; done or operated by hand. **n.** A book of instructions; a guidebook; a handbook.

MANUFACTURE.   **1.** To make or process raw materials into a finished product by machine or industrial operation. **2.** To invent fictitiously; to fabricate; to concoct. *Example*: The manufactured evidence did not fool the jury.

MANY.   Amounting to a large unspecified number; numerous.

MAP PROGRAM.   Abbreviation for MUTUAL AGREEMENT PROGRAM.

MAPP v. OHIO.   The U.S. Supreme Court decision that held that the EXCLUSIONARY RULE was applicable in state criminal prosecutions. The citation for *Mapp v. Ohio* is 367 U.S. 643, 81 S.Ct. 1684, 6 L.Ed.2d 1081 (1961). See EXCLUSIONARY RULE for a list of related terms.

MARIHUANA.   Same as MARIJUANA.

MARIJUANA.   21 U.S.C. 802 (16) defines marijuana as "all parts of the plant Cannabis sativa L., whether growing or not; the seeds thereof; the resin extracted from any part of such plant; and every compound, manufacture, salt, derivative, mixture, or preparation of such plant, its seeds or resin. Such term does not include the mature stalks of such plant, fiber produced from such stalks, oil or cake made from the seeds of such plant, any other compound, manufacture, salt, derivative, mixture, or preparation of such mature stalks (except the resin extracted therefrom), fiber, oil, or cake, or the sterilized seed of such plant which is incapable of germination." *Also spelled*: **marihuana.**

MARSHAL.   **n.** *See*: UNITED STATES MARSHALS SERVICE. **v.** To arrange or set in methodical order. *Example*: The prosecutor marshaled the facts for his closing argument.

MARSHALS SERVICE, UNITED STATES.   *See*: UNITED STATES MARSHALS SERVICE.

MASOCHISM.   A sexual perversion that manifests itself in the desire to have oneself beaten, maltreated, or humiliated by another person.

MASTER.   A **judicial officer** of the court to whom certain matters may be referred, such as examining **witnesses**, taking **testimony**, computing damages, and taking **oaths** and **affidavits**. A master makes a report of findings to the **judge** upon which a **decree** is formulated.

MATERIAL.   **1.** Important; influential; substantial; significant. **2.** Having substantial probative value toward establishing the truth or falsity of a proposition. *Example*: In order to be admissible, evidence must be competent, relevant, and material. See EVIDENCE for a list of related terms. **3.** Essential; necessary. *Example*: The defendant's state of mind is a material fact in a murder case.

MATERIAL WITNESS. A **witness** whose testimony is crucial or indispensable to either the **prosecution's** or the **defense's** case. In an important case a material witness may be required to post an appearance bond or may be confined or held against his or her will until the witness testifies. See WITNESS for a list of related terms.

MATHEMATICAL. Certain; exact; precise; absolute.

MATRICIDE. **1.** The killing of one's mother. **2.** One who kills his or her mother.

MATTER. **1.** The object of consideration or attention; something to be done or dealt with; the subject to be treated. *Example*: The time of death was the primary matter in dispute in the murder case. **2.** Thing; affair; concern; event; business. *Example*: This is a serious matter.

MATTER OF COURSE. An action allowed and approved by a **court** as a matter of right or routine procedure with no requirement of formal application or request. *Also called*: **matter of right**.

MATTER OF RIGHT. Same as MATTER OF COURSE.

MATTER OF RECORD. A **judicial** fact or event that has been recorded by the court and that can be proved by producing the court **record**.

MAXIMUM. The highest amount, number, degree, or value. *Example*: The violent prisoner was placed in a maximum security cell. *See*: MINIMUM.

MAXIMUM SENTENCE. The maximum **penalty** provided by **statute** for a given criminal offense, usually stated as a maximum term of imprisonment or a maximum fine. The maximum sentence as stated by the **court** is usually the maximum period of **confinement** applicable to a specific offender for a specific offense, as selected by the court within the limits prescribed by statute, before jail time or any other irrevocable **sentence credit time** has been subtracted. See SENTENCE for a list of related terms.

MAY. **1.** To be permitted, allowed, or authorized to do something. In statutes, rules, and court decisions may signifies the granting of power, permission, or authority as opposed to the imposing of a duty or the issuing of a command or order. *Example*: A person may hunt deer only during the open season on deer. *See*: MUST; SHALL; SHOULD. **2.** To have a possibility, ability, or opportunity to do or be something. *Example*: A mistrial may prevent a retrial because of the double jeopardy doctrine.

MAYHEM. The intentional inflicting of injury on another that causes the removal of, seriously disfigures, renders useless, or seriously impairs the function of any member or organ of the body. Under the **common law**, the crime of mayhem was limited to maliciously maiming or crippling a person so as to make the person unable to fight or defend him or herself. See ASSAULT for a list of related terms.

McNABB-MALLORY RULE. A rule applicable to federal courts that any **admission** or **confession** obtained during an unreasonable delay between the **arrest** of a person and his or her **initial appearance** before a **committing magistrate** will be inadmissible in court. The decisions in *McNabb v. U.S.*, 318 U.S. 332, 63 S.Ct. 608, 87 L.Ed. 819 (1943) and *Mallory v. U.S.*, 354 U.S. 449, 77 S.Ct. 1356, 1. L.Ed.2d 1479 (1957) were based not on violations of the Constitution but on the U.S. Supreme Court's supervisory power over federal courts and its power to implement and interpret federal statutes or rules governing procedures in federal courts.

McNABB v. U.S. *See*: McNABB-MALLORY RULE.

MEANS. A method, course of action, or instrument used to accomplish a purpose. *Example*: He will use any means to escape.

MEASURE. A general term for any **law** proposed or enacted by a legislature. See ACT for a list of related terms.

MEDICAL EVIDENCE. **Evidence** provided by the **expert testimony** of persons trained and skilled in the practice of medicine or by standard medical texts or treatises. See EVIDENCE for a list of related terms.

MEDICAL EXAMINER. A public medical officer whose primary duties are (1) to establish the cause, manner, time, and place of death, and the identity of the deceased in instances of death by violence or poisoning, unexpected death, unattended death, or death under unusual conditions or where suspicion might be entertained; and (2) to provide further information necessary for criminal **prosecution**, clearing innocent suspects, documenting public health hazards, and processing vital statistics. (The cause of death is the medical pathology, e.g., asphyxiation or hemorrhage; the manner of death is whether the death is accidental, suicidal, homicidal, or natural.) Medical examiner records may also assist in settling insurance and civil liability matters. *See*: CORONER; CORONER'S INQUEST; DEATH.

MEDICAL JURISPRUDENCE. Same as FORENSIC MEDICINE.

MEDICO-LEGAL. Pertaining to the **law** as it relates to medical matters.

MEMBER. **1.** One of the persons constituting a group, association, or other body of persons. **2.** A part or organ of the human or animal body, especially a limb or a part other than the trunk.

MEMORANDUM. A brief, informal note or record written as a reminder.

MEMORANDUM DECISION. A **court**'s **decision** that is unaccompanied by an **opinion** stating the reasons for the decision. A memorandum decision has no value as a precedent and may not be **appealed**. See DECISION and JUDGMENT for lists of related terms.

MEMORANDUM OF LAW. A written **argument** in support of a legal position, similar to a **brief**, but in a less formal style.

MEMORY. The recollection of past events.

MENACE. A threat.

MENS. *Latin.* "Mind"; intention.

MENS REA. *Latin.* Guilty mind; criminal **intent**. Most crimes consist of a forbidden act or **actus reus** accompanied by a certain mental state or mens rea. The mens rea may be different for different crimes. Also, the mens rea for the same or similar crimes may differ from state to state. Typical terms used to describe the mens rea are **intentionally**, **willfully**, **maliciously**, with **malice aforethought**, **knowingly**, and **recklessly**. *Example*: The mens rea for murder is malice aforethought. *See*: CRIME; CULPABILITY; GENERAL INTENT; SPECIFIC INTENT; STRICT LIABILITY STATUTE.

MENTAL. Relating to the mind.

MENTAL CAPACITY. *See*: CAPACITY.

MENTAL COMPETENCE. *See*: COMPETENCE.

MENTAL DISEASE OR DEFECT. *See*: DURHAM RULE; SUBSTANTIAL CAPACITY TEST.

MERCY. A **judge's** discretionary power to cancel or mitigate the punishment to which a convicted person is liable. *Example*: He threw himself at the mercy of the court.

MERCY KILLING. *See*: EUTHANASIA.

MERE EVIDENCE. **Evidence** of **crime** that does not fall into the categories of **contraband** or **fruits** or **instrumentalities** of crime. Examples of mere evidence might include clothing, hair, or business records. Before 1967, under the so-called **mere evidence rule**, mere evidence could not be seized by **law enforcement officers** either with or without a warrant. The U.S. Supreme Court case of *Warden v. Hayden*, 387 U.S. 294, 87 S.Ct. 1647, 18 L.Ed.2d 782 (1967), did away with the mere evidence rule, holding that mere evidence could be seized and was **admissible** in court in a criminal **prosecution**. See EVIDENCE for a list of related terms.

MERE EVIDENCE RULE. *See*: MERE EVIDENCE.

MERGER. The legal process by which, when a single criminal act constitutes two distinct offenses, the less serious offense is absorbed by the more serious offense. In order to merge into the more serious offense, the less serious offense must necessarily be established by proof of the more serious offense. The less serious offense is called a **lesser included offense**. *Example*: The crime of rape includes the lesser offense of sexual abuse, both of which are merged into a single prosecution for rape.

MERITS. The intrinsic right and wrong or substance of a matter as determined by analysis of factual issues as opposed to the procedural, technical, or other extraneous aspects of the matter. *Example*: The court decided the case on its merits.

MESNE. Intermediate; intervening; in the middle.

MESNE PROCESS. A **writ** or other **process** issued between the commencement of an **action** and the final process in the action.

MIND. **1.** The part or aspect of a person that thinks, perceives, wills, remembers, understands, judges, and imagines. *Example*: His act was the product of a diseased mind. **2.** The intellect as opposed to the emotions or the will. *Example*: She has a good mind. **3.** Purpose; intention. *Example*: Most crimes require a guilty mind.

MINIMUM. The least or lowest amount, number, degree, or value. *Example*: The judge gave him the minimum sentence.

MINIMUM PAROLE ELIGIBILITY DATE. *See*: ELIGIBLE FOR PAROLE.

MINIMUM SENTENCE. The minimum **penalty** provided by **law** for a given offense. Like the **maximum sentence**, the minimum potential term of **confinement** applicable to a person at time of commitment can be provided by **statute**, or determined by a **court** or **paroling authority** within statutory limits. In some jurisdictions there is no officially stated minimum sentence. A formally declared minimum sentence is also a time value affected by various statutory rules and discretionary executive actions. For example, in some jurisdictions an offender is eligible for parole after a certain fraction of the minimum sentence has been served. See SENTENCE for a list of related terms.

MINISTER. A person acting as an **agent** for another by carrying out specified orders or functions.

MINISTERIAL. Involving or relating to obedience to the mandate of a legal authority and requiring no **discretion** or judgment. *Example*: Serving a summons is a ministerial duty.

MINISTERIAL ACT.   An act involving obedience to instructions or legal authority but not requiring the exercise of **discretion** or judgment. *Example*: The officer's giving a receipt for property seized under a search warrant is a ministerial act. *See*: JUDICIAL ACT.

MINISTERIAL OFFICER.   An officer whose duties are entirely **ministerial** and who exercises no **executive**, **judicial**, or **legislative** functions.

MINOR.   adj. Lesser in importance, seriousness, rank, size, or amount. *Example:* Jaywalking is a minor offense. **n.** A person under the age of MAJORITY or full legal age. *Example*: It is illegal to sell liquor to a minor.

MINOR IN NEED OF SUPERVISION.   Same as CHILD IN NEED OF SUPER-VISION. *Abbreviation*: **M.I.N.S.**

MINORITY.   1. The state of being a MINOR; the period during which a person is a minor. **2.** A number of people, votes, or other things that is less than half of the total number.

M.I.N.S.   Abbreviation for MINOR IN NEED OF SUPERVISION.

MIRANDA v. ARIZONA.   A landmark decision of the U.S. Supreme Court that held as follows: "[T]he **prosecution** may not use statements, whether exculpatory or inculpatory, stemming from **custodial interrogation** of the defendant unless it demonstrates the use of procedural safeguards effective to secure the privilege against **self-incrimination**. By custodial interrogation, we mean questioning initiated by law enforcement officers after a person has been taken into custody or otherwise deprived of his freedom of action in any significant way. As for the procedural safeguards to be employed, unless other fully effective means are devised to inform accused persons of their right of silence and to assure a continuous opportunity to exercise it, the following measures are required. Prior to any questioning, the person must be warned that he has a right to remain silent, that any statement he does make may be used as **evidence** against him, and that he has a right to the presence of an **attorney**, either retained or appointed. The defendant may **waive** effectuation of these rights provided the waiver is made voluntarily, knowingly, and intelligently. If, however, he indicates in any manner and at any stage of the process that he wishes to consult with an attorney before speaking there can be no questioning. Likewise, if the individual is alone and indicates in any manner that he does not wish to be interrogated, the police may not question him. The mere fact that he may have answered some questions or volunteered some statements on his own does not deprive him of the right to refrain from answering any further inquiries until he has consulted with an attorney and thereafter consents to be questioned." *Miranda v. Arizona*, 384 U.S. 436, 444-45, 86 S.Ct. 1602, 1612, 16 L.Ed.2d 694, 706-07 (1966). *See*: CONFESSION; VOLUNTARY.

MIRANDA WARNINGS. *See*: MIRANDA v. ARIZONA.

MISADVENTURE. An instance of ill fortune; an accident; a mishap. *See*: HOMICIDE BY MISADVENTURE.

MISALLEGE. To give a false or misleading citation of authority in support of one's position.

MISAPPLICATION. Same as MISAPPROPRIATION.

MISAPPROPRIATION. The use of the funds or property of another for a wrongful purpose. The term misappropriation is often applied to the acts of a **fiduciary** in wrongfully using the funds or property of his or her **beneficiary** for the fiduciary's own benefit. See ABSTRACTION for a list of related terms.

MISCARRIAGE OF JUSTICE. A legal proceeding or other official action that causes substantial prejudice to the rights of a party amounting to an injustice.

MISCEGENATION. The mixing of the races, especially the marriage or sexual union between white and black people. The U.S. Supreme Court held that state laws prohibiting marriage between persons of different races were unconstitutional. *Loving v. Virginia*, 388 U.S. 1, 87 S.Ct. 1817, 18 L.Ed.2d 1010 (1967).

MISCHIEF. *See*: MALICIOUS MISCHIEF.

MISCONDUCT. Behavior not conforming to established laws or standards; improper conduct; misbehavior.

MISCONDUCT IN OFFICE. Corrupt behavior by a public official while exercising the duties of office or while acting under color of office. Misconduct in office may involve **malfeasance**, **misfeasance**, or **nonfeasance**. *Also called*: **official misconduct**.

MISDEMEANANT. A person who is guilty of, or has been convicted of, a MISDEMEANOR. *See*: FELON.

MISDEMEANOR. In general, a CRIME of less serious nature than those designated as FELONIES. In jurisdictions that recognize the felony-misdemeanor distinction, a misdemeanor is any crime that is not a felony. Misdemeanors are usually punished by **fine** or by **incarceration** in a local **confinement facility** rather than a state **prison** or penitentiary. The maximum period of confinement that may be imposed for a misdemeanor is defined by statute and is usually less than one year. Court procedures for handling misdemeanors are usually different from those for felonies. See CRIME for a list of related terms.

MISDIRECTION. An erroneous **instruction** to the **jury** by a **judge**. See IN-STRUCTION for a list of related terms.

MISFEASANCE. The performance of a lawful act in an unlawful or inadequate manner. See: FEASANCE; MALFEASANCE; NONFEASANCE.

MISIDENTIFICATION. An identification of the wrong person as the perpetrator of a crime at a **confrontation** with witnesses.

MISJOINDER. An improper JOINDER.

MISLEAD. To lead into error or confusion; to deceive.

MISNOMER. An error in naming a person or thing.

MISPLEADING. An error in **pleading**, such as a misjoinder of parties or an omission of an essential fact or allegation. See ERROR and PLEADING for lists of related terms.

MISPRISION. Failure to perform a public duty. Misprision includes improper administration of a public office and failure to report a crime.

MISPRISION OF FELONY. Concealment of and failure to disclose a known FELONY committed by another. The person committing the misdemeanor of misprision of felony must not have given such assistance or aid as to make him or her a **principal** or an **accessory** before or after the fact.

MISPRISION OF TREASON. Concealment of and failure to disclose an act of **treason** by another.

MISREPRESENTATION. A false or incorrect statement. An **innocent misrepresentation** is one made with reasonable grounds for believing it to be true. A **negligent misrepresentation** is one made carelessly and without reasonable grounds for believing it to be true. A **false** or **fraudulent misrepresentation** is one made intentionally and with knowledge of its falsity.

MISTAKE. An unintentional error in action or thought.

MISTAKE OF FACT. An erroneous conclusion on or misunderstanding of a matter of **fact** not attributed to negligence in finding out the truth. A mistake of fact may be a **defense** to a **crime** if it negates the existence of a mental state required for the crime.

MISTAKE OF LAW. An erroneous conclusion on or misunderstanding of the **legal** consequences of a situation with full knowledge of the facts surrounding the situation.

A mistake of law is usually not a **defense** to a **crime** unless the defendant relied on a court **decision**, **statute**, or administrative rule that was later declared to be invalid or the defendant relied on erroneous advice from a person charged with administering the statute defining the crime.

MISTRIAL.   A **trial** that has been terminated and declared invalid by the **court** because of some circumstance that creates a substantial and uncorrectable prejudice to the conduct of a fair trial, or that makes it impossible to continue the trial in accordance with prescribed procedures. Commonly cited grounds for the declaring of a mistrial include lack of **jurisdiction**, incurable **error**, illness of the **defendant** or the **presiding judge**, and misconduct on the part of the **jury**, the **defense**, the **prosecution**, or the court. In some jurisdictions, a **hung jury** can be grounds for a mistrial. The declaration of a mistrial can be followed by **retrial** on the original charges, or by a **dismissal** of the case. The judicial decision to declare a mistrial can be **appealed** by either the defense or the prosecution. See TRIAL for a list of related terms.

MITIGATED SENTENCE.   A SENTENCE in which the penalty is less than the norm for the offense. See SENTENCE for a list of related terms.

MITIGATING CIRCUMSTANCES.   Circumstances surrounding the commission of a **crime** that do not in law justify or excuse the crime, but that tend to make the crime less reprehensible or outrageous and in fairness may be considered as reducing the blameworthiness of the defendant. Mitigating circumstances may be taken into account when setting **bail**, deciding what crime the defendant will be **charged** with in court, or in determining a **penalty**. Examples of mitigating circumstances are extreme youth or old age, **diminished responsibility**, lack of a prior criminal record, willingness to pay **restitution**, voluntary **confession**, and **provocation**. *Also called*: **extenuating circumstances**; **mitigation**. *See*: AGGRAVATING CIRCUM-STANCES.

MITIGATION.   **1.** Abbreviation or reduction of a penalty or punishment. **2.** Same as MITIGATING CIRCUMSTANCES.

MITTIMUS.   *Latin.* "We send." **1.** A court **order** directing a **law enforcement officer** to commit a person to **prison**. **2.** A **writ** for transferring a **record** or **suit** from one **court** to another. See ARREST WARRANT for a list of related terms.

MIXED LARCENY.   Same as COMPOUND LARCENY.

M'NAGHTEN RULE.   A rule used to determine whether a person accused of a crime was sane at the time of its commission and therefore criminally responsible. Under the M'Naghten Rule, an accused is not criminally responsible if, at the time the unlawful act was committed, the person was laboring under such a defect of reason, from disease of the mind, as not to know the nature and quality of his or her act. Even if the person knew the nature and quality of the act performed, the person is not responsible for a crime if, because of a defect of reason, the person did not know that the act was wrong. Also, if the person acted under an insane **delusion**, although not insane in other respects, the responsibility for the crime is the same as if the facts were as they seemed to the person. Therefore if the person's insane delusion was that the act was done in **self-defense** or was carrying out the will of God, the person is not criminally responsible. *Also called*: **right-wrong test**. *See*: INSANITY.

M.O. Abbreviation for MODUS OPERANDI.

MOB. A violent and disorderly crowd, causing or threatening to cause injury to person or property.

MOCK. **v.** To treat with contempt; to ridicule; to deride. **adj.** Simulated; false; sham; imitative.

MODE. The method or manner of doing something.

MODEL PENAL CODE. A generalized modern codification of that which is considered basic to criminal law, published by the American Law Institute in 1962. The Model Penal Code differed from almost all state codes at the time of its publication, in that such matters as the general principles of **culpability** and **justification**, formerly defined mainly in case law, were explicitly codified. Many states have enacted completely revised penal codes since 1962. The formal arrangement of and definition of crimes in these statutes is very different from earlier criminal law in many instances, although the actions that the language defines as **crimes** are essentially the same actions forbidden by earlier penal codes. The content and arrangement of the recently revised codes often reflect the Model Penal Code approach. See CRIME for a list of related terms.

MODEL PENAL CODE INSANITY TEST. Same as SUBSTANTIAL CAPACITY TEST.

MODIFICATION. *See*: MODIFY.

MODIFICATION OF PROBATION. A change in the terms and **conditions** of a **probation order**, making them more restrictive or less restrictive, as determined by a **court**. Modifications of probation may be requested by the **probation officer**, the **prosecuting attorney**, the **defense attorney**, the **defendant**, or other persons. Probation terms and conditions may be modified for a number of reasons—for example, to provide extra time for payment of **fines** or **restitution**, to shorten a jail term, to permit a change of residence to out of state or to require treatment for alcoholism or drug abuse. See PROBATION for a list of related terms.

MODIFY. **v.** To change or alter in one or more details, usually toward leniency or moderation; to temper. *Example*: He asked the court to modify his sentence. **n.** MODIFICATION.

MODUS. *Latin.* "Manner; method; way."

MODUS OPERANDI. *Latin.* "Mode of operating." A characteristic pattern of behavior repeated in a series of offenses that coincides with the pattern evidenced by a particular single person, or by a particular group of persons working together. Modus operandi information can enable police to determine that the pattern does not fit any previously arrested or investigated person. It may also be a portion of the **evidence** used to establish **guilt** in criminal proceedings. Most law enforcement agencies maintain modus operandi files. *Example*: The modus operandi of the kidnapping was by snatching children on their way home from school. *Abbreviation*: **M.O.**

MOLEST. To interfere with or meddle with a person, usually for sexual purposes.

MONITION. **1.** A court **order** in the nature of a **summons** directing a person to **appear** and answer. See ARREST WARRANT for a list of related terms. **2.** An official warning or notice.

MOOT. **1.** Arguable; debatable; unsettled; undecided. *Example*: That is a moot point. **2.** Without legal significance.

MOOT CASE. A case proposed for discussion to determine abstract issues, but that is without legal significance.

MOOT COURT. A fictitious **court** set up to argue **moot cases**, usually as an instrument of learning for law students. See COURT for a list of related terms.

MORAL. **1.** Of or concerned with the distinction between right and wrong in relation to human action or character. *Example*: Your decision involves moral as well as legal considerations. **2.** Conforming to or founded on the fundamental rules of right conduct. *Example*: She has a reputation as a moral person.

MORAL CERTAINTY. A very high degree of **probability**. "Moral certainty is a reasonable certitude or conviction based on convincing reasons and excluding all doubts that a contrary or opposite conclusion can exist based on any reasons. One having such a state of mind is said to be convinced **beyond reasonable doubt**. Such state of mind is more than an opinion, or an ordinary conviction. It is a higher state of conviction called moral certitude, which is the firm assent of the mind to one of two contraries without any reasonable fear of error, i.e., beyond a reasonable doubt." *State v. Johnson*, 104 N.W.2d 379, 382 (Wis. 1960).

MORAL EVIDENCE.   Evidence that is not **mathematical** or **demonstrative**, but whose **probability** or persuasiveness is founded on human experience, the general tendencies of human nature, or the character of particular individuals. See EVIDENCE for a list of related terms.

MORAL FRAUD.   Same as ACTUAL FRAUD.

MORAL TURPITUDE.   Depravity; baseness; vileness; wickedness. In some juris-dictions, a person convicted of a **crime** involving moral turpitude may lose certain rights and privileges, such as that of holding office. Examples of crimes involving moral turpitude are **rape**, **forgery**, and **robbery**. *Also called*: **turpitude**.

MORATORIUM.   A postponement or delay of some action.

MOREOVER.   In addition; furthermore; besides.

MORGUE.   A place in which bodies of the dead are kept for identification and arrangement for burial.

MORS.   *Latin.* "Death."

MORTAL.   Causing death; deadly; fatal. See DEATH for a list of related terms.

MOTION.   An oral or written request made to a **court** at any time before, during, or after court proceedings, asking the court to make a specified **finding**, **decision**, or **order**. In criminal proceedings a motion can be made by the **prosecution**, the **defense**, or the **court** itself. *See*: PETITION; PLEA.

MOTION FOR ACQUITTAL.   A MOTION made at the end of the **prosecution's** case requesting that the case be **dismissed** because there is insufficient **evidence** to sustain a **conviction** on the offense charged. See DISMISSAL for a list of related terms.

MOTION FOR DIRECTED VERDICT.   *See*: DIRECTED VERDICT.

MOTION IN ARREST OF JUDGMENT.   *See*: ARREST OF JUDGMENT.

MOTION TO DISMISS.   A MOTION, usually made before **trial**, requesting **dis-missal** of the case because of an insufficiency in the **pleadings** of the opposing party. See DISMISSAL and PLEADING for a list of related terms.

MOTION TO SET ASIDE JUDGMENT.   A MOTION to have a **judgment** set aside because of **errors** appearing on the **face** of the **record**. It has the same effect as a **motion in arrest of judgment**, but a motion in arrest of judgment must be made during the term of the court that rendered the judgment, whereas a motion to set aside judgment can be made at any time within the applicable **statute of limitations**. See ERROR and JUDGMENT for lists of related terms.

MOTION TO SUPPRESS. A MOTION to have certain **evidence** declared inadmissible at trial made by a defendant who believes his or her constitutional rights have been violated, for example by an unlawful **search and seizure** or an unlawfully obtained **admission** or **confession**. The purposes of a motion to suppress are (1) to enable the defendant to invoke the **exclusionary rule** and prevent the use of illegally obtained evidence at trial; and (2) to enable the **court** to resolve the issue of the legality of a search and seizure or confession without interrupting the trial. See EVIDENCE and EXCLUSIONARY RULE for a list of related terms.

MOTIVE. The reason that leads the mind to desire and seek a particular result; the cause that moves or stimulates a person's will to do an act; why a person does something. *See*: INTENT.

MOTOR VEHICLE. Any self-propelled wheeled vehicle in or on which a person or thing may be carried and which does not run on rails. Generally, the term motor vehicle includes automobiles, trucks, motorcycles, and any other motorized vehicles legally allowed on public roads and highways. In some contexts, non-wheeled vehicles such as motorboats and snowmobiles are included within the definition of motor vehicle.

MOTOR VEHICLE THEFT. Stealing or unauthorized taking of a **motor vehicle** owned by another with the intent to deprive the owner of possession either permanently or temporarily.

MOVABLE PROPERTY. Section 223.0 (4) of the **Model Penal Code** defines movable property as "property the location of which can be changed, including things growing on, affixed to, or found on land, and documents although the rights represented thereby have no physical location."

MOVANT. One who makes a MOTION.

MOVE. To make a MOTION.

MOVING CAUSE. Same as PROXIMATE CAUSE.

MUGGING. A type of **unarmed robbery** in which the offender suddenly approaches the victim from behind. In some areas of the country, mugging has a broader meaning, including any **assault** by a stranger in a public place. See ASSAULT for a list of related terms.

MULCT. A **fine** or similar penalty for a minor offense.

MULTIFARIOUSNESS.   The improper **joinder** of **causes of action, defendants,** or other matters.

MULTIPLE OFFENDER.   Same as HABITUAL CRIMINAL.

MULTIPLE SENTENCE.   Two or more **concurrent sentences** or **consecutive sentences,** or a combination of both types. It is possible for a person to be serving one of a set of consecutive sentences while also serving time on a concurrent sentence. See SENTENCE for a list of related terms.

MULTIPLICITY.   "[T]he practice of **charging** the commission of a single offense in several **counts.**" *U.S. v. Allied Chemical Corp.*, 420 F.Supp. 122, 123 (E.D.Va. 1976). The evil of multiplicity is that it may lead to multiple **sentences** for the same offense, or it may have some psychological effect upon a **jury** by suggesting that the defendant has committed not one but several crimes. The Federal Rules of Criminal Procedure and state rules of criminal procedure have been drafted to discourage the practice. See PLEADING for a list of related terms.

MULTIPLICITY OF ACTIONS.   Several unnecessary attempts to litigate the same claim or issue.

MUNICIPAL.   Of or relating to a city or town.

MUNICIPAL COURT.   A **court** whose **territorial jurisdiction** is limited to a particular city or town. *See*: COURT OF LIMITED JURISDICTION.

MUNICIPAL ORDINANCE.   *See*: ORDINANCE.

MURDER.   Under the common law, murder is the unlawful killing of another human being with **malice aforethought,** or the unlawful killing of another human being during the commission or attempted commission of a **felony** (see **felony-murder rule**). The definition of murder has been changed or refined by **statute** in many states. Also, some states have established different **degrees** of murder by statute. See HOMICIDE for a list of related terms.

MUST.   To be required or obligated. The word must is usually used in legal drafting to create a condition precedent. *Example*: To be eligible to run for Governor, a person must be 30 years of age. *See*: MAY; SHALL; SHOULD.

MUTE.   *See*: STAND MUTE.

MUTILATE.   **1.** To deprive a person of the use of a limb or other essential bodily part. *See*: MAYHEM. **2.** To make imperfect or ineffective by removing or damaging a part. *Example*: The mutilated document was of no legal effect.

MUTINY.   Revolt or rebellion against constituted authority, especially by soldiers or seamen. *See*: SEDITION.

MUTUAL.   Experienced or shared equally by each of two persons or things with respect to each other; reciprocal.

MUTUAL AGREEMENT PROGRAM.   A program providing for a form of contract between a **prisoner** and state prison and parole officials wherein the prisoner undertakes to complete specified self-improvement programs in order to receive a definite **parole** date, and the agency promises to provide the necessary educational and social services. The overall purposes of mutual agreement programs are to provide prisoners with explicit choices regarding steps toward preparation for **release**, to objectify the mutual obligations of prisoners and officials, and to provide a framework for focus upon problems impeding successful completion of contracts. *Also called*: **contract parole**. *Abbreviation:* **MAP program**. See PAROLE for a list of related terms.

NAMELY. That is to say; specifically; to wit.

NARCOTIC. Any of a class of substances that in small doses dull the senses, relieve pain, and induce sleep, but that in large doses are poisonous and that with prolonged use become addictive. Opium and morphine are examples of narcotics. See DRUG for a list of related terms.

NARRATE. To give a detailed account of an event or experience in the nature of a story. See ADDRESS for a list of related terms.

NATIONAL CRIME SURVEY. The National Crime Survey (NCS) is a statistical program instituted in 1972 providing information on the extent to which persons 12 years of age and older and households have been victimized by selected crimes. Data are collected on the incidence of crimes, circumstances under which the events occurred, effects on the victim, and whether or not incidents were reported to the police. The NCS program is currently administered by the **Bureau of Justice Statistics** and the data are collected by the Bureau of the Census. See CRIME for a list of related terms.

NATIONAL CRIMINAL JUSTICE REFERENCE SERVICE. *See*: NATIONAL INSTITUTE OF JUSTICE.

NATIONAL INSTITUTE FOR JUVENILE JUSTICE AND DELINQUENCY PREVENTION. *See*: JUVENILE JUSTICE AND DELINQUENCY PREVENTION, OFFICE OF.

NATIONAL INSTITUTE OF CORRECTIONS. *See*: BUREAU OF PRISONS.

NATIONAL INSTITUTE OF JUSTICE. The National Institute of Justice, in the **Office of Justice Programs**, is the primary federal sponsor of research on crime and its control and is a central resource for information on innovative approaches in criminal justice. As mandated by the Justice Assistance Act of 1984, as amended, the institute sponsors and conducts research, evaluates policies and practices, demonstrates promising new approaches, provides training and technical assistance, assesses new technology for criminal justice, and disseminates its findings to state and local practitioners and policymakers.

The institute emphasizes policy-relevant research that responds to the practical needs of those in the criminal justice system. Working with state and local practitioners and researchers across the country, the institute sponsors research efforts through grants and contracts that are carried out by universities, private institutions, and state and local agencies. In addition, it directs a small in-house research program to provide quick, reliable data on emerging policy issues. The institute gives priority to such critical policy concerns as combatting drugs and crime, deterring career criminals and violent crime, advocating fairness to crime victims, controlling family violence, and easing prison and jail capacity problems.

The institute also operates an international information clearinghouse, the **National Criminal Justice Reference Service**. The service maintains a computerized data base of more than 85,000 books, reports, articles, and audiovisual materials. Its information specialists answer queries on a wide range of subjects and facilitate the exchange of information among criminal justice practitioners and researchers.

NATIONAL PRISONER STATISTICS. National Prisoner Statistics (NPS) is a national data program that publishes statistical information on federal and state prisons and prisoners. There are two annual publications. *Prisoners in State and Federal Institutions* contains summary counts for each state and for the federal government of year-end prison system populations and of additions to and subtractions from these populations. These are categorized by type of movement. *Capital Punishment* contains statistics on persons under sentence of death, persons executed, and descriptions of changes in capital punishment statutes. The program was established in 1926 and is currently sponsored by the **Bureau of Justice Statistics**. The data are collected by the Bureau of Census.

NATURAL. Based upon innate human and moral feelings as opposed to **legal** considerations. *Example*: Even a fool has a rough sense of natural justice.

NATURAL DEATH. A death resulting from natural causes, without the aid or assistance of any intervening means such as accident or violence. See DEATH for a list of related terms.

NATURAL PERSON. A human being, as distinguished from an artificial or fictitious person such as a corporation.

NATURAL RIGHTS. Those innate rights that belong to each person inherently as a human being, such as the rights to life, liberty, property, and the pursuit of happiness. Natural rights are to be distinguished from rights created by the enactment of laws by governments to establish an orderly civilized society, such as the right to make a will.

N.B. Abbreviation for NOTA BENE.

NCS. Abbreviation for NATIONAL CRIME SURVEY.

NEAR. Close to; at or within a short distance or time of. See PROXIMITY for a list of related terms.

NECESSARY. Indispensable; essential; required; inevitable.

NECESSARY INFERENCE. An INFERENCE that is inescapable or unavoidable from a given set of facts. See FACT for a list of related terms.

NECESSITY. Something that is NECESSARY.

NECROPSY. Same as AUTOPSY.

NEEDLESS. Unnecessary; unwanted; uncalled for.

NE EXEAT. The title of a **writ** that forbids the person to whom it is addressed to leave the country, the state, or the jurisdiction of the court. See ARREST WARRANT for a list of related terms.

NEGATE. To deny; to nullify; to make ineffective.

NEGATIVE. **adj.** Expressing, containing, or consisting of contradiction, opposition, refusal, or denial. **n.** A **negative** (adj.) statement or act. **v. 1.** To deny; to contradict. **v. 2.** To counteract; to neutralize; to disprove. **v. 3.** To veto; to refuse to approve or agree to.

NEGATIVE PREGNANT. A denial that **implies** an **admission** of a substantial **fact** or **allegation**. An example would be a person charged with killing another with a knife who denies using a knife. Such a denial is a negative pregnant because it implies that the person committed the killing, but with something other than a knife. See FACT for a list of related terms.

NEGATIVE PROOF. Proof that establishes a fact or matter in question by showing that its opposite is not or cannot be true. See FACT for a list of related terms. *See also*: POSITIVE PROOF.

NEGLECT. **1.** To fail to give proper attention or care to; to disregard. *Example*: A person neglects the law at his own risk. **2.** To fail to perform or do something through carelessness or oversight. *Example*: She neglected to file the motion on time.

NEGLIGENCE. A state of mind accompanying a person's conduct such that he or she is not aware, though a reasonable person should be aware, that there is a risk that the conduct might cause a particular harmful result. The distinction between criminal negligence (also called **culpable negligence** or **gross negligence**) and lesser negligence figures in the definition of some serious crimes, such as **negligent**

manslaughter and different **degrees** of **arson**. The exact states of mind and the circumstances required to establish criminal negligence cannot be simply defined. The amount of negligence required to constitute a **cause of action** in a **criminal action** is said to be more than the ordinary negligence that will justify a **civil action**. See CULPABILITY for the **Model Penal Code** definition of negligently.

NEGLIGENT MANSLAUGHTER. Unintentionally causing the death of another by **recklessness** or **gross negligence**, including by reckless or grossly negligent operation of a **motor vehicle**. See HOMICIDE for a list of related terms.

NEGLIGENT MISREPRESENTATION. *See*: MISREPRESENTATION.

NEGOTIABLE. **1.** Capable of being legally transferred from one person to another by delivery, with or without endorsement. *Example*: A check is a negotiable instrument. **2.** Capable of being arranged or settled by discussion and compromise. *Example*: A mandatory sentence is not negotiable.

NEGOTIABLE INSTRUMENT. A written and signed unconditional promise or order to pay a specified amount of money on demand or at a specified time payable to order of a specified person or to the bearer of the instrument. For a writing to be negotiable under §3-104 of the Uniform Commercial Code, it must "(a) be signed by the maker or drawer; and (b) contain an unconditional promise or order to pay a sum certain in money and no other promise order, obligation or power given by the maker or drawer . . . (c) be payable on demand or at a definite time; and (d) be payable to order or to bearer."

NEGOTIATED PLEA. *See*: PLEA BARGAINING.

NEIGHBORHOOD. **1.** The area near or immediately surrounding some place or thing; vicinity; locality. **2.** The community in which a person is well known and has established a reputation.

NEMO. *Latin.* "No one."

NEMO EST SUPRA LEGIS. *Latin.* "No one is above the law."

NEUTRAL. Not inclining toward or actively favoring either side in a controversy; impartial. *Example*: A search warrant must be issued by a neutral magistrate.

NEW COURT COMMITMENT. The entry into **prison** of a person who is being admitted on one or more new **sentences** to **confinement** and is not being readmitted on any previous sentence still in effect. A new court commitment excludes all returns from **parole** or other **conditional release** with or without a new sentence for a new offense, all transfers in from other jurisdictions unless the inmate is beginning to serve time on a new sentence, and all returns from **escape** or other unauthorized departure. A new court commitment includes persons who have violated **probation** and are being committed to prison for the first time in relation to a given **conviction**. See COMMITMENT and SENTENCE for lists of related terms.

NEWLY DISCOVERED EVIDENCE.   **Evidence** relating to an issue in a **trial** that is discovered after the trial is completed. A **court** will grant a **motion** for a **new trial** based on newly discovered evidence if the court is convinced that the evidence will probably change the result; that it could not have been discovered before trial by the exercise of due diligence; that it is **material** to the issue; and that it is not merely **cumulative** or **impeaching**. *Also called*: **after-discovered evidence**. See EVIDENCE for a list of related terms.

NEW MATTER.   Generally, **facts** not previously alleged or introduced by either party to an **action**. See FACT for a list of related terms.

NEW TRIAL.   A reexamination in a **court** of an **issue** or issues decided by that same court at an earlier trial. A new trial can be ordered by that same court or by a higher appellate court. A new trial can be ordered for various reasons, including **reversible error**, **bribing** a **juror**, introduction of **inadmissible evidence**, failure to produce a necessary **witness**, and **newly discovered evidence** that could have led to a different **judgment** if presented at the earlier trial. *Also called*: **retrial**. *See*: ERROR; NEWLY DISCOVERED EVIDENCE; TRIAL; TRIAL DE NOVO.

NEXT.   **1.** Nearest in space or position; closest. **2.** Immediately following in time or sequence. See PROXIMITY for a list of related terms.

NEXT FRIEND.   A person who represents a **minor**, an **incompetent** person, or another person who does not have the legal **capacity** to act on his or her own behalf. *Also called*: **prochain ami**; **prochein ami**.

NEXUS.   A means of connection; a bond; a link.

NIC.   Abbreviation for NATIONAL INSTITUTE OF CORRECTIONS.

NIGHTTIME.   The time period between sunset and sunrise during which there is insufficient natural sunlight to be able to recognize a person's facial features. The term nighttime has been given various other definitions by different courts and legislatures. *See*: DAYTIME.

NIGHTWALKER.   A **prostitute** who walks the streets at night.

NIHIL.   *Latin.* **1.** "Nothing." **2.** Abbreviated form of NIHIL HABET.

NIHIL HABET.   *Latin.* "He has nothing." The name of a **return** made by a **sheriff** or other officer after an unsuccessful attempt to serve a **summons** or other **writ**.

NIL. *Latin.* A contracted form of NIHIL.

NISI. *Latin.* "Unless." The word nisi is often attached to the words **order**, **judgment**, or **decree** to indicate that the order, judgment, or decree is not absolute and final but will become so unless the party affected by it appears to **show cause** against it, to **appeal** it, or otherwise attempt to avoid it.

NISI PRIUS. *Latin.* "Unless before." A term indicating a **court** in which a case is first tried before a **judge** and **jury**, as distinguished from an **appellate court**.

NITROGLYCERIN CHARGE. Same as ALLEN CHARGE.

NO BILL. Same as NO TRUE BILL.

NOCUOUS. Harmful; injurious; noxious.

NOLLE. *See*: NOLLE PROSEQUI.

NOLLE PROSEQUI. *Latin.* A formal entry on the **record** of the **court** indicating that the **prosecutor** declares that he or she will proceed no longer in the **action**. Nolle prosequi is a type of **defendant disposition** occurring after filing of a case in court and before judgment. In **felony** cases it often occurs after the initial **complaint** is filed in a lower court, and before an **information** or **indictment** is filed in a higher court. In some jurisdictions felony cases can be dismissed on the prosecutor's motion in a lower court but filed anew in a higher court. Some jurisdictions require the approval of the court for nolle prosequi. *Also called*: **nolle**. *Abbreviation*: **nol. pros.** See DISMISSAL and PROSECUTE for lists of related terms.

NOLO CONTENDERE. *Latin.* "I do not wish to contest." A defendant's PLEA to a criminal **charge** in which the defendant states that he or she does not contest the charge, but neither admits **guilt** nor claims innocence. A plea of nolo contendere subjects the defendant to the same legal consequences as a **guilty plea**. Both pleas can be followed by a judgment of **conviction** without a **trial** or **verdict**, and by a **sentencing disposition**. The major difference between the two pleas is that a plea of nolo contendere cannot constitute **evidence** in a **civil action** that relevant facts have been admitted; a guilty plea can. A court may not accept a plea of nolo contendere unless the court is satisfied, after inquiry, that the defendant committed the crime charged and that the plea is made **voluntarily** with an understanding of the nature of the charge. *Also called*: **non vult contendere**.

NOL. PROS. Abbreviation for NOLLE PROSEQUI.

NOMINAL. Existing in name only; not real or actual; trifling.

NOMINAL PARTY. A party who has no real interest in the subject matter of an **action** but is joined in the action because the technical rules of **pleading** require it. See PLEADING for a list of related terms.

NON. *Latin.* "Not."

NON-. A prefix meaning "not" or "failure to," depending on the word to which it is attached. For example, nonnegotiable means not **negotiable**; nonappearance means failure to **appear**.

NONAGE. Same as MINORITY.

NO NAME WARRANT. *See*: ARREST WARRANT.

NONAPPEARANCE. Failure to **appear**.

NON COMPOS MENTIS. *Latin.* "Not of sound mind"; insane. Non compos mentis is a general term used to describe varying degrees of mental **incapacity**.

NON CULPABILIS. *Latin.* "Not guilty."

NONDEADLY FORCE. Any physical force that is not DEADLY FORCE. See FORCE for a list of related terms.

NONDISCLOSURE. Failure to reveal facts.

NONFEASANCE. Neglect or intentional failure to perform a required act or duty. *See*: FEASANCE; MALFEASANCE; MISFEASANCE.

NONJURY TRIAL. A TRIAL in which there is no **jury** and in which a **judicial officer** determines all issues of **fact** and **law**. *Also called*: **bench trial**; **court trial**; **judge trial**; **trial by court**; **trial by judge**; **trial by witnesses**; **trial per testes**. See JURY and TRIAL for lists of related terms.

NONNEGLIGENT MANSLAUGHTER. Same as VOLUNTARY MAN-SLAUGHTER.

NON OBSTANTE. *Latin.* "Notwithstanding."

NON OBSTANTE VEREDICTO. *Latin.* "Notwithstanding the verdict." *See*: JUDGMENT NOTWITHSTANDING THE VERDICT.

NONRUN TIME. Same as DEAD TIME.

NON SEQUITUR. *Latin.* "It does not follow." Something that does not follow logically from or is unrelated to things preceding it.

NONSUFFICIENT FUNDS CHECK. Same as CHECK FRAUD. *Abbreviation:* **n.s.f. check**.

NONSUPPORT. Failure to provide for the **support** (n.) of one's spouse, child, or other dependent as required by law. Nonsupport is a crime in some states.

NON VULT CONTENDERE. *Latin.* "He does not wish to contest it." Same as NOLO CONTENDERE.

NOTA BENE. *Latin.* "Note well." An indication in a document calling attention to a particular part of the document. *Abbreviation:* **N.B.**

NOTARY PUBLIC. A public officer authorized by law to administer **oaths, certify documents**, take **affidavits** and **depositions**, and perform certain other commercial acts.

NOT A TRUE BILL. Same as NO TRUE BILL.

NOTE. **n. 1.** A brief, informal written statement or record. **n. 2.** A PROMISSORY NOTE. **v.** To take notice of.

NOTE OF ISSUE. A **notice** stating that a **case** is ready for **trial**.

NOT FOUND. Same as NO TRUE BILL.

NOT GUILTY. *See:* NOT GUILTY BY REASON OF INSANITY; NOT GUILTY PLEA; NOT GUILTY VERDICT.

NOT GUILTY BY REASON OF INSANITY. The PLEA of a **defendant** or the **verdict** of a **jury** or **judge** in a criminal proceeding, that the defendant is not **guilty** of the offense charged because at the time the crime was committed the defendant did not have the mental **capacity** to be held criminally responsible for his or her actions. A plea or verdict of not guilty by reason of insanity differs from other not guilty pleas and verdicts in that the claim or finding is not based on what the defendant is alleged or determined to have done, but rather on the issue of whether he or she possessed the mental capacity to be held responsible for a criminal act. A verdict of not guilty by reason of insanity differs from a court finding that the defendant is **incompetent to stand trial**, which concerns only the defendant's mental fitness at the time of trial, and is not related to the question of guilt. *See:* CIVIL COMMITMENT; INCOMPETENT TO BE EXECUTED; INCOMPETENT TO STAND TRIAL; INSANITY; NOT GUILTY PLEA; PLEA; VERDICT.

NOT GUILTY PLEA. A defendant's PLEA to criminal **charges** contained in a **complaint, information**, or **indictment**, claiming that he or she did not commit the offense listed. In this plea the defendant denies the charge and puts in issue all the material facts alleged in the complaint, indictment, or information. If the defendant exercises his or her right to refuse to plead, the court must enter a plea of not guilty. *See*: NOT GUILTY BY REASON OF INSANITY; PLEA.

NOT GUILTY VERDICT. A **verdict**, on the basis of the **evidence** presented at trial, that the defendant is not **guilty** of the offense for which he or she has been tried. A not guilty verdict indicates that the evidence left at least a reasonable doubt as to the defendant's guilt. A not guilty verdict entitles the defendant to a judgment of **acquittal**, which frees the defendant forever from further **prosecution** for that crime. The court cannot enter a judgment of **conviction** unless the defendant has been found guilty or the defendant has pled guilty or **nolo contendere**. See VERDICT for a list of related terms.

NOTICE. 1. Information or knowledge of the existence of a fact or facts. 2. Formal advice or warning to inform a person of a proceeding in which his or her interests are involved or of a fact that the person is entitled to know. *Example*: An indictment must provide a defendant with sufficient notice of the specific charges against him or her. 3. A handbill, poster, placard, or the like conveying information or warning. *See*: ACTUAL NOTICE; CONSTRUCTIVE NOTICE; EXPRESS NOTICE; FACT; IMPLIED NOTICE; JUDICIAL NOTICE; LEGAL NOTICE; NOTICE OF APPEAL; NOTICE TO APPEAR.

NOTICE OF APPEAL. The first **notice** to the **appellate court** from a lower court or an attorney indicating that a **case** is being **appealed**. See APPEAL and NOTICE for lists of related terms.

NOTICE TO APPEAR. *See*: CITATION.

NOTIFY. To give NOTICE to; to inform.

NOTORIOUS. Widely known and discussed; universally recognized. Sometimes notorious carries the connotation of infamous or unfavorably regarded. *Example:* Courts may take judicial notice of notorious facts.

NO TRUE BILL. Words written across the face of a **bill of indictment** indicating the decision by a **grand jury** that it has failed to find **probable cause** to justify the **prosecution** of the person accused of a **crime**, on the basis of the **allegations** and **evidence** presented by the **prosecutor**. *Also called*: **ignoramus**; **no bill**; **not a true bill**; **not found**. See GRAND JURY for a list of related terms.

NOT TRANSFERABLE. When written across the face of a **negotiable instrument**, the words not transferable operate to destroy the negotiability of the instrument.

N.O.V. Abbreviation for NON OBSTANTE VEREDICTO.

NOVUS HOMO. *Latin.* "New man." A person who has been **pardoned** of a **crime**.

NOW. **1.** At the present time or moment. **2.** Immediately; at once; forthwith.

NOXIOUS. Harmful or injurious to health, well-being, or morals.

N.P. Abbreviation for NOTARY PUBLIC.

NPS. Abbreviation for NATIONAL PRISONER STATISTICS.

NSF CHECK. Abbreviation for NONSUFFICIENT FUNDS CHECK.

NUDE. **1.** Lacking some legal requirement. **2.** Naked; without clothing.

NUGATORY. Of no force or effect; inoperative. *See*: VOIDABLE.

NUISANCE. Generally, a use of property or course of conduct that interferes with the legal rights of another or others by causing inconvenience, annoyance, danger, or damage. Depending on the nature of the nuisance and the provisions of individual statutes, a nuisance may be remedied by private lawsuit, public prosecution, or both.

NUL. *French.* No; none.

NULL. Void; invalid; of no legal effect.

NULL AND VOID. Same as NULL.

NULLITY. A **null** act, proceeding, document, or other thing.

NUMBERS GAME. An unlawful **game of chance** in which money is wagered on the occurrence of a chosen number and in which a winner is usually paid at odds. In a numbers game, a person usually bets however much money he or she chooses on a single number. Any number of people can bet on the same number. The amount to be won is variable, depending on factors such as the amount of the person's bet, the total amount of all bets on the winning number, etc. The winning number is not randomly selected from the numbers bet on, but consists of a set of digits taken from an external source, such as pari-mutuel race track reports, stock exchange reports, clearinghouse balances, or the like. *Also called*: **policy.** See GAMBLING for a list of related terms.

NUNC PRO TUNC. *Latin.* "Now for then." A phrase used to describe acts allowed to be done after the time when they should have been done and given retroactive effect as if done on time.

OATH. A solemn appeal to God, or some other sacred object, in witness of the truth of a statement or the binding nature of a promise or undertaking. If a person makes a false statement under oath or **affirmation**, he or she may be subject to a **prosecution** for **perjury**, **false swearing**, or a related crime. An oath, in its broadest sense, includes forms of attestation by which a party signifies that he or she is bound in conscience to perform an act faithfully and truthfully. See AFFIRMATION for a list of related terms.

OB. *Latin.* "On account of."

OBITER. *Latin.* Incidentally; in passing; by the way.

OBITER DICTUM. *Latin.* "A remark by the way." A statement by a **judge** in deciding a case that is not essential to the decision and is therefore not binding as a **precedent**. An obiter dictum is used for the purposes of illustration, analogy, or argument on collateral legal matters only remotely related to the essential facts of the case. *See*: HOLDING.

OBJECT. **n. 1.** Anything perceptible by the senses, especially something seen or touched; a material thing. *Example*: Objects to be seized under authority of a search warrant must be specifically described in the affidavit. **n. 2.** Aim; purpose; goal. *Example*: What is the object of your line of argument? **n. 3.** A person or thing to which attention, thought, discussion, or action is directed. *Example*: His children were the unfortunate objects of his violent tantrums.

OBJECT. **v.** To assert opposition to an action by the opposing party or by the court because it is illegal or improper, and to refer the question of its legality or propriety to the court. The assertion is usually made by a lawyer and is called an **objection**. The purposes of an objection are to correct **errors** of the court, to keep something from being admitted into **evidence**, and to preserve errors for evaluation on **appeal**. *Example:* I object to the admission of the confession in evidence. *See*: ERROR; EVIDENCE; EXCEPTION; GENERAL OBJECTION; SPECIFIC OBJECTION.

OBJECTION. The act of objecting or the statement made when objecting. *See*: OBJECT.

OBLIGATE. To legally bind.

OBLIGATION. A duty; anything that a person is legally required to do because of a promise, a contract, an oath, or a law.

OBLITERATE. **1.** To destroy so as to leave no trace. **2.** To erase, wipe out, or blot out written words or marks. See CANCEL for a list of related terms.

OBLIVIOUS. Forgetful; unmindful.

OBNOXIOUS. Offensive; objectionable; distasteful.

OBSCENE MATERIAL. Material that is so offensive or objectionable to accepted standards of decency that it is not protected by the freedom of speech guarantee of the First Amendment. The U.S. Supreme Court in the 1973 case of *Miller v. California* set out the basic guidelines for the **trier of fact** in determining whether material is obscene. Those guidelines are: "(a) whether 'the average person applying contemporary community standards' would find that the work, taken as a whole, appeals to the prurient interest . . . ; (b) whether the work depicts or describes, in a patently offensive way, sexual conduct specifically defined by the applicable state law; and (c) whether the work, taken as a whole lacks serious literary, artistic, political, or scientific value." 413 U.S. 15, 24, 93 S.Ct. 2607, 2615, 37 L.Ed.2d 419, 431.

OBSCURE. Not clearly expressed; difficult to understand.

OBSERVE. **1.** To see; to notice; to perceive. **2.** To obey; to comply with; to adhere to. *Example*: She carefully observed the traffic laws. **3.** To remark; to comment.

OBSOLESCENT. Passing out of use or usefulness; becoming OBSOLETE.

OBSOLETE. No longer in use or useful. *Example*: The statute is obsolete because the reason for its passage no longer exists.

OBSTANTE. *See*: NON OBSTANTE.

OBSTRUCT. To block, interrupt, or hinder someone or something in motion or in progress.

OBSTRUCTING JUSTICE. A class of offenses, sometimes so named in statutes, that at its broadest consists of all unlawful acts committed with intent to prevent or hinder the administration of justice, either civil or criminal, including **law enforcement**, **judicial**, and **corrections** functions. Obstructing justice may include influencing or intimidating a **party**, **juror**, or **witness**, destroying **evidence**, hindering a **law enforcement officer** in the performance of his or her duties, failing to report or falsely reporting a **crime**, harboring a **fugitive**, and failing or refusing to obey a court **order**. See ABUSE OF PROCESS for a list of related terms. *See also*: RESISTING AN OFFICER; RESISTING ARREST.

OBSTRUCTING PROCESS. Hindering or impeding the execution of PROCESS (definition 2).

OBTAIN. To get possession of through effort; to acquire; to procure. Under Section 223.0 (5) of the **Model Penal Code** obtain means "(a) in relation to property, to bring about a transfer or purported transfer of a legal interest in the property, whether to the obtainer or another; or (b) in relation to labor or service, to secure performance thereof." *See*: RECEIVE.

OBTS. Abbreviation for OFFENDER-BASED TRANSACTION STATISTICS.

OBVIOUS. Easily seen or understood; plain; clear; apparent.

OCCASION. **n. 1.** An event; a happening. **n. 2.** Opportunity; set of favorable circumstances. *Example*: I took the occasion to congratulate him. **n. 3.** Ground; reason. *Example*: I had no occasion to object to the witness. **n. 4.** The incidental or immediate cause of some event. *Example*: What was the occasion for her violent outburst? **v.** To bring about; to give rise to; to produce.

OCCUPANT. A person who has actual physical possession, control, or use of premises or of a thing; a tenant. *See*: OWNER.

OCCUPATION. A person's regular employment, trade, business, or profession.

OCCUPIED STRUCTURE. Section 221.0 (1) of the **Model Penal Code** defines occupied structure as "any structure, vehicle or place adapted for overnight accommodation of persons, or for carrying on business therein, whether or not a person is actually present."

OCCUPY. **1.** To take or hold possession of. **2.** To be an OCCUPANT. **3.** To fill up or take up space or time. *Example*: He occupied his evenings studying.

OCCUR. **1.** To happen; to take place; to come about. **2.** To come to mind; to present itself in thought. *Example*: It never occurred to me.

ODIOUS. Exciting or deserving of hatred; detestable; disgusting; highly offensive.

ODIUM. Hatred; strong dislike; contempt.

OF COUNSEL. A phrase used to describe an **attorney** who is employed to assist in the preparation or management of a case, but is not the principal **attorney of record**. Of counsel is also used to describe an attorney who is associated with a law firm but is neither a partner nor an associate.

OF COURSE. *See*: MATTER OF COURSE.

OFF-CALENDAR CASES. **Cases** that have not reached **judgment** or other definite conclusion such as **dismissal**, but for other reasons (both within and beyond the control of the court) cannot be scheduled.

OFFENDER. An **adult** who has been **convicted** of a criminal offense. The term offender is ambiguous and its meaning may include **alleged offender**, **suspect**, or **ex-offender** in some contexts. See ACCUSED for a list of related terms.

OFFENDER-BASED TRANSACTION STATISTICS. Offender-Based Transaction Statistics are derived from information concerning **law enforcement**, **court**, and **corrections** proceedings recorded in such a way that the system identity of the person subject to the proceedings is preserved throughout data collection and analysis. The use of the individual **offender** or **alleged offender** as the basic unit tracked by the statistical system provides the mechanism for linking events in the different parts of the criminal justice system. The output of one agency can be linked to the input of another agency, and the flow of alleged offenders and offenders through the system can be observed over long periods of time. This capability permits study of the relationships between **decisions** and **dispositions** made at one point and decisions and dispositions made at another point in the criminal justice process. *Abbreviation*: **OBTS.**

OFFENSE. An act committed or omitted in violation of a law forbidding or commanding it. The term offense is sometimes used restrictively as a synonym of CRIME. In its broadest usage, however, offense may include **crimes**, **delinquent acts**, **status offenses**, **infractions**, **civil violations**, and **private wrongs** and injuries. See CRIME for a list of related terms.

OFFENSIVE. Causing discomfort or displeasure; annoying; irritating; disagreeable.

OFFENSIVE WEAPON. **1.** Same as DEADLY WEAPON. **2.** Section 5.07 of the **Model Penal Code** defines offensive weapon as "any **bomb**, **machine gun**, sawed-off shotgun, **firearm** specially made or specially adapted for concealment or silent discharge, any **blackjack**, sandbag, metal knuckles, **dagger**, or other implement for the infliction of **serious bodily injury** that serves no common lawful purpose."

OFFER. **1.** To present for acceptance or rejection; to propose; to put forth; to introduce. See ADDRESS for a list of related terms. *Example*: The murder weapon was offered in evidence. **2.** To express or exhibit an intention; to attempt. *Example*: She offered to bribe the judge.

OFFICE. **1.** A position of authority, trust, or duty in governmental service or in the administration of a corporation or other organization. *Example*: She holds a high office in state government. **2.** A place or room where public or private business is transacted. *Example*: He works in the Attorney General's office. **3.** The officers and staff of a public agency or private organization considered as a whole. *Example*: The District Attorney's office is very effective.

OFFICE FOR VICTIMS OF CRIME.   The Office for Victims of Crime (OVC), in the **Office of Justice Programs**, serves as the federal focal point for addressing the needs and improving the treatment of crime **victims**. This includes carrying out the activities mandated by the Victims of Crime Act of 1984 (V.O.C.A.), as amended; monitoring compliance with the provisions regarding assistance for federal crime victims of the Victim and Witness Protection Act of 1982; and implementing the recommendations of the President's Task Force on Victims of Crime, the Attorney General's Task Force on Family Violence, and the President's Child Safety Partnership Program.

The act (V.O.C.A.) created a Crime Victims Fund in the U.S. Treasury to provide federal financial assistance to state governments to compensate and assist victims of crime. Monies in the fund come from fines and penalties assessed on convicted federal defendants. The office awards grants to states to compensate crime victims for expenses, such as medical costs, resulting from their victimization. Grants also are awarded to state governments to support state and local programs that provide direct assistance to crime victims and their families. Priority for victim assistance funds is given to programs providing direct services to victims of sexual assault, spouse abuse, and child abuse. States also must use grant funds to assist previously underserved victim populations, such as victims of drunk drivers or the families of homicide victims. One percent of the Crime Victims Fund is available to support services for victims of federal crimes. Programs under this initiative have focused on developing victim assistance services for federal crime victims on Native American lands, creating an emergency fund for use by U.S. Attorneys Offices to pay for emergency services for federal crime victims, and assistance to Native American child abuse victims.

In collaboration with other agencies and groups, OVC administers numerous projects serving the victims of drug-related crimes. The office also supports national programs to improve and coordinate services to crime victims and sponsors conferences and training for criminal justice practitioners, medical and mental health personnel, the clergy, and others who work with crime victims and their families. The National Victims Resource Center, which provides information concerning victims' issues to victims' advocates, criminal justice practitioners, and the public, is funded by OVC.

OFFICE OF JUSTICE PROGRAMS.   *See*: JUSTICE PROGRAMS, OFFICE OF.

OFFICE OF JUVENILE JUSTICE AND DELINQUENCY PREVENTION.   *See*: JUVENILE JUSTICE AND DELINQUENCY PREVENTION, OFFICE OF.

OFFICER.   **1.** A person who holds an OFFICE (definition 1). **2.** A LAW ENFORCEMENT OFFICER.

OFFICER OF THE COURT. A general term for any type of court employee including **judges, clerks of court, bailiffs, sheriffs, marshals,** and **constables.** **Attorneys** are also considered officers of the court and therefore must obey **rules of court.** See COURT for a list of related terms.

OFFICIAL. n. Same as OFFICER. **adj. 1.** Relating to or done by an OFFICE or OFFICER. **adj. 2.** Derived from or formally approved by an OFFICER; authoritative; authorized.

OFFICIAL MISCONDUCT. Same as MISCONDUCT IN OFFICE.

OFFICIAL PROCEEDING. Section 240.0 (4) of the **Model Penal Code** defines official proceeding as "a proceeding heard or which may be heard before any legislative, judicial, administrative or other governmental agency or official authorized to take evidence under oath, including any referee, hearing examiner, commissioner, notary or other person taking testimony or deposition in connection with any such proceeding."

OFFICIO. *See*: EX OFFICIO.

OFF THE RECORD. Not for publication or quotation as something authoritative or official.

OF RECORD. Entered or existing on the official RECORD of a court in connection with a particular case, judgment, or proceeding. *Example*: Mr. Seitzinger is the attorney of record.

OF RIGHT. *See*: MATTER OF RIGHT.

OJP. Abbreviation for OFFICE OF JUSTICE PROGRAMS.

O.K. or **OK.** Correct; approved; all right.

OMISSION. 1. The act, process, or result of omitting. *See*: OMIT. **2.** A failure to perform an **act.** Under Section 2.01 (3) of the **Model Penal Code** "[l]iability for the commission of an offense may not be based on an omission unaccompanied by **action** unless: (a) the omission is expressly made sufficient by the law defining the offense; or (b) a duty to perform the omitted act is otherwise imposed by law."

OMIT. v. 1. To leave out; to fail to include. **v. 2.** To fail to do something. **n.** OMISSION.

OMNIBUS. *Latin.* "For all." Relating to or including many separate and distinct things or situations at once. *Example*: The legislature is debating a complicated omnibus bill.

OMNIBUS HEARING.   *See*: PRETRIAL CONFERENCE.

Oo

ON ALL FOURS.   A phrase used to describe a **case** whose facts are similar to and whose legal issues are substantially the same as those of another case. *Example*: Your fact situation is on all fours with *State v. Pankus*.

ON OR ABOUT.   **1.** Near; approximately; in close proximity to. *Example:* The robbery occurred on or about February 8, 1979. **2.** Either attached or connected to or conveniently accessible to. *Example*: It is unlawful to carry a weapon on or about the person in some places.

ON POINT.   Directly applicable to or dispositive of the matter under consideration. *Example*: Her research provided a case on point with respect to the issue being appealed.

ON RECORD.   Known, published, or documented. *Example*: The judge's views are on record.

ON THE PERSON.   In contact with the body or in clothing or containers worn on the body.

ONUS.   *Latin*. "Burden; weight."

ONUS PROBANDI.   Latin. "Burden of proof."

OPEN.   **v. 1.** To begin; to initiate; to commence; to begin operation of. *Example*: The bailiff's formal announcement opened traffic court. **v. 2.** To uncover; to unseal; to disclose; to expose; to make accessible or visible. *Example*: The court ordered the attorney to open the sealed documents. **v. 3.** To recall a **judgment** or **ruling** in an **action** for a reexamination of the **merits** of the action. *Example*: The judge opened the judgment on the basis of the new evidence. **v. 4.** To make an **opening statement**. **adj. 1.** Exposed; available; accessible; uncovered; unconcealed; unrestricted. **adj. 2.** Undecided. *Example*: That is an open question. **adj. 3.** Ready or available for the transaction of business.

OPEN COURT.   **1.** A **court** ready or available for the transaction of judicial business. **2.** A court accessible to and not closed off to public spectators. See COURT for a list of related terms.

OPEN FACILITY.   *See*: JUVENILE FACILITY.

OPEN FIELDS.   The portions of a person's premises lying outside the CURTILAGE of his or her home or business. The open fields doctrine states that "the special protection accorded by the Fourth Amendment to the people in their 'persons houses, papers, and effects,' is not extended to the open fields. *Hester v. U.S.* 265 U.S. 57, 59, 44 S.Ct. 445, 446, 68 L.Ed. 898, 900 (1924). This doctrine simply means that a law enforcement officer may search for and seize items of evidence lying in the open fields without **probable cause**, **search warrant**, or other legal justification without violating a person's Fourth Amendment rights.

OPENING ARGUMENT.   Same as OPENING STATEMENT.

OPENING STATEMENT.   The part of a **trial** before the presentation of **evidence** in which the **attorney** for each party gives an outline of what that party intends to prove by the evidence it will present. The primary purpose of the opening statement is to acquaint the **judge** and **jury** in a general way with the nature of the case. *Also called*: **opening argument**. See EVIDENCE and TRIAL for lists of related terms.

OPEN SEASON.   The time period during which fish and game laws permit the taking or killing of certain species of fish or game.

OPEN VIEW.   *See*: IN OPEN VIEW.

OPERATE.   **1.** To control the function of; to conduct the workings of; to manage. *Example*: She operated the vehicle in a reckless manner. **2.** To bring about an effect; to exert an influence. *Example*: This statute operates to repeal the old one.

OPERATING UNDER THE INFLUENCE.   Same as DRIVING UNDER THE INFLUENCE OF ALCOHOL.

OPERATION OF LAW.   The manner in which a person's rights or liabilities are determined through the automatic application of the law to a situation or transaction, without any direct act of the person himself or herself.

OPINION.   **1.** The official announcement of a **decision** of a **court** together with the reasons for that decision. A **judge** can deliver an opinion about any aspect of a case at almost any time, but the term opinion is generally used only in connection with final decisions in **appeal** proceedings. *See*: ADVISORY OPINION; CONCURRING OPINION; DECISION; DECLARATORY JUDGMENT; DISSENTING OPINION; FULL OPINION; JUDGMENT; MAJORITY OPINION; MEMORANDUM DECISION; PER CURIAM; PLURALITY OPINION; SIGNED OPINION; SLIP OPINION; SUB SILENTIO. **2.** Same as OPINION EVIDENCE. **3.** A document prepared by an **attorney** for a client stating his or her understanding and conclusions on the application of the **law** to a particular set of **facts**.

OPINION EVIDENCE.   **Evidence** of a **witness's inferences** or **conclusions** about **facts**, as opposed to evidence of his or her knowledge of the facts as perceived directly through the witness's five senses. See EVIDENCE and FACT for lists of related

O o

terms. *See also*: COMMENT ON THE EVIDENCE; EXPERT WITNESS; FACT; HYPOTHETICAL QUESTION; OPINION RULE; WITNESS.

OPINION RULE.   The opinion rule of evidence states that a **witness** may testify only to **facts** that the witness has directly perceived through one or more of his or her five senses, not to conclusions or opinions based upon those facts. The basis for this rule is that once the **jury** has the facts, they are as able as the witness to draw the proper conclusions. There are two major exceptions to the opinion rule. One exception allows an **expert witness** to testify under certain conditions to his or her opinions on questions within the person's area of expertise. The basis for this exception is that the jury, even with the pertinent facts, does not have sufficient knowledge or expertise to formulate a rational conclusion in technical matters. The other exception allows opinion testimony on certain matters of common observation that would be impossible to describe except in the form of an opinion. Examples of such matters about which any witness may state an opinion are sobriety, mental condition, speed, size, distance, voice identification, age, taste, and smell. See EVIDENCE, FACT, and WITNESS for lists of related terms.

OPPRESSION.   An illegal act of a public officer, done under color of office, that causes harm, injustice, or disadvantage to a person.

OPUS.   *Latin.* "Work."

ORAL.   **1.** Spoken, as distinguished from written. **2.** Of or pertaining to the mouth.

ORDAIN.   To decree; to enact; to establish.

ORDER.   **v.** To issue a command or instruction. **n. 1.** A mandate, command, or direction issued by a **judicial officer** in the exercise of judicial authority and entered in the court **record**. A court order is sometimes viewed as a **judgment**, but it is rather the mechanism by which the court, having reached conclusions as to matters of fact and law in a controversy, directs the course of a proceeding, settles intervening matters, or ensures that the actions implementing the judgment occur. **Writs** and **injunctions** are orders. *Example*: The judge issued a gag order for the remainder of the proceeding. See JUDGMENT for a list of related terms. **n. 2.** Conformity to law or constituted authority; absence of riot, insurrection, or revolt.

ORDINANCE.   **1.** A legislative enactment of a municipal government, similar in effect to a **statute**. Ordinances regulate such local matters as speed of vehicles, parking, refuse disposal, loitering, and zoning. **2.** An enactment serving as an **organic law** but not of the stature of a **constitution**. An ordinance is similar to but broader in scope than a **statute**. *Example*: The Ordinance of 1787 provided for just treatment of Indians in the Northwest Territory. See ACT for a list of related terms.

ORDINARY.   Regular; normal; usual.

ORDINARY CARE.   Such care as a reasonably prudent person would exercise under the same or similar circumstances. *Also called*: **ordinary diligence**; **proper care**; **reasonable care**.

ORDINARY DILIGENCE.   Same as ORDINARY CARE.

ORDINARY NEGLIGENCE.   The failure to exercise ORDINARY CARE.

ORDINARY PRUDENT PERSON.   Same as REASONABLE PERSON.

ORGANIC LAW.   The essential or fundamental law or the **constitution** of a nation, state, or other governmental unit that establishes the manner in which its government will be organized. *See*: ORDINANCE (definition 2).

ORGANIZATION.   A general term for a group or association of people joined together either formally or legally. Examples of an organization are a government, a corporation, a partnership, and a civic or political association.

ORGANIZED CRIME.   A complex pattern of activity that includes the commission of statutorily defined offenses, in particular the provision of illegal goods and services, such as **gambling**, **prostitution**, **loansharking**, and **narcotics**, and other carefully planned and coordinated **fraud**, **theft**, and **extortion**-type offenses. Organized crime is uniquely characterized by the planned use of both legitimate and criminal professional expertise, and the use for criminal purposes of organizational features of legitimate business, including availability of large capital resources, disciplined management, division of labor, and focus upon maximum profit. The term organized crime also refers to the persons engaged in this pattern of activity. See CRIME for a list of related terms.

ORGASM.   Sexual climax.

ORIGINAL EVIDENCE.   **Evidence** consisting of a writing or material object itself as distinguished from a **copy** of it or **testimony** about it. See EVIDENCE for a list of related terms.

ORIGINAL JURISDICTION.   JURISDICTION of a **court** or administrative agency to hear or act upon a case from its beginning and to pass judgment on the **law** and the **facts**. See JURISDICTION for a list of related terms.

OS.   *Latin*. "The mouth."

OSTENSIBLE.   Presented or displayed as actual or real; apparent.

OSTENSIBLE AUTHORITY.   Same as APPARENT AUTHORITY.

OUTBUILDING. A small building, usually separate from the main house and located a short distance from it, used in connection with the main house for the convenience or necessity of the occupants. Examples of outbuildings are a barn, a garage, a toolhouse, and a stable.

OUTHOUSE. Same as OUTBUILDING

OUTLAW. **n. 1.** A habitual criminal. **n. 2.** A person excluded from normal legal benefits and protection. **v.** To make illegal; to prohibit.

OUT OF COURT. Not made or done before an **open court**; without being referred to a court for approval or authorization. *Example*: The prosecutor and defense attorney made an out-of-court agreement about the sentence recommendation. See COURT for a list of related terms.

OUT OF TERM. At a time when the **court** is on vacation or is not holding a **term**.

OUTRAGE. An extremely offensive act or insult.

OUTRIGHT. Downright; unqualified; unrestrained; direct; complete. *Example*: That is outright fraud.

OUTSTANDING WARRANT. A WARRANT that has not yet been **executed**.

OVC. Abbreviation for OFFICE FOR VICTIMS OF CRIME.

OVERBROAD. A term used to describe a **statute** that prohibits not only conduct that may be constitutionally prohibited, but also conduct that is constitutionally protected. For example, a statute that prohibits any publication of pictures of the nude human body would be unconstitutionally overbroad. See STATUTE for a list of related terms.

OVERREACH. To take unfair advantage of another by **cheating**, trickery, or **fraud**.

OVERRULE. **1.** To overturn the **holding** of a prior **case** by deciding a point of law exactly opposite to the decision in the prior case. A court's **decision** can only be overruled by itself or by a higher court with the same **subject matter jurisdiction**. **2.** To deny a **motion**, **objection**, or other request made to the **court** during the course of a **trial**. *Example*: Your objection is overruled.

OVERT. Open to view or knowledge; manifest; not concealed or hidden.

OVERT ACT. An outward act done toward the accomplishment of a **crime** from which an **intent** to commit the crime may be **inferred**. More than mere words, intention, or design is needed to constitute an overt act. An overt act is required to find a person criminally liable for **attempt**, **conspiracy**, or **treason**. Article III, Section 3, Clause 1 of the U.S. Constitution states: "No Person shall be convicted of Treason unless on the Testimony of two Witnesses to the same overt Act."

OWN.   To have legal or rightful title to; to have; to possess.

OWNER.   A person who has legal or rightful title to and the right to dispose of real or personal property, whether or not the person has actual physical possession, control, or use of the property. *See*: OCCUPANT.

OYER AND TERMINER.   *French.* "Hear and determine." A term used to describe some state **courts** with **criminal jurisdiction** over **felonies**.

OYEZ.   "Hear ye." A word cried out in some courtrooms to get attention when an announcement is about to be made.

PACIFIST. One who is opposed to using war or violence as a means of settling disputes and who demonstrates that opposition by refusing to participate in military service.

PACK. To rig or put together a **jury** or other deliberating body in an unlawful or improper manner in order to secure favorable treatment.

PACT. An agreement; a compact.

PACTUM. *Latin.* "Pact."

PAIN. Any suffering or distress of the body or mind.

PAIS. *French.* "Country." *See*: TRIAL PER PAIS.

PALPABLE. Easily or plainly perceived; obvious. *Example*: That was a palpable lie.

PANDER. **n.** One who supplies another with the means of gratifying lustful or base sexual desires; a pimp. *Also called*: **panderer**; **pimp**; **procurer**. **v.** To act as a PANDER (n.).

PANDERER. Same as PANDER (n.).

PANEL. **1.** The list of persons summoned for **jury** service. **2.** The body of persons selected from the list to compose the jury.

PANEL OF JUDGES. A group of three or more **judges** of a court who jointly hear and decide a case. Proceedings conducted by a panel of judges rather than by a single judge are most common in **appellate courts**. Sentencing decisions are also sometimes made by a group of judges. A case heard jointly by all judges of a particular court is said to be heard **en banc**.

PAPER. Any written or printed **document** or **instrument**, including letters, memoranda, legal or business documents, and account books. The Fourth Amendment to the U.S. Constitution guarantees the right of the people to be secure in their persons, houses, papers, and effects.

PAR. *Latin.* "Equal."

PARAJUDGE. A **judicial officer** with less authority than a **judge**. Parajudges are given various names such as **masters**, **commissioners**, **referees**, **magistrates**, and **hearing officers**. As a rule, parajudges have no **original jurisdiction**, but receive cases on an assignment basis from a judge. Parajudges perform basic functions of the judicial process such as setting **bail**, conducting **hearings**, analyzing **evidence**, and examining **witnesses** and submit their report to the court. These reports may contain findings of **fact**, conclusions of **law**, and recommendations for **disposition**. The judge, after reviewing the parajudge's report, issues the court's decree.

Other parajudges specialize in or are limited to a particular type of proceeding such as probate, juvenile matters, traffic, or domestic relations. Still others are officials, such as **paroling authority** members and certain **probation officers**, holding specified, limited judicial powers in relation to the powers and duties of the administrative agencies to which they belong. The authority of parajudges in any given jurisdiction depends upon the combination of statutory and administrative rules and customs governing practice in the particular jurisdiction. *Also called*: **parajudicial personnel**.

PARAJUDICIAL PERSONNEL. Same as PARAJUDGE.

PARALEGAL. A person who is not a **lawyer** but who has legal skills and uses those skills under the supervision of a lawyer or in a manner otherwise authorized by law.

PARALYSIS. Loss or impairment of sensation, function, or movement of a bodily part as a result of injury or disease.

PARAMOUNT. Superior; preeminent; foremost.

PARAMOUR. A lover, of either sex, especially an illicit lover of a married person.

PARAPHERNALIA. Articles or objects used in some activity; equipment; apparatus. *Example*: The search warrant authorized the seizure of gambling paraphernalia.

PARCEL. To divide into pieces or allotments and give out to members of a group. See ALLOCATE for a list of related terms.

PARDON. An act of an executive official of the government releasing a person from punishment for a **crime** he or she has committed. The two types of pardon are **full pardon** and **conditional pardon**. Article II, Section 2, Clause 1, of the U.S. Constitution states that the president "shall have Power to grant Reprieves and Pardons for Offences against the United States, except in cases of Impeachment." See CLEMENCY for a list of related terms.

PARDON ATTORNEY. The Office of the Pardon Attorney in the **Department of Justice** in consultation with the United States **Attorney General** or designee, assists the President in the exercise of executive **clemency** as authorized under Article II, Section 2, of the Constitution. Generally, all requests for executive clemency are directed to the Pardon Attorney for investigation and review. Executive clemency may take several forms, including **pardon**, **commutation**, **remission** of fine, and **reprieve**.

Pp

PARENS PATRIAE. *Latin.* "Parent of the country." The doctrine of parens patriae holds that the government has inherent power and authority to protect the person and property of **minors**, insane persons, and other persons under a legal **disability**. *Also called*: **pater patriae**.

PARENTICIDE. **1.** The killing of one's parent. **2.** One who kills his or her parent.

PARI DELICTO. *See*: IN PARI DELICTO.

PARI MATERIA. *See*: IN PARI MATERIA.

PARI-MUTUEL. A form of betting (usually on horses or dogs) in which those who bet on a winner share the total stakes, minus a fixed percentage for the management, in proportion to the amounts of their respective bets.

PARITY. Equality; equivalence; correspondence.

PAROL. Oral or verbal, as opposed to written.

PAROLE. A **conditional release** from prison by discretion of a **paroling authority** entitling the person released to serve the remainder of his or her **sentence** outside the prison if the person complies with all the terms and conditions of the **parole** order. A person on parole is placed under the **supervision** of a **parole agency**. Conditions of parole, as set forth by the paroling authority, frequently include requirements such as maintaining regular employment, not committing another offense, abstaining from drugs and alcohol, not associating with known offenders or other specified persons, regularly reporting to a **parole officer** or other designated person, and/or remaining within a designated geographic area. Violation of the conditions of parole can result in parole revocation by a paroling authority. The length of time of parole is determined by the length of the sentence less the length of time served in a **confinement facility**. **Juveniles** as well as **adults** can be placed on parole, although juvenile parole is often called **aftercare**. *See*: ABSCOND; AFTERCARE; CONDITION; CONDITIONAL RELEASE; COURTESY SUPERVISION; DISCHARGE; ELIGIBLE FOR PAROLE; MANDATORY SUPERVISED RELEASE; MUTUAL AGREEMENT PROGRAM; PAROLE AGENCY; PAROLEE; PAROLE REVOCATION; PAROLE SUPERVISION; PAROLE SUSPENDED;

PAROLE VIOLATION; PAROLING AUTHORITY; PROBATION; RELEASE; RELEASE TO PAROLE; REPAROLE; RESCISSION; REVOCATION HEARING; SENTENCE; STREET TIME; SUPERVISORY CUSTODY; TEMPORARY RELEASE; TIME SERVED; UNCONDITIONAL RELEASE; UNITED STATES PAROLE COMMISSION.

PAROLE AGENCY. A **correctional agency**, which may or may not include a **paroling authority**, and of which the principal functions are prerelease investigations and **parole** plan preparation for prospective **parolees**, and the **supervision** of **adults** or **juveniles** placed on parole. Supervision typically includes making sure the parolee adheres to the conditions of his or her parole, regularly reports to a **parole officer** or other designated person, and engages in behavior appropriate to a parolee. Authority and supervisory responsibility for juvenile parole (**aftercare**) is variously located and organized in different jurisdictions. See PAROLE for a list of related terms.

PAROLE BOARD. *See*: PAROLING AUTHORITY.

PAROLE COMMISSION. *See*: PAROLING AUTHORITY.

PAROLE COMMISSION, UNITED STATES. *See*: UNITED STATES PAROLE COMMISSION.

PAROLEE. A person who has been granted a **conditional release** from prison by a **paroling authority** prior to the expiration of his or her **sentence**, and placed under the **supervision** of a **parole agency**, and who is required to observe **conditions** of **parole**. This definition excludes (1) persons discharged from **prison** without conditions and without **supervision** (usually because of expiration of **sentence** or **clemency**); (2) persons subject to **conditional release** from prison other than parole (e.g., **mandatory supervised release**), although they may be considered part of the **parole supervisory caseload**; and (3) persons paroled from **jails** and other local **confinement facilities** who have not been under the jurisdiction of a state-level **corrections agency**. A parolee differs from a **probationer** in that a parolee has been placed on parole status either by a paroling authority or by **statute**, after confinement, whereas a probationer has been placed on **probation** status by a court. See PAROLE for a list of related terms.

PAROLE ELIGIBILITY. *See*: ELIGIBLE FOR PAROLE.

PAROLE REVOCATION. The administrative act of a **paroling authority** removing a person from **parole** status in response to a violation of lawfully required **conditions** of parole, including the prohibition against commission of a new offense, and usually resulting in a return to **prison**. The parole revocation process occurs in two steps, and each step can end with a decision to take no further action or to continue. The first step is a preliminary hearing (often called a "Morrissey hearing" after *Morrissey v. Brewer*, 408 U.S. 471, 92 S.Ct. 2593, 33 L.Ed.2d 484 [1972]), which centers around the issue of whether there is **probable cause** to believe an alleged violation of conditions of parole did occur. A finding of probable cause may result in a return to prison pending completion of proceedings. The second step, if probable cause is found, is a parole revocation hearing, at which the issues are whether the violation did in fact occur and whether an actual violation necessitates revocation of parole. This is the final administrative hearing on the question of whether or not a person's parole status should be revoked. During each of these processes, the legal rights of the parolee are similar though not identical to the rights of defendants in the initial stages of **prosecution**. Parole status can usually be revoked only by the authority that granted it. Parole revocation may result in a short **confinement** in a local facility or return to a federal or state **confinement facility**. See HEARING and PAROLE for lists of related terms.

PAROLE SUPERVISION. Guidance, treatment, or regulation of the behavior of a convicted **adult** who is obliged to fulfill **conditions** of parole or other **conditional release** from prison, authorized and required by statute, performed by a **parole agency**, and occurring after a period of **prison confinement**. The supervisory responsibilities of parole agencies normally include both persons on parole and persons with other conditional release statuses such as **mandatory supervised release**. See PAROLE for a list of related terms.

PAROLE SUSPENDED. The withdrawal by a **paroling authority** or parole agent of a person's effective **parole** status, usually accompanied by a return to **confinement**, pending a determination of whether parole should be revoked, or pending resolution of some problem that may require a temporary return to confinement. Parole can be effectively suspended while the parolee is awaiting the results of **parole revocation** procedures or when a parolee from one state is **arrested** in another state and held for **prosecution** or other **disposition** of his or her case. See PAROLE for a list of related terms.

PAROLE VIOLATION. An act or a failure to act by a **parolee** that does not conform to the **conditions** of parole. A parole violation will not necessarily result in **parole revocation** and return to **prison**. A parole violation that does not consist of commission of a **crime**, or is not prosecuted or adjudicated as a crime, is usually called a **technical violation** to indicate that it is behavior forbidden by the conditions of parole and not by **statute**, or is treated as if not forbidden by statute. See PAROLE for a list of related terms.

PAROLING AUTHORITY. A board or commission that has the authority to release on **parole adults** committed to **prison**, to revoke parole or other **conditional release**, and to **discharge** from parole or other conditional release status. Parole board authority includes all **grants of parole** and may include granting of other types of conditional release from prison, with the exception of **mandatory supervised release**. Parole boards also perform investigative and advisory functions regarding grants of

clemency—for example, **pardons**, which in most states are granted by the governor. The precise extent of parole board authority varies among the states, depending upon statutory provisions concerning sentencing, eligibility for parole, authority to discharge before end of maximum sentence period, and related matters. Typical names for paroling authorities are board of parole, board of pardons and parole, parole board, parole commission, and, in jurisdictions where probation is administered by the state, board of probation and parole. A paroling authority may or may not be administratively separate from the **parole agency** that supervises **parolees**. See PAROLE for a list of related terms.

PARRICIDE.   Same as PATRICIDE.

PARTIAL.   Biased or prejudiced in favor of one person or side over another.

PARTIAL INSANITY.   1. Same as DIMINISHED RESPONSIBILITY. **2.** The condition of a person who is insane (see **insanity**) as to a particular subject but sane as to all other subjects.

PARTIAL RESPONSIBILITY.   Same as DIMINISHED RESPONSIBILITY.

PARTIAL VERDICT.   A **verdict** of **acquittal** on part of a **charge** and of **conviction** on the rest of it. See VERDICT for a list of related terms.

PARTICEPS CRIMINIS.   *Latin.* "A participant in a crime." An ACCOMPLICE.

PARTICULAR.   1. A separate or distinct part of a whole. **2.** A specific item; a detail. *See*: BILL OF PARTICULARS.

PARTICULARITY.   Attention to detail; special carefulness.

PARTICULARLY.   In detail; with special care. *Example*: An affidavit for a search warrant must particularly describe the place to be searched.

PARTNER.   A member of a PARTNERSHIP.

PARTNERSHIP.   A contract between two or more persons to carry on a business together, in which each person agrees to furnish a part of the capital and labor and to share in some fixed proportion of the profits and losses.

PART-TIME TEMPORARY RELEASE.   *See*: TEMPORARY RELEASE.

PARTY.   1. A person who takes part in a criminal offense, whether before, during, or after the offense. Under the **common law**, parties to crime are classified according to the degree or nature of their participation in the crime. The parties to a **felony** are classified as

(1) **principal** in the first degree;

(2) principal in the second degree;

(3) **accessory** before the fact; and

(4) accessory after the fact.

These common-law classifications apply only to felonies. All parties to a **misdemeanor** are classified as principals, except that conduct which would make a person an accessory after the fact to a felony is not criminal when applied to a misdemeanor. Also, all parties to the crime of **treason** are classified as principals.

The modern approach to the subject of parties to the crime is to do away with common-law terminology and distinctions and to hold a person legally accountable for the conduct of another if he or she is an **accomplice** of the other person in the commission of the crime. An example of this approach is the **Model Penal Code**, which provides that "a person is an accomplice of another person in the commission of an offense if, with the purpose of promoting or facilitating the commission of the offense, he solicits the other person to commit it, or aids or agrees or attempts to aid the other person in planning or committing it, or (having a legal duty to prevent the crime) fails to make proper effort to prevent it." *See*: ABET; ACCESSORY; ACCOMPLICE; AID; ATTEMPT; COMPLICITY; CONFEDERATE; CON-SPIRACY; CRIMINAL FACILITATION; PRINCIPAL; SOLICITATION; THREAT.

2. A person who is directly interested in the subject matter of a case and who may assert a claim, make a **defense**, control proceedings, examine and cross-examine **witnesses**, or **appeal** from the **judgment**.

PARTY IN INTEREST. Same as REAL PARTY IN INTEREST.

PASS. **1.** To utter; to pronounce; to render; to enter. *Example*: The court passed sentence on the defendant. **2.** To sanction; to approve; to adopt; to enact. *Example*: The legislature passed the bill. **3.** To sit for the purpose of investigation or adjudication. *Example*: The jury passed on the issue of the defendant's insanity.

PASSION. *See*: HEAT OF PASSION.

PAST RECOLLECTION RECORDED. An exception to the **hearsay rule** that allows the reading into **evidence** of a record or memorandum about which a **witness** on the stand once had knowledge, but about which the witness now has insufficient recollection to enable him or her to testify fully and accurately. In order to be admissible, the record or memorandum must be shown to have been made when the matter was fresh in the witness's memory and to have been truthfully recorded.

Under this exception the record or memorandum itself is not **admissible** in evidence by its proponent. "Under past recollection recorded the witness is unable to testify from memory even after reviewing writings, diagrams, or any other stimuli which might refresh his memory. . . . Under past recollection recorded, since the witness cannot testify from memory, the facts being elicited must be put into evidence by means of the writing. This can be done by having the witness read the writing to the **jury**." *State v. Corn*, 296 S.E.2d 261, 264 (N.C. 1982). See HEARSAY RULE for a list of other exceptions.

PATENT.   Open to view or knowledge; evident; manifest; plain.

PATERNITY.   Fatherhood.

PATER PATRIAE.   *Latin.* "Father of the country." Same as PARENS PATRIAE.

PATHOLOGICAL INTOXICATION.   Section 2.08 (5) of the **Model Penal Code** defines pathological intoxication as "**intoxication** grossly excessive in degree, given the amount of the intoxicant, to which the actor does not know he is susceptible." See INTOXICATION for a list of related terms.

PATHOLOGY.   The science of the cause, nature, and development of diseases.

PATRICIDE.   **1.** The killing of one's father. **2.** One who kills his or her father.

PATROLMAN.   A **police officer** assigned to patrol a certain district. See LAW ENFORCEMENT OFFICER for a list of related terms.

PATRONIZING PROSTITUTES.   Under Section 251.2 (5) of the **Model Penal Code** a person is guilty of patronizing prostitutes "if he hires a **prostitute** to engage in sexual activity with him, or if he enters or remains in a **house of prostitution** for the purpose of engaging in sexual activity." See SEX OFFENSES for a list of related terms.

PAUPER.   A very poor person who must be supported at public expense. *See*: IN FORMA PAUPERIS.

PEACE.   A state of public security and tranquility characterized by conformity to law and order and an absence of disturbance or violence. *Also called*: **public peace**.

PEACEABLE.   Without force, violence, or other disturbance.

PEACE BOND.   The deposit of money in **court**, as ordered by a **judge** or **magistrate**, the return of which is conditioned on a person's not committing a **breach of the peace** for a specific period of time. A peace bond may be required of a person if there are reasonable grounds to believe that the **release** of the person would endanger other persons or property.

PEACE OFFICER.   Same as LAW ENFORCEMENT OFFICER. The term peace officer is often used in a broader sense than law enforcement officer to include prison guards, probation officers, court personnel, forest rangers, and game wardens in addition to **law enforcement agency** personnel. See LAW ENFORCEMENT OFFICER for a list of related terms.

Pp

PECULATION.   Same as EMBEZZLEMENT.

PECULIAR.   **1.** Unusual; strange; odd. **2.** Special; particular.

PECUNIARY.   Relating to or consisting of money; financial.

PECUNIARY BENEFIT.   Section 240.0 (6) of the **Model Penal Code** defines pecuniary benefit as "benefit in the form of money, property, commercial interests or anything else the primary significance of which is economic gain."

PEDDLER.   A person who sells small goods which he or she carries from place to place.

PEDERASTY.   Anal intercourse between a man and a young boy. See SEX OFFENSES for a list of related terms.

PEDESTRIAN.   One who travels on foot.

PEEPING TOM.   A person who trespasses for the purpose of observing persons inside a dwelling or other inhabited building without visible or lawful business with the owner or occupant of the building.

PEER.   A person of equal standing before the law; a fellow citizen. *Example*: He is entitled to a trial by a jury of his peers.

PENAL.   Relating to or denoting **penalty** or **punishment**. *Example*: The state enacted a new penal code.

PENAL ACTION.   An **action** to enforce or recover a penalty for an offense set by statute.

PENAL INSTITUTION.   Any place of **confinement** for convicted criminals.

PENAL LAW.   A law that creates an **offense** and establishes a **penalty** for its violation. *Also called*: **penal statute**. See CRIME and STATUTE for a list of related terms.

PENAL STATUTE. Same as PENAL LAW.

PENALTY. The sanction, loss, or deprivation of right or property imposed or determined by **law** or **court decision** for the commission of a particular **offense**. Examples of penalties are **death, incarceration, fine, forfeiture**, and loss of civil privileges. The penalty imposed by the court upon a person convicted of a crime is called a **sentence**. See SENTENCE for a list of related terms.

PENDENCY. The state of an **action** after it has begun and before it has been finally disposed of.

PENDENS. *Latin.* "Pending."

PENDENTE LITE. *Latin.* "Pending the litigation." During the progress of an **action**; during litigation. *See*: LIS PENDENS.

PENDENT JURISDICTION. JURISDICTION that a federal **court** may, in its **discretion**, take over nonfederal matters if they arise from the same common nucleus of operative facts as a federal **case** before the court. See JURISDICTION for a list of related terms.

PENDING. **adj.** Awaiting decision; begun but not yet concluded or disposed of. *Example*: He has several cases pending against him. **prep.** Until; while awaiting. *Example*: She was admitted to bail pending trial.

PENDING CASELOAD. The number of **cases** at any given point in time that are before a given **court** or **judicial officer**, but have not reached **disposition**. *See*: BACKLOG; CASELOAD.

PENETRATION. In prosecutions for **rape, sodomy**, and the like, penetration means any entry, however slight, of the **penis** into the **vagina, anus,** or mouth of another person. Mere touching without entry is not sufficient to constitute penetration, but emission is not required. See SEX OFFENSES for a list of related terms.

PENIS. The male sex organ.

PENITENTIARY. *See*: PRISON.

PENITENTIARY MISDEMEANOR. *See*: SERIOUS MISDEMEANOR.

PENOLOGY. The study of **criminal** punishment and rehabilitation, deterrence of crime, and **prison** management. See CRIME for a list of related terms.

PEN REGISTER. "A pen register is a mechanical device that records the numbers dialed on a telephone by monitoring the electrical impulses caused when the dial on the telephone is released. It does not overhear oral communications and does not indicate whether calls are actually completed." *United States v. New York Tel. Co.*, 434 U.S. 159, 161 n.1., 98 S.Ct. 364, 366 n.1., 54 L.Ed.2d 376, 382 n. 1. (1977). A pen register is usually installed at a central telephone facility and records on a paper tape all numbers dialed from the line to which it is attached. In *Smith v. Maryland*, 442 U.S. 735, 99 S.Ct. 2577, 61 L.Ed.2d 220 (1979), the U.S. Supreme Court held that the installation and use of a pen register is not a **search** and is therefore not subject to the Fourth Amendment.

Pp

PEOPLE. **1.** All persons in a nation or state considered as a whole; the public. *Example*: The Fourth Amendment protects the right of the people to be free from unreasonable searches and seizures. **2.** The state as a governmental or political entity. People is used in some states to indicate the government or prosecution in a criminal case, e.g., People v. Peedum.

PER. **1.** By; by means of; through. *Example*: A crime against nature per os means the crime committed by means of the mouth. **2.** By each; for each. *Example*: She was traveling 80 miles per hour.

PER ANNUM. *Latin.* By the year; through the year; in any one year; annually.

PER CAPITA. By individuals; for each individual. A division per capita means a division by which each individual gets an equal share of the whole.

PERCEIVE. To obtain knowledge or discover through any of the senses. *Example:* The officer perceived several indications of criminal activity.

PER CENT. For, in, or out of every hundred; by the hundred.

PER CURIAM. *Latin.* "By the court." Per curiam is a term used to describe a **court decision** or **opinion** upon which all **judges** of the court agree and whose author is unidentified. See JUDGMENT and OPINION for lists of related terms.

PER DIEM. *Latin.* By the day; in any one day; daily.

PEREMPTORY. Decisive; final; absolute; unconditional; not subject to debate or question; not requiring explanation or justification.

PEREMPTORY CHALLENGE. A formal **objection** to a prospective **juror** for which no reason need be given. The **judge** will automatically dismiss a juror to whom a peremptory challenge is made. The number of peremptory challenges available to each party is limited by statute or court rule. See CHALLENGE for a list of related terms.

PER EUNDEM. *Latin.* "By the same."

PERFECT. **v.** To finish; to complete; to accomplish; to satisfy all legal requirements of. *Example*: He was released after perfecting bail.

PERFECT. **adj.** Complete; finished.

PERFIDY. A deliberate violation of a promise or trust; treachery.

PERFORM. To carry out; to fulfill; to execute; to do; to accomplish.

PERIOD. An interval or portion of time.

PERJURY. Generally, all false statements, oral and written, knowingly made under **oath** or made in any of various contexts where a **penalty** for false statement is provided by **law**. The more restricted meaning of perjury is the intentional making of a false statement as part of **testimony** by a **sworn witness** in a judicial proceeding on a matter **material** to the inquiry. Some jurisdictions define two or more **degrees** of perjury; others define a series of separately labeled offenses, for example, perjury, **false swearing**, and **unsworn falsification**. Distinctions may be drawn on the basis of whether or not the statement is made under oath, whether or not the information contained is material, and whether the proceeding is judicial, administrative, or legislative. See AFFIRMATION and WITNESS for lists of related terms.

PERMANENT. Lasting or intended to last indefinitely; enduring.

PERMISSION. Consent, authorization, or leave to do something.

PERMIT. **n.** An official written **certificate** of permission, similar to a **license**, allowing someone to do a lawful act that would not be allowed without the certificate.

PERMIT. **v.** To allow; to grant permission or **license**; to authorize.

PERPETRATE. To commit, perform, or carry out a **crime** or evil act.

PERPETRATOR. The chief actor in the commission of a **crime**; the person who directly commits the criminal act. See ACCUSED for a list of related terms.

PERPETUATION OF EVIDENCE. A procedure to ensure that **evidence** is available for possible use at a later **trial**. See EVIDENCE and TRIAL for lists of related terms.

PER SE. *Latin.* "By, of, or in itself." Inherently; intrinsically; without connection or reference to anything else.

PERSON. In legal usage, a human being, or a group of human beings considered a legal unit, having the lawful **capacity** to defend rights, incur obligations, prosecute claims, or be prosecuted or adjudicated. Examples of a legal unit constituting a legal person are a state, a territory, a government, a country, a partnership, a public or private corporation, or an unincorporated association. *See*: ARTIFICIAL PERSON; NATURAL PERSON.

Pp

PERSONAL. Closely or intimately related to a human being.

PERSONAL EFFECTS. Movable articles having a more or less intimate relation to a person, such as clothing, jewelry, handbags, wallets, and luggage.

PERSONAL KNOWLEDGE. KNOWLEDGE obtained by a person firsthand through perception or experience. Personal knowledge is to be distinguished from **hearsay** (see **hearsay evidence**) or secondhand knowledge, i.e., knowledge that is obtained from other sources. See HEARSAY RULE for a list of related terms.

PERSONAL NOTICE. Same as EXPRESS NOTICE.

PERSONAL PROPERTY. All property that is not REAL PROPERTY. Personal property can be divided into two major categories: (1) **corporeal** personal property including money, goods, vehicles, books, papers, animals, and other movable things; and (2) **incorporeal** personal property, including rights such as stocks, bonds, patents, and copyrights.

PERSONAL RECOGNIZANCE. Same as RECOGNIZANCE.

PERSONAL RIGHTS. Rights that appertain to the person, such as the rights of personal security, personal liberty, and private property. *Also called*: **private rights**.

PERSONAL SERVICE. SERVICE accomplished by actually delivering a legal **writ** or **notice** to someone in person or leaving a copy at the person's home or usual place of residence with a responsible person. *See*: CONSTRUCTIVE SERVICE.

PERSONATION. *See*: FALSE IMPERSONATION.

PERSON IN NEED OF SUPERVISION. Same as CHILD IN NEED OF SUPERVISION. *Abbreviation*: **P.I.N.S.**

PERSUADE. To win over or induce another, by argument, reasoning, or urging, to do something or to follow a recommended course.

PERSUASION BURDEN. Same as BURDEN OF PERSUASION.

PERSUASIVE AUTHORITY. Any source of law, such as related cases and legal encyclopedias, that a **court** may, but is not required to, use in deciding a **case**. *See*: BINDING AUTHORITY.

PERTAIN. **v.** To have reference to; to relate to; to have a connection to; to belong to. *Example*: The district attorney was required to turn over certain evidence pertaining to the case. **adj.** PERTINENT.

PERTINENT. **adj.** Relating to a specific matter; relevant; applicable. **n.** PERTAIN.

PERVERSION. A sexual act or practice considered abnormal or deviant. See SEX OFFENSES for a list of related terms.

PETIT. Of lesser importance; minor; small. *Also spelled*: PETTY. *See*: PETIT JURY; PETIT LARCENY.

PETITION. A written request made to a **court** asking for the exercise of its judicial powers, or asking for permission to perform some act where the authorization of a court is required. A petition is a formal **document** filed in court that initiates a **case**, in contrast to a **motion**, which is a request made in the course of proceedings and which is often oral. **Charging documents (complaints, informations, indictments)** are technically petitions, but they are not so called in common usage. In criminal cases the filing of a document called a petition is the usual method of requesting leave to make an **appeal** or of requesting a **postconviction remedy** or **sentence review.** Juvenile court cases are initiated by petitions (see **juvenile petition**) requesting the court to make a determination as to the juvenile's status. The person who files a petition in court is called a **petitioner**, and the person who answers a petition is generally called a **respondent**. Some petitions, such as a petition for a **writ**, do not require a respondent. *See*: ASSEMBLY AND PETITION.

PETITIONER. The person who files a PETITION in court. See ACCUSED for a list of related terms.

PETITION NOT SUSTAINED. The finding by a **juvenile court** in an **adjudicatory hearing** that there is not sufficient evidence to sustain an allegation that a **juvenile** is a **delinquent, status offender,** or **dependent.** This type of **juvenile court judgment** corresponds to an **acquittal** or **dismissal** in a criminal proceeding. In delinquency cases, the allegation is that the juvenile has committed a **delinquent act** or a **status offense**. In dependency cases, the allegation is about the behavior of the parent or guardian, not the behavior of the juvenile. See DISMISSAL and JUVENILE for lists of related terms.

PETIT JURY. Same as TRIAL JURY.

PETIT LARCENY. LARCENY in which the value of the property stolen falls below a set statutory limit. See ABSTRACTION for a list of related terms.

PETTY. Same as PETIT.

PHOTOGRAPHIC IDENTIFICATION. The pretrial showing of a photograph or photographs to a **witness** for the purpose of allowing the witness to attempt to **identify** the **perpetrator** of a **crime**. With respect to photographic identifications, the U.S. Supreme Court held that "each case must be considered on its own facts, and that convictions based on eyewitness identification at trial following a pretrial identification by photograph will be set aside on that ground only if the photographic identification procedure was so impermissibly suggestive as to give rise to a very substantial likelihood of irreparable misidentification." *Simmons v. U.S.*, 390 U.S. 377, 384, 88 S.Ct. 967, 984, 19 L.Ed.2d 1247, 1253 (1968). In a later case, the U.S. Supreme Court held that "the Sixth Amendment does not grant the right to **counsel** at photographic displays conducted by the Government for the purpose of allowing a witness to attempt an identification of the offender." *U.S. v. Ash*, 413 U.S. 300, 321, 93 S.Ct. 2568, 2579, 37 L.Ed.2d 619, 633 (1973). *See*: LINEUP.

PHYSICAL CUSTODY. **1.** *See*: CUSTODY. **2.** In the **corrections** context, direct control of and responsibility for the body of a confined person. A correctional agency may have physical custody over a person, but may or may not have **jurisdictional control**. *See*: SUPERVISORY CUSTODY.

PHYSICAL EVIDENCE. Same as REAL EVIDENCE.

PHYSICAL FACT. A **fact** that can be seen heard, smelled, tasted, or touched, as distinguished from a conception of the mind. See FACT for a list of related terms.

PHYSICAL FORCE. FORCE or violence applied to the body or to material things as distinguished from moral force, persuasive force, or the like.

PHYSICAL INJURY. An injury to the **body**, as distinguished from a mental or emotional injury.

PICKLOCK. **1.** An instrument or device for opening locks without a key. **2.** A person who opens locks without a key, especially a **thief**.

PICKPOCKET. One who steals from the pockets of others.

PICKUP ORDER. *See*: WANTED PERSON.

PILFER. To **steal** (especially small amounts).

PILLAGE. To take another's goods by ruthless force.

PILLORY. A wooden framework on a post with holes for the head and hands in which criminals were formerly locked to expose them to public ridicule.

PIMP. Same as PANDER.

P.I.N.S. Abbreviation for PERSON IN NEED OF SUPERVISION.

PIRACY. The attacking of a ship, accompanied by acts of violence or plunder, by persons aboard another ship on the high seas without authority from any sovereign nation. Under international law, those committing piracy may be apprehended on the high seas by the authorities of any nation and punished as provided by that nation's law. *See*: AIRCRAFT PIRACY.

PIRATE. One who practices or is guilty of PIRACY.

PISTOL. A short firearm designed to be aimed and fired with one hand.

P.J. Abbreviation for PRESIDING JUDGE or PRESIDING JUSTICE.

PLACE. Any region, locality, or site, regardless of how large or small.

PLACEMENT. The **commitment** or assignment of a person to a facility, or to any supervisory or treatment program, as the result of official or unofficial actions. This term has acquired a broad meaning in current usage, ranging from the judicial action of commitment to a **confinement facility**, to such unofficial actions as the assignment of a **runaway** to a private facility or temporary foster home by a private community service agency. Because of this broad range of meaning, use of the term placement should indicate the kind of person or agency making the placement, the legal authority under which it is done, and the judicial status of the subject. See COMMITMENT for a list of related terms.

PLAIN ERROR RULE. The rule that an **appellate court** may, on its own **motion**, take notice of **error** in the proceedings even if the error was not objected to at the time it was made. The rule applies to errors that are obvious, that affect substantial rights of the accused, and that, if uncorrected, will seriously affect the fairness, integrity, or public reputation of judicial proceedings. The plain error rule may also apply to a **trial court** passing on motions made after trial. See ERROR for a list of related terms.

PLAIN LARCENY. Same as SIMPLE LARCENY.

PLAINTIFF. A person who initiates a court action. Plaintiff is the customary name for the person who initiates a **civil action**. In some states the **prosecution** in a **criminal**

action (i.e., the people, as represented by the government) is called the plaintiff. See ACCUSED for a list of related terms.

PLAINTIFF IN ERROR.   The party who **appeals** by means of a **writ of error** from an adverse judgment in a lower court. The plaintiff in error could have been either the plaintiff or the defendant in the lower court. The plaintiff in error corresponds to the **appellant** in modern practice. See ACCUSED for a list of related terms.

Pp

PLAIN VIEW DOCTRINE.   The rule stating that the observation of items lying open to view by a **law enforcement officer** who has a right to be in a position to have that view is not a **search**, and that the officer may **seize** the **evidence** without a **search warrant**. The plain view doctrine has five requirements, all of which must be satisfied before seizure of an item of evidence can be legally justified.

1. The officer, as a result of a prior valid intrusion into a **constitutionally protected area**, must be in a position in which he or she has a legal right to be, such as effecting an **arrest**, executing a search warrant, or responding to an **emergency**.
2. The officer must not unreasonably intrude on any person's reasonable expectation of privacy. *See*: RIGHT OF PRIVACY.
3. The officer must actually observe the item of evidence. Mere **probable cause** to believe an item is in a particular place is insufficient.
4. The item of evidence must be lying in the open. The officer may use mechanical or electrical aids, such as a flashlight or binoculars, to assist in observing the item, so long as this does not unreasonably intrude on someone's reasonable expectation of privacy.
5. The officer must have probable cause to believe that the item observed is subject to seizure, i.e., legally allowed to be seized under the law of the officer's jurisdiction. *See*: ITEMS SUBJECT TO SEIZURE.

PLEA.   A defendant's formal answer in court to the **charge** contained in a **complaint**, **information**, or **indictment**, that he or she is guilty or not guilty of the offense charged, or does not contest the charge. The pleas in a criminal case are **guilty, nolo contendere, not guilty**, and **not guilty by reason of insanity**. *See*: FINAL PLEA; INITIAL PLEA.

PLEA BARGAINING.   The exchange of prosecutorial or judicial concessions, or both, in return for a **guilty plea**. Common concessions include a lesser **charge**, the **dismissal** of other pending charges, a recommendation by the prosecutor for a **reduced sentence**, or a combination of these. The guilty plea arrived at through the process of plea bargaining is sometimes called a **negotiated plea**.

Plea bargaining has been approved by the U.S. Supreme Court and is governed by **rules of court** in federal and in many state courts. The U.S. Supreme Court stated:

"The disposition of criminal charges by agreement between the **prosecutor** and the **accused**, sometimes loosely called 'plea bargaining,' is an essential component of the administration of justice. Properly administered, it is to be encouraged. If the criminal **charge** were subjected to a full-scale **trial**, the States and the Federal Government would need to multiply by many times the number of **judges** and **court** facilities.

"Disposition of charges after plea discussions is not only an essential part of the process but a highly desirable part for many reasons. It leads to prompt and largely final disposition of most criminal cases; it avoids much of the corrosive impact of enforced idleness during pretrial confinement for those who are denied release pending trial; it protects the public from those accused persons who are prone to continue criminal conduct even while on pretrial release; and, by shortening the time between charge and disposition, it enhances whatever may be the rehabilitative prospects of the guilty when they are ultimately imprisoned." *Santobello v. N.Y.*, 404 U.S. 257, 260-61, 92 S.Ct. 495, 498, 30 L.Ed.2d 427, 432 (1971).

PLEAD.   **1.** To enter a PLEA or an allegation. **2.** To assert or urge as a **defense**, **justification**, or **excuse**. *Example*: He will plead the Fifth Amendment. **3.** To address a court as an advocate.

PLEADING.   **1.** A formal written statement by which a party sets forth the **cause of action** or **defense** in a legal **action**. The purposes of the pleadings are (1) to give notice of the claim or defense; (2) to set out the facts of the case; (3) to formulate the issues to be resolved; and (4) to direct the flow of cases to the proper court. *See*: AIDER BY VERDICT; ALLEGATION; ALTERNATIVE PLEADING; ARGUMENTATIVE PLEADING; ARTICULATED PLEADING; ASSIGNMENT OF ERRORS; AVERMENT; CAPTION; CONFESSION AND AVOIDANCE; DEFAULT; DEMURRER; DUPLICITY; MISPLEADING; MOTION TO DISMISS; MULTIPLICITY; NOMINAL PARTY; PRAYER; RECITAL; SCANDAL; SCILICET; SEVERANCE; TRANSCRIPT; TRIAL. **2.** The act of one who **pleads**.

PLENARY.   Full; complete, entire.

PLUNDER.   To take another's goods by force or as an enemy. Plunder often suggests robbing or looting on an extensive scale.

PLURALITY OPINION.   A court **opinion** to which a majority agree as to result, but to which less than a majority agree as to reasoning. A plurality opinion carries less weight as a **precedent** than a **majority opinion** under the rule of **stare decisis**. See OPINION for a list of related terms.

PLURALITY REQUIREMENT.   The requirement, to constitute the crime of CONSPIRACY, that there must be a combination of two or more persons.

P.M.   **1.** Abbreviation for POST MERIDIEM. **2.** Abbreviation for POST MORTEM.

POACH. To unlawfully enter upon another's land to take or destroy fish or game.

POENA. *Latin.* "Punishment; penalty."

POINT. **n.** A particular proposition, argument, or question of law arising in a case. *Example*: The defense attorney raised the point of the legality of the police entry onto the premises. **v.** To turn or direct at or toward a person or object. *Example*: It is illegal to point a gun at a person. *See*: AIM.

Pp

POLICE. *See*: LAW ENFORCEMENT.

POLICE COURT. An inferior **court** with power to try minor criminal offenses and to examine persons charged with more serious offenses and hold them over for **trial** in a superior court. *See*: COURT OF LIMITED JURISDICTION.

POLICE DEPARTMENT. Generally, a municipal (city, town, village) **law enforcement agency** directed by a chief of police or commissioner. *Also called*: **police force**. *See*: LOCAL LAW ENFORCEMENT AGENCY.

POLICE FORCE. Same as POLICE DEPARTMENT.

POLICE MAGISTRATE. An inferior JUDICIAL OFFICER whose jurisdiction is confined to minor criminal matters.

POLICE OFFICER. A local LAW ENFORCEMENT OFFICER employed by a **police department**.

POLICE POWER. The power inherent in a government to enact laws, within constitutional limits, to promote the order, safety, health, morals, and general welfare of society. A state, in exercise of its police power, may create **law enforcement agencies** to protect its citizens against crime and other threats to the public welfare. "The term 'police power', as understood in American constitutional law means simply the power to impose such restrictions upon private rights as are practically necessary for the general welfare of all. . . . And it must be confined to such restrictions and burdens as are thus necessary to promote the public welfare, or, in other words, to prevent the infliction of public injury. . . . And in the exercise of its police powers a state is not confined to matters relating strictly to the public health, morals, and peace, but . . . there may be interference whenever the public interest demands it; and in this particular, a large discretion is necessarily vested in the legislature, to determine not only what the interests of the public require, but what measures are necessary for the protection of such interests. . . . It is not limited to regulations necessary for the preservation of good order or the public health and safety but the prevention of fraud and deceit, cheating, unfair competition, and imposition are equally within the power." *State v. Cromwell*, 9 N.W.2d 914, 919-20 (N.D. 1943). *See*: LAW ENFORCEMENT.

POLICE WITNESS. A **police officer** who is a WITNESS. He or she may be the arresting officer, an officer who assisted in the arrest, or an investigating officer. See LAW ENFORCEMENT OFFICER and WITNESS for lists of related terms.

POLICY. **1.** The general principles adopted by a government or governmental body in managing its public affairs. *Example*: The governor established a strict law-and-order policy. **2.** Same as NUMBERS GAME.

POLICY OF THE LAW. The principle of **law** which holds that acts contrary to the public welfare, morals, or order are invalid. *Also called*: **public policy**.

POLITICAL. Pertaining or relating to the management of governmental affairs.

POLITICAL LIBERTY. Same as POLITICAL RIGHTS.

POLITICAL QUESTIONS. Questions that **judicial courts** will refuse to decide because they are within the **jurisdiction** of the **executive** or **legislative** branches of government.

POLITICAL RIGHTS. Rights of a **citizen** to participate in the formation and administration of government, including the right to vote. *Also called*: **political liberty**. *See*: CIVIL RIGHTS.

POLL THE JURY. *See*: JURY POLL.

POLLUTE. To make dirty or unclean; to contaminate.

POLYGAMY. The offense of having more than one spouse at the same time.

POLYGRAPH. "[A]n electromechanical instrument which simultaneously measures and records certain physiological changes in the human body, which it is believed are involuntarily caused by an examinee's conscious attempts to deceive an interrogator while responding to a carefully prepared set of questions. Commonly, the machine records three items of information : (1) rate and depth of respiration, (2) blood pressure and pulse rate, and (3) galvanic skin response (G.S.R.). The latter is a measurement of increased sweating of the palmar surfaces of the hand." *United States v. De Betham*, 348 F.Supp. 1377, 1380-81 (1972). Results of polygraph tests are generally held **inadmissible** as **evidence**, although some courts have held them admissible on the stipulation of the parties. *Also called*: **lie detector**.

POOL. In certain **gambling** games, a common fund consisting of the bets of all players, the fund to be taken or shared by the winner or winners. See GAMBLING for a list of related terms.

POOR. So destitute of property or means of **support** as to require public assistance.

P p

POPULATION MOVEMENT. Entries and exits of **adjudicated** persons, or persons subject to judicial proceedings, into or from **correctional facilities** or programs.

PORNOGRAPHY. Written, graphic, or other forms of communication that are obscene. *See*: OBSCENE MATERIAL.

PORTION. To give out in more or less equal shares to members of a group. See ALLOCATE for a list of related terms.

POSE. To put forth a question or proposition for discussion with the implication that no immediate answer is available. See ADDRESS for a list of related terms.

POSITIVE. **1.** Certain; undisputed; admitting of no doubt. *Example*: I am positive the liquor is on the premises. **2.** Explicitly stated, expressed, or formally laid down as distinguished from **constructive** or **implied**. **3.** Direct; absolute.

POSITIVE EVIDENCE. Same as DIRECT EVIDENCE.

POSITIVE FRAUD. Same as ACTUAL FRAUD.

POSITIVE LAW. **Law** enacted by a **legislative** body.

POSITIVE PROOF. Proof that establishes a fact or matter in question by **direct evidence**. See FACT for a list of related terms. *See also*: NEGATIVE PROOF.

POSSE. **1.** Possible; potential. **2.** Shortened form of POSSE COMITATUS.

POSSE COMITATUS. *Latin.* "Force of the country." The body of persons called, or available to be called, by a **sheriff** or other **peace officer** to assist in making **arrests** and preserving the peace, usually in **emergencies**.

POSSESS. *See*: POSSESSION.

POSSESSION. "The word 'possession' is often ambiguous in its meaning. It is used to describe actual possession and also to describe constructive possession. Actual and constructive possession are often so blended that it is difficult to see where one ends and the other begins. . . . Actual possession exists where the thing is in the physical control, or immediate occupancy of the party. Constructive possession is that which exists in contemplation of law without actual personal occupation.

Constructive possession often refers to the person lawfully entitled to immediate physical possession and control. In criminal law possession usually means care, management, physical control, or the secret hiding or protection of something forbidden or stolen. . . .

"Possession is synonymous with occupied, held, or controlled; possession is the fact or condition of having such control of property that a person may enjoy it to the exclusion of all others who have no better right to it than himself; physical control of a thing is possession of it." *State v. Gellers,* 282 A.2d 173, 178 (Me. 1971).

POSSIBILITY.   Something POSSIBLE.

POSSIBLE.   Capable of existing, happening, or being done.

POST.   *Latin.* "After."

POSTCONVICTION REMEDY.   The procedure or set of procedures by which a person who has been **convicted** of a **crime** can challenge in **court** the validity or legality of a judgment of **conviction** or **penalty** or of a **correctional agency** action, and thus obtain relief in situations where this cannot be done by a direct **appeal**. Although postconviction remedy most properly refers only to relief actually granted by the court, the term is often used as above, to refer to the entire process by which such relief can be sought. Depending on the jurisdiction, application for postconviction remedy can be made either to the same court in which the original proceedings were conducted, or to a higher court. Reasons why the appeal process may be unavailable in a given case include: the time limits within which an appeal must be made have been exceeded; the appeal process has been exhausted; or the decision or action being challenged was by an administrative agency rather than a court, and cannot be challenged by appeal. In situations where the law in a given jurisdiction would allow a challenge to be made either through appeal or through application for postconviction remedy, there is usually a procedural requirement that the appeal process be used.

The federal postconviction review statute is 28 U.S.C. §2255. Many states have adopted similar statutes or rules of court dealing with constitutional challenges to judgments of conviction. The rules governing statutory postconviction remedies are similar to **habeas corpus** and the availability of statutory relief generally precludes federal or state habeas corpus relief. Among the most common nonstatutory forms of postconviction remedies are the writ of habeas corpus and the writ of **coram nobis**.

POST FACTO.   *See:* EX POST FACTO.

POST MERIDIEM.   *Latin.* "After noon." Post meridiem is usually abbreviated P.M. or p.m. *Example*: The murder occurred at approximately 3 p.m.

POST MORTEM. **adj.** *Latin.* "After death." *Abbreviation*: **P.M. n.** A POST MORTEM EXAMINATION.

POST MORTEM EXAMINATION. Same as AUTOPSY.

POSTPONE. To put off to a future time; to defer.

POTENTIAL. Possible but not yet realized or actually existing.

POWER. The right or ability to do something.

POWER OF ATTORNEY. A written instrument authorizing another person to act as one's **agent** or **attorney**.

PRACTICABLE. Capable of being done or used; feasible.

PRACTICAL. **1.** Actually useful or serviceable; available or valuable in practice or action. *Example*: Come up with a practical solution. **2.** Of or relating to practice or action, as distinguished from theoretical, speculative, or ideal. *Example:* Law enforcement officers think in practical terms.

PRACTICE. **1.** The act or process of doing something; performance; action. *Example*: His shady practices were being investigated. **2.** Habitual or customary performance or action. *Example*: She made a practice of driving after drinking. **3.** The exercise of an occupation or profession. *Example*: A disbarred lawyer may not engage in the practice of law. **4.** The form, manner, and order of initiating and conducting **lawsuits** or **prosecutions** in the **courts**, through successive stages to a final determination or settlement. *Example*: The Supreme Court establishes rules of practice in the lower courts.

PRAECIPE. A written **order** commanding a **clerk of court** to take some action. See JUDGMENT for a list of related terms.

PRAYER. The request, in a **petition** or **pleading**, for the aid or relief desired from the **court**.

PREADJUDICATED. The status of an **adult defendant** or a **juvenile** who is subject to court proceedings that have not reached **judgment** or **dismissal**.

PREAMBLE. A statement at the beginning of a **constitution**, **statute**, or other formal **document** explaining the reasons for and purposes of what follows.

PREARRAIGNMENT LOCKUP. A **confinement facility** for **arrested adults** awaiting **arraignment**, consideration for **pretrial release**, return to another jurisdiction, or other immediate disposition. The duration of stay in a pre-arraignment lockup is usually limited by statute to 48 hours, or until the next **session** of the appropriate **court**. The prearraignment detention function is also performed by **jails**, which hold persons detained for trial and also committed persons. *See*: CORRECTIONAL FACILITY; DETENTION.

PRECEDE. To come before in time, place, order, or importance.

PRECEDENCE. The act, state, or right of preceding (see **precede**); priority.

PRECEDENT. A previous judicial decision or method of proceeding that is recognized as an authority or rule for disposition of future similar or analogous cases. *See*: STARE DECISIS.

PRECEDING. Existing or coming before; previous.

PRECEPT. A written order; a writ; a warrant. See ARREST WARRANT for a list of related terms.

PRECINCT. A small geographic subdivision of a city government patrolled by a unit of the police force.

PRECISE. Clearly expressed; exact; strictly defined.

PRECLUDE. To make impossible; to prevent; to bar.

PREDICATE. To base or establish. *Example*: She predicates her argument on the following facts.

PREDISPOSITION INVESTIGATION. An investigation by a **probation agency** or other designated authority, at the request of a **juvenile court**, into the past behavior, family background, and personality of a **juvenile** who has been adjudicated a **delinquent**, **status offender**, or **dependent**, to help the court determine the most appropriate **juvenile disposition**. The predisposition investigation and resulting **predisposition report** is usually made by a **probation agency** or special **intake unit** or intake officer attached to a juvenile court. The investigations often form a substantial part of a probation agency's or intake unit's workload. A predisposition investigation generally corresponds to an adult **presentence investigation**. See JUVENILE for a list of related terms.

PREDISPOSITION REPORT. A document submitted to a **juvenile court** consisting of the results of a PREDISPOSITION INVESTIGATION. The investigation and report is usually made by a **probation agency** or special **intake unit** attached to a juvenile court. A predisposition report corresponds to an adult **presentence report**. See JUVENILE for a list of related terms.

PREEMPTION. A judicially created doctrine, based on the **supremacy clause** of the U.S. Constitution, providing that certain matters are of such a national, as opposed to local, character that federal laws relating to these matters take precedence over state laws. "Preemption is . . . a doctrine which ousts a state or other government from the exercise of its **police power** in an area in which the power of the federal government is, by law or by implication, preeminent." *Owen v. City of Atlanta*, 277 S.E.2d 338, 340 (Ga.App. 1981).

Pp

PREFER. To formally bring before or present to a **judicial officer** for consideration, approval, or sanction. *Example*: She preferred charges against him for robbery.

PREJUDICE. A preconceived judgment or opinion formed without knowledge or examination of facts. *See*: BIAS.

PREJUDICIAL ERROR. Same as REVERSIBLE ERROR.

PREJUDICIAL PRETRIAL PUBLICITY. "Prejudicial pretrial publicity is that which contains inflammatory material which would not be admissible at the **defendant's trial** or contains misstatements or distortions of the **evidence** given at trial." *Burdine v. State*, 515 N.E.2d 1085, 1092 (Ind. 1987).

PRELIMINARY. Preceding the main matter or business; introductory; preparatory.

PRELIMINARY EXAMINATION. Same as PRELIMINARY HEARING.

PRELIMINARY HEARING. The proceeding before a **judicial officer** in which three matters must be decided: whether a **crime** was committed; whether the crime occurred within the **territorial jurisdiction** of the **court**; and whether there is **probable cause** to believe that the **defendant** committed the crime.

A chief purpose of the preliminary hearing is to protect the accused from an inadequately based **prosecution** in **felony** cases by making a judicial test of the existence of probable cause early in the proceedings. In felony cases in states where a felony trial can be initiated by the filing of an **information** by the **prosecutor**, the preliminary hearing (usually in a lower court) is a key step at which it is determined whether proceedings will continue. If the court does find probable cause, **bail** may be set or reset, and the defendant will be **bound over** or held to answer the **charge** in the **trial court**.

In felony cases in states where the **grand jury indictment** is used to initiate proceedings in the trial court, defendants often **waive** the preliminary hearing, because the grand jury will make the probable cause determination. But some defendants request a preliminary hearing because it affords opportunity to acquire information about the basis of the prosecution's case or to **move** for **dismissal** of the case.

Whether the defendant has the right to a preliminary hearing in a **misdemeanor** case depends upon the jurisdiction. *Also called*: **examining trial**; **felony preliminary**; **preliminary examination**; **probable cause hearing**. See EXAMINATION and HEARING for lists of related terms.

PRELIMINARY SCREENING.   Same as INTAKE.

PREMEDITATED.   Thought of or reflected upon beforehand for at least a short period of time. Under some state statutes, premeditation is one of the elements of first-degree **murder**.

PREMISES.   Land and the buildings and structures on it. Premises is a vague term with different meanings in different contexts.

PREPARATION.   Planning or arranging the means or measures necessary for the commission of an **offense** without going far enough toward its accomplishment to constitute an **attempt**.

PREPONDERANCE OF THE EVIDENCE.   **Evidence** that outweighs evidence offered to oppose it; the more convincing evidence; the greater **weight of the evidence**. Preponderance of the evidence is the standard of proof in **civil actions**. It simply means that the **plaintiff** must convince the **trier of fact** that the evidence in support of his or her case outweighs the evidence offered by the defendant to oppose it. It is a less strict standard than proof **beyond a reasonable doubt**. See EVIDENCE for a list of related terms.

PREROGATIVE.   An exclusive right or privilege of a person, group, or class.

PREROGATIVE WRIT.   A **writ** issued only at the discretion of the issuing authority for good cause shown. *Example*: A writ of certiorari is a prerogative writ granting the petitioner an opportunity to appeal the decision of a lower court where the petitioner has no absolute right to appeal. See ARREST WARRANT for a list of related terms.

PRESCRIBE.   To lay down or establish a rule, guide, or direction; to ordain. *Example*: The judge prescribed rules for the conduct of the hearing.

PRESENCE.   The state or fact of being PRESENT (adj.).

PRESENCE OF AN OFFICER.   An offense is committed in the presence of a **law enforcement officer** if the officer is able to perceive the offense through any of his or her five senses: sight, hearing, smell, touch, and taste. In most states, unless otherwise provided by statute, a law enforcement officer may **arrest** without a **warrant** for a **misdemeanor** only if the misdemeanor is committed in the arresting officer's presence. An officer may not arrest without a warrant if he or she comes upon the scene of a misdemeanor after the offense has been completed, even if the alleged offender is still at the scene. An officer may arrest for a **felony** without a warrant, however, if the felony is committed in the officer's presence or if he or she has **probable cause** to believe a person committed the felony. Some state statutes have changed the meaning of presence of an officer and have established a new classification scheme for crimes, doing away with the felony-misdemeanor distinction. See ARREST and LAW ENFORCEMENT OFFICER for lists of related terms.

Pp

PRESENT. **v.** To submit for action or consideration; to lay before; to offer.

PRESENT. **adj.** At or within the immediate proximity of a certain place, person, or group at a certain time. Opposite of **absent**. *Example*: She was present at the scene of the crime. **n. 1.** The here and now; the moment or period in time between past and future. **n. 2.** (plural) The **document** or **writing** in question or under consideration. *Example*: Be it known by these presents. (These presents refers to the document in which the phrase itself occurs.)

PRESENTENCE INVESTIGATION. An investigation undertaken by a **probation agency** or other designated authority, at the request of a **court**, into the past behavior, family circumstances, and personality of an **adult** who has been convicted of a **crime**, in order to assist the court in determining the most appropriate **sentence**. The report resulting from such an investigation is usually called a **presentence report**. The investigations often form a substantial part of an adult **probation agency's** workload. Presentencing information may reach the court in various ways. For example, a confidential report may be prepared in addition to the usually public presentence report. Or the defendant may submit his or her own information to the court. A presentence investigation generally corresponds to a juvenile **predisposition investigation**. *Also called*: **social investigation**. See SENTENCE for a list of related terms.

PRESENTENCE REPORT. A document submitted to a court consisting of the results of a PRESENTENCE INVESTIGATION. A presentence report corresponds to a juvenile **predisposition report**. *Also called*: **court report**; **social history**; **social study**. See SENTENCE for a list of related terms.

PRESENTLY. **1.** In a little while; after a short time; soon; shortly. **2.** Now; at this time.

PRESENTMENT. **1.** A written statement presented to a **court** by a **grand jury**, based on the grand jury's own knowledge or observation, that an **offense** has been committed and that there is **probable cause** to believe that a particular person committed it. A presentment is made on a grand jury's own initiative without a **bill of indictment** being laid before it. It is the result of the grand jury's "investigation on its own without the consent or participation of a **prosecutor**. The grand jury holds broad power over the terms of **charges** it returns, and its decision not to bring charges is unreviewable. Furthermore, the grand jury may insist that prosecutors prepare whatever accusations it deems appropriate and may return a draft **indictment** even though the government attorney refuses to sign it." *In re Report and Recommendation of June 5, 1972 Grand Jury*, 370 F.Supp. 1219, 1222 (D.D.C. 1974). See ACCUSATION and GRAND JURY for lists of related terms. **2.** The act of presenting a formal statement of some matter to a **court** or other legal authority for its action or consideration. For example, in some jurisdictions, presentment means any of several presentations of alleged facts and charges to a **court** or **grand jury** by a **prosecutor**.

PRESENT RECOLLECTION REFRESHED. A rule of evidence that allows the consultation of notes, documents, or books by a witness while testifying to remind himself or herself of the details of past events or transactions. Courts generally allow such consultation when the witness cannot recollect or is unclear about certain facts and when his or her recollection would be refreshed by referring to a writing. The witness may not rely completely on the writing, nor may the witness read from the writing directly while testifying. Also, the writing itself is not admissible in evidence. "Under present recollection refreshed the witness' memory is refreshed or jogged through the employment of a writing, diagram, smell or even touch. . . . When a witness' recollection is refreshed the testimony comes from his memory and not from the writing or diagram." *State v. Corn*, 296 S.E.2d 261 (N.C. 1982). *Also called*: **present recollection revived**; **refreshing recollection**; **refreshing memory**. *See*: PAST RECOLLECTION RECORDED.

PRESENT RECOLLECTION REVIVED. Same as PRESENT RECOLLECTION REFRESHED.

PRESIDE. To hold or exercise authority or control.

PRESIDING JUDGE. **1.** A judge who **presides** over or conducts a legal proceeding. If more than one judge sits at a legal proceeding, each may be considered a presiding judge. **2.** The title of the **judicial officer** formally designated for some period as the chief judicial officer of a court having two or more judicial officers. *Also called*: **chief judge**; **chief justice**; **presiding justice**.

PRESIDING JUSTICE. Same as PRESIDING JUDGE.

PRESS. **1.** The publication of one's opinions and feelings by means of the printed word. *Example*: The Constitution guarantees freedom of the press. **2.** Newspapers and periodicals and the people associated with them such as reporters and editors. *Example*: The D.A. had bad relations with the press.

PRESUME. To assume or accept as true beforehand, in the absence of proof.

PRESUMPTION.   A conclusion that is required by law to be drawn, from given facts or common experience or as a matter of public policy, and accepted as true in the absence of proof. *See*: CONCLUSIVE PRESUMPTION; DEDUCTION; DIRECT EVIDENCE; EVIDENCE; FACT; INFERENCE; PRESUMPTION OF FACT; PRESUMPTION OF INNOCENCE; PRESUMPTION OF LAW; PRIMA FACIE EVIDENCE; PROOF EVIDENT; REBUTTABLE PRESUMPTION; VIOLENT PRESUMPTION.

Pp

PRESUMPTION GREAT.   *See*: PROOF EVIDENT.

PRESUMPTION OF FACT.   A conclusion that a particular **fact** exists or is true that naturally arises from the existence or truth of another fact or facts because of common experience or general knowledge. See FACT and PRESUMPTION for lists of related terms.

PRESUMPTION OF INNOCENCE.   A hallowed principle of the criminal law that a person charged with a **crime** is innocent of the crime until his or her **guilt** is proved by the **prosecution beyond a reasonable doubt** and that the defendant has no burden to prove innocence. It is not a true **presumption** because the defendant is not required to come forward with proof of innocence once evidence of guilt is introduced to avoid a **directed verdict** of **guilty**. The term presumption of innocence "succinctly conveys the principle that no person may be convicted of a crime unless the government carries the burden of proving his guilt beyond a reasonable doubt. To be sure, this means that no criminal penalties may follow from the mere fact of **indictment**. It does not, however, mean that no significance at all may be attached to the indictment." *U.S. v. Friday*, 404 F.Supp. 1343, 1344-45 (E.D.Mich. 1975).

PRESUMPTION OF LAW.   A **legal** conclusion required to be drawn from particular **facts** in the absence of evidence to the contrary. *Example:* The presumption of innocence is a presumption of law. See PRESUMPTION for a list of related terms.

PRESUMPTIVE EVIDENCE.   Same as PRIMA FACIE EVIDENCE.

PRESUMPTIVE NOTICE.   Same as IMPLIED NOTICE.

PRETEND.   **1.** To assert or allege falsely or with intent to **deceive**. **2.** To hold out or display something false as something real; to feign; to affect.

PRETENSE.   *See*: FALSE PRETENSE.

PRETEXT.   Something put forward to conceal the real purpose or object of an action; an ostensible but false justification for an action. *Example*: An officer may not make a sham arrest as a pretext for making a search.

PRETRIAL CONFERENCE. A meeting of the opposing parties in a **case** with the **judicial officer** prior to **trial**, for the purposes of stipulating those things that are agreed upon and thus narrowing the trial to the things that are in dispute, disclosing the required information about **witnesses** and **evidence**, making **motions**, and generally organizing the presentation of motions, witnesses, and evidence. The matters dealt with in a pretrial conference may instead be taken up in a procedure called an **omnibus hearing**. The name of the proceeding and the precise range of matters included in it depend upon the statutes, court rules, and customs of a given jurisdiction. In criminal proceedings, this type of pretrial activity occurs before the trial judge after an **arraignment** in which the **defendant** has entered a **not guilty plea**. It may include consideration of **reduced charges**. *Also called*: **pretrial hearing**. See HEARING for a list of related terms.

PRETRIAL DETENTION. Any period of **confinement** occurring between **arrest** or other holding to answer a **charge** and the conclusion of **prosecution**. Pretrial detention is usually shortened or eliminated by some form of **pretrial release**. See DETENTION for a list of related terms.

PRETRIAL DISCOVERY. *See*: DISCOVERY.

PRETRIAL HEARING. Same as PRETRIAL CONFERENCE.

PRETRIAL RELEASE. The **release** of an **accused** person from **custody**, for all or part of the time before or during **prosecution**, upon his or her promise to appear in **court** when required. Pretrial release policies and procedural requirements are sometimes spelled out in statutes or judicial rules. The release of a given **arrestee** is authorized by a **magistrate** or other **judicial officer**, or by another official to whom authority has been delegated. An accused person who has been arrested ordinarily has the right to be taken before a magistrate, with more or less dispatch according to the rules of each jurisdiction, to be set free upon guarantee of reappearance to hear the **charges** against him or her and submit to **judgment** (see **initial appearance**). The usual procedure is for the magistrate to set **bail**, which means that a sum of money or other thing of value is pledged by the accused or another person that will be forfeited if the accused fails to appear. The pretrial release can be reconsidered and bail reset at later stages of adjudication.

The three major types of pretrial release are RELEASE ON BAIL; RELEASE ON OWN RECOGNIZANCE; and RELEASE TO THIRD PARTY. See RELEASE for a list of related terms.

PREVAIL. To predominate; to be superior or victorious; to be effective or successful.

PREVAILING PARTY. The party that wins a favorable **judgment** in a legal **action**.

PREVENT. To keep something from happening; to keep someone from doing something; to thwart; to hinder; to impede.

PREVENTIVE DETENTION. The court-ordered **pretrial detention** of a person charged with certain types of **crime** for a substantial period of time on the ground that the person is likely to commit crimes endangering the safety of the community if **released** prior to **trial**. See DETENTION for a list of related terms.

Pp

PREVIOUS. Coming or happening before something else; prior; antecedent.

PREVIOUSLY RECORDED TESTIMONY. Recorded testimony of a **witness** given at an earlier judicial **proceeding** or **deposition**. Previously recorded testimony is **admissible** in a second proceeding as an exception to the **hearsay rule** if: (1) the testimony was given under **oath** or **affirmation**; (2) both proceedings involved substantially the same parties and issues; and (3) the particular witness's testimony is UNAVAILABLE at the time the previously recorded testimony is offered. The reason for this exception is that the witness was under oath and either subject to or available for **cross-examination** at the prior proceeding. See HEARSAY RULE for a list of other exceptions.

PRIMA FACIE. *Latin.* "At first sight or appearance." Sufficient or adequate on its face without further investigation or inquiry.

PRIMA FACIE CASE. A **case** established by **prima facie evidence**, and which will prevail until contradicted and overcome by other sufficient **evidence**.

PRIMA FACIE EVIDENCE. "[E]vidence sufficient to establish a given fact and which, if not rebutted or contradicted, will remain sufficient." *State v. Williams*, 400 So.2d 575, 579 (La. 1981). *Also called*: **presumptive evidence**. See EVIDENCE for a list of related terms.

PRIMARY. First in rank, order, or time; principal; basic; fundamental.

PRIMARY AUTHORITY. *See*: AUTHORITY (definition 5).

PRIMARY CAUSE. Same as PROXIMATE CAUSE.

PRIMARY EVIDENCE. Same as BEST EVIDENCE.

PRIMARY FACT. Same as EVIDENTIARY FACT.

PRIME. First in authority, power, quality, or importance.

PRINCIPAL. **n. 1.** A principal in the first degree is the chief actor in or **perpetrator** of a **crime**; the person whose acts directly cause the criminal result. A principal in the second degree is a person who **aids and abets** the principal in the first degree and is present, either actually or constructively, at the commission of the crime. "The principal in the second degree differs from the principal in the first degree only in that he does not do the felonious deed himself or with the aid of an innocent agent, but rather he aids, commands, counsels or encourages a culpable party to perpetrate the crime. To convict a principal in the second degree, the State must prove actual or constructive presence, intent, and some form of participation in the perpetration of the crime." *State v. Mower*, 317 A.2d 807, 811 (Me. 1974). See PARTY for a list of related terms. **n. 2.** A person who authorizes an AGENT to represent the person or to act for the person. **adj.** Chief; most important; highest; foremost.

PRINCIPLE. **1.** An accepted rule of action or procedure. **2.** A fundamental truth or doctrine which provides a basis for other truths or for action.

PRIOR. Preceding in time, order, or importance.

PRIORITY. The state or right of coming before in time, order, or importance.

PRISON. A state or federal **confinement facility** having custodial authority over **adults** sentenced to **confinement** for more than one year. A small proportion of prison **inmates** may be allowed to participate in **work release** or other **temporary release** programs. Common names for prisons are **conservation camp**, **correctional facility**, **correctional institution**, and **penitentiary**. *See*: CORRECTIONAL FACILITY.

PRISON BREACH. Same as PRISON BREAKING.

PRISON BREAKING. The unauthorized departure or escape, by use of force, of a prisoner from legal custody. *Also called*: **breach of prison**; **prison breach**.

PRISON COMMITMENT. A **sentence** of **commitment** to the **jurisdiction** of a state or federal **confinement facility** system for **adults**, of which the custodial authority extends to persons sentenced to more than a year of confinement, for a term expressed in years or for life, or to await execution. There are four types of prison commitment: (1) DEFINITE SENTENCE; (2) INDEFINITE SENTENCE; (3) LIFE SENTENCE; and (4) DEATH SENTENCE. *Also called*: **prison sentence**. See COMMITMENT and SENTENCE for lists of related terms.

PRISONER. **1.** A person in physical **custody** in a **confinement facility**, or in the personal physical custody of a **law enforcement officer** while being transported to or between confinement facilities. **2.** An **arrestee** who is in the custody of a law enforcement officer or a court. See ACCUSED for a list of related terms.

PRISONER AT THE BAR. A person accused of **crime** who is actually on **trial** before the **court**.

PRISONS, BUREAU OF. *See*: BUREAU OF PRISONS.

PRISON SENTENCE. Same as PRISON COMMITMENT.

PRIVACY. *See*: ABORTION; CONSTITUTIONALLY PROTECTED AREA; CURTILAGE; EAVESDROP; FREEDOM OF INFORMATION ACT; GOVERNMENT IN THE SUNSHINE ACT; PLAIN VIEW DOCTRINE; PRIVACY ACT OF 1974; PRIVATE PLACE; RIGHT OF PRIVACY; SEARCH; STANDING; WIRETAPPING.

PRIVACY ACT of 1974. A federal statute (5 U.S.C. §552a) that reasserts the fundamental right to privacy as derived from the Constitution of the United States and provides a series of basic safeguards for the individual to prevent the misuse of personal information by agencies of the federal government.

The act provides for making known to the public the existence and characteristics of all personal information systems kept by every federal agency. The act permits a person to have access to records containing personal information on him or her, to have copies made, and to control the transfer of that information to other federal agencies for nonroutine uses. The act also requires all federal agencies to keep accurate accountings of transfers of personal records to other agencies and outsiders, and to make the accountings available to the person requesting them. The act further provides for civil remedies for the person whose records are kept or used in contravention of the requirements of the act.

The Privacy Act also requires the agencies to adopt regulations that list and describe routine transfers of their personal records and to establish procedures for access to and amendment of such records. Virtually all agencies of the federal government have issued regulations implementing the Privacy Act. These regulations generally inform the public how to determine if a system of records contains information on themselves, how to gain access to such records, how to request amendment of such records, and the method of internal appeal of an adverse agency determination on such a request. See PRIVACY for a list of related terms.

PRIVATE. **1.** Belonging to or concerning a particular person or persons as distinguished from the general public or the government. **2.** Not holding public office. *Example*: He became a private person after losing the election. **3.** Personal; confidential; intimate; secret. See PRIVACY for a list of related terms.

PRIVATE BILL. A legislative bill that deals with or affects an individual person, a group, or a locality, as opposed to the general public. *See*: PUBLIC BILL.

PRIVATE NUISANCE. A NUISANCE that affects one or a small number of particular persons, as opposed to the public in general, a whole community or neighborhood, or an indefinite number of people. *See*: PUBLIC NUISANCE.

PRIVATE PERSON. **1.** A person who is not holding public office. **2.** Under the law of **arrest**, a person who is not a **law enforcement officer**. *Example*: Arrests by private persons are governed by different rules than arrests by law enforcement officers.

PRIVATE PLACE. Section 250.12 of the **Model Penal Code** defines private place as "a place where one may reasonably expect to be safe from casual or hostile intrusion or surveillance, but does not include a place to which the public or a substantial group thereof has access." See PRIVACY for a list of related terms.

PRIVATE PROSECUTOR. Same as PROSECUTING WITNESS.

PRIVATE REHABILITATION AGENCY. A private organization providing care and treatment services, which may include housing, to convicted persons, juvenile offenders, or persons subject to judicial proceedings. Private rehabilitation agency includes residential facilities, juvenile shelters, and the like, operated by private agencies. It is to be distinguished from public **correctional agencies** (**jails**, **prisons**, **probation agencies**, and **parole agencies**), which may offer rehabilitative services, but also have officially established control and **supervision** responsibilities. The major distinguishing characteristic of public versus private agencies is that public agencies are authorized and required by law to carry out certain criminal justice functions, while private agencies are only *permitted* by law to perform criminal justice functions.

PRIVATE RIGHTS. Same as PERSONAL RIGHTS.

PRIVATE SECURITY AGENCY. An independent or proprietary commercial organization whose activities include employee clearance investigations, maintaining the security of persons or property, and/or performing the functions of detection and investigation of crime and criminals and apprehension of offenders. The major distinguishing characteristic between public **law enforcement agencies** and private security agencies is that public agencies are authorized and required by law to carry out certain criminal justice functions, while private agencies are only permitted by law to perform criminal justice functions.

PRIVATE WRONG. A wrong committed against one or more persons or organizations, as distinguished from a wrong committed against society (a **crime**). *Also called*: **civil wrong**.

PRIVILEGE. A special right, benefit, or immunity granted to a certain person or class.

PRIVILEGED COMMUNICATION. Same as CONFIDENTIAL COMMUNICATION.

PRIVILEGES AND IMMUNITIES. Article IV of the U.S. Constitution provides that "The Citizens of each State shall be entitled to all Privileges and Immunities of Citizens in the several States." This provision prohibits discrimination against citizens of other states for no substantial reason other than citizenship in another state. Examples of protected privileges and immunities are the right of access to and protection from the state government, the right to acquire and possess all kinds of property, the privilege of **habeas corpus**, the right to reside in or travel through any state for trade, agricultural, or professional purposes, and the right to sue and defend **actions** in court.

The 14th Amendment to the Constitution states that "No State shall make or enforce any law which shall abridge the privileges or immunities of citizens of the United States." This provision protects U.S. citizens against unreasonable state action or interference with respect to the fundamental rights that owe their existence to the federal government, its national character, its constitution, or its laws. Examples of such rights are the right to travel from state to state, the right to vote for federal officeholders, the right to enter public lands, the right to petition Congress for redress of grievances, the right to access to the federal courts, and the privilege of habeas corpus.

PRO. *Latin.* "For; on account of; in behalf of."

PRO AND CON. For and against.

PROBABILITY. Likelihood; the state of being **probable**.

PROBABLE. Likely; having more evidence in favor than against; appearing to be true but leaving some room for doubt.

PROBABLE CAUSE. Probable cause exists when the facts and circumstances within a person's knowledge and of which he or she has reasonably trustworthy information are sufficient in themselves to justify a person of reasonable caution and prudence in believing that something is true. It means something less than certainty, but more than mere suspicion, speculation, or possibility.

Probable cause is required to justify the issuance of an **arrest warrant** or **search warrant**, all **arrests** made without a warrant, and most **searches** made without a warrant. The quality and amount of information needed to establish probable cause to arrest or search are the same in either case. The kind of information needed to justify an arrest, however, is different from that to justify a search. Probable cause to arrest arises from facts tending to show that a specific **crime** has been or is being committed and that a particular person committed or is committing it. Probable cause to search arises from facts tending to show that the items searched for are **items subject to seizure** and that they will be located in a particular place at a particular time.

Information to establish probable cause may come to a person through any of his or her five senses or through a third person or informant. When the information comes through an informant, the information must satisfy the "totality of the circumstances" test set out in the U.S. Supreme Court case of ILLINOIS v. GATES. Even though the *Gates* case dealt with a search warrant, the "totality of the circumstances" test must be satisfied to establish probable cause for a warrantless search and for arrests made both with and without a warrant.

Probable cause to believe that a particular person committed a particular crime is also required to initiate **prosecution**. In **felony** cases the existence of probable cause will be established in court in a hearing usually called a **preliminary hearing**, or by a **grand jury**, before felony trial proceedings begin. Whether the defendant has the right to a preliminary hearing in a misdemeanor case depends upon the jurisdiction. *Also called*: **reasonable cause**; **sufficient cause**. See ARREST WARRANT, EVIDENCE, FACT, and SEARCH for lists of related terms.

PROBABLE CAUSE HEARING.   Same as PRELIMINARY HEARING.

PROBABLE CONSEQUENCE.   A consequence that is more likely than not to follow from a given cause or given set of facts.

PROBABLE EVIDENCE.   Same as PRIMA FACIE EVIDENCE.

PROBATE COURT.   *See*: COURT OF LIMITED JURISDICTION.

PROBATION.   The conditional freedom without imprisonment granted by a **judicial officer** to an alleged or adjudicated **adult** or **juvenile** offender, as long as the person meets certain conditions of behavior. Probation differs from **parole,** in that it is conditional freedom ordered by a court, whereas parole is conditional freedom granted by a **paroling authority** after **commitment** to a period of **confinement**. Probation is usually a continuation of freedom previously granted by the court during court proceedings. It may be granted after **conviction**, but also may be granted before **adjudication**, as when the defendant concedes **guilt**, **prosecution** is suspended, and the subject placed on probation.

Probation is usually granted to young offenders and first offenders who have committed minor crimes. Typical conditions of adult probation, as set forth by the court that granted the probation, frequently include such admonishments as maintaining regular employment, abstaining from drugs and alcohol, not associating with known offenders or other specified persons, regularly reporting to a **probation officer** or other designated person, and/or remaining within a designated geographic area. Not committing another offense is always a condition of probation. A grant of probation after conviction often includes another kind of **sentencing disposition** as a condition: confinement in **jail**, payment of **restitution** in the form of money or public service, a **fine**, etc. Conditions of probation unique to a person may also be imposed, such as payment of personal debts. Some courts commit offenders to prison with a period of probationary status, instead of parole, to follow. This is often called **shock probation**.

The limits of probationary periods are usually set by **statute** and can be longer than the **maximum sentence** of confinement, or series of sentences to confinement, provided by law for a given offense. Some jurisdictions limit probationary periods for **felonies** to the maximum possible period of imprisonment for the offense.

Violation of any of the conditions of probation may lead to **probation revocation** and the execution of a **suspended sentence** or the imposition and execution of a sentence if one has not already been imposed.

Juvenile probation is often designated as informal or formal, depending upon the authority granting it and the nature of the conditions. Juveniles may be placed on informal probation by a probation officer in lieu of the filing of a **juvenile petition**. *See*: ABSCOND; CONDITION; COURTESY SUPERVISION; COURT PROBATION; DISCHARGE; INTAKE; MODIFICATION OF PROBATION; PAROLE; PREDISPOSITION INVESTIGATION; PREDISPOSITION REPORT; PRESENTENCE INVESTIGATION; PRESENTENCE REPORT; PROBATION AGENCY; PROBATION COUNSELOR; PROBATIONER; PROBATION OFFICER; PROBATION ORDER; PROBATION REVOCATION; PROBATION TERMINATION; PROBATION VIOLATION; PROBATION WORKLOAD; RESIDENTIAL COMMITMENT; REVOCATION HEARING; SENTENCE; SPLIT SENTENCE; SUPERVISED PROBATION; SUPERVISORY CUSTODY; SUSPENDED SENTENCE; UNCONDITIONAL RELEASE.

PROBATION AGENCY. A **correctional agency** whose principal functions are juvenile **intake**, the **supervision** of **adults** and **juveniles** placed on **probation**, and the investigation of adults or juveniles for the purpose of preparing **presentence reports** or **predisposition reports** to assist the **court** in determining the proper **sentence** or **juvenile disposition**. State-level adult and juvenile probation agencies are often separate governmental units. However, probation agencies organized at local levels of government usually operate under the authority of a court. In many states a single state agency performs both probation and parole supervision functions for adults, but juvenile probation functions are typically local and performed under the guidance of a **juvenile court**.

A probation agency's concern with adults is usually limited to those who have pled **guilty** or have been **convicted** of an offense. Its discretionary powers regarding juveniles are much greater, in that it usually administers the **intake unit** that can make a decision to close a case at intake, to take other actions that preclude or defer the intervention of the juvenile court, or to file a petition asking the court to assume jurisdiction over the juvenile. Some agencies administer juvenile shelter facilities. The juvenile concern is also broad in that the intake function and subsequent

supervision and care authority may apply to **dependent** juveniles, especially those in custody pending court disposition. *Also called*: **probation department**. See PROBATION for a list of related terms.

PROBATION COUNSELOR. **1.** In the narrowest sense, a **probation officer** whose chief duties relate to client **intake** and screening, and assistance and treatment of **probationers**. **2.** A private person who assists or advises probationers. See PROBATION for a list of related terms.

PROBATION DEPARTMENT. Same as PROBATION AGENCY.

PROBATIONER. A person who is placed on PROBATION status and required by a **court** or **probation agency** to meet certain **conditions** of behavior, and who may or may not be placed under the **supervision** of a probation agency. See PROBATION for a list of related terms.

PROBATION INTAKE. Same as INTAKE.

PROBATION OFFICER. An employee of a PROBATION AGENCY whose primary duties include one or more of the probation agency functions. The **intake** function of a juvenile probation agency may include the exercise of **judicial** authority in disposing of juvenile referrals (see **referral to intake; intake decision**). Probation officers who exercise judicial authority may be considered **judicial officers** in some jurisdictions. In some jurisdictions probation officers have some **law enforcement** powers, but are not generally considered to be **law enforcement officers**. See PROBATION for a list of related terms.

PROBATION ORDER. A **court** action requiring that a person fulfill certain conditions of behavior for a specified period of time, often with assignment to a **probation agency** for **supervision**, either in lieu of **prosecution** or **judgment**, or after **conviction**, usually in lieu of a **sentence** to **confinement**. *Also called*: **grant of probation**. See PROBATION for a list of related terms.

PROBATION REVOCATION. A **court order** in response to a violation of **conditions** of PROBATION, taking away a person's probationary status, and usually withdrawing the conditional freedom associated with the status. If the **grant of probation** was awarded after **conviction**, revocation may be followed by execution of a previously set **penalty**, or the pronouncement and execution of a previously unpronounced penalty. If the person was placed on probation before adjudication was completed by **judgment** (see **adjudication withheld**), then violation of probation conditions may result in pronouncement of judgment and execution of a **sentence**. The person can be committed or recommitted to **confinement** without conviction for a new offense, but only on evidence presented during a **revocation hearing** that he or she had violated conditions of probation.

Not all alleged violations of probation conditions result in revocation hearings or revocations. Also a court may in some circumstances revoke probation, order the probationer to appear in court, and reinstate probationary status. However, probation revocation often results in commitment to a **confinement facility** to serve a previously **suspended sentence**.

Various legal rights pertain to the probation revocation process, such as right to **counsel** and advance **notice** of charges, but the level of proof required is less than that required to **convict**. A probationer may be detained in **jail** while awaiting a court hearing concerning an alleged violation of probation conditions. See HEARING and PROBATION for lists of related terms.

PROBATION SCREENING.   Same as INTAKE.

PROBATION SUPERVISION.   *See*: SUPERVISED PROBATION.

PROBATION TERMINATION.   The ending of the **probation** status of a given person by routine expiration of probationary period, by special early termination by **court**, or by **probation revocation**. See PROBATION for a list of related terms.

PROBATION VIOLATION.   An act or a failure to act by a PROBATIONER that does not conform to the **conditions** of his or her PROBATION. A probation violation may lead to probation revocation, but not necessarily. If it is alleged that the probationer committed a new **crime**, the court may revoke probation because of the violation of the conditions of probation, or may initiate **prosecution** for the new offense, and occasionally will do both. A probation violation that does not consist of commission of a crime or is not prosecuted as such is usually called a **technical violation**, to indicate that it is behavior forbidden by the court order granting probation, and not forbidden by **statute**, or treated as if not forbidden by statute. See PROBATION for a list of related terms.

PROBATION WORKLOAD.   The total set of activities required in order to carry out the basic **probation agency** functions of **intake** screening of juvenile cases, referral of cases to other service agencies, investigation of **juveniles** and **adults** for the purpose of preparing **predisposition reports** or **presentence reports**, **supervision** or treatment of juveniles and adults granted **probation**, assisting in the enforcement of court orders concerning family problems such as abandonment and nonsupport cases, and such other functions as may be assigned by statute or court order. Additional responsibilities assigned by law or by a court vary greatly from one jurisdiction to another and include such duties as monitoring collection of **restitution** payment or **fines**, screening **arrestees** for release on own **recognizance**, and administering juvenile shelter or confinement facilities or adult residences. See PROBATION for a list of related terms.

PROBATIVE.   Affording proof of some proposition; tending to convince one of the truth of some proposition.

PROBATIVE FACTS.   **Facts** that can be used to prove the ultimate fact or facts in issue. See FACT for a list of related terms.

PROBATIVE VALUE.   Same as WEIGHT OF THE EVIDENCE.

PRO BONO ET MALO.   *Latin.* "For good and bad."

PRO BONO PUBLICO.   *Latin.* "For the public good." **Attorneys** who take on **cases** without compensation as a public service are said to be acting pro bono publico.

PROCEDURAL DUE PROCESS.   Generally, procedural due process requires a fair and reasonable procedure and "certain minimal standards of notice, hearing, and opportunity to respond adequately before a governmental agency may effectively deprive an individual of life, liberty or property." *State v. Manocchio*, 448 A.2d 761, 764 n.3 (R.I. 1982). *See*: DUE PROCESS OF LAW; SUBSTANTIVE DUE PROCESS.

PROCEDURAL LAW.   **1.** The law governing PROCEDURE as distinguished from **substantive law**. Procedural law provides a method of enforcing rights, duties, and obligations created by the substantive law. Procedural law governs the conduct of proceedings to bring parties into court and the conduct of the court after they are brought in. Examples of procedural laws are laws of **pleading**, **evidence**, and **practice**. *Also called*: **adjective law**. **2.** The body of such laws. *See*: SUBSTANTIVE LAW.

PROCEDURE.   The method, form, and order of conducting judicial or legal business, as distinguished from the definition of rights and duties and the establishment of penalties. *See*: ADMINISTRATIVE PROCEDURE; CIVIL PROCEDURE; CRIMINAL PROCEDURE; PROCEDURAL LAW.

PROCEED.   To institute and carry on a legal **action**.

PROCEEDING.   **1.** A legal **action** (definition 2) or **process**. **2.** Any step or measure taken in a legal action by either party or by the court. **3.** The instituting or carrying on of a legal action. **4.** An event or course of action taking place at a particular place or time. *Example*: They went to the state house to observe the legislative proceedings. *See*: OFFICIAL PROCEEDING.

PROCESS.   **1.** The series of progressive and interdependent steps or stages that make up the whole of a legal **action**. *See*: DUE PROCESS **2.** A **writ**, **warrant**, **mandate**, or other written order issued by a court such as an **arrest warrant**, a **search warrant**, or a **summons**. Sometimes the word process is used in a more limited sense to mean the written **order** by which a court exercises its **jurisdiction** over a particular person or property. *Also called*: **judicial process**. See ARREST WARRANT for a list of related terms.

PROCESS SERVER. One who **serves** legal **documents**, such as **warrants**, **writs**, **subpoenas**, and **summonses**.

Pp

PROCHAIN AMI. *French.* Same as NEXT FRIEND.

PROCHEIN AMI. *French.* Same as NEXT FRIEND.

PROCLAMATION. **1.** An official public announcement. **2.** The announcement by the crier that something is about to happen or be done in the courtroom. *See*: OYEZ.

PROCURE. To PANDER (v.).

PROCURER. Same as PANDER (n.).

PROCURING CAUSE. Same as PROXIMATE CAUSE.

PRODUCE. To bring forward; to present; to exhibit. *Example*: The witness was required to produce the records for the court's examination.

PRODUCING CAUSE. Same as PROXIMATE CAUSE.

PRODUCTION BURDEN. Same as BURDEN OF PRODUCTION OF EVIDENCE.

PROFANITY. Abusive disrespect or irreverence toward God or sacred things by word or deed.

PROFESS. **1.** To state or declare positively from a personal or emotional involvement or commitment. See ADDRESS for a list of related terms. **2.** To claim knowledge of or skill in.

PROFESSION. **1.** An occupation requiring special knowledge or skill in some area of learning or science, such as law or medicine. **2.** The act of professing. *See*: PROFESS.

PROFESSIONAL CRIMINAL. A person who has made **crime** his or her livelihood, that is, a person who depends upon criminal activities for at least a substantial portion of his or her income, and who has developed special, related skills. See CRIME for a list of related terms.

PROFFER. To put before; to offer; to tender; to present for acceptance. See ADDRESS for a list of related terms.

PRO FORMA. *Latin.* As a matter of form; according to form. A pro forma judicial **decree** or **judgment** is one that was rendered, not on conviction that it is right, but merely to facilitate further **appellate** proceedings.

PRO HAC VICE. *Latin.* For this occasion only.

PROHIBIT. **1.** To forbid by legal command or statute. **2.** To prevent; to preclude; to hinder.

PROHIBITION. *See*: WRIT OF PROHIBITION.

PROLICIDE. The destruction of the human offspring either before or soon after birth. *See*: ABORTION; INFANTICIDE.

PROMISSORY NOTE. A written promise to pay a specified sum of money at a specified time or on demand.

PROMOTE. To further the progress, growth, or development of; to encourage; to advance.

PROMOTION OF PROSTITUTION. The soliciting or aiding in any manner of another to engage in **prostitution**, or the soliciting or aiding of another to secure the services of a prostitute, or knowingly receiving any money or other thing of value that is the proceeds of prostitution. Promotion of prostitution typically includes offenses of varying names and content, such as **pimping**, **pandering**, **procuring** for prostitution, maintaining a **house of prostitution**, and living off the earnings of a **prostitute**. See SEX OFFENSES for a list of related terms.

PROMPT. Done at once or immediately. The exact meaning of prompt depends on the context in which it is used. In a legal sense, it often means done as soon as possible under the circumstances.

PROMULGATE. To put into effect or operation by formal public announcement. *Example*: The court promulgated new rules of practice.

PRONOUNCE. To announce formally and officially. *Example*: The court pronounced sentence on the defendant.

PRONOUNCEMENT OF JUDGMENT. Same as RENDITION OF JUDGMENT.

PROOF. The establishment of the truth of or belief in a **fact** by means of EVIDENCE; the effect or result of evidence; the conclusion drawn from evidence. The terms evidence and proof are sometimes used interchangeably. See EVIDENCE and FACT for lists of related terms.

PROOF EVIDENT. Under the constitutional provision in some states that the accused is entitled to **bail** as of right except in **capital** cases where the "proof is evident" or the "presumption great," the quoted phrases mean that the **evidence** is clear and strong that the offense has been committed as charged, that the accused committed it, and that the accused would probably be punished capitally if the law were administered. See BAIL for a list of related terms.

Pp

PROPER. Conforming to established standards; suitable; appropriate; fitting.

PROPER CARE. Same as ORDINARY CARE.

PROPERTY. 1. Anything of value that may be owned, whether tangible or intangible. Section 223.0 (6) of the **Model Penal Code** defines property as "anything of value, including real estate, tangible and intangible personal property, contract rights, choses-in-action and other interests in or claims to wealth, admission or transportation tickets, captured or domestic animals, food and drink, electric or other power." The two types of property are REAL PROPERTY and PERSONAL PROPERTY. 2. The right to possess, use, and dispose of **property** (1) in every legal way to the exclusion of others.

PROPERTY CRIMES. A category used in some crime classification schemes to include crimes such as **robbery**, **burglary**, **larceny**, **motor vehicle theft**, and **arson**. See CRIME for a list of related terms.

PROPONENT. One who offers or **proposes**.

PROPOSAL. 1. A scheme or plan of action offered for consideration. 2. The act of proposing. *See*: PROPOSE.

PROPOSE. To put forth or present for consideration, discussion, acceptance, or other action; to suggest. See ADDRESS for a list of related terms.

PROPOSITION. 1. A formal statement offered for discussion, argument, proof, or disproof. 2. A PROPOSAL.

PROPOUND. To put forth a question or proposition for discussion. See ADDRESS for a list of related terms.

PROPRIETOR. A person who has an exclusive right or title to something; an owner.

PRORATE. To give out shares or portions to members of a group with the suggestion of a proportional division based on authoritative decision or agreement of members of the group. See ALLOCATE for a list of related terms.

PROSCRIBE. To prohibit; to outlaw; to condemn.

PRO SE. *Latin.* "For himself or herself; on his or her own behalf." Acting as one's own **defense attorney** in criminal proceedings; representing oneself without retaining an **attorney**. *Also called*: **in propria persona**.

PROSECUTE. To initiate and maintain a **criminal action** against a person alleged to have committed an **offense** against the law in order to obtain a **conviction**. In a broader sense, prosecute means to initiate and maintain any legal **action** against someone. *See*: ATTORNEY AT LAW; BILL OF INDICTMENT; BILL OF PARTICULARS; BURDEN OF PROOF; COMPLAINT; COMPLAINT DENIED; COMPLAINT GRANTED; COMPLAINT REQUESTED; COMPOUNDING CRIME; COUNTY ATTORNEY; CRIME; CRIMINAL ACTION; CRIMINAL DIVISION; DEFENDANT DISPOSITION; DISMISSAL FOR WANT OF PROSECUTION; DOUBLE JEOPARDY; GRAND JURY; INDICTMENT; INFORMATION; MALICIOUS PROSECUTION; NOLLE PROSEQUI; PLAINTIFF; PLEA BARGAINING; PROSECUTING WITNESS; PROSECUTION; PROSECUTION AGENCY; PROSECUTOR; PROSECUTORIAL DISCRETION; PROSECUTORIAL SCREENING DECISION; STATUTE OF LIMITATIONS; UNITED STATES ATTORNEY.

PROSECUTING ATTORNEY. Same as PROSECUTOR.

PROSECUTING WITNESS. The private person whose **complaint** or information is the basis for a criminal **accusation** and who is the principal **witness** at the **trial**. Usually the prosecuting witness is the **victim** who is chiefly injured by the alleged crime. *Also called*: **complaining party**; **complaining witness**. See PROSECUTE and WITNESS for lists of related terms.

PROSECUTION. **1.** The act or process of prosecuting. *See*: PROSECUTE. **2.** Same as PROSECUTOR. *Example*: The prosecution rests its case. See PROSECUTE for a list of related terms.

PROSECUTION AGENCY. A federal, state, or local **criminal justice agency** or subunit of which the principal function is the **prosecution** of alleged offenders. Typical prosecution agencies are county district attorney offices, criminal divisions of state attorney general offices, U.S. attorney offices, and organized crime units in federal and state departments of justice. *Also called*: **prosecutorial agency**. See PROSECUTE for a list of related terms.

PROSECUTOR. **1.** An **attorney** employed by a government agency whose official duty is to initiate and maintain **criminal actions** on behalf of the government against persons accused of committing **crimes**. A prosecutor may be called **county attorney**, **D.A.**, **district attorney**, **prosecuting attorney**, **prosecution**, **public prosecutor**, **state's attorney**, or **United States attorney**. See PROSECUTE for a list of related terms. **2.** *See*: PRIVATE PROSECUTOR.

PROSECUTORIAL AGENCY. Same as PROSECUTION AGENCY.

PROSECUTORIAL DISCRETION. The **prosecutor's** power to decide whether or not to **prosecute** a person for a **crime**, and if so, what crime to prosecute the person for. The prosecutor is given wide discretion in making this decision. "In our system, so long as the prosecutor has **probable cause** to believe that the **accused** committed an **offense** defined by **statute**, the decision whether or not to prosecute, and what charge to file or bring before a **grand jury**, generally rests entirely in his discretion." *Bordenkircher v. Hayes*, 434 U.S. 357, 364, 98 S.Ct. 663, 668, 54 L.Ed.2d 604 (1978). Courts have consistently held that the exercise of this discretion is not subject to direct **judicial review** except in cases of abuse for discriminatory or vindictive reasons. Review of an affirmative decision to prosecute may be afforded by the **preliminary examination** or the **grand jury**. No effective procedure exists, however, to review a decision not to prosecute. Prosecutorial discretion may also refer to decisions relating to **plea bargaining**, trial strategy, **sentence** recommendations, etc. See PROSECUTE for a list of related terms.

PROSECUTORIAL SCREENING DECISION. The decision of a **prosecutor** to submit a **charging document** to a **court**, or to seek a **grand jury indictment**, or to decline to prosecute. See PROSECUTE for a list of related terms.

PROSPECTIVE. Looking forward in time; operative with respect to the future. *Example*: The court's decision has only prospective effect. *See*: RETRO-SPECTIVE.

PROSTITUTE. A person who engages in PROSTITUTION.

PROSTITUTION. Offering or agreeing to engage in, or engaging in, a **sexual act** with another in return for a fee. Prostitution is commonly codified as a single offense. In some jurisdictions the offense so named is more narrowly defined as offering or agreeing to engage in, or engaging in **sexual intercourse** by a woman in return for a fee. In some jurisdictions the offense is more broadly defined such that clients as well as **prostitutes** are guilty of an offense. A few jurisdictions now have a separately codified offense of **patronizing prostitutes**. See SEX OFFENSES for a list of related terms.

PRO TANTO. *Latin.* "For so much"; so far; to such an extent.

PROTECTIVE CUSTODY. The safeguarding of a person by law enforcement authorities in a place other than the person's home because his or her safety is seriously threatened. A material **witness** to a **crime** may be held in protective custody if the alleged **perpetrator** or others have made **threats** against the witness.

PRO TEMPORE. *Latin.* "For the time being"; temporarily.

PROTEST.   To state positively and emphatically in the face of doubt or contradiction. *Example*: She protested her innocence. See ADDRESS for a list of related terms.

PROVE.   To establish a **fact** as true by putting forth **evidence**. See EVIDENCE and FACT for lists of related terms.

PROVIDE.   **1.** To furnish; to supply; to afford. **2.** To make a stipulation; to set a condition.

PROVIDED.   On the condition; with the stipulation; if. *Example*: You may file your motion late, provided you do so within 10 days.

PROVISIONAL.   Temporary; tentative; taking the place of something regular or permanent.

PROVISIONAL EXIT.   Same as TEMPORARY RELEASE.

PROVISO.   A clause in a legal document making some condition, stipulation, or exception. Such a clause is often introduced by the word **provided**.

PROVOCATION.   Any action, language, or other conduct that **provokes** another. *See*: ADEQUATE PROVOCATION.

PROVOKE.   To excite or arouse to anger or passion; to enrage; to irritate.

PROXIMATE CAUSE.   The real, dominant, or direct cause; the cause that sets in motion a continuous series of events, unbroken by any major independent intervening cause, producing a result. The proximate cause is not necessarily the closest cause in time or space, nor the cause that initially sets other causes in operation, but the effective moving or producing cause. In practical legal terms, a proximate cause is one sufficiently related or connected to a result to justify imposing liability for that result on the person who produced the cause. *Also called*: **direct cause**; **dominant cause**; **efficient adequate cause**; **efficient cause**; **jural cause**; **legal cause**; **moving cause**; **procuring cause**; **producing cause.**

PROXIMATE CONSEQUENCE.   Same as PROXIMATE RESULT.

PROXIMATE RESULT.   A result or consequence that an ordinary **prudent** person might reasonably expect to follow. *Also called*: **proximate consequence**.

PROXIMITY.   Nearness; closeness. *See*: ABUTTING; ADJACENT; ADJOINING; BESIDE; BORDERING; BOUNDING; BY; CLOSE; CONTERMINOUS; CONTIGUOUS; JUXTAPOSED; NEAR; NEXT; TANGENT.

PRUDENCE.   The fact, state, or quality of being **prudent**.

PRUDENT. Wisely cautious; having or using good judgment; practically sensible; careful.

PSEUDO. False; counterfeit; sham; fake.

PSYCHOLOGICAL FACT. A fact that can only be perceived mentally and not by any of the five senses. *Example*: Criminal intent is a psychological fact. See FACT for a list of related terms.

PSYCHOPATH. A person with a mental disorder, especially one that manifests itself in aggressively antisocial behavior.

PSYCHOSIS. A severe mental disease or disorder characterized by intellectual and social malfunctioning and withdrawal from reality.

PUBLIC. **n. 1.** The whole nation, state, or community; the people as a whole. **n. 2.** The view, knowledge, or accessibility of all. *Example*: They demonstrated in public. **adj. 1.** Relating to, belonging to, directed to, or affecting the **public** (definition n1). Section 250.2 of the **Model Penal Code** defines public as "affecting or likely to affect persons in a place to which the public or a substantial group has access; among the places included are highways, transport facilities, schools, prisons, apartment houses, places of business or amusement, or any neighborhood." *Example:* Their rowdy behavior caused public inconvenience. **adj. 2.** Open to or common to the public (definition n1). *Example*: The town hall is a public building. **adj. 3.** Governmental. *Example*: She is running for public office.

PUBLICATION. **1.** The act of publishing (see **publish**); the state or fact of being published; something that is published, like a book or magazine. **2.** The printing and distribution of written materials. **3.** Any form of intentional or negligent communication of a defamatory (see **defamation**) statement to a third person, i.e., to someone other than the originator and the person defamed.

PUBLIC BILL. A legislative **bill** that deals with matters of concern to the PUBLIC (definition n1). *See:* PRIVATE BILL.

PUBLIC DEFENDER. A **defense attorney** employed by a **public defender agency** or by a private organization under contract to a unit of government for the purpose of representing in **court** persons **accused** or **convicted** of a **crime** who are unable to hire private counsel. Court decisions establishing the right to **assistance of counsel** for persons subject to **incarceration** as a consequence of conviction have led to a considerable increase in the number of publicly funded **defense attorneys**. Some are regular full- or part-time employees of government units, but in some jurisdictions defense of indigents is provided by a legal aid society.

The Criminal Justice Act (18 U.S.C. §3006A) establishes the procedure for the appointment of counsel in federal criminal cases for persons who are unable to afford adequate representation under plans adopted by each district court. The act also permits the establishment by the district courts of a Federal Public Defender Organization (staffed by one or more full-time salaried attorneys) or a Federal Community Defender Organization (a nonprofit defense counsel service established and administered by authorized groups and eligible to furnish attorneys and receive payments under the law). See ATTORNEY AT LAW for a list of related terms.

PUBLIC DEFENDER AGENCY. A federal, state, or local **criminal justice agency** or subunit of which the principal function is to represent in **court** persons **accused** or **convicted** of a **crime** who are unable to hire private **counsel**. *See*: PUBLIC DEFENDER.

PUBLIC DOMAIN. Land owned or controlled by the government.

PUBLIC DRUNKENNESS. *See*: PUBLIC INTOXICATION.

PUBLIC ENEMY. A notorious offender against the criminal laws who is still **at large** (definition 2).

PUBLIC INTOXICATION. The offense of being in a public place while intoxicated through consumption of **alcohol** or intake of a **controlled substance** or **drug**. Public intoxication resulting from alcohol, or **public drunkenness**, has been decriminalized in many jurisdictions. The behavior or condition is no longer a penal code violation, but is usually treated as a health problem. In other jurisdictions, the statutes explicitly give law enforcement personnel discretion to treat these cases as health matters or **crimes**.

Where a person who is publicly intoxicated performs acts that cause a disturbance, he or she may be charged with **disorderly conduct**. Operation of a motor vehicle while intoxicated is usually a separate statutory offense. *See*: DRIVING UNDER THE INFLUENCE OF ALCOHOL. See INTOXICATION for a list of related terms.

PUBLIC LAW. The area of law concerned with the organization of the government, the relations between the government and its citizens, the powers, capacities, rights, and duties of government officials, and the relations between political entities.

PUBLIC NUISANCE. A NUISANCE that affects the **public** in general, a whole community or neighborhood, or an indefinite number of people, as opposed to a nuisance that affects one or a small number of particular persons. *Also called*: **common nuisance**. *See*: PRIVATE NUISANCE.

PUBLIC OFFICE. A position in public employment requiring the exercise of some portion of the sovereign power, whether great or small. The Supreme Court of Iowa said: "[F]ive essential elements are required by most courts to make a public employment a public office. They are : (1) The position must be created by the constitution or legislature. (2) A portion of the sovereign power of government must be delegated to that position. (3) The duties and powers must be defined, directly or impliedly, by the legislature or through legislative authority. (4) The duties must be performed independently and without control of a superior power other than the law. (5) The position must have some permanency and continuity, and not be only temporary and occasional." *State v. Taylor*, 144 N.W.2d 289, 292 (Iowa, 1966).

Pp

PUBLIC PEACE. Same as PEACE.

PUBLIC POLICY. Same as POLICY OF THE LAW.

PUBLIC PROSECUTOR. Same as PROSECUTOR (definition 1).

PUBLIC SAFETY DEPARTMENT. An agency organized at the state or local level of government incorporating at a minimum various law enforcement and emergency service functions. A local public safety agency may bring under one central administration functions otherwise assigned to separate police, sheriff's, fire, and county communications departments. The administrative scope of state-level agencies of this type may include **state police** and **state highway patrol** units, law enforcement support services, fire control units, road safety units, and **correctional agency** functions.

PUBLIC SERVANT. Section 240.0 (7) of the **Model Penal Code** defines public servant as "any officer or employee of government, including legislators and judges, and any person participating as juror, advisor, consultant or otherwise, in performing a governmental function; but the term does not include witnesses."

PUBLIC TRIAL. A TRIAL that is open to the view, knowledge, or judgment of the **public** or in a location readily accessible and open to the attendance of the general public or those who may be properly admitted. The Sixth Amendment to the U.S. Constitution guarantees that "[i]n all criminal **prosecutions**, the **accused** shall enjoy the right to a speedy and public trial." This guarantee benefits the accused in that the public may observe that he or she is dealt with fairly and the **judicial officers**, **attorneys**, and other criminal justice personnel are closely scrutinized and made more keenly aware of their responsibilities. See TRIAL for a list of related terms.

PUBLIC VERDICT. A VERDICT delivered by the **jury** in open **court**. See VERDICT for a list of related terms.

PUBLIC WRONGS. Offenses that affect the whole community; **crimes**.

PUBLISH. **1.** To make known to the public or to people in general; to formally announce. **2.** To make known or communicate defamatory matter (see **defamation**) to one or more persons other than the person being defamed.

PUNISH. To subject someone to a **penalty** for committing an offense.

PUNISHMENT. Same as PENALTY.

PUNITIVE. Relating to, involving, or inflicting a **penalty** or **punishment**.

PURGE. **1.** To wipe out, completely remove, or obliterate **arrest**, **criminal**, or **juvenile** record information from a given records system. Purge differs from **seal** in that sealing only transfers information from routinely available access to greatly restricted access. *Example*: He demanded that the record of his arrest be purged from the police files. See CANCEL for a list of related terms. **2.** To exonerate; to clear from **guilt** or **accusation**.

PURLOIN. To commit theft; to steal.

PURPORT. **n.** The substance or meaning as it appears on the face; the apparent import. *See*: TENOR.

PURPORT. **v.** To convey to the mind; to give the impression or have the appearance of being; to profess outwardly; to claim.

PURPORTED. Alleged; professed; reputed; rumored.

PURPOSE. Intention; aim; end; goal; object. *Example*: What is the purpose of the law?

PURPOSELY. Intentionally; deliberately; designedly. See CULPABILITY for the **Model Penal Code** definition of purposely.

PURSUANT. In accordance with; proceeding in conformity to.

PURSUE. **1.** To follow with the intent to overtake or catch; to chase. **2.** To follow the course of. **3.** To strive to gain or accomplish. **4.** To proceed in accordance or compliance with a plan or method. **5.** To carry on; to engage in; to practice.

PURSUIT. The act or process of pursuing. *See*: PURSUE.

PURSUIT OF HAPPINESS. An inherent, natural, and inviolable right protected by governments through its incorporation into various constitutions. The term pursuit of happiness is a comprehensive, general term that includes an aggregation of many particular rights. Among the rights included within the term pursuit of happiness are personal freedom, exemption from oppression or invidious discrimination, liberty of conscience, enjoyment of domestic relations, acquisition and use of private property, and pursuit of any lawful business or occupation in a manner not inconsistent with the equal rights of others. The right to the pursuit of happiness is not an absolute right but is subject to governmental restriction under the **police power** for the promotion of the general welfare.

PURVIEW. **1.** The body of a **statute** following directly after the preamble and beginning with the words "Be it enacted," or words of like import. **2.** The full scope or range of application or meaning of any statute, document, book, or subject. *Example*: Does his conduct fall within the purview of the statute? See STATUTE for a list of related terms.

PUTATIVE. Commonly thought or regarded; supposed; reputed. A putative father is the person alleged to be the father of an illegitimate child.

QUA. *Latin.* As; in the character or capacity of.

QUAERE. Same as QUERY.

QUALIFICATION. **1.** The act, process, or result of qualifying. *See*: QUALIFY. **2.** The state of being qualified. **3.** That which is needed to qualify. *Example*: The qualifications for the job are as follows. **4.** A limitation; a modification; a restriction.

QUALIFY. **1.** To make legally suitable or capable. *Example*: The defense attorney was unable to qualify his expert witness. **2.** To limit; to modify; to restrict. *Example*: Let me qualify my last statement.

QUARE. *Latin.* "Wherefore"; for what cause or reason.

QUASH. To annul; to make void; to set aside; to throw out; to put an end to.

QUASI. *Latin.* "As if"; like; resembling; almost; somewhat. The term quasi is often used in combination with other words to indicate something that is sufficiently similar to another thing for certain purposes, but is not the same as or equivalent to that thing. *See*: QUASI-CRIME for example.

QUASI-CRIME. An offense against the public that is like a **crime**, but is not declared to be a crime, and that is dealt with in a **civil action** for **forfeiture** or other penalty rather than a **criminal action**. See CRIME for a list of related terms.

QUASI-JUDICIAL. Like or almost JUDICIAL. The term quasi-judicial is usually applied to a nonjudicial person or body, such as an administrative agency, that performs **judicial** functions such as investigating facts, examining witnesses, and determining rights and obligations.

QUERY. **n.** A question; an inquiry; a doubt. **v.** To ask; to inquire; to question. *Example*: Query, whether a seven-year-old is capable of murder. *Also spelled*: **quaere**.

QUESTION. A subject of inquiry, investigation or controversy; an unsettled issue; a problem.

QUESTIONED DOCUMENT. A paper or any other surface on which appears handwriting, typewriting, printing, or other communicative symbols, whose genuineness is in dispute. The dispute may involve authorship or possible alterations to or erasures of the document. A document will not be admissible in court unless its genuineness has been established.

QUESTIONED SPECIMEN. *See*: KNOWN SPECIMEN.

QUESTION OF FACT. A disputed factual issue that is traditionally decided by the **jury** or the **judge** as **fact-finder** in a **nonjury trial**. See FACT for a list of related terms.

QUESTION OF LAW. A disputed legal issue that is traditionally decided by the **judge**, because it involves the application or interpretation of the **law** (definition 5).

QUI. *Latin.* "Who; he (or she) who."

QUICK CHILD. An unborn child that has developed to the stage that it moves within the mother's womb.

QUID PRO QUO. *Latin.* "Something for something"; one thing in exchange for another. *Example*: The reduction in the charge was the quid pro quo for the defendant's plea of guilty.

QUOD VIDE. *Latin.* "Which see." Usually abbreviated q.v., the term quod vide is used to refer a reader to another named part of the book or document, or to another named source of information outside the book or document, for further information.

QUORUM. The number of members of a body required to be present for the proper or valid transaction of business.

QUOTATION. **1.** That which is **quoted**. **2.** The act of quoting.

QUOTE. To repeat or copy the exact words of another from a book, document, speech, etc., usually with an acknowledgment of the source. Quote differs from **cite** in that cite does not require the use of exact words, but allows for paraphrasing the source. See ADDRESS for a list of related terms.

QUO WARRANTO. *Latin.* "By what authority." A **writ** to determine the right of a **court**, a corporation, an official, or some other person or entity to use or exercise an office, franchise, or power and to prevent the continuing use or exercise of an authority unlawfully asserted. In modern practice, quo warranto proceedings are usually brought by a **prosecuting attorney** by means of an **information** in the nature of quo warranto. The information in the nature of quo warranto was originally primarily criminal in nature but is now substantially a civil proceeding. See ARREST WARRANT for a list of related terms.

Q.V. Abbreviation for QUOD VIDE.

RACKET. An organized illegal commercial scheme or activity such as **gambling**, bootlegging, or obtaining money from legitimate businessmen by **fraud**, **extortion**, or **threat** of violence. *See*: RACKETEER INFLUENCED AND CORRUPT ORGANIZATIONS ACT.

RACKETEER. A person engaged in a RACKET. *See*: RACKETEER INFLUENCED AND CORRUPT ORGANIZATIONS ACT.

RACKETEER INFLUENCED AND CORRUPT ORGANIZATIONS ACT. The Racketeer Influenced and Corrupt Organizations Act (RICO), 18 U.S.C. §§1961-1968, was enacted in 1970 to allow federal law enforcement officials to target the infiltration of **organized crime** into the regular business marketplace. To win a RICO case, the plaintiff must prove that there is an "ongoing criminal enterprise" and that the defendants have conspired to participate in it. Over time, courts have typically defined a "racketeer" under RICO to be any person or business that commits two connected **felonies** within ten years. The felonies can range from violent crimes such as **murder** and **robbery** to **confidence games** involving **fraud**, or many other forms of using the mail or communications for illegal purposes. Criminal RICO penalties include up to twenty years in prison, $25,000 in fines, and/or the forfeiture of any illegally obtained gains.

In recent years, the often previously overlooked civil provisions of RICO have been increasingly employed both by the government and by private individuals to obtain **forfeiture** of private property. Under the civil sanctions of RICO, private individuals can prosecute and recover triple their actual damages from business competitors, investment swindlers, or their employers or unions in contract disputes.

RAFFLE. A LOTTERY in which a number of persons buy equal shares in a prize and the winner is determined by chance. See GAMBLING for a list of related terms.

RAISE. To produce; to put forward; to bring up. *Example*: Did you raise that issue in your brief?

RANCH. *See*: JUVENILE FACILITY.

RANSACK. To **search** thoroughly, often with the implication of careless haste, improper motive, or lack of regard for the rights of others.

RANSOM. **1.** The **release** of a captured person or property in return for payment of a specified price. **2.** The price paid or demanded for the release of a captured person or property.

RAPE. Unlawful **sexual intercourse** with a female, by **force** or without legal or factual **consent**. Historically, rape meant only **forcible rape**, but it is currently used in statutes as a general term for forcible rape together with other sexual acts codified as criminal because of the victim's inability to give legal consent because underage (see **statutory rape**), or because of mental or physical defect, unconsciousness, or **intoxication** (see **rape without force or consent**). Some jurisdictions include both homosexual and heterosexual conduct under the definition of rape and define rape as the carnal knowledge of another person of the same or opposite sex, by force or threat of force. This offense between males is more commonly punished as **sodomy**. See SEX OFFENSES for a list of related terms.

RAPE WITHOUT FORCE OR CONSENT. **Sexual intercourse** without **force** or **threat** of force with a female legally of the age of consent, but who is unconscious, or whose ability to judge or control her conduct is inherently impaired by mental defect, or impaired by intoxicating substances. See SEX OFFENSES for a list of related terms.

RAPINE. The **felonious** taking of the personal property of another, openly, by **force**, and against the other's will.

RATIFICATION. The act, process, or result of ratifying. *See*: RATIFY.

RATIFY. To make valid or legal by formal official approval.

RATIO DECIDENDI. *Latin.* "Reason for deciding." Same as RATIONALE.

RATION. To give out scarce items equitably to members of a group by a method that limits individual portions. See ALLOCATE for a list of related terms.

RATIONAL DOUBT. Same as REASONABLE DOUBT.

RATIONALE. The fundamental reason or basic principle underlying a judicial **opinion**, **decision**, or **action**. The rationale creates binding **precedent**, as compared to **dictum**, which is a general argument or observation unnecessary to the decision and which has no force as precedent. *Also called*: **ratio decidendi**.

RAVISH. **1.** To RAPE. **2.** To forcibly seize and carry away.

RE. *Latin.* Concerning; in reference to; in the case of. *See*: IN RE.

REAL. **1.** Actual, true, authentic, genuine, existing in fact, or tangible, as distinguished from apparent, ostensible, imaginary, artificial, or fictitious. **2.** Relating to the land and things on the land, as opposed to personal property.

REAL ESTATE. Same as REAL PROPERTY.

REAL EVIDENCE. **Evidence** consisting of tangible items or objects which can be viewed or inspected, offered as **proof** in a **trial**, as distinguished from oral **testimony**. When objects are identified and associated with a **crime**, they constitute proof of facts that bear upon the matters in issue. For example, a shoe identified as belonging to the defendant that is shown to match a footprint found at the scene of a crime is real evidence that the defendant was at the place where the crime was committed. Other examples of real evidence are weapons, wounds, documents, fingerprints, hairs, maps, photographs, charts, models, X rays, etc. *Also called*: **demonstrative evidence**; **physical evidence**; **tangible evidence**. See EVIDENCE for a list of related terms.

REALIZE. **1.** To understand or comprehend completely or clearly. *Example*: She realized her mistake. **2.** To obtain; to achieve. *Example*: They realized heavy profits from their illegal activity.

REAL PARTY IN INTEREST. A **party** who stands to actually gain or lose something substantial from being a part of a **case**, as opposed to a party with only a nominal, formal, or technical interest. *See*: NOMINAL PARTY.

REAL PROPERTY. Land, whatever is erected on, attached to, or growing on it, and rights associated with it. *See*: PERSONAL PROPERTY.

REALTY. Same as REAL PROPERTY.

REASONABLE. **1.** Exhibiting sound judgment or common sense; sensible; prudent. **2.** Fair; moderate; appropriate; suitable. *Example*: An officer may use reasonable force to arrest an offender.

REASONABLE CARE. Same as ORDINARY CARE.

REASONABLE CAUSE. Same as PROBABLE CAUSE, but probable cause is the preferred term.

REASONABLE DOUBT. *See*: BEYOND A REASONABLE DOUBT. *Also called*: **rational doubt**.

REASONABLE EXPECTATION OF PRIVACY. *See*: RIGHT OF PRIVACY.

REASONABLE PERSON. A hypothetical person who exercises average or sufficient care, skill, or judgment in conducting his or her affairs, protecting self-interest, and the interests of others. The reasonable person is used as a comparative interest, and the interests of others. The reasonable person is used as a comparative standard in the law for determining liability and in various legal tests. *Example*: "[A] person has been 'seized' within the meaning of the Fourth Amendment only if, in view of all the circumstances surrounding the incident, a reasonable person would have believed that he was not free to leave." *U.S. v. Mendenhall*, 446 U.S. 544, 554, 100 S.Ct. 1870, 1877, 64 L.Ed.2d 497, 509 (1980). *Also called*: **ordinary prudent person**; **reasonably prudent person**.

REASONABLY PRUDENT PERSON.   Same as REASONABLE PERSON.

REBUT.   To refute or disprove by offering opposing **evidence** or **arguments**.

REBUTTABLE PRESUMPTION.   A PRESUMPTION that may be accepted and acted upon until refuted by opposing **evidence** or **arguments**. *Example*: In order to refute the rebuttable presumption of innocence in favor of the accused, the prosecution must establish beyond a reasonable doubt that the accused committed the crime with which he or she is charged. *Also called*: **disputable presumption**. See PRESUMPTION for a list of related terms.

REBUTTAL.   **1.** Same as REBUTTAL EVIDENCE. **2.** The stage of a trial at which rebuttal evidence may be introduced.

REBUTTAL EVIDENCE.   **Evidence** that refutes or contradicts evidence given by an **adverse** party or witness or that counteracts or opposes a **presumption of fact**. See EVIDENCE for a list of related terms.

RECALL A JUDGMENT.   To revoke or vacate a **judgment** because of **errors** of **fact**. *See*: ERROR; JUDGMENT; REVERSE.

RECANT.   To formally withdraw or disavow something that has been openly professed. *Example*: The witness recanted his testimony. *See*: ABJURE; RE-NOUNCE.

RECEIVER.   A person who knowingly obtains possession of stolen property.

RECEIVING.   Section 223.6 (1) of the **Model Penal Code** defines receiving as "acquiring possession, control or title, or lending on the security of property."

RECEIVING STOLEN PROPERTY.   The crime of receiving property with knowl-edge that it was unlawfully obtained and with the **intent** to deprive the rightful owner of the property. This crime is defined in different ways by different state statutes. See ABSTRACTION for a list of related terms.

RECESS.   A short time interval during which a **court** or **legislative session** suspends business, but does not **adjourn**.

RECIDIVISM.   The repetition of criminal behavior; habitual criminality. *See*: RECIDIVIST.

RECIDIVIST.   1. A person who has been **convicted** of one or more **crimes**, and who is alleged or found to have subsequently committed another crime or series of crimes. **2.** A HABITUAL CRIMINAL. **3.** In **corrections** usage, the term recidivist generally refers to an offender who has been released on **probation, parole**, or other **conditional release** and who is alleged or found to have committed one or more additional crimes while in that status, usually within a specified period of time after release. The National Advisory Commission on Criminal Justice Standards and Goals recommended a standard definition of recidivism in its volume *Corrections* (1973): "Recidivism is measured by (1) criminal acts that resulted in conviction by a court, when committed by individuals who are under correctional supervision or who have been released from correctional supervision within the previous three years, and by (2) technical violations of probation or parole in which a sentencing or paroling authority took action that resulted in an adverse change in the offender's legal status." The exact criteria used in identifying recidivists may vary between jurisdictions, between agencies, and according to the purpose of particular statistical presentations.

RECIPROCITY.   A relationship between persons, states, or nations in which favors or privileges granted by one are returned by the other or others.

RECITAL.   1. A formal statement in a legal **document** that explains the reasons or facts upon which a transaction is based or, in **pleading**, introduces a positive **allegation**. A recital usually begins with the word "whereas." **2.** A particularized account.

RECITE.   1. To give a detailed account, usually from memory, with a description or enumeration of particulars. **2.** To state formally in a legal document. See ADDRESS for a list of related terms.

RECKLESS.   1. Carelessly indifferent to consequences or to the rights or safety of others, although no harm is intended. *Example*: He was convicted of reckless driving. See CULPABILITY for the **Model Penal Code** definition of recklessly.

RECOGNIZANCE.   A PRETRIAL RELEASE in which an **accused** person enters into an obligation before a proper **judicial officer** or a **law enforcement officer** and secures his or her own **release** from custody by agreeing to appear in **court** when required. Under federal law, in determining whether to allow release on an accused's own recognizance, the court must "take into account the nature and circumstances of the offense charged, the **weight of the evidence** against the accused, the accused's family ties, employment, financial resources, character and mental condition, the length of his residence in the community, his record of **convictions**, and his record of appearance at court proceedings or of flight to avoid **prosecution** or failure to **appear** at court proceedings." Release on recognizance differs from release on unsecured bail (see **release on bail**) in that release on recognizance usually requires no payment by the accused and no **sureties** or promised sums of money or property. If, however, the person fails to appear in court as agreed, he or she may be subject to **arrest** or may be required to pay to the court a specified amount of money. In jurisdictions where release on recognizance is not provided for, release on unsecured bail may fulfill a similar function. Release on recognizance is often abbreviated R.O.R. *Also called*: **personal recognizance**; **release on own recognizance**; **release on recognizance**.

RECOGNIZE.   **1.** To enter into a RECOGNIZANCE. **2.** To acknowledge. See BAIL and RELEASE for a list of related terms.

RECORD.   n. **1.** An officially written account of an act or transaction designed to be preserved as **evidence** of the act or transaction. **n. 2.** An officially written account of judicial or legislative proceedings designed to be preserved as evidence of those proceedings. The record of a court case includes the history of actions taken, papers filed, rulings made, and all written opinions. As stated by the court in *State v. Willis*, 193 So.2d 775, 776 (La. 1967), the record in a criminal case "includes the **caption** in the case, a statement of the time and place of holding court, the **indictment** or **information** with the endorsement, the **arraignment**, the **plea** of the **accused**, mention of the impaneling of the **jury**, **verdict**, and **judgment** of the court." **n. 3.** The documents or volumes containing the accounts in definitions 1 and 2. *See*: ARREST RECORD; CRIMINAL RECORD.

RECORD.   v. To set down in writing or other permanent manner in order to preserve as evidence.

RECORD NOTICE.   Same as IMPLIED NOTICE.

RECOUNT.   To give a detailed account with a description or enumeration of particulars. See ADDRESS for a list of related terms.

RECROSS-EXAMINATION.   A **cross-examination** of a witness after the prosecuting attorney has conducted a **redirect examination**. See EXAMINATION and WITNESS for lists of related terms.

RECTIFY.   To correct; to remedy; to make or set right.

RECUSAL.   **1.** Refusal; rejection; objection; exception. **2.** The process by which a **judge** is disqualified from hearing a case because of alleged interest, **prejudice**, or other incompetency. *Also called*: **recusation**.

RECUSATION. Same as RECUSAL.

REDIRECT EXAMINATION. A reexamination of a witness by a **prosecuting attorney** in order to **rehabilitate** him or her after **cross-examination**. *Also called*: **re-examination**. See EXAMINATION and WITNESS for lists of related terms.

REDRESS. **v.** To correct; to remedy; to rectify. **n.** Satisfaction or restitution for harm or injury.

REDUCED CHARGE. A new **charge**, which is entered by prosecutorial action during the course of proceedings, and which replaces the original greater charge. The reduced charge is then the only one to be considered by **judge** or **jury**. The reduced charge need not be an **included offense** with respect to the original charge. It can be an offense that has one or more elements (see **element of a crime**) that are not elements of the more serious offense.

REDUCED SENTENCE. A **sentence** to **confinement** of which the time duration has been shortened by **judicial** action, or a **fine** or other material penalty that has been reduced by judicial action. Reduction of sentence can occur at many points in the criminal justice process, beginning with the **sentencing disposition** after **conviction**. See CLEMENCY and SENTENCE for lists of related terms.

REDUCTIBLE FELONY. A FELONY for which, upon **conviction**, a **jury** may recommend punishment as if it were a **misdemeanor**.

REDUCTIO AD ABSURDUM. *Latin.* The method of disproving an argument or proposition by showing that it leads to an absurd result.

REDUNDANT. Superfluous; exceeding what is necessary.

REEXAMINATION. Same as REDIRECT EXAMINATION.

REFER. To present supporting **evidence** for an argument or discussion by directing one to another source for help or information. Refer is indefinite as to the extent or specificity of the supporting evidence. See ADDRESS for a list of related terms.

REFEREE. A **judicial officer** to whom an action is referred by a court for the purpose of taking testimony, resolving factual disputes, and reporting the findings to the court.

REFERENCE STATUTE. A **statute** that refers to and adopts, wholly or partially, a preexisting statute. See STATUTE for a list of related terms.

REFERRAL TO INTAKE. In juvenile proceedings, a written request by a **law enforcement agency**, parent, or other agency or person, that an **intake unit** or officer take appropriate action concerning a **juvenile** alleged to have committed a **delinquent act** or **status offense**, or alleged to be **dependent**. See JUVENILE for a list of related terms.

REFRESHING MEMORY. Same as PRESENT RECOLLECTION REFRESHED.

REFUSE. To decline; to reject.

REGULAR. **1.** Customary; usual; normal. **2.** Conforming to law, principle, or ordinary practice.

REGULATE. To control, direct, or govern according to rules.

REGULATION. A principle, standard, or rule prescribed by a **court** or other proper authority for the control or management of an organization or system, sometimes having the force of law. *Example*: The Fisheries and Wildlife Department promulgated new hunting regulations. See ACT for a list of related terms.

REHABILITATE. **1.** To restore the **credibility** of a **witness** after it has been destroyed or put in question by the opposing party through **impeachment** or **cross-examination**. See WITNESS for a list of related terms. **2.** To restore a **criminal** or **delinquent** to a productive life through education, training, therapy, or other method.

REHEARING. A second or new consideration of an **issue** or issues in a case by the same **court** or body.

REINSTATE. To restore a person or thing to a previous condition or position. *Example*: The court has the power to reinstate a dismissed case.

RELATE. To give a detailed or orderly account of something one has experienced or witnessed. See ADDRESS for a list of related terms.

RELATOR. *See*: EX RELATIONE.

RELEASE. **1.** To set free or liberate from **confinement**, **restraint**, bondage, or obligation. *See*: ABSENT WITHOUT LEAVE; ACQUIT; AGGREGATE MAXIMUM RELEASE DATE; BAIL; BALANCE OF SENTENCE SUSPENDED; COMMITMENT; CONDITIONAL RELEASE; DETENTION; DISCHARGE; ELIGIBLE FOR PAROLE; EXPIRATION OF SENTENCE; FURLOUGH; MANDATORY RELEASE DATE; MANDATORY SUPERVISED RELEASE; PAROLE; PRETRIAL RELEASE; RANSOM; RECOGNIZANCE; RELEASE AFTER INSANITY COMMITMENT; RELEASE ON BAIL; RELEASE TO PAROLE; RELEASE TO THIRD PARTY; SENTENCE; SENTENCED TO TIME SERVED; STREET TIME; TEMPORARY RELEASE; TIME SERVED; UNCON-

DITIONAL RELEASE; WORK RELEASE PROGRAM. **2.** To give up or relinquish a right or claim, especially to another person.

RELEASE AFTER INSANITY COMMITMENT. A person committed to a mental institution after being found **not guilty by reason of insanity** may be later **released**. The decision to release is made by a **court**, a prison administrator, or an administrative agency. The determination whether a person should be released depends on the person's sanity and dangerousness to self or others. Definitions and interpretations of sanity and dangerousness differ from jurisdiction to jurisdiction. See RELEASE for a list of related terms.

RELEASE ON BAIL. A PRETRIAL RELEASE in which reappearance is guaranteed by a pledge that money or property will be forfeited upon nonappearance, with or without payment of a bondsman's fee or deposit of some or all of the pledge with the court. **Bail** is usually secured not by the deposit of the total amount to be forfeited, but by a percentage thereof. When the accused is released on a promise to pay a certain sum, but where no money or property at all is required to be deposited in advance, this is spoken of as release on **unsecured bail** or **unsecured bond**. Release on unsecured bail differs from release on **recognizance** in that release on recognizance does not require the security of even a promised sum of money or property. In jurisdictions where release on recognizance is not provided for, release on unsecured bail may fulfill a similar function. See BAIL and RELEASE for lists of related terms.

RELEASE ON OWN RECOGNIZANCE. *See*: RECOGNIZANCE.

RELEASE ON RECOGNIZANCE. *See*: RECOGNIZANCE.

RELEASE TO PAROLE. A **release** from prison by discretionary action of a **paroling authority**, conditional upon the parolee's fulfillment of specified conditions of behavior. Release to parole and **mandatory supervised release** are the two major classes of **conditional releases** from prison. The length of time of **parole** is usually determined by the length of the **sentence** less the length of time served in a confinement facility. The original sentence can, of course, be reduced by executive **clemency**, **good time** deductions for good behavior in prison or on parole, or other means. Violation of the conditions of parole (see **parole violation**) can result in **parole revocation**. *Also called*: **grant of parole**; **entry to parole**. See PAROLE and RELEASE for lists of related terms.

RELEASE TO THIRD PARTY. A PRETRIAL RELEASE without financial guarantee in which a person or organization other than the **defendant** assumes responsibility for returning the defendant to **court** when required. Release to third party is sometimes used in conjunction with some form of **bail**. See BAIL and RELEASE for lists of related terms.

RELEVANT EVIDENCE. Evidence that tends to prove or disprove the truth of a **fact** or matter in issue. Relevant evidence has a tendency to make the existence of any fact that is of consequence to the determination of the action more probable than it would be without the evidence. While evidence offered only to prove a merely **collateral fact** is not generally considered relevant, any evidence that tends to either add probability or improbability to a **material** fact is relevant. *Example*: Evidence must be relevant in order to be admissible. See EVIDENCE for a list of related terms.

RELIABLE. Trustworthy; worthy of confidence; dependable.

RELIEF. The remedy or assistance that a **party** seeks from a **court** in a lawsuit.

RELIGIOUS LIBERTY. Same as FREEDOM OF RELIGION.

RELINQUISH. To abandon; to surrender; to give up; to renounce.

Rr

REMAND. **1.** To send a **case** back to a lower **court** from which it was **appealed** with instructions as to what further action should be taken. When an **appellate court** reverses a **judgment** of a lower court, it will often remand the case to the lower court for further proceedings not inconsistent with the appellate court's opinion. **2.** To send a **prisoner** or **accused** person back into **custody** to await further proceedings after a **preliminary hearing**.

REMEDY. The means of enforcing a right or of preventing or redressing a wrong.

REMISSION OF FINE OR FORFEITURE. The forgiving of or release from payment of a **fine** or **forfeiture**. See CLEMENCY for a list of related terms.

REMIT. **1.** To send; to transmit. **2.** To refrain from enforcing or inflicting a punishment; to cancel a punishment. **3.** To REMAND (definition 1.).

REMOTE. **1.** Far off; distant; removed. **2.** Distant in relationship or connection. **3.** Slight; faint; inconsiderable; barely discernible.

REMOVAL. **1.** The transfer of a person or thing from one place to another. **2.** The transfer of a **case** from one **court** to another. In this sense, removal generally refers to a transfer from a court in one **jurisdiction** to a court in another or a transfer from a state court to a federal court.

RENDER. **1.** To deliver officially; to pronounce; to formally announce. *Example:* The court is about to render judgment. **2.** To give up; to yield; to surrender.

RENDITION. A procedure, less cumbersome than that of **extradition**, for effectuating the return of a person who has been **accused** of **crime** and **released** from **custody**

prior to final judgment by a court of one state (**demanding state**) and whose presence in another state (**asylum state**) constitutes a violation of the terms of release.

RENDITION OF JUDGMENT. The pronouncement or declaration of the court's JUDGMENT in a particular case. *Also called*: **pronouncement of judgment**. See JUDGMENT for a list of related terms.

RENDITION WARRANT. Same as EXTRADITION WARRANT.

RENEW. To revive; to begin again; to make or do again; to reestablish.

RENOUNCE. **v.** To disclaim; to disown; to repudiate; to reject; to abandon. **n.** RENUNCIATION. *See*: ABJURE; RECANT.

RENUNCIATION. The voluntary and complete abandonment of the purpose to commit a **crime** before its commission or an act otherwise preventing the commission of the crime. Section 5.01 (4) of the **Model Penal Code** recognizes renunciation of criminal purpose as an **affirmative defense**. Under that section of the code "renunciation of criminal purpose is not voluntary if it is motivated, in whole or in part, by circumstances, not present or apparent at the inception of the actor's course of conduct, that increase the probability of detection or apprehension or that make more difficult the accomplishment of the criminal purpose. Renunciation is not complete if it is motivated by a decision to postpone the criminal conduct until a more advantageous time or to transfer the criminal effort to another but similar objective or victim."

REPARATION. Generally, compensation for an injury; redress for a wrong done. In the criminal law context, reparation means reimbursement to **victims** of **crime** for actual loss flowing from the charged offense or from related misconduct. In *State v. Stalheim*, 552 P.2d 829, 832 (Or. 1976), the court construed reparation as "encompassing only reimbursement for the victim's liquidated or easily measurable damages resulting from the charged offense. This construct would embrace medical expenses, wages actually (not prospectively) lost, and reimbursement for easily measurable property damage." *See*: RESTITUTION.

REPAROLE. A **release to parole** occurring after a return to **prison** from an earlier release to parole, on the same **sentence** to **confinement**. See PAROLE for a list of related terms.

REPEAL. To **revoke** or **annul** formally or officially. A legislative act expressly repeals another act when it does so by direct language. A legislative act impliedly repeals another act when the new act contains provisions so contrary to or irreconcilable with the old act that only one can remain in effect. *See*: AMEND; DEROGATION.

REPEATER. A person who has been **convicted** of a **crime** more than once.

REPEAT OFFENDER. Same as HABITUAL CRIMINAL.

REPORT. **v.** To give a detailed account of what has been learned from observation or investigation. See ADDRESS for a list of related terms. **n. 1.** An official or formal account of facts or proceedings that is written or announced. **n. 2.** Same as RE- PORTER (definition 2).

REPORTER. **1.** *See*: COURT REPORTER. **2.** A published collection of the de- cisions of a court or group of courts. *Example*: Decisions of the Wyoming Supreme Court are published in the *Pacific Reporter*.

REPOSITORY. A place where things may be put for safekeeping or preservation.

Rr

REPRESENT. **1.** To state or set forth with a view toward influencing conduct or judgment. *Example*: He represented himself to be a police officer. **2.** To act as a person's lawyer or agent. *Example*: She was represented by the public defender.

REPRESENTATION. The act of representing (see **represent**) or the thing repre- sented.

REPRIEVE. An **executive** act temporarily **suspending** the **execution** of a **sentence**, usually a death sentence. A reprieve differs from other suspensions of sentence (see **suspended sentence**) not only in that it almost always applies to the temporary withdrawing of a death sentence, but also in that it is usually an act of **clemency** intended to provide the prisoner with time to secure amelioration of the sentence. *Example*: The Governor granted the condemned prisoner a reprieve. See CLEMENCY for a list of related terms.

REPRIMAND. A formal or official rebuke or censure.

REPUDIATE. To reject; to refuse; to disown.

REPUGNANT. **1.** Distasteful; objectionable; offensive. **2.** Contradictory; inconsis- tent; incompatible. Two parts of a **pleading**, **statute**, or other **document** that are inconsistent with each other are said to be repugnant.

REPUTABLE. Honorable; respectable.

REPUTATION. The qualities and traits that are attributed to a person by others in the community; the opinion of others in the community about a person's CHAR- ACTER.

REPUTED.   Generally supposed or considered. *Example*: He is reputed to be involved in organized crime.

REQUEST.   To ask for.

REQUIRE.   To order; to compel; to command; to demand.

REQUISITION.   **1.** A formal written request for something needed. **2.** A formal demand by the governor of one state (**demanding state**) upon the governor of another state (**asylum state**) for the surrender of a **fugitive from justice**. *See*: EXTRADITION.

RES.   *Latin.* "A thing; an object."

RES ADJUDICATA.   Same as RES JUDICATA.

RESCIND.   To void, cancel, or annul something previously granted or agreed to.

RESCISSION.   **1.** The act or result of rescinding. *See*: RESCIND. **2.** The cancellation of a prison **inmate's** tentative **parole** date.

RESCUE.   The **common-law crime** of knowingly and forcibly freeing another from legal **confinement** or **custody**. Rescue is also a **statutory** crime in some jurisdictions. *See*: ESCAPE.

RES DERELICTA.   *Latin.* Abandoned property.

RESERVE.   To hold back, delay, or save for future use or consideration. *Example*: The court reserved decision on that point until the end of the trial.

RES GESTAE.   *Latin.* "Things done." Everything said or done as part of an event or **transaction**. "Acts or events are a proof of the res gestae if they occur in the same transaction as the **crime**, are substantially contemporaneous with the commission of the crime and are part of one continuous transaction in the accomplishment of a common design." *State v. Winton*, 657 S.W.2d 399, 401 (Mo.App. 1983). A res gestae declaration (also called a **verbal act**) is an impulsive or spontaneous statement made at the time of an event that relates to the event and in some manner explains or characterizes the event. Such a statement is considered to be an integral part of the event and is admissible as an exception to the **hearsay rule**. This exception to the hearsay rule "is broad and includes not only spontaneous utterances and declarations made before or after commission of crime, but also testimony of witnesses and police officers pertaining to what they heard or observed before, during or after commission of the crime, if the continuous chain of events is evident under the circumstances." *State v. Leason*, 477 So.2d 771, 777 (La.App. 1 Cir. 1985). Res gestae declarations are considered reliable because one who speaks before he or she has time to reflect or deliberate is considered likely to tell the truth. See HEARSAY RULE for a list of other exceptions.

RESIDE. To live or dwell in a place.

RESIDENCE. **1.** The place where one lives or dwells at a given time, without necessarily intending to make the place his or her **domicile**. **2.** The National Crime Survey defines residence as a separate living quarters that is occupied by a conventional household.

RESIDENT. **1.** A person who lives or dwells in a place. **2.** A person required by official action, or his or her own acceptance of placement, to reside in a public or private facility established for purposes of **confinement**, **supervision**, or care. In some jurisdictions, the term resident may be used as a synonym for **inmate** or **prisoner**. See ACCUSED for a list of related terms.

RESIDENTIAL COMMITMENT. A sentence of **commitment** to a RESIDENTIAL FACILITY for **adults**. A residential commitment is usually a type of **sentencing disposition**, but is occasionally a **disposition** made when adjudication is withheld in order that the defendant receive, for example, treatment for drug addiction. The disposition is usually combined with **probation** status. See COMMITMENT for a list of related terms.

RESIDENTIAL FACILITY. A **correctional facility** in which residents are required to reside at night, but from which residents are regularly permitted to depart, unaccompanied by any official, for the purpose of daily use of community resources such as schools or treatment programs, and seeking or holding employment. Residential facility includes facilities variously called **community facility**, **halfway house**, and **residential treatment center**. *See*: CONFINEMENT FACILITY.

RESIST. To actively or forcefully oppose.

RESISTING AN OFFICER. The offense of opposing or obstructing a **law enforcement officer** in the lawful discharge of his or her duties. This type of offense is variously named and defined in state statutes. Its elements often include the use of **force** in resistance, or behavior that requires the use of force by the officer to overcome it. The resistance need not be only on the part of one whose **arrest** is being attempted; anyone who interferes with the law enforcement officer's purpose can be charged. *See*: ASSAULT ON A LAW ENFORCEMENT OFFICER; RESISTING ARREST.

RESISTING ARREST. The offense of opposing or obstructing a **law enforcement officer** effecting one's **arrest**. In some jurisdictions, resisting arrest is an offense only if the arrest is lawful and a person may use **nondeadly force** to resist an unlawful arrest. *See*: ASSAULT ON A LAW ENFORCEMENT OFFICER; RESISTING AN OFFICER.

RES JUDICATA. *Latin.* "The matter has been decided." The doctrine that a final **judgment** by a **competent court** on a particular matter or **issue** is conclusive upon the parties in any subsequent litigation involving the same matter or issue. *Also spelled*: **res adjudicata**.

RES NOVA. *Latin.* "A new matter; a new case."

RESOLUTION. A formal statement of decision or expression of opinion adopted by vote of a legislature or other assembled body. A resolution does not have the enforceability of a **law**. *Example*: The legislature adopted a joint resolution censuring the senator.

RESORT. Someone or something turned to for relief; recourse. *Example:* The U.S. Supreme Court is the court of last resort in a criminal case.

RESPECTIVE. Relating to two or more persons or things considered individually. *Example*: The judge examined the respective records of the three defendants.

RESPITE. Same as REPRIEVE.

RESPOND. To reply; to answer.

RESPONDENT. Generally, the person or party who answers or responds in certain legal proceedings, including **appeals**, **motions**, and **petitions**. In criminal proceedings, the respondent to an appeal is usually the **prosecution**. See ACCUSED and APPEAL for lists of related terms.

RESPONSIBILITY. **1.** Duty; obligation. **2.** Accountability; answerability.

RESPONSIVE. Directly answering; constituting a complete answer. *Example*: A motion to dismiss is not a responsive pleading.

REST. To voluntarily terminate the introduction of **evidence**, except potentially in **rebuttal**. *Example*: The defense rests.

RESTITUTION. **1.** In a strict sense, the return "of a sum of money, an object, or the value of an object which a defendant wrongfully obtained in the course of committing the crime." *State v. Stalheim*, 552 P.2d 829, 832 (Or. 1976). Restitution implies the restoration of the status quo and putting the **victim** in as good a position as he or she would have been in if no **crime** had been committed. **2.** In a broader sense, restitution is a **court** requirement that an **alleged** or **convicted offender** pay money or provide services to the victim of the crime or provide services to the community. Besides being a condition of **probation**, restitution can be a requirement combined with a **commitment** to **prison** or **jail**, or with confinement followed by probation status. When restitution is a condition of probation, failure to comply can lead to reappearance in court and **probation revocation**. Although restitution can be viewed as a means of compensating a victim for loss, the term **victim compensation** is usually used to describe a governmentally administered program intended to provide at least a partial reimbursement of a victim's losses, and does not necessarily depend on the offender being identified or prosecuted. The terms may be used differently in different jurisdictions. *See*: REPARATION.

RESTRAIN. **v.** To restrict one's freedom of action; to hold one back; to deprive one of personal liberty. **n.** RESTRAINT.

RESTRAINING ORDER. An **order** granted upon the application of a **plaintiff**, without **notice** or **hearing**, forbidding a **defendant** from taking an action or threatened action until a hearing can be held to determine whether a temporary or permanent INJUNCTION should issue. A restraining order is always temporary and is often called a **temporary restraining order** or TRO.

RESTRICT. To set bounds on or around; to confine; to limit.

RESULT. A consequence; an effect; an outcome.

RETAIN. **1.** To continue to have, hold, or use. **2.** To hire a lawyer.

RETAINED COUNSEL. A **defense attorney** selected and compensated by the defendant or offender, or by other private persons. See ATTORNEY AT LAW for a list of related terms.

RETAINER. **1.** The contract between an **attorney** and client specifying the nature and cost of the services to be rendered. **2.** The fee paid to engage the services of an attorney.

RETIRE. Spoken of a **jury**, to depart or withdraw to deliberate on a **verdict**.

RETRACT. To take back; to withdraw; to disavow.

RETREAT. To withdraw or flee to a position of safety. In the law of **self-defense**, a person threatened with **bodily injury** who can safely retreat need not do so before using **nondeadly force**. Jurisdictions differ, however, on the extent to which **deadly force** may be used in self-defense. Some jurisdictions hold that a person need not retreat, even though a retreat may be accomplished safely, before using deadly force upon an assailant whom the person reasonably believes will kill or do serious bodily harm to the person. Other jurisdictions require a person to retreat, sometimes called **retreat to the wall**, before using deadly force, if the person can do so in complete safety.

RETREAT TO THE WALL. *See*: RETREAT.

RETRIAL. *See*: NEW TRIAL.

RETRO-. *Latin.* "Back; backward; behind." A prefix meaning back or backwards in space or time.

RETROACTIVE. Influencing or applying to matters that have occurred in the past. *Also called*: **retrospective**.

RETROACTIVE LAW. A **law** that gives different legal effect to rights, obligations, acts, transactions, or conditions that existed or occurred before the law came into effect. *Also called*: **retrospective law**. *See*: EX POST FACTO.

RETROSPECTIVE. Same as RETROACTIVE.

RETROSPECTIVE LAW. Same as RETROACTIVE LAW.

RETURN. The delivering back of a **writ, warrant**, or other document or **process**, by a **sheriff** or other **law enforcement officer**, after **serving** or **executing** it or attempting to do so, to the **court** from which it was issued. The return is usually accompanied by a **report** of the officer on the time and manner of execution of service or the failure to accomplish it. *Also called*: **return of process**. *See*: FALSE RETURN; NIHIL HABET.

RETURNABLE. Legally required to be returned. *See*: RETURN. *Example:* The search warrant was returnable on July 23.

RETURN DAY. The day indicated on a **writ, warrant**, or other document or **process**, on which the officer is required to make the RETURN.

RETURN OF PROCESS. Same as RETURN.

REVERSAL. The act, process, or result of **reversing**. *See*: REVERSE.

REVERSE. To overthrow, set aside, or revoke by a contrary **decision**, usually because of **errors** of **law**. An **appellate court** reverses a lower court's **decision** either by substituting its own decision or by **remanding** the case to the lower court with instructions for a **new trial**. *See*: ERROR; JUDGMENT; RECALL A JUDGMENT.

REVERSIBLE ERROR. A substantial ERROR made during lower **court** proceedings that is so prejudicial to the **appellant's** legal rights and obligations that the **appellate court** is required to REVERSE the judgment of the lower court. *Also called*: **fatal error**; **harmful error**; **prejudicial error**. See ERROR for a list of related terms.

REVIEW. A **judicial** reexamination of an action or determination in order to correct possible **errors**. *See*: JUDICIAL REVIEW.

REVISE. To amend; to change; to modify.

REVIVE. To restore the validity or effectiveness of; to renew.

REVOCABLE. Capable of being revoked. *See*: REVOKE.

REVOCATION. *See*: PAROLE REVOCATION; PROBATION REVOCATION.

REVOCATION HEARING. An administrative or judicial hearing on whether a person's **probation** or **parole** should be revoked. A revocation hearing occurs as a response to a **probation violation** or **parole violation**. Not all probation or parole violations necessarily result in revocation hearings, and not all revocation hearings necessarily result in revocation. See HEARING, PAROLE, and PROBATION for lists of related terms.

REVOKE. To void or annul by taking back or recalling; to cancel; to rescind.

REVOLVER. A **handgun** with a cylinder of several chambers, each of which is brought successfully into line with the barrel and discharged with the same hammer.

REWARD. A payment promised to the public in general or to a particular class of persons to induce the single performance of a special service (such as the apprehension of a criminal or the recovery of stolen property). Only the single person who performs the requested act is entitled to the promised compensation. *See*: BOUNTY.

RICO. Abbreviation for RACKETEER INFLUENCED AND CORRUPT ORGANIZATIONS ACT.

RIDER. An amendment or addition to a **document**, often attached to it on a separate piece of paper. Riders are deemed to be incorporated into the terms of the document to which they are attached, making a redrafting of the document unnecessary.

RIFLE. **n.** A **firearm** with spiral grooves on the surface of its bore designed to be fired from the shoulder. **v.** To **ransack** and **steal** by **force**. Rifle often implies a breaking into a place or receptacle. *Example*: The burglars rifled the safe.

RIGHT. adj. 1. Just; morally good; legal; fitting; proper. **adj. 2.** Correct; in conformity with truth, reason, or fact. **n. 1.** That which is just, morally good, legal, fitting, or proper. *Example*: Does he know the difference between right and wrong. **n. 2.** A just claim, based on moral or legal grounds, to be allowed certain behavior or to demand certain behavior of others.

RIGHT OF PRIVACY. The general right of a person to be let alone by other people and by the government. This right has received judicial recognition in many cases, most important of which is *Katz v. U.S.*, in which the U.S. Supreme Court stated that "the Fourth Amendment protects people, not places. What a person knowingly exposes to the public, even in his own home or office, is not a subject of Fourth Amendment protection. . . . But what he seeks to preserve as private, even in an area accessible to the public may be constitutionally protected." 389 U.S. 347, 351-52, 88 S.Ct. 507, 511, 19 L.Ed.2d 576, 582 (1967). The *Katz* decision and many decisions following it have established a new formula for applications of the Fourth Amendment: "[W]herever an individual may harbor a reasonable 'expectation of privacy' . . . he is entitled to be free from unreasonable governmental intrusion." *Terry v. Ohio*, 392 U.S. 1, 9, 88 S.Ct. 1868, 1873, 20 L.Ed.2d 889, 899 (1968). This formula has been applied to a great variety of cases arising under the Fourth Amendment.

Note that privacy, as one of the basic rights guaranteed to individuals in our society, encompasses much more than the protections offered by the Fourth Amendment, even as interpreted under the *Katz* formula.

"[T]he Fourth Amendment cannot be translated into a general constitutional 'right to privacy.' That Amendment protects individual privacy against certain kinds of governmental intrusion, but its protections go further, and often have nothing to do with privacy at all. Other provisions of the Constitution protect personal privacy from other forms of governmental invasion. But the protection of a person's general right to privacy—his right to be let alone by other people—is, like the protection of his property and of his very life, left largely to the law of individual States." 389 U.S. at 350-51, 88 S.Ct. at 510-11, 19 L.Ed.2d at 581.

See PRIVACY for a list of related terms.

RIGHT-WRONG TEST. Same as M'NAGHTEN RULE.

RIGOR MORTIS. *Latin.* "The stiffness of death." The stiffening of the body that sets in a few hours after death. See DEATH for a list of related terms.

RIOT. An UNLAWFUL ASSEMBLY that has either done an unlawful act or has done a lawful act in an unlawful, violent, or tumultuous manner, to the disturbance of others. The term riot ordinarily does not apply to brief disturbances. The minimum number of persons who must be acting together in order to constitute a riot is usually specified by statute. It varies from as few as two to as many as ten. The offenses named riot, **disorderly conduct**, and unlawful assembly have various and overlapping meanings in the penal codes of different states. See AFFRAY for a list of related terms.

RIPENESS DOCTRINE. The constitutional law doctrine under which a federal **court** will not decide a **case** unless the case has matured to the point where the legal issues involved are definite and concrete enough and sufficiently evolved and presented that the court can make a clear **decision**. Under the ripeness doctrine, federal courts are precluded from adjudicating cases in which the alleged injury or threat of injury is neither real nor immediate and is conjectural or hypothetical. The doctrine arises from the limitation of Article III, Section 2, of the U.S. Constitution, which confines federal court jurisdiction to cases and **controversies**.

RISING. The breaking up or adjournment of a court or assembly, especially at the end of a **term** or **session**. *See*: SITTING.

RISK. A possibility or chance of suffering injury or loss; danger; hazard.

ROAD BLOCK. A structure, device, or other means used by duly authorized **law enforcement officers** to control all traffic through a point of the highway, whereby all vehicles may be slowed or stopped. Road blocks are commonly used to enforce motor vehicle laws, to apprehend fleeing violators of the law, to search for contraband, or to make inquiries and investigations for the effective prevention of crime and enforcement of the law. The constitutionality of a roadblock is tested by "balancing [the] intrusion on the individual's Fourth Amendment interests against [the] promo-tion of legitimate governmental interests." *Delaware v. Prouse*, 440 U.S. 648, 654, 99 S.Ct. 1391, 1396, 59 L.Ed.2d 660 (1979).

ROAD CAMP. *See*: COUNTY FARM.

ROBBER. One who commits or has committed ROBBERY.

ROBBERY. The unlawful taking of property that is in the immediate possession or presence of another, by **force** or **threat** of force. **Armed robbery** is robbery with the use or threatened use of a **deadly weapon. Unarmed robbery** (also called **strongarm robbery**) is robbery without the use of a weapon. See ABSTRACTION for a list of related terms.

ROGATORY LETTERS. Same as LETTERS ROGATORY.

ROLL. To **steal** from a person who is asleep or intoxicated by turning the victim over to go through his or her pockets.

R.O.R. Abbreviation for RELEASE ON RECOGNIZANCE. *See*: RECOGNIZANCE.

ROUT. An UNLAWFUL ASSEMBLY that has taken steps toward the commission of an unlawful act, without committing such an act. See AFFRAY for a list of related terms.

RULE. **n. 1.** An established law, standard, principle, or guide governing conduct, procedure, or action. **n. 2.** Same as REGULATION. **n. 3.** Same as HOLD-ING. *Example*: What is the rule of the *Miranda* case? See ACT for a list of related terms. **v. 1.** To settle or decide a point of law at a trial or hearing. *Example*: The judge ruled on the motion to dismiss. **v. 2.** To command; to require. *Example*: The court ruled the sheriff to serve the summons.

RULE OF FOUR. The U.S. Supreme Court's practice of granting **certiorari** on the vote of four justices.

RULE OF LAW. The principle that the **law**, and not one person or group of persons, is the highest authority. *Also called*: **supremacy of the law**.

RULES OF COURT. **Rules** or **regulations**, usually established by the highest **court** in a court system, governing practice and procedure in a court or court system. See COURT for a list of related terms.

RULING. A settlement of or **decision** on a point of **law** at a **trial** or **hearing**.

RUMOR. Unverified information of uncertain source or authority, usually spread by word of mouth; gossip.

RUN. **1.** To have legal validity or applicability in a particular place or during a prescribed period of time. *Example*: The arrest warrant runs throughout the state. **2.** To conduct; to manage; to control; to operate. *Example*: They were running an illegal gambling operation.

RUN AT LARGE. To wander, rove, or stroll about at will, without constraint or confinement. *Example*: The statute prohibits allowing animals to run at large.

RUNAWAY. A **juvenile** who has been **adjudicated** by a **judicial officer** of a **juvenile court** as having committed the **status offense** of leaving the custody and home of his or her parents, guardians or custodians without permission and failing to return within a reasonable length of time. Statutes defining the status offense usually specify either a length of time that the juvenile must be away or declare habitual running away a status offense. The codification of this offense varies greatly among different states. See JUVENILE for a list of related terms.

RUNNING OF THE STATUTE OF LIMITATIONS. The passing of the time mentioned in the STATUTE OF LIMITATIONS.

SABBATH.   Another name for Sunday.

SABOTAGE.   The willful and malicious injury to or destruction of an employer's property or obstruction and interference with the employer's business by employees or their agents to force the employer to accede to demands. The term sabotage also applies to similar activity directed toward disrupting the production or operations of a nation by enemy agents during wartime.

SADISM.   A sexual perversion that manifests itself in the desire to inflict pain or humiliation on others. *See*: MASOCHISM.

SAID.   Same as AFORESAID.

SALOON.   Same as TAVERN.

SAME.   Identical with something previously mentioned.

SAME OFFENSE.   *See*: DOUBLE JEOPARDY.

SAMPLE.   A small quantity or piece of a substance presented or regarded as a fair representative of the whole. *Example*: He tested the blood sample for alcohol content.

SANCTION.   **n.** A penalty or punishment to enforce obedience to a law or rule. **v.** To approve; to confirm; to ratify; to authorize; to legitimate.

SANE.   Of sound mental health. *See*: INSANITY.

SANITY.   Soundness of mental health; the opposite or reverse of INSANITY.

SANS.   *French*. "Without."

SATISFACTORY EVIDENCE.   The term satisfactory evidence has different meanings in different contexts, but in general means evidence that produces moral certainty in an unprejudiced mind or that satisfies an unprejudiced mind beyond a reasonable doubt. *Also called*: **sufficient evidence**. See EVIDENCE for a list of related terms.

SATISFY. **1.** To free from doubt or uncertainty; to set at rest the mind of; to convince. *Example*: She was unable to satisfy the jury as to her innocence. **2.** To fulfill or discharge an obligation or demand. **3.** To gratify or fulfill a need, desire, or expectation.

SAVE THE STATUTE OF LIMITATIONS. To prevent or suspend the running or operation of the STATUTE OF LIMITATIONS.

SAVING CLAUSE. **1.** An exception or reservation in a **statute**. **2.** A provision in a statute stipulating that if one or more parts of the statute are declared unconstitutional, the balance of the statute that is constitutional continues in force. *Also called*: **severability clause**. See STATUTE for a list of related terms.

SC. Abbreviation for SCILICET.

SCANDAL. Unnecessary matter in **pleading** that reflects adversely on a person's moral character or is unbecoming to the dignity of the court. See PLEADING for a list of related terms.

SCANDALIZE. To offend the moral sense or conscience of; to shock.

SCHEDULE. **1.** A formal written list of items or details. **2.** A program of future events; a timetable. **3.** An appendix to a legal document containing a statement of details that could not conveniently be placed in the body of the document.

SCHEME. **1.** A design or plan of action. **2.** A SYSTEM.

SCHMERBER v. CALIFORNIA. The 1966 U.S. Supreme Court case which held that there was no denial of **due process of law** in the warrantless taking of a blood sample for a blood-alcohol test from an **arrested** person who is unconscious and unable to give **consent**, and no unreasonable **search** and **seizure** or violation of the person's privilege against **self-incrimination** when such a specimen is taken without consent while the person is in lawful custody. In the *Schmerber* case, the blood sample was taken in a hospital by a physician following accepted medical procedures. Also, there was a need for immediate action because the alcoholic content in the blood would quickly dissipate. The Court said:

> "[W]e reach this judgment only on the facts in the present record. The integrity of an individual's person is a cherished value of our society. That we today hold that the Constitution does not forbid the State's minor intrusions into an individual's body under stringently limited conditions in no way indicates that it permits more substantial intrusions or intrusions under other conditions." 384 U.S. 757, 772, 86 S.Ct. 1826, 1836, 16 L.Ed.2d 908, 920.

OTH v. BUSTAMONTE. *See*: CONSENT SEARCH.

SFY—SCHNECKLOTH v. BUSTAMONTE

SCIENTER. *Latin.* "Knowingly." Guilty knowledge; such knowledge as to make a person legally responsible for the consequences of his or her acts.

SCIL. Abbreviation for SCILICET.

SCILICET. *Latin.* To wit; namely. The term scilicet is used in **pleadings** and other documents to introduce a more particular statement of matters that have been previously mentioned in general terms. *Abbreviations*: **sc.**; **scil.**; **SS**.

SCINTILLA. *Latin.* "Spark." A barely perceptible amount; the slightest trace. *Example*: A mere scintilla of evidence is not enough to require submission of the issue to the jury.

SCIRE FACIAS. *Latin.* "Made known." A judicial **writ** founded upon some matter of **record**, such as a **recognizance** or **judgment**, requiring the party against whom it is issued to appear and show cause why the matter of record should not be enforced, vacated, or annulled. See ARREST WARRANT for a list of related terms.

Ss

SCOPE. **1.** The range or area of operation, application, or effectiveness of an activity. *Example*: The scope of a search incident to arrest is limited. **2.** The intention or meaning of a law or proposal. *Example*: Her actions fall within the scope of the law.

SCORN. Extreme contempt; disdain.

SCREENING. *See*: INTAKE; PROSECUTORIAL DISCRETION.

SCURRILOUS. Vile; vulgar; foul.

SE. *Latin.* "Himself; herself; itself."

SEAL. **v. 1.** To remove, for the benefit of the subject, **arrest**, **criminal**, or **juvenile record** information from routinely available status to a status requiring special procedures for access. Seal differs from **purge** in that purging is the total removal of information within a given system. Sealing is typically done to prevent general access to information concerning juvenile offenses, minor offenses committed by young adults, or **criminal history record information** concerning persons who have been outside the jurisdiction of the criminal justice system for a given period of time. Records may be sealed by court order or because of a statute requiring, for example, all juvenile records to be sealed when the subject reaches a certain age. Sealing may or may not extend to information contained in precinct arrest books, other original entry records, chronological court files, and reported court opinions. **v. 2.** To affix a SEAL (n.) to a legal document. **n.** A mark or symbol made of some substance such as wax or paper or as an impression affixed to a legal document to prove its authenticity. Seals are used much less frequently today than in the past.

SEALED VERDICT. A **verdict** that is agreed upon by a **jury** but, because the **court** is not is session at the time, is put in writing and sealed in an envelope rather than being returned in open court. A sealed verdict does not become final until it is read into the record and the jury is discharged. See VERDICT for a list of related terms.

SEARCH. Under the Fourth Amendment prohibition against unreasonable searches and seizures, a search can be defined as an examination or inspection of a location, vehicle, or person by a law enforcement officer or other authorized person for the purpose of locating objects relating to or believed to relate to criminal activities or wanted persons. Mere observation of objects lying open to view by a law enforcement officer who is in a position in which he or she has a legal right to be does not constitute a search. In recent years courts have increasingly analyzed search and seizure issues in terms of violation of the **right of privacy** and have expanded the definition of search to include any official intrusion into matters and activities as to which a person has exhibited a reasonable expectation of privacy. "A 'search' occurs when an expectation of privacy that society is prepared to consider reasonable is infringed." *U.S. v. Jacobsen*, 466 U.S. 109, 113, 104 S.Ct. 1652, 1656, 80 L.Ed.2d 85, 94 (1984).

The general rule is that any search conducted without a SEARCH WARRANT is unreasonable. Courts have fashioned several well-defined exceptions to this rule, however. A warrant is not required, therefore, for a SEARCH INCIDENT TO ARREST; a CONSENT SEARCH; an observation of evidence falling under the PLAIN VIEW DOCTRINE; an emergency search of a motor vehicle under the CARROLL DOCTRINE; searches conducted in the OPEN FIELDS; observations of abandoned property (see ABANDON); and frisks conducted as a part of an investigative stop (see STOP AND FRISK). *See*: AFFIDAVIT; CURTILAGE; EXCLUSIONARY RULE; FRISK; FRUIT OF THE POISONOUS TREE DOCTRINE; GENERAL WARRANT; HOT PURSUIT; ILLINOIS v. GATES; INVENTORY SEARCH; ITEMS SUBJECT TO SEIZURE; MOTION TO SUPPRESS; PEN REGISTER; PRIVACY; PROBABLE CAUSE; RANSACK; SEARCH INCIDENT TO ARREST; SEARCH WARRANT; SEIZURE; SILVER PLATTER DOCTRINE; STANDING; SUPPRESSION HEARING; WRIT OF ASSISTANCE; ZONE SEARCH.

SEARCH AND SEIZURE. *See*: SEARCH; SEIZURE.

SEARCH INCIDENT TO ARREST. A recognized exception to the SEARCH WARRANT requirement, allowing a **law enforcement officer** who legally **arrests** a person to conduct a warrantless **search** of that person contemporaneous with the arrest. The basic legal requirements of a search incident to arrest are stated in the 1969 U.S. Supreme Court case of *Chimel v. California*:

> "When an arrest is made, it is reasonable for the arresting officer to search the person arrested in order to remove any **weapons** that the latter might seek to use in order to resist arrest or effect his escape. Otherwise, the officer's

safety might well be endangered, and the arrest itself frustrated. In addition, it is entirely reasonable for the arresting officer to search for and seize any **evidence** on the arrestee's person in order to prevent its concealment or destruction. And the area into which an arrestee might reach in order to grab a weapon or evidentiary items must, of course, be governed by a like rule. A gun on a table or in a drawer in front of one who is arrested can be as dangerous to the arresting officer as one concealed in the clothing of the person arrested. There is ample justification, therefore, for a search of the arrestee's person and the area 'within his immediate control'—construing that phrase to mean the area from within which he might gain possession of a weapon or destructible evidence." 395 U.S. 752, 762-63, 89 S.Ct. 2034, 2040, 23 L.Ed.2d 685, 694.

See SEARCH for a list of related terms. *See also*: CUSTODIAL ARREST.

SEARCH WARRANT. An **order** in writing, issued by a **magistrate** or other proper **judicial officer** in the name of the people of a state or of the nation, directed to a **law enforcement officer** and commanding him or her to search a specified person or premises for specified property and to bring it before the judicial authority named in the warrant. Generally, the types of property for which a search warrant may be issued, as set out in statutes or rules of court, are **weapons, contraband, fruits** of crime, **instrumentalities** of crime, and other **evidence** of crime (see **items subject to seizure**). The Fourth Amendment to the U.S. Constitution states that "no warrants shall issue, but upon **probable cause**, supported by **Oath** or **affirmation**, and particularly describing the place to be searched and the persons or things to be seized." The judicial officer, before issuing the warrant, must determine whether there is **probable cause** to **search** based on information supplied in an **affidavit** by a law enforcement officer or other person. See ARREST WARRANT and SEARCH for lists of related terms.

Ss

SEASONABLE. Timely; performed or occurring at the proper time.

SEC. Abbreviation for SECURITIES AND EXCHANGE COMMISSION.

SECOND. A person who aids and assists another who is fighting a duel.

SECONDARY. Inferior; minor; lesser; subordinate.

SECONDARY AUTHORITY. *See*: AUTHORITY (definition 5).

SECONDARY EVIDENCE. Evidence that is not **primary evidence** of some fact or thing and that is inferior to primary evidence. Copies of a document and testimony as to its contents are secondary evidence of the actual document and its contents. Under the **best evidence rule**, secondary evidence is admissible as proof in a judicial proceeding if primary evidence is shown to be inaccessible. *Also called*: **substitutionary evidence**. See EVIDENCE for a list of related terms.

SECOND-HAND EVIDENCE.   Same as HEARSAY EVIDENCE.

SECOND JEOPARDY.   Same as DOUBLE JEOPARDY.

SECOND OFFENSE.   An offense committed after a **conviction** for a first offense under a **habitual criminal** statute.

SECRET.   Kept from general or public knowledge or view; hidden; concealed.

SECRETE.   To make or keep SECRET; to hide; to conceal.

SECRET SERVICE, UNITED STATES.   The mission of the United States Secret Service in the **Department of the Treasury** includes the authority and responsibility:

— to protect the President, the Vice President, the President-elect, the Vice President-elect, and members of their immediate families; major Presidential and Vice Presidential candidates; former Presidents and their spouses, except that protection of a spouse shall terminate in the event of remarriage; minor children of a former President until the age of 16; visiting heads of foreign states or governments; other distinguished visitors to the United States; and official representatives of the United States performing special missions abroad, as directed by the President;

— to provide security at the White House complex and other Presidential offices, the temporary official residence of the Vice President in the District of Columbia, and foreign diplomatic missions in the Washington, D.C., metropolitan area and throughout the United States, its territories and possessions, as prescribed by statute;

— to detect and arrest any person committing any offense against the laws of the United States relating to currency, coins, obligations, and securities of the United States or of foreign governments;

— to suppress the forgery and fraudulent negotiation or redemption of federal government checks, bonds, and other obligations or securities of the United States; and

— to detect and arrest offenders of laws pertaining to electronic funds transfer frauds, credit and debit card frauds, false identification documents or devices, computer access fraud, and U.S. Department of Agriculture food coupons, including authority-to-participate cards.

SECTION.   A paragraph or other subdivision of a statute, code, or other writing. *Example*: Burglary is prohibited by section 401 of the criminal code.

SECTOR SEARCH.   Same as ZONE SEARCH.

SECUNDUM.   *Latin.* "According to."

SECURE. **adj.** Safe; not exposed to danger. **v. 1.** To make safe; to guard from danger. **v. 2.** To fasten; to make firm. **v. 3.** To get possession of; to obtain; to acquire. **v. 4.** To seize and confine. *Example*: The officer secured the prisoner.

SECURITY. The restriction of **inmate** movement within a **correctional facility**, usually divided into maximum, medium and minimum levels. Security level is not solely a physical characteristic of correctional facilities but a type of physical custodial status of inmates, relating both to restrictive architectural features of buildings or areas and to human regulation of inmate movement within the facility. No standard definition of security levels is given in this dictionary because the defining physical and behavioral restrictive features vary greatly among jurisdictions. *See*: PRIVATE SECURITY AGENCY.

SED. *Latin*. "But."

SE DEFENDENDO *Latin*. "In defending himself or herself." In **self-defense**.

SEDITION. Advocacy of resistance to, disruption of, or overthrow of the government through speech, publications, or other acts, short of overt acts of **treason**.

Ss

SEDUCE. To entice, persuade, solicit, or otherwise induce a previously chaste woman to have unlawful **sexual intercourse** without the use of **force**. The offense of seduction is variously defined by **statute** in different states, but is not a criminal offense in all states.

SED VIDE. *Latin*. "But see." A phrase used to direct a reader to a conflicting or contradictory statement or principle.

SEE v. CITY OF SEATTLE. *See*: CAMARA v. MUNICIPAL COURT.

SEIZABLE ITEMS. Same as ITEMS SUBJECT TO SEIZURE.

SEIZE. *See*: SEIZURE.

SEIZURE. **1.** Under the Fourth Amendment prohibition against unreasonable searches and seizures, a seizure of the **person** can be defined as follows: "[A] person has been 'seized' within the meaning of the Fourth Amendment only if, in view of all of the circumstances surrounding the incident, a reasonable person would have believed that he was not free to leave. Examples of circumstances that might indicate a seizure even where the person did not attempt to leave, would be the threatening presence of several officers, the display of a weapon by an officer, some physical touching of the person of the citizen, or the use of language or tone of voice indicating that compliance with the officer's request might be compelled. . . . In the absence of some such evidence, otherwise inoffensive contact between a member of the public and the police cannot, as a matter of law, amount to a seizure of that person." *U.S. v. Mendenhall*, 446 U.S. 544, 554-55, 100 S.Ct. 1870, 1877, 64 L.Ed.2d 497, 509 (1980).

The least intrusive type of seizure of the person governed by the Fourth Amendment is the so-called *Terry*-type investigative stop (see **stop and frisk**). A stop is a brief detention of a person for investigative purposes that is intrusive to the extent that a reasonable person would have believed that he or she was not free to leave. Officers may stop a person only if they have a reasonable suspicion that criminal activity is afoot. Officers may conduct a **frisk** (a limited pat-down search of the outer clothing) of a person they have stopped only if the officers have reason to believe that they are dealing with an armed and dangerous person. Both the stop and frisk must be reasonable under the circumstances.

At a still higher level of intensity are police contacts with members of the public involving a detention or temporary seizure of a person that is more intrusive on a person's freedom of action than a brief investigatory stop, but that does not satisfy the four elements of a formal **arrest**. An example would be an officer's handcuffing a suspect and transporting him or her to the station for questioning without formally arresting the person. In this type of situation, a court may find that the officer's actions are tantamount to an arrest if they are indistinguishable from an arrest in important respects. The seizure or detention will be ruled illegal unless it is supported by **probable cause**. This type of seizure is sometimes referred to as a **seizure tantamount to arrest**.

The highest level of seizure of the person governed by the Fourth Amendment is the formal arrest.

2. Under the Fourth Amendment's prohibition against unreasonable searches and seizures, a seizure of **property** "occurs when there is some meaningful interference with an individual's possessory interests in that property." *U.S. v. Jacobsen*, 466 U.S. 109, 113, 104 S.Ct. 1652, 1656, 80 L.Ed.2d 85, 94 (1984). Usually a seizure involves the taking into custody by a **law enforcement officer** of an item of property relating to or believed to relate to criminal activity. Ordinarily property is seized after a **search** conducted pursuant to a **search warrant** or pursuant to one of the recognized exceptions to the warrant requirement. In certain situations, however, such as seizures of items under the **plain view doctrine**, seizures of items found in the **open fields**, and seizures of abandoned property (see **abandon**), the seizure may be made without any preceding search. Because a search and seizure are often combined in one transaction, they are often referred to together by the term "search and seizure," and the legal principles applicable to searches and seizures are referred to as the law of search and seizure.

See: ABANDON; APPREHENSION; ARREST; ATTACH; BODY EXECUTION; CONFISCATE; DETAIN; EXCLUSIONARY RULE; INTERCEPTION; ITEMS SUBJECT TO SEIZURE; MERE EVIDENCE; SEARCH; SECURE; STOP; STOP AND FRISK; TAKE; USURP; WIRETAPPING.

SELECT.   To choose in preference to another or others; to pick out. *Example*: They are in the process of selecting a jury.

SELECTIVE INCORPORATION. The doctrine under which some, but not all, of the rights in the Bill of Rights are incorporated into the Fourteenth Amendment to the U.S. Constitution and thus made applicable to the states. The U.S. Supreme Court has held that the Fourteenth Amendment's due process clause (see **due process of law**) incorporates those rights in the Bill of Rights that are "fundamental to the American scheme of justice." *Duncan v. Louisiana*, 391 U.S. 145, 149, 18 S.Ct. 1444, 1447, 20 L.Ed.2d 491, 496 (1968). Among the rights that have been incorporated are freedoms of speech, press, religion, and assembly; separation of church and state; freedom from unreasonable searches and seizures; the privilege against compelled self-incrimination; freedom from double jeopardy; the right to a fair, speedy, and public trial; and the freedom from cruel and unusual punishment. Furthermore, provisions of the Bill of Rights applicable to the states apply to state and local actions in the same manner as they do to federal action. Thus, rulings on the meaning of incorporated provisions of the Bill of Rights apply equally to both state and federal laws.

SELF-DEFENSE. The right of a person to use **force** upon another person in order to protect him or herself, a third person, or sometimes his or her property from the imminent use of unlawful force by the other person. The degree of force that may be used in self-defense varies in different jurisdictions. In general, however, a person may use a reasonable degree of **nondeadly force** upon another person when he or she reasonably believes the other person is about to use unlawful nondeadly force and when he or she reasonably believes it necessary to prevent **bodily injury**. A person may use **deadly force** upon another person when he or she reasonably believes it necessary to prevent **death** or **serious bodily injury**, and when he or she reasonably believes that the other person is about to use unlawful deadly force. In some jurisdictions, a person must retreat, if he or she can safely do so, before using deadly force, except that a person is not required to retreat from his or her home or place of business. A person may never use more force than is reasonably necessary to repel the attack. The force used must be reasonably related to the harm it seeks to avoid.

Self-defense is **defense** (definition 2) to a criminal **charge** for crimes such as **murder**, **manslaughter**, and **assault and battery**. An initial **aggressor**, however, may not ordinarily avail him or herself of the defense of self-defense.

In general, the same rules apply to a person's use of force to defend a third person from the unlawful use of force as apply to the defense of self. In some states, however, a person is justified in using force in defense only of others who bear a stated relationship to the defender. A person may use reasonable nondeadly force to protect his or her real or personal property if the person reasonably believes that the property is in immediate danger of unlawful trespass, entry, or carrying away and if the person reasonably believes that the use of force is necessary to avoid this danger. In general, deadly force is not justifiable to protect property. Some jurisdictions, however, allow the use of deadly force to protect an occupied dwelling when the defender reasonably believes that the trespasser intends to commit a felony in the dwelling or to harm one of the occupants of the dwelling.

See FORCE for a list of related terms.

SELF-EXECUTING.   Providing for its own enforcement or legal effectiveness and needing no further act of a **court** or **legislature** to enforce it or make it legally effective.

SELF-INCRIMINATION.   The Fifth Amendment to the U.S. Constitution provides that no person "shall be compelled in any criminal case to be a **witness** against himself." This so-called privilege against compelled self-incrimination, taken in its most literal sense, gives a person the right to refuse to **testify** against him or herself once the person has been put on trial on a criminal **charge**.

The privilege against self-incrimination has been extended by statutory and case law well beyond the literal language of the Fifth Amendment. For example, a defendant in a criminal case may refuse even to be sworn in and take the stand in his or her own defense. And if a defendant does so refuse, neither the **prosecution** nor the trial **judge** may comment on the refusal to testify, nor may the **fact-finder** properly draw an **inference** of **guilt** from the refusal.

The privilege against self-incrimination applies not only to testimony but to any **evidence** of a testimonial or communicative nature. It applies therefore to writings and communicative gestures. It does not apply, however, to **real evidence** that derives from a person's body. The U.S. Supreme Court stated that "both federal and state courts have usually held that it offers no protection against compulsion to submit to fingerprinting, photographing, or measurements, to write or speak for identification, to appear in court, to stand, to assume a stance, to walk, or to make a particular gesture." *Schmerber v. California*, 384 U.S. 757, 764, 86 S.Ct. 1866, 1832, 16 L.Ed.2d. 908, 916 (1966). Other unprotected activities are the taking of samples of blood, urine, breath, or other bodily extractions.

The eventuality protected against by the privilege against self-incrimination is the risk that one's communication will be used as evidence in a criminal **prosecution**. The risk of prosecution must be real and substantial for the privilege to be applicable. The privilege does not apply in essentially noncriminal situations. Furthermore, a person may not claim the privilege if he or she has been granted **immunity** from the use of the compelled testimony and evidence derived from it (**use immunity**) or immunity from prosecution for crimes to which the compelled testimony relates (**transactional immunity**).

The privilege against self-incrimination extends to out-of-court as well as in-court situations. Therefore a pretrial **admission** or **confession** obtained through the use of **force** or **threat** of force would be inadmissible because it violates the privilege against self-incrimination. Furthermore, because of sophisticated police interrogation methods and the compulsion inherent in police custodial surroundings, any pretrial admissions or confessions resulting from **interrogation** of a person who is in **custody** or deprived of his or her freedom of action in a significant way will be held inadmissible unless certain safeguards have been provided the defendant. (See MIRANDA v. ARIZONA for a discussion of those safeguards.) The privilege against self-incrimination is also available at such proceedings as legislative hearings, **coroner's inquests**, and **grand jury** investigations.

The Fifth Amendment privilege against compelled self-incrimination is applicable to both the federal government and the states through the due process clause of the Fourteenth Amendment. Also the states must enforce the privilege according to the following federal standard: "The privilege afforded not only extends to answers that would in themselves support a conviction . . . but likewise embraces those which would furnish a link in the chain of evidence needed to prosecute." *Malloy v. Hogan*, 378 U.S. 1, 11, 84 S.Ct. 1489, 1495, 12 L.Ed.2d 653, 661 (1964). See WITNESS for a list of related terms.

SELF-INDUCED INTOXICATION. The **Model Penal Code** defines self-induced intoxication as "intoxication caused by substances that the actor knowingly introduces into his body, the tendency of which to cause intoxication he knows or ought to know, unless he introduces them pursuant to medical advice or under such circumstances as would afford a defense to a charge of crime." See INTOXICATION for a list of related terms.

SELF-SERVING DECLARATION. An **extrajudicial** statement made by a party in his or her own interest. Self-serving declarations are inadmissible unless part of the **res gestae**.

SEMEN. The whitish fluid produced in an adult male's reproductive organ.

SEMINAL. Containing or contributing to the possibility of future development. *Example:* The *Miranda* case was a seminal decision in the area of confessions.

SEMPER. *Latin.* "Always."

SENATE OF THE UNITED STATES. *See*: CONGRESS OF THE UNITED STATES.

SENIOR. Above others in rank, importance, or length of service.

SENTENCE. 1. The penalty imposed by a **court** upon a person **convicted** of a **crime**. The types of sentences are **death, commitment** to **confinement, probation** or a **suspended sentence**, and a **fine**. The determination of the sentence is perhaps the most sensitive and difficult decision the **judge** has to make because of the effect it will have on the defendant's life. For this reason, most states have laws directing and guiding the judge in this determination. A typical provision requires the judge to impose sentence without unreasonable delay. This protects the defendant from a prolonged period of uncertainty about the future. In addition, before imposing sentence, the judge is usually required to address the defendant personally and ask if the defendant desires to be heard before the imposition of sentence. The defendant may be heard personally or by **counsel** or both. The purpose of this provision is to enable the defendant to present any information that may be of assistance to the court in determining punishment.

Another typical statutory provision that is designed to assist the court in fixing sentence allows the court, in its discretion, to direct the state probation and parole board to make a **presentence investigation** and **presentence report** to the court before the imposition of sentence. This report will contain any prior criminal record of the defendant and such other information on personal characteristics, financial condition, and the circumstances affecting the defendant's behavior as may be helpful to the court in reaching its decision.

The court has a number of alternatives open to it with respect to sentencing, depending largely on individual state criminal statutes. Some criminal statutes have **mandatory sentences**, some have fixed **maximum sentences**, some have fixed **minimum sentences**, and others leave the matter of sentencing to the judge. Therefore, depending upon the offense for which the defendant has been convicted, the court may have a very broad discretion in fixing sentence, or no discretion whatsoever. In a few states, the **jury** has the power to fix the sentence as well as to determine guilt or innocence. *See*: ACCUMULATIVE JUDGMENT; AGGRAVATED SENTENCE; AGGRAVATING CIRCUMSTANCES; AGGREGATE MAXIMUM RELEASE DATE; ALLOCUTION; BALANCE OF SENTENCE SUSPENDED; BIFURCATED TRIAL; CLEMENCY; COMMITMENT; CONCURRENT SENTENCE; CONDITIONALLY SUSPENDED SENTENCE; CONSECUTIVE SENTENCE; COURT DISPOSITION; DEAD TIME; DEATH SENTENCE; DETERMINATE SENTENCE; DISPOSITION; ELIGIBLE FOR PAROLE; EXPIRATION OF SENTENCE; GOOD TIME; HABITUAL CRIMINAL; HARD LABOR; INDETERMINATE SENTENCE; INTERMITTENT SENTENCE; JAIL COMMITMENT; JEOPARDY; JUDGMENT; JURY SENTENCING; JUVENILE COURT JUDGMENT; JUVENILE DISPOSITION; LIFE SENTENCE; MANDATORY RELEASE DATE; MANDATORY SENTENCE; MANDATORY SUPERVISED RELEASE; MAXIMUM SENTENCE; MINIMUM SENTENCE; MITIGATED SENTENCE; MITIGATING CIRCUMSTANCES; MULTIPLE SENTENCE; NEW COURT COMMITMENT; PAROLE; PENALTY; PLEA BARGAINING; PRESENTENCE INVESTIGATION; PRESENTENCE REPORT; PRISON COMMITMENT; PROBATION; REDUCED SENTENCE; RELEASE; SENTENCE CREDIT TIME; SENTENCED TO TIME SERVED; SENTENCE EFFECTIVE DATE; SENTENCE REVIEW; SENTENCING CONTINUED; SENTENCING DISPOSITION; SENTENCING HEARING; SENTENCING POSTPONED; SPLIT SENTENCE; STREET TIME; SUSPENDED SENTENCE; TIME SERVED.

2. The court **judgment** specifying the penalty imposed upon a person convicted of a crime.

SENTENCE CREDIT TIME.   Time already spent in **confinement** in relation to a given offense, deducted at the point of admission on a **sentence** to **jail** or **prison**

from the maximum jail or prison liability of the sentence for the offense. Sentence credit time can be deducted by the court or in accord with a **statute** from the jail or prison time to be served on a given sentence. The time may have been spent in jail awaiting trial or sentencing, or under **diagnostic commitment**. Credit time is not the same as **good time**, which is calculated with respect to time spent in prison, which can vary according to the particular statutory penalty, and which is often dependent upon good behavior. See SENTENCE for a list of related terms.

SENTENCED TO TIME SERVED. A **sentencing disposition** consisting of a **sentence** to **prison** or **jail**, which credits the defendant for an amount of time already spent in **confinement** equal to the amount of the sentence, and results in **release** from confinement of the defendant. See RELEASE and SENTENCE for lists of related terms.

SENTENCE EFFECTIVE DATE. With respect to a term of **confinement**, the date from which **time served** is calculated, not necessarily coincident with the date sentence was pronounced or the date of entry to confinement after sentencing. **Sentence credit time** for time spent in detention awaiting and during trial is usually deducted from a sentence to a term of confinement, and the sentence effective date can therefore predate **conviction**. Events such as **appeal** proceedings can delay entry to any confinement so that the sentence effective date can postdate conviction by months or years. See SENTENCE for a list of related terms.

SENTENCE REVIEW. The reconsideration of a **sentence** imposed on a person **convicted** of a crime either by the same **court** that imposed the sentence or by a higher court. Sentence review is usually requested on the grounds that the **penalty** is harsh or excessive, either in relation to circumstances of the specific case or in relation to sentences imposed in similar cases. An application for sentence review can be part of an **appeal** or application for **postconviction remedy** that raises other issues as well, or it can be a separate action. See SENTENCE for a list of related terms.

SENTENCING CONTINUED. A delay of the court's pronouncement of **sentence** for practical reasons including the following: the court has not received the **presentence report**; the defendant cannot be present in the courtroom for the hearing because he or she is testifying in another trial or is in another geographical jurisdiction; illness of any of the major participants in the case (e.g., the judicial officer, the prosecutor, the defense attorney, the defendant). See SENTENCE for a list of related terms.

SENTENCING DISPOSITION. A **court disposition** of a defendant after a judgment of **conviction**, expressed as **penalties**, such as **incarceration** or payment of **fines**; or any of a number of alternatives to actually executed penalties, such as suspended sentences, grants of probation, or orders to perform restitution; or various combinations of the above. Following is a list of possible sentencing dispositions.

—**sentencing postponed**

—**suspended sentence** (either unconditionally or conditionally)

—**balance of sentence suspended** or **sentenced to time served**

—**probation order** (either **court probation** or **supervised probation**)

—**restitution**

—**fine, forfeit,** court costs

—**residential commitment**

—**jail commitment**

—**prison commitment** (**determinate sentence, indeterminate sentence, life sentence,** or **death sentence**)

See DISPOSITION and SENTENCE for lists of related terms.

SENTENCING HEARING. A **hearing** during which the **court** or **jury** considers relevant information, such as evidence concerning **aggravating circumstances** or **mitigating circumstances,** for the purpose of determining a **sentencing disposition** for a person **convicted** of an offense. A sentencing hearing is held after a judgment of **conviction** has been entered, the **presentence investigation** (if any) has been conducted, and the **presentence report** (if any) has been submitted to the court. Sentencing hearings can include arguments made by the **defense** in favor of a lesser sentence than that recommended in the presentence report; arguments made by the **prosecution** for or against the recommendations in the presentence report; the court's consideration of the mitigating or aggravating circumstances brought out by the defense and prosecution; and announcement of the court's decision. See HEARING and SENTENCE for lists of related terms.

SENTENCING POSTPONED. The delay for an unspecified period of time, or to a remote date, of the court's pronouncement of **sentencing disposition** for a person **convicted** of an **offense,** in order to place the defendant in some status contingent on good behavior in the expectation that a **penalty** need never be pronounced or executed. Sentencing postponed is the court's decision as a matter of policy to delay pronouncing a sentencing disposition, as opposed to **sentencing continued,** which is a delay for practical reasons. *Also called*: **deferred sentence. NOTE:** Sentencing postponed is called a **suspended sentence** in some jurisdictions, but the terms are distinguished in this dictionary. See SENTENCE for a list of related terms.

SEPARABLE. Capable of being separated or divided.

SEPARATE. Set apart from others; not connected; detached; distinct.

SEPARATE TRIAL. Where several persons are jointly accused of a **crime,** the **trial** of one or more of the codefendants apart from the other codefendants. See TRIAL for a list of related terms.

SEPARATION OF POWERS. The balancing of governmental power among the **executive**, **legislative**, and **judicial** branches of government. The legislative branch makes the laws. The executive branch implements and carries out the laws. The judicial branch interprets the laws and decides controversies that arise under the laws. One branch may not encroach upon the domains of the others, but an effective government requires that all branches cooperate with each other whenever possible.

SEQUESTER. To set apart; to segregate; to separate. To sequester a **jury** means to keep a jury together but separate from the general public throughout the **trial** and **deliberations** until discharged, in order to protect them from improper contact. To sequester **witnesses** means to keep witnesses at a trial separate from one another and outside the courtroom when not testifying, in order to prevent the testimony of one witness from being influenced by that of another witness.

SERGEANT-AT-ARMS. An officer appointed by a legislative, judicial, or social body to enforce its commands and to preserve order.

SERIATIM. *Latin.* One after another; in a series; successively; individually.

Ss

SERIOUS. Grave; great; important; weighty.

SERIOUS BODILY INJURY. Section 210.0 (3) of the **Model Penal Code** defines serious bodily injury as "**bodily injury** which creates a substantial risk of **death** or which causes serious, permanent disfigurement, or protracted loss or impairment of the function of any bodily member or organ." The term serious bodily injury may be defined differently in different jurisdictions.

SERIOUS MISDEMEANOR. A class of MISDEMEANOR having more severe penalties than other misdemeanors but not constituting a **felony** for technical reasons; sometimes a statutory name for a type of misdemeanor having a possible maximum penalty much greater than the customary one-year incarceration for misdemeanors. In some jurisdictions the term serious misdemeanor is the official penal code name of a class of offenses. In others, it is the unofficial name for higher penalty range misdemeanors, or for offenses that can be charged as either misdemeanors or as felonies. The term can also be officially or unofficially used to designate misdemeanors that are prosecuted only in a particular **court** or by a particular agency. Other terms with similar meaning and also with variable usage are **aggravated misdemeanor**, **high crimes and misdemeanors**, **high misdemeanor**, **indictable misdemeanor**, and **penitentiary misdemeanor**. See CRIME for a list of related terms.

SERVE. To deliver or present a legal **writ** or **notice** to a person in order to officially charge the person with **notice** of some pending action or proceeding, and to advise the person of what action he or she should take to comply with the law or to protect or defend rights. *Example*: The officer served him with a summons.

SERVICE.   Same as SERVICE OF PROCESS.

SERVICE OF PROCESS.   The serving (see **serve**) of a legal **writ** or **notice** upon a person. *See*: CONSTRUCTIVE SERVICE; PERSONAL SERVICE.

SERVICES.   Under Section 223.7 (1) of the **Model Penal Code** services "includes labor, professional service, transportation, telephone or other public service, accommodation in hotels, restaurants or elsewhere, admission to exhibitions, use of vehicles or other movable property."

SERVITUDE.   Any subjection of one person to another person as a servant, whether voluntary or involuntary.

SESSION.   **1.** A particular meeting or **sitting** of a **court**, **legislature**, or other deliberative body for the transaction of business.   **2.** The period of time in a **term** during which a court, legislature, or other deliberative body sits for the transaction of business.

SESSION LAWS.   **Statutes** enacted by a state legislature at one of its **sessions**. Session laws are usually published in the order that they were passed in pamphlet form periodically during a legislative session and are published in a more permanent bound format at the end of the session. See STATUTE for a list of related terms.

SESSIONS.   A **court** of **criminal jurisdiction** in some states. See COURT for a list of related terms.

SET ASIDE.   To annul; to invalidate; to cancel. *Example*: The judge set aside the verdict.

SET DOWN.   **1.** To put into writing or print.   **2.** To enter a **case** on a **calendar** or **docket** for trial or hearing.

SET FORTH.   To describe; to narrate; to relate.

SET OUT.   To recite or describe in detail. *Example*: The facts were carefully set out in the brief.

SETTLE.   To finally decide a question or point of dispute. *Example*: That issue was settled by the Supreme Court in a recent case.

SET UP.   To offer or propose for acceptance. *Example*: She set up an alibi as her defense.

SEVER.   To separate; to divide into parts. *See*: SEVERANCE.

SEVERABILITY CLAUSE.   Same as SAVING CLAUSE (definition 2).

SEVERABLE. Capable of being separated from another thing or things to which it was joined, yet maintaining an independent existence and validity.

SEVERABLE STATUTE. A **statute** that, even though a portion of it is invalidated, the portion remaining is still valid and enforceable. See STATUTE for a list of related terms.

SEVERAL. **1.** More than one. **2.** Separate; individual; independent; distinct. **3.** Held by, obligating, or affecting each party separately. *See*: JOINT; JOINT AND SEVERAL.

SEVERALLY. Separately; distinct from and apart from others.

SEVERANCE. **1.** The act of severing; the state of being severed (see **sever**). **2.** The separation, for purposes of **pleading** and/or **trial**, of one or more **defendants** from others charged in the same **charging document** or one or more **charges** against a particular defendant listed in a single charging document. A **motion** requesting severance of defendants or charges can be made at any time before or during trial. The most common reason for requesting severance is to prevent prejudice to a defendant. For example, a defendant who has no prior record can request that his or her case be severed from that of a codefendant who does have a prior record.

Ss

SEVERE. Grave; serious; extreme; harsh.

SEX OFFENSES. All unlawful **sexual intercourse**, unlawful **sexual contact**, and other unlawful behavior intended to result in sexual gratification or profit from sexual activity. *See*: ADULTERY; BESTIALITY; BUGGERY; CUNNILINGUS; DEBAUCH; FELLATIO; FORCIBLE RAPE; HOUSE OF PROSTITUTION; INCEST; INDECENT ASSAULT; INDECENT EXPOSURE; PATRONIZING PROSTITUTES; PEDERASTY; PERVERSION; PROMOTION OF PROSTITUTION; PROSTITUTION; RAPE; RAPE WITHOUT FORCE OR CONSENT; SEXUAL ACT; SEXUAL ASSAULT; SEXUAL CONTACT; SEXUAL INTERCOURSE; SODOMY; STATUTORY RAPE.

SEXUAL ACT. Any act between two persons or between a person and an animal involving direct physical contact between the genitals of one and the genitals, anus, or mouth of the other; or any act involving direct physical contact between the genitals or anus of one and an instrument or device manipulated by another person when the act is done for the purpose of arousing or gratifying sexual desire or for the purpose of causing bodily injury or offensive physical contact. See SEX OFFENSES for a list of related terms.

SEXUAL ASSAULT. Section 213.4 of the **Model Penal Code** defines sexual assault as follows:

"A person who has sexual contact with another not his spouse, or causes such other to have sexual conduct with him, is guilty of sexual assault, a misdemeanor, if:

(1) he knows that the contact is offensive to the other person; or

(2) he knows that the other person suffers from a mental disease or defect which renders him or her incapable of appraising the nature of his or her conduct; or

(3) he knows that the other person is unaware that a sexual act is being committed; or

(4) the other person is less than 10 years old; or

(5) he has substantially impaired the other person's power to appraise or control his or her conduct, by administering or employing without the other's knowledge drugs, intoxicants or other means for the purpose of preventing resistance; or

(6) the other person is less than [16] years old and the actor is at least [four] years older than the other person; or

(7) the other person is less than 21 years old and the actor is his guardian or otherwise responsible for general supervision of his welfare; or

(8) the other person is in custody of law or detained in a hospital or other institution and the actor has supervisory or disciplinary authority over him."

See ASSAULT and SEX OFFENSES for lists of related terms.

SEXUAL CONTACT. Section 213.4 of the **Model Penal Code** defines sexual contact as "any touching of the sexual or other intimate parts of the person for the purpose of arousing or gratifying sexual desire." See SEX OFFENSES for a list of related terms.

SEXUAL INTERCOURSE. Sexual union between a man and a woman involving the penetration of the female sex organ by the male sex organ; carnal knowledge; coitus. Section 213.0 (2) of the **Model Penal Code** expands the definition of sexual intercourse to include "intercourse per **os** or per **anum**, with some penetration however slight; emission is not required." See SEX OFFENSES for a list of related terms.

SHALL. To be required, ordered, or directed to do something. In statutes, rules, and court decisions shall signifies the imposing of a **duty** or the issuing of a command or order as opposed to the granting of power, permission, or discretionary authority. *Example*: Law enforcement officers shall bring arrested persons before a magistrate without necessary delay. *See*: MAY; MUST; SHOULD.

SHAM. False; pretended; counterfeit.

SHANGHAI. To drug, intoxicate, or otherwise render a person insensible in order to **kidnap** him or her for compulsory service aboard a ship.

SHELTER. A short-term **juvenile facility** that provides temporary care similar to that of a **detention center**, but in a physically unrestricting environment. See JUVENILE for a list of related terms.

SHERIFF. The elected or appointed chief officer of a county **law enforcement agency**, usually responsible for law enforcement in unincorporated areas and for the operation of the county **jail**. Other law enforcement related duties of the sheriff may include **service of process**, the transfer of **convicts** to state penal institutions, and the summoning of **jurors**. See LAW ENFORCEMENT OFFICER for a list of related terms.

SHERIFF'S DEPARTMENT. A **law enforcement agency** organized at the county level, directed by a **sheriff**, which exercises its law enforcement functions at the county level, usually within unincorporated areas, and operates the county **jail** in most jurisdictions. Some sheriff's departments have contractual arrangements with cities or districts to perform law enforcement duties within incorporated areas, municipalities, or special districts.

SHIELD LAW. A state law allowing a news reporter to refuse to disclose to the court or law enforcement officials the names of confidential informants, notes, and other sources of information obtained while gathering the news.

SHIFT. To move from one place, position, or person to another. *Example*: The burden of proof shifted to the defendant.

SHOCK PROBATION. *See*: SPLIT SENTENCE (2.).

SHOOT. 1. To strike or hit with something discharged or propelled from a **weapon** such as a **firearm** or bow. *Example*: She shot her husband. **2.** To discharge or propel something from a weapon such as a firearm or bow. *Example*: You may not shoot a gun near a dwelling.

SHOPLIFTING. A crime whose essential elements are "(1) wilful taking of possession of any goods, wares, or merchandise offered for sale by any wholesale or retail store or other mercantile establishment; (2) without the knowledge or consent of the seller; (3) with the intention of converting such goods, wares, or merchandise to his own use and (4) without having paid the purchase price." *State v. White*, 576 P.2d 138, 139 (Ariz.App. 1978). See ABSTRACTION for a list of related terms.

SHORT. 1. Having little length or height; not long; not tall. **2.** Brief; not extensive; not lasting long. **3.** Not meeting a requirement or standard; inadequate; insufficient.

SHORT-TERM FACILITY. *See*: JUVENILE FACILITY.

Ss

SHOTGUN.   A shoulder-held, smoothbored firearm that fires multiple pellets and is designed to kill birds and small animals at close range.

SHOTGUN INSTRUCTION.   Same as ALLEN CHARGE.

SHOULD.   Ought to. The term should is used to convey a sense of duty or obligation, but is not as strong as **must** or **shall**. Should conveys a sense of moral obligation or preferred conduct as opposed to legal obligation.

SHOW.   **1.** To indicate; to exhibit; to allege; to represent. **2.** To reasonably satisfy; to establish; to prove; to make apparent or clear by evidence.

SHOW CAUSE ORDER.   A court **order**, made upon the **motion** of an applicant, requiring the adverse party to appear in court and explain why a certain thing should not be done or permitted. If the responding party fails to meet the **prima facie case** made out by the applicant's **affidavit** or declaration, the court will grant the relief sought by the applicant.

SHOWUP.   A CONFRONTATION involving the presentation of a single **suspect** to a **victim** or **witness** of a **crime** for the purpose of identifying the **perpetrator** of the crime. *See*: EYEWITNESS IDENTIFICATION; IDENTIFICATION; LINEUP.

SI.   *Latin.* "If."

SIC.   *Latin.* Thus; so; in such manner. The term sic is often used parenthetically to indicate that something has been copied exactly from an original and should be read as it stands.

SIDE.   **1.** Aspect; phase. *Example*: The court considered all sides of the issue. **2.** One of two or more opposing parties or positions in a case or dispute. *Example*: I have to support the defendant's side on that issue.

SIGN.   To affix one's name or mark upon a writing or instrument to authenticate it or to indicate knowledge, approval, acceptance, or obligation with regard to its contents.

SIGNATURE.   The mark made by a person who **signs** a writing or instrument.

SIGNED OPINION.   An OPINION bearing the name of the individual **judge** who authored it, whether or not issued on behalf of the whole court. See OPINION for a list of related terms.

SIGNIFY.   To make known, to express, or to communicate through signs, words, gestures, or acts.

SILVER PLATTER DOCTRINE. The doctrine that **evidence** of a federal **crime** obtained in a **search** by state law enforcement officers by means which, if used by federal law enforcement officers, would constitute a violation of the Fourth Amendment, is admissible in a federal prosecution. The silver platter doctrine was abolished by the U.S. Supreme Court in *Elkins v. U.S.*, 364 U.S. 206, 80 S.Ct. 1437, 4 L.Ed.2d 1669 (1960). The *Elkins* Court held that the foundation upon which the admissibility of state-seized evidence in a federal trial originally rested—that unreasonable state searches did not violate the U.S. Constitution—had disappeared with the holding of **Wolf v. Colorado,** 338 U.S. 25, 69 S.Ct. 1359, 93 L.Ed. 1782 (1949). See SEARCH for a list of related terms.

SIMILAR. Resembling in a general way; somewhat like though not identical.

SIMILITER. *Latin.* "Likewise."

SIMPLE. Mere; ordinary; common; not aggravated; not compound.

SIMPLE ASSAULT. **1.** An ASSAULT committed without the intention of committing any other **crime** or inflicting any other injury. **2.** An ASSAULT committed without aggravating circumstances. **3.** Under modern statutes that include **battery** within the definition of assault, simple assault may include unlawful intentional threatening, attempted inflicting or inflicting of less than **serious bodily injury,** or offensive physical contact upon another, without the use of a dangerous or **deadly weapon**. The **Model Penal Code** defines simple assault as follows:

"A person is guilty of assault if he:

(a) attempts to cause or purposely, knowingly or recklessly causes bodily injury to another; or

(b) negligently causes bodily injury to another with a deadly weapon; or

(c) attempts by physical menace to put another in fear of imminent serious bodily injury."

See ASSAULT for a list of related terms.

SIMPLE BATTERY. **1.** A BATTERY committed without **aggravating circumstances**. **2.** A battery not resulting in **serious bodily injury**.

SIMPLE LARCENY. LARCENY committed without such **aggravating circumstances** as violence, taking from one's person, or taking from one's house. *Also called*: **plain larceny**. See ABSTRACTION for a list of related terms.

SIMULATE. To falsely assume the appearance of; to feign; to counterfeit; to pretend; to imitate.

SIMULTANEOUS. Existing, occurring, or operating at substantially the same time. *Example*: Simultaneous shots rang out from both sides of the street.

SINE. *Latin.* "Without."

SINE DIE. *Latin.* "Without day." Without assigning a time for further meeting, hearing, or action. *See*: ADJOURN.

SINE QUA NON. *Latin.* "Without which not." An essential or indispensable element or condition.

SINGLE. Unitary; individual; one only; separate; not multiple; not combined or united with another or others.

SIT. **1.** To hold a **session** of a **court**, **legislature**, or other deliberative body. *Example*: The court will sit next Wednesday. **2.** To officially occupy a seat as a member of a deliberative body. *Example*: She sits on the highest court of the state.

SITTING. The holding of a **term** or **session** of a **court**, **legislature**, or other deliberative body. *See*: RISING.

SITUATION. **1.** State of affairs; combination of circumstances. *Example:* This is a serious situation. **2.** The position of a person with regard to surrounding conditions and circumstances. *Example*: The court refused to consider the juvenile's living situation.

SITUS. The place where something is for purposes of exercising power or **jurisdiction** over it; location; position.

SKILLED WITNESS. Same as EXPERT WITNESS.

SLANDER. The malicious **publication** (definition 3) of DEFAMATION by spoken words, bodily gestures, or other transitory means. Slander gives rise only to a **civil action** unless it has been specifically made **criminal** by **statute**. *See*: LIBEL.

SLATING. Same as BOOKING.

SLAY. Same as KILL.

SLIGHT. Of little importance or consideration; trifling.

SLIP OPINION. A copy of the OPINION of a court or other tribunal that is published and distributed very soon after the opinion is handed down. See OPINION for a list of related terms.

SLOT MACHINE. A coin-operated **gambling device** by which a person may, by chance, obtain something of value either directly or indirectly. Slot machine is variously defined in different jurisdictions. See GAMBLING for a list of related terms.

SMALL CLAIMS COURT. *See*: COURT OF LIMITED JURISDICTION.

SMUGGLING. Unlawful movement of goods across a national or state boundary or into or out of a **correctional facility**. Smuggling offenses are of two general types. One type prohibits the movement of ordinary goods without observing special conditions, such as payment of import duties. The other type prohibits the movement of particular goods across particular boundaries and/or by particular persons. Examples of smuggling offenses include goods moved across a boundary with intent to avoid payment of import duties or excise taxes, or with intent to avoid special restrictions such as quarantine requirements for plants and animals. Movement may also be prohibited because of the nature of the material (e.g., pornographic photographs), or because of the source, such as the import into the United States of foreign goods in violation of a trade embargo.

SOCIAL HISTORY. *See*: PRESENTENCE REPORT.

SOCIAL INVESTIGATION. *See*: PRESENTENCE INVESTIGATION.

SOCIAL STUDY. *See*: PRESENTENCE REPORT.

S s

SODOMY. Broadly speaking, sodomy consists of any unnatural sexual act between two human beings or between a human being and an animal. It may include any act of penetration between sexual organs, the mouth, or the anus. Sodomy is often referred to as the **infamous crime against nature** and is variously defined by statute in different jurisdictions. *Also called*: **crime against nature**; **deviate sexual conduct**; **deviate sexual intercourse**; **sexual abuse**; **unnatural act**; **unnatural intercourse**; **unnatural offense**. See SEX OFFENSES for a list of related terms.

SOLE. Only; exclusive; unique. *Example*: The district court has sole jurisdiction over misdemeanor trials.

SOLEMN. Formal.

SOLICITATION. **1.** Generally, seeking to obtain something by persuasion, entreaty, petition, or formal application. **2.** Under Section 5.02 (1) of the **Model Penal Code** "[a] person is guilty of solicitation to commit a crime if with the purpose of promoting or facilitating its commission he commands, encourages or requests another person to engage in specific conduct that would constitute such crime or an attempt to commit such crime or would establish his complicity in its commission or attempted commission." The crime solicited need not actually be committed to convict a person of solicitation. See INCHOATE OFFENSE and PARTY for lists of related terms.

SOLICITOR. The chief law officer of a city, town, municipality, or government department.

SOLICITOR GENERAL. The Solicitor General in the **Department of Justice** represents the U.S. Government in cases before the Supreme Court. The Solicitor General's duties include the following:

—deciding what cases the Government should ask the Supreme Court to review and what position the Government should take in cases before the Court;

—supervising the preparation of the Government's Supreme Court briefs and other legal documents and the conduct of the oral arguments in the Court;

—arguing most of the Government's cases in the Supreme Court; and

—deciding whether the United States should appeal in all cases it loses before the lower courts.

SOLITARY CONFINEMENT. Confinement of a prisoner in which he or she has little or no human contact.

SOON. Within a reasonable time.

SOUND. **1.** Healthy; normal; in good condition; unimpaired by disease, defect, or injury. *Example*: He was of sound mind. **2.** Fair; equitable; reasonable; not arbitrary or capricious. *Example*: You must exercise sound judicial discretion.

SOUND SPECTOGRAPH. *See*: VOICEPRINT IDENTIFICATION.

SOURCE. A person, place, or thing from which something comes or derives. *Example*: The reporter tried to protect his sources of information.

SOUTH DAKOTA v. OPPERMAN. *See*: IMPOUND; INVENTORY SEARCH.

SOVEREIGN. Having superior or supreme rank, power, or authority.

SOVEREIGN PEOPLE. The entire citizenry, considered as a whole, who exercise their supreme political power through their elected representatives.

SPEAKER. The chairman or presiding officer of certain legislative bodies, such as the United States House of Representatives.

SPECIAL. **1.** Limited or confined to a particular person, class, subject matter, or purpose. **2.** Unusual; extraordinary; peculiar.

SPECIAL ACT. Same as SPECIAL LEGISLATION.

SPECIAL AGENT. An AGENT who has SPECIAL AUTHORITY.

SPECIAL APPEARANCE. An APPEARANCE made only for the purpose of attacking the **jurisdiction** of the **court** over the defendant's person. See JURISDICTION for a list of related terms.

SPECIAL AUTHORITY. AUTHORITY (definition 1) conferred by a PRINCIPAL upon an AGENT to act for or represent him or her in one or more transactions but not involving continuous service to the principal. Special authority may involve particular instructions in a particular matter.

SPECIAL INTERROGATORIES. Written questions submitted to a **jury** on one or more material issues of fact to test the correctness of the **general verdict**. See INTERROGATORIES and JURY for lists of related terms.

SPECIAL JUDGE. A **judge** who is appointed to hear and exercise all judicial functions for a specific **case**. Special judges are appointed in addition to, not in lieu of, regularly appointed or elected judges. They conduct all criminal proceedings pertaining to a specific case only.

SPECIAL JURISDICTION. *Also called*: **limited jurisdiction**. *See*: COURT OF LIMITED JURISDICTION.

Ss

SPECIAL JURY. Same as STRUCK JURY.

SPECIAL LAW. Same as SPECIAL LEGISLATION.

SPECIAL LEGISLATION. Legislation that operates only on particular persons, places, or things, as distinguished from legislation that operates generally on all persons, places, and things. Many state constitutions have provisions prohibiting the enactment of special legislation. Courts have held that these provisions do not prevent the legislature from enacting laws making reasonable classifications. Only arbitrary and unreasonable classifications that exclude one or more of a class without a reasonable basis will make a law void. *Also called*: **special act**; **special law**; **special statute**. See STATUTE for a list of related terms.

SPECIAL MALICE. MALICE directed toward a particular person.

SPECIAL SESSION. A **sitting** of a **court**, **legislature**, or other deliberative body on an extraordinary occasion, as distinguished from its regularly scheduled sittings.

SPECIAL STATUTE. Same as SPECIAL LEGISLATION.

SPECIAL TERM. A period of time for conducting court business during which the court deals with matters other than **trial**, such as **motions**, **arguments**, various types of formal business, or a special class of cases. *See*: GENERAL TERM (definition 2).

SPECIAL VERDICT. A VERDICT consisting of answers to specific questions relating to all material **facts** in a **case**. The **court** then applies the **law** to the facts as found by the **jury** and renders **judgment**. See VERDICT for a list of related terms.

SPECIFIC. Definite; particular; explicit; precise.

SPECIFICATION. A detailed enumeration of particular points or matters.

SPECIFIC INTENT. An additional **intent**, required by the definition of some **crimes**, above and beyond the intent to commit the **actus reus** of the crime. For example, the specific intent in the common law crime of **burglary** is the intent to commit a **felony** in the dwelling house of another, which is required in addition to the intent to break and enter the dwelling in the nighttime. *Also called*: **specific mens rea**. *See*: GENERAL INTENT.

SPECIFIC MENS REA. Same as SPECIFIC INTENT.

SPECIFIC OBJECTION. An OBJECTION that identifies the ground of the objection.

SPECIFY. To state explicitly or in detail.

SPECIMEN. Same as SAMPLE.

SPECTROGRAM. *See*: VOICEPRINT IDENTIFICATION.

SPECTROGRAPH. *See*: VOICEPRINT IDENTIFICATION.

SPEEDY TRIAL. The right of a **defendant** to have a prompt **trial** as guaranteed by the Sixth Amendment to the U.S. Constitution: "In all criminal prosecutions, the accused shall enjoy the right to a speedy and public trial. . . ." Although the U.S. Constitution and the constitutions of almost all the states provide that the accused shall enjoy the right to a speedy trial, the requirements vary among the jurisdictions. Generally, whether a criminal defendant has been denied his constitutional right to a speedy trial depends not upon the application of an inflexible rule but upon a balancing of certain factors in the particular context of his or her case. Among the relevant factors are the length of and reason for the delay, the defendant's assertion of the right, and the prejudice inuring to the defendant. *Barker v. Wingo,* 407 U.S. 514, 92 S.Ct. 2182, 33 L.Ed.2d 101 (1972). Most states and the federal government have enacted statutes establishing the time within which a defendant must be tried following the date of **arrest**, **initial appearance**, or the filing of **charges** in **court**. If the defendant is not brought to trial within the specified period, the case must be dismissed. Jurisdictions differ, however, on whether **dismissal** on these grounds constitutes a **bar** to subsequent **prosecution** for the same offense.

Most speedy trial statutes provide a method for computing **excludable delay**, delay not included in calculations of elapsed time for purposes of determining speedy trial. Examples of excludable delay are periods of time spent on other proceedings concerning the defendant, such as a hearing on mental **competency** to stand trial, trial on other **charges**, or **probation revocation** or **parole revocation** hearings. Other examples are delays due to **continuances** granted at the request of the defendant, the **absconding** of the defendant, or the execution of procedures necessary to obtain the presence of a confined prisoner. See TRIAL for a list of related terms.

SPEEDY TRIAL ACT. A 1974 federal statute setting time limits for carrying out the major steps in the **prosecution** of a federal criminal case. The citation for this act is 18 U.S.C. §3161 et seq. See TRIAL for a list of related terms.

SPINELLI v. UNITED STATES. *See*: ILLINOIS v. GATES.

SPLIT SENTENCE. **1.** A sentence of a **fine** and **imprisonment** in which only the fine is enforced and the imprisonment is suspended. **2.** A sentence explicitly requiring the convicted person to serve a period of **confinement** in a local, state, or federal facility followed by a period of **probation**. In this sense, a split sentence is frequently called **shock probation**. The theory behind this procedure is that the experience of incarceration will shock the person into responding positively to the subsequent probation. See PROBATION and SENTENCE for lists of related terms.

SPONTANEOUS DECLARATION. A statement is admissible under the spontaneous declaration exception to the **hearsay rule** under the following conditions: "1) an occurrence sufficiently startling to produce a spontaneous and unreflecting statement; 2) absence of time to fabricate; and 3) the statement must relate to the circumstances of the occurrence." *People v. Was*, 318 N.E.2d 309, 313 (Ill.App. 1974). Spontaneous declarations are sometimes said to be part of the **res gestae**. *Also called*: **spontaneous exclamation**. See HEARSAY RULE for a list of other exceptions.

SPONTANEOUS EXCLAMATION. Same as SPONTANEOUS DECLARATION.

SPOUSE. A wife or husband.

SPURIOUS. Not genuine; not authentic; counterfeit; false.

SS. Abbreviation for SCILICET.

STAB. To pierce or wound with a pointed instrument.

STALE. Having lost legal force or effectiveness through passage of time or inaction. **Probable cause** to **search** for certain objects may become stale if there is too long a delay between the time when the information upon which probable cause is based is gathered and the time when the search is executed. Depending on the nature of the object, the nature of the criminal activity, the criminal suspects, and other factors, there may no longer be good reason to believe that the property is still at the same location.

STAND. n. The place in the courtroom from which **witnesses** give their testimony. v. **1.** To remain valid; to continue in force. *Example*: The judge's ruling was allowed to stand. **v. 2.** To endure; to undergo; to submit to. *Example*: You will stand trial for your crime. **v. 3.** To become or remain inactive or stationary. **v. 4.** To take or assume a position, attitude, or course.

STANDARD OF PROOF. The measure or level of **proof** required in a particular type of case. In a **criminal case**, the standard of proof required to convict a person is proof **beyond a reasonable doubt**.

STAND DOWN. To leave the witness **stand**.

STANDING. The legal right of a person to judicially challenge the conduct of another person or the government. In general, standing depends on whether the person seeking relief has a legally sufficient personal interest at stake to obtain judicial resolution of the **merits** of the dispute. The "gist of the question of standing" is whether the party seeking relief has "alleged such a personal stake in the outcome of the controversy as to assure that concrete adverseness which sharpens the presentation of issues upon which the court so largely depends for illumination of difficult constitutional questions." *Baker v. Carr*, 369 U.S. 186, 204, 82 S.Ct. 691, 703, 7 L.Ed.2d 663, 678 (1962).

To invoke the **exclusionary rule** to challenge the admissibility of **evidence**, a defendant must have standing. A defendant has standing when his or her own constitutional rights have been violated.

" 'Fourth Amendment rights are personal rights which, like some other constitutional rights, may not be vicariously asserted.' . . . A person who is aggrieved by an illegal search and seizure only through the introduction of damaging evidence secured by a search of a third person's premises or property has not had any of his Fourth Amendment rights infringed. . . . And since the exclusionary rule is an attempt to effectuate the guarantees of the Fourth Amendment, . . . it is proper to permit only defendants whose Fourth Amendment rights have been violated to benefit from the rule's protections." *Rakas v. Illinois*, 439 U.S. 128, 133-34, 99 S.Ct. 421, 425, 58 L.Ed.2d 387, 394-95 (1978).

In determining whether a defendant's Fourth Amendment rights have been violated, courts will analyze whether the defendant had a reasonable expectation of privacy in the area **searched** or the item **seized**. See EXCLUSIONARY RULE, PRIVACY, and SEARCH for lists of related terms.

STAND MUTE. To refuse to **plead** to a criminal **charge**. Courts will consider standing mute a **not guilty plea**.

STARE DECISIS. *Latin.* "To stand by that which was decided." The doctrine that when a principle of **law** has been decided by a **court**, that principle will be adhered to by that court and by inferior courts in future cases in which the facts are substantially the same, even though the parties may be different. The object of the doctrine of stare decisis is uniformity, certainty, and stability in the law. Stare decisis is a compelling but not absolute doctrine. Principles announced in former decisions may be overturned only on a showing of good cause or if they conflict with a statutory or constitutional provision. Stare decisis differs from **res judicata** in that:

—stare decisis relates only to questions of law, whereas res judicata relates to both the law and facts;

—stare decisis operates on all persons, whereas res judicata operates merely on the parties to the particular proceeding and their privies; and

—stare decisis is persuasive but not absolute, whereas res judicata is imperative and compels judgment.

See: LAW OF THE CASE; PRECEDENT.

Ss

STAT. Abbreviation for UNITED STATES STATUTES AT LARGE.

STATE. **n. 1.** In general, a body of people occupying a defined territory and politically organized under a sovereign government. **n. 2.** One of the commonwealths or political units, each more or less autonomous regarding internal affairs, comprising the federal union of the United States of America. *See*: UNITED STATES. **n. 3.** The territory, government, or people in their collective governmental capacity of one of the states (definition n2). *Example*: The court handed down its opinion in the case of *State v. Angus*. **n. 4.** The condition of a person or thing. *Example*: She was in a state of shock. **v.** To say or set forth clearly and definitely. See ADDRESS for a list of related terms.

STATE ACTION. Under the 14th Amendment due process and equal protection clauses and other similar constitutional prohibitions against state deprivations of individual rights, state action means an action taken by an agent or instrumentality of a **state** (definition n2) under authority or **color** of state law.

STATE COURT. A **court** established or authorized under the constitution or laws of a **state** (definition n2) and concerned primarily with judicial administration of state and local laws; any court other than a federal court. See COURT for a list of related terms.

STATED. Fixed; settled.

STATE HIGHWAY PATROL.   A state **law enforcement agency** whose principle functions are the prevention, detection, and investigation of motor vehicle offenses, and the apprehension of traffic offenders. In some states, **state police** functions include highway patrol; in other states the state police and the state highway patrol are separate organizational units with identifiably separate functions.

STATE HIGHWAY PATROL OFFICER.   An employee of a **state highway patrol** who is an officer sworn to carry out law enforcement duties, primarily traffic code enforcement. See LAW ENFORCEMENT OFFICER for a list of related terms.

STATE LAW ENFORCEMENT AGENCY.   A **law enforcement agency** that is an organizational unit or subunit of **state** (definition n2) government. Examples of state law enforcement agencies are **state police** agencies, **state highway patrols**, state park ranger agencies, and campus police agencies of colleges and universities that are financed and administered by state government.

STATEMENT.   An oral or written declaration.

STATEMENT OF PARTICULARS.   Same as BILL OF PARTICULARS.

STATE OF MIND EXCEPTION.   An exception to the **hearsay rule** under which an out-of-court declaration of a then-existing intention to do something in the future is admissible as circumstantial proof that the declarant later accomplished the intended act. The theory justifying this exception is that people generally do what they say they intend to do. See HEARSAY RULE for a list of other exceptions.

STATE POLICE.   A state **law enforcement agency** whose principal functions usually include criminal investigation, aiding local police, maintaining statewide police communications, police training, and guarding state property, and may include highway patrol. In some states the duties of traffic code enforcement are performed by the state police; in others there is a separate **state highway patrol**. State police may also perform local law enforcement functions in incorporated areas or in support of local police.

STATE POLICE OFFICER.   An employee of a **state police** agency who is an officer sworn to carry out **law enforcement** duties, sometimes including traffic enforcement duties. See LAW ENFORCEMENT OFFICER for a list of related terms.

STATE'S ATTORNEY.   *See*: PROSECUTOR.

STATE'S EVIDENCE.   **1. Evidence** given by an **accomplice** or joint participant in a **crime** who becomes a **witness** for the **prosecution** against the other defendants in the crime, sometimes in return for **clemency** or a grant of **immunity** from prosecution. **2.** Evidence given by or on behalf of the prosecution in a criminal case. See EVIDENCE for a list of related terms.

STATIM. *Latin.* Forthwith; immediately.

STATUS. The legal state or condition of a person or thing.

STATUS CRIME. Same as STATUS OFFENSE (definition 2).

STATUS OFFENDER. A **juvenile** who has been adjudicated by a judicial officer of a juvenile court as having committed a STATUS OFFENSE (definition 1). In some jurisdictions a status offender who commits repeated status offenses can be adjudged a **delinquent**. A status offender is sometimes called a child, person, minor, or juvenile in need of supervision. See JUVENILE for a list of related terms.

STATUS OFFENSE. **1.** An act or conduct that is declared by **statute** to be an offense, but only when committed or engaged in by a **juvenile**, and that can be adjudicated only by a **juvenile court**. Typical examples of status offenses are violation of curfew, running away from home, truancy, possession of an alcoholic beverage, incorrigibility, having delinquent tendencies, leading an immoral life, and being in need of supervision. See CRIME and JUVENILE for lists of related terms. **2.** An adult offense that consists not of a specific prohibited act or omission but of the accused's having a certain personal condition or being a person of a specified character. Typical examples of status offenses are **vagrancy**, being an **addict**, and being an **habitual criminal**. *Also called*: **status crime**.

STATUS QUO. The existing state or condition of affairs at a particular time. *Example*: The police tried to maintain the status quo.

STATUTE. A written law enacted by a **legislature** declaring, commanding, or prohibiting something. The term statute may refer to a single **act** of a legislature or an organized body of such acts. See ACT for a list of related terms. *See also*: AFFIRMATIVE STATUTE; AUTHORITY; CASE LAW; COMMON LAW; COMMON-LAW CRIME; DECLARATORY STATUTE; ENABLING CLAUSE; ENABLING STATUTE; ENACT; EQUITABLE; EXPOSITORY STATUTE; JUDGE-MADE LAW; LEGISLATION; LEGISLATIVE INTENT RULE; LETTER OF THE LAW; OVERBROAD; PENAL LAW; PREAMBLE; PURVIEW; REFERENCE STATUTE; RUNNING OF THE STATUTE OF LIMITATIONS; SAVE THE STATUTE OF LIMITATIONS; SAVING CLAUSE; SECTION; SESSION LAWS; SEVERABLE STATUTE; SPECIAL LEGISLATION; STATUTE OF LIMITATIONS; STATUTORY; STATUTORY ARSON; STATUTORY LAW; STATUTORY RAPE; STRICT LIABILITY STATUTE; UNITED STATES CODE; UNITED STATES CODE ANNOTATED; UNITED STATES STATUTES AT LARGE; UNWRITTEN LAW; VAGUE; VIOLATION.

STATUTE OF LIMITATIONS. A **statute** that sets out the time period within which a certain type of **action** must be brought or the right to bring the action will be lost.

Generally **prosecutions** for all **crimes** except **murder** are subject to different statutes of limitations, the time periods of which vary from jurisdiction to jurisdiction. There is no statute of limitations for murder. The statute of limitations generally starts to run when every **element** of the crime has occurred, regardless of when the crime was discovered. The running of the statute of limitations may be suspended during any time when the accused is absent from the jurisdiction or during any time when a prosecution against the accused for the same crime based on the same conduct is pending in the jurisdiction. *Also called*: **limitation of actions**.

STATUTORY.   **1.** Relating to a STATUTE. **2.** Created, defined, regulated, required, or authorized by statute. See STATUTE for a list of related terms.

STATUTORY ARSON.   A term used to describe **statutes** that proscribe conduct analogous to but not technically constituting ARSON. An example of statutory arson would be the exploding of another person's house.

STATUTORY LAW.   The body of law created by **legislative** enactment as distinguished from **judge-made law** or law created by administrative decision-making. *Also called*: **written law**. See STATUTE for a list of related terms.

STATUTORY RAPE.   **Sexual intercourse**, without **force** or **threat** of force, with a female who has consented in fact but is deemed to be legally incapable of **consent** because she is below a statutorily designated age. The **prosecution** is not required to prove lack of consent by the female, because the law presumes her to be incapable of consent because of her tender age. Statutory rape is sometimes called **carnal knowledge of a child**. It is no **defense** to statutory rape that the defendant was unaware or mistaken as to the victim's age. See SEX OFFENSES for a list of related terms.

STAY.   To stop; to hold in abeyance; to refrain from enforcing; to suspend. *Example*: The Governor stayed the execution to permit the defendant to take further appeals.

STAY OF PROCEEDINGS.   The postponement or suspension of all proceedings in a **case** by order of the **court** to await the happening of a particular event.

STEAL.   **1.** To wrongfully take and carry away the property of another with the **intent** to deprive the owner of the property and to appropriate it to one's own use. **2.** To commit LARCENY. **3.** In a broad and colloquial sense, to unlawfully take anything from another. See ABSTRACTION for a list of related terms.

STEALTH.   A secret, clandestine, or furtive action or manner. *Example*: The statute prohibited the taking of personal property accomplished by stealth or fraud.

STICK UP.   To rob at gunpoint.

STILL.   An apparatus used for distilling alcoholic liquor.

STILLBORN. Born dead.

STIPULATE. To formally agree.

STIPULATION. An agreement between parties or their attorneys with respect to business before the court, which is designed to simplify, shorten, or settle litigation.

STOLEN. Obtained by **stealing**.

STONE v. POWELL. The U.S. Supreme Court case which held that "where the State has provided an opportunity for full and fair litigation of a Fourth Amendment claim, a state prisoner may not be granted federal **habeas corpus** relief on the ground that **evidence** obtained in an unconstitutional **search** or **seizure** was introduced at his trial." 428 U.S. 465, 494, 96 S.Ct. 3037, 3052, 49 L.Ed.2d 1067, 1088 (1976).

STOP. The least intrusive type of SEIZURE governed by the Fourth Amendment. *See*: FRISK; STOP AND FRISK.

Ss

STOP AND FRISK. A shorthand term for the law enforcement practice involving the temporary investigative **seizure** of a person and the pat-down **search** of the person's outer clothing for weapons. A stop and frisk is a much less severe and less extensive restraint on a person than that of an **arrest** and search. A stop and frisk may be initiated on a lesser justification than **probable cause** for the purposes of crime prevention and investigation and for the protection of the **law enforcement officer** carrying out the investigation. In order to protect society's interest in effective crime prevention or detection, a law enforcement officer may stop or temporarily detain a person for the purpose of investigating possibly criminal behavior, even though there is no probable cause to make an arrest. The officer making the stop, however, must have an **articulable suspicion**—specific and articulable **facts** that, taken together with rational **inferences** from those facts, reasonably warrant that intrusion. Also, the extent of the officer's interference with the person must be reasonable under the circumstances.

In order to protect the officer and others from possible violence by persons being investigated for crime, a law enforcement officer may frisk or pat-down the outer clothing of a person for **weapons**. The officer conducting the frisk must have reason to believe that he or she is dealing with an armed and dangerous person and must be able to justify the stop by pointing to specific facts and specific reasonable inferences that the officer is entitled to draw from the facts in light of his or her experience. Also, the frisk must be limited to what is minimally necessary for self-protection and the protection of others and therefore must be limited initially to a pat-down of the outer clothing for weapons. If a weaponlike object is felt, the officer may seize it. If a weaponlike object is not felt, the officer must discontinue the search immediately.

The basic principles of the law of stop and frisk are discussed in the U.S. Supreme Court case of TERRY v. OHIO, 392 U.S. 1, 88 S.Ct. 1868, 20 L.Ed.2d 889 (1968). Note that these basic principles have been applied to other limited detention and search situations involving objects such as motor vehicles and packages in the mail. *See*: STOP; FRISK.

STREET CRIME. A class of offenses, sometimes defined with some degree of formality as those that occur in public locations, are visible and assaultive, and thus constitute a group of offenses that are a special risk to the public and a special target of law enforcement preventive efforts and prosecutorial attention. Crimes typically included in street crime are **robbery**, purse snatching, and any kind of **assault** outside a residence. See CRIME for a list of related terms.

STREET TIME. Time spent on **conditional release** from prison. If **parole** or other conditional release is revoked, and the person is reconfined, all or part of this time may become **dead time** in calculations of **time served** under correctional jurisdiction, according to administrative or court decision. See RELEASE and SENTENCE for lists of related terms.

STRICT. Precise, accurate, exact; rigorous; stringent; narrowly and specifically limited.

STRICT CONSTRUCTION. A CONSTRUCTION of language limited to the exact and technical meanings of the words and considering no other equitable or reasonable implications beyond the fair meaning of the language used. *Also called*: **literal construction**. *See*: LIBERAL CONSTRUCTION.

STRICT LIABILITY STATUTE. "A strict liability statute is one which imposes criminal sanction for an unlawful act without requiring a showing of criminal **intent**." *State v. Lucero*, 531 P.2d 1215, 1217 (N.M.App. 1975). A person may be **guilty** under such a statute even though he or she had no knowledge that the act was criminal and had no thought of committing a **crime**. All that is required under a strict liability statute is that the **act** is **voluntary**, since involuntary acts cannot be criminal. The usual rationale for such statutes is that the public interest in the matter is so compelling or that the potential for harm is so great that the interests of the public must override the interests of the individual. See STATUTE for a list of related terms.

STRIKE. **1.** To hit with force. **2.** To eliminate; to expunge. *Example*: Strike that from the record. See CANCEL for a list of related terms.

STRONG. Forceful; cogent; persuasive. *Example*: There was strong evidence in the defendant's favor.

STRONGARM ROBBERY. See ROBBERY.

STRONG HAND. A criminal degree of **force** used in the entry of lands.

STRUCK JURY. A special **jury** selected by each party striking a certain number from the panel of jurors, so as to leave a number required by law to try the case. See JURY for a list of related terms.

STRUCTURE. Something constructed or built; an edifice or building of any kind. Examples of structures are a house, a garage, a bridge, and a dam. Whether or not something is a structure may depend on the context in which the word is used.

SUA SPONTE. *Latin.* "Of itself or oneself." Through its, his, or her own volition or **motion**; voluntarily. When a **court** takes action on its own motion rather than at the request of one of the parties to an action, it is said to be acting sua sponte.

SUB. *Latin.* "Under."

SUB CURIA. *Latin.* "Under the law."

SUBJECT. n. A person, thing, or matter about which something is said or to which something is done. **adj. 1.** Under the power or authority of another. *Example:* You are now subject to the jurisdiction of this court. **adj. 2.** Dependent or contingent on something. *Example:* His release was subject to his maintaining good behavior. **adj. 3.** Open; exposed. *Example:* The statute was subject to misinterpretation.

SUBJECT. v. To cause to undergo or experience. *Example:* The prisoner was subjected to torture.

SUBJECT MATTER. The thing in dispute; the issue under consideration.

SUBJECT MATTER JURISDICTION. The power of a **court** to hear and determine **cases** of the general category to which the case under consideration belongs. *Example:* A tax court does not have subject matter jurisdiction over criminal cases. See JURISDICTION for a list of related terms.

SUB JUDICE. *Latin.* Under judicial consideration.

SUBMIT. **1.** To yield to the opinion or authority of another; to acquiesce; to surrender. *Example:* The kidnapper submitted to the authorities. **2.** To refer or commit to the consideration or judgment of another. *Example:* The judge submitted the case to the jury for their deliberation and verdict. **3.** To offer or present, as an opinion. *Example:* I submit that the charge was not proven. See ADDRESS for a list of related terms.

SUB NOMINE. *Latin.* "Under the name of."

SUBORDINATE. Secondary; minor; belonging to a lower or inferior class, rank, or order.

S s

SUBORN.   To procure or induce another to commit an unlawful act, especially **perjury**.

SUBORNATION OF PERJURY.   The crime of intentionally causing another person to commit PERJURY. See AFFIRMATION for a list of related terms.

SUBPOENA.   A written **order** issued by a **judicial officer** requiring a specified person to appear in a designated **court** at a specified time in order to **testify** in a case under the jurisdiction of that court, or to bring a **document**, piece of **evidence** or other thing for use or inspection by the court. Subpoenas can be served in various ways. They may be served in person by a **law enforcement officer**, or by another person authorized to do so. In some jurisdictions some types of subpoenas may be served by mail or by telephone. Failure to obey a subpoena is **contempt of court**.

A subpoena to serve as a **witness** is called a **subpoena ad testificandum**. A subpoena to bring a document, piece of evidence, or other thing into court is called a **subpoena duces tecum**. A subpoena issued for the appearance of a hostile witness or person who has failed to appear in answer to a previous subpoena, and which authorizes a law enforcement officer to bring that person to the court, is often called an **instanter**. See ARREST WARRANT and WITNESS for lists of related terms.

SUBPOENA AD TESTIFICANDUM.   *See*: SUBPOENA.

SUBPOENA DUCES TECUM.   *See*: SUBPOENA.

SUB ROSA.   *Latin.* Confidentially; privately.

SUBSCRIBE.   To sign one's name at the end of a **document** as a **witness**, to show consent, or to bind oneself to the terms of the document.

SUBSCRIBING WITNESS.   A person who signs his or her name as a **witness** to another person's signature. See WITNESS for a list of related terms.

SUBSEQUENT.   Following in time or order; coming later or after; succeeding.

SUB SILENTIO.   *Latin.* "Under silence." Silently. When a court **opinion** reaches a conclusion contrary to that of a previously controlling court opinion without mentioning the earlier opinion, the later opinion is said to have overruled sub silentio the prior opinion by necessary implication. See OPINION for a list of related terms.

SUBSTANCE.   **1.** Essence; the primary or basic component or element of a thing. **2.** Matter or material of a definite chemical composition. *Example*: Heroin and cocaine are controlled substances. *See*: CONTROLLED SUBSTANCE.

SUBSTANTIAL.   **1.** Ample or considerable in value, importance, amount, or degree. **2.** Real; actual; not imaginary. **3.** Relating to the essence of something; essential.

SUBSTANTIAL CAPACITY TEST.   A test developed by the American Law Institute's **Model Penal Code** project to determine a person's mental capacity to commit crime. Section 4.01 of the Model Penal Code reads:

"(1) A person is not responsible for criminal conduct if at the time of such conduct as a result of mental disease or defect he lacks substantial capacity either to appreciate the criminality [wrongfulness] of his conduct or to conform his conduct to the requirements of law.

"(2) As used in this Article, the terms "mental disease or defect" do not include an abnormality manifested only by repeated or otherwise antisocial conduct."

Also called: **ALI insanity test**; **Model Penal Code insanity test**. *See*: INSANITY.

SUBSTANTIAL COMPLIANCE.   Compliance with the essential requirements and purposes of a constitution, statute, contract, or other law or agreement.

SUBSTANTIAL EVIDENCE.   Such relevant, credible **evidence** that a reasonable, unprejudiced mind might accept as adequate to support a particular conclusion. Whether a reviewing court will sustain the decision of a court, jury, or administrative agency often involves a determination of whether there is substantial evidence to support the decision. Substantial evidence is more than a mere **scintilla** of evidence but may be less than a **preponderance of evidence**. See EVIDENCE for a list of related terms.

SUBSTANTIAL JUSTICE.   Each party to a case having received a **fair trial** on the merits. *See*: SUBSTANTIAL JUSTICE RULE.

SUBSTANTIAL JUSTICE RULE.   The rule that an **appellate court** will not order a **new trial** where each of the parties has had a **fair trial** in the lower court and where a new trial is not likely to produce a different result or any **error** complained of will not affect the result. See TRIAL for a list of related terms.

SUBSTANTIAL QUESTION.   A question that is not frivolous but is fairly debatable.

SUBSTANTIATE.   To establish or support by competent **evidence**; to verify.

SUBSTANTIVE.   **1.** Same as SUBSTANTIAL. **2.** Relating to rights and duties and **causes of action** arising therefrom, as distinguished from the procedures to protect and enforce those rights and duties. *See*: SUBSTANTIVE LAW. **3.** Having an independent existence or function; not dependent on or referable to something else; not subordinate.

SUBSTANTIVE DUE PROCESS.   "Substantive due process may be broadly defined as the constitutional guaranty that no person shall be arbitrarily deprived of his life, liberty, or property. The essence of substantive due process is protection from arbitrary and unreasonable action." *Babineaux v. Judiciary Commission*, 341 So.2d 396, 400 (La. 1976). Substantive due process means that state action that deprives a person of life, liberty, or property must have a rational basis. The reason for deprivation may not be so inadequate that it would be characterized as arbitrary. *See*: DUE PROCESS OF LAW; PROCEDURAL DUE PROCESS.

SUBSTANTIVE EVIDENCE. **Evidence** offered to establish the truth of a **fact** or proposition in issue as distinguished from evidence offered to discredit or corroborate a witness's testimony or for some other incidental or collateral purpose. See EVIDENCE for a list of related terms.

SUBSTANTIVE ISSUE. In a criminal case, an issue that concerns the guilt or innocence of the **accused**, as distinguished from collateral procedural issues.

SUBSTANTIVE LAW. **1.** A law that creates, defines, and regulates rights and duties. In criminal law, a substantive law is one that declares what acts are **crimes** and prescribes **punishments** for committing them. *Example*: Criminal laws defining arson, kidnapping, and robbery are substantive laws. *See*: PROCEDURAL LAW. **2.** The body of such laws.

SUBSTANTIVE OFFENSE. An **offense** that is complete in and of itself and is not dependent on another offense.

SUBSTITUTE. A person or thing that takes the place of another; a replacement.

SUBSTITUTED SERVICE. Same as CONSTRUCTIVE SERVICE.

SUBSTITUTIONARY EVIDENCE. Same as SECONDARY EVIDENCE.

SUBTERFUGE. An evasive tactic or trick used for escape or concealment, to justify conduct or opinions, or to avoid unfavorable consequences. *Example*: The arrest was a mere subterfuge to enable the officers to search the defendant's car.

SUCCEEDING. Immediately following.

SUCCESSIVE. Following in uninterrupted order or regular sequence; consecutive.

SUCCESSOR. A person or thing that follows another in order, office, or position.

SUDDEN. Happening quickly and without adequate warning or preparation; abrupt; unexpected.

SUDDEN AFFRAY. A fight or brawl suddenly resulting from the mutual agreement of two or more parties. *See*: SUDDEN HEAT OF PASSION.

SUDDEN HEAT OF PASSION. *See*: HEAT OF PASSION.

SUDDEN PASSION. Same as SUDDEN HEAT OF PASSION.

SUE. To institute or carry on a legal **action**, especially a **civil action**, against another.

SUE OUT. To apply for and obtain a **writ** or other legal **process**.

SUFFER. **1.** To allow; to permit; to tolerate. **2.** To experience physical or mental pain or distress. **3.** To undergo; to experience; to endure.

SUFFICIENT. Adequate or enough for a given purpose.

SUFFICIENT CAUSE. Same as PROBABLE CAUSE.

SUFFICIENT EVIDENCE. **1.** Same as SUBSTANTIAL EVIDENCE. **2.** Same as SATISFACTORY EVIDENCE. **3.** Evidence legally adequate or satisfactory for a given purpose.

NOTE: The term sufficient evidence has varying meanings depending on the context in which it is used. See EVIDENCE for a list of related terms.

SUFFICIENT EVIDENCE TO SUPPORT CONVICTION. An amount of credible **evidence** that would justify a **jury**, or a **judge** in a **nonjury trial**, in believing **beyond a reasonable doubt** that the defendant was **guilty** of the **crime** charged. An **appellate court** may overturn a **conviction** if it finds that there was not sufficient evidence to support the conviction. See EVIDENCE and TRIAL for lists of related terms.

SUFFICIENT PROVOCATION. Same as ADEQUATE PROVOCATION.

SUFFOCATE. To kill by depriving of oxygen, such as by strangling or by asphyxiation.

SUGGEST. **1.** To propose an idea or plan for consideration or action. **2.** To present indirectly to the mind; to hint; to imply.

SUICIDE. The intentional taking of one's own life. Attempted suicide is a **crime** in some states, but suicide is not. **Aiding** or **abetting** suicide is a crime in all jurisdictions, but prosecutions are rare, especially where the suicide is committed by a terminally ill person.

SUI GENERIS. *Latin.* "Of its own kind." Unique; peculiar.

SUI JURIS. *Latin.* "Of one's own right." Capable of managing one's own affairs.

SUIT. A **civil action** or proceeding to enforce a **right** or to obtain compensation for an **injury**. The term suit may also be used in relation to **criminal** proceedings, but this use is infrequent.

SUITABLE. Appropriate; fit; proper; adapted.

SUMMARY. **adj.** Conducted quickly, briefly, and without formal procedures or ceremony. *Example*: He was punished for contempt of court in a summary proceeding. **n.** A short, concise restatement of the main points or substance of a larger work; an abstract; a synopsis. See ABSTRACT for a list of related terms.

SUMMARY JURISDICTION. The authority of a **court** to give a **judgment** or make an **order** without delay or formality. See JURISDICTION for a list of related terms.

SUMMARY PROBATION. Same as COURT PROBATION.

SUMMARY PROCESS. A **writ**, **warrant**, or other **order** that issues from a court instantaneously and without intermediate applications and that takes effect without delay.

SUMMATION. Same as CLOSING ARGUMENT.

SUMMON. To serve a SUMMONS.

SUMMONS. A written **order** issued by a **judicial officer** requiring a person accused of a criminal offense to **appear** in a designated **court** at a specified time to answer the **charge** or charges. Rules of court and statutes usually provide that if a defendant fails to appear in response to a summons, an **arrest warrant** will be issued for his or her **arrest**. The summons is usually used when the offense charged in a **complaint** is a violation of a municipal **ordinance** or some other **misdemeanor** or petty offense. If the offender is a citizen with "roots firmly established in the soil of the community," and thus can be easily found for service of a warrant if the summons is ignored, the summons procedure is a much easier and better way of inducing a defendant to appear in court than is arresting the defendant and taking him or her into custody. See ARREST WARRANT for a list of related terms.

SUNDRIES. Small miscellaneous items that need not be individually identified but may be considered together.

SUO NOMINE. *Latin.* "In his or her own name."

SUPER. *Latin.* Over; above; higher; more than.

SUPERIOR. **adj.** Higher in degree, rank, grade, or authority. **n.** Someone or something entitled to command, influence, or control.

SUPERIOR COURT. In most states of the United States, a **court of general jurisdiction** intermediate between **courts of limited jurisdiction** (such as magistrate courts and district courts) and higher **appellate courts**. In some states superior courts are courts of limited jurisdiction. See COURT and JURISDICTION for lists of related terms.

SUPERSEDE. To set aside something and replace it with something of a higher value or authority. *Example*: The newly enacted statute superseded the old law.

SUPERSEDEAS. A **writ** commanding a **stay** of legal proceedings. See ARREST WARRANT for a list of related terms.

SUPERSEDING CAUSE. Same as INTERVENING CAUSE.

SUPERVENING CAUSE. Same as INTERVENING CAUSE.

SUPERVISED PROBATION. Guidance, treatment, or regulation by a **probation agency** of the behavior of a person who is subject to **adjudication** or who has been **convicted** of an offense, resulting from a formal **court order** or a probation agency decision. Supervision of adults may be in lieu of **prosecution**, in lieu of **judgment**, or after a judgment of **conviction**. Supervised probation may be a substitute for **confinement** or may occur after a period of confinement in **jail** or **prison**.

Ss

Probation supervision differs according to the degree of intensity of supervision and amount of services provided to subjects. A common broad distinction, known by a variety of names, is between **active supervision** and **inactive supervision**. Active supervision involves contact between the agency and the client on a regular basis. Under inactive supervision, contact occurs only when initiated by the client or other interested party outside the probation agency, and is not on a regular basis. Inactive cases are sometimes called **banked cases**. More detailed levels of service distinctions are made by some probation agencies.

Probation supervision is not a necessary feature of probationary status. A court may place an offender on **probation** without assignment to a probation agency's supervisory caseload (see **court probation**), or may request a private citizen to assume specified responsibilities in connection with the probationer. See PROBATION for a list of related terms. *See also*: PAROLE SUPERVISION.

SUPERVISION. Authorized and required guidance, treatment, and/or regulation of the behavior of a person either before or after **adjudication**, performed by a **correctional agency**. Supervision may but need not be accompanied by other supportive efforts on the part of the agency. *See*: PAROLE SUPERVISION; SUPERVISED PROBATION; SUPERVISORY CUSTODY.

SUPERVISORY CUSTODY. In the **corrections** context, responsibility for SUPERVISION of a **probationer, parolee,** or other member of a nonincarcerated correctional caseload. Supervisory custody represents the type of custodial responsibility assigned to **probation agencies**, which have neither full **jurisdictional control** over their clients nor immediate **physical custody** over their persons.

Parole agencies may have only supervisory custody of their caseloads, or may have jurisdictional control also, depending upon whether the **paroling authority** and the field service function are in a single agency. A **judicial officer** who places a person on **probation**, but without assignment to an agency caseload, may be said to have both jurisdictional control and supervisory custody of the probationer if the judicial officer both sets probation conditions and requires the subject to report compliance to him or her. See PAROLE and PROBATION for lists of related terms.

SUPPLEMENT. **1.** An addition to something to complete, correct, or update it. **2.** Material added after the end of a book (either as part of the book or as a separate volume) that corrects errors or provides later information. A supplement is usually necessary to the current usefulness of a book. *See*: ADDENDUM; APPENDIX.

SUPPLEMENTAL. Serving as a SUPPLEMENT (definition 1). *Example:* The officer filed a supplemental affidavit to provide additional information for the magistrate.

SUPPLIANT. A petitioner.

SUPPLICANT. A petitioner.

SUPPLY. To furnish; to provide.

SUPPORT. **v. 1.** To sustain or maintain by supplying money or other things necessary to existence. **v. 2.** To uphold or maintain the validity or authority of something; to corroborate; to verify; to substantiate; to strengthen. *Example*: "[N]o warrants shall issue, but upon probable cause, supported by oath or affirmation." **n.** The means of livelihood; sustenance; maintenance. Support includes food, shelter, clothing, and other necessary care and may, depending on the jurisdiction or situation, include transportation expenses, utility expenses, medical and drug expenses, household expenses, income tax liability, and the like.

SUPPOSE. **1.** To believe; to think; to deem; to esteem. *Example*: It is supposed that the wound was accidental. **2.** To assume as true for the purpose of argument or tracing consequences. **3.** To believe on slight grounds or with insufficient proof; to presume; to guess.

SUPPRESS. **1.** To keep from being disclosed, published, or circulated. *Example:* The prosecution suppressed information favorable to the defendant. **2.** With respect to **evidence**, to suppress means to invoke the **exclusionary rule** and prevent the use of illegally obtained evidence at **trial**. *Example*: The defendant filed a motion to suppress the gun seized from his automobile by the police. **3.** To put an end to; to subdue; to quell; to prohibit. *Example*: We will not allow the government to suppress our freedoms.

SUPPRESSION HEARING.   A **hearing** in a criminal case in which a defendant attempts to prevent specified statements, documents, or objects from being introduced into **evidence** in a **trial**. The kinds of issues considered in a suppression hearing include the legality of a **search and seizure**, the legality of the obtaining of a **confession**, and the legality of an **identification** procedure. Suppression hearings are commonly initiated before trial on a **motion** by the defendant, although occasionally a **court** will initiate a suppression hearing. If the court suppresses evidence critical in proving the **charge**, the **prosecution** may drop the case and it may be **dismissed**. If the evidence is not critical, the case may proceed. See EXCLUSIONARY RULE and HEARING for lists of related terms. *See also*: MOTION TO SUPPRESS.

SUPRA.   *Latin.* "Above." The term supra refers a reader to a previous part of a written work. *See*: INFRA.

SUPREMACY CLAUSE.   The clause in Article VI, Section 2, of the U.S. Constitution that reads as follows:

> "This Constitution, and the Laws of the United States which shall be made in Pursuance thereof; and all Treaties made, or which shall be made, under the Authority of the United States, shall be the supreme Law of the Land; and the Judges in every State shall be bound thereby, any Thing in the Constitution or Laws of any State to the Contrary notwithstanding."

The supremacy clause is the basic foundation of the federal government's power over the states. This clause has been interpreted to mean that the states may not interfere in any manner with the functioning of the federal government and that federal statutes, treaties, court decisions, administrative acts, and other actions must prevail over state actions that are inconsistent with them.

In situations where there may be an apparent conflict between state and federal law, the following criteria are used to determine whether **preemption** is appropriate.

> "Where . . . Congress has not stated specifically whether a federal statute has occupied a field in which States are otherwise free to legislate, different criteria have furnished touchstones for decision. . . .
>
> First, '[t]he scheme of federal regulation [is] so pervasive as to make reasonable the inference that Congress left no room for the States to supplement it.' . . .
>
> Second, the federal statutes 'touch a field in which the federal interest is so dominant that the federal system [must] be assumed to preclude enforcement of state laws on the same subject.' . . .
>
> Third, enforcement of state . . . acts presents a serious danger of conflict with the administration of the federal program." *Pennsylvania v. Nelson*, 350 U.S. 497, 501-06, 76 S.Ct. 477, 479-82, 100 L.Ed. 640, 651-54 (1956).

Ss

SUPREMACY OF THE LAW.   Same as RULE OF LAW.

SUPREME.   Highest in rank or authority.

SUPREME COURT.   The highest **appellate court** in the United States federal court system and in the court systems of most of the states. See COURT for a list of related terms.

SUPREME JUDICIAL COURT.   *See*: APPELLATE COURT.

SUPREME LAW OF THE LAND.   *See*: SUPREMACY CLAUSE.

SURETY.   **1.** Generally, a person who becomes responsible to pay a sum of money or to perform an obligation for another, if the other person fails to act. **2.** A person who arranges, sometimes for a fee, for the **release** of an **arrested** or **imprisoned** person by posting a **bail bond** guaranteeing the **appearance** of the person in **court** as required. A surety can be either a professional **bail bondsman** or a private individual. See BAIL for a list of related terms.

SURFACE.   The superficial or outer appearance of something, as distinguished from its real or inner substance.

SURMISE.   To guess; to conjecture.

SURNAME.   A person's family name or last name, as distinguished from the given name or first name.

SURPLUSAGE.   Extraneous, irrelevant, superfluous, or unnecessary material.

SURPRISE.   A situation at **trial** in which a party, through no fault of his or her own, is unforeseeably and unexpectedly placed in a detrimental condition.

SURRENDER.   To yield or deliver someone or something to the power or authority of another because of demand or compulsion.

SURREPTITIOUS.   Secret; clandestine; stealthy.

SUSCEPTIBLE.   Capable of being acted upon, impressed, affected, or moved.

SUSPECT.   **n.** An **adult** or **juvenile**, believed by a criminal justice agency to have committed a specific criminal offense, but who has not been **arrested** or **charged**. See ACCUSED for a list of related terms.

SUSPECT. **v. 1.** To believe someone **guilty** of a **crime** based on information not sufficient to constitute **probable cause.** **v. 2.** To surmise; to imagine to be true; to have a slight idea or notion about.

SUSPEND. To render ineffective or inoperative for a time; to stop, interrupt, or stay temporarily with an expectation or possibility of resumption; to hold in abeyance.

SUSPENDED SENTENCE. A **court disposition** of a **convicted** person pronouncing a penalty of a **fine** or **commitment** to **confinement**, but:

(1) unconditionally **discharging** the defendant of all obligations and restraints (unconditionally suspended sentence); or

(2) holding **execution** of the penalty in abeyance upon good behavior (conditionally suspended sentence). Whether a conditionally suspended sentence is considered equivalent or complementary to a **probation order**, or is considered an entirely distinct legal action depends on the jurisdiction.

In some jurisdictions a postponement of sentence (see **sentencing postponed**) is also considered to be a suspended sentence, but the terms are distinguished in this dictionary. See PROBATION and SENTENCE for lists of related terms.

Ss

SUSPICION. A belief or opinion that a person has committed a crime, based on information that is not sufficient to constitute **probable cause**.

SUSTAIN. **1.** To uphold as valid, just, or correct; to affirm; to approve. *Example*: The appellate court sustained the lower court decision. **2.** To support; to warrant; to justify. *Example*: The verdict is not sustained by sufficient evidence. **3.** To endure; to experience; to undergo. *Example*: The victim sustained multiple injuries. **4.** To carry on; to maintain; to keep up.

SWEAR. **1.** To give evidence or testimony on **oath** or **affirmation**. **2.** To administer a legal oath or affirmation to someone.

SWEEPING. Wide-ranging; comprehensive; extensive.

SWINDLE. To make an intentional **false representation** to obtain money or any other thing of value, where the deception is accomplished through the **victim's** belief in the validity of some statement or object presented by the offender. The term swindle is sometimes used as a synonym for **confidence game**, but in this dictionary trust in a person as opposed to belief in the validity of some statement or object distinguishes a confidence game from a swindle.

SWORN. Made or done under **oath** or **affirmation**; bound by oath or affirmation. *Example*: An affidavit is a sworn statement.

SYLLABUS. **1.** A short statement, appearing at the beginning of a reported court decision, summarizing the facts and legal principles established in the decision. *Also called*: **headnote**. **2.** A brief statement or outline of the main points of a treatise, lecture, course of study, or the like. See ABSTRACT for a list of related terms.

SYNDICALISM. *See*: CRIMINAL SYNDICALISM.

SYNONYMOUS. Having the same or substantially the same meaning.

SYNOPSIS. A brief statement or outline providing a general view or condensation of some subject. See ABSTRACT for a list of related terms.

SYSTEM. An orderly combination of interacting or interdependent elements forming a uniting whole. *Example*: The court system needs to be overhauled.

TABLE. An orderly list or arrangement of numbers, words, or items.

TABLE OF CASES. An alphabetized list of the judicial decisions cited, referred to, or explained in a book, with references to the pages or sections where they are found.

TACIT. Implied, indicated, or understood without being openly expressed or stated.

TACIT ADMISSION. Same as ADOPTIVE ADMISSION.

TAINT. A touch or trace of something contaminated or offensive. *See*: FRUIT OF THE POISONOUS TREE DOCTRINE.

TAINTED EVIDENCE. **Evidence** indirectly obtained by exploitation of some prior illegal police activity under the FRUIT OF THE POISONOUS TREE DOCTRINE. See EVIDENCE for a list of related terms.

TAKE. To obtain possession of; to assume ownership of; to get hold or control of; to seize; to apprehend. The exact shade of meaning of take depends on the context in which it is used.

TAKE AN APPEAL. To complete or perfect an **appeal**. See APPEAL for a list of related terms.

TAKE CHARGE. To assume control or command.

TAKE EFFECT. To become operative.

TAKE ISSUE. To adopt or assume an opposing viewpoint or position.

TAKE PART IN. To engage in; to carry on.

TAKE PLACE. To happen; to occur.

TALESMAN. A person chosen to serve on a **jury** from the bystanders in **court**, when the original **panel** has become deficient in number.

TAMPER. **1.** To illegally or improperly interfere or meddle with something for the purpose of altering or misusing it. *Example*: It is illegal to tamper with an odometer on an automobile. **2.** To improperly influence in a secret or underhanded manner. *Example*: He tampered with the jury by attempting to bribe one of the jurors.

TANGENT. Touching at a single point. See PROXIMITY for a list of related terms.

TANGIBLE. **1.** Capable of being touched; having physical substance; corporeal; material. **2.** Real; substantial; palpable; objective; definite; concrete.

TANGIBLE EVIDENCE. Same as REAL EVIDENCE.

TAVERN. A place licensed to sell liquor, wine, and beer to be drunk on the premises. *Also called*: **dramshop**; **grogshop**; **tippling house**; **saloon**.

TAX DIVISION. The Tax Division of the **Department of Justice** has responsibility for representing the United States and its officers in all civil and criminal litigation arising under the internal revenue laws, other than proceedings in the United States Tax Court. While the division's primary client is the **Internal Revenue Service**, it also represents federal officials and employees in actions arising out of the performance of their official duties, as well as representing other federal departments and agencies in their dealings with state and local tax authorities.

With respect to criminal tax litigation, the division has the responsibility of prosecuting or supervising the prosecution of all criminal offenses committed under the internal revenue laws, including attempts to evade and defeat taxes, willful failure to file returns and to pay taxes, filing false returns and other deceptive documents, making false statements to revenue officials, and other miscellaneous offenses involving internal revenue matters. These duties include the institution of criminal proceedings and collaboration with **United States attorneys** in the control and supervision of the actions in the trial and appellate courts. Further, Tax Division attorneys frequently conduct grand jury investigations and actual trials of criminal tax cases, often as a result of requests for assistance by the appropriate United States attorney. In its efforts to deter willful deception through prosecution of criminal offenders, the Tax Division has played a significant role in curbing organized crime.

TECHNICAL. **1.** Not involving substantial rights or issues. *Example*: It was merely a harmless technical error. **2.** Peculiar to a particular art, science, profession, or trade. *Example*: The doctor used technical medical terms in his testimony. **3.** Characterized by a **strict construction**. *Example*: Constitutional provisions guaranteeing rights should not be read in too technical a manner.

TECHNICAL VIOLATION. *See*: PAROLE VIOLATION; PROBATION VIOLATION.

TEMPORARY. Lasting, serving, or effective for a limited time; not permanent.

TEMPORARY RELEASE. An authorized **release** from a **confinement facility** for **appearance** in **court**, participation in a **work release program**, hospital treatment, **appeal** proceedings, education, personal or family welfare, or other purposes that require departure from prison but with expectation of return. A temporary release differs from a **conditional release** from prison in that the released person's return under a conditional release depends upon his or her behavior. In a temporary release, return is officially intended and expected, unless some other official action such as a **court decision** supersedes correctional agency authority over the released person. A **full-time temporary release** is a release for a period of 24 hours or more. This term is used when it is necessary to distinguish between extended leaves of absence of a full day or more and regular, short absences of part of a day for the same purposes. The less-than-24-hour release is called a **part-time temporary release**. *Also called*: **provisional exit.** See RELEASE for a list of related terms.

TEMPORARY RESTRAINING ORDER. Same as RESTRAINING ORDER.

TEND. To be directed or to have an inclination toward some object or purpose. *Example*: The defendant offered evidence tending to show an alibi.

TENDER. To offer to the court or to a person for formal acceptance or approval. See ADDRESS for a list of related terms.

TENOR. **1.** In a technical legal sense, the exact meaning, an exact copy, or the actual wording of a document. **2.** General sense or meaning; substance; purport; effect.

TENURE. The time period during which a person has a right to occupy a public or private office. *Example*: The tenure of a federal judge is during life and good behavior.

TERM. **1.** A fixed period of time. *Example*: The judge sentenced her to a five year prison term. **2.** The legally prescribed time period during which a **court**, **legislature**, or other official body may be in **session**. Term and session are sometimes used interchangeably. **3.** The time during which an appointed or elected official may hold the office, exercise its functions, and enjoy its rights and privileges. **4.** Same as TERM OF ART. *Example*: Try to avoid using technical terms in your testimony.

TERMINATE. To bring to an end; to complete; to finish.

TERM OF ART. A word or group of words with a particular meaning in a particular profession, science, or discipline. The terms **appellant**, **plea**, and **probable cause** are terms of art in the legal profession.

TERMS. Conditions; stipulations; provisos. *Example*: He violated the terms of his probation.

TERRITORIAL JURISDICTION. JURISDICTION over cases, persons, or subject matter within a given territory such as a county, a district, or a state. See JURISDICTION for a list of related terms.

TERRITORY. An area of land of undefined size; a region; a district.

TERRITORY OF A JUDGE. The area or region within which a **judge** may exercise **judicial** authority.

TERROR. Intense or extreme fear or dread.

TERRORISTIC THREAT. Section 211.3 of the **Model Penal Code** defines terroristic threat as threatening " to commit any crime of violence with purpose to terrorize another or to cause evacuation of a building, place of assembly, or facility of public transportation, or otherwise to cause serious public inconvenience, or in reckless disregard of the risk of causing such terror or inconvenience."

TERRORIZE. To cause TERROR by use of **violence** or **threats**. The crime of terrorizing is defined by statute in some states.

TERRY v. OHIO. The 1968 U.S. Supreme Court case that upheld the validity of **stop and frisk** procedures. The case held that a law enforcement officer may detain a person briefly for questioning even though the officer does not have **probable cause** to believe that the person has committed a **crime** and may conduct a limited **search** of the person for weapons for the protection of the officer and others. A **stop** of a person is justified if the officer has a reasonable suspicion of impending criminal behavior supported by specific facts and circumstances. "[I]n justifying the particular intrusion the police officer must be able to point to specific and articulable facts which, taken together with rational inferences from those facts, reasonably warrant that intrusion." 392 U.S. 1, 21, 88 S.Ct. 1868, 1880, 20 L.Ed.2d 889, 906. A **frisk** is permitted only if the officer has reason to believe he or she is dealing with an armed and dangerous individual. A frisk is required to be "a reasonable search for weapons for the protection of the police officer" (392 U.S. at 27, 88 S.Ct. at 1883, 20 L.Ed.2d at 909) and, therefore, must initially be limited to a pat-down of the outer clothing. If during the pat-down the officer detects an object that feels like a weapon, the officer may then reach inside the clothing or pocket and seize it. The Court held that "where a police officer observes unusual conduct which leads him reasonably to conclude that in light of his experience that criminal activity may be afoot and that the persons with whom he is dealing may be armed and presently dangerous, where in the course of investigating this behavior he identifies himself as a policeman and makes reasonable inquiries, and where nothing in the initial stages of the encounter serves to dispel his reasonable fear for his own or other's safety, he is entitled for the protection of himself and others in the area to conduct a carefully limited search of the outer clothing of such persons in an attempt to discover weapons which might be used to assault him." 392 U.S. at 30, 88 S.Ct. at 1884-85, 20 L.Ed.2d at 911.

TEST. A process or method for determining the presence, quality, or truth of something. *Example*: The Durham test is one of the ways to determine a person's mental capacity to commit crime.

TEST CASE. A legal **action** whose outcome is likely to determine the constitutionality of a **statute**, set a **precedent**, or establish an important legal principle.

TESTE. The witnessing or concluding clause of a **writ**.

TESTES. *See*: TRIAL PER TESTES.

TESTIFY. To give oral EVIDENCE as a **witness** under **oath** or **affirmation**. See ADDRESS, EVIDENCE, and WITNESS for lists of related terms.

TESTIMONIAL. Relating to or in the nature of TESTIMONY.

TESTIMONY. Oral EVIDENCE consisting of the statements of **competent witnesses** given under **oath** or **affirmation**, as distinguished from **documentary evidence** or **real evidence**. See EVIDENCE and WITNESS for lists of related terms.

THEFT. Same as LARCENY. Under some modern penal statutes, the single crime of theft may embrace such formerly separate crimes as **larceny, larceny by bailee, larceny by trick, embezzlement**, obtaining property by **false pretenses, extortion, blackmail, shoplifting, check fraud**, and **receiving stolen property**. See ABSTRACTION for a list of related terms.

THEFT-BOTE. The offense of taking some payment from a thief to secure him or her from **prosecution**. The offense may consist of the receiving back of stolen goods by the owner or the taking of a **bribe** by a **judge** or other person who ought to have brought the thief to justice. See ABUSE OF PROCESS for a list of related terms.

THEFT OF SERVICES. Under Section 223.7 of the **Model Penal Code** a person is guilty of theft of services "if he purposely obtains **services** which he knows are available only for compensation, by deception or threat, or by false token or other means to avoid payment for the service" or "having control over the disposition of services of others, to which he is not entitled, he knowingly diverts such services to his own benefit or to the benefit of another not entitled thereto." See ABSTRACTION for a list of related terms.

THEN. **1.** At that time. **2.** Soon or immediately afterward. **3.** In that case; under those circumstances.

THEN AND THERE. At the last previously mentioned time and place.

THEORY. An analysis or explanation of the **facts** of a **case** designed to form the basis of a **cause of action** or a **defense**. See FACT for a list of related terms.

THERE. At that place.

THEREAFTER. After that time; afterwards; subsequently.

THEREBY. By that means; as a result; in consequence of that.

THEREFOR. For that; for this; for it.

THEREFORE. Consequently; for that reason; as a result.

THEREFROM. From that place.

THEREIN. In that place.

THEREOF. Of that; of this; of it.

THEREON. On that; on this; on it.

THERETOFORE. Before that time.

THEREUPON. **1.** Immediately or directly following that; forthwith. **2.** In consequence of. **3.** Upon that; upon this; upon it.

THIEF. A person who commits or has committed **theft** or **larceny**.

THIRD DEGREE. The use of mental or physical torture to obtain information or a confession from a person.

THIRD-DEGREE INSTRUCTION. Same as ALLEN CHARGE.

THIRD PARTY. A person not directly involved in an **action** or **transaction**, but who might be affected by it.

THREAT. An expression of intention or determination to injure another's person, property, or rights by some unlawful act. A threat may be made orally, in writing, or by gesture or other action. In some jurisdictions, the making of a threat, or of a certain kind of threat, constitutes a statutory offense variously entitled **criminal threatening**, **menacing**, or **terrorizing**. Threat is an element in such offenses as **extortion** and **robbery**. A threat is implied in an **attempt** to commit a **crime**, but a threat is less than an attempt because it does not require that an overt act directed toward immediate accomplishment of a crime take place. See INCHOATE OFFENSE and PARTY for lists of related terms.

THRUST. To push, shove, or drive with force.

THUS. **1.** In the manner previously indicated. **2.** Therefore; consequently.

TICKET. A **citation** or **summons** issued for minor **violations** or **infractions** of the motor vehicle laws.

TIMELY. Occurring or done at a suitable or opportune time; seasonable. *Example*: Questions regarding the legality of a search must be timely raised.

TIME SERVED. Generally, time spent in **confinement** in relation to **conviction** and **sentencing** for a given **offense**, calculated in accordance with the rules and conventions specific to a given jurisdiction; also total time served under **correctional agency** jurisdiction. Time served is calculated in order to determine, for example, when a particular prisoner will be **eligible for parole** or have served his or her **maximum sentence**. For a person committed to prison all or some portion of the time spent in confinement pending conviction or sentencing may be credited as confinement time served on the sentence, depending upon statute or judge's decision. All time spent in the legal status of prisoner may be counted towards time served in confinement, although the person may be participating in a **work release program**, in the hospital, or otherwise not in the **physical custody** of the prison. Time on **parole** or other **conditional release** counts as total time served under correctional agency jurisdiction, but this can be discounted if conditional release status is revoked, and thus will delay the date of expiration of sentence. See RELEASE and SENTENCE for lists of related terms.

TIP. Private or confidential information. *Example*: The officer acted on an informant's tip.

TIPPLING HOUSE. Same as TAVERN.

TIPSTER. An INFORMER.

TITLE. **1.** The distinctive name by which a **case** is known and distinguished from others. *Example*: The title of the case is *State v. Rankermanns.* **2.** The heading or preliminary clause of a **statute** that gives a brief summary of its purpose or subject matter and distinguishes it from others. *Example*: The title of the statute is "An act to amend the arson law." **3.** A division of a **statute**, book, or other work that is larger than an article, chapter, or section. *Example*: The criminal laws can be found in Title 16 of the Nevada Revised Statutes. **4.** Same as CAPTION. **5.** An established legal right or legal ground of claim to something. **6.** A document serving as evidence of ownership.

TOLERATE. To allow to exist or to be done without interfering; to endure.

TOLL. **1.** To stop temporarily; to suspend. *Example*: The running of the statute of limitations was tolled during the defendant's absence from the country. **2.** To take away; to bar; to defeat; to annul.

TOOL. An instrument; an implement.

TORMENT. To inflict continued or repeated annoyance, suffering, or distress.

TORT. A private or **civil wrong** or injury, other than a breach of contract, resulting from a violation of a duty and for which courts will provide relief in the form of **damages**. The essential elements of a tort are a legal duty owed by the defendant to the plaintiff, a violation of that duty, and a sufficient causal connection between the defendant's conduct and the resulting damage to the plaintiff. Examples of torts are **negligence, false arrest**, invasion of privacy, and **trespass**. Some wrongs, such as an **assault**, may be both a **crime** and a tort.

TORT-FEASOR. One who commits or has committed a TORT.

TORTIOUS. Of the nature of or pertaining to a TORT.

TORTURE. To inflict severe mental or physical pain.

TOTAL. Whole; complete; entire.

TO WIT. Namely; that is to say. To wit is used in legal documents to call attention to a more particular statement of what has preceded.

TOXIC. Poisonous.

TOXICOLOGY. The study of poisons and their effects on living organisms.

TOXIN. A poisonous substance.

TRAFFIC. **v.** To exchange goods, commodities, or merchandise for the equivalent in goods or money; to carry on trade; to have commercial dealings. **n.** The coming and going of persons, vehicles, or messages along routes of transportation or communication.

TRAFFIC COURT. *See*: COURT OF LIMITED JURISDICTION.

TRAFFIC OFFENSES. In common usage, a group of offenses including **infractions** and very minor **misdemeanors** relating to the operation of self-propelled **motor vehicles,** such as parking violations, violations of equipment standards, speeding, and improper turns. Traffic offenses have in common the feature that they are not likely to be contested and in many or most jurisdictions are handled by administrative or quasi-judicial bodies or procedures quite separate from the major business of the courts. The majority of traffic offenses are dealt with by **citations** permitting forfeit of money as an alternative to **appearance** in court. Failure to respond to such citations, however, may result in the issuing of a court order for appearance.

TRAINING SCHOOL. A long-term specialized type of JUVENILE FACILITY that provides strict confinement for its residents. See JUVENILE for a list of related terms.

TRAITOR. A person who has committed TREASON.

TRAMP. Same as VAGRANT.

TRANSACT. To carry on, perform, or conduct business or affairs.

TRANSACTION. **1.** In rules or statutes relating to **sentencing** for or **joinder** of offenses based on the same act or transaction, transaction is a word of flexible meaning conveying the idea of a **crime** or series of crimes, committed by a defendant at a single time or in temporally continuous actions, that are logically related, are part of a common scheme, or are connected by a single guilty **intent.** "Spree" crimes are not considered part of the same transaction unless they occurred as continuous actions not separated in time by law-abiding behavior. For example, in *Commonwealth v. Fries*, 523 A.2d 1134 (Pa.Super. 1987), a defendant's convictions for kidnapping, rape, and burglary constituted a single transaction for sentencing purposes, where the defendant abducted the victim and held her captive for three days during which he burglarized cabins and repeatedly raped the victim. *See*: MERGER. **2.** The act, process, or result of transacting. *See*: TRANSACT.

TRANSACTIONAL IMMUNITY. A type of WITNESS IMMUNITY under which a **witness** may be compelled to testify despite the privilege against **self-incrimination,** but the witness is protected from any **prosecution** for **crimes** to which his or her compelled testimony relates. *See*: USE IMMUNITY.

TRANSCRIBE. To reproduce in writing or print. *Example*: The court reporter needed time to transcribe his notes.

TRANSCRIPT. **1.** A written, typewritten, or printed reproduction of an original. **2.** A printed copy of the entire **record** of the **pleadings** and proceedings of a **trial** or **hearing**. See ABSTRACT and TRIAL for lists of related terms.

TRANSFER. **1.** To convey or shift from one person, place, or thing to another. **2.** To convey or give over possession, control, right, or title. **3.** To remove a **cause of action** from one **court**, **jurisdiction**, or **venue** to another. *Example*: The case was transferred from district court to superior court for a trial de novo. *See*: BIND OVER; TRANSFER HEARING; TRANSFER TO ADULT COURT. **4.** In the **corrections** context, the movement of a person from one **correctional facility** or **caseload** to another.

TRANSFER HEARING. A preadjudicatory **hearing** in **juvenile court** to determine whether juvenile court **jurisdiction** should be retained over a **juvenile** alleged to have committed a **delinquent act**, or whether it should be **waived** and the juvenile transferred to **criminal court** for **prosecution** as an **adult**. A transfer hearing determines whether a juvenile is amenable to rehabilitation or treatment within the juvenile justice system. If the juvenile court certifies that neither the facilities nor the programs are appropriate for that juvenile, then he or she is transferred to criminal court for prosecution as an adult. *Also called*: **certification hearing**; **fitness hearing**; **waiver hearing**. See HEARING and JUVENILE for lists of related terms.

TRANSFER TO ADULT COURT. The decision by a **juvenile court**, resulting from a **transfer hearing**, that **jurisdiction** over an alleged **delinquent** will be **waived** and that he or she should be **prosecuted** as an **adult** in a **criminal court**. Juvenile courts usually waive jurisdiction over alleged delinquents only when a serious felony has been alleged, and when the juvenile is near the statutory age limit between **juvenile** and **adult**. At a transfer hearing, **probable cause** to believe that the juvenile committed the offense must be shown. After a transfer to adult court, the prosecutor decides whether prosecution will take place and what offense will be charged. Transfer to adult court is sometimes called **waiver** or **certification**. A juvenile whose case has been transferred to a criminal court is sometimes called a **certified juvenile**.

Recent revisions of criminal and juvenile law have, in some instances, reduced juvenile court **original jurisdiction** over cases resulting from certain serious crimes, or allowed for waiver in more kinds of cases. See JUVENILE for a list of related terms.

TRANSIENT. **adj.** Temporary; not permanent; of short duration. **n.** A person who is passing through or temporarily living in a place but is not a **resident** of the place.

TRANSITORY. Inherently short-lived or impermanent; fleeting.

TRANSITORY ACTION. An **action** that may be brought in any place where personal **service of process** can be made on the **defendant**. See: LOCAL ACTION.

TRANSPORT. **1.** To carry from one place to another. **2.** To **punish** a **criminal** by banishing the criminal from his or her own country to exile in another country.

TRAUMA. **1.** A wound or injury produced by violence or some other outside force such as heat, electricity, or poison. **2.** An emotional shock causing substantial and lasting damage to a person's psychological development.

TRAUMATIC. Caused by or resulting from a TRAUMA.

TRAVEL. To go from one place to another; to make a journey.

TRAVERSE. **1.** To formally deny the **charges** in an **indictment**. **2.** To pass across, over, or through.

TRAVERSE JURY. Same as TRIAL JURY.

TREACHERY. Willful betrayal of trust, confidence, or allegiance.

TREASON. Article III, Section 3, of the United States Constitution defines treason as follows: "Treason against the United States, shall consist only in levying war against them, or in adhering to their enemies, giving them aid and comfort." "[A]dhering to their enemies, giving them aid and comfort" has been interpreted to mean committing an **overt act** or engaging in a course of conduct that gives assistance, support, or encouragement to an enemy with an intent to betray the United States. No other acts can be declared to constitute treason. Therefore Congress can neither extend, restrict, nor redefine the crime.

Many states have constitutional or statutory provisions defining treason against a state, which are often patterned after the national provision. *See*: AID AND COMFORT.

TREASURY, DEPARTMENT OF THE. *See*: DEPARTMENT OF THE TREA-SURY.

TREATISE. A book or other publication containing a systematic exposition of all the **law** in a particular area of the law.

TRESPASS. **1.** Generally, an unlawful act committed with **force**, either express or implied, that damages another's person, property, or rights. **2.** In the criminal law, the offense of **knowingly** or **intentionally** and without **license** or **privilege** entering or remaining upon or in the property, structure, or vehicle of another, having notice that the entering or remaining was forbidden. Penalties may be increased if the trespass involves violence or injury to person or property.

TRESPASS DE BONIS ASPORTATIS. The unlawful taking and carrying away of the goods of another without his or her consent.

TRIAL. The examination in **court** of issues of **fact** and **law** in a **case** for the purpose of reaching a **judgment**. A trial begins when the jury has been selected in a **jury trial**, or when the first **witness** is sworn or the first **evidence** introduced in a **nonjury trial**. A trial concludes when a judgment is entered or the case is **dismissed**. *See*: ACQUITTAL; ADJUDICATION; ADJUDICATORY HEARING; ADVERSARY SYSTEM; APPEAL; ARRAIGNMENT; BAIL; BIND OVER; BURDEN OF PROOF; CALENDAR; CALENDAR CALL; CALL THE DOCKET; CASE AGREED ON; CLOSING ARGUMENT; CONSOLIDATED TRIAL; CONTINUANCE; CONVICTION; COURT; DEPOSITION; DIRECT EXAMINATION; DISCOVERY; DISMISSAL; ERROR; EVIDENCE; FAIR TRIAL; GENERAL TERM; HEARING; INCOMPETENT TO STAND TRIAL; INSTRUCTION; JOINDER; JURISDICTION; JURY; JURY TRIAL; MISTRIAL; MOTION; NEW TRIAL; NONJURY TRIAL; OPENING STATEMENT; PERPETUATION OF EVIDENCE; PLEA BARGAINING; PLEADING; PRELIMINARY HEARING; PRETRIAL CONFERENCE; PRETRIAL DETENTION; PRETRIAL RELEASE; PUBLIC TRIAL; SEPARATE TRIAL; SEVERANCE; SPECIAL TERM; SPEEDY TRIAL; SPEEDY TRIAL ACT; STAY OF PROCEEDINGS; SUBSTANTIAL JUSTICE RULE; SUPPRESS; TRANSCRIPT; TRIAL CALENDAR; TRIAL COURT; TRIAL DE NOVO; TRIAL JUDGE; TRIAL JURY; TRIAL LAWYER; TRIAL LIST; TRIAL ON THE MERITS; TRIAL ON TRANSCRIPT; TRIER OF FACT; VENUE; VERDICT; VOIR DIRE; WITNESS.

TRIAL BY COURT. Same as NONJURY TRIAL.

TRIAL BY JUDGE. Same as NONJURY TRIAL.

TRIAL BY JURY. Same as JURY TRIAL.

TRIAL BY THE RECORD. Same as TRIAL ON TRANSCRIPT.

TRIAL BY WITNESSES. Same as NONJURY TRIAL.

TRIAL CALENDAR. A list of **cases** awaiting **trial** including the dates of the trials and other basic information about the cases. *Also called*: **trial docket**; **trial list**. See TRIAL for a list of related terms.

TRIAL COURT. A **court** whose primary function is to conduct **trials**. In most states, there are two levels of trial court: **courts of limited jurisdiction** and **courts of general jurisdiction**. *Also called*: **court of original jurisdiction**. See COURT, JURISDICTION, and TRIAL for lists of related terms.

TRIAL DE NOVO. A **new trial** or **retrial** in which the whole **case** is gone into again as if no trial whatever had been held before. In a trial de novo, matters of

fact as well as **law** may be considered, **witnesses** may be heard, and new **evidence** may be presented, regardless of what happened at the first trial. See TRIAL for a list of related terms.

TRIAL DOCKET. Same as TRIAL CALENDAR.

TRIAL JUDGE. **1.** A **judicial officer** who is authorized to conduct **jury trials** and **nonjury trials**, and who may or may not be authorized to hear **appeals**. **2.** The judicial officer who conducts a particular **trial** and whose rulings are reviewed on **appeal**. See TRIAL for a list of related terms.

TRIAL JURY. A JURY of a statutorily defined number of persons selected according to law and sworn to determine, in accordance with the law as **instructed** by the **court**, certain matters of **fact** based on the **evidence** presented at **trial** and to render a **verdict**. A trial jury's powers and duties ordinarily are to determine matters of fact only. The presiding **judicial officer**'s power and duty is to interpret the **law** of the case. In certain circumstances, however, in accordance with the law as instructed by the court, a trial jury may also advise the court regarding **sentencing** or recommend a specific sentence (which the court may or may not be required to act upon, depending upon the jurisdiction). The size of a trial jury is set by **statute** and, depending upon jurisdiction, is 12 or a number less than 12. Some jurisdictions require a minimum of 6 jurors but allow for fewer if a juror falls ill. *Also called*: **petit jury**; **traverse jury**. See JURY and TRIAL for lists of related terms.

TRIAL LAWYER. A **lawyer** engaged primarily in the **trial** of **cases** before trial courts. See ATTORNEY AT LAW and TRIAL for lists of related terms.

TRIAL LIST. Same as TRIAL CALENDAR.

TRIAL ON THE MERITS. A **trial** of the **substantive issues** of a **case** as distinguished from a hearing on a **motion** or other interlocutory, procedural, or technical matters. See TRIAL for a list of related terms.

TRIAL ON TRANSCRIPT. A NONJURY TRIAL in which the **judicial officer** makes a decision on the basis of the **record** of pretrial proceedings in a lower **court**. *Also called*: **trial by the record**. See TRIAL for a list of related terms.

TRIAL PER PAIS. Same as JURY TRIAL.

TRIAL PER TESTES. Same as NONJURY TRIAL.

TRIBUNAL. A **court** or forum of justice; a person or body with authority to adjudicate matters.

TRICK. **1.** A professional engagement of a **prostitute**. **2.** A man with whom a prostitute engages in an act of **sexual intercourse**.

TRICKERY. Achieving an end by deceptive (see **deceive**) or **fraudulent** means.

TRIER OF FACT. The person or persons who weigh the **evidence**, determine the **credibility** of **witnesses**, and find the **facts** in a judicial or administrative proceeding. In a **jury trial**, the **jury** is the trier of fact. In an **nonjury trial**, the **judge** is the trier of both fact and law. *Also called*: **fact-finder**. See EVIDENCE, FACT, and TRIAL for lists of related terms.

TRIVIAL. Of little importance; insignificant.

TRO. Abbreviation for TEMPORARY RESTRAINING ORDER.

TRUANT. A **juvenile** who has been **adjudicated** by a **judicial officer** of a **juvenile court** as having committed the **status offense** of violating a compulsory school attendance law. Compulsory attendance statutes may specify the number of days of continuous absence that constitute a violation or provide a more general definition of truancy, such as habitual absence. The codification of this offense varies greatly among different states. See JUVENILE for a list of related terms.

TRUE. **1.** Correct; conforming with reality or fact; not false, erroneous, or inaccurate. *Example*: She swore that her testimony was true. **2.** Conforming exactly to a rule, standard, or pattern; accurate. *Example*: The clerk testified that the transcript of the record was a true and correct copy. **3.** Honest; sincere; not fraudulent.

TRUE ADMISSION. A formal act done in the course of judicial proceedings whereby one party **waives** or dispenses with the production of **evidence** by another party by conceding for the purposes of litigation that the proposition of **fact** alleged by the other party is true.

TRUE BILL. **1.** The endorsement made by a **grand jury** upon a bill of **indictment** when they find sufficient evidence (**probable cause**) to warrant a **prosecution**. **2.** Same as INDICTMENT. See GRAND JURY for a list of related terms.

TRUE VERDICT. A VERDICT arrived at by a **jury** voluntarily and after deliberate consideration. A verdict is not a true verdict if it is the result of an arbitrary rule or order or of **coercion**. See VERDICT for a list of related terms.

TRUSTY. An **inmate** of a **jail** or **prison** who has been entrusted with some custodial responsibilities, or who performs other services assisting in the operation of the facility. Trusties have special privileges and freedoms, including more physical mobility than other inmates. Trusty status is usually given as a reward for good behavior. Satisfactory performance of trusty duties can, in some jurisdictions, result in a shortening of time to be served.

A trusty in most cases performs duties that would otherwise be performed by a correctional officer or other facility staff. Thus, by providing extra manpower the use of trusties can reduce the workload of regular employees, and consequently reduce facility budgetary needs. A trusty can in effect have quasi-correctional officer status, when he or she performs duties that would otherwise be the responsibility of a correctional officer.

TRUTH. **1.** Conformity with reality or fact. **2.** Conformity to a rule, standard, or pattern; accuracy. **3.** A fact or proposition proven to be or accepted as correct or accurate. **4.** Veracity; honesty; integrity. *Example*: He has a good reputation for truth.

TRY. **1.** To examine and determine by judicial process. **2.** To put an accused person on **trial** in order to determine his or her guilt or innocence. *See*: TRIAL.

TUMULT. A noisy and disorderly commotion or disturbance.

TURNKEY. A person, under the supervision of a jailer, who has charge of the keys of a prison or jail. "A turnkey's primary duty is the retention of custody of male prisoners and he keeps the keys to the cell block and cell; he wears a regulation uniform and is armed; he receives prisoners from policemen, records in a register the data on all those received and released, and keeps copies of the arrest sheets and removal orders; he provides generally for the feeding and care of the prisoners, and performs some cleaning or so-called 'housekeeping' function within the cells. He may not receive, release, or transfer a prisoner except in the presence of a police officer; he is subject to other police assignments (an infrequent occurrence in fact) and to the discipline provided for police officers. . . ." *State v. Gunn*, 326 S.W.2d 314, 318-19 (Mo. 1959). See LAW ENFORCEMENT OFFICER for a list of related terms.

Tt

TURPITUDE. Same as MORAL TURPITUDE.

TWICE IN JEOPARDY. *See*: DOUBLE JEOPARDY.

UBI. *Latin.* "Where; when."

UCR. Abbreviation for UNIFORM CRIME REPORTING.

ULTERIOR. Beyond what is openly stated, avowed, or manifest; intentionally concealed. *Example*: She had an ulterior motive for her actions.

ULTIMATE. **1.** Final; last; conclusive. **2.** Fundamental; elemental.

ULTIMATE FACTS. Facts necessary and essential for a **court's** decision and towards which **evidence** is offered; logical conclusions from primary or **evidentiary facts**. In a criminal case, the ultimate facts are those that establish the essential **elements** of the **crime charged** or of the **defense** to the charges. The evidentiary facts are those that prove the ultimate facts. See EVIDENCE and FACT for lists of related terms.

ULTIMATE ISSUE. The issue that must finally be determined. *Example:* The guilt or innocence of the accused is the ultimate issue in a criminal case.

ULTRA. *Latin.* "Beyond; in excess of."

UN-. A prefix meaning "not."

UNALIENABLE. Same as INALIENABLE.

UNANIMOUS. In complete accord of one mind; having the agreement or consent of all concerned. *Example*: The verdict of the jurors was unanimous.

UNARMED ROBBERY. *See*: ROBBERY.

UNAUTHORIZED PRACTICE. The performance of professional services, such as medical or legal services, by a person not licensed by the state to do so. Unauthorized practice is a **crime**, but is defined and punished variously among the states.

UNAUTHORIZED USE OF A MOTOR VEHICLE. *See*: JOYRIDING.

UNAVAILABLE. In the law of **evidence**, if the **testimony** of a **witness** is shown to be unavailable, **previously recorded testimony** of that witness may be admissible under certain conditions as an exception to the HEARSAY RULE. Different statutes or rules in different jurisdictions variously define when a witness's testimony is unavailable. A witness's testimony may be unavailable if the witness (1) is unable to be present or to testify because of death, insanity, physical illness, or infirmity; (2) has a **privilege** permitting him or her to refuse to testify; (3) persists in refusing to testify concerning the subject matter of prior testimony despite a court **order** to do so; (4) claims failure of memory with respect to the subject matter of prior testimony; or (5) is absent from the proceeding and the proponent of his or her prior testimony demonstrates an inability, despite due diligence, to procure the witness's attendance by **subpoena** or other reasonable means.

A witness's testimony is not unavailable, however, if his or her inability to testify, refusal to testify, claim of failure of memory, or absence from the proceeding is brought about by the device or connivance of the proponent of the witness's previously recorded testimony.

UNA VOCE. *Latin.* "With one voice"; unanimously.

UNCONDITIONAL. Without limitations or conditions; absolute.

UNCONDITIONAL RELEASE. The final **release** of an offender from the jurisdiction of a **court** or **correctional agency**. An unconditional release is a release without **probation**, **parole**, or other **conditional release** status to follow. See RELEASE for a list of related terms.

UNCONSCIONABLE. **1.** Not controlled by **conscience**; not in accord with what is right or reasonable; unscrupulous. **2.** Unreasonably excessive; unusually harsh; shocking to the conscience; grossly unfair.

UNCONSCIOUS. Temporarily lacking conscious awareness.

UNCONSTITUTIONAL. In conflict with or unauthorized by some provision of a constitution.

UNCONTROLLABLE IMPULSE. Same as IRRESISTIBLE IMPULSE.

UNDER. **1.** Beneath; below; lower than; less than. **2.** Subject to; subordinate to; inferior to. **3.** According to; in view of; by virtue of.

UNDER-SHERIFF. The chief deputy sheriff.

UNDERSTAND. To know; to appreciate; to comprehend the meaning of.

UNDERTAKE. To enter upon; to set about; to attempt; to engage in.

UNDER THE INFLUENCE OF INTOXICATING LIQUOR. Physically or mentally affected by the consumption of intoxicating liquor so as to deprive one of the clearness of intellect and control of oneself that one would otherwise have. *See*: DRIVING UNDER THE INFLUENCE OF ALCOHOL.

UNDISPUTED. Unchallenged; unquestioned.

UNDUE. Improper; unwarranted; unjustifiable; unreasonably excessive.

UNEQUIVOCAL. Clear; plain; not ambiguous.

UNERRING. Consistently accurate; without error; certain; infallible.

UNFOUNDED COMPLAINT. Same as UNFOUNDED REPORTED OFFENSE.

UNFOUNDED REPORTED OFFENSE. A reported occurrence of an **offense** that is found by investigation not to have occurred or not to constitute an offense, or that must be reclassified as another offense. A reported incident of **criminal homicide** later determined to have been a **justifiable homicide** or an **excusable homicide** is an unfounded reported offense. A reported incident of **aggravated assault**, where the victim later dies of the injuries received in the incident, is an unfounded reported offense and should be reported as an offense of criminal homicide. Other examples of circumstances commonly causing reported offenses to be unfounded are changes in alleged victim statements or discovery that a witness lacking full knowledge of the event incorrectly assumed that a crime was being committed. *Also called*: **baseless complaint**; **baseless offense**; **unfounded complaint**.

UNIFORM. Conforming to one standard, rule, or pattern; applying alike to all persons or in all places; consistent; undiversified; invariable.

UNIFORM CRIME REPORTING. A national crime reporting program of the **Federal Bureau of Investigation**, which produces a major annual report called *Crime in the United States*. The bulk of the information in this report relates to reported instances (offenses known to the police) of the FBI's **Crime Index** offenses, reported **arrests** for all crimes, and **law enforcement agency** employee data. The detail includes information concerning crimes cleared by arrest, arrests and **dispositions** of arrested persons, and dispositions of **juveniles** taken into custody. The reported crime and reported arrest data are categorized by geographical area and related to various factors. The Uniform Crime Reporting program also produces three other annual publications: *Law Enforcement Officers Killed*, *Assaults on Federal Officers*, and *Bomb Summary*. See CRIME for a list of related terms.

UNIFORM CRIMINAL EXTRADITION ACT. A uniform law, adopted by most states, that requires the executive authority of an **asylum state**, subject to the U.S.

Constitution and controlling federal laws, to have **arrested** and delivered up to the executive authority of any other state a person who is **charged** with a **crime** in the latter state (**demanding state**) and who has fled from justice and is found in the asylum state. *See*: EXTRADITION.

UNILATERAL.   Affecting or involving only one side or **party**; performed by or undertaken by only one side or party.

UNINTELLIGIBLE.   Not capable of being understood.

UNINTENTIONAL HOMICIDE.   A HOMICIDE committed without **intent** to cause death. Unintentional homicide includes **involuntary manslaughter**, which is criminal, and those entirely **accidental homicides** that lack any element of gross or criminal **negligence**, and are thus noncriminal. See HOMICIDE for a list of related terms.

UNITED STATES.   "A **state**, in the ordinary sense of the Constitution, is a political community of free citizens, occupying a territory of defined boundaries, and organized under a government sanctioned and limited by a written constitution, and established by the consent of the governed. It is the union of such states, under a common constitution, which forms the distinct and greater political unit, which that Constitution designates as the United States, and makes of the people and states which compose it one people and one country." *Texas v. White*, 74 U.S. 700, 721, 19 L.Ed. 227, 236 (1868).

UNITED STATES ATTORNEY.   A United States attorney is appointed by the President for each judicial district for a term of four years. The **Attorney General** may appoint one or more assistant United States attorneys in any district when the public interest so requires. 28 U.S.C. §547 sets out the duties of the United States attorney:

"Except as otherwise provided by law, each United States attorney, within his district, shall—

(1) **prosecute** for all **offenses** against the United States;

(2) prosecute or **defend**, for the Government, all **civil actions**, suits or proceedings in which the United States is concerned;

(3) appear in behalf of the defendants in all civil actions, suits or proceedings pending in his district against collectors, or other officers of the revenue or customs for any act done by them or for the recovery of any money exacted by or paid to these officers, and by them paid into the Treasury;

(4) institute and prosecute proceedings for the collection of **fines, penalties**, and **forfeitures** incurred for violation of any revenue law, unless satisfied

Uu

on investigation that justice does not require the proceedings; and

(5) make such reports as the Attorney General may direct."

See PROSECUTE for a list of related terms.

UNITED STATES CODE.   A multivolume publication containing the complete text of all public and general laws enacted by the United States Congress. *Abbreviation*: **U.S.C.** See STATUTE for a list of related terms.

UNITED STATES CODE ANNOTATED.   A multivolume work published by West Publishing Company that contains the complete text of federal laws enacted by Congress that are included in the **United States Code**, together with annotations of state and federal decisions that interpret and apply specific sections of federal statutes, plus the text of presidential proclamations and executive orders. *Abbreviation*: **U.S.C.A.** See STATUTE for a list of related terms.

UNITED STATES CONGRESS.   *See*: CONGRESS OF THE UNITED STATES.

UNITED STATES COURTS.   Under Article III, Section 1, of the U.S. Constitution, "The judicial Power of the United States, shall be vested in one supreme Court, and in such inferior courts as the Congress may from time to time ordain and establish. The Judges, both of the supreme and inferior Courts, shall hold their Offices during good behaviour, and shall, at stated Times, receive for their Services a Compensation which shall not be diminished during their Continuance in Office." The U.S. Supreme Court has held that these constitutional courts "share in the exercise of the judicial power defined in that section, can be invested with no other jurisdiction, and have judges who hold office during good behavior, with no power in Congress to provide otherwise." *Glidden Company v. Zdanok,* 370 U.S. 530, 593, 82 S.Ct. 1459, 1495, 8 L.Ed.2d 671, 712 (1962). Examples of inferior United States Courts are the Courts of Appeals, the District Courts, the Court of Claims, the Customs Court, and the Court of Customs and Patent Appeals. *See*: UNITED STATES COURTS OF APPEALS; UNITED STATES DISTRICT COURTS; UNITED STATES SUPREME COURT.

UNITED STATES COURTS OF APPEALS.   The United States Courts of Appeals are **intermediate appellate courts** created by act of March 3, 1891 (28 U.S.C. ch. 3), to relieve the **United States Supreme Court** of considering all **appeals** in cases originally decided by the federal **trial courts**. They are empowered to review all final decisions and certain interlocutory decisions of **United States District Courts**. They also are empowered to review and enforce orders of many federal administrative bodies. The decisions of the courts of appeals are final except as they are subject to **discretionary review** or appeal in the Supreme Court.

The United States is divided geographically into 12 judicial circuits, including the District of Columbia. Each circuit has a court of appeals (28 U.S.C. §§41, 1294). Each of the 50 states is assigned to one of the circuits, and the territories are assigned variously to the 1st, 3rd, and 9th circuits. There is also a Court of Appeals for the Federal Circuit, which has nationwide jurisdiction defined by subject matter, including patent and contract appeals. At this writing, each court of appeals has from 6 to 28 permanent circuit judgeships (168 in all), depending upon the amount of judicial work in the circuit. Circuit judges hold their offices during good behavior as provided by Article III, Section 1, of the Constitution. One of the justices of the Supreme Court is assigned as circuit justice for each of the 13 judicial circuits. Each court normally hears cases in panels consisting of three judges, but may sit **en banc** with all judges present. See APPEAL and COURT for lists of related terms.

UNITED STATES CUSTOMS SERVICE. *See*: CUSTOMS SERVICE, UNITED STATES.

UNITED STATES DEPARTMENT OF JUSTICE. *See*: DEPARTMENT OF JUSTICE.

UNITED STATES DISTRICT COURTS. The United States District Courts are the federal **courts of general jurisdiction**. Each state has at least one district court, while some of the larger states have as many as four. Altogether there are 89 district courts in the 50 states, plus the one in the District of Columbia. In addition, the Commonwealth of Puerto Rico has a district court with jurisdiction corresponding to that of district courts in the various states.

At this writing, each district court has from 2 to 27 federal district judgeships, depending upon the amount of judicial work within its territory. Only one **judge** is usually required to hear and decide a case in a district court, but in some limited cases it is required that three judges be called together to constitute the court (28 U.S.C. §2284). District judges hold their offices during good behavior as provided by Article III, Section 1, of the Constitution. However, Congress may create temporary judgeships for a court with the provision that when a vacancy occurs in that district, the vacancy shall not be filled. Each district court has a clerk, a **United States attorney**, a **United States marshal**, one or more **United States magistrates**, and bankruptcy judges, **probation officers**, **court reporters**, and their staffs. The **jurisdiction** of the district courts is set forth in 28 U.S.C. ch. 85 and at 18 U.S.C. §3231. Cases from the district courts are reviewable on appeal by the applicable **United States Court of Appeal**. See COURT for a list of related terms.

UNITED STATES HOUSE OF REPRESENTATIVES. *See*: CONGRESS OF THE U.S.

UNITED STATES MAGISTRATE. A **judicial officer** of the federal government who performs certain low-level **judicial** functions for the federal **courts** such as issuing **search warrants**, conducting **preliminary examinations**, and receiving

affidavits and fees. The decisions of magistrates are subject to **review** by the federal **judges** for whom they work. The court must approve the findings and orders of a magistrate before they can be regarded as final and official. United States magistrates are appointed as needed by district court judges.

UNITED STATES MARSHAL. *See*: MARSHAL; UNITED STATES MAR-SHALS SERVICE.

UNITED STATES MARSHALS SERVICE. The United States Marshals Service in the **Department of Justice** is the nation's oldest federal **law enforcement agency**, having served as a vital link between the **executive** and **judicial** branches of the government since 1789. Today, the Presidentially appointed **marshals** and their support staff of just over 3,000 deputy marshals and administrative personnel operate from 427 office locations in all 94 federal judicial districts.

The Marshals Service performs tasks that are essential to the operation of virtually every aspect of the federal justice system. The service is responsible for:

—providing support and protection for the federal courts, including security for 560 judicial facilities and nearly 1,900 **judges** and **magistrates**, as well as countless other trial participants such as **jurors** and **attorneys**;

—apprehending most federal fugitives;

—operating the Federal Witness Security program, ensuring the safety of endangered government **witnesses**;

—maintaining custody of and transporting thousands of federal prisoners annually;

—executing **court orders** and **arrest warrants**;

—seizing, managing, and selling property forfeited to the government by drug traffickers and other criminals, and operating the Justice Department's National Asset Seizure and Forfeiture Program; and

—responding to emergency circumstances, including civil disturbances, terrorist incidents, and other crisis situations, through its Special Operations Group, and restoring order in riot and mob-violence situations.

See LAW ENFORCEMENT OFFICER for a list of related terms.

UNITED STATES NATIONAL CENTRAL BUREAU. The United States National Central Bureau (USNCB) in the **Department of Justice** represents the United States in the **International Criminal Police Organization** (INTERPOL). Also known as Interpol-Washington, the USNCB provides an essential communications link between the United States police community and their counterparts in the foreign member countries.

The bureau operates through cooperative efforts with federal, state, and local **law enforcement agencies**. New programs and initiatives, such as the State Liaison

Program, the Airport/Seaport Program, and the Canadian Interface Project, broaden the scope of U.S. investigative resources to include the international community, thus forming an integral part of the United States' efforts to confront the problem of international crime.

Federal and state law enforcement agencies represented at the USNCB include the **Federal Bureau of Investigation**; **U.S. Marshals Service**; **Drug Enforcement Administration**; **Immigration and Naturalization Service**; **Criminal Division, U.S. Customs Service**; **U.S. Secret Service**; **Internal Revenue Service**; **Bureau of Alcohol, Tobacco and Firearms**; Office of the Comptroller of the Currency; **Federal Law Enforcement Training Center**; Office of the Inspector General, Department of Agriculture; Inspection Service, U.S. Postal Service; Diplomatic Security Service, Department of State; and the Illinois State Police.

The State Liaison Program invites states to establish an office within their own law enforcement community to serve as liaison to USNCB. International leads developed in criminal investigations being conducted by a state or local police entity can be pursued through the INTERPOL Liaison Office, and criminal investigative requests from abroad are funneled through the relevant state liaison office for action by the appropriate state or local agency. Thirty-eight states now participate in the liaison program, which is currently coordinated by a representative from the Illinois State Police.

UNITED STATES PAROLE COMMISSION. The granting, denying, modifying or revocation of **parole** for eligible federal offenders rests in the discretion of the United States Parole Commission in the **Department of Justice**. The Parole Commission consists of nine members, appointed by the President with the advice and consent of the Senate. The commission will be abolished on November 1, 1992, five years after the implementation of the U.S. Sentencing Guidelines. (The Comprehensive Crime Control Act of 1984 abolished the United States Parole Commission and instituted mandatory sentencing for all offenders whose crimes were committed after November 1, 1987.) The commission is also responsible for the **supervision** of paroled or otherwise released offenders until expiration of their terms, including determination of supervisory conditions, and may discharge parolees early from supervision. U.S. **probation officers** supervise parolees and persons released under mandatory supervised release under the direction of the commission. See PAROLE for a list of related terms.

UNITED STATES REPORTS. The official printed record of **cases** heard and **decided** by the U.S. Supreme Court, usually including for each case, a **syllabus**, the Court's **opinion, concurring opinions** and **dissenting opinions**, if any, and the Courts **disposition**. The U.S. Reports are cited 41 U.S. 234, for example, with 41 representing the volume number and 234 representing the page number.

UNITED STATES SECRET SERVICE. *See*: SECRET SERVICE, UNITED STATES.

UNITED STATES SENATE. *See*: CONGRESS OF THE UNITED STATES.

UNITED STATES STATUTES AT LARGE. An official compilation, issued annually in bound volumes, of the acts and resolutions of each session of the **Congress of the United States**. It contains all public and private laws and concurrent resolutions enacted during a **session** of Congress, reorganization plans, proposed and ratified amendments to the Constitution, and Presidential proclamations. See STATUTE for a list of related terms.

UNITED STATES SUPREME COURT. The United States Supreme Court was created by the authority of the Judiciary Act of September 24, 1789 (1 Stat. §73). It was organized on February 2, 1790. The Supreme Court comprises the Chief Justice of the United States and such number of Associate Justices as may be fixed by Congress. Under that authority, and by virtue of act of June 25, 1948 (28 U.S.C. §1), the number of Associate Justices is eight. Power to nominate the Justices is vested in the President of the United States, and appointments are made with the advice and consent of the Senate. Article III, Section 1, of the Constitution further provides that "[t]he judges, both of the supreme and inferior courts, shall hold their Offices during good Behaviour, and shall, at stated Times, receive for their Services, a Compensation, which shall not be diminished during their continuance in Office." The term of the Court begins, by law, the first Monday in October of each year and continues as long as the business before the Court requires, usually until about the end of June. Six members constitute a quorum.

According to Article III, Section 2, of the Constitution, "[t]he judicial Power shall extend to all Cases, in Law and Equity, arising under this Constitution, the Laws of the United States, and Treaties made, or which shall be made, under their Authority; —to all Cases affecting Ambassadors, other public Ministers and Consuls; —to all Cases of admiralty and maritime jurisdiction; —to **Controversies** to which the United States shall be a Party; —to Controversies between two or more States; — between a State and Citizens of another State; —between Citizens of different States; —between Citizens of the same State claiming Lands under Grants of different States, and between a State, or the Citizens thereof, and foreign States, Citizens or Subjects.

"In all Cases affecting Ambassadors, other public Ministers and Consuls, and those in which a State shall be Party, the supreme Court shall have **original jurisdiction**. In all the other Cases before mentioned, the supreme Court shall have **appellate jurisdiction**, both as to Law and Fact with such Exceptions, and under such Regulations as the Congress shall make."

Appellate jurisdiction has been conferred upon the Supreme Court by various statutes, under the authority given Congress by the Constitution. The basic statutes effective at this writing in conferring and controlling jurisdiction of the Supreme Court may be found in 28 U.S.C. §§1251, 1253, 1254, 1257-59, and various special statutes. Congress has no authority to change the original jurisdiction of the Supreme Court.

Congress has from time to time conferred upon the Supreme Court power to prescribe rules of procedure to be followed by the lower courts of the United States. Pursuant to these statutes there are now in force **rules** promulgated by the Court to govern **civil** and **criminal cases** in the **United States District Courts**, bankruptcy proceedings, admiralty cases, **appellate** proceedings, and the trial of **misdemeanors** before **United States magistrates**. See APPEAL and COURT for lists of related terms.

UNITED STATES v. WADE. *See*: LINEUP.

UNIVERSAL. Affecting, concerning, or involving all, without exception.

UNLAWFUL. Not LAWFUL.

UNLAWFUL ASSEMBLY. The meeting together of three or more persons with the purpose of committing an unlawful act, but without taking any steps toward the commission of the act. See AFFRAY for a list of related terms.

UNLAWFUL FORCE. Section 3.11 (1) of the **Model Penal Code** defines unlawful force as "force, including confinement, that is employed without the consent of the person against whom it is directed and the employment of which constitutes an offense or actionable tort or would constitute such offense or tort except for a defense (such as the absence of intent, negligence, or mental capacity; duress; youth; or diplomatic status) not amounting to a privilege to use the force." See FORCE for a list of related terms.

UNNATURAL ACT. *See*: SODOMY.

UNNATURAL INTERCOURSE. *See*: SODOMY.

UNNATURAL OFFENSE. *See*: SODOMY.

UNPRECEDENTED. Without **precedent**; new; novel.

UNPROFESSIONAL CONDUCT. Conduct that violates professional **ethics** or that is unbecoming a member of a profession in good standing.

UNREASONABLE SEARCH AND SEIZURE. *See*: SEARCH; SEIZURE.

UNSECURED BAIL. *See*: RELEASE ON BAIL.

UNSECURED BOND. *See*: RELEASE ON BAIL.

UNSOUNDNESS OF MIND.   Incapability of understanding and acting in the ordinary personal, property, and business affairs of life. The term "unsoundness of mind" is sometimes used in a broader sense as a synonym for **insanity**.

UNSUPERVISED PROBATION.   Same as COURT PROBATION.

UNSWORN FALSIFICATION.   An offense variously defined, which may include making **false** written statements or omitting necessary information with **intent** to **deceive** on official forms or applications or making false written or oral statements with intent to deceive a public servant in the performance of official duties. This deception may include submitting or inviting reliance on a writing that is known to be forged, altered, or otherwise lacking in authenticity or on a sample, specimen, map, boundary mark, or other object known to be false. See AFFIRMATION for a list of related terms.

UNTIL.   Up to the time of.

UNUSUAL.   Not ordinary; uncommon; rare.

UNWRITTEN LAW.   The part of the **law** that has not been enacted or promulgated in the form of **statutes** or **rules** and **regulations**, but that is nevertheless observed and administered in the **courts**. The unwritten law includes the unenacted portion of the **common law**, **customs** having the force of law, and rules and principles established by judicial **precedent**.

U.S.   Abbreviation for UNITED STATES.

USAGE.   A long continued procedure, practice, or course of conduct that has become so established that it serves as a guide or determinant of action or choice.

U.S.C.   Abbreviation for UNITED STATES CODE.

U.S.C.A.   Abbreviation for UNITED STATES CODE ANNOTATED.

USE.   **1.** To apply to or employ for some purpose; to put into service; to utilize. **2.** To expend; to consume; to deplete; to exhaust.

USE IMMUNITY.   A type of WITNESS IMMUNITY under which a **witness** may be compelled to testify despite the privilege against **self-incrimination**, but the witness is protected from the use of the compelled testimony and any **evidence** derived from it. Use immunity would still permit **prosecution** for related offenses based upon evidence derived from independent sources. *See*: TRANSACTIONAL IMMUNITY.

USNCB.   Abbreviation for UNITED STATES NATIONAL CENTRAL BUREAU.

USUAL.   Ordinary; normal; common; customary.

USURP.   To seize and hold the office, power, or right of another by force and without legal right.

USURY.   The charging of interest greater than that permitted by law in return for the loan of money. Usury is prohibited by **statute** in all states. Rate restrictions vary from state to state and different limits are set for different kinds of loans. *See*: LOAN SHARK.

UTTER.   **v. 1.** To put something into circulation or to offer or pass it to another in trade, representing it to be good or genuine. *Example*: He was convicted of uttering a forged instrument. **v. 2.** To express audibly; to speak. **adj.** Complete; absolute; total. *Example*: That is utter nonsense.

V. 1. Abbreviation for VERSUS. *Example*: The court handed down its opinion in the case of *State v. Runger*. **2.** Abbreviation for VIDE.

VACANT. Empty; unoccupied; having no contents; unfilled.

VACANTIA BONA. Same as BONA VACANTIA.

VACATE. 1. To make VACANT; to give up; to relinquish. **2.** To annul; to make void; to set aside; to cancel. *Example*: The court vacated the judgment.

VACATION. The period of time between the end of one **term** of **court** and the beginning of the next term. *See*: RECESS.

VAGABOND. Same as VAGRANT.

VAGINA. The female sex organ.

VAGRANCY. *See*: VAGRANT.

VAGRANT. Under the **common law**, an idle person who wanders about from place to place, has no lawful or visible means of support, subsists on charity, and does not work, though able to do so. Modern state statutes and municipal ordinances differ in their definitions of vagrancy, many having been declared unconstitutional for vagueness or for punishing conduct that is not criminal. *Also called*: **tramp**; **vagabond**. See AFFRAY for a list of related terms.

VAGUE. Imprecise; uncertain; ambiguous. Vague is a term used to describe a **statute** whose language is so unclear or ambiguous that it fails to give fair **notice** of what is prohibited or required so that "men of common intelligence must necessarily guess at its meaning and differ as to its application." *Connally v. General Construction Co.*, 269 U.S. 385, 391, 46 S.Ct. 126, 127, 70 L.Ed. 322, 328 (1926). A criminal statute is **void** as a violation of the due process clause of the Fifth Amendment (see **due process of law**) if it is vague as to what conduct is prohibited, what persons are covered, or what punishment may be imposed. *See*: OVERBROAD; STATUTE; SUBSTANTIVE DUE PROCESS.

VALID. Legally effective, sufficient, or binding; having legal force or strength.

VALUE. The worth, merit, importance, usefulness, desirability, or excellence of a thing, expressed in monetary terms.

VANDALISM. Same as CRIMINAL MISCHIEF.

VARIANCE. A difference or discrepancy between the **allegations** in a **complaint**, **indictment**, or **information** and the **proof** offered in support. A variance is best illustrated where one **crime** is alleged and a different crime proved. *See*: FATAL VARIANCE.

VEHICLE. A container or device, in or on which persons or things may be carried or conveyed from one place to another. *See*: MOTOR VEHICLE.

VEHICULAR MANSLAUGHTER. Unintentional homicide by the grossly **negligent** operation of a **motor vehicle**. Vehicular manslaughter is a type of **involuntary manslaughter**. See HOMICIDE for a list of related terms.

VEL NON. *Latin.* "Or not." *Example*: We must consider the merits vel non of this appeal.

VEND. To sell.

VENEREAL. Of or relating to **sexual intercourse** or the genitals.

VENIRE. **n. 1.** The **panel** of prospective **jurors** from which a **jury** is selected. **n. 2.** Same as VENIRE FACIAS. **v.** *Latin.* "To come"; to appear in court.

VENIRE DE NOVO. Under the **common law**, a new **writ** of VENIRE FACIAS, summoning another **jury** for another **trial**, issued because of some irregularity or defect in the **verdict** or finding of the court appearing on the face of the record. The venire de novo is now sometimes used to denote the submission of a case to another jury for a **new trial**. *Also called*: **venire facias de novo**. See ARREST WARRANT for a list of related terms.

V

VENIRE FACIAS. Under the **common law**, a judicial **writ** ordering a **sheriff** to cause a certain number of qualified persons to **appear** in **court** at a specified time to serve as **jurors**. *Also called*: **venire**. See ARREST WARRANT for a list of related terms.

VENIRE FACIAS DE NOVO. Same as VENIRE DE NOVO.

VENIREMAN. A member of a **panel** of prospective **jurors**.

VENUE. The geographical area from which the **jury** is drawn and in which a **court** with **jurisdiction** may hear and determine a **case**. Venue is usually the county or district in which the **crime** is alleged to have been committed. The Sixth Amendment to the U.S. Constitution grants an accused "the right to a speedy and public trial, by an impartial jury of the State and district wherein the crime shall have been committed, which district shall have been previously ascertained by law. . . ." *See*: CHANGE OF VENUE; JURISDICTION; REMOVAL; TRIAL.

VERACITY.   Truth; honesty.

VERBA.   *Latin.* "Words."

VERBAL.   **1.** Pertaining to or expressed in words, whether written or spoken. **2.** Spoken or **oral**, as opposed to written. **NOTE:** Because the difference between the two meanings of verbal can cause confusion, great caution should be taken in using or interpreting the word. The term oral is preferred when referring to the spoken word.

VERBAL ACT.   *See*: RES GESTAE.

VERBI GRATIA.   *Latin.* For example. *Abbreviation*: **v.g.**

VERBUM.   *Latin.* "Word."

VERDICT.   **1.** The decision made by a **jury** in a **jury trial**, or by a **judicial officer** in a **nonjury trial**, that a defendant is either **guilty** or not guilty of the offense for which he or she has been tried. In entering a **judgment**, a judicial officer has the power to reject a jury verdict of guilty, but must accept a jury verdict of not guilty. Thus a jury verdict of not guilty results in a judgment of **acquittal**, but a verdict of guilty does not necessarily result in a judgment of **conviction**. **2.** Any decision by a **jury**, or a **judicial officer** acting as a **jury**, on a question of **fact**. *See*: ACQUITTAL; AIDER BY VERDICT; ARREST OF JUDGMENT; CHANCE VERDICT; COMPROMISE VERDICT; CONTRARY TO LAW; CONVICTION; DIRECTED VERDICT; FALSE VERDICT; GENERAL VERDICT; GUILTY VERDICT; HUNG JURY; IMPARTIAL JURY; INSTRUCTION; JUDGMENT; JUDGMENT NOTWITHSTANDING THE VERDICT; JURY; JURY POLL; JURY TRIAL; NOT GUILTY BY REASON OF INSANITY; NOT GUILTY VERDICT; PARTIAL VERDICT; PUBLIC VERDICT; RETIRE; SEALED VERDICT; SPECIAL INTERROGATORIES; SPECIAL VERDICT; TRIAL; TRIAL JURY; TRUE VERDICT; VENIRE DE NOVO.

VERIFY.   **1.** To make certain; to substantiate; to confirm; to establish the truth or correctness of. **2.** To confirm or substantiate formally by **oath**, **affirmation**, or **affidavit**.

VERILY.   Truly; really; certainly.

VERITY.   **1.** The quality of being true, accurate, or real; conformity to fact. **2.** A true statement, doctrine, or belief; an established fact.

VERSUS. *Latin.* "Against." *Example*: She argued the case of *State versus Beedum* before the appellate court. *Abbreviation*: **v.**; **vs.**

VEST. To give an immediate fixed right to present or future enjoyment.

VESTED GOOD TIME. *See*: GOOD TIME.

VESTED RIGHT. An absolute, unconditional, and fixed right of which a person cannot be divested without his or her consent.

VETO. The power of a chief **executive**, such as a president or governor, to reject a **bill** passed by a **legislature** and thus prevent or delay its enactment into law. An absolute veto destroys a bill finally. A qualified veto prevents a bill from becoming law unless it is passed again by a stated proportion of votes of the legislature or by some other required formalities.

VEX. To bring trouble, distress, or agitation to; to annoy; to disquiet.

VEXATIOUS. Without sufficient grounds or reasonable cause and serving only to cause annoyance or embarrassment. *Example*: Vexatious actions or proceedings are frequently found to be frivolous by the court and are dismissed.

V.G. Abbreviation for VERBI GRATIA.

VIABLE. Capable of living or surviving.

VIABLE CHILD. An unborn child that has developed to the point that it is capable of surviving independently outside its mother's womb.

VICE. **1.** Depravity; corruption; wickedness; immoral conduct. Vice is sometimes used to describe such illegal and immoral practices as **gambling**, **prostitution**, and **pornography**. **2.** A fault; a defect; an imperfection.

Vv

VICE SQUAD. A police unit charged with the control of VICE.

VICINAGE. Neighborhood; vicinity; district. Vicinage may have different meanings in different contexts.

VICINITY. **1.** The state of being near; proximity. *Example*: The suspect was seen in the vicinity of the bank at the time of the robbery. **2.** A nearby, adjoining, or surrounding region.
NOTE: Vicinity does not express any definite idea of distance, its meaning depending on the context in which it is used.

VICTIM. A person who has suffered death, physical or mental suffering, or loss of property, as the result of an actual or attempted criminal offense committed by another person. A victim can be a single human being or a group of human beings considered as a unit. *See*: CRIME; DEATH; OFFICE FOR VICTIMS OF CRIME; REPARATION; RESTITUTION.

VICTIM COMPENSATION. *See*: RESTITUTION.

VIDE. *Latin.* "See." Vide is commonly used in making references to parts of a text. *Abbreviation*: **v.**

VIDELICET. Namely; to wit; that is to say. *Abbreviation*: **viz.**

VIEW. **1.** Sight; vision. *Example*: The stolen goods were lying open to view. **2.** The inspection by a fact-finding tribunal of an object or scene that cannot be produced in court because of immovability or inconvenience, such as a piece of real property or a crime scene. The purpose of a view is to help the **fact-finder** visualize and more clearly understand the **facts** involved in a case.

VILIFY. To speak evil of; to malign; to defame.

VIOLATE. **1.** To break, transgress, or disregard a law, rule, duty, or agreement. **2.** To commit rape on; to ravish.

VIOLATION. **1.** The performance of an act forbidden by a **statute** or the failure to perform an act commanded by a statute. **2.** An act contrary to a local government **ordinance**. **3.** *See*: INFRACTION (definition 1). **4.** PAROLE VIOLATION. **5.** PROBATION VIOLATION.
NOTE: Violation is an ambiguous word with varying definitions depending on the context in which it is used.

VIOLENCE. Unjust or unwarranted physical **force**.

VIOLENT. Acting with or characterized by unjust or unwarranted physical **force**.

VIOLENT CRIMES. A category used in some crime classification schemes to include crimes such as **murder**, **voluntary manslaughter**, **forcible rape**, **robbery**, and **assault**. See CRIME for a list of related terms.

VIOLENT DEATH. A death caused by violent external means, such as an accident or the violent actions of another person. See DEATH for a list of related terms.

VIOLENT PRESUMPTION. A very strong PRESUMPTION. See PRESUMPTION for a list of related terms.

VIS. *Latin.* "Force."

VISIBLE.   Capable of being seen.

VITAL STATISTICS.   Public records of significant dates and events relating to human life, such as births, deaths, and marriages.

VITIATE.   To make legally ineffective; to invalidate.

VIVA VOCE.   *Latin.* "With the living voice." Orally; by word of mouth.

VIZ.   Abbreviation for VIDELICET.

VOICEPRINT.   *See*: VOICEPRINT IDENTIFICATION.

VOICEPRINT IDENTIFICATION.   The comparison of a recording of a questioned voice with a known speech sample. The comparison is made using a **sound spectrograph**, an electromagnetic instrument that can produce a graphic picture of the human voice, called a voiceprint or **spectrogram**. The sound spectrograph "separates the sounds of human voices into the three component elements of time, frequency and intensity. Using a series of lines or bars, the machine plots these variables across electronically sensitive paper. The result is a spectrogram of the acoustical signal of the speaker, with the horizontal axis representing time lapse, the vertical axis indicating frequency, and the thickness of the lines disclosing the intensity of the voice. . . . Spectrograms are taken of certain cue words, such as 'the,' 'me,' 'on,' 'is,' 'I,' and 'it,' spoken by a known voice and an unknown voice. An examiner then visually compares the spectrograms of the same words, as spoken, and also listens to the two voices. Based upon these visual and aural comparisons, the examiner states his opinion whether or not the voices, known and unknown, are the same. . . . Since the identification process is essentially an exercise in pattern matching, the examiner's opinion is to a large extent a subjective one based upon the relative aural similarity or dissimilarity of the two voices and visual comparison of their spectrograms." *People v. Kelly*, 130 Cal.Rptr. 144, 147, 549 P.2d 1240, 1243 17 Cal. 3rd 24, 29-30 (Cal. 1976).

VOID.   Without legal force or effect; not legally binding; unenforceable.

VOIDABLE.   Valid and effectual, but capable of being made VOID later by some act.

VOID FOR VAGUENESS.   *See*: VAGUE.

VOIR DIRE.   *French.* "To speak the truth." **1.** An examination conducted by the **court** or by the **attorneys** of a prospective **juror** or **witness** to determine if he or she is **competent** or qualified for service. **2.** During a **trial**, a **hearing** conducted by the court out of the presence of the **jury** on some issue upon which the court must make an initial determination as a matter of law. See HEARING and JURY for lists of related terms.

VOLATILE. **1.** Evaporating readily or rapidly. **2.** Changeable; fleeting; transitory.

VOLUNTARY. Done or given intentionally, understandingly, and of one's own free will, and not induced by **force**, **coercion**, fear, promise, persuasion, or deception. When the prosecutor attempts to introduce into court a **confession** or **evidence** obtained as a result of a **consent search**, the court requires proof that under the totality of the circumstances, the confession or the consent was voluntary. With respect to confessions, the U.S. Supreme Court said that "while mental condition is surely relevant to an individual's susceptibility to police coercion, mere examination of the confessant's state of mind can never conclude the due process inquiry. . . . [C]oercive police activity is a necessary predicate to the finding that a confession is not 'voluntary' within the meaning of the Due Process Clause of the Fourteenth Amendment." *Colorado v. Connelly*, 479 U.S. 157, 165-67, 107 S.Ct. 515, 521-22, 93 L.Ed.2d 473, 483-84 (1986).

With respect to consent searches, the Court said:

"Just as was true with confessions the requirement of 'voluntary' consent reflects a fair accommodation of the constitutional requirements involved. In examining all the surrounding circumstances to determine if in fact the consent to search was coerced, account must be taken of subtly coercive police questions, as well as the possibly vulnerable subjective state of the person who consents. Those searches that are the product of police coercion can thus be filtered out without undermining the continuing validity of consent searches." *Schneckloth v. Bustamonte*, 412 U.S. 218, 229, 93 S.Ct. 2041, 2048-49, 36 L.Ed.2d 854, 864 (1973).

VOLUNTARY ACT. *See*: ACT.

VOLUNTARY COMMITMENT. In the **corrections** context, admission to a correctional, residential, or medical facility or program for care or treatment without a **court** commitment and by personal choice. Voluntary commitment to a treatment program is often made an alternative to **prosecution** or **conviction** and **sentencing**, or may be a condition of **probation**. See COMMITMENT for a list of related terms.

VOLUNTARY MANSLAUGHTER. The **intentional** killing of a human being in the sudden **heat of passion** caused by **adequate provocation**. The provocation must be of a nature to cause a reasonable person to lose his or her self-control. *Also called*: **nonnegligent manslaughter**. See HOMICIDE for a list of related terms.

VOYEUR. A person who derives sexual satisfaction from observing the sexual organs or sexual acts of others, usually from a secret vantage point.

VS. Abbreviation for VERSUS.

WAGER. An agreement between two or more parties that a certain sum of money or other thing shall be paid or delivered to the one proved right about the outcome of an uncertain event.

WAIVER. **1.** "[T]he intentional relinquishment or abandonment of a known right or privilege." *Johnson v. Zerbst*, 304 U.S. 458, 464, 58 S.Ct. 1019, 1023, 82 L.Ed. 1461, 1466 (1938). The *Miranda* decision (see MIRANDA v. ARIZONA) held that the defendant may waive the rights conveyed in the *Miranda* warnings "provided the waiver is made voluntarily, knowingly and intelligently." 384 U.S. at 475, 86 S.Ct. at 1628, 16 L.Ed.2d at 724. The inquiry whether the defendant has made a full and effective waiver has two distinct dimensions:

"First the relinquishment of the right must have been **voluntary** in the sense that it was the product of a free and deliberate choice rather than **intimidation**, **coercion** or **deception**. Second, the waiver must have been made with a full awareness both of the nature of the right being abandoned and the consequences of the decision to abandon it. Only if the 'totality of the circumstances surrounding the interrogation' reveal both an uncoerced choice and the requisite level of comprehension may a court properly conclude that the *Miranda* rights have been waived." *Moran v. Burbine*, 475 U.S. 412, 421, 106 S.Ct. 1135, 1141, 89 L.Ed.2d 410, 421 (1986).

2. Same as TRANSFER TO ADULT COURT.

WAIVER HEARING. Same as TRANSFER HEARING.

WANT. Lack; absence. *Example*: The court cannot act in this case for want of jurisdiction.

WANTED PERSON. A person sought by law enforcement authorities because an **arrest warrant** has been issued or because the person has **escaped** from **custody**. Wanted persons may be crime **suspects**, escapees, **absconders** from **supervised probation** or **parole supervision**, or persons avoiding **prosecution**, **confinement**, or giving **testimony** in criminal proceedings.

No warrant is necessary to arrest persons who have escaped from lawful confinement or failed to return after authorized leave. The message requesting apprehension transmitted to law enforcement officials is sometimes called a **pickup order**. It need not be in writing. See ABSCOND and ACCUSED for lists of related terms.

WANTON. Utterly disregardful of consequences or of the rights or safety of others; extremely reckless; malicious. Wanton sometimes implies conscious knowledge of probable consequences, whereas **reckless** implies merely careless indifference to consequences.

WARD. A child or incompetent person who has been legally placed under the care or protection of a guardian or court.

WARDEN. **1.** The chief administrative officer of a **prison**; the prison superintendent. **2.** An officer charged with special supervisory duties and with enforcement of certain laws, rules, and regulations. *Example*: A game warden arrested him for night hunting. See LAW ENFORCEMENT OFFICER for a list of related terms.

WARN. To notify; to give notice; to caution. *Example*: The officer failed to warn her of her *Miranda* rights.

WARRANT. A written **order** or **writ** issued by a **judicial officer** or other authorized person commanding a **law enforcement officer** to perform some act incident to the administration of justice. See ARREST WARRANT for a list of related terms.

WAY. A path, road, street, or other means of passage from one place to another.

WEAPON. An object, instrument, material, or substance used or designed to be used in destroying, defeating, or injuring another person or as an instrument of offensive or defensive combat. The term weapon is variously defined in statutes depending on the purpose of the statute and the jurisdiction. Section 5.06 (2) of the **Model Penal Code** defines weapon as "anything readily capable of lethal use and possessed under circumstances not manifestly appropriate for lawful uses it may have; the term includes a **firearm** that is not loaded or lacks a clip or other component to render it immediately operable, and components that can readily be assembled into a weapon." *See*: DEADLY WEAPON.

WEAPONS OFFENSES. Offenses involving the unlawful sale, distribution, manufacture, alteration, transportation, possession, or use, or the attempted sale, distribution, manufacture, alteration, transportation, possession, or use of a deadly or dangerous **weapon**.

WEEKEND SENTENCE. Same as INTERMITTENT SENTENCE.

WEIGH. To ponder in mind; to consider or examine in order to form an opinion or reach a conclusion; to evaluate. *Example*: The jury was instructed to weigh the evidence to determine which evidence was more persuasive.

WEIGHT OF THE EVIDENCE. **1.** The believability or persuasiveness of **evidence**; the probative value of evidence; the effect of evidence in influencing belief. *See*:

CONTRARY TO THE EVIDENCE. **2.** Same as PREPONDERANCE OF THE EVIDENCE. See EVIDENCE for a list of related terms.

WHARTON RULE. The rule that an agreement between two persons to commit a particular **crime** cannot be prosecuted as **conspiracy** when the crime logically requires the participation of two persons. Examples of crimes which logically require the participation of two persons are **dueling** and **adultery**.

WHEREAS. Considering that; being the case that; due to. The term "whereas" placed at the beginning of a legislative bill means because, and is followed by an explanation for the enactment of the legislation.

WHEREBY. By which; through which.

WHEREUPON. Upon which; after which; in consequence of which.

WHILE. **1.** During the time that; as long as. *Example*: He received credit for time served while he was awaiting trial. **2.** At the same time that. *Example*: He operated a vehicle while under the influence of intoxicating liquor.

WHISKEY. A distilled alcoholic liquor made from grain such as corn, rye, or barley and usually containing from 43 to 50 percent of alcohol by weight.

WHITE-COLLAR CRIME. Nonviolent **crime** for financial gain committed by means of **deception** by:

—persons whose occupational status is entrepreneurial, professional, or semiprofessional and utilizing their special occupational skills and opportunities; or

—anyone having special technical and professional knowledge of business and government, irrespective of the person's occupation.

The objectives of white-collar crime may be to obtain money, property, or services, to avoid payment or loss of money, property, or services, or to obtain some business or personal advantage. White-collar crime may be committed by individuals of any socioeconomic level or by organizations, associations, or other combinations of persons. Actual instances of white-collar crime are prosecuted as the offenses defined in statutes under such headings as **theft, fraud,** and **embezzlement**. The kinds of crime designated as business crime, **consumer fraud, confidence games**, tax violations, bankruptcy fraud, insurance fraud, and the like are often regarded as equivalent to or included within the general range of white-collar crime. Some of these types of activity also fall within categories of **organized crime** operations. See CRIME for a list of related terms.

WHITE SLAVE TRAFFIC ACT. An act of Congress, passed June 25, 1910, making it a criminal offense to knowingly transport or to procure the transportation of

women or girls for immoral purposes in interstate or foreign commerce. *Also called*: **Mann Act**.

WHOLE. Entire; complete; total.

WHOLLY. Entirely; completely; totally.

WILFUL. Same as WILLFUL.

WILL. The mental faculty or power that directs a person's actions; volition.

WILLFUL. **1.** Done **purposely**; **intentional**; deliberate; voluntary. A willful act or omission is to be distinguished from one that is done accidentally, inadvertently, or innocently. **2.** Done with bad purpose or evil intent.

WILLFUL HOMICIDE. A **homicide** committed **intentionally**, with or without legal justification. The term willful homicide is often used when criminal homicide is meant. Willful homicide embraces **murder** and **voluntary manslaughter**, both of which are criminal, and **justifiable homicide**, which is not criminal. See HOMICIDE for a list of related terms.

WILLINGLY. Voluntarily; readily; without reluctance; of one's own free choice.

WINE. The fermented juice of grapes or of various other fruits or plants.

WIRETAPPING. A form of electronic eavesdropping consisting of the **seizing** or overhearing of communications by means of a concealed recording or listening device connected to the transmission line. The Crime Control and Safe Streets Act (18 U.S.C.A. Sect. §2510 et seq.) and various state statutes govern the circumstances and procedures under which law enforcement officials may conduct wiretapping. See PRIVACY for a list of related terms.

WIT. *See*: TO WIT.

WITHDRAW. **1.** To take back; to retract; to remove. *Example*: The defense attorney withdrew his motion. **2.** To move back; to retreat; to disengage or remove oneself; to retire; to resign. **3.** To remove a **juror** from the **panel** with the result that the proceedings are ended because the jury is incomplete. **4.** In the law of **self-defense**, same as **retreat**. **5.** In the law of **conspiracy**, to abandon a conspiracy by communicating one's abandonment in a manner reasonably calculated to inform all other conspirators in time for them also to effectively abandon the conspiracy.

WITHHOLD. **1.** To hold back; to restrain; to keep in check. **2.** To refrain from giving, granting, or allowing; to retain; to keep for oneself.

WITHOUT CONSENT. Same as AGAINST THE WILL.

WITHOUT DAY. *See*: SINE DIE.

WITHOUT DELAY. **1.** Immediately; at once; forthwith. **2.** As soon as possible under the circumstances.

WITHOUT PREJUDICE. *See*: DISMISSAL WITHOUT PREJUDICE.

WITH PREJUDICE. *See*: DISMISSAL WITH PREJUDICE.

WITNESS. **1.** A person who directly sees or perceives an event or thing (see **eye-witness**), or who has expert knowledge relevant to a case (see **expert witness**). **2.** A person who **testifies** to what he or she has seen or perceived or what he or she knows. **3.** A person who signs his or her name to a document to attest to its authenticity. Such a person is sometimes called an **attesting witness**. *See*: ACCOMPLICE WITNESS; ADVERSE WITNESS; ATTEST; COMPETENCE; COMPETENT EVIDENCE; COMPULSORY PROCESS; CONFRONTATION; CREDIBILITY; CRIMEN FALSI; CROSS-EXAMINATION; DEMEANOR; DEPOSITION; DIRECT EXAMINATION; DISINTERESTED; EAR WITNESS; EVIDENCE; EXAMINATION; EXPERT WITNESS; EYEWITNESS; EYEWITNESS IDENTIFICATION; FALSE WITNESS; FOUNDATION; HEARING; HEARSAY EVIDENCE; HEARSAY RULE; HYPOTHETICAL QUESTION; IDENTIFICATION; IMPEACH; INTERROGATORIES; LAY WITNESS; LEADING QUESTION; LETTERS ROGATORY; LINEUP; MATERIAL WITNESS; OPINION EVIDENCE; OPINION RULE; PAST RECOLLECTION RECORDED; PERJURY; PHOTOGRAPHIC IDENTIFICATION; POLICE WITNESS; PRESENT RECOLLECTION REFRESHED; PREVIOUSLY RECORDED TESTIMONY; PROSECUTING WITNESS; PROTECTIVE CUSTODY; RECROSS-EXAMINATION; REDIRECT EXAMINATION; REHABILITATE; SELF-INCRIMINATION; SEQUESTER; SHOWUP; STAND; STAND DOWN; STATE'S EVIDENCE; SUBPOENA; SUBSCRIBING WITNESS; TESTIFY; TESTIMONY; TRIAL; UNAVAILABLE; VOIR DIRE; WITNESS IMMUNITY; ZEALOUS WITNESS.

WITNESS AGAINST HIM OR HERSELF. *See*: SELF-INCRIMINATION.

WITNESS IMMUNITY. Freedom or exemption from **prosecution** granted to a **witness** to compel answers to questions or the production of **evidence**, which the witness might otherwise refuse to do on the grounds of the Fifth Amendment privilege against **self-incrimination**. Two types of immunity that may be granted are TRANSACTIONAL IMMUNITY and USE IMMUNITY. Witness immunity granted by a state also prevents the use of the evidence provided by the witness or its fruits in a subsequent prosecution against the witness by the federal government. Similarly, witness immunity granted by the federal government prevents the use of the evidence provided by the witness or its fruits in a subsequent prosecution against the witness by a state government. A witness's failure to answer questions or produce evidence within the subject of the investigation as ordered by the court constitutes **contempt of court**. See WITNESS for a list of related terms.

WOLF v. COLORADO. The 1949 U.S. Supreme Court case which held that freedom from unreasonable **searches and seizures** was such a fundamental right as to be protected against state violations by the due process clause of the Fourteenth Amendment (see **due process of law**), but that the right thus guaranteed required no **exclusionary rule** to be applied in the state courts as it was in the federal courts, since there were other means to observe and enforce the right. The Court said: "Granting that in practice the exclusion of evidence may be an effective way of deterring unreasonable searches, it is not for this Court to condemn as falling below the minimal standards assured by the Due Process Clause a State's reliance upon other methods which, if consistently enforced, would be equally effective." 338 U.S. 25, 31, 69 S.Ct. 1359, 1362-63, 93 L.Ed. 1782, 1787.

NOTE: See MAPP v. OHIO, which overruled *Wolf v. Colorado* and held that the exclusionary rule should and did apply to the states. See EXCLUSIONARY RULE for a list of related terms.

WORD OF ART.   Same as TERM OF ART.

WORK CAMP.   *See*: COUNTY FARM.

WORK PRODUCT DOCTRINE.   The doctrine that grants a qualified exemption from **discovery** to material prepared in anticipation of litigation that reflects an attorney's mental impressions, conclusions, opinions, personal beliefs, or legal theories. The doctrine recognizes that "[i]n performing his various duties . . . it is essential that a lawyer work with a certain degree of privacy, free from unnecessary intrusion by opposing parties and their counsel. Proper preparation of a client's case demands that he assemble information, sift what he considers to be the relevant from the irrelevant facts, prepare his legal theories and plan his strategy without undue and needless interference." *Hickman v. Taylor*, 329 U.S. 495, 510-11, 67 S.Ct. 385, 393, 91 L.Ed. 451, 462 (1947). In *U.S. v. Nobles*, 422 U.S. 225, 238-39, 95 S.Ct. 2160, 2170, 45 L.Ed.2d 141, 154 (1975), the U.S. Supreme Court said:

> "[T]he work product doctrine shelters the mental processes of the attorney, providing a privileged area within which he can analyze and prepare his client's case. But the doctrine is an intensely practical one, grounded in the realities of litigation in our adversary system. One of those realities is that attorneys often must rely on the assistance of investigators and other agents in the compilation of materials in preparation for trial. It is therefore necessary that the doctrine protect material prepared by agents for the attorney as well as those prepared by the attorney himself. Moreover, the concerns reflected in

the work product doctrine do not disappear once trial has begun. Disclosure of an attorney's efforts at trial, as surely as disclosure during pretrial discovery, could disrupt the orderly development and presentation of his case."

Although what constitutes the work product of an attorney eludes exact definition and differs from jurisdiction to jurisdiction, examples of the types of materials that may be included are witness interview notes, investigative reports, trial analysis and strategies, and other private memoranda of mental impressions, conclusions, opinions, and legal theories.

WORK RELEASE PROGRAM.　A correctional program allowing an **inmate** to maintain regular employment outside the **correctional institution** on weekdays but requiring the inmate to return to the institution at night and on weekends. See RELEASE for a list of related terms.

WOUND.　To inflict a cut, laceration, bruise, fracture, or other injury on the body of a person or animal.

WRATH.　Strong or violent anger; rage.

WRIT.　A written **order** issued by a **judicial officer** commanding the person to whom it is addressed to perform or cease performing a specified act. The kinds of writs that are normally issued in connection with **criminal trial** proceedings are **arrest warrants**, **bench warrants**, **search warrants**, **subpoenas**, and **summonses**. The majority of writs are primarily or exclusively **civil** in application, although a few kinds of writs are used in connection with posttrial proceedings related to criminal cases. The writ of **habeas corpus** is a fundamental means of seeking postconviction relief when **appeal** is not possible. In some jurisdictions and in some circumstances two other kinds of writs are used in posttrial criminal matters: the writ of **certiorari** and the writ of error **coram nobis**. See ARREST WARRANT for a list of related terms. *See also*: ALTERNATIVE WRIT; CONSTRUCTIVE SERVICE; MESNE PROCESS; PERSONAL SERVICE; POSTCONVICTION PROCESS; REMEDY; SERVE; SUE OUT.

WRITING.　The California Evidence Code Sect. 250 provides a comprehensive definition of a writing as "handwriting, typewriting, printing, photostating, photographing, and every other means of recording upon any tangible thing any form of communication or representation, including letters, words, pictures, sounds, or symbols, or combinations thereof." Writing may have different meanings in different contexts and in different jurisdictions. Its meaning may be limited to written or printed papers or documents or may be expanded to include such things as phonograph records, compact disks, tape recordings, computer disks, motion pictures, and videotapes.

WRIT OF ASSISTANCE.　A form of **general warrant** issued by the British Colonial courts against the American colonists in the mid-18th century to enforce the Trade

Acts. Writs of assistance authorized royal customs officers to **search** houses and ships at will in order to discover and seize smuggled goods or goods on which the required duties had not been paid. The reaction of the colonists against the writs of assistance was strong and was one of the major causes of the American Revolution. See ARREST WARRANT and SEARCH for lists of related terms.

WRIT OF CAPIAS. *See*: CAPIAS.

WRIT OF CERTIORARI. A discretionary **writ** issued from an **appellate court** for the purpose of obtaining from a lower court the record of its proceedings in a particular case. In the U.S. Supreme Court, and in some states, this writ is the mechanism for **discretionary review**. A request for review is made by petitioning for a writ of certiorari, and granting of review is indicated by issuance of the writ. See APPEAL and ARREST WARRANT for lists of related terms.

WRIT OF CORAM NOBIS. *See*: CORAM NOBIS.

WRIT OF ERROR. A **writ** issued from an **appellate court** to a **trial court** requiring the trial court to submit to the appellate court the **record** of a case adjudged by it, in order that the appellate court may review the record for alleged **errors** of law. The writ of error is an outmoded method of appeal. See APPEAL, ARREST WARRANT, and ERROR for lists of related terms.

WRIT OF ERROR CORAM NOBIS. *See*: CORAM NOBIS.

WRIT OF EXECUTION. *See*: EXECUTION.

WRIT OF HABEAS CORPUS. *See*: HABEAS CORPUS.

WRIT OF MANDAMUS. *See*: MANDAMUS.

WRIT OF PROBABLE CAUSE. A **writ** designed to **stay execution** of a **judgment** pending an **appeal**. See ARREST WARRANT for a list of related terms.

WRIT OF PROHIBITION. A **writ** issued by a superior court directing an inferior court or other tribunal to cease particular proceedings because the tribunal either lacks **jurisdiction** or exceeds its jurisdiction. See ARREST WARRANT for a list of related terms.

WRIT OF QUO WARRANTO. *See*: QUO WARRANTO.

WRIT OF REVIEW. Any **writ** issued by an **appellate court** to bring up for **review** the **record** or **decision** of an inferior court. See ARREST WARRANT for a list of related terms.

WRIT OF RIGHT. A **writ** issued as a matter of right merely on the filing of an application in proper form. See ARREST WARRANT for a list of related terms.

WRIT OF SCIRE FACIAS. *See*: SCIRE FACIAS.

WRIT OF SUMMONS. Same as SUMMONS.

WRIT OF SUPERSEDEAS. *See*: SUPERSEDEAS.

WRITTEN LAW. Same as STATUTORY LAW.

WRONG. A violation of another person's legal right.

WRONGDOER. One who commits a WRONG.

WRONGFUL. **1.** Violative of another person's legal rights. **2.** Unlawful; illegal; unjust; unfair; injurious.

XYY CHROMOSOMES. An abnormal arrangement of the chromosomes in the human cell that, some scientists claim, produces aggressive, antisocial behavior in persons with the abnormality. The XYY chromosome theory has not yet achieved sufficient acceptance to provide a **defense** to a criminal charge.

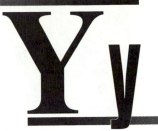

Y CHROMOSOMES. *See*: XYY CHROMOSOMES.

YEAR-AND-A-DAY RULE.   The rule that a person cannot be guilty of **murder** (or sometimes **manslaughter**) if the **victim** lives for a year and a day after the injury was inflicted.

YIELD.   To give way; to submit; to surrender; to concede; to relinquish.

YOUTHFUL OFFENDER.   A person, adjudicated in **criminal court**, who may be above the statutory age limit for **juveniles** but is below a specified upper age limit, for whom special **correctional commitments** and special record **sealing** procedures are made available by statute. The special correctional commitment may be to a **juvenile facility**, to a special section of an adult facility, or to a separate facility for the confinement of persons between the age limits specified in the particular statute. Such provisions exist in federal law and in the laws of several states. Many jurisdictions permit **arrest** and court information concerning young adults to be sealed according to the record-sealing procedures that apply to juveniles. See JUVENILE for a list of related terms.

ZEALOUS WITNESS. A **witness** who shows partiality for the **party** that first calls him or her to the stand and who is eager to volunteer what the witness thinks will be advantageous to that party. See WITNESS for a list of related terms.

ZIP GUN. A nonprofessionally made **gun** constructed from a toy pistol or length of pipe, and having a firing pin usually powered by a rubber band.

ZONE OF PRIVACY. Same as CONSTITUTIONALLY PROTECTED AREA.

ZONE SEARCH. A method of **searching** a crime scene in which the area to be searched is divided into sectors and each sector is carefully examined. *Also called*: **sector search**. See SEARCH for a list of related terms.